D0875317

THE PAPERS
OF
JOHN MARSHALL

Sponsored by
The College of William and Mary
and
The Omohundro Institute of Early American History and Culture
under the auspices of
The National Historical Publications and Records
Commission

JOHN MARSHALL
Oil on canvas by Rembrandt Peale, 1825.
Courtesy of the Office of the Curator, Supreme Court of the United States.

THE PAPERS
OF
JOHN MARSHALL

Volume X

Correspondence, Papers, and Selected Judicial Opinions
January 1824–March 1827

CHARLES F. HOBSON, *Editor*

SUSAN HOLBROOK PERDUE   ROBERT W. SMITH

The University of North Carolina Press, Chapel Hill
in association with the
Omohundro Institute of Early American History and Culture
Williamsburg, Virginia

*The Omohundro Institute of Early American History and Culture
is sponsored jointly by
The College of William and Mary in Virginia
and The Colonial Williamsburg Foundation.
On November 15, 1996, The Institute adopted the present
name in honor of a bequest from Malvern H. Omohundro, Jr.*

*The paper in this book meets the guidelines for permanence and durability of the Committee on
Production Guidelines for Book Longevity of the Council on Library Resources.*
*The ornament on the title page is based upon John Marshall's personal seal, as it appears on a gold
watch fob that also bears the seal of his wife, Mary Willis Marshall. It was drawn by Richard J.
Stinely of Williamsburg, Virginia, from the original, now owned by the Association for the
Preservation of Virginia Antiquities, Richmond, Virginia, and is published with the
owner's permission.*

The Library of Congress has cataloged Vols. 1 and 2 as follows:

Marshall, John, 1755–1835.
  *The papers of John Marshall / Herbert A. Johnson, editor; Charles T. Cullen, associate editor;
Nancy G. Harris . . . [et al.], assistant editors.*
  *"Sponsored by the College of William and Mary and the Institute of Early American History and
Culture under the auspices of the National Historical Publications Commission."*
  Includes bibliographical references and indexes.

  *1. Marshall, John, 1755–1835 — Manuscripts.   2. United States — Politics and government —
1775–1783 — Sources.   3.   United   States — Politics   and   government — 1783–1865 —
Sources.   4.   Statesmen — United   States — Manuscripts.   5.   Judges — United   States — Manuscripts.   6.   Manuscripts, American.   7.   Judicial opinions.   I.   Johnson,   Herbert   Alan.
II. Cullen, Charles T., 1940–   .   III. Hobson, Charles F., 1943–   .   IV. Institute of Early American History and Culture (Williamsburg, Va.)   V. Title.*
E302.M365   347.73'2634 — dc19   [347.3073534]   74-9575 CIP r986
                                       ISBN 0-8078-1233-1 (v. 1)
                                       ISBN 0-8078-1302-8 (v. 2)
                                       ISBN 0-8078-1337-0 (v. 3)
                                       ISBN 0-8078-1586-1 (v. 4)
                                       ISBN 0-8078-1746-5 (v. 5)
                                       ISBN 0-8078-1903-4 (v. 6)
                                       ISBN 0-8078-2074-1 (v. 7)
                                       ISBN 0-8078-2221-3 (v. 8)
                                       ISBN 0-8078-2404-6 (v. 9)
                                       ISBN 0-8078-2520-4 (v. 10)

*Publication of this volume has been assisted by grants from the
National Endowment for the Humanities, the National Historical Publications
and Records Commission, the Robert G. III & Maude Morgan Cabell
Foundation, the William Nelson Cromwell Foundation,
and the Earhart Foundation.*

CONTENTS

JANUARY 1824–MARCH 1827

1824

1825

1826

1827

ILLUSTRATIONS

Preface

In the summer of 1825 John Adams wrote that it was "the pride of my life that I have given to this nation a Chief Justice equal to Coke or Hale, Holt or Mansfield" (from John Adams, 17 August 1825). Unlike the eminent English jurists named, Adams's appointee, John Marshall, achieved his fame in the novel field of constitutional law. During the period covered by this volume (January 1824-March 1827) — the last year of James Monroe's presidency and the first two years of the administration of John Quincy Adams — Chief Justice Marshall further enhanced his reputation as the expositor of the Constitution. The series of "great" cases that began at the 1819 term had not yet played itself out. In *Gibbons* v. *Ogden* and *Osborn* v. *Bank of the United States,* both decided at the 1824 term, the Marshall Court's constitutional nationalism perhaps reached its peak. At the 1827 term the Court issued another pair of notable pronouncements, *Ogden* v. *Saunders* and *Brown* v. *Maryland,* but by then a crack in the nationalist consensus had revealed itself.

Each of these cases required the Court to perform the delicate task of determining the limits on state powers, either by deciding whether those powers conflicted with a federal power or whether they fell within an express prohibition of the Constitution. In *Gibbons* the Court for the first time expounded Congress's power to regulate commerce while considering the validity of New York's steamboat monopoly laws. Marshall gave an expansive reading to the commerce clause that came close to adopting the view that Congress's power was exclusive. The Court struck down the monopoly, though ultimately basing its decision not on the commerce clause but on the narrower ground of collision with a federal statute. In *Osborn* the chief justice recapitulated the nationalist themes of *McCulloch* v. *Maryland* (1819) and *Cohens* v. *Virginia* (1821) while invalidating Ohio's attempt to tax the Second Bank of the United States. He reaffirmed a broad reading of the jurisdiction of the federal courts (along with a narrow reading of the Eleventh Amendment) and restated the principle of national supremacy to uphold the bank's exemption from state taxation.

As in 1819 and 1821, states' rights proponents deplored these decisions as another fateful step toward consolidation, though opposition was more muted on this occasion. *Gibbons,* indeed, was regarded as a popular victory over an entrenched monopoly and yielded almost immediate economic benefits by opening the nation's waterways to unfettered commercial traffic. *Osborn* came down relatively unnoticed, as hostility toward the national bank had subsided by 1824, even in Ohio. Proposals to reform the federal judiciary, including measures to require a supermajority of the Supreme Court justices to concur in setting aside state laws, were regularly introduced in Congress during these years. All attempts to curb the Supreme Court's powers failed, but so too did such reforms as abolishing circuit riding, increasing the number of circuits, and adding a second term. The only change Congress brought about was to lengthen the Court's term by having it commence the second Monday in January, effective at the 1827 term.

A sign that the Court's unanimity, if not unity, was beginning to break down occurred in *Gibbons,* when Justice William Johnson announced that henceforth he would give his own opinion in major constitutional cases. Two new justices who joined the Court during these years also served notice that they would follow an independent course. Smith Thompson of New York took his seat in 1824, replacing Brockholst Livingston; and Robert Trimble of Kentucky succeeded Thomas Todd in 1826. Johnson, Thompson, and Trimble were part of the four-to-three majority in *Ogden* v. *Saunders* that upheld the validity of prospective state bankruptcy laws at the 1827 term. For the first and only time during his tenure, Chief Justice Marshall was compelled to dissent in a constitutional case. His opinion for the minority was his last and most powerfully reasoned exposition of the contract clause. In *Brown* v. *Maryland,* also decided at the 1827 term, the chief justice resumed his accustomed role of delivering the Court's opinion, this time voiding a state law imposing a license fee on importers. Thompson's dissent, however, hinted at the difficulty of restoring the nationalist consensus of earlier years.

Marshall also delivered notable opinions in two nonconstitutional cases. *The Antelope* (1825) dealt with the status and disposition of Africans on board a captured slave ship and brought into dramatic conflict "the sacred rights of liberty and of property" (Opinion, 15 March 1825). A less dramatic but equally revealing specimen of Marshall's jurisprudence was *Bank of the United States* v. *Dandridge* (1827), which overruled a judgment given by the chief justice on circuit in 1823. Apart from the dry legal question concerning corporations on which the case turned, Marshall's dissenting opinion was an expression of professional pride, an attempt to explain to the world at large that his circuit judgment was not a "rash and hasty decision" but the result of a reasoned consideration of a host of "imposing authorities" (Opinion, 28 February 1827).

Elias B. Caldwell, the Court's longtime clerk, died in June 1825, precipitating a flurry of applications for that post. Choosing a successor proved to be an unexpectedly protracted and disagreeable task. To Marshall's chagrin the list of applicants contained not only a great number of respectable candidates but "many of my highly valued personal friends, and the sons of others with whom I have been connected by ties of close affection & esteem." In this "distressing situation," the chief justice decided to support the "one of the many I could wish to assist" who could obtain enough votes to be elected (to James Monroe, 31 July 1826). The Court's first choice, William Griffith, died before he could assume his duties, and the vexing process began again. "If patronage be always so painful," complained Marshall, "those who possess it are much better entitled to our pity than our envy. God in his mercy defend me from being ever again called to its exercise" (to Joseph Hopkinson, 31 July 1826). His prayer was answered. With the appointment of William T. Carroll in 1827, the Court had a clerk who would remain in office for many years.

In contrast to his Supreme Court opinions, Marshall's circuit court opinions dealt with mundane questions of private law, typically arising in equity suits for the recovery of a debt or legacy from a decedent's estate. Several of these cases involved debts contracted by Virginians to British merchants before the Revolution. "I have some long & troublesome suits in chancery which occupy me very closely," Marshall wrote in 1825, "one of which is particular[ly] unpleasant because between old friends, and one of those unfortunate cases that the ruin or nearly the ruin of one or the other must be the consequence" (to Bushrod Washington, 12 June 1825). He evidently referred to *Garnett, Brooke's Executor* v. *Macon* (1825), which considered whether a tract of land in King and Queen County was liable for an ancient debt. Marshall prepared a lengthy opinion that exhibits his mastery of the principles of equity law and his adept handling of the numerous English cases cited by counsel (Opinion, 25 November 1825).

Another thorny equity suit was enlivened by a question of legitimacy arising from claims to the estate of a man who had children by two wives. In *Stegall* v. *Stegall's Administrator* (1825), Marshall "determined that the conclusion of the law in favour of legitimacy may be rebutted by strong circumstances although access of the husband to the wife was not impossible." The particular issue to be decided, he explained, was "the legitimacy of two children of a woman residing in North Carolina in the free indulgence of her natural appetites, whose husband resided in Virginia with another woman whom he married between the two births. Our best lawyers are engaged in it" (to Bushrod Washington, 12 June 1825; to Joseph Story, 31 May 1826; Opinion, 22 June 1825). A libel case on the North Carolina circuit in Raleigh also engrossed the chief justice's attention, though no opinion survives. The parties were two New England clergymen, one of whom accused the other of "very serious crimes." The testimony, which consisted of "depositions of almost all New England" was "very contradictory." Marshall was struck by the "obstinacy" of these "gentlemen of th⟨e⟩ sacred profession" in pursuing this case until he "was informed that it was Presbyterian vs. Unitarian" (to Story, 31 May 1826).

Off the bench, Marshall worked on two longstanding projects: revising his *Life of George Washington* and preparing an edition of Washington's correspondence. Although he had completed substantive revisions of the *Life,* he continued to make corrections to the fifth volume, which covered the period from the end of the war through the end of Washington's presidency. When a newspaper reported that he was writing a general history of the United States for these years, Marshall publicly denied the rumor, explaining that it probably arose from communications among his friends that he was revising the *Life*. That work, he ruefully confessed, "was composed with too much precipitation, and I have been engaged in correcting its language where it has been negligently written, and in pruning a minuteness of detail which gives a wearisome tediousness to the narrative now, though the facts were at the time of immense importance" (to Gales & Seaton, 22 February 1825). Plans for publishing a revised edition had not yet matured, however, though he did publish the original introductory part as *A History of the Colonies* in 1824.

For some years Marshall had collaborated with Bushrod Washington in selecting and copying General Washington's correspondence for publication. Early in 1826 Jared Sparks approached them with his own ambitious plan of preparing a comprehensive annotated edition, for which he hoped to gain access to the papers at Mount Vernon. Bushrod Washington was initially cold to this project, but when Sparks sweetened the deal by offering an equal interest in the copyright and profits of sale, Marshall "instantly advised his acceptance of it." The two jurists and friends also apparently abandoned their own publication plans, though three volumes were ready for the press by the summer of 1826. For his part, the chief justice told Sparks that he believed Washington's correspondence "would appear to more advantage if published according to your views of the subject." The edition he and Judge Washington had in mind did not go beyond a selective publication "unaccompanied by comment or notes of any description" (to Jared Sparks, 10 December 1826). With a financial stake in Sparks's enterprise, there was all the more reason to put aside their own work.

As author of the *Life*, Marshall was drawn into a controversy with William B. Giles, who in the 1790s had been one of the most outspoken opponents of the administration. In 1825 Giles, then attempting a political comeback in Virginia, publicly accused the author of misrepresenting a speech he had made thirty years earlier. Marshall had cited no source for the speech, but Giles's complaint prompted him (with the aid of friends) to track down the Philadelphia newspaper he had used in paraphrasing Giles (from William B. Giles, 26 November 1825; to William B. Giles, 29 November 1825). In revising the *Life* for the second edition, he made sure to cite the newspaper and for good measure to quote Giles's speech as reported in an opposition newspaper to demonstrate the fidelity of his own account. Evidently before receiving Marshall's conciliatory response concerning this episode, Giles delivered another public censure of a passage in the *Life*. Again, after extensive communications with his Philadelphia friends, Marshall found the source on which he based his account and took care to include this information in his revised edition (to Joseph Hopkinson, 11 December 1825).

A good portion of Marshall's correspondence for these years can be aptly described as revisiting the past, particularly the Revolutionary era. This looking backward was prompted in great measure by the publication of biographies, memoirs, and letters of the founding generation that occurred with increasing frequency during the 1820s. Marshall's own work on Washington reflected his generation's broader campaign to preserve the record of its military and civil achievements as an enduring legacy for posterity. Such a legacy, of course, could never fully compensate the inevitable loss of memory across generations. "Those who follow us will know very little of the real transactions of our day," the chief justice observed, "and will have very untrue impressions respecting men & things. Such is the lot of humanity" (to Timothy Pickering, 20 March 1826). Among the topics Marshall and his friends discussed were the causes of the Revolution, various battles and generals, and the character of General Washington. In response to an oration commemorating the fiftieth anniversary of the Declaration of Independence, Marshall praised its realistic view of the causes of the break with England while implicitly criticizing the passage of the Declaration listing the "tyrannical acts" of the monarch. The truth could now be declared that the "war was a war of principle, against a system hostile to political liberty, from which oppression was to be dreaded, not against actual oppression" (to Edward Everett, 2 August 1826).

None of Marshall's correspondents exceeded Timothy Pickering in garrulous recollections of past military and civil events, whereby the embittered high Federalist sought to set the record straight. The chief justice cordially replied to Pickering's lengthy communications, commenting circumspectly on the New Englander's quarrel with the Adams family, his attack on William Johnson's biography of General Greene, and his low opinion of General Washington's abilities as a military leader. On the last subject, Marshall admitted that his own impression of Washington was not based on close observation, having "seen him only at a distance," though it was formed "on a very attentive consideration of his character[,] his conduct, and his papers." Pickering, a former staff officer, was able to "take a closer view of him, especially as a military man than was in my power, and have consequently better means of judging correctly than I possess" (to Timothy Pickering, 15 March 1827).

Marshall continued to profess his serene indifference to current party politics, a posture that age and his judicial character would dictate even if he were not predisposed to adopt it. "I am as calm an observer of passing events & controversies as a man can be," he wrote, "who feels & to his latest breath will feel an ardent wish for the prosperity of his country" (to John Randolph, 5 May 1826). Except for some shrewd observations about the presidential election of 1824, his letters are largely devoid of political commentary. To Henry Clay, accused of obtaining the post of secretary of state by a "corrupt bargain" with newly elected president

John Quincy Adams, Marshall remarked: "There is unquestionably a party determined to oppose Mr. Adams at the next election, and this party will attack him through you. It is an old and has been a successful Stratagem" (to Henry Clay, 14 April 1825). Marshall's and the nation's attention to politics was pleasantly diverted by the visit of Lafayette in 1824 and 1825, which consisted of a series of nostalgic reunions of war veterans throughout the country. During the general's progress through Virginia, the chief justice gave ceremonial speeches and toasts at Yorktown, Richmond, and Warrenton.

Over the years Marshall had been party to a number of lawsuits concerning tracts of land within the former Fairfax estate, of which he and his brother James M. Marshall were principal purchasers. In 1826 the Marshalls were sued in the chancery court at Winchester, this time not about land but concerning the payment of annuities directed by Lord Fairfax's will. The Marshalls assumed payment of these annuities as a condition of their purchase of the estate. The case of *Catlett* v. *Marshall* was complicated, turning on the construction of a clause in Fairfax's will designating the remainder of an annuity to go to the fourth child of Bryan Fairfax. Marshall drew upon his thorough knowledge of the law of legacies, executory devises, and contingent remainders in preparing an answer to this suit and in advising his nephew, who was to argue the case in court. Although the chancery court ruled in the Marshalls' favor in 1827, the case went to the state Court of Appeals, where it was still pending at Marshall's death in 1835.

As he approached and passed his seventieth year, Marshall continued to enjoy remarkably good health. In February 1824 he suffered a concussion and dislocated his shoulder after falling in the darkness over the cellar door of his Washington lodgings. He mended quickly, and within two weeks he was back in court. Two years later he endured "a pretty severe attack of the influenza" but soon resumed his regimen of rising early and walking "three miles by seven." In letters to his wife, he wrote light-heartedly about his ailments, growing old, the kind attentions of the Cabinet secretaries' wives during his recovery, and his confinement within doors that kept him from "gazing at the ⟨numerous⟩ belles" who flocked to the capital during the winter. The attractions of the Washington social scene, he was quick to reassure Polly, were nothing to an old man who "feels that his home is his place of most comfort, and his old wife the companion in the world in whose society he is most happy." The enforced idleness following his accident left him with plenty of time on his hands. "How do you think I beguile it?" he asked her by way of introducing a charming recollection of their courtship (to Mary W. Marshall, 23 February 1824, 12 February 1826, 12 March 1826).

In 1826 Edward Carrington Marshall, the chief justice's youngest son, graduated from Harvard College. Soon thereafter he informed his parents that had become engaged to a young lady from Cambridge, the daughter of Judge Samuel Fay. Without having actually discussed the engagement in person with Edward, Marshall wrote a friendly letter to Judge Fay welcoming his daughter to the family. To his acute embarrassment, the chief justice received a reply that conveyed Judge Fay's "positive and deliberate" refusal to consent to the marriage. This produced a second letter to Judge Fay, which Marshall crafted with the exacting attention he gave to composing his judicial opinions. The result was a literary gem, worthy of Jane Austen, whose novels he was reading at the time. Cast in the form of an apology for a gross impropriety, it expressed his deep mortification while communicating a subtle reproach to the Cambridge judge. Acknowledging the "intrinsic weight" of Fay's objections to the marriage "independent of their authority," Marshall hoped the judge's decision was "made with the approbation of Mrs. & Miss Fay" (to Samuel Fay, 15 October 1826).

Acknowledgments

We gratefully acknowledge the assistance of the staffs of the Earl Gregg Swem Library and the Marshall-Wythe Law Library, College of William and Mary. Conley Edwards and his staff at the archives division of the Library of Virginia, Richmond, courteously attended to our requests for materials from that institution's collections. Special thanks are due to Dale F. Harter of the archives staff. Dane Hartgrove and Michael T. Meier of the National Historical Publications and Records Commission supplied documents from various record groups of the National Archives. The following persons also provided information or documents used in preparing this volume: Wayne Cutler, the Papers of James K. Polk, University of Tennessee; John K. Gott, Fauquier Heritage Society; Marie E. Lamoureux, American Antiquarian Society; Harold Moser, the Papers of Andrew Jackson, University of Tennessee; R. Kent Newmyer, University of Connecticut; Margaret Nichols, Rare and Manuscript Collections, Cornell University Library; Paul W. Romaine, the Gilder Lehrman Collection, New York City; Celeste Walker, Adams Papers, Massachusetts Historical Society; and Melanie Wisner, Houghton Library, Harvard University. Robert W. Smith was a valued colleague on the Marshall Papers staff from September 1994 to September 1997. His research contributed significantly to the making of this volume.

Without the support of our sponsors, the College of William and Mary and the Omohundro Institute of Early American History and Culture, this edition would not be possible. In addition to the college's generous financial and in-kind assistance, the project benefits from the Institute's prestigious book publishing program. Fredrika J. Teute and Gilbert Kelly of the publications staff offered helpful editorial suggestions. The National Endowment for the Humanities provided major funding for the preparation of this volume. The National Historical Publications and Records Commission, the Robert G. Cabell III and Maude Morgan Cabell Foundation, the William Nelson Cromwell Foundation, and the Earhart Foundation also supplied timely assistance.

The Plan of the Volume
and
Editorial Policy

Volume X is composed of 177 documents published in full and another 73 that are either calendared or listed. Most of the documents fall into two broad categories, correspondence and judicial papers. Documents that do not belong to either of these classifications include two speeches, two interviews, two legal pleadings, and the author's preface to *A History of the Colonies.* Together, these documents record Marshall's public and private activities from January 1824 through March 1827.

CORRESPONDENCE

Large portions of Marshall's correspondence have been lost or destroyed. What survives does not form a continuous record and consists overwhelmingly of letters Marshall wrote to others. Of a total of 150 letters published in full in Volume X, 110 are from Marshall to various recipients. Fifteen are to Bushrod Washington, his most frequent correspondent. Other multiple correspondents include Joseph Hopkinson and Timothy Pickering. Fifteen letters are addressed to family members, including 8 to Mary W. Marshall ("Polly").

JUDICIAL PAPERS

Over the course of his long judicial tenure, Marshall delivered nearly 700 reported opinions in the Supreme Court and in the U.S. Circuit Courts for Virginia and North Carolina. From 1801 on, judicial opinions constitute an ever-increasing proportion of the documentary record of his career. The editors have adopted the following policy with respect to this voluminous material.

This edition is not a documentary history of the Supreme Court from 1801 to 1835. Nor does its scope entail reproducing all 550 opinions Marshall delivered on the Supreme Court, the full texts of which are accessible in the official *United States Reports.* The original drafts of the great majority of his opinions have not survived, and their loss precludes rendering more accurately the texts that we now have. Only 88 of Marshall's manuscript opinions (16 percent of the total) are extant, most of them dating from his last years in office. (For a fuller description of the sources documenting Marshall's Supreme Court career, see the *Papers of John Marshall,* VI, 69-73.) Yet an edition of Marshall's papers cannot omit altogether such a large and important group of documents. As a workable compromise between total inclusion and total exclusion, this edition is publishing in full most of the constitutional opinions (about 30) and a small but representative selection of nonconstitutional opinions. It also presents calendar entries for all the opinions given by the chief justice during the years covered by a volume. (See Appendix I for a list of the opinions from 1824 through 1827.)

Selecting from the huge mass of nonconstitutional opinions presents an editorial problem that admits of no fully satisfactory solution. Even eliminating many relatively insignificant cases that were disposed of in a brief opinion still leaves a sizable body of judicial literature. From this corpus the editors have attempted to provide a sampling of Marshall's jurisprudence in the several fields that occupied the major share of the Court's attention, including procedure, real property, contracts and commercial law, admiralty, and international law. With this general purpose in mind, they have flexibly applied several other criteria to shorten the list of potential choices. Priority is given to opinions that illuminate Marshall's broader views on politics, society, and economy; that reflect an important public issue or policy of the time; and that can be amply documented from the official case file and other sources, especially if the supplementary materials provide new information about the case not found in the printed report. Another important consideration is the availability of the original manuscript opinion, though this criterion will not often come into play until the last seven years of Marshall's chief justiceship. There is an unavoidable element of arbitrariness in the selection process. For every opinion chosen for inclusion, many others could equally suffice as examples of the chief justice's style, mode of reasoning, and learning in a particular field of law.

Although publishing in full only a small fraction of the Supreme Court opinions, this edition presents complete texts of all extant opinions given in the U.S. Circuit Courts for Virginia and North Carolina. Marshall spent much the greater part of his judicial life on circuit, yet this side of his career is relatively unknown, and the documents are less accessible. His circuit court papers include more than 60 autograph opinions delivered in the Virginia court. The one previous edition of Marshall's circuit opinions, prepared by John W. Brockenbrough in 1837, is extremely rare. Although Brockenbrough's reports have been reprinted in *Federal Cases*, the alphabetical arrangement of that work scatters Marshall's opinions over many volumes. Brockenbrough also took certain liberties with Marshall's drafts, regularizing his spelling and punctuation, for example, and occasionally improving what he regarded as infelicitous phrasing. The editors believe that bringing these opinions together and presenting texts that more faithfully adhere to the original drafts serve a sound documentary purpose. By comparison with the Virginia materials, judicial papers from the North Carolina court are scanty—no manuscript opinions and only a handful of published reports of cases. (Marshall's circuit court papers are described at greater length in the *Papers of John Marshall,* VI, 126-29, 142-44.)

Eight Supreme Court opinions are published in the main body of Volume X, 6 of which belong to the category of constitutional law. The volume presents 12 circuit opinions, 11 given in the U.S. Circuit Court for Virginia and 1 in the U.S. Circuit Court for North Carolina.

OMITTED PAPERS

As a general editorial policy, dinner invitations and routine documents arising from Marshall's financial transactions — bills of exchange, promissory notes, bank drafts, and the like — are omitted entirely, though they may be referred to in the annotation. The same holds true for land deeds, even though in previous volumes these have been calendared and sometimes printed in full.

Editorial Apparatus

Editorial Method

The editors have applied modern historical editing standards in rendering the texts of documents. Transcriptions are as accurate as possible and reflect format and usage as nearly as is feasible, with the following exceptions. The first letter of a sentence is capitalized, and redundant or confusing punctuation has been eliminated. Superscript letters have been brought down to the line. Words abbreviated by a tilde ($\sim$) have not been expanded, but the tilde has been omitted and a period added. Layout and typography attempt to replicate the appearance of the originals. The location of the dateline in letters, however, has been standardized, placed on the first line of the letter, flush to the right margin. The salutation has been set flush to the left margin. The complimentary closing has been run into the last paragraph of letters. Signatures, regardless of whether they are autograph, have been set in large and small capital letters and indented one space from the right margin. Other names at the foot of a document (for example, those of witnesses, sureties, and pledges) are rendered in the same distinctive type as signatures and are placed approximately where they appear in the originals.

Obvious slips of the pen, usually repeated words, have been silently corrected, as have typographical errors in printed sources. Words or parts of words illegible or missing because of mutilation are enclosed in angle brackets; letters or punctuation added by the editors for clarity's sake are set off by square brackets. If the editors are uncertain about their rendition, the words are enclosed within brackets followed by a question mark. If a portion of the manuscript is missing, the lacuna is shown by ellipsis points within angle brackets. Undecipherable words or phrases are indicated by the word "illegible" set in italics within angle brackets.

This volume follows the format first adopted in Volume V. Footnotes follow immediately at the end of the document, and identification of the source occurs in an unnumbered provenance note (referred to as "n." in cross-references) preceding the first numbered footnote. This note also supplies information on other copies, endorsements, dating, description, or peculiarities of the original. The provenance contains a full citation for the source of each document, except that the symbols listed in the Library of Congress's *Symbols of American Libraries* (14th ed.; Washington, D.C., 1992) are used throughout. Elsewhere the editors have employed abbreviated titles for the most frequently cited public collections of manuscripts and secondary sources. These appear below in the lists of symbols and short titles. For other publications, a full citation is given the first time a source is cited in a document.

For books, periodicals, and articles, the editors follow the style of citation used in standard academic history. Reports of cases, however, are
given in legal citation form. The name of the case is followed by the
volume number and abbreviated title (usually the reporter's last name);
the page number on which the case begins; and, if needed, the court and
year within parentheses. For the old English cases, the volume number
and page of the reprint of the case in the *English Reports* (abbreviated
"Eng. Rep.") are also given. Full titles of all reports cited in this volume
are provided in the short-title list. References to statutes also follow the
historical style. In citing English statutes, the editors use the standard
abbreviated form giving the regnal year, chapter and section (if appropriate), and year of enactment (if not otherwise indicated), e.g., 13 Edw. I,
c. 31 (1285); 4 and 5 Anne, c. 3, sec. 12 (1705).

Annotation consists of footnotes to documents, occasional editorial
notes preceding a document or group of documents, and short contextual notes preceding Marshall's court opinions. The guiding principle
is to supply enough information and explanation to make the document
intelligible to the general reader. The editors prefer to let the documents
speak for themselves as much as possible. This laissez-faire policy is more
easily followed in the case of personal correspondence. Legal materials
by nature require denser annotation. Without presuming any knowledge
of law on the reader's part, the editors attempt to strike a balance between too little and too much commentary.

The provenance note is followed, if needed, by one or more numbered
footnotes that address matters arising immediately from the document:
identifications of persons, places, technical words and phrases, statutes,
authorities, cases, pamphlets, newspaper articles, and the like. If the information is available in a standard reference or secondary work, the
note is brief, often no more than a citation to that source. Three standard
reference works are not cited: *Dictionary of American Biography, Dictionary
of National Biography,* and *Biographical Directory of Congress.* If the source is a
manuscript collection or archival record group that is relatively inaccessi-
ble, the information derived from it is reported in greater detail. Cross-
references to other documents or notes in the same volume are kept to a
minimum, relying on the index to bring them all together. Editorial
notes provide more extensive information or interpretation than can be
conveniently included in footnotes. They serve to introduce documents
of unusual significance or important subjects or episodes that are reflected in a number of documents. In Volume VII the editors adopted the
practice of supplying brief contextual notes to introduce court opinions.
Unlike editorial notes, these notes are concerned only with setting the
immediate context of the opinion to follow. They typically provide the
full names of the parties, the essential facts of the dispute (including, in
the case of Supreme Court appellate opinions, the history of the case in

the lower federal court or in the state court), and the particular point or motion addressed by the opinion.

Textual Notes

Marshall's manuscript drafts of judicial opinions receive special editorial treatment. With these documents, Marshall's intent as author takes on additional importance, for he meant them to be officially promulgated. In his opinions, Marshall made many deletions and insertions, which reveal his thought process at work; his choice of words and redrafting of phrases show a careful consideration of meaning. The final result was what he intended the public to hear, and, in keeping with that object, the editors have followed their standard rules of transcription and editorial method in presenting nearly clear texts of these documents as the main entries. In order to provide an inclusive list of Marshall's alterations in the manuscript, however, they have appended a set of textual notes, following the annotation, to each of these autograph opinions and drafts. By this means, a genetic text can be reconstructed, and a complete record of Marshall's revisions is preserved.

Marshall made changes in his text in a variety of ways: he struck through words, erased them, wrote over them, added words above the line, or indicated by means of a superscript symbol an addition to be inserted from the margin or a separate sheet. In recording Marshall's alterations, the editors have not distinguished among his various modes of deleting words, or between words inserted above the line as opposed to altered on the line. Marshall made many of his changes on the line, indicating that he amended as he was writing. The editors believe that the alterations were part of his process of refining his opinions and that he incorporated them into his final statement from the bench. He apparently did not go back later and revise his opinion as delivered orally in court.

Deletions are indicated by canceled type (~~ease~~), and insertions are surrounded by up and down arrows (↑court↓). Deleted punctuation will appear below the strike-through rule (~~, appeal~~). Illegible erasures or deletions are denoted by "*erasure*" within square brackets. Uncertain renderings are followed by a question mark within square brackets. Insertions within insertions are not indicated, but deletions within insertions are. Insertions within a deletion appear in canceled type and are set off by arrows.

Characteristically, in changing a preposition, article, indefinite pronoun, or verb ending, Marshall wrote over the end of the existing word to alter it to a new form. For instance, he transformed "that" to "this" by writing "is" over "at" and "on" to "in" by writing "i" over "o." Rather than placing internal marks within words to replicate Marshall's process of altering them, the editors have represented the change in substance by entering complete words. Canceled type shows his first version; up and down arrows indicate his substitution. Thus, a change from "that" to "this" will appear in the text notes as ~~that~~ ↑this↓, rather than ~~that~~ ↑is↓. Although this method sacrifices the exact recording of how Marshall entered a change, it does make clear the alteration of the content of what he wished to say. Marshall's intentions are not always self-evident; irregularities in pen, ink, and manuscript preclude certainty in some instances. Sometimes it is not possible to know whether he added or erased a word, or whether he had crowded words on a line or blotted a drop of ink. Where Marshall inadvertently repeated a word or words, the repetition is left out in the main text but is recorded verbatim in the textual notes.

All deletions and insertions, as the editors have been best able to determine from appearance and context of the manuscript, are listed by paragraph and line numbers of the printed document. (Paragraph numbers appear in the margin of the main text to facilitate use.) A word or two before and after the alteration is included to aid the reader in finding the phrase and following the change. The succeeding designations indicate alterations made in places other than in the middle of the text: "Title," in the title of an opinion; "mar.," in a marginal note; "footnote," in a note at the bottom of the manuscript page; "beg.," at the beginning of a paragraph before the first word of the main text. To avoid confusion, footnote numbers in the document have been dropped from words appearing in the textual notes.

Descriptive Symbols

AD	Autograph Document
ADf	Autograph Draft
ADS	Autograph Document Signed
ALS	Autograph Letter Signed
Df	Draft
DS	Document Signed
JM	John Marshall
LS	Letter Signed
MS	Manuscript
Tr	Transcript

All documents in an author's hand are designated as autograph items (e.g., ALS). If the attribution of autograph is conjectural, a question mark within parentheses follows the designation. Documents can be in the hand of someone else but signed by persons under whose names they are written (e.g., DS). If the signature has been cropped or obliterated, the "S" appears within square brackets (e.g., AL[S]). Copies are contemporary replications of documents; if they are made by the author, the type of document will be indicated by one of the above symbols followed by "copy" or "letterbook copy" within parentheses. For instance, an unsigned copy of a letter retained by the writer will be described as AL (copy). Transcripts are transcribed versions of documents made at a later time by someone other than the author.

Location Symbols

CoCCC	Colorado College, Colorado Springs, Colo.
Ct	Connecticut State Library, Hartford, Conn.
DLC	Library of Congress, Washington, D.C.
DNA	National Archives, Washington, D.C.
GEpFRC	Federal Records Center, East Point, Ga.
Ia-HA	Iowa State Department of History and Archives, Des Moines, Iowa
ICABF	American Bar Foundation, Chicago, Ill.
ICHi	Chicago Historical Society, Chicago, Ill.
ICU	University of Chicago, Chicago, Ill.
KHi	Kansas State Historical Society, Topeka, Kans.
MB	Boston Public Library, Boston, Mass.
MeB	Bowdoin College, Brunswick, Maine
MH	Harvard University, Cambridge, Mass.
MH-L	Harvard University, Law School, Cambridge, Mass.
MHi	Massachusetts Historical Society, Boston, Mass.
MiU-C	University of Michigan, Clements Library, Ann Arbor, Mich.
MoSW	Washington University, St. Louis, Mo.
NcD	Duke University, Durham, N.C.
NcU	University of North Carolina, Chapel Hill, N.C.
NhHi	New Hampshire State Historical Society, Concord, N.H.
N	New York State Library, Albany, N.Y.
NHi	New-York Historical Society, New York, N.Y.
NIC	Cornell University, Ithaca, N.Y.
NjP	Princeton University, Princeton, N.J.
NjMoHiP	Morristown National Historical Park, Morristown, N.J.
NjR	Rutgers University, New Brunswick, N.J.
NN	New York Public Library, New York, N.Y.
NNC	Columbia University, New York, N.Y.
NNPM	Pierpont Morgan Library, New York, N.Y.
NRU	University of Rochester, Rochester, N.Y.
OHi	Ohio Historical Society, Columbus, Ohio
PHi	Historical Society of Pennsylvania, Philadelphia, Pa.
PP	Free Library of Philadelphia, Philadelphia, Pa.
PPAmP	American Philosophical Society, Philadelphia, Pa.

TxU   University of Texas, Austin, Tex.
Vi   Library of Virginia, Richmond, Va.
ViHi   Virginia Historical Society, Richmond, Va.
ViU   University of Virginia, Charlottesville, Va.
ViW   College of William and Mary, Williamsburg, Va.

Record Groups in the National Archives

RG 15   Records of the Veterans Administration
RG 21   Records of the District Courts of the United States
RG 45   Naval Records Collection of the Office of Naval Records
           and Library
RG 59   General Records of the Department of State
RG 77   Records of the Office of the Chief of Engineers
RG 94   Records of the Adjutant General's Office, 1780's–1917
RG 267   Records of the Supreme Court of the United States

Abbreviations for Court and Other Records

App. Cas.   Appellate Case
                       RG 267, National Archives

U.S. Circ. Ct., N.C.   U.S. Circuit Court, N.C.
   Min. Bk.   Minute Book
                       RG 21, National Archives

U.S. Circ. Ct., Va.   U.S. Circuit Court, Va.
   Ord. Bk.   Order Book
   Rec. Bk.   Record Book
                       Library of Virginia

U.S. Dist. Ct., Va.   U.S. District Court, Va.
   Ord. Bk.   Order Book
                       Library of Virginia

U.S. Sup. Ct.   U.S. Supreme Court
   Minutes   Minutes
   Dockets   Dockets
                       RG 267, National Archives

Va. Ct. App. Ord. Bk. Virginia Court of Appeals Order Books
                       Library of Virginia

After the first citation of legal papers in a case, the court reference is omitted, and the suit record is designated simply by the names of plaintiff v. defendant. The exception is the provenance note, where complete depository information will be given for the document printed.

Abbreviations for English Courts

Ch.   Chancery
C.P.   Common Pleas
Crown   Crown Cases
Ex.   Exchequer
K.B.   King's Bench
N.P.   Nisi Prius
P.C.   Privy Council

Short Titles

Acton
   Thomas Harman Acton, *Reports of Cases Argued and Determined before the Most Noble and Right Honorable the Lords Commissioners of Appeals in Prize Causes* (2 vols.; London, 1811–19).
Amb.
   Charles Ambler, *Reports of Cases Argued and Determined in the High Court of Chancery, with Some Few in Other Courts* (Dublin, 1790).
Anst.
   Alexander Anstruther, *Reports of Cases Argued and Determined in the Court of Exchequer* (3 vols.; London, 1796–97).
ASP
   American State Papers. Documents, Legislative and Executive, of the Congress of the United States . . . (38 vols.; Washington, D.C., 1832–61).
Atk.
   John Tracy Atkyns, *Reports of Cases Argued and Determined in the High Court of Chancery, in the Time of Lord Chancellor Hardwicke* (3d ed.; London, 1794).
Bacon, *Abridgment*
   Matthew Bacon, *A New Abridgment of the Law* (1st Am. ed. from 6th London ed.; 7 vols.; Philadelphia, 1811).
Barn. C.
   Thomas Barnardiston, *Reports of Cases Determined in the High Court of Chancery* (London, 1742).
Barn. & Cress.
   Richard V. Barnewall and Robert N. Cresswell, *Reports of Cases Ar-*

gued and Determined in the Court of King's Bench (10 vols.; London, 1823–32).

Blackstone, *Commentaries*

William Blackstone, *Commentaries on the Laws of England* (13th ed.; 4 vols.; Dublin, 1796).

Black. W.

William Blackstone, *Reports of Cases Determined in the Several Courts of Westminster Hall, from 1746 to 1779* (2 vols.; London, 1780).

Brock.

John W. Brockenbrough, *Reports of Cases Decided by the Honorable John Marshall . . . in the Circuit Court of the United States for the District of Virginia and North Carolina, from 1802 to 1833 [1836] Inclusive* (2 vols.; Philadelphia, 1837).

Bro. C.C.

William Brown, *Reports of Cases Argued and Determined in the High Court of Chancery* (4 vols.; London, 1785–94).

Call

Daniel Call, *Reports of Cases Argued and Adjudged in the Court of Appeals of Virginia* (6 vols.; Richmond, Va., 1801–33). Beginning with vol. IV, the title reads: *Reports of Cases Argued and Decided. . . .*

Cranch

William Cranch, *Reports of Cases Argued and Adjudged in the Supreme Court of the United States (1801–15)* (9 vols.; New York and Washington, D.C., 1804–17).

Conn.

Connecticut, *Reports of Cases, Argued and Determined in the Supreme Court of Errors of the State of Connecticut* (21 vols.; Hartford, Conn., 1814–1852).

Cowp.

Henry Cowper, *Reports of Cases Adjudged in the Court of King's Bench: from . . . 1774, to . . . 1778 . . .* (London, 1783).

Cox

Samuel Compton Cox, *Cases Determined in the Courts of Equity from 1783 to 1796, . . .* (2 vols. in 1; London, 1816).

Desaus.

Henry William Desaussure, *Reports of Cases Argued and Determined in the Court of Chancery of the State of South Carolina* (3 vols.; Columbia, S.C., 1817).

Dods.

John Dodson, *Reports of Cases Argued and Determined in the High Court of Admiralty: Commencing with the Judgments of Sir William Scott* (2 vols.; London, 1815–28).

East

Edward Hyde East, *Reports of Cases Argued and Determined in the Court of King's Bench* (16 vols.; London, 1801–14).

Eq. Ca. Abr.
> *General Abridgment of Cases in Equity Argued and Adjudged in the High Court of Chancery* . . . (2 vols.; London, 1732–56).

Eng. Rep.
> *The English Reports* (176 vols.; reprint of all the early English reporters).

Hening, *Statutes*
> William Waller Hening, ed., *The Statutes at Large; Being a Collection of All the Laws of Virginia, from the First Session of the Legislature* . . . (13 vols.; 1819–23; Charlottesville, Va., 1969 reprint: vols. I–IV from 2d ed.; vols. V–XIII from 1st ed.).

Johns.
> William Johnson, *Reports of Cases Argued and Determined in the Supreme Court of Judicature and in the Court for the Trial of Impeachments and the Correction of Errors in the State of New-York* (20 vols.; Albany, N.Y., 1793–1823).

Johns. Ch.
> William Johnson, *Reports of Cases Adjudged in the Court of Chancery of New York* (4 vols.; Albany, N.Y., 1816–21).

Leach
> Thomas Leach, *Cases in Crown Law* (4th ed.; 2 vols.; London, 1815).

Leigh
> Benjamin Watkins Leigh, *Reports of Cases Argued and Determined in the Court of Appeals* (12 vols.; Richmond, Va., 1830–44).

Mass.
> Massachusetts, *Reports of Cases Argued and Determined in the Supreme Judicial Court of the Commonwealth of Massachusetts* (100 vols.; Boston, 1837–78).

Mer.
> John Herman Merivale, *Reports of Cases Argued and Determined in the High Court of Chancery* (3 vols.; London, 1818).

Mod.
> Thomas Leach, *Modern Reports; or, Select Cases Adjudged in the Courts of King's Bench, Chancery, Common Pleas, and Exchequer* (5th ed.; 12 vols.; London, 1793–96).

Mos.
> William Mosely, *Reports of Cases Argued and Determined in the High Court of Chancery: During the Time of Lord Chancellor King* (London, 1803).

Munf.
> William Munford, *Reports of Cases Argued and Determined in the Supreme Court of Appeals of Virginia* (6 vols.; New York, Philadelphia, Fredericksburg, Richmond, 1812–21).

Nels.
> William Nelson, *Reports of Special Cases Argued and Decreed in the Court of Chancery* (London, 1717).

Paxton, *Marshall Family*
> W. M. Paxton, *The Marshall Family* . . . (1885; Baltimore, 1970 reprint).

Pet.
> Richard Peters, Jr., *Reports of Cases Argued in the Supreme Court of the United States (1828–42)* (16 vols.; Philadelphia, 1828–[45]).

Pick.
> Octavius Pickering, *Reports of Cases Argued and Determined in the Supreme Judicial Court of Massachusetts* (24 vols.; Boston, 1824–42).

PJM
> Herbert A. Johnson et al., eds., *The Papers of John Marshall* (10 vols. to date; Chapel Hill, N.C., 1974–).

Prec. Ch.
> *Precedents in Chancery: Being Cases Argued and Adjudged in the High Court of Chancery . . . from 1689–1722* (2d ed.; London, 1750).

P. Wms.
> William Peere Williams, *Reports of Cases Argued and Determined in the High Court of Chancery, and of Some Special Cases Adjudged in the Court of King's Bench* (2 vols.; London, 1740–49).

Rand.
> Peyton Randolph, *Reports of Cases Argued and Determined in the Supreme Court of Appeals of Virginia* (6 vols.; Richmond, Va., 1823–29).

Raym. Ld.
> Robert Raymond, *Reports of Cases Argued and Adjudged in the Courts of King's Bench and Common Pleas . . .* (3 vols.; London, 1743–90).

Revised Code of Va.
> *The Revised Code of the Laws of Virginia . . .* (2 vols.; Richmond, Va., 1819).

Richmond Portraits
> *Richmond Portraits in an Exhibition of Makers of Richmond, 1737–1860* (Richmond, Va., 1949).

S and R
> Thomas Sergeant and William Rawle, *Reports of Cases Adjudged in the Sup. Ct. of Pennsylvania, 1814–1828* (17 vols.; Philadelphia, 1818–29).

Salk.
> William Salkeld, *Reports of Cases in the Court of King's Bench with Some Special Cases in the Courts of Chancery, Common Pleas and Exchequer . . .* (3 vols.; London, 1717–24).

Story, *Life and Letters*
> William W. Story, ed., *Life and Letters of Joseph Story . . .* (2 vols.; Boston, 1852).

Str.
> John Strange, *Reports of Adjudged Cases in the Courts of Chancery, King's Bench, Common Pleas and Exchequer* (2 vols.; London, 1755).

Taunt.

William Pyle Taunton, *Reports of Cases Argued and Determined in the Court of Common Pleas* (8 vols.; London, 1814–23).

T.R.

Charles Durnford and Edward Hyde East, *Term Reports in the Court of King's Bench* (8 vols.; London, 1787–1800).

Tucker, *Blackstone's Commentaries*

St. George Tucker, *Blackstone's Commentaries: With Notes of Reference, to the Constitution and Laws, of the Federal Government of the United States; and of the Commonwealth of Virginia* (5 vols.; Philadelphia, 1803).

U.S. *Statutes at Large*

The Public Statutes at Large of the United States of America, 1789–1873 (17 vols.; Boston, 1845–73).

Vent.

Peyton Ventris, *The Reports of Sir Peyton Ventris, Kt., Late One of the Justices of Common Pleas: In Two Parts* (4th ed.; 2 vols. in 1; London, 1726).

Vern.

Thomas Vernon, *Cases Argued and Adjudged in the High Court of Chancery* (2 vols.; London, 1726–28).

Ves. sen.

Francis Vesey, *Cases Argued and Determined, in the High Court of Chancery, in the time of Lord Chancellor Hardwicke, from the Year 1746–7, to 1755* (2 vols.; London, 1771).

Ves. jun. or Ves. (after vol. II)

Francis Vesey, Jr., *Reports of Cases Argued and Determined in the High Court of Chancery* . . . (20 vols.; London, 1795–1822).

Ves. & Bea.

Francis Vesey, Jr., and John Beames, *Reports of Cases Argued and Determined in the High Court of Chancery, in the Time of Lord Chancellor Eldon* . . . (2d ed.; 3 vols.; London, 1818).

VMHB

Virginia Magazine of History and Biography.

Warren, *Supreme Court*

Charles Warren, *The Supreme Court in United States History* (2 vols.; Cambridge, Mass., 1926).

Wash.

Bushrod Washington, *Reports of Cases Argued and Determined in the Court of Appeals of Virginia* (2 vols.; Richmond, Va., 1798–99).

Wheat.

Henry Wheaton, *Reports of Cases Argued and Adjudged in the Supreme Court (1816–27)* (12 vols.; Philadelphia, 1816–27).

Wils. K.B.

George Wilson, *Reports of Cases Argued and Adjudged in the King's Courts at Westminster* (2 vols.; London, 1770–75).

Wms. Saund.
>Edmund Saunders, *The Reports of the Most Learned Sir Edmund Saunders, . . . of Several Pleadings and Cases in the Court of King's Bench* (1st Am. ed., with notes and references to the pleadings and cases by John Williams; 2 vols.; London, 1807).

MARSHALL CHRONOLOGY

2 February 1824–28 March 1827

1824

2 February–24 March	At Washington, attends Supreme Court.
19 February	Dislocates shoulder in fall (absent from court until 2 March).
2 March	Delivers opinion in *Gibbons* v. *Ogden.*
19 March	Delivers opinion in *Osborn* v. *Bank of the United States.*
Ca. 4 May	Returns to Richmond after visit to Fauquier.
12–13 May	At Raleigh, attends U.S. Circuit Court.
24 May–28 June	At Richmond, attends U.S. Circuit Court.
17–20 October	At Williamsburg and Yorktown for Lafayette's visit.
27 October	At Richmond, gives speech in honor of Lafayette's visit.
12–13 November	At Raleigh, attends U.S. Circuit Court.
22 November–16 December	At Richmond, attends U.S. Circuit Court.

1825

7 February–21 March	At Washington, attends Supreme Court.
13 April	Leaves Richmond for visit to Fauquier.
Ca. 1 May	Returns to Richmond.
12–13 May	At Raleigh, attends U.S. Circuit Court.
23 May–22 June	At Richmond, attends U.S. Circuit Court.
23 August	At Warrenton (Fauquier County), gives speech during Lafayette's visit.
26 August	At Oak Hill, Fauquier County .
12–14 November	At Raleigh, attends U.S. Circuit Court.
22 November–15 December	At Richmond, attends U.S. Circuit Court.

1826

6 February–21 March	At Washington, attends Supreme Court.

1 April	At Richmond, visited by Jared Sparks.
9 May	At Monroe, N.C., meets with Jared Sparks.
12–13 May	At Raleigh, attends U.S. Circuit Court.
22 May–8 June	At Richmond, attends U.S. Circuit Court.
24 August	In Fauquier County.
13–17 November	At Raleigh, attends U.S. Circuit Court.
22 November–23 December	At Richmond, attends U.S. Circuit Court.

1827

8 January–16 March	At Washington, attends Supreme Court.
19 February	Delivers dissenting opinion in *Ogden* v. *Saunders.*
12 March	Delivers opinion in *Brown* v. *Maryland.*
28 March	At Richmond.

CORRESPONDENCE, PAPERS,

AND

SELECTED JUDICIAL OPINIONS

January 1824–March 1827

To Don Pablo Chacon

Sir   Richmond Jany. 9th. 1824

On receiving your letter[1] enclosing an application for a writ of habeas corpus for the liberation of two Spaniards said to be held in confinement by Captain Warrington I mentioned the subject to Mr. Stannard who informed me that the Secretary of the Navy had determined to discharge them.[2] He added that lest any delay should take place he would write immediately to remind the secretary of his purpose. I have therefore no doubt but that these persons will be discharged sooner than they could be if brought before me; and that it will be desirable to them to avoid an useless voyage to Richmond. Should any circumstance prevent their discharge the writ will of course be awarded.[3] Very respectfully, I am Sir, your obedt

J MARSHALL

ALS, ViHi. Addressed to Chacon, "Consul of his Catholic Majesty," in Norfolk; postmarked Richmond, 10 Jan. Endorsed.

1. Letter not found. Don Pablo Chacon was the Spanish consul at Norfolk.

2. The enclosed petition was on behalf of Pedro Castro and Ysidro Romero, Spanish subjects, who were then confined to prison at the Gosport navy yard on suspicion of piracy. Their petition set forth that sometime in 1822 they had been captured within one hundred yards of the coast of Cuba by crewmen of the U.S. schooner *Shark* and brought to Norfolk, where they had been imprisoned for about fourteen months. Capt. Lewis Warrington was the commandant of the navy yard (petition, 5 Jan. 1824, Papers of the Spanish Consulate at Norfolk, ViHi).

3. Secretary of the Navy Samuel L. Southard (1787–1842) issued an order for the prisoners' release on 12 Jan. 1824 (Lewis Warrington to Chacon, 17 Jan. 1824; Southard to Chacon, 19 Jan. 1824, ibid.).

To James Monroe

Sir   Washington Feb. 4, 1824

The sentiments you were pleased to express at the commencement of this term have led us to believe that an application on the subject of a library would not be received unfavourably.[1]

Law is well known to be a system of rules drawn from many sources; and the strongest reasoning powers will not enable an individual to apply them in a manner that will be satisfactory to the public, and especially to that intelligent profession which is intermixed with the whole community, has great influence on its judgement, and is intimately connected with the jurisprudence of the country, unless he has access to those precedents which contain the reasonings and decisions of the wise whose opinions the world respects, as well as to those legislative acts which, in many cases, constitute the rule by which he is to be governed.

The cases brought before the supreme court are frequently of such a character as to require extensive researc⟨h.⟩ In addition to those duties which are common to all cour⟨ts⟩ the Judges of the United States have some to perform whi⟨ch⟩ are peculiar to themselves. Not only is common law, equ⟨ity⟩ and admiralty jurisdiction united in them; but, in the exe⟨r⟩cise of that jurisdiction they are frequently compelled t⟨o⟩ refer to the laws, usages, and decisions of the several states. The difficulty of obtaining this information in a form to command confidence has more than once delay⟨ed⟩ the business of the court to the great injury of the suitors, and has often embarassed the Judges. It would very much promote the administration of justice, if a public library could be procured which, among other valuable books, should contain the laws of all the states, and the reports of the cases decided in their several courts. We shall not, we trust be considered by you as assuming too much if we suggest that an appropriation of about $3000 — in the first instance aided by small annual appropriations afterwards, might furnish such a law library as would, in addition to the law books now in possession of the government, in a great measure remove the difficulties which have heretofore embarassed the Judges of the supreme court in the performance of their duties. With the utmost respect we remain Sir, Your Obedt. Servts.

J MARSHALL
BUSH. WASHINGTON
WILLM JOHNSON
THOMAS TODD
G DUVALL.
JOSEPH STORY
SMITH THOMPSON

ALS, RG 59, DNA. Addressed to the president. Endorsed by Monroe "The Judges." Another endorsement in unknown hand.

1. Congress did not create a law library for the Supreme Court until 1832; previous attempts in 1816, 1826 and 1830 failed (Edward G. Hudon, "The Library Facilities of the Supreme Court of the United States: A Historical Study," *University of Detroit Law Journal,* 34 [1956], 193–94).

To Mary W. Marshall

My dearest Polly   Washington Feby. 23d. 1824

I was made extremely uneasy to day by being informed that you had heard of my fall before my letter reached you and had supposed me to be hurt much worse than I was in reality.[1] I had hoped that my letter would be the first communication you would receive on the subject.

I have been disappointed in being kept longer from court than I expected. Old men I find do not get over sprains and hurts quite as quickly as young ones. Although I feel no pain when perfectly still, yet I cannot get up and move about without difficulty, & cannot put on my coat. Of course I cannot go to court. I believe confidently however that I shall go the beginning of next week. Altho I do not get well as immediately as I expected myself, the doctors say I mend a great deal faster than they expected. Everything is certainly in the best possible train. The swelling has gone entirely down, and I have not the slightest appearance of fever.

I have been treated with a degree of kindness and attention which is very flattering. All my friends have called to see me. The President himself has visited me and has expressed his wish to serve me in any manner that may be in his power. I have however in reserve a still higher compliment which would very much surprize you and all others who know me. All the Ladies of the Secretaries have called on me, some more than once, and have brought me more jelly than I can eat, and have offered me a great many good things. I thank them but stick to my barly broth.

Notwithstanding these attentions I have a plenty of time on my hands in the night as well as in the day. How do you think I beguile it? I am almost tempted to leave you to guess till I write again. But as I suppose you will have rather more curiosity in my absence than you usually show to hear my stories when I am present, I will tell you without waiting to be asked. You must know then that I begin with the ball at York, and with the dinner on the fish at your house the next day: I then retrace my visit to York, our splendid assembly at the Palace in Williamsburg, my visit to Richmond where I acted Pa for a fortnight, my return the ensuing fall and the very welcome reception you gave me on your arrival from Dover, our little tiffs & makings up, my feelings while Major Dick[2] was courting You, my trip to the cottage,[3] the lock of hair, my visit again to Richmond the ensuing fall, and all the thousand indescribable but deeply affecting instances of your affection or coldness which constituted for a time th⟨e⟩ happiness or misery of my life and will alway⟨s⟩ be recollected with a degree of interest which can never be lost while recollection remains.[4]

Thus is it that I find amusement for those hours which I pass without company or books.

Farewell my dearest Polly. I beg you beleive that tho confined I am free from pain & shall soon be free from confinement. Yours ever

J MARSHALL

ALS, Marshall Papers, ViW. Addressed to Mrs. Marshall in Richmond; postmarked Washington, 25 Feb.

1. Returning to his lodgings on the evening of 19 Feb., JM stumbled over a cellar door. He dislocated his shoulder, suffered a concussion, and was unconscious for fifteen minutes. After recuperating for two weeks, the chief justice was able to return to court on 2 Mar. with his arm in a sling (Joseph Story to Sarah W. Story, 19, 22 Feb., 6 Mar. 1824, Joseph Story Papers, TxU; Warren, *Supreme Court,* I, 608 and n. 1).

2. Maj. Alexander Dick, an officer of the Va. Continental Line during the Revolution.

3. The Cottage was the residence of John Ambler in Hanover County, where JM and Polly were married in 1783.

4. JM's first attempt to court Polly was unsuccessful, but cousin John Ambler intervened by sending the disappointed lover a lock of her hair. JM, thinking that Polly herself had sent the lock, renewed his suit. For the story, as related by Edward C. Marshall, see Sallie E. Marshall Hardy, "John Marshall, Third Chief Justice of the United States, As Son, Brother, Husband and Friend," *The Green Bag*, VIII (1896), 481. The lock is now on display at the Marshall House in Richmond.

To Henry Jackson

Sir   Washington Feby.   1824

I have just received your letter of the 28th. of January, and should feel real pleasure in giving Mrs. Jackson all the information she wishes were it in my power to do so.[1]

I was connected with Mr. Rootes by marriage, had a real regard for him and his family, and con⟨ti⟩nued in habits of friendship with him to the time of his death.[2] For several years however I have seldom seen him. He removed to a part of the country which I never visit and the situation of my own family ha⟨s⟩ withdrawn me so much from society, that I know but little of what is passing even among my friends. I knew generally that Mr. Rootes was much embarassed, but had no particular knowledge of the true state of his affairs. He was in possession of a large and valuable estate, and I supposed him to be much more than able to meet all his engagements. While entertaining this opinion I was surprized and grieved to hear that his estate was sold and that he had himself taken the oath of an insolvent debtor. Mr. Tabb a gentleman of character and fortune who was married to the daughter of Mrs. Rootes by a former husband, became the purchaser at a price supposed to be below the full value of the land; but he was the highest bidder at a sale made under a deed of trust.

Whether this purchase was entirely for the benefit of Mr. Tabb, or with an understanding that there should be any resulting trust to Mr. Rootes, is a matter on which I have no information. I never saw Mr. Rootes after the sale, and his death soon followed his insolvency. I left Richmond for this place within a very few days after hearing of his death, and have no means of knowing whether it may be practicable to save any thing from the wreck of his once valuable esta⟨te⟩. Our law directs it to be sold by the sheriff, and I fear, tho⟨u⟩gh I have no means at present of speaking with any confidence on the subject, that the whole will be absorbed by his debts.

After my retu⟨rn⟩ to Richmond, it may be in my power to obtain farther information respecting ⟨the⟩ affairs of Mr. Rootes; and if my enquiries should result in any thing which may be advantageous to Mrs. Jackson, I shall make a point of communicating it. I cannot howe⟨v⟩er conceal my fears that the case is almost hopeless. With my co⟨m⟩pliments to Mrs. Jackson, I am Sir very respectfully, Your Obedt. Servt

J MARSHALL

ALS, Marshall Papers, NcD. Addressed to Jackson in Georgia. Endorsed by Jackson. Cover torn, partially obscuring address.

1. Letter not found. Henry Jackson (1778–1840), a native of England, obtained his medical degree at the University of Pennsylvania in 1802. After serving as secretary to William H. Crawford while the latter was minister to France (1813–15), he became a professor at the University of Georgia in Athens, where for many years he held the chair of natural sciences. In 1819 he married Martha Jaquelin Rootes Cobb (b. 1786), widow of Howell Cobb of Georgia (*VMHB*, IV [1896], 209; Louise Pecquet du Bellet, *Some Prominent Virginia Families* [1907; 4 vols. in 2; Baltimore, 1976 reprint], III, 27, 54–55).

2. Martha Jackson was the eldest child of Thomas Reade Rootes (1763–1824), who lived first at Federal Hill near Fredericksburg and then at White Marsh in Gloucester County. Mary Marshall and Rootes were related to each other as descendants of the Jaquelin family (*VMHB*, IV [1896], 208–9; Pecquet du Bellet, *Some Prominent Virginia Families*, III, 27).

Gibbons v. Ogden
Opinion and Decree
U.S. Supreme Court, 2 March 1824

EDITORIAL NOTE

Gibbons v. *Ogden* was another in a series of Marshall Court decisions dealing with the competing claims of federal power and state sovereignty. Having previously pronounced decisions concerning Congress's implied powers and the reach of federal judicial power, the Court in *Gibbons* for the first time discussed the nature and extent of one of the general government's enumerated powers, the regulation of commerce with foreign nations and "among the several States." No part of the Constitution has proved a more fertile source of national power than the commerce clause, under which Congress has enacted the federal regulatory and welfare state of the twentieth century. Although *Gibbons* has often been cited as a landmark judicial precedent for extensive national power, the principal question it raised at the time was how far an affirmative grant of power to Congress operated to abridge state power.

The case originated in legal efforts to break a monopoly on steam navigation in New York waters, which the state legislature had first granted in 1787 to the inventor John Fitch.[1] In 1798, after Fitch's death, Robert R. Livingston (1746–1813), a prominent New York politician and longtime chancellor, obtained a legislative act transferring to him Fitch's rights. Livingston subsequently entered into partnership with Robert Fulton (1765–1815) to build a steamboat, which had a successful trial run on the Hudson River in 1807. The following year the legislature extended the Livingston-Fulton monopoly for thirty years and in 1811 strengthened enforcement by providing for immediate seizure of steam vessels operating in New York waters without a license from the monopoly.

AARON OGDEN

Oil on canvas by Asher B. Durand, 1833. *Courtesy of The New-York Historical Society.*

Although efforts to expand the monopoly to the West were largely unsuccessful, in New York the Livingston-Fulton interests withstood legal and political challenges to their privileges during the years preceding the Supreme Court case. The case against the monopoly in its early proceedings rested as much on being an unconstitutional interference with Congress's power over patents as in usurping Congress's power to regulate commerce. In 1811 Livingston sought an injunction in the state chancery court against an Albany businessman who had begun to operate a steamboat line between that city and New York City. After this request was denied, Livingston appealed to the New York Court of Errors, which upheld the monopoly by granting the injunction. The case was notable for the opinion of Chief Justice James Kent (1763–1847), who maintained that Congress's power over both patents and commerce was concurrent with that of the states. He conceded that in a direct collision between state and national legislation the state must yield, but found no such conflict in this case.[2]

Instead of pressing its legal rights to the utmost, the monopoly sought to buy off competitors by offering franchises to operate steamboats in designated waters. Challenges continued to arise, however, the most serious coming from Aaron Ogden (1756–1839) of New Jersey, a Revolutionary war veteran, lawyer, and politician. After serving as governor in 1812–13, Ogden turned his attention to establishing a profitable steamboat ferry service between his home in Elizabethtown and New York City. Blocked by the Livingston group, he worked through both the New Jersey and New York legislatures in an effort to defeat the monopoly. Ultimately, he failed, and to keep his ferry line operating he paid heavily for a license from the monopoly. Having become a licensee, Ogden now found himself challenged by a fellow resident of Elizabethtown, Thomas Gibbons (1757–1826), a Georgia native who despite being a Loyalist during the Revolution had enjoyed a successful career as a politician, lawyer, and judge in that state before moving to New Jersey.

Gibbons and Ogden were originally partners in the ferry business, but relations between them broke over a series of legal and personal quarrels. At one point Gibbons challenged Ogden to a duel, but Ogden instead sued for trespass and won a judgment against Gibbons. Out of revenge Gibbons started his own ferry line between New Jersey and New York City with his steamboats *Stoudinger* and the *Bellona,* the latter piloted by future railroad magnate Cornelius Vanderbilt. In October 1818 Kent, who was now the chancellor of New York, issued a temporary injunction on Ogden's behalf against Gibbons. This was the beginning of the case that eventually came to the Supreme Court. Gibbons decided to contest the injunction by filing an answer to the bill of complaint in September 1819—in the meantime frequently ignoring the court's order by having Vanderbilt run the *Bellona* into New York City. The answer was noteworthy for asserting Gibbons's right to operate his steamboats by virtue of a license obtained under the 1793 act of Congress for enrolling and licensing vessels employed in the coasting trade.

Chancellor Kent rejected Gibbons's claim and awarded a permanent injunction. In his accompanying opinion Kent denied that the federal coasting statute granted any right that superseded the rights of property conferred by the New York laws to the Livingston-Fulton monopoly. The federal act, he said, did nothing more than designate a coasting vessel as "American," so that it would not have to pay the same tariff and tonnage duties as foreign vessels. Congress, the chancellor maintained, did not intend the act to be a regulation of interstate commerce or an interference with rights of property acquired under state laws. Again conceding the principle of federal supremacy, Kent concluded that there was no collision between the federal law and the state acts creating the monopoly. In January 1820 the New York Court of Errors affirmed Kent's decree, and Gibbons decided to appeal his case to the Supreme Court.[3]

The case was docketed as early as June 1820 and set for argument at the following term by Daniel Webster and David B. Ogden for Gibbons and Thomas A. Emmet (1764–1827) and William Pinkney for Ogden. In March 1821, however, the Supreme Court dismissed the appeal because the record failed to show that a final decree had been pronounced by the state court as provided by section 25 of the Judiciary Act.[4] The case was reinstated in time for the 1822 term, but the absence of Emmet and the death of Pinkney further postponed a hearing. The increasingly frustrated Gibbons urged his counsel to press the case, complaining that there was "something wrong in our Judiciary, that this important tribunal should convene but once a year."[5] The appeal finally came on at the 1824 term, Attorney General Wirt now joining Webster as counsel for Gibbons and Thomas J. Oakley (1783–1857) joining Emmet as counsel for Ogden. As Wirt predicted, the argument extending over five days between 4 and 9 February was "a combat worth witnessing." The throng of spectators who crowded into the Supreme Court chamber were treated to an unsurpassed "display of legal learning, ability and eloquence." On the day Emmet spoke the House of Representatives lacked a quorum, most of the members having deserted the legislative hall for the courtroom. His speech also attracted an "extraordinary influx of ladies" that "seemed to indicate an irresistible disposition in them to be *courted*."[6]

Six Supreme Court justices sat in this case: Marshall, Washington, Duvall, Johnson, Story, and Todd. Smith Thompson, the new justice, did not arrive until after the close of arguments owing to the death of his daughter. Webster opened by observing that if the general government could not control the "extreme belligerent legislation" concerning steamboat navigation enacted by New York and the neighboring states of Connecticut and New Jersey, "the powers of the government were essentially deficient, in a most important and interesting particular." He rested his case principally on the idea that Congress's power to regulate commerce in its "higher branches" — including monopolies of trade or navigation — was necessarily exclusive. "Henceforth," said Webster, "the commerce of the States was to be an *unit;* and the system by which it was to exist and be governed, must necessarily be complete, entire, and uniform." As a navigation monopoly, the New York laws were accordingly null and void even in the absence of federal legislation on the subject. Webster conceded that the states retained a great mass of powers that indirectly affected commerce as shown by acts concerning turnpikes, bridges, ferries, pilotage, and health. Such laws were not evidence of a concurrent power to regulate commerce but were "rather regulations of police." Webster also argued that Gibbons's license under the federal coasting act of 1793 conferred a right to the free navigation of United States waters. This was a case of "actual collision" between federal law and state monopoly laws in which the latter must yield.[7]

Oakley, in reply, presented the case for concurrent powers in a tightly reasoned, analytical argument replete with definitions and distinctions. The state of New York, he said, was sovereign and independent, with no restrictions on its legislative power that "in any manner relate to the present controversy." The

Constitution, by contrast, was "a delegation of power, and not a restriction of power previously possessed." It accordingly must "be construed strictly, as regards the powers *expressly granted,* and the objects to which those powers are to be applied." Citing *The Federalist,* statements by Chief Justice Marshall in *Sturgis* v. *Crowninshield* and Justice Story in *Houston* v. *Moore,* and other authorities, Oakley elaborated a theory of concurrent powers in which he contended that the states could legislate even if Congress had acted under the same power on the same subject and that the collision between federal and state legislation "must be direct and positive" to invoke the supremacy principle. He then applied this theory to Congress's power to grant patents and to regulate commerce and found no repugnancy or conflict between these powers and the New York laws. If considered to be a regulation of commerce, the New York laws concerned only the state's internal trade or navigation, to which Congress's power did not reach. Oakley also defined "commerce" narrowly as "the transportation and sale of commodities," which did not include the business of transporting passengers for hire. Gibbons was not engaging in interstate commerce properly understood and therefore could claim no right under the coasting law.[8]

Emmet covered much the same ground as his co-counsel, demonstrating an unrivaled knowledge of the history of the controversy and a great depth of research. The repeated sanction of the New York monopoly laws by distinguished jurists on the state's council of revision and in a number of state judicial decisions, he said, created a strong presumption in favor of the constitutionality of these laws. The framers of the Constitution "must have felt the difficulty of designating the limits of what ought to be permitted to State authority" and did not "attempt the limitation, except in some plain cases, which they marked by restrictions and prohibitions." Where there were no express limits, the supremacy clause "guarded against any practical abuse" of state power. Emmet denied that the affirmative grant of the commerce power swept away state legislation on this subject. He undertook an exhaustive demonstration that the regulation of commerce belonged to the class of concurrent powers, citing various clauses of the Constitution, early proceedings that led to the federal convention, and a host of state laws that were "very material regulations respecting commerce." That many of these laws fell into the police category did not make them any less regulations of commerce. Like Oakely, he cited *The Federalist,* Marshall, Story, and Chancellor Kent as authorities for the proposition that there had to be a direct and positive interference or collision, not " 'a mere possibility of inconvenience,' " in order to invalidate a state exercise of concurrent power. No such collision could be shown between the New York laws and any federal regulation concerning patents or commerce. He repeated Kent's construction of the federal coasting act as merely defining a vessel's character as American and not conferring any right to navigate. Emmet closed with a glowing recital of the benefits flowing from the Livingston-Fulton steamboat monopoly not only to New York but to the American union and indeed to the "the whole civilized world."[9]

By prior arrangement with Webster, Wirt focused his primary attention to showing that the New York laws conflicted with Congress's power over patents, but he also bolstered his colleague's exclusive power argument by answering objections raised by Oakley and Emmet. That argument had been misrepresented, he said, as claiming the whole field of commerce as Congress's exclusive domain. In fact, the subject was "susceptible of division," leaving to the states the immense field of police regulations affecting commerce and vesting in Congress those parts of the power, such as navigation, that were exclusive in their nature. He also urged an expansive definition of commerce as embracing the authority to regulate passenger vessels, the term always implying "intercommunication and intercourse." Wirt's most effective contribution was to counteract Emmet's peroration with his own, returning to the theme of commercial discord with which Webster had begun five days earlier. Far from being a blessing to the American union and to mankind, the steamboat monopoly, Wirt declaimed, had sown "the seeds of anarchy" that would eventuate in civil war, the destruction of "republican institutions," the fall of the Constitution, and the disappearance of the "last hope of nations."[10]

Three weeks elapsed between the close of arguments and the delivery of the Court's opinion. Chief Justice Marshall reportedly had nearly finished writing the opinion when he fell and dislocated his shoulder on 19 February. Although a rumor circulated that Story was completing the opinion, Story himself informed one of the lawyers that after the accident Marshall "occupies all the time that he is able to write in completing it."[11] In the meantime speculation on the outcome leaned strongly to the view that the steamboat monopoly would fall. A correspondent informed Ogden that he had "not seen a man who heard the argument, and the Court room was crowded," who had "a doubt about the unconstitutionality of the laws." Webster was supremely confident that the Court would rule against the monopoly so far as it operated on interstate traffic between New Jersey and New York and possibly even on navigation wholly within New York waters. He told his client's son "*confident[i]ally*" that until the case had been argued, the majority of the Court considered the case as "merely a Question of collission" between rights derived from state and federal laws. Now "they have changed that opinion" and view it as "a broad constitutional question upon which scarcely any doubt exists." For his part Oakley was hopeful that his client's intrastate rights on the Hudson River would remain intact.[12]

On 2 March, his first day back on the bench since his accident, a numerous audience gathered close by Chief Justice Marshall to hear him deliver his opinion "in a low, feeble voice."[13] As many had predicted, the Supreme Court upheld Gibbons's right to operate his steamboat ferry service and struck down the New York laws. Beyond this immediate result, the decision ensured that steamboat navigation on the coastal and inland waters of the United States would no longer be controlled by state-oriented monopolies and would henceforth be opened to free competition. State jealousy had threatened to disrupt the free development of interstate trade by this new technology. The monopoly laws and accompanying retaliatory legislation were reminiscent of the commercial warfare that occurred under the Confederation. In striking down the steamboat monopoly, the chief justice and his brethren could with good reason claim to be applying the Constitution to those very abuses it was intended to remedy.

Still, the case was not so easy in terms of expounding the commerce clause in relation to the perplexing problem of federalism: where to draw the line between respective powers of the general and state governments. Counsel had presented two contrasting theories of the commerce power, one that it was exclusive in its nature and prohibited all state legislation on the subject, the other that it was concurrent and permitted state legislation until superseded by federal legislation. From these arguments Marshall fashioned a synthesis that leaned toward exclusive power while recognizing as a practical matter the states' concurrent power in this area. In denying strict construction as the rule for interpreting the powers of the general government, in defining commerce broadly to include navigation, in contending that the extent of the commerce power did not stop at state boundary lines but could reach into the interior of a particular state, and in describing the power as "plenary" and "vested in Congress as absolutely as it would be in a single government," the chief justice laid the groundwork for asserting the exclusive power doctrine.[14] Moreover, in one of the longest sections of the opinion, he denied that counsel's citations of the Constitution, acts of Congress, and state laws demonstrated that the states could concurrently exercise the power to regulate interstate and foreign commerce.

Marshall, however, stopped short of accepting the argument for exclusive power, content to say only that the Court was "not satisfied that it has been refuted." And while refusing to concede the case for concurrent power, the chief justice did recognize a vast area of state authority to enact legislation concerning internal trade and police that could affect interstate and foreign commerce. In the end the Court avoided choosing between exclusive or concurrent power by deciding the case on the narrower ground of collision between the monopoly laws and the federal coasting statute. It was accordingly "immaterial" whether the state laws emanated from an asserted concurrent power to regulate interstate and foreign commerce or an acknowledged power to regulate internal trade and police.[15]

Pragmatic considerations no doubt influenced the Court majority to hold back from declaring the nullity of the New York laws as interfering with Congress's exclusive power to regulate interstate commerce. No such motives prevented Justice Johnson in a concurring opinion from endorsing the exclusive power doctrine, just as he had done seven months earlier on circuit. On that occasion Johnson had voided a South Carolina law requiring detention in jail of free black sailors while their ships lay in port, a decision denounced by angry spokesmen for states' rights as another act of consolidating usurpation by the federal judiciary. With this incident in mind and "not fond of butting against a wall in sport," the chief justice was not prepared to pronounce the full nationalizing potential of the commerce clause if he did not have to. Given the unpopularity of recent Supreme Court decisions and resulting attempts to curb its jurisdiction, the wiser course was to proceed with caution.[16]

The authority of past Supreme Court decisions seemed also to argue against a precipitate adoption of the exclusive power theory. Marshall, to be sure, had declared in *Sturgis* v. *Crowninshield* (1819), that if the terms or nature of a power granted to Congress "require that it should be exercised exclusively by Congress, the subject is as completely taken from the State Legislatures, as if they had been expressly forbidden to act on it." Yet in that case he denied that Congress's power over bankruptcy was exclusive, observing that it was "not the mere existence of the power, but its exercise, which is incompatible with the exercise of the same power by the States."[17] Likewise, Justice Story, the chief justice's nationalist coadjutor, in *Houston* v. *Moore* (1820) adopted the concurrent power doctrine with respect to the militia power. Congress's affirmative powers, he said, were "never exclusive of similar powers existing in the States, unless where the constitution has expressly in terms given an exclusive power to Congress, or the exercise of a like power is prohibited to the States, or there is a direct repugnancy or incompatibility in the exercise of it by the States."[18] These passages, which Ogden's counsel repeatedly cited, may well have reinforced the Court's determination to decide the steamboat case on the ground of the state laws' incompatibility with an actual exercise of the federal commerce power. Although perhaps not wholly satisfied with resorting to "esoteric statutory construction" to bring down the monopoly,[19] Marshall and his brethren embraced this alternative as preferable to making a definitive pronouncement concerning the extent to which the commerce clause by itself operated as a negative upon state legislation.

1. For background, see Maurice G. Baxter, *The Steamboat Monopoly: Gibbons v. Ogden, 1824* (New York, 1972), 3–37.

2. Livingston v. Van Ingen, 9 Johns. 507 (1812); Baxter, *Steamboat Monopoly*, 21–25; Thomas P. Campbell, Jr., "Chancellor Kent, Chief Justice Marshall and the Steamboat Cases," *Syracuse Law Review*, XXV (1974), 502–6.

3. Campbell, "Chancellor Kent," 508–13; Ogden v. Gibbons, 4 Johns. Ch. 150 (N.Y. Ch., 1819); Gibbons v. Ogden, 17 Johns. 488 (N.Y. Ct. Err. & App., 1820).

4. Ogden v. Gibbons, App. Cas. No. 1001, U.S. Sup. Ct. Dockets; Gibbons v. Ogden, 6 Wheat. 448–50; Joseph Story to William Fettyplace, 28 Feb. 1821, Story, *Life and Letters*, I, 397.

5. Gibbons v. Ogden, App. Cas. No. 1148; Daniel Webster to Thomas Gibbons, 2 Mar. 1822; Gibbons to Webster, 14 Jan. 1823, Charles M. Wiltse and Harold Moser, eds., *The Papers of Daniel Webster: Correspondence, Volume 1, 1798–1824* (Hanover, N.H., 1974), 308–9, 320.

6. William Wirt to Dabney Carr, 1 Feb. 1824, in John P. Kennedy, *Memoirs of the Life of William Wirt* (2 vols.; Philadelphia, 1854), II, 144; *Enquirer* (Richmond, Va.), 26 Feb., 2 Mar. 1824; Warren, *Supreme Court*, I, 602–6.

7. 9 Wheat. 5, 14, 19, 31.

8. 9 Wheat. 33, 34, 42, 76.

9. 9 Wheat. 101, 107, 129, 158.

10. 9 Wheat. 180, 182–83, 185.

11. Warren, *Supreme Court*, I, 608; William Gibbons to Thomas Gibbons, 23 Feb. 1824, MH-L.

12. David B. Ogden to Aaron Ogden, [9 Feb. 1824], Ogden Papers, NjR; Webster to Joseph Hopkinson, 14 Feb. 1824; to Jeremiah Mason, 15 Feb. 1824, Wiltse and Moser, eds., *Papers of Webster: Correspondence, Volume 1*, 353, 354; William Gibbons to Thomas Gibbons, 23 Feb. 1824, MH-L; Baxter, *Steamboat Monopoly*, 47.

13. Warren, *Supreme Court*, I, 609.

14. Opinion and Decree, 2 Mar. 1824 (21, below).

15. Opinion and Decree, 2 Mar. 1824 (27, below).

16. Baxter, *Steamboat Monopoly*, 58–60; JM to Story, 26 Sept. 1823, *PJM*, IX, 338, 339 n. 2.

17. Sturgis v. Crowninshield, 4 Wheat. 193, 196; *PJM*, VIII, 245, 246.

18. Houston v. Moore, 5 Wheat. 49.

19. Felix Frankfurter, *The Commerce Clause under Marshall, Taney, and Waite* (Chapel Hill, N.C., 1937), 20.

This is a writ of error to a decree of the highest court of law or equity in the State of New York, affirming a decree pronounced by the Chancellor of that State.

The Legislature of New York has enacted several laws for the purpose of securing to Robert R. Livingston and Robert Fulton the exclusive navigation of all the waters within the jurisdiction of that State, with boats moved by fire or steam, for a term of years, which has not yet expired; and has authorized the Chancellor to award an injunction, restraining any person whatever from navigating those waters with boats of that description.

This bill was filed by Aaron Ogden, claiming as assignee of Livingston and Fulton, suggesting that Thomas Gibbon, the plaintiff in error, was in possession of two steam-boats, the Stoudinger and Bellona, which were actually employed in running between New York and Elizabethtown in New Jersey, in violation of the exclusive privilege conferred on the plaintiff, and praying an injunction to restrain the said Gibbon from using the said boats, or any others propelled by fire or steam, in navigating the waters within the territory of New York.

The injunction having been awarded, the answer of Gibbon was filed, in which he stated that the boats employed by him were duly enrolled and licensed, according to the act of Congress, to carry on the coasting trade of the United States; and insisted on his right, in virtue of that license, to navigate the waters between Elizabethtown and New York, the acts of the Legislature of New York notwithstanding.

The Chancellor perpetuated the injunction, being of opinion that the acts conferring the privilege were not repugnant to the Constitution and laws of the United States, and were valid. This decree was affirmed, in the Court for the trial of impeachments and correction of errors, which is the highest tribunal before which the cause could be carried in the State.

The plaintiff in error[1] contends that this decree is erroneous, because the laws which purport to give the exclusive privilege it sustains, are repugnant to the Constitution and laws of the United States.

They are said to be repugnant —

1st. To that clause in the Constitution which authorizes Congress to regulate commerce.

2d. To that which authorizes Congress to promote the progress of science and useful arts.

The State of New York maintains the constitutionality of these laws; and their Legislature, their Council of Revision, and their Judges, have repeatedly concurred in this opinion. It is supported by great names — by names which have all the titles to consideration that virtue, intelligence, and office, can bestow. No tribunal can approach the decision of this question, without feeling a just and real respect for that opinion which is sustained by such authority; but it is the province of this Court, while it respects, not to bow to it implicitly; and the Judges must exercise, in the examination of the subject, that understanding which Providence has bestowed upon them, with that independence which the people of the United States expect from this department of the government.

As preliminary to the very able discussions of the Constitution, which we have heard from the bar, and as having some influence on its construction, reference has been made to the political situation of these States, anterior to its formation. It has been said, that they were sovereign; were completely independent, and were connected with each other only by a league. This is true. But, when these allied sovereigns converted their league into a government — when they converted their Congress of Ambassadors, deputed to deliberate on their common concerns, and to recommend measures of general utility, into a Legislature empowered to enact laws on the most interesting subjects, the whole character, in which the States appear, underwent a change, the extent of which must be determined by a fair consideration of the instrument by which that change was effected.

This instrument contains an enumeration of powers expressly granted by the people to their government. It has been said, that these powers ought to be construed strictly. But why ought they to be so construed? Is there one sentence in the Constitution which gives countenance to this rule? In the last of the enumerated powers, that which grants, expressly, the means for carrying all others into execution, Congress is authorized "to make all laws which shall be necessary and proper" for the purpose. But this limitation on the means which may be used, is not extended to the powers which are conferred; nor is there one sentence in the Constitution, which has been pointed out by the gentlemen of the bar, or which we have been able to discern, that prescribes this rule. We do not, therefore, think ourselves justified in adopting it. What do gentlemen mean by a strict construction? If they contend only against that enlarged construction which would extend words beyond their natural and obvious import, we might question the application of the term, but should not controvert the principle. If they contend for that narrow construction which, in support of some theory not to be found in the Constitution, would deny to the government those powers which the words of the grant, as usually understood, import, and which are consistent with the general views and objects of the instrument, for that narrow construction which would cripple the government, and render it unequal to the objects for which it is declared to be instituted, and to which the powers given, as fairly understood, render it competent, then we cannot perceive the propriety of this strict construction, nor adopt it as the rule by which the Constitution is to be expounded. As men, whose intentions require no concealment, generally employ the words which most directly and aptly express the ideas they intend to convey, the enlightened patriots who framed our Constitution, and the people who adopted it, must be understood to have employed words in their natural sense, and to have intended what they have said. If, from the imperfection of human language, there should be serious doubts respecting the extent of any given power, it is a well settled rule, that the objects for which it was given, especially when those objects are expressed in the instrument itself, should have great influence in the construction. We know of no reason for excluding this rule from the present case. The grant does not convey power which might be beneficial to the grantor if retained by himself, or, which can enure solely to the benefit of the grantee; but is an investment of power for the general advantage, in the hands of agents selected for that purpose, which power can never be exercised by the people themselves, but must be placed in the hands of agents or lie dormant. We know of no rule for construing the extent of such powers, other than is given by the language of the instrument which confers them, taken in connexion with the purposes for which they were conferred.

The words are — "Congress shall have power to regulate commerce with foreign nations, and among the several states, and with the Indian tribes."

The subject to be regulated is commerce; and our constitution being, as was aptly said at the bar, one of enumeration, and not of definition, to ascertain the extent of the power, it becomes necessary to settle the meaning of the word. The counsel for the appellee would limit it to traffic, to buying and selling, or the interchange of commodities, and do not admit that it comprehends navigation. This would restrict a general term, applicable to many objects, to one of its significations. Commerce undoubtedly is traffic, but it is something more: It is intercourse. It describes the commercial intercourse between nations, and parts of nations, in all its branches, and is regulated by prescribing rules for carrying on that intercourse. The mind can scarcely conceive a system for regulating commerce between nations which shall exclude all laws concerning navigation, which shall be silent on the admission of the vessels of the one nation into the ports of the other, and be confined to prescribing rules for the conduct of individuals in the actual employment of buying and selling, or of barter.

If commerce does not include navigation, the government of the Union has no direct power over that subject, and can make no law prescribing what shall constitute American vessels, or requiring that they shall be navigated by American seamen. Yet this power has been exercised from the commencement of the government, has been exercised with the consent of all, and has been understood by all to be a commercial regulation. All America understands, and has uniformly understood, the word "commerce" to comprehend navigation. It was so understood, and must have been so understood, when the Constitution was framed. The power over commerce, including navigation, was one of the primary objects for which the people of America adopted their government, and must have been contemplated in forming it. The convention must have used the word in that sense, because all have understood it in that sense; and the attempt to restrict it comes too late.

If the opinion that "commerce," as the word is used in the Constitution, comprehends navigation also, require any additional confirmation, that additional confirmation is, we think, furnished by the words of the instrument itself.

It is a rule of construction acknowledged by all, that the exceptions from a power mark its extent; for it would be absurd, as well as useless, to except from a granted power that which was not granted — that which the words of the grant could not comprehend. If, then, there are, in the constitution plain exceptions from the power over navigation, plain inhibitions to the exercise of that power in a particular way, it is proof that those who made these exceptions, and prescribed these inhibitions, understood the power to which they applied as being granted.

The 9th section of the 1st article declares, that "no preference shall be given by any regulation of commerce or revenue, to the ports of one state over those of another." This clause cannot be understood as applicable to those laws only which are passed for purposes of revenue, because it is expressly applied to commercial regulations; and the most obvious preference which can be given to one port over another, in regulating commerce, relates to navigation. But the subsequent part of the sentence is still more explicit. It is, "nor shall vessels bound to or from one state, be obliged to enter, clear, or pay duties, in another." These words have a direct reference to navigation.

The universally acknowledged power of the government to impose embargoes, must also be considered as showing that all America is united in that construction which comprehends navigation in the word commerce. Gentlemen have said, in argument, that this is a branch of the war-making power, and that an embargo is an instrument of war, not a regulation of trade.

That it may be, and often is used as an instrument of war, cannot be denied. An embargo may be imposed for the purpose of facilitating the equipment or manning of a fleet, or for the purpose of concealing the progress of an expedition preparing to sail from a particular port. In these, and in similar cases, it is a military instrument, and partakes of the nature of war. But all embargoes are not of this description. They are, sometimes, resorted to without a view to war, and with a single view to commerce. In such case an embargo is no more a war-measure than a merchantman is a ship of war, because both are vessels which navigate the ocean with sails and seamen.

When Congress imposed that embargo, which, for a time, engaged the attention of every man in the United States, the avowed object of the law was the protection of commerce and the avoiding of war. By its friends and its enemies it was treated as a commercial, not as a war measure. The persevering earnestness and zeal with which it was opposed, in a part of our country which supposed its interests to be vitally affected by the act, cannot be forgotten. A want of astuteness in discovering objections to a measure to which they felt the most deep rooted hostility, will not be imputed to those who were arrayed in opposition to this. Yet they never suspected that navigation was no branch of trade, and was, therefore, not comprehended in the power to regulate commerce. They did, indeed, contest the constitutionality of the act, but on a principle which admits the construction for which the appellant contends. They denied that the particular law in question was made in pursuance of the constitution, not because the power could not act directly on vessels, but because a perpetual embargo was the annihilation, and not the regulation of commerce. In terms, they admitted the applicability of the words used in the Constitution to vessels; and that, in a case which produced a degree and an extent of excitement calculated to draw forth every principle on which legitimate resistance could be sustained. No example could more strongly illustrate the universal understanding of the American people on this subject.

The word used in the Constitution, then, comprehends, and has been always understood to comprehend, navigation within its meaning; and a power to regulate navigation is as expressly granted, as if that term had been added to the word "commerce."[2]

To what commerce does this power extend? The Constitution informs us to commerce "with foreign nations, and among the several states, and with the Indian tribes."

It has, we believe, been universally admitted, that these words comprehend every species of commercial intercourse between the United States and foreign nations. No sort of trade can be carried on between this country and any other, to which this power does not extend. It has been truly said, that commerce, as the word is used in the constitution, is a unit, every part of which is indicated by the term.

If this be the admitted meaning of the word, in its application to foreign nations, it must carry the same meaning throughout the sentence, and remain a unit, unless there be some plain intelligible cause which alters it.

The subject to which the power is next applied, is to commerce "among the several states." The word "among" means intermingled with. A thing which is among others, is intermingled with them. Commerce among the states cannot stop at the external boundary line of each state, but may be introduced into the interior.

It is not intended to say that these words comprehend that commerce, which is completely internal, which is carried on between man and man in a state, or between different parts of the same state, and which does not extend to, or affect other states. Such a power would be inconvenient, and is certainly unnecessary.

Comprehensive as the word "among" is, it may very properly be restricted to that commerce which concerns more states than one. The phrase is not one which would probably have been selected to indicate the completely interior traffic of a state, because it is not an apt phrase for that purpose; and the enumeration of the particular classes of commerce to which the power was to be extended, would not have been made, had the intention been to extend the power to every description. The enumeration presupposes something not enumerated; and that something, if we regard the language or the subject of the sentence, must be the exclusively internal commerce of a state. The genius and character of the whole government seem to be, that its action is to be applied to all the external concerns of the nation, and to those internal concerns which affect the states generally; but not to those which are completely within a particular state, which do not affect other states, and with which it is not necessary to interfere for the purpose of executing some of the general powers of the government. The completely internal commerce of a state, then, may be considered as reserved for the state itself.

But, in regulating commerce with foreign nations, the power of Congress does not stop at the jurisdictional lines of the several states. It would be a very useless power if it could not pass those lines. The commerce of the United States with foreign nations is that of the whole United States. Every district has a right to participate in it. The deep streams which penetrate our country in every direction, pass through the interior of almost every state in the Union, and furnish the means of exercising this right. If Congress has the power to regulate it, that power must be exercised wherever the subject exists. If it exists within the states, if a foreign voyage may commence or terminate at a port within a state, then the power of Congress may be exercised within a state.

This principle is, if possible, still more clear when applied to commerce "among the several states." They either join each other, in which case they are separated by a mathematical line; or they are remote from each other, in which case other states lie between them. What is commerce "among" them, and how is it to be conducted? Can a trading expedition between two adjoining states, commence and terminate outside of each? And if the trading intercourse be between two states remote from each other, must it not commence in one, terminate in the other, and probably pass through a third? Commerce among the states must, of necessity, be commerce within the states. In the regulation of trade with the Indian tribes, the action of the law, especially when the constitution was made, was chiefly within a state. The power of Congress, then, whatever it may be, must be exercised within the territorial jurisdiction of the several states. The sense of the nation on this subject is unequivocally manifested by the provisions made in the laws for transporting goods, by land, between Baltimore and Providence, between New York and Philadelphia, and between Philadelphia and Baltimore.

We are now arrived at the inquiry—What is this power?

It is the power to regulate, that is, to prescribe, the rule by which commerce is to be governed. This power, like all others vested in Congress, is complete in itself; may be exercised to its utmost extent; and acknowledges no limitations, other than are prescribed in the constitution. These are expressed in plain terms, and do not affect the questions which arise in this case, or which have been discussed at the bar. If, as has always been understood, the sovereignty of Congress, though limited to specified objects, is plenary as to those objects, the power over commerce with foreign nations and among the several states, is vested in Congress as absolutely as it would be in a single government, having in its constitution the same restrictions on the exercise of the power as are found in the constitution of the United States. The wisdom and the discretion of Congress, their identity with the people, and the influence which their constituents possess at elections, are, in this, as in many other instances, as that, for example, of declaring war, the sole restraints on which they have relied to secure them from its abuse. They are the restraints on which the people must often rely solely in all representative governments.

The power of Congress, then, comprehends navigation within the limits of every state in the Union; so far as that navigation may be, in any manner, connected with "commerce with foreign nations, or among the several states, or with the Indian tribes." It may, of consequence, pass the jurisdictional line of New York, and act upon the very waters to which the prohibition now under consideration applies.

But it has been urged with great earnestness that, altho' the power of Congress to regulate commerce with foreign nations and among the several states be co-extensive with the subject itself, & have no other limits than are prescribed in the constitution, yet the states may severally exercise the same power within their respective jurisdictions. In support of this argument, it is said, that they possessed it as an inseparable attribute of sovereignty before the formation of the constitution and still retain it, except so far as they have surrendered it by that instrument; that this principle results from the nature of the government, and is secured by the tenth amendment; that an affirmative grant of power is not exclusive, unless in its own nature it be such that the continued exercise of it by the former possessor is inconsistent with the grant, and that this is not of that description.

The plaintiff,[3] conceding these postulates, except the last, contends, that full power to regulate a particular subject, implies the whole power, and leaves no residuum; that a grant of the whole is incompatible with the existence of a right in another to any part of it.

Both parties have appealed to the constitution, to legislative acts, and judicial decisions; and have drawn arguments from all these sources to support and illustrate the propositions they respectively maintain.

The grant of the power to lay and collect taxes is, like the power to regulate commerce, made in general terms, and has never been understood to interfere with the exercise of the same power by the states; and hence has been drawn an argument which has been applied to the question under consideration. But the two grants are not, it is conceived, similar in their terms or their nature. Although many of the powers formerly exercised by the states are transferred to the government of the Union, yet the state governments remain, and constitute a most important part of our system. The power of taxation is indispensable to their existence, and is a power which, in its own nature, is capable of residing in, and being exercised by, different authorities at the same time. We are accustomed to see it placed, for different purposes, in different hands. Taxation is the simple operation of taking small portions from a perpetually accumulating mass, susceptible of almost infinite division, and a power in one to take what is necessary for certain purposes is not, in its nature, incompatible with a power in another to take what is necessary for other purposes. Congress is authorized to lay and collect taxes, &c. to pay the debts and provide for the common defence and general welfare of the United States. This does not interfere with the power of the states to tax for the support of their own governments; nor is the exercise of that power by the states an exercise of any portion of the power that is granted to the United States. In imposing taxes for state purposes, they are not doing what Congress is empowered to do. Congress is not empowered to tax for those purposes which are within the exclusive province of the states. When, then, each government exercises the power of taxation, either is exercising the power of the other. But when a state proceeds to regulate commerce with foreign nations, or among the several states, it is exercising the very power that is granted to Congress, and is doing the very thing which Congress is authorized to do. There is no analogy, then, between the power of taxation and the power of regulating commerce.

In discussing the question whether this power is still in the states, in the case under consideration, we may dismiss from it the inquiry whether it is surrendered by the mere grant to Congress, or is retained until Congress shall exercise the power. We may dismiss that inquiry, because it has been exercised, and the regulations which Congress deemed it proper to make, are now in full operation. The sole question is, can a state regulate commerce with foreign nations and among the states, while Congress is regulating it?

The counsel for the appellee[4] answered this question in the affirmative, and rely very much on the restrictions in the 10th section as supporting their opinion. They say, very truly, that limitations of a power furnish a strong argument in favour of the existence of that power, and that the section which prohibits the states from laying duties on imports or exports proves that this power might have been exercised had it not been expressly forbidden; and, consequently, that any other commercial regulation, not expressly forbidden, to which the original power of the state was competent, may still be made.

That this restriction shows the opinion of the Convention, that a state might impose duties on exports and imports, if not expressly forbidden, will be conceded; but that it follows as a consequence, from this concession, that a state may regulate commerce with foreign nations and among the states, cannot be admitted.

We must first determine, whether the act of laying "duties or imposts

on imports or exports," is considered in the constitution as a branch of
the taxing power, or of the power to regulate commerce. We think it very
clear, that it is considered as a branch of the taxing power. It is so treated
in the first clause of the 8th section: "Congress shall have power to lay and
collect taxes, duties, imposts, and excises;" and before commerce is mentioned, the rule by which the exercise of this power must be governed, is
declared. It is, that all duties, imposts, and excises, shall be uniform. In a
separate clause of the enumeration, the power to regulate commerce is
given, as being entirely distinct from the right to levy taxes and imposts,
and as being a new power, not before conferred. The Constitution, then,
considers these powers as substantive, and distinct from each other; and
so places them in the enumeration it contains. The power of imposing
duties on imports, is classed with the power to levy taxes, and that seems
to be its natural place. But the power to levy taxes could never be considered as abridging the right of the states on that subject; and they might,
consequently, have exercised it by levying duties on imports or exports,
had the Constitution contained no prohibition on this subject. This prohibition, then, is an exception from the acknowledged power of the states
to levy taxes, not from the questionable power to regulate commerce.

"A duty of tonnage," is as much a tax, as a duty on imports or exports;
and the reason which induced the prohibition of those taxes, extends to
this also. This tax may be imposed by a state, with the consent of Congress; and it may be admitted, that Congress cannot give a right to a state,
in virtue of its own powers. But a duty of tonnage being part of the power
of imposing taxes, its prohibition may certainly be made to depend on
Congress, without affording any implication respecting a power to regulate commerce. It is true, that duties may often be, and in fact often are,
imposed on tonnage, with a view to the regulation of commerce; but they
may be also imposed with a view to revenue; and it was, therefore, a
prudent precaution, to prohibit the states from exercising this power.
The idea that the same measure might, according to circumstances, be
arranged with different classes of power, was no novelty to the framers
of our Constitution. Those illustrious statesmen and patriots had been,
many of them, deeply engaged in the discussions which preceded the war
of our Revolution, and all of them were well read in those discussions.
The right to regulate commerce, even by the imposition of duties, was not
controverted; but the right to impose a duty for the purpose of revenue,
produced a war as important, perhaps, in its consequences to the human
race, as any the world has ever witnessed.

These restrictions, then, are on the taxing power, not on that to regulate commerce; and presuppose the existence of that which they restrain,
not of that which they do not purport to restrain.

But, the inspection laws are said to be regulations of commerce, and
are certainly recognized in the Constitution, as being passed in the exercise of a power remaining with the states.

That inspection laws may have a remote and considerable influence on commerce, will not be denied; but that a power to regulate commerce is the source from which the right to pass them is derived cannot be admitted. The object of inspection laws is to improve the quality of articles produced by the labor of a country; to fit them for exportation, or, it may be, for domestic use. They act upon the subject before it becomes an article of foreign commerce, or of commerce among the states, and prepare it for that purpose. They form a portion of that immense mass of legislation which embraces every thing within the territory of a state, not surrendered to the general government: all which can be most advantageously exercised by the states themselves. Inspection laws, quarantine laws, health laws, of every description, as well as laws for regulating the internal commerce of a state, and those which respect turnpike roads, ferries, &c. are component parts of this mass.

No direct general power over these objects is granted to Congress; and, consequently, they remain subject to state legislation. If the legislative power of the Union can reach them, it must be for national purposes; it must be where the power is expressly given for a special purpose, or is clearly incidental to some power which is expressly given. It is obvious, that the government of the Union, in the exercise of its express powers — that, for example, of regulating commerce with foreign nations and among the states — may use means that may also be employed by a state, in the exercise of its acknowledged powers — that, for example, of regulating commerce within the state. If Congress license vessels to sail from one port to another, in the same state, the act is supposed to be necessarily incidental to the power expressly granted to Congress, and implies no claim of a direct power to regulate the purely internal commerce of a state, or to act directly on its system of police. So, if a state, in passing laws on subjects acknowledged to be within its control, and with a view to those subjects, which shall adopt a measure of the same character with one which Congress may adopt, it does not derive its authority from the particular power which has been granted, but from some other, which remains with the state, and may be executed by the same means. All experience shows, that the same measures, or measures scarcely distinguishable from each other, may flow from distinct powers; but this does not prove, that the powers themselves are identical. Although the means used in their execution may sometimes approach each other so nearly as to be confounded, there are other situations in which they are sufficiently distinct to establish their individuality.

In our complex system, presenting the rare and difficult scheme of one general government, whose action extends over the whole, but which possesses only certain enumerated powers; and of numerous state governments, which retain and exercise all powers not delegated to the Union, contests respecting power must arise. Were it even otherwise, the measures taken by the respective governments to execute their acknowledged powers, would often be of the same description, and might, sometimes, interfere. This, however, does not prove, that the one is exercising, or has a right to exercise, the powers of the other.

The acts of Congress, passed in 1796 & 1799, empowering and directing the officers of the general government to conform to, and assist in the execution of, the quarantine and health laws of a state, proceed, it is said, upon the idea that these laws are constitutional.[5] It is undoubtedly true, that they do proceed upon that idea; and the constitutionality of such laws has never, so far as we are informed, been denied. But they do not imply an acknowledgement that a state may rightfully regulate commerce with foreign nations, or among the states; for they do not imply that such laws are an exercise of that power, or enacted with a view to it. On the contrary, they are treated as quarantine and health laws, are so denominated in the acts of Congress, and are considered as flowing from the acknowledged power of a state, to provide for the health of its citizens. But, as it was apparent that some of the provisions made for this purpose, and in virtue of this power, might interfere with, and be affected by the laws of the United States, made for the regulation of commerce, Congress, in that spirit of harmony and conciliation which ought always to characterize the conduct of governments standing in the relation which that of the Union and those of the States bear to each other, has directed its officers to aid in the execution of these laws; and has, in some measure, adapted its own legislation to this object, by making provisions in aid of those of the states. But, in making these provisions, the opinion is unequivocally manifested, that Congress may control the state laws, so far as it may be necessary to control them for the regulation of commerce.

The act passed in 1803, prohibiting the importation of slaves into any state which shall itself prohibit their importation, implies, it is said, an admission that the states possessed the power to exclude or admit them; from which it is inferred that they possess the same power with respect to all other articles.[6]

If this inference were correct, if this power was exercised, not under any particular clause in the constitution, but in virtue of a general right over the subject of commerce, to exist as long as the constitution itself, it might now be exercised. Any state might now import African slaves into its own territory. But, it is obvious that the power of the states over this subject, previous to the year 1808, constitutes an exception to the power of Congress to regulate commerce, and the exception is expressed in such words as to manifest clearly the intention to continue the pre-existing right of the states to admit or exclude for a limited period. The words are, "the migration or importation of such persons as any of the states now existing *shall* think proper to admit, shall not be prohibited by the Congress prior to the year 1808." The whole object of the exception is to preserve the power to those states which might be disposed to exercise it and its language seems to the court to convey this idea unequivocally. The possession of this particular power, then, during the time limited in the constitution, cannot be admitted to prove the possession of any other similar power.

It has been said that the act of August 7, 1789, acknowledges a concurrent power in the states to regulate the conduct of pilots, and hence is inferred an admission of their concurrent right with Congress to regulate commerce with foreign nations, and among the states.[7] But, this inference is not, we think, justified by the fact.

Although Congress cannot enable a state to legislate, Congress may adopt the provisions of a state on any subject. When the government of the Union was brought into existence, it found a system for the regulation of its pilots in full force in every state. The act which has been mentioned adopts this system, and gives it the same validity as if its provisions had been specially made by Congress. But the act, it may be said, is prospective also, and the adoption of laws to be made in future presupposes the right in the maker to legislate on the subject.

The act unquestionably manifests an intention to leave this subject entirely to the states, until Congress should think proper to interpose; but the very enactment of such a law indicates an opinion that it was necessary; that the existing system would not be applicable to the new state of things unless expressly applied to it by Congress. But this section is confined to pilots within the "bays, inlets, rivers, harbours, and ports of the United States," which are, of course, in whole or in part, also within the limits of some particular state. The acknowledged power of a state to regulate its police, its domestic trade, and to govern its own citizens, may enable it to legislate on this subject to a considerable extent; and the adoption of its system by Congress, and the application of it to the whole subject of commerce, does not seem to the court to imply a right in the states so to apply it of their own authority. But, the adoption of the state system being temporary, being only "until further legislative provision shall be made by Congress," shews, conclusively an opinion that Congress could control the whole subject, and might adopt the system of the states, or provide one of its own.

A state, it is said, or even a private citizen, may construct light houses. But gentlemen must be aware, that, if this proves a power in a state to regulate commerce, it proves that the same power is in the citizen. States, or individuals, who own lands, may, if not forbidden by law, erect on those lands what buildings they please; but this power is entirely distinct from that of regulating commerce, and may, we presume, be restrained, if exercised so as to produce a public mischief.

These acts were cited at the bar for the purpose of shewing an opinion in Congress that the states possess, concurrently with the legislature of the Union, the power to regulate commerce with foreign nations and among the states. Upon reviewing them, we think they do not establish the proposition they were intended to prove. They shew the opinion that the states retain powers enabling them to pass the laws to which allusion has been made, not that those laws proceed from the particular power which has been delegated to Congress.

It has been contended by the counsel for the appellant, that, as the word "to regulate" implies in its nature full power over the thing to be regulated, it excludes necessarily the action of all others that would perform the same operation on the same thing. That regulation is designed for the entire result, applying to those parts which remain as they were, as well as to those which are altered. It produces a uniform whole, which is as much disturbed and deranged by changing what the regulating power designs to leave untouched, as that on which it has operated.

There is great force in this argument, and the court is not satisfied that it has been refuted.

Since, however, in exercising the power of regulating their own purely internal affairs, whether of trade or police, the states may sometimes enact laws, the validity of which depends on their interfering with, and being contrary to, an act of Congress passed in pursuance of the Constitution, the court will enter upon the inquiry, whether the laws of New York, as expounded by the highest tribunal of that state, have, in their application to this case, come into collision with an act of Congress, and deprived a citizen of a right to which that act entitles him. Should this collision exist, it will be immaterial whether those laws were passed in virtue of a concurrent power "to regulate commerce with foreign nations and among the several states," or in virtue of a power to regulate their domestic trade and police. In the one case and the other, the acts of New York must yield to the law of Congress; and the decision sustaining the privilege they confer, against a right given by a law of the Union, must be erroneous.

This opinion has been frequently expressed in this court, and is founded as well on the nature of the government as on the words of the Constitution. In argument, however, it has been contended that, if a law passed by a state, in the exercise of its acknowledged sovereignty, comes into conflict with a law passed by congress in pursuance of the Constitution, they affect the subject and each other like equal opposing powers.

But the framers of our Constitution foresaw this state of things, and provided for it, by declaring the supremacy not only of itself, but of the laws made in pursuance of it. The nullity of any act inconsistent with the Constitution, is produced by the declaration, that the Constitution is the supreme law. The appropriate application of that part of the clause which confers the same supremacy on laws and treaties, is to such acts of the state legislatures as do not transcend their powers, but, though enacted in the execution of acknowledged state powers, interfere with, or are contrary to, the laws of Congress, made in pursuance of the Constitution, or some treaty made under the authority of the United States. In every such case, the act of Congress, or the treaty, is supreme; and the law of the state, though enacted in the exercise of powers not controverted, must yield to it.

In pursuing this inquiry at the bar, it has been said that the Constitution does not confer the right of intercourse between state and state. That right derives its source from those laws whose authority is acknowledged by civilized man throughout the world. This is true. The Constitution found it an existing right, and give to Congress the power to regulate it. In the exercise of this power, Congress has passed "An act for enrolling or licensing ships or vessels to be employed in the coasting trade, and fisheries, and for regulating the same."[8] The counsel for the appellee contend that this act does not give the right to sail from port to port, but confines itself to regulating a pre-existing right so far only as to confer certain privileges on enrolled and licensed vessels in its exercise.

It will at once occur, that, when a legislature attaches certain privileges and exemptions to the exercise of a right over which its control is absolute, the law must imply a power to exercise the right. The privileges are gone if the right itself be annihilated. It would be contrary to all reason, and to the course of human affairs, to say that a state is unable to strip a vessel of the particular privileges attendant on the exercise of a right, and yet may annul the right itself; that the State of New York cannot prevent an enrolled and licensed vessel, proceeding from Elizabeth town, in N. Jersey, to N. York, from enjoying, in her course, and, on her entrance into port, all the privileges conferred by the act of Congress, but can shut her up in her own port, and prohibit altogether her entering the waters and ports of another state. To the court it seems very clear, that the whole act on the subject of the coasting trade, according to those principles which govern the construction of statutes, implies unequivocally, an authority to licensed vessels to carry on the coasting trade.

But we will proceed briefly to notice those sections which bear more directly on the subject.

The first section declares, that vessels enrolled by virtue of a previous law, and certain other vessels enrolled as described in that act, and having a license in force as is by the act required, "and no others, shall be deemed ships or vessels of the United States, entitled to the privileges of ships or vessels employed in the coasting trade."

This section seems to the court to contain a positive enactment that the vessels it describes shall be entitled to the privileges of ships or vessels employed in the coasting trade. These privileges cannot be separated from the trade, and cannot be enjoyed unless the trade may be prosecuted. The grant of the privilege is an idle, empty form, conveying nothing, unless it convey the right to which the privilege is attached, and in the exercise of which its whole value consists. To construe these words otherwise than as entitling the ships or vessels described to carry on the coasting trade, would be, we think, to disregard the apparent intent of the act.

The fourth section directs the proper officer to grant to a vessel quali-fied to receive it, "a license for carrying on the coasting trade;" and prescribes its form. After reciting the compliance of the applicant with the previous requisites of the law, the operative words of the instrument are, "license is hereby granted for the said steam boat Bellona, to be employed in carrying on the coasting trade for one year from the date hereof, and no longer."

These are not the words of the officer—they are the words of the legislature; and convey as explicitly the authority the act intended to give, and operate as effectually, as if they had been inserted in any other part of the act than in the license itself.

The word "license" means permission or authority; and a license to do any particular thing is a permission or authority to do that thing; and if granted by a person having power to grant it, transfers to the grantee the right to do whatever it purports to authorize. It certainly transfers to him all the right which the grantor can transfer, to do what is within the terms of the license.

Would the validity or effect of such an instrument be questioned by the appellee, if executed by persons claiming regularly under the laws of New York?

The license must be understood to be what it purports to be, a legisla-tive authority to the steam boat Bellona "to be employed in carrying on the coasting trade for one year from its date."

It has been denied that these words authorize a voyage from New Jersey to New York. It is true that no ports are specified; but it is equally true that the words used are perfectly intelligible, and do confer such authority as unquestionably as if the ports had been mentioned. The coasting trade is a term well understood. The law has defined it; and all know its meaning perfectly. The act describes, with great minuteness, the various opera-tions of a vessel engaged in it; and it cannot, we think, be doubted, that a voyage from New Jersey to New York is one of those operations.

Notwithstanding the decided language of the license, it has also been maintained, that it gives no right to trade, and that its sole purpose is to confer the American character.

The answer given to this argument, that the American character is conferred by the enrolment, and not by the license, is, we think, founded too clearly in the words of the law, to require the support of any addi-tional observations. The enrolment of vessels designed for the coasting trade, corresponds precisely with the registration of vessels designed for the foreign trade, and requires every circumstance which can constitute the American character. The licence can be granted only to vessels al-ready enrolled, if they be of the burthen of twenty tons, and upwards; and requires no circumstance essential to the American character. The object of the license, then, cannot be to ascertain the character of the vessel, but to do what it professes to do—that is, to give permission to a vessel already proved by her enrolment to be American, to carry on the coasting trade.

But, if the license be a permit to carry on the coasting trade, the appellee denies that these boats were engaged in that trade, or that the decree under consideration has restrained them from prosecuting it. The boats of the appellant were, we are told, employed in the transportation of passengers; and this is no part of that commerce which Congress may regulate.

If, as our whole course of legislation on this subject shows, the power of Congress has been universally understood in America, to comprehend navigation, it is a very persuasive, if not a conclusive argument, to prove that the construction is correct; and, if it be correct, no clear distinction is perceived between the power to regulate vessels employed in transporting men for hire, and property for hire. The subject is transferred to Congress and no exception to the grant can be admitted, which is not proved by the words or the nature of the thing. A coasting vessel employed in the transportation of passengers, is as much a portion of the American marine, as one employed in the transportation of a cargo: and no reason is perceived why such vessel should be withdrawn from the regulating power of that government which has been thought best fitted for the purpose generally. The provisions of the law respecting native seamen, and respecting ownership, are as applicable to vessels carrying men, as to vessels carrying manufactures; and no reason is perceived why the power over the subject should not be placed in the same hands. The argument urged at the bar, rests on the foundation that the power of Congress does not extend to navigation, as a branch of commerce; and can only be applied to that subject incidentally and occasionally. But if that foundation be removed, we must show some plain intelligible distinction, supported by the constitution, or by reason, for discriminating between the power of Congress over vessels employed in navigating the same seas. We can perceive no such distinction.

If we refer to the constitution, the inference to be drawn from it is rather against the distinction. The section which restrains Congress from prohibiting the migration or importation of such persons as any of the States may think proper to admit, until the year 1808, has always been considered as an exception from the power to regulate commerce, and certainly seems to class migration with importation. Migration applies as appropriately to voluntary, as importation does to involuntary, arrivals; and, so far as an exception from a power proves its existence, this section proves that the power to regulate commerce applies equally to the regulation of vessels employed in transporting men who pass from place to place voluntarily, and to those who pass involuntarily.

If the power reside in Congress, as a portion of the general grant to regulate commerce, then acts applying that power to vessels generally, must be construed as comprehending all vessels. If none appear to be excluded by the language of the act, none can be excluded by construction. Vessels have always been employed to a greater or less extent in the transportation of passengers, and have never been supposed to be, on that account, withdrawn from the control or protection of Congress. Packets which ply along the coast, as well as those which make voyages between Europe and America, consider the transportation of passengers as an important part of their business. Yet, it has never been suspected that the general laws of navigation did not apply to them.

The duty act, sections 23 and 46, contains provisions respecting passengers, and shows that vessels which transport them, have the same rights and must perform the same duties, with other vessels.[9] They are governed by the general laws of navigation.

In the progress of things, this seems to have grown into a particular employment, and to have attracted the particular attention of government. Congress was no longer satisfied with comprehending vessels engaged specially in this business within those provisions which were intended for vessels generally, and, on the 2d of March, 1819, passed "An act regulating passenger ships and vessels."[10] This wise and humane law provides for the safety and comfort of passengers, and for the communication of every thing concerning them, which may interest the Government, to the Department of State, but makes no provision concerning the entry of the vessel, or her conduct in the waters of the United States. This, we think, shows conclusively the sense of Congress, (if, indeed, any evidence to that point could be required,) that the pre-existing regulations comprehended passenger ships, among others; and, in prescribing the same duties, the Legislature must have considered them as possessing the same rights.

If, then, it were even true, that the Bellona and the Stoudinger were employed exclusively in the conveyance of passengers between New York and New Jersey, it would not follow, that this occupation did not constitute a part of the coasting trade of the United States, and was not protected by the license annexed to the answer. But we cannot perceive how the occupation of these vessels can be drawn into question, in the case before the court. The laws of New York, which grant the exclusive privilege set up by the appellee, take no notice of the employment of vessels, and relate only to the principle by which they are propelled. Those laws do not inquire, whether vessels are engaged in transporting men or merchandise, but whether they are moved by steam or wind. If by the former, the waters of New York are closed against them, though their cargoes be dutiable goods, which the laws of the United States permit them to enter and deliver in New York. If by the latter, those waters are free to them, though they should carry passengers only. In conformity with the law, is the bill of the plaintiff in the state court. The bill does not complain that the Bellona and the Stoudinger carry passengers, but that they are moved by steam. This is the injury of which he complains, and is the sole injury against the continuance of which he asks relief. The bill does not even allege, specially, that those vessels were employed in the transportation of passengers, but says, generally, that they were employed "in the transportation of passengers, or otherwise." The answer avers, only, that they were employed in the coasting trade, and insists on the right to carry on any trade authorized by the license. No testimony is taken, and the writ of injunction and decree restrain these licensed vessels, not from carrying passengers, but from being moved through the waters of New York by steam, for any purpose whatever.

The questions, then, whether the conveyance of passengers be a part of the coasting trade, and whether a vessel can be protected in that occupation by a coasting license, are not, and cannot be, raised in this case. The real and sole question seems to be, whether a steam machine, in actual use, deprives a vessel of the privileges conferred by a license.

In considering this question, the first idea which presents itself, is, that the laws of Congress for the regulation of commerce, do not look to the principle by which vessels are moved. That subject is left entirely to individual discretion; and, in that vast and complex system of legislative enactment concerning it, which embraces every thing that the Legislature thought it necessary to notice, there is not, we believe, one word respecting the peculiar principle by which vessels are propelled through the water, except what may be found in a single act, granting a particular privilege to steam boats. With this exception, every act, either prescribing duties, or granting privileges, applies to every vessel, whether navigated by the instrumentality of wind or fire, or sails or machinery. The whole weight of proof, then, is thrown upon him who would introduce a distinction to which the words of the law give no countenance.

If a real difference could be admitted to exist between vessels carrying passengers, and others, it has already been observed, that there is no fact in this case which can bring up that question. And, if the occupation of steam boats be a matter of such general notoriety, that the Court may be presumed to know it, although not specially informed by the record, then we deny that the transportation of passengers is their exclusive occupation. It is a matter of general history, that, in our Western waters, their principal employment is the transportation of merchandise; and all know that, in the waters of the Atlantic they are frequently so employed.

But all inquiry into this subject seems to the Court to be put completely at rest, by the act already mentioned, entitled "An act for the enrolling and licensing of steam boats."[11]

This act authorizes a steam boat employed, or intended to be employed, only in a river or bay of the United States, owned wholly or in part by an alien, resident within the United States, to be enrolled and licensed as if the same belonged to a citizen of the United States.

This act demonstrates the opinion of Congress, that steam boats may be enrolled and licensed, in common with vessels using sails. They are, of course, entitled to the same privileges, and can no more be restrained from navigating waters and entering ports which are free to such vessels, than if they were wafted on their voyage by the winds, instead of being propelled by the agency of fire. The one element may be as legitimately used as the other, for every commercial purpose authorized by the laws of the Union, and the act of a State, inhibiting the use of either, to any vessel having a license under the act of Congress, comes, we think, in direct collision with that act.

As this decides the cause, it is unnecessary to enter into an examination of that part of the constitution which empowers Congress to promote the progress of science and the useful arts.

The Court is aware that, in stating the train of reasoning by which we have been conducted to this result, much time has been consumed in the attempt to demonstrate propositions which may have been thought axioms. It is felt that the tediousness inseparable from the endeavour to prove that which is already clear, is imputable to a considerable part of this opinion. But it was unavoidable. The conclusion to which we have come, depends on a chain of principles which it was necessary to preserve unbroken; and, although some of them were thought nearly self-evident, the magnitude of the question, the weight of character belonging to those from whose judgment we dissent, and the argument at the bar, demanded that we should assume nothing.

Powerful and ingenious minds, taking, as postulates, that the powers expressly granted to the Government of the Union, are to be contracted by construction into the narrowest possible compass, and that the original powers of the States are retained, if any possible construction will retain them, may, by a course of well-digested, but refined and metaphysical reasoning, founded on these premises, explain away the constitution of our country, and leave it, a magnificent structure, indeed, to look at, but totally unfit for use. They may so entangle and perplex the understanding, as to obscure principles which were before thought quite plain, and induce doubts where, if the mind were to pursue its own course, none would be perceived. In such a case, it is peculiarly necessary to recur to safe and fundamental principles, to sustain those principles, and, when sustained, to make them the test of the arguments to be examined.

[Decree]

Thomas Gibbons
v
Aaron Ogden

This cause came on to be heard on the transcript of the record of the court For the trial of Impeachments, and correction of Errors of the state of New York and was argued by counsel, on consideration whereof this court is of opinion that the several licenses to the steamboats The Stoudinger and The Bellona to carry on the coasting trade which are set up by the appellant Thomas Gibbons in his answer to the bill of the Appellee Aaron Ogden filed in the court of chancery for the state of New York which were granted under an act of Congress passed in pursuance of the constitution of the United States gave full authority to those vessels to navigate the waters of the United States by steam or otherwise for the purpose of carrying on the coasting trade any law of the state of New York to the contrary notwithstanding; and that so much of the several laws of the state of New York as prohibits vessels licensed according to the laws of the United States from navigating the waters of New York by means of fire or steam is repugnant to the constitution and void. This court is therefore of opinion that the decree of the court of the state of New York For the trial of Impeachments and the correction of Errors, affirming the decree of the chancellor of that state which perpetually injoins the said Thomas Gibbons the appellant from navigating the waters of the state of New York with the steam boats the Stoudinger and the Bellona by steam or fire is erroneous and ought to be reversed and the same is hereby reversed and annulled. And this court doth farther direct order and decree that the bill of the said Aaron Ogden be dismissed and the same is hereby dismissed accordingly.[12]

Printed, *Daily National Intelligencer* (Washington, D.C.), 5 March 1824. Decree, AD, Gibbons v. Ogden, Appellate Case No. 1148, RG 267, DNA.

1. Wheaton omitted JM's statement of the case and began his report of the opinion at this point, substituting "appellant" for "plaintiff in error."

2. On circuit in 1820 JM had also maintained that commerce embraced navigation. See Brig Wilson v. U.S., 1 Brock. 431–32; *PJM*, IX, 33.

3. Wheaton has "appellant."

4. Here and below Wheaton substitutes "respondent" for "appellee."

5. *U.S. Statutes at Large*, I, 474, 619.

6. Ibid., II, 205.

7. Ibid., I, 53–54.

8. JM cited the act of 1793 (ibid., I, 305–18).

9. This was the 1799 act to regulate the collection of import and tonnage duties (ibid., I, 627, 644–45, 661–62).

10. Ibid., III, 488.

11. This act was adopted in 1812 (ibid., II, 694).

12. After their defeat in the Supreme Court, the monopolists returned to the New York courts in an effort to preserve their privileges of steamboat navigation on the Hudson River within the boundaries of New York. In regard to this question, the meaning of Gibbons v. Ogden was not entirely clear. The opinion itself evidently embraced only interstate navigation between New York and New Jersey, though the official decree seemed to declare that the New York laws could not prevent a vessel holding a federal coasting license from engaging in intrastate navigation on the Hudson. In 1825 the New York Court of Errors struck down the remaining privileges of the monopoly through a broad reading of the Gibbons decision. See Baxter, *Steamboat Monopoly*, 62–68.

To Gales & Seaton

Gentlemen [3 March 1824]

I have received your note respecting the opinion in the Steamboat case and have certainly for myself not the slightest objection to its publication. I beleive the court has none except this. There is no copy of the opinion, and the rough draft has, as will always happen when an opinion on an extensive & complex question is written without previous arrangement, frequent insertions of arguments which are supposed to belong properly to a part which has been passed, in sepa⟨ra⟩te papers with letters of reference. Without great care this will le⟨ad⟩ to blunders in printing of a serious extent. Mr. Wheaton is accustomed to copying our opinions & will be enabled to be of great service to you should you proceed to print it. Yours &c

J MARSHALL

ALS, Collection of Henry N. Ess III, New York, N.Y. Addressed to Gales & Seaton. Date supplied by endorsement.

To Rembrandt Peale

Washington, March 10, 1824.

SIR:

I have received your letter of yesterday, and shall, with much pleasure, communicate the impression I received from viewing your Washington.[1]

I have never seen a Portrait of that great man which exhibited so perfect a resemblance of him. The likeness in features is striking, and the character of the whole face is preserved and exhibited with wonderful accuracy. It is more Washington, himself, than any Portrait of him I have ever seen.[2] With great respect, I am, sir, your obedient,

J. MARSHALL.

Printed, *Daily National Intelligencer* (Washington, D.C.), 12 Mar. 1824.

1. Letter not found. Rembrandt Peale (1778–1860), the premier portrait painter of his era, had just completed his portrait of Washington (*Patriae Pater*), which he was then exhibiting in Washington (Lillian B. Miller, et als., eds., *The Selected Papers of Charles Willson Peale and His Family*, IV [New Haven, Conn., 1996], 384–85).

2. Peale included the text of JM's letter in a lecture delivered in 1858, preceded by his account of JM's viewing of the portrait. Referring to JM's injury from his recent fall, Peale recalled: "He came with his Arm in a sling, and as he raised his eyes to look at the Portrait, exclaimed with emotion — 'It seems as if I were looking at the living Man! It is more like WASHINGTON than anything I have ever seen.' " Peale went on to note that JM advised him to procure written testimonials from Washington's close friends and relatives about the quality of the portrait. Peale accordingly solicited a letter from JM and published it in the *Daily National Intelligencer* with this introduction: "If any doubt existed of the veri-semblance

of Peale's Portrait of WASHINGTON, the following testimony of his Biographer and intimate friend, the Chief Justice of the United States, would, we should think, entirely remove it" (Gustavus A. Eisen, *Portraits of Washington,* I [New York, 1932], 297, 315; *Daily National Intelligencer,* 12 Mar. 1824; Miller, et al., eds., *Selected Papers of Charles Willson Peale,* IV, 384).

Osborn v. Bank of the United States
Opinion and Decree
U.S. Supreme Court, 19 March 1824

EDITORIAL NOTE

Osborn v. *Bank of the United States* was the judicial culmination of the efforts of the Second Bank of the United States to protect itself against hostile state actions. This hostility had intensified with the onset of the Panic of 1819 and ensuing economic depression. In Ohio, where branch offices had been established in 1817 at Cincinnati and Chillicothe, antagonism against the bank was particularly acute. There the bank's policy of contraction, the result in large part of its own initial folly in overextending credit, forced the suspension or closing of local banks and inflicted distress on debtors. In February 1819, a month before the Supreme Court's decision in *McCulloch* v. *Maryland,* the Ohio legislature adopted a law laying a tax of $50,000 per year on each branch office. It directed the state auditor to assess the tax on 15 September of each year and in case of default authorized him to search the bank's offices and seize specie and notes. The Ohio tax, similar to taxes on the bank laid in other states at this time, was enacted after careful deliberation and was an extension of earlier legislation taxing the state's banks. Even after the decision in *McCulloch,* the majority of the legislature continued to insist upon the constitutional right of the state to tax the national bank. From its perspective, the state's subsequent action in collecting the tax was not a willful defiance of the Supreme Court but a legal and peaceful means to resolve a controversy that was by no means fully settled by *McCulloch.*[1]

The Ohio legislature expected the bank to close its operations in the state as a result of the tax. The bank's decision to stay and the state's determination to collect the tax precipitated a legal and constitutional dispute that lasted for five years. The tax was to go into effect on 15 September 1819. On the previous day the bank had initiated process in the federal circuit court to enjoin Ralph Osborn, the state auditor, from proceeding under the state law. On the morning of the fifteenth Osborn received a copy of a bill of injunction along with a subpoena summoning him to appear in court to answer the bill. After obtaining legal advice to the effect that these papers did not in themselves constitute an injunction, Osborn issued a warrant to John L. Harper to collect the tax. Harper, on 17 September, went to the Chillicothe branch office and on the cashier's refusal to pay the tax forcibly seized money and notes amounting to more than $120,000. Eventually, $98,000 of this amount was deposited in the state treasury, the remainder (except for $2,000 retained by Harper as his fee) being returned to the bank. On 18 September, after the tax had been collected, an injunction was served upon Osborn and Harper, who were ordered to appear at the next term to answer the bill.[2]

Following a continuance at the January 1820 term, the bank in September

1820 filed a supplemental bill naming Hiram M. Curry, former treasurer, Samuel Sullivan, present treasurer, defendants along with Osborn and Harper. A year later, on 5 September 1821, the circuit court pronounced a decree ordering the defendants to deliver $100,000 to the bank, with interest on the specie amount ($19,830) of that sum. The decree also perpetually enjoined the defendants from proceeding to collect any further tax under the act of February 1819. By agreement of counsel, the decree went into effect immediately against Sullivan by means of a writ of sequestration. Commissioners appointed to execute this writ accordingly took from Sullivan the keys to the treasury and removed the $98,000 that had been deposited there a year earlier. At the request of the defendants the court allowed an appeal of this decree to the Supreme Court. The appeal was to operate as a suspension of the execution of the decree only as to the $2,000 taken by Harper, interest, and costs.[3]

While these proceedings were pending in the federal court, a joint committee of the Ohio legislature presented a report in December 1820 defending the actions of the state's officials and the constitutionality of the tax imposed on the bank. The chairman of the committee was Charles Hammond, counsel for the defendants in the circuit court and also in the appeal to the Supreme Court.[4] The report contained a number of arguments Hammond later employed in his brief for the Supreme Court, though in a different form and much toned down. The report's principal contention was that the proceeding by injunction against Osborn and others was substantially a suit against the state and that jurisdiction was therefore barred by the Eleventh Amendment. Quoting with approval the Virginia and Kentucky Resolutions of 1798, the report denied the federal judiciary's claim to decide cases involving the political power and authority of the states.[5]

While denying federal jurisdiction, the report also sought to vindicate the state's right to tax the national bank. It rejected the binding authority of *McCulloch* v. *Maryland* on two principal grounds. First, the case was collusive, contrived to obtain a decision favorable to the bank and thus shore up the credit of an institution then verging on bankruptcy. "If, by the management of a party, and through the inadvertence or connivance of a State," the report stated, "a case be made, presenting to the Supreme Court . . . for decision important and interesting questions of State power and State authority, upon no just principle ought the States to be concluded by any decision had upon such a case." Second, though the Court was correct in affirming Congress's power to charter a bank, the principle of supremacy asserted in that case was incorrectly applied to deny the state's right to tax the bank. In support of this proposition the report maintained that the bank was a private trading company and that its federal charter did not confer any implied exemption from taxation. In no sense could the bank be considered an instrument of government like the mint or the post office.[6]

Although insisting that the bank was subject to the taxing power of the states, the report did propose a compromise whereby the state would return the money collected as tax if the bank would drop its suit against the state officials and give assurance that the branch offices would be withdrawn from the state. If the compromise were not accepted, the report recommended legislation that would completely exclude the bank from the protection and use of state officers in carrying on its business. Such a measure would "leave the bank exclusively to the protection of the Federal Government, and its constitutional power to preserve it in the sense maintained by the Supreme Court may thus be fairly, peaceably, and constitutionally tested."[7] The report concluded with a series of resolutions summarizing the propositions asserted in the text and recommending that the governor transmit copies of the report and resolutions to the state legislatures and to the president and Congress.

The Ohio legislature adopted the report in January 1821 and soon thereafter passed legislation depriving the bank of the protection and aid of the state's laws unless the bank discontinued its suit against the state officers and submitted to an annual tax or removed its branch offices from the state. The bank ignored the provisions of this law, which evidently remained a dead letter until its repeal in 1826. No other states besides Virginia and Kentucky endorsed Ohio's position in its controversy with the bank, and the subject received no attention in Congress. By the time the case came to be argued in the Supreme Court in 1824, the economic and financial situation of the state had improved and agitation over the issue had largely subsided.[8]

Chief Justice Marshall was thoroughly acquainted with the issues of the case before the Court heard the appeal. Late in 1823 Hammond, who did not argue the appeal orally at the 1824 term, published a lengthy argument that he sent to Marshall (and perhaps to the other justices as well). The chief justice read it "with that pleasure which I always feel in reading or hearing one in which the subject is discussed with real ability, whether I concur or not in opinion with the person who makes it." He found it "less vulnerable" to a charge of "disrespect to the court" than Hammond's joint committee report of 1820, "which however was far from being deficient in vigour."[9] Indeed, in presenting the case to the Supreme Court, Hammond recast the argument of the 1820 committee report, stripping away much of its garb of states' rights doctrine. As in the report, he urged two principal reasons for reversing the circuit court's decree: (1) that the case was in fact against the state of Ohio and therefore the circuit court had no jurisdiction; (2) that the states had power to tax the national bank notwithstanding the opinion in *McCulloch* v. *Maryland*.

On the first point Hammond, in contrast to the report, did not rely on the Eleventh Amendment and maintain that federal jurisdiction was completely ousted because the defendant was a state. Instead, he asserted the doctrine of sovereign immunity only to the extent that a state could not be sued in an inferior federal court. Conceding on the authority of *Cohens* v. *Virginia* (decided after the report) that a state could be made a party in a case arising under the Constitution or federal law, Hammond argued that such a case was one of original jurisdiction and that "by the express letter of the constitution, the Supreme Court alone are authorized to take jurisdiction."[10] Whether or not federal jurisdiction attached by the character of the party or because the case arose under the Constitution or federal law, if a state was a party jurisdiction had to be original and the case could originate only in the Supreme Court. Employing Chief Justice Marshall's own preferred mode of literal construction of the Constitution's words, Hammond insisted that the phrase "all cases" in the clause distributing the Supreme Court's original and appellate jurisdiction allowed of no exception by which an original suit could be brought against a state in an inferior federal court. It was a powerfully reasoned argument, but it hinged on the Court's agreeing that the bank's suit was against the state of Ohio rather than the individuals named in the record.

Hammond gave most of his attention to demonstrating the constitutionality of the state's tax on the bank, which he regarded as "the most important point in the case." The question of the bank's exemption from state taxation, he said, "depends upon the nature and character of the institution." If it was a public institution like the mint or the post office, then it was "entitled to the exemption it claims."[11] The true character of the bank, however, was that it was a company engaged in private trade for private profit. This argument had received little attention in *McCulloch,* and for that reason alone Hammond felt justified in requesting the Court's reconsideration of that decision.

The bank's incorporation under an act of Congress, Hammond said, did not change its essential nature as a private company. True, it performed public functions and conferred public benefits by facilitating the government's fiscal operations, but in this respect it was no different from a private individual or company that contracts with the government to provide certain services such as transporting the mail. Hammond drew support for his contention from the Court's own words in *Dartmouth College* v. *Woodward,* quoting both Marshall's and Story's opinions in that case. Immunity from taxation was not incident to a private corporation and was not to be implied in the charter creating the corporation. That the charter in this instance was granted by the national government made no difference. The *Dartmouth* decision and the history of private corporations down to *McCulloch* demonstrated that "exemption from taxation for public purposes, by an inferior legislative power, is not incident to a corporation created by the supreme power." Such an exemption, if intended by Congress, would have to be specially inserted in the charter. The very attempt to create this exemption, however, would produce a constitutional inquiry into Congress's power to do it that "would still further elucidate the" error of regarding the exemption as "an incident of the charter, independent of special grant."[12]

The lawyers who argued the case in court at the 1824 term were Henry Clay for the bank and John C. Wright (1783–1861) and Ethan A. Brown (1776–1852) for Osborn. Wright was then a member of the House of Representatives from Ohio; Brown, recently governor of Ohio, was then serving in the Senate. Clay, who had also received a copy of Hammond's printed argument, presented his response on 10 February. As to the state's right to tax the bank, he considered that question fully settled by *McCulloch,* while noting that Ohio was in fact asserting a right to expel the bank. Surely, he said, the federal judiciary could exercise its jurisdiction to prevent a single state from defeating a measure adopted by the whole nation. Federal jurisdiction could not be ousted even if the state was a party because this was a case arising under the Constitution and federal laws. "There the nature of the controversy, and not the character of the parties, must determine the question of jurisdiction," said Clay.[13] Wright on 11 February added little to the case stated by Hammond, though going beyond him in holding that the Eleventh Amendment barred suits against states even if the case arose under the Constitution or federal law.

At this point another jurisdictional question arose, whether the bank had a general right to sue in the federal circuit courts under the 1816 act granting the charter. Osborn's counsel had not contested jurisdiction on this ground, perhaps reasoning that if the state was not a party federal jurisdiction would attach because the case concerned the constitutionality of the tax. The issue did arise in a case certified from Georgia, *Bank of the United States* v. *Planters' Bank of Georgia,* but the Court wished to hear argument before deciding *Osborn.* Clay arranged to have the cases heard together on this point on 10 and 11 March. John Sergeant and Daniel

Webster for the bank argued in favor of the jurisdiction; Brown and Wright for Osborn and Robert G. Harper for the Planters' Bank argued against jurisdiction.[14]

For the jurisdiction it was contended that the 1816 act expressly conferred the right to sue in the circuit courts. Although the Court in *Bank of the United States* v. *Deveaux* (1809) ruled that the first bank had no right to sue in the circuit courts by virtue of its charter, the act creating the first bank did not specifically mention federal courts. Congress, however, had constitutional authority to enable the bank to sue in the circuit courts and exercised this authority in establishing the second bank. Such authority, it was argued, derived from the clause extending federal jurisdiction to all cases arising under the Constitution and laws of the United States. Since all the bank's rights, privileges, and capacities existed under its charter, every case in which it was a party arose under federal law. In support of the jurisdiction counsel also invoked the maxim that the judicial power should be commensurate with the legislative power.[15]

Opposing counsel denied any difference in the legal effect of the acts creating the first and second banks, insisting that under both the bank could sue only in those courts that were otherwise competent to take jurisdiction. Under the *Deveaux* precedent the bank could only come into the federal circuit court by virtue of diversity jurisdiction. If every suit by the bank was deemed to arise under the laws of the United States because the bank's existence and powers derived from federal law, then every naturalized citizen could claim a right to sue in the federal courts. Suits by the bank concerning bills of exchange and promissory notes depended on the local law of contract or law of evidence and had nothing to do with federal law.[16]

Marshall delivered the Court's opinion on 19 March, first taking up the jurisdictional issue raised by the act of 1816. As in *Cohens* he gave a broad reading of the "arising under" clause to sustain Congress's constitutional power to confer original jurisdiction on the circuit courts to hear cases involving the bank. Such a construction had much to recommend it in terms of policy and expediency, for it gave the bank frontline legal protection. If the bank were forced to seek redress in the first instance in the state courts, the consequence might be the postponement of justice until the case came before the federal Supreme Court on appeal. Yet expediency and constitutional principle were not opposed to each other in this instance, the chief justice concluded. In giving the bank immediate access to the federal courts, Congress was not bestowing any jurisdiction that was not already fully conferred by the Constitution. Just as Congress under the "necessary and proper" clause had broad discretion to select the means of executing its express powers, so under the "arising under" clause it could choose to extend or not to extend federal jurisdiction to the full limit allowed by the Constitution. Although agreeing with the "policy" of the decision, Justice Johnson dissented from this part of the opinion, contending that the Constitution did not authorize Congress to give the bank a right to sue in the circuit courts "merely on the ground that a question might *possibly* be raised in it, involving the constitution, or constitutionality of a law, of the United States."[17]

On the two principal questions arising on the merits of Osborn's case, the Court also upheld the bank. Although admitting that the state of Ohio had a "direct interest" in the suit, Chief Justice Marshall held that the circuit court could act upon the state's agents. Here again he invoked the argument from necessity, pointing to the dire consequences if federal jurisdiction was to be ousted because the real party in this case was a state. It would mean that an individual state could with impunity prevent the execution of federal laws, while the federal government "stands naked, stripped of its defensive armour."[18] Hammond had attempted to blunt the force of this argument by conceding that a state was amenable to the Supreme Court's original jurisdiction. A concession that required the bank to seek original legal redress in the Supreme Court against actions occurring in a distant state amounted to little, and evidently for this reason the chief justice did not respond to it. Instead, he focused on the question whether a suit against an individual could be considered a suit against a state as understood by the Constitution. Construction yielded a rule "that in all cases where jurisdiction depends on the party, it is the party named in the record."[19] Where the Constitution refers to suits in which a state is a party, the state must be a party of record. In this case, then, the jurisdiction of the federal circuit court was not excluded by the Eleventh Amendment. It was unnecessary to add that the rule also covered Hammond's modified immunity argument that ousted the circuit court's original jurisdiction but not that of the Supreme Court.

In so restricting the reach of the Eleventh Amendment, Marshall conceded that in a suit against a state's agents those individuals must have "a real interest" and could not merely be "nominal parties."[20] In this case the Court was fully satisfied of the individual responsibility and liability of the Ohio officials who were concerned in the removal and detaining of the bank's money. The amendment could not be evaded merely by naming a state officer as a party, as was attempted in a case that arose four years later. In that case the Court determined that a suit against the governor of Georgia was in his official character and that the state itself was to be considered as a party of record.[21]

The opinion concluded by reaffirming *McCulloch,* pronouncing the "much more objectionable" Ohio tax void as repugnant to the federal law creating the bank. Marshall used this occasion to conduct a more thorough inquiry into the nature of the bank than he had done in the earlier case. To each of Hammond's arguments endeavoring to show that the bank was an essentially private institution that could not claim exemption from state taxation, the chief justice offered a cogent reply. The bank, he insisted, retained its character as a public corporation, even though it had the capacity to transact private business. This capacity, indeed, was indispensable to the bank's public purposes, enabling it to be "a machine for the fiscal operations of the government." It was therefore unnecessary for Congress to have expressly declared the bank's exemption from taxation. To construe the act granting the charter as if it had conferred the exemption in express terms was not an act of judicial will, said Marshall in the opinion's most celebrated passage, but an exercise of "meer legal discretion" in "giving effect to the will of the legislature; or, in other words, to the will of the law."[22]

Unlike *McCulloch* five years earlier, the decision in *Osborn* attracted little public notice. Opposing counsel Clay and Hammond cooperated to work out a satisfactory means of carrying into effect the Court's mandate. In December 1824, the Ohio legislature signified its acquiescence by appropriating a sum necessary to cover the decree.[23]

A Note on the Text

The opinion in *Osborn* is one of a handful of Marshall's constitutional opinions that have survived in manuscript. Not until 1834 did the Supreme Court adopt a

1

Osborn &al
The "Bank of the US.

on the ~~14th~~ of September 1819, a bill was presented to the circuit
court of the United States for the District of Ohio, by gentlemen who
were practising attornies at that bar, praying an injunction to restrain
Ralph Osborne auditor of the state of Ohio, from proceeding against
the complainants under an act passed by the legislature of
the state, entitled an act to levy and collect a tax from all banks
and individuals, and companies and associations of individuals
that may transact banking business in this state without
being authorized to do so by the laws thereof."
            This act after reciting that the bank pursued its
operations contrary to a law of the state, enacted that if, after the first
day of the following September, the said Bank or any other
should continue to transact business within the state, it should
be liable to an annual tax of $50.000 on each office. And that,
on the 15th day of Septr the Auditor should charge such tax
to the Bank, and should make out his warrant under his seal
of office, directed to any person, commanding him to collect the said
tax, who should enter the banking house and demand the same; and
if payment be not made, should levy the amount on the money or other
goods of the Bank; — the money to be retained, and the goods sold
as if taken on a fi. fa. If no effects should be found in the banking
room, the person having the warrant was authorized to go into every
room, vault, &c and to open every chest &c for search of which might sa
tisfy his warrant.
            after reciting this act
            The bill, states that Ralph Osborn is the Audi
tor, and gives out in speeches that he will execute the law. It was
exhibited in open court on the 14th of September; and, notice of the applica
having been given to the defendant Osborne, an order was made
on the execution of bond & security in the penalty of $10,000; the order
ing the injunction, after which a subpoena was issued, on which
that had been made for
the injunction was indorsed by the attorneys for the plaintiff;
and a memorandum that bond with security had been given by the plain
tiff was indorsed by the clerk; and a power to James McDowell to serve
the same was indorsed by the Marshal. It appears

DRAFT OF OSBORN V. BANK OF THE UNITED STATES

First page of Marshall's draft opinion. *Courtesy of the Gilder Lehrman
Collection at the Pierpont Morgan Library, New York, GLC 3653.*

rule ordering original opinions to be filed in the clerk's office after publication by the reporter. Before that time the Court's opinions remained the property of the reporter, who in many instances must have destroyed them after they were set in type.[24] In this case Henry Wheaton preserved the original, but the history of the manuscript from the time he possessed it until it was offered for sale in 1977 cannot be reconstructed. The reporter may have sold or donated the manuscript to gratify the wishes of a nineteenth-century autograph collector. From 1977 until it was sold again in 1993 the document was in the hands of a California collector. The present owner is the Gilder Lehrman Collection at the Pierpont Morgan Library in New York City.

The manuscript consists of twenty-two folio leaves, which until recently were bound in a leather-backed board volume with a lettering-piece "MARSHALL" on the front cover.[25] The writing is on both sides and is paginated "1" to "42." Marshall's autograph decree follows on an unnumbered page. There are numerous emendations, most of them in Marshall's hand but some evidently made by Wheaton. In a few instances it is not possible to state with certainty that Marshall made the correction. Marshall began his opinion with a statement of the case that fills nearly three manuscript pages. As published in the Washington *Daily National Intelligencer* on 22 March 1824, the opinion includes the statement of the case. In his report Wheaton summarized Marshall's statement and began the opinion at the tenth paragraph of the manuscript.

1. Ernest L. Bogart, "Taxation of the Second Bank of the United States by Ohio," *American Historical Review*, XVII (1911–12), 312–31.

2. Osborn v. Bank of the United States, App. Cas. No. 1135; Bogart, "Taxation of the Second Bank of the United States," 323–24.

3. Ibid., 325; Henry Clay to Langdon Cheves, 8 Sept. 1821, James F. Hopkins and Mary W. M. Hargreaves, eds., *The Papers of Henry Clay*, III (Lexington, Ky., 1963), 111–14.

4. *PJM*, IX, 367, 368 n. 3.

5. *ASP, Miscellaneous*, II, 643–47.

6. Ibid., II, 647.

7. Ibid., II, 653.

8. Bogart, "Taxation of the Second Bank of the United States," 329–30; Warren, *Supreme Court*, I, 537–38.

9. JM to Charles Hammond, 28 Dec. 1823, *PJM*, IX, 367.

10. 9 Wheat. 757.

11. 9 Wheat. 765, 765–66.

12. 9 Wheat. 780, 794–95.

13. 9 Wheat. 798.

14. Bank of the U.S. v. Planters' Bank of Georgia, Opinion, 20 Mar. 1824; Clay to Nicholas Biddle, 17 Feb. 1824, Hopkins and Hargreaves, eds., *Papers of Clay*, III, 646–47; U.S. Sup. Ct. Minutes, 10, 11 Mar. 1824.

15. 9 Wheat. 805–11.

16. 9 Wheat. 811–16.

17. 9 Wheat. 871–72, 874.

18. Opinion and Decree, 19 Mar. 1824 (61, below).

19. Opinion and Decree, 19 Mar. 1824 (66, below).

20. Opinion and Decree, 19 Mar. 1824 (66, below).

21. Governor of Georgia v. Madrazo, 1 Pet. 110 (1828); Clyde E. Jacobs, *The Eleventh Amendment and Sovereign Immunity* (Westport, Conn., 1972), 97–105.

22. Opinion and Decree, 19 Mar. 1824 (71, below).

23. Bogart, "Taxation of the Second Bank of the United States," 330–31; Henry Clay to Charles Hammond, 21 June 1824, Hopkins and Hargreaves, eds., *Papers of Clay*, III, 782; *Acts of a General Nature, . . . of the State of Ohio* (Columbus, Ohio, 1825), 8–9.

24. *PJM*, VI, 70.

25. The binding was removed in 1994 to permit safe handling of the manuscript (communication from Paul W. Romaine, Curator and Executive Director of the Gilder Lehrman Collection).

Osborne & al

v

The Bank of the U.S.

¶1   In September 1819, a bill was presented to the circuit court of the United States for the District of Ohio in the name of the Bank of the U.S., signed by gentlemen who were practising attornies at that bar, praying an injunction to restrain Ralph Osborne Auditor of the state of Ohio, from proceeding against complainants under an act passed the preceding February by the legislature of the state, entitled "an act to levy and collect a tax from all banks and individuals, and companies and associations of individuals that may transact banking business in this state without being authorized to do so by the laws thereof."

¶2   This act after reciting that the Bank pursued its operations contrary to a law of the state, enacted that if, after the first day of the following September, the said Bank or any other should continue to transact business within the state, it should be liable to an annual tax of $50000 on each office. And that, on the 15th. day of September, the Auditor should charge such tax to the Bank, and should make out his warrant under his seal of office, directed to any person, commanding him to collect the said tax, who should enter the banking house and demand the same; and if payment be not made, should levy the amount on the money or other goods of the Bank; the money to be retained, and the goods sold as if taken on a fi. fa. If no effects should be found in the Banking room, the person having the warrant was authorized to go into every room, vault, &c and to open every chest &c in search of what might satisfy his warrant.

¶3   The bill after reciting this act states that Ralph Osborne is the Auditor, and gives out in speeches that he will execute the law. It was exhibited in open court on the 14th. of September; and, notice of the application having been given to the defendant Osborne, an order was made awarding the injunction, on the execution of bond & security in the penalty of $100,000; after which a subpœna was issued, on which the order that had been made for the injunction was indorsed by the attorneys for the plaintiff; and a memorandum that bond with security had been given by the plaintiff was indorsed by the clerk; and a power to James MDowell to serve the same was indorsed by the Marshal. It appears from the affidavit of MDowell that both the subpœna and indorsment were served on Ralph Osborne early in the morning of the 15th. On the 18th. of the same month of September, a writ of injunction was issued on the same bill which was served on the same day on Ralph Osbourne, and on John L. Harper. The affidavit of MDougal states that he served the writ on Harper while on his way to Columbus with the money and funds which were the subject matter on which the same were to operate as he understood; and that the writ was served on Osborne before Harper reached Columbus.

In September 1820 leave was given to file a supplemental and amended ¶4 bill, and to make new parties.

This bill charges that subsequent to the service of the subpœna and ¶5 injunction, to wit on the 17th. of Septr. 1819, John L. Harper, who was employed by Osborne to collect the tax and well knew that an injunction had been allowed, proceeded by violence to the office of the Bank at Chilicothe, and took therefrom $100 000 in specie and bank notes belonging to or in deposite with the complainants. That this money was delivered either to H. M Curry, who was then Treasurer of the state, or to the defendant Osborne, both of whom had notice of the illegal seizure, and paid no consideration for the amount, but received it to keep on safe deposit. That Curry did keep the same until he delivered it over to one Samuel Sullivan, his successor as Treasurer. That neither Curry nor Sullivan held the said money in their character as Treasurer, but as individuals. The bill prays that the said H. M. Curry late Treasurer, Samuel Sullivan the present Treasurer and Ralph Osborne in their official and private characters, and the said John L Harper may be made defendants, that they may make discovery, and may be enjoined from using or paying away the coin and notes taken from the bank, may be decreed to restore the same and may be enjoined from proceeding farther under the said act.

The defendant Curry filed his answer admitting that the defendant ¶6 Harper delivered to him about the 20th. of September 1819 the sum of $98000 which he was informed and beleived was a tax levied of the Branch Bank of the United States. He passed this sum to the credit of the state as revenue; but kept it separate in fact from other money, until January or February 1820 when the monies in the treasury were seized upon by a committee of the House of Representatives, soon after which he resigned his office and the monies and bank notes in the bill mentioned, still separate from other monies in the Treasury, came to the hands of S. Sullivan, the present Treasurer, who gave a receipt for the same.

The defendant Sullivan failing to answer an attachment for contempt ¶7 was issued on which he was taken into custody. He then filed his answer and was discharged.

This answer denies all personal knowledge of the levying collecting ¶8 and paying over the money in the bill mentioned. It admits that he was appointed Treasurer as successor of Curry, on the 17th. of Feb. 1820, and that he entered the Treasury on the 23d and began examining the funds, among which he found the sum of $98000 which he understood was the same that is charged in the bill, but this he does not know of his own knowledge. He gave a receipt as Treasurer, and the money has remained in his hands as Treasurer and not otherwise. The sum of $98000 remained untouched out of respect for an injunction said to have been allowed by the circuit court on a bill since dismissed. He admits the sum in his hands to correspond with the description in the bill so far as that description goes, and annexes a schedule of the residue to his answer. He has no individual interest in the money and holds it only as state Treasurer. Admits notice from general report and from the late Treasurer that the said sum of $98000 was levied as a tax from the Bank, and that the Bank alleged it to be illegal and violent.

¶9   The cause came on to be heard upon these answers and upon the decrees nisi against Osborn and Harper; and the court pronounced a decree directing them to restore to the Bank the sum of $100000, with interest on $19830, the amount of the specie in the hands of Sullivan. From this decree an appeal was prayed to this court.

¶10   At[1] the close of the argument a point was suggested of such vital importance as to induce the court to request that it might be particularly spoken to. That point is, the right of the Bank to sue in the courts of the United States. It has been argued and ought to be disposed of before we proceed to the actual exercise of jurisdiction by deciding on the rights of the parties.

¶11   The appellants contest the jurisdiction of the court on two grounds
    1st. That the act of Congress has not given it.
    2d. That, under the constitution Congress cannot give it.
    1. The first part of the objection depends entirely on the language of the act. The words are that the Bank shall be "made able and capable in law" "to sue and be sued, plead and be impleaded, answer and be answered, defend and be defended, in all state courts having competent jurisdiction, and in any circuit court of the United States."[2]

¶12   These words seem to the court to admit of but one interpretation. They cannot be made plainer by explanation. They give expressly the right "to sue and be sued," "in any circuit court of the United States," and it would be difficult to substitute other terms which would be more direct and appropriate for the purpose. The argument of the appellants is founded on the opinion of this court in The Bank of the United States v Deveaux, Cranch   .[3] In that case, it was decided that the former Bank of the United States was not enabled by the act which incorporated it, to sue in the federal courts. The words of the 3d. sec. of that act are that the Bank may "sue and be sued" &c "in courts of record, or any other place whatsoever."[4] The court was of opinion, that these general words, which are usual in all acts of incorporation, gave only a general capacity to sue, not a particular privilege to sue in the courts of the United States; and this opinion was strengthened by the circumstance that the 9th. rule of the 7th. Sec. of the same act, subjects the Directors, in case of excess in contracting debt, to be sued in their private capacity "in any court of record of the United States, or either of them."[5] The express grant of jurisdiction to the federal courts in this case was considered as having some influence on the construction of the general words of the 3d. Sec. which does not mention those courts. Whether this decision be right or wrong, it amounts only to a declaration that a general capacity in the Bank to sue, without mentioning the courts of the Union, may not give a right to sue in those courts; To infer from this that words expressly conferring a right to sue in those courts, does not give the right, is surely a conclusion which the premises do not warrant.

The act of incorporation then confers jurisdiction on the circuit courts of the United States, if Congres can confer it. ¶13

2d. We will now consider the constitutionality of the clause in the act of incorporation which authorizes the Bank to sue in the federal courts. ¶14

In support of this clause it is said that the Legislative, Executive and Judicial powers of every well constructed government, are coextensive with each other. That is, they are potentially coextensive. The Executive department may constitutionally execute every law which the legislature may constitutionally make, and the judicial department may receive from the legislature the power of construing every such law. All governments which are not extremely defective in their organization, must possess within themselves the means of expounding as well as enforcing their own laws. If we examine the constitution of the United States we find that its framers kept this great political principle in view. The 2d. art. vests the whole executive power in the President; and the 3d. declares that "the judicial power shall extend to all cases in law and equity arising under this constitution, the laws of the United States, and treaties made or which shall be made under their authority." ¶15

This clause enables the judicial department to receive jurisdiction to the full extent of the constitution, laws, & treaties, of the United States, when any question respecting them shall assume such a form that the judicial power is capable of acting on it. That power is capable of acting only when the subject is submitted to it by a party who asserts his rights in the form prescribed by law. It then becomes a case, and the constitution declares that the judicial power shall extend to all cases arising under the constitution laws and treaties of the United States. ¶16

The suit of the Bank of the United States v Osborne and others is a case, and the question is whether it arises under a law of the United States. ¶17

The appellants contend that it does not, because several questions may arisc in it, which depend on the general principles of law, not on any act of Congress. ¶18

If this were sufficient to withdraw a case from the jurisdiction of the federal courts, almost every case though involving the construction of a law would be withdrawn; and a clause in the constitution relating to a subject of vital importance to the government, and expressed in the ¶19 most comprehensive terms, would be construed to mean almost nothing. There is scarcely any case, every part of which depends on the constitution, laws, or treaties of the United States. The questions whether the fact alleged as the foundation of the action be real or fictitious, whether the conduct of the plaintiff has been such as to entitle him to maintain his action, whether his right is barred, whether he has received satisfaction, or has in any manner released his claim, are questions some or all of which may occur in almost every case; and if their existence be sufficient to arrest the jurisdiction of the court, words which seem intended to be as extensive as the constitution laws, and treaties of the union, which seem designed to give the courts of the government the construction of all its acts, so far as they affect the rights of individuals would be reduced to almost nothing.

¶20   In those cases in which original jurisdiction is given to the supreme court, the judicial power of the United States cannot be exercised in its appellate form. In every other case the power is to be exercised in its original or appellate form or both as the wisdom of Congress may direct. With the exception of those cases in which original jurisdiction is given to this court, there is none to which the judicial power extends, from which the original jurisdiction of the inferior courts is excluded by the constitution. Original jurisdiction, so far as the constitution gives a rule, is coextensive with the judicial power. We find in the constitution no prohibition to its exercise in every case in which the judicial power can be exercised. It would be a very bold construction to say that this power could be applied in its appellate form only, to the most important class of cases to which it is applicable.

¶21   The constitution establishes the supreme court and defines its jurisdiction. It enumerates cases in which its jurisdiction is original and exclusive; and then defines that which is appellate, but does not insinuate that in any such case the power cannot be exercised in its original form by courts of original jurisdiction. It is not insinuated that the judicial power, in cases depending on the character of the cause, cannot be exercised in the first instance in the courts of the union, but must first be exercised in the tribunals of the state; tribunals over which the government of the union has no adequate controul, and which may be closed to any claim asserted under a law of the United states.

¶22   We perceive then no ground on which the proposition can be maintained that Congress is incapable of giving the circuit courts original jurisdiction in any case to which the appellate jurisdiction, extends.

¶23   We ask then if it can be sufficient to exclude this jurisdiction that the case involves questions depending on general principles? A cause may depend on several questions of fact and law. Some of these may depend on the construction of a law of the United States, others on principles unconnected with that law. If it be a sufficient foundation for jurisdiction that the title or right set up by the party may be defeated by one construction of the constitution or law of the United States, and sustained by the opposite construction, provided the facts necessary to support the action be made out, then all the other questions must be decided as incidental to this which gives that jurisdiction. Those other questions cannot arrest the proceedings. Under this construction the judicial power of the union extends effectively and beneficially to that most important class of cases which depend on the character of the cause. On the opposite construction, the judicial power never can be extended to a whole case, as expressed by the constitution, but to those parts of cases only which present the particular question involving the construction of the constitution or the law. We say it never can be extended to the whole case, because, if the circumstance that other points are involved in it shall disable congress from authorizing the courts of the Union to take jurisdiction of the original cause, it equally disables congress from authorizing those courts to take jurisdiction of the whole cause on an appeal; and thus words which in their plain sense apply to a whole cause,[6] will be restricted to a single question in that cause, and words obviously intended to secure to those who claim rights under the constitution laws or treaties of the United states a trial in the federal courts, will be restricted to the insecure remedy of an appeal upon an insulated point, after it has received that shape which may be given to it by another tribunal into which he is forced against his will.

We think then that when a question to which the judicial power of the Union is extended by the constitution forms an ingredient of the original cause, it is in the power of Congress to give the circuit courts jurisdiction of that cause, although other questions of fact or of law may be involved in it. ¶24

The case of the Bank is, we think, a very strong case of this description. The charter of incorporation not only creates it, but gives it every faculty which it possesses. The power to acquire rights of any description, to transact business of any description, to make contracts of any description, to sue on those contracts, is given and measured by its charter, and that charter is a law of the United States. This being can acquire no right, make no contract, bring no suit, which is not authorized by a law of the United States. It is not only itself the meer creature of a law, but all its actions and all its rights are dependent on the same law. Can a being thus constituted have a case which does not arise literally as well as substantially under the law? ¶25

Take the case of a contract which is put as the strongest against the Bank. ¶26

When a bank sues, the first question which presents itself, and which lies at the foundation of the cause, is, has this legal entity a right to sue? Has it a right to come, not into this court particularly, but into any court? This depends on a law of the United States. The next question is, has this being a right to make this particular contract? If this question be decided in the negative, the cause is determined against the plaintiff; and this ¶27 question to[o] depends entirely on a law of the United States. These are important questions and they exist in every possible case. The right to sue, if decided once is decided forever; but the power of Congress was exercised antecedently to the first decision on that right, and if it was constitutional then it cannot cease to be so, because the particular question is decided. It may be revived at the will of the party and most probably would be renewed were the tribunal to be changed. But the question respecting the right to make a particular contract, or to acquire a particular property, or to sue on account of a particular injury, belongs to every particular case, and may be renewed in every case. The question forms an original ingredient in every cause. Whether it be in fact relied on or not in the defence, it is still a part of the cause and may be relied on. The right of the plaintiff to sue cannot depend on the defence which the defendant may chuse to set up. His right to sue is anterior to that defence, and must depend on the state of things when the action is brought. The questions which the case involves then, must determine its character, whether those questions be made in the cause or not.

¶28   The appellants say that the case arises in the contract, but the validity of the contract depends on a law of the United States and the plaintiff is compelled in every case to show its validity. The case arises emphatically under the law. The act of Congress is its foundation. The contract could never have been made but under the authority of that act. The act itself is the first ingredient in the case, is its origin, is that from which every other part arises. That other questions may also arise, as the execution of the contract, or its performance, cannot change the case or give it any other origin than the charter of incorporation. The action still originates in and is sustained by that charter.

¶29   The clause giving the Bank a right to sue in the circuit courts of the United States stands on the same principle with the acts authorizing officers of the United States who sue in their own names, to sue in the courts of the United States. The Post Master General for example, cannot sue under that part of the constitution which gives jurisdiction to the federal courts in consequence of the character of the party, nor is he authorized to sue by the judicial act. He comes into the courts of the union under the authority of an act of Congress the constitutionality of which can only be sustained by the admission that his suit is a case arising under a law of the United States. If it be said that it is such a case, because a law of the United States authorizes the contract and authorizes the suit, the same reasons exist with respect to a suit brought by the Bank. That too is such a case, because that suit too is itself authorized, and is brought on a contract authorized, by a law of the United States. It depends absolutely on that law, and cannot exist a moment without its authority.

¶30   If it be said that a suit brought by the Bank may depend in fact altogether on questions unconnected with any law of the United States, it is equally true with respect to suits brought by the Post Master General. The plea in bar may be payment, if the suit be brought on a bond, or non-assumpsit if it be brought on an open account, and no other question may arise than what respects the complete discharge of the demand. Yet the constitutionality of the act authorizing the Post Master General to sue in the courts of the United States, has never been drawn into question. It is sustained singly by an act of congress standing on that construction of the constitution which asserts the right of the legislature to give original jurisdiction to the circuit courts in cases arising under a law of the United States.

The clause in the patent law, authorizing suits in the circuit courts ¶31 stands we think on the same principle. Such a suit is a case arising under a law of the United States. Yet the defendant may not at the trial question the validity of the patent, or make any point which requires the construction of an act of Congress. He may rest his defence exclusively on the fact that he has not violated the right of the plaintiff. That this fact becomes the sole question made in the cause cannot oust the jurisdiction of the court, or establish the position that the case does not arise under a law of the United States.

It is said that a clear distinction exists between the party and the cause; ¶32 that the party may originate under a law with which the cause has no connexion, and that Congress may with the same propriety give a naturalized citizen who is the meer creature of law a right to sue in the courts of the United States as give that right to the Bank.

This distinction is not denied; and if the act of Congress was a simple ¶33 act of incorporation, and contained nothing more, it might be entitled to great consideration. But the act does not stop with incorporating the Bank. It proceeds to bestow upon the being it has made all the faculties and capacities which that being possesses. Every act of the Bank grows out of this law and is tested by it. To use the language of the constitution every act of the Bank arises out of this law.

A naturalized citizen is indeed made a citizen under an act of congress, ¶34 but the act does not proceed to give, to regulate, or to prescribe his capacities. He becomes a member of the society, possessing all the rights of a native citizen, and standing, in the view of the constitution, on the footing of a native. The constitution does not authorize Congress to enlarge or abridge those rights. The simple power of the national legislature is to prescribe a uniform rule of naturalization, and the exercise of this power exhausts it, so far as respects the individual. The constitution then takes him up, and among other rights, extends to him the capacity of suing in the courts of the United States precisely under the same circumstances under which a native might sue. He is distinguishable in nothing from a native citizen, except so far as the constitution makes the distinction. The law makes none.

There is then no resemblance between the act incorporating the Bank, ¶35 and the general naturalization law.

¶36   Upon the best consideration we have been able to bestow on this subject, we are of opinion that the clause in the act of incorporation enabling the Bank to sue in the courts of the United States is consistent with the constitution and to be obeyed in all courts.

¶37   We will now proceed to consider the merits of the cause.

¶38   The appellants contend that the decree of the circuit court is erroneous,

¶39   1st. Because no authority is shown in the record from the Bank, authorizing the institution or prosecution of the suit.

¶40   2d. Because as against the defendant Sullivan, there are neither proofs nor admissions sufficient to sustain the decree.

¶41   3d. Because, upon equitable principles the case made in the bill does not warrant a decree against either Osborne or Harper for the amount of coin and notes in the bill specified to have passed through their hands.

¶42   4th. Because the defendants are decreed to pay interest upon the coin when it was not in the power of Osborne or Harper, and was stayed in the hands of Sullivan by injunction.

¶43   5th Because the case made in the bill does not warrant the interference of a court of chancery by injunction or otherwise.[7]

¶44   6th. Because if any case is made in the bill proper for the interference of a court of chancery, it is against the state of Ohio, in which case the circuit court could not exercise jurisdiction.

¶45   7th. Because the decree assumes that the Bank of the United States is not subject to the taxing power of the State of Ohio, and decides that the law of Ohio, the execution of which is injoined, is unconstitutional.

¶46   These points will be considered in the order in which they are made.

¶47   1st. It is admitted that a corporation can only appear by attorney, and it is also admitted that the attorney must receive the authority of the corporation to enable him to represent it. It is not admitted that this authority must be under seal. On the contrary, the principle decided in the cases of the Bank of Columbia v Paterson and   is supposed to apply to this case and to show that the seal may be dispensed with.[8] It is however unnecessary to pursue this enquiry since the real question is whether the non appearance of the power in the record be error, not whether the power was insufficient in itself.

¶48   Natural persons may appear in court either by themselves or by their attorney; but no man has a right to appear as the attorney of another without the authority of that other. In ordinary cases the authority must be produced, because there is in the nature of things no prima facie evidence that one man is in fact the attorney of another. The case of an attorney at law, an attorney for the purpose of representing another in court, and prosecuting or defending a suit in his name, is somewhat different. The power must indeed exist, but its production has not been considered as indispensable. Certain gentlemen, first licensed by government, are admitted by order of court to stand at the bar, with a general capacity to represent all the suitors in the court. The appearance of any one of these gentlemen in a cause, has always been received as evidence of his authority; and no additional evidence, so far as we are informed, has ever been required. This practice we beleive has existed from the first establishment of our courts and no departure from it has been made in those of any state or of the union.

The argument supposes some distinction in this particular, between a natural person and a corporation; but the court can perceive no reason for this distinction. A corporation, it is true, can appear only by attorney, while a natural person may appear for himself. But when he waives this privilege, and elects to appear by attorney, no reason is perceived why the same evidence should not be required that the individual professing to represent him has authority to do so, which would be required if he were incapable of appearing in person. The universal and familiar practice then of permitting gentlemen of the profession to appear without producing a warrant of attorney forms a rule which is as applicable in reason to their appearance for a corporation as for a natural person. Were it even otherwise, the practice is as uniform and as ancient with regard to corporations as to natural persons. No case has ever occurred, so far as we are informed, in which the production of a warrant of attorney has been supposed a necessary preliminary to the appearance of a corporation either as plaintiff or defendant, by a gentleman admitted to the bar of the court. The usage then is as full authority for the case of a corporation as of an individual. If this usage ought to be altered it should be by a rule to operate prospectively, not by the reversal of a decree pronounced in conformity with the general course of the court in a case in which no doubt of the legality of the appearance had ever been suggested. ¶49

In the statutes of jeofails and amendment which respect this subject, the non appearance of a warrant of attorney in the record has generally been treated as matter of form, and the 32d. Sec of the judicial act may very well be construed to comprehend this formal defect in its general terms, in a case at law.[9] No reason is perceived why the courts of chancery should be more rigid in exacting the exhibition of a warrant of attorney than a court of law; and, since the practice has, in fact, been the same in both courts, an appellate ought, we think, to be governed in both by the same rule. ¶50

2d. The second point is one on which the productiveness of any decree in favor of the plaintiffs most probably depends; for, if the claim be not satisfied with the money found in possession of Sullivan, it is at best uncertain whether a fund out of which it can be satisfied is to be found elsewhere. ¶51

In enquiring whether the proofs or admissions in the cause be sufficient to charge Sullivan, the court will look into the answer of Currie as well as into that of Sullivan. In objection to this course, it is said that the answer of one defendant cannot be read against another. This is gener- ¶52 ally but not universally true. Where one defendant succeeds to another, so that the right of the one devolves on the other, and they become privies in estate, the rule is not admitted to apply. Thus if an ancester die pending a suit, and the proceedings be revived against his heir, or if a suit be revived against an exr. or admr., the answer of the deceased person, or any other evidence establishing any fact against him, might be read also against the person who succeeds to him. So a pendente lite purchaser is bound by the decree without being even made a party to the suit; a fortiori he would, if made a party, be bound by the testimony taken against the vendor.

¶53   In this case, if Currie received the money taken out of the Bank and passed it over to Sullivan, the establishment of this fact in a suit against Currie would seem to bind his successor Sullivan both as a privy in estate and as a person getting possession pendente lite, if the original suit had been instituted against Currie. We can perceive no difference, so far as respects the answer of Currie, between the case supposed and the case as it stands. If Currie who was the predecessor of Sullivan admits that he received the money of the Bank, the fact seems to bind all those coming in under him as completely as it binds himself. This therefore appears to the court to be a case in which, upon principle, the answer of Currie may be read.

¶54   His answer states that on or about the 19th. or 20th. of September 1819, the defendant Harper delivered to him in coin and notes, the sum of $98000, which he was informed and beleived to be the money levied on the Bank as a tax, in pursuance of the law of the state of Ohio. After consulting counsel on the question whether he ought to retain this sum within his individual controul, or pass it to the credit of the state on the books of the treasury, he adopted the latter course, but retained it carefully in a trunk, separate from the other funds of the treasury. The money afterwards came to the hands of Sullivan the gentleman who succeeded him as treasurer and gave him a receipt for all the money in the Treasury including this which was still kept separate from the rest.

¶55   We think no reasonable doubt can be entertained but that the $98000 delivered by Harper to Currie were taken out of the Bank. Currie understood & beleived it to be the fact. When did he so understand and beleive it? At the time when he received the money. And from whom did he derive his understanding and beleif? The inference is irresistible that he derived it from his own knowledge of circumstances, for they were all of public notoriety, and from the information of Harper. In the necessary course of things, Harper, who was sent as Currie must have known, on this business, brings with him to the Treasurer of the state a sum of money which by the law was to be taken out of the bank, pays him $98000 thereof, which the treasurer receives and keeps as being money taken from the Bank, and so enters it on the books of the Treasury. In a suit brought against Mr. Currie for this money by the state of Ohio, if he had failed to account for it, could any person doubt the competency of the testimony to charge him? We think no mind could hesitate in such a case.

Currie then being clearly in possession of this money, and clearly liable for it, we are next to look into Sullivans answer for the purpose of enquiring whether he admits any facts which show him to be liable also. ¶56

Sullivan denies all personal knowledge of the transaction. That is, he was not in office when it took place, and was not present when the money was taken out of the Bank, or when it was delivered to Currie. But when he entered the Treasury office he received this sum of $98000, separate from the other money of the Treasury, which he understood from report, and was informed by his predecessor from whom he received it, was the money taken out of the bank. This sum has remained untouched ever since from respect to the injunction awarded by the court. ¶57

We ask if a rational doubt can remain on this subject? ¶58

Mr. Currie as Treasurer of the state of Ohio receives $98000 as being the amount of a tax imposed by the legislature of that state on the Bank of the United States, enters the same on the books of the Treasury, and, the legality of the act by which the money was levied being questioned, puts it in a trunk & keeps it apart from the other money belonging to the public. He resigns his office and is succeeded by Mr. Sullivan to whom he delivers the money informing him at the same time that it is the money raised from the Bank, and Mr. Sullivan continues to keep it apart, and abstains from the use of it out of respect to an injunction forbidding him to pay it away or in any manner to dispose of it. Is it possible to doubt the identity of this money? ¶59

Even admitting that the answer of Currie, though establishing his liability as to himself, could not prove even that fact as to Sullivan, the answer of Sullivan is itself sufficient we think to charge him. He admits that these $98000 were delivered to him as being the money which was taken out of the Bank, and that he so received it; for he says that he understood this sum was the same as charged in the bill; that his information was from report and from his predecessor; and that the money has remained untouched from respect to the injunction. This declaration then is a part of the fact. The fact as admitted in his answer is not, simply, that he received $98000, but that he received $98000 as being the money taken out of the bank, the money to which the writ of injunction applied. ¶60

In a common action between two private individuals such an admission would at least be sufficient to throw on the defendant the burthen of proving that the money which he acknowledges himself to have received and kept as the money of the plaintiff, was not that which it was declared to be on its delivery. A declaration accompanying the delivery, and constituting a part of it, gives a character to the transaction, and is not to be placed on the same footing with a declaration made by the same person at a different time. The answer of Sullivan then is, in the opinion of the court sufficient to show that these $98000 were the specific dollars ¶61 for which this suit was brought. This sum having come to his possession with full knowledge of the fact, in a separate trunk, unmixed with other money, and with notice that an injunction had been awarded respecting it, he would seem to be responsible to the plaintiff for it, unless he can show sufficient matter to discharge himself.

¶62   3d. The next objection is to the decree against Osgood[10] and Harper, as to whom the bill was taken for confessed.

¶63   The bill charges that Osborne employed John L Harper to collect the tax who proceeded by violence to enter the office of discount and deposite at Chilicothe and forcibly took therefrom $100000 in specie and bank notes; and that at the time of the seizure Harper well knew and was duly notified that an injunction had been allowed, which money was delivered either to Currie or Osborne.

¶64   So far as respects Harper and Osborne these allegations are to be considered as true. If the act of the legislature of Ohio, and the official character of Osborne, constitute a defence, neither of these defendants are liable, and the whole decree is erroneous; but if the act be unconstitutional and void, it can be no justification, and both these defendants are to be considered as individuals who are amenable to the laws. Considering them, for the present, in this character, the fact as made out in the bill is that Osborne employed Harper to do an illegal act, and that Harper has done that act. That they are jointly responsible for it is supposed to be as well settled as any principle of law whatever.

¶65   We think it unnecessary in this part of the case to enter into the enquiry respecting the effect of the injunction. No injunction is necessary to attach responsibility on those who conspire to do an illegal act, which this is if not justified by the authority under which it was done.

¶66   4th. The next objection is to the allowance of interest on the coin which constituted a part of the sum decreed to the complainants. Had the complainants, without the intervention of a court of equity, resorted to their legal remedy for the injury sustained, their right to principal and interest would have stood on equal ground. The same rule would be adopted in a court of equity had the subject been left under the controul of the party in possession, while the right was in litigation. But the subject was not left under the controul of the party. The court itself interposed, and forbad the person in whose possession the property was to make any use of it. This order, having been obeyed, places the defendant in the same situation, so far as respects in[te]rest, as if the court had taken the money into its own custody. The defendant, in obeying the mandate of the court, becomes its instrument as entirely as the Clerk of the court would have been, had the money been placed in his hands. It does not appear reasonable that a decree which proceeds upon the idea that the injunction of the court was valid, ought to direct interest to be paid on the money which that injunction restrained the defendant from using.

5th. The 5th. objection to the decree is that the case made in the bill ¶67 does not warrant the interference of a court of Chancery.

In examining this question, it is proper that the court should consider ¶68 the real case, and its actual circumstances. The original bill prays for an injunction against Ralph Osborne Auditor of the state of Ohio, to restrain him from executing a law of that state to the great oppression and injury of the complainants, and to the destruction of rights and privileges conferred on them by their charter, and by the constitution of the United States. The true enquiry is whether an injunction can be issued to restrain a person who is a state officer from performing any official act enjoined by statute and whether a court of equity can decree restitution if the act be performed. In pursuing this enquiry, it must be assumed, for the present, that the act is unconstitutional, and furnishes no authority or protection to the officer who is about to proceed under it. This must be assumed because in the arrangement of his argument, the counsel who opened the cause has chosen to reserve that point for the last, and to contend that, though the law be void, no case is made out against the defendants. We suspend also the consideration of the question whether the interest of the state of Ohio, as disclosed in the bill shows a want of jurisdiction in the circuit court which ought to have arrested its proceedings. That question too is reserved by the appellants, and will be subsequently considered. The sole enquiry for the present, is, whether, stripping the case of these objections, the plaintiffs below were entitled to relief in a court of equity against the defendants, and to the protection of an injunction. The appellants expressly waive the extravagant proposition that a void act can afford protection to the person who executes it, and admits the liability of the defendants to the plaintiffs to the extent of the injury sustained, in an action at law. The question then is reduced to the single enquiry whether the case is cognizable in a court of equity. If it is, the decree must be affirmed so far as it is supported by the evidence in the cause.

The appellants allege that the original bill contains no allegation ¶69 which can justify the application for an injunction, and treat the declarations of Ralph Osborne, the auditor, that he should execute the law, as the light and frivolous threats of an individual that he would commit an ordinary trespass. But surely this is not the point of view in which the application for an injunction is to be considered. The legislature of Ohio had passed a law for the avowed purpose of expelling the Bank from the state, and had made it the duty of the Auditor to execute it, as a ministerial officer. He had declared that he would perform this duty. The law, if executed, would unquestionably effect its object, and would deprive the Bank of its chartered privileges, so far as they were to be exercised in that state. It must expel the Bank from the state; and this is we think, a conclusion which the court might rightfully draw from the law itself. That the declarations of the Auditor would be fulfilled, did not admit of reasonable doubt. It was to be expected that a person continuing to hold an office would perform a duty injoined by his government which was completely within his power. This duty was to be repeated until the Bank should abandon the exercise of its chartered rights.

¶70   To treat this as a common casual trespass would be to disregard entirely its true character and substantial merits. The application to the court was, to interpose its writ of injunction to protect the bank, not from the casual trespass of an individual who might not perform the act he threatened, but from the total destruction of its franchise, of its chartered privileges, so far as respected the state of Ohio. It was morally certain that the Auditor would proceed to execute the law, and it was morally certain that the effect must be the expulsion of the bank from the state. An annual charge of $100000 would more than absorb all the advantages of the privilege, and would consequently annul it.

¶71   The appellants admit that injunctions are often awarded for the protection of parties in the enjoyment of a franchise; but deny that one has ever been granted in such a case as this. But, although the precise case may never have occurred, if the same principle applies, the same remedy ought to be afforded. The interference of the court in this class of cases has most frequently been to restrain a person from violating an exclusive privilege by participating in it. But if, instead of a continued participation in the privilege, the attempt be to disable the party from using it, is not the reason for the interference of the court rather strengthened than weakened? Had the privilege of the Bank been exclusive, the argument admits that any other person or company might have been injoined, according to the regular course of a court of chancery, from using or exercising the same business. Why would such person or company have been enjoined? To prevent a permanent injury from being done to the party entitled to the franchise or privilege, which injury, the appellants say, cannot be estimated in damages. It requires no argument to prove that the injury is greater if the whole privilege be destroyed than if it be divided; and, so far as respects the estimate of damages, although precise accuracy may not be attained, yet a reasonable calculation may be made of the amount of the injury so as to satisfy the court and jury. It will not be pretended that, in such a case, an action at law could not be maintained, or that the materials do not exist on which a verdict might be found, and a judgement rendered. But in this, and many other cases of continuing injuries, as in the case of repeated ejectments, a court of chancery will interpose. The injury done by denying to the Bank the exercise of its franchise in the state of Ohio is as difficult to calculate as the injury done by participating in an exclusive privilege. The single act of levying the tax in the first insta⟨nce⟩ is the cause ⟨of⟩ an action at law, but that affords a remedy only for the single act, and is not equal to the remedy in chancery which prevents its repetition, and protects the privilege. The same conservative principle which induces the court to interpose its authority for the protection of exclusive privileges, to prevent the commission of waste, even in some cases of trespass, and in many cases of destruction, will, we think, apply to this. Indeed trespass is destruction where there is no privity of estate.

If the state of Ohio could have been made a party defendant, it can ¶72 scarcely be denied that this would be a strong case for an injunction. The objection is that as the real party cannot be brought before the court, a suit cannot be sustained against the agents of that party; and cases have been cited to show that a court of chancery will not make a decree unless all those who are substantially interested be made parties to the suit.

This is certainly true where it is in the power of the plaintiff to make ¶73 them parties; but if the person who is the real principal, the person who is the true source of the mischief, by whose power and for whose advantage it is done, be himself above the law, be exempt from all judicial process, it would be subversive of the best established principles to say that the laws could not afford the same remedies against the agent employed in doing the wrong which they would afford against him could his principal be joined in the suit. It is admitted that the privilege of the principal is not communicated to the agent, for the appellants acknowledge that an action at law would lie against the agent in which full compensation ought to be made for the injury. It being admitted then that the agent is not privileged by his connexion with his principal, that he is responsible for his own act to the full extent of the injury, why should not the preventive power of the court also be applied to him? Why may it not restrain him from the commission of a wrong which it would punish him for committing? We put out of view the character of the principal as a sovereign state because that is made a distinct point, and consider the question singly as respects the want of parties. Now if the party before the court would be responsible for the whole injury, why may he not be restrained from its commission if no other party can be brought before the court. The appellants found their distinction on the legal principle that all trespasses are several as well as joint. Without enquiring into the validity of this reason if true, we ask if it be true? Will it be said that the action of trespass is the only remedy given for this injury? Can it be denied that an action on the case for money had and received to the plaintiffs use might be maintained? We think it cannot: and if such an action might be maintained, no plausible reason suggests itself to us for the opinion that an injunction may not be awarded to restrain the agent, with as much propriety as it might be awarded to restrain the principal, could the principal be made a party.

We think the reason for an injunction is much stronger in the actual, ¶74 than it would be in the supposed case. In the regular course of things the agent would pay over the money immediately to his principal and would thus place it beyond the reach of the injured party, since his principal is not amenable to the law. The remedy for the injury would be against the agent only; and what agent could make compensation for such an injury? The remedy would have nothing real in it. It would be a remedy in name only, not in substance. This alone would in our opinion be a sufficient reason for the interference of[11] a court of equity. The injury would in fact be irreparable; and the cases are innumerable in which injunctions are awarded on this ground.

¶75   But, were it even to be admitted that the injunction in the first instance was improperly awarded and that the original bill could not be maintained, that would not, we think materially affect the case. An amended and supplemental bill making new parties has been filed in the cause; and on that bill with the proceedings under it, the decree was pronounced. The question is whether that bill and those proceedings support the decree.

¶76   The case they make is that the money and notes of the plaintiffs in the circuit court, have been taken from them without authority, and are in possession of one of the defendants, who keeps them separate and apart from all other money and notes. It is admitted that this defendant would be liable for the whole amount in an action at law; but it is denied that he is liable in a court of equity.

¶77   We think it a case in which a court of equity ought to interpose, and that there are several grounds on which its jurisdiction may be placed.

¶78   One which appears to us to be ample for the purpose is that a court will always interpose to prevent the transfer of a specific article which, if transferred, will be lost to the owner. Thus the holder of negotiable securities indorsed in the usual manner, if he has acquired them fraudulently, will be injoined from negotiating them, because if negotiated, the maker or indorser must pay them.[a] Thus too a transfer of stock will be restrained in favor of a person having the real property in the article. In these cases the injured party would have his remedy at law, and the probability that this remedy would be adequate is stronger in the cases put in the books than in this where the sum is so greatly beyond the capacity of an ordinary agent to pay. But it is the province of a court of equity in such cases, to arrest the injury and prevent the wrong. The remedy is more beneficial and complete than the law can give. The money of the Bank if mingled with the other money in the treasury and put into circulation would be totally lost to the owners, and the reason for an injunction is at least as strong in such a case as in the case of a negotiable note.

¶79   6 We proceed now to the 6th. point made by the appellants which is, that if any case is made in the bill proper for the interference of a court of chancery, it is against the state of Ohio, in which case the circuit court could not exercise jurisdiction.

¶80   The bill is brought, it is said, for the purpose of protecting the bank in the exercise of a franchise granted by a law of the United States, which

---

[a] 1st Maddock 154.5[12]

franchise the state of Ohio asserts a right to invade, and is about to invade. It prays the aid of the court to restrain the officers of the state from executing the law. It is then a controversy between the Bank & the state of Ohio. The interest of the state is direct and immediate, not consequential. The process of the court though not directed against the state by name, acts directly upon it by restraining its officers. The process therefore is substantially though not in form against the state, and the court ought not to proceed without making the state a party. If this cannot be done, the court cannot take jurisdiction of the cause.

The full pressure of this argument is felt, and the difficulties it presents ¶81 are acknowledged. The direct interest of the state in the suit as brought is admitted, and, had it been in the power of the Bank to make it a party, perhaps no decree ought to have been pronounced in the cause until the state was before the court. But this was not in the power of the Bank. The 11th. amendment of the constitution has exempted a state from the suits of citizens of other states, or aliens, and the very difficult question is to be decided whether, in such a case, the court may act upon the agents employed by the state, and on the property in their hands.

Before we try this question by the constitution, it may not be time ¶82 misapplied, if we pause for a moment, and reflect on the relative situation of the Union with its members should the objection prevail.

A denial of jurisdiction forbids all enquiry into the nature of the case. It ¶83 applies to cases perfectly clear in themselves, to cases where the government is in the exercise of its best established and most essential powers, as well as to those which may be deemed questionable. It asserts that the agents of a state, alleging the authority of a law void in itself because repugnant to the constitution, may arrest the execution of any law of the United States. It maintains that if a state shall impose a fine or penalty on any person employed in the execution of any law of the United States, it may levy that fine or penalty by a ministerial officer, without the sanction even of its own courts, and that the individual, though he perceives the approaching danger, can obtain no protection from the judicial department of the government. The carrier of the mail, the collecter of the revenue, the marshal of a district, the recruiting officer, may all be inhibited under ruinous penalties from the performance of their respective duties; the warrant of a ministerial officer may authorize the collection of these penalties; and the person thus obstructed in the performance of his duty, may indeed resort to his action for damages after the infliction of the injury, but cannot avail himself of the preventive justice of the nation, to protect him in the performance of his duties. Each member of the union is capable, at its will, of attacking the nation, of arresting its progress at every step, of acting vigorously and effectually in the execution of its designs; while the nation stands naked, stripped of its defensive armour, and incapable of shielding its agent or executing its laws otherwise than by proceedings which are to take place after the mischief is perpetrated, and which must often be ineffectual, from the inability of the agents to make compensation.

¶84   These are said to be extreme cases, but the case at bar, had it been put by way of illustration in argument, might have been termed an extreme case; and if a penalty on a revenue officer for performing his duty be more obviously wrong than a penalty on the Bank, it is a difference in degree not in principle. Public sentiment would be more shocked by the infliction of a penalty on a public officer for the performance of his duty, than by the infliction of this penalty on a bank which, while carrying on the fiscal operations of the government, is also transacting its own business; but, in both cases, the officer levying the penalty acts under a void authority, and the power to restrain him is denied as positively in the one as in the other.

¶85   The distinction between any extreme case and that which has actually occurred, if indeed any difference of principle can be supposed to exist between them, disappears when considering the question of jurisdiction. For, if the courts of the United States cannot rightfully protect the agents who execute every law authorized by the constitution from the direct action of state agents in the collection of penalties, they cannot rightfully protect those who execute any law.

¶86   The question then is whether the constitution of the United states has provided a tribunal which can peacefully and rightfully protect those who are employed in carrying into execution the laws of the union from the attempts of a particular state to resist the execution of those laws.

¶87   The state of Ohio denies the existence of this power, and contends that no preventive proceedings whatever, or proceedings against the very property which may have been seized by the agent of a state, can be sustained against such agent, because they would be substantially against the state itself, in violation of the 11th. amendment of the constitution.

¶88   That the courts of the union cannot entertain a suit brought against a state by an alien or the citizen of another state, is not to be controverted. Is a suit brought against any individual for any cause whatever, a suit against a state in the sense of the constitution?

¶89   The 11th. amendment is the limitation of a power supposed to be granted in the original instrument; and to understand accurately the extent of the limitation, it seems proper to define the power that is limitted.

¶90   The words of the constitution, so far as they respect this question, are "The judicial power shall extend" "to controversies between two or more states, between a state and citizens of another state" "and between a state and foreign states citizens or subjects."

¶91   A subsequent clause distributes the power previously granted and assigns to the supreme court original jurisdiction in those cases in which "a state shall be a party."

The words of the 11th. amendment are "The judicial power of the ¶92 United States shall not be construed to extend to any suit in law or equity commenced or prosecuted against one of the United States by citizens of another state, or by citizens or subjects of a foreign state."

The Bank of the United states contends that in all cases in which ¶93 jurisdiction depends on the character of the party, reference is made to the party on the record, not to one who may be interested, but is not shown by the record to be a party.

The appellants admit that the jurisdiction of the court is not ousted by ¶94 any incidental or consequential interest which a state may have in the decision to be made, but is to be considered as a party where the decision acts directly and immediately upon the state through its officers.

If this question were to be determined on the authority of English ¶95 decisions, it is believed that no case can be adduced where any person has been considered as a party who is not made so in the record. But the court will not review those decisions because it is thought that a question growing out of the constitution of the United States requires rather an attentive consideration of the words of that instrument, than of the decisions of analogous questions by the courts of any other country.

Do the provisions then of the American constitution respecting con- ¶96 troversies to which a state may be a party, extend, on a fair construction of that instrument, to cases in which the state is not a party on the record.

The first in the enumeration is a controversy between two or more ¶97 states.

There are not many questions in which a state would be supposed to ¶98 take a deeper or more immediate interest than in those which decide on the extent of her territory. Yet the constitution, not considering the state as a party to such controversies if not plaintiff or defendant on the record, has expressly given jurisdiction, in those between citizens claiming lands under grants of different states. If each state in consequence of the influence of a decision on her boundary, had been considered by the framers of the constitution as a party to that controversy, the express grant of jurisdiction would have been useless. The grant of it certainly proves that the constitution does not consider the state as a party in such a case.

Jurisdiction is expressly granted in those cases only where citizens of ¶99 the same state claim lands under grants of different states. If the claimants be citizens of different states, the court takes jurisdiction for that reason. Still the right of the state to grant is the essential point in dispute; and in that point the state is deeply interested. If that interest converts the state into a party there is an end of the cause; and the constitution will be construed to forbid the circuit courts to take cognizance of questions to which it was thought necessary expressly to extend their jurisdiction even when the controversy arose between citizens of the same state.

¶100   We are aware that the application of these cases may be denied, because the title of the state comes on incidentally, and the appellants admit the jurisdiction of the court where its judgement does not act directly upon the property or interests of the state; but we deemed it of some importance to show that the framers of the constitution contemplated the distinction between cases in which a state was interested and those in which it was a party, and makes no provision for a case of interest without being a party on the record.

¶101   In cases where a state is a party on the record, the question of jurisdiction is decided by inspection. If jurisdiction depend, not on this plain fact, but on the interest of the state, what rule has the constitution given by which this interest is to be measured? If no rule be given is it to be settled by the court? If so, the curious anomaly is presented of a court examining the whole testimony of a cause, enquiring into and deciding on the extent of a state's interest, without having a right to exercise any jurisdiction in the case. Can this enquiry be made without the exercise of jurisdiction?

¶102   The next in the enumeration is a controversy between a state and the citizens of another state.

¶103   Can this case arise if the state be not a party on the record? If it can the question recurs: What degree of interest shall be sufficient to change the parties, and arrest the proceeding against the individual? Controversies respecting boundary have lately existed between Virginia and Tenessee, between Kentucky & Tenessee, and now exist between New-York & New Jersey. Suppose, while such a controversy is pending, the collecting officer of one state should seize property for taxes belonging to a man who supposes himself to reside in the other state, and who seeks redress in the federal court of that state in which the officer resides. The interest of the state is obvious, yet it is admitted that in such a case the action would lie, because the officer might be treated as a trespasser, and the verdict and judgement against him would not act directly on the property of the state. That it would not so act may perhaps depend on circumstances. The officer may retain the amount of the taxes in his hands, and on the proceedings of the state against him may plead in bar the judgement of a court of competent jurisdiction. If this plea ought to be sustained, and it is far from being certain that it ought not, the judgement so pleaded would have acted directly on the revenue of the state in the hands of its officer, and yet the argument admits that the action in such a case would be sustained. But suppose, in such a case, the party supposing[13] himself to be injured instead of bringing an action sounding in damages, should sue for the specific thing while yet in possession of the seizing officer. It being admitted in argument that the action sounding in damages would lie, we are unable to perceive the line of distinction between that and the action of detinue. Yet the latter action would claim the specific article seized for the tax, and would obtain it should the seizure be deemed unlawful.

It would be tedious to pursue this part of the enquiry farther, and it would be useless, because every person will perceive that the same reasoning is applicable to all the other enumerated controversies to which a state may be a party. The principle may be illustrated by a reference to those other controversies where jurisdiction depends on the party. But before we review them, we will notice one where the nature of the controversy is in some degree blended with the character of the party. ¶104

If a suit be brought against a foreign minister the supreme court alone has original jurisdiction, and this is shown on the record. But suppose a suit be brought which affects the interest of a foreign minister, or by which the person of his secretary, or of his servant is arrested. The minister does not by the meer arrest of his secretary or his servant become a party to this suit, but the actual defendant pleads to the jurisdiction of the court and asserts his privilege. If the suit affects a foreign minister it must be dismissed, not because he is a party to it, but because it affects him. The language of the constitution in the two cases is different. This court can take cognizance of all cases "affecting" foreign ministers, and therefore jurisdiction does not depend on the party named in the record; but this language changes when the enumeration proceeds to states. Why this change? The answer is obvious. In the case of foreign Ministers, it was intended, for reasons which all comprehend, to give the national courts jurisdiction over all cases by which they were in any manner affected. In the case of states, whose immediate or remote interests were mixed up with a multitude of cases, and who might be affected in an almost infinite variety of ways, it was intended to give jurisdiction in those cases only to which they were actual parties. ¶105

In proceeding with the cases in which jurisdiction depends on the character of the party, the first in the enumeration is "controversies to which the United States shall be a party.["] ¶106

Does this provision extend to cases where the United States are not named in the record but claim and are actually entitled to the whole subject in controversy? ¶107

Let us examine this question. ¶108

Suits brought by the Post master General are for money due to the United States. The nominal plaintiff has no interest in the controversy, and the United States are the only real party. Yet these suits could not be instituted in the courts of the Union under that clause which gives jurisdiction in all cases to which the United States are a party, and it was found necessary to give the Court jurisdiction over them as being cases arising under a law of the United States. ¶109

The judicial power of the union is also extended to controversies between citizens of different states, and it has been decided that the character of the parties must be shown on the record. Does this provision depend on the character of those whose interest is litigated, or of those who are parties on the record? In a suit for example brought by or against an ¶110 executor, The creditors or legatees of his testator are the persons really concerned in interest; but it has never been suspected that, if the executor be a resident of another state, the jurisdiction of the federal court could be ousted by the fact that the creditors or legatees were citizens of the same state with the opposite party. The universally received construction in this case is that jurisdiction is neither given nor ousted by the relative situation of the parties concerned in interest, but by the relative situation of the parties named on the record. Why is this construction universal? No case can be imagined in which the existence of an interest out of the party on the record is more unequivocal than in that which has been just stated. Why then is it universally admitted that this interest in no manner affects the jurisdiction of the court? The plain and obvious answer is because the jurisdiction of the court depends, not upon this interest, but upon the actual party in the record.

¶111   Were a state to be the sole legatee It will not we presume be alleged that the jurisdiction of the court in a suit against the executor would be more affected by this fact, than by the fact that any other person not suable in the courts of the union was the sole legatee. Yet in such a case the court would decide directly and immediately on the interest of the state.

¶112   This principle might be further illustrated by showing that jurisdiction where it depends on the character of the party, is never conferred in consequence of the existence of an interest in a party not named; and by showing that under the distributive clause of the 2d. Sec. of the 3d. art. the supreme court could never take original jurisdiction in consequence of an interest in a party not named in the record.

¶113   But the principle seems too well established to require that more time should be devoted to it. It may we think be laid down as a rule which admits of no exception, that in all cases where jurisdiction depends on the party, it is the party named in the record. Consequently the 11th. amendment which restrains the jurisdiction granted by the constitution over suits against States, is of necessity limited to those suits in which a state is a party on the record. The amendment has its full effect if the constitution be construed as it would have been construed had the jurisdiction of the court never been extended to suits brought against a state by the citizens of another state, or by aliens.

¶114   The state not being a party on the record, and the court having jurisdiction over those who are parties on the record, the true question is not one of jurisdiction, but whether in the exercise of its jurisdiction, the court ought to make a decree against the defendants: Whether they are to be considered as having a real interest or as being only nominal parties.

¶115   In pursuing the arrangement which the appellants have made for the argument of the cause, this question has already been considered. The responsibility of the officers of the state for the money taken out of the bank was admitted, and it was acknowledged that this responsability might be enforced by the proper action. The objection is to its being enforced against the specific article taken, and by the decree of this court. But it has been shown we think that an action of detinue might be maintained for that article, if the Bank had possessed the means of describing it, and that the interest of the state would not have been an obstacle to the suit of the Bank against the individual in possession of it. The judgement in such a suit might have been enforced had the article been found in possession of the individual defendant. It has been shown that the danger of its being parted with, of its being lost to the plaintiff, and the necessity of a discovery justified the application to a court of equity. It was in a court of equity alone that the relief would be real, substantial, and effective. The parties must certainly have a real interest in the case since their personal responsability is acknowledged, and if denied, could be demonstrated.

It was proper then to make a decree against the defendants in the circuit court, if the law of the state of Ohio be repugnant to the constitution, or to a law of the United States made in pursuance thereof, so as to furnish no authority to those who took or to those who received the money for which this suit was instituted. ¶116

7th. Is that law unconstitutional? ¶117

This point was argued with great ability, and decided by this court, after mature and deliberate consideration, in the case of MCullough vs. The State of Maryland. A revision of that opinion has been requested; and many considerations combine to induce a review of it. ¶118

The foundation of the argument in favour of the right of a state to tax the bank is laid in the supposed character of that institution. The argument supposes the corporation to have been originated for the management of an individual concern, to be founded upon contract between individuals, having private trade and private profit for its great end and principal object. ¶119

If these premises were true, the conclusion drawn from them would be inevitable. This meer private corporation, engaged in its own business, with its own views, would certainly be subject to the taxing power of the state, as any individual would be, and the casual circumstance of its being employed by the government in the transaction of its fiscal affairs would no more exempt its private business from the operation of that power, than it would exempt the private business of any individual employed in the same manner. But the premises are not true. The Bank is not considered as a private corporation, whose principal object is individual trade and individual profit; but as a public corporation created for public and national purposes. That the meer business of banking is in its own nature a private business, and may be carried on by individuals or companies having no political connexion with the government, is admitted; but the Bank is not such an individual or company. It was not created for its own sake, or for private purposes. It has never been supposed that Congress could create such a corporation. The whole opinion of the court in the ¶120 case of MCullough v The state of Maryland is founded on, and sustained by, the idea that the Bank is an instrument which is "necessary and proper" for carrying into effect the powers vested in the government of the United States. It is not an instrument which the government has found ready made, and has supposed to be adapted to its purposes, but one which was created in the form in which it now appears, for national purposes only. It is undoubtedly capable of transacting private as well as public business. While it is the great instrument by which the fiscal operations of the government are effected, it is also trading with individuals for its own advantage. The appellants endeavour to distinguish between this trade, and its agency for the public, between its Banking operations and those qualities·which it possesses in common with every corporation, such as individuality, immortality, &c. While they seem to admit the right to preserve this corporate existence, they deny the right to protect it in its trade and business.

¶121   If there be any thing in this distinction, it would tend to show that so much of the act as incorporates the Bank is constitutional, but so much of it as authorizes its Banking operations is unconstitutional. Congress can make the inanimate body, and employ the machine as a depositary of, and vehicle for, the convey[ance] of, the treasure of the nation, if it be capable of being so employed, but cannot breathe into it the vital spirit which alone can bring it into useful existence.

¶122   Let this distinction be considered.

¶123   Why is it that Congress can incorporate or create a Bank? This question was answered in the case of MCullough v The State of Maryland. It is an instrument which is "necessary and proper" for carrying on the fiscal operations of government. Can this instrument, on any rational calculation, effect its object unless it be endowed with that faculty of lending and dealing in money which is conferred by its charter? If it can, if it be as competent to the purposes of government without as with this faculty, there will be much difficulty in sustaining that essential part of the charter. If it cannot, then this faculty is necessary to the legitimate operations of government, and was constitutionally[14] engrafted on the institution. It is in that view of the subject, the vital part of the corporation, it is its soul, and the right to preserve it originates in the same principle with the right to preserve the skeleton or body which it animates. The distinction between destroying what is denominated the corporate franchise, and destroying its vivifying principle, is precisely as incapable of being maintained, as a distinction between the right to sentence a human being to death, and a right to sentence him to a total privation of sustenance during life. Deprive a Bank of its trade and business which is its sustenance, and its immortality, if it have that property, will be a very useless attribute.

¶124   This distinction then has no real existence. To tax its faculties, its trade, and occupation is to tax the Bank itself. To destroy or preserve the one, is to destroy or preserve the other.

It is urged that Congress has not by this act of incorporation created ¶125
the faculty of trading in money. That it had anterior existence, and may
be carried on by a private individual or company, as well as by a corporation. As this profession or business may be taxed regulated or restrained
when conducted by an individual, it may likewise be taxed regulated or
restrained when conducted by a corporation.

The general correctness of these propositions need not be contro- ¶126
verted. Their particular application to the question before the court is
alone to be considered. We do not maintain that the corporate character
of the Bank exempts its operations from the action of state authority. If
an individual were to be endowed with the same faculties for the same
purposes, he would be equally protected in the exercise of those faculties.
The operations of the Bank are beleived not only to yield the compensation for its services to the government, but to be essential to the performance of those services. Those operations give its value to the currency in
which all the transactions of the government are conducted. They are
therefore inseparably connected with those transactions. They enable
the bank to render those services to the nation for which it was created,
and are therefore of the very essence of its character as a national instrument. The business of the Bank constitutes its capacity to perform its
functions as a machine for the money transactions of the government. Its
corporate character is meerly an incident which enables it to transact that
business more beneficially.

Were the Secretary of the Treasury to be authorized by law to appoint ¶127
agencies throughout the union to perform the public functions of the
Bank, and to be endowed with its faculties as a necessary auxiliary to
those functions, the operations of those agents would be as exempt from
the controul of the states as the Bank, and not more so. If instead of the
Secretary of the Treasury, a distinct office were to be created for the
purpose, filled by a person who should receive as a compensation for his
time, labor, and expense, the profits of the banking business instead of
other emoluments to be drawn from the Treasury, which banking business was essential to the operations of the government, would each state
in the union possess a right to controul these operations? The question
on which this right would depend must always be, are these faculties so
essential to the fiscal operations of the government as to authorize Congress to confer them. Let this be admitted, and the question does the
right to preserve them exist must always be answered in the affirmative?

Congress was of opinion that these faculties were necessary to enable ¶128
the Bank to perform the services which are exacted from it, and for
which it was created. This was certainly a question proper for the consideration of the national legislature. But, were it now to undergo revision,
who would have the hardihood to say that, without the employment of a
banking capital, those services could be performed? That the exercise of
these faculties greatly facilitates the fiscal operations of the government

is too obvious for controversy, and who will venture to affirm that the suppression of them would not materially affect those operations, and essentially impair, if not totally destroy the utility of the machine to the government? The currency which it circulates by means of its trade with individuals is beleived to make it a more fit instrument for the purposes of government than it could otherwise be; and if this be true, the capacity to carry on this trade is a faculty indispensable to the character and objects of the institution.

¶129   The appellants admit that, if this faculty be necessary to make the bank a fit instrument for the purposes of the government, Congress possesses the same power to protect the machine in this as in its direct fiscal operations; but they deny that it is necessary to those purposes, and insist that it is granted solely for the benefit of the members of the corporation. Were this proposition to be admitted all the consequences which are drawn from it might follow. But it is not admitted. The court has already stated its conviction that without this capacity to trade with individuals the Bank would be a very defective instrument when considered with a single view to its fitness for the purposes of government. On this point the whole argument rests.

¶130   It is contended that, admitting Congress to possess this power the exemption ought to have been expressly asserted in the act of incorporation; and not being expressed ought not to be implied by the court.

¶131   It is not unusual for a legislative act to involve consequences which are not expressed. An officer, for example, is ordered to arrest an individual. It is not necessary nor is it usual to say that he shall not be punished for obeying this order. His security is implied in the order itself. It is no unusual thing for an act of Congress to imply without expressing this very exemption from state controul which is said to be so objectionable in this instance. The collectors of the revenue, the carriers of the mail, the mint establishment, and all those institutions which are public in their nature are examples in point. It has never been doubted, that all who are employed in them are protected while in the line of duty; and yet this protection is not expressed in any act of Congress. It is incidental to and is implied in the several acts by which these institutions are created, and is secured to the individuals employed in them by the judicial power alone. That is, the judicial power is the instrument employed by the government in administering this security.

¶132   That department has no will in any case. If the sound construction of the act be that it exempts the trade of the Bank as being essential to the character of a machine necessary to the fiscal operations of the government, from the controul of the states, courts are as much bound to give it that construction as if the exemption had been established in express terms. Judicial power as contradistinguished from the power of the laws has no existence. Courts are the meer instruments of the law and can will nothing. When they are said to exercise a discretion it is a meer legal

discretion — a discretion to be exercised in discerning the course prescribed by law; and when that is discerned, it is the duty of the court to
follow it. Judicial power is never exercised for the purpose of giving effect
to the will of the Judge, always for the purpose of giving effect to the will
of the legislature; or, in other words, to the will of the law.

The appellants rely greatly on the distinction between the Bank and a   ¶133
public institution, such as the mint or the post office. The agents in those
offices are, it is said, officers of government, and are excluded from a seat
in Congress. Not so the Directors of the Bank. The connexion of the
government with the Bank is likened to that with contracters.

It will not be contended that the Directors or other officers of the Bank   ¶134
are officers of government. But it is contended that, were their resemblance to contractors more perfect than it is, the right of the state to
controul its operations, if those operations be necessary to its character
as a machine employed by the government cannot be maintained. Can a
contracter for supplying a military post with provisions be restrained
from making purchases within any state, or from transporting the provisions to the place at which the troops were stationed, or could he be fined
or taxed for doing so? We have not yet heard these questions answered in
the affirmative.

It is true that the property of the contracter may be taxed as the   ¶135
property of other citizens; and so may the[15] property of the Bank. But we
do not admit that the act of purchasing or of conveying the articles
purchased can be under state controul.

If the trade of the Bank be essential to its character as a machine for   ¶136
the fiscal operations of the government, that trade must be as exempt
from state controul as the actual conveyance of the public money. Indeed
a tax bears upon the whole machine, as well upon the faculty of collecting
and transmitting the money of the nation, as on that of discounting the
notes of individuals. No distinction is taken between them.

Considering the capacity of carrying on the trade of banking as an im-   ¶137
portant feature in the character of this corporation, which was necessary
to make it a fit instrument for the objects for which it was created, the
court adheres to its decision in the case of MCullough against The state of
Maryland, and is of opinion that the act of the state of Ohio, which is
certainly much more objectionable than that of the state of Maryland, is
repugnant to a law of the United States made in pursuance of the constitution, and therefore void. The counsel for the appellants are too intelligent, and have too much self respect, to pretend that a void act can
afford any protection to the officers who execute it. They expressly admit
that it cannot.

It being then shown, we think conclusively, that the defendants could   ¶138
derive neither authority nor protection from the act which they executed, and that this suit is not against the state of Ohio within the view of
the Constitution, the state being no party on the record, the only real

question in the cause is whether the record contains sufficient matter to justify the court in pronouncing a decree against the defendants. That this question is attended with great difficulty, has not been concealed or denied. But when we reflect that the defendants Oswold[16] & Harper are incontestably liable for the full amount of the money taken out of the bank; that the defendant Currie is also responsible for the sum received by him, it having come to his hands with full knowledge of the unlawful means by which it was acquired; that the defendant Sullivan is also responsible for the sum specifically delivered to him with notice that it was the property of the bank, unless the form of having made an entry on the books of the treasury can countervail the fact that it was in truth kept untouched in a trunk by itself as a deposit to await the event of the pending suit respecting it; we may lay it down as a proposition safely to be affirmed that all the defendants in the cause were liable in an action at law for the amount of this decree. If the original injunction was properly awarded for the reasons stated in the preceding part of this opinion, the money having reached the hands of all those to whom it afterwards came with notice of that injunction, might be pursued so long as it remained a distinct deposit, neither mixed with the money of the treasury, nor put into circulation. Were it to be admitted that the original injunction was not properly awarded, still the amended and supplemental bill which brings before the court all the parties who had been concerned in the transaction, was filed after the cause of action had completely accrued. The money of the bank had been taken without authority by some of the defendants, and was detained by the only person who was not an original wrong doer, in a specific form, so that detinue might have been maintained for it had it been in the power of the bank to prove the facts which were necessary to establish the identity of the property sued for. Under such circumstances, we think a court of equity may afford its aid on the ground that a discovery is necessary, and also on the same principle that an injunction issues to restrain a person who has fraudulently obtained possession of negotiable notes from putting them into circulation, or a person having the apparent ownership of stock really belonging to another, from transferring it. The suit then might be as well sustained in a court of equity as in a court of law, and the objection that the interests of the state are committed to subordinate agents, if true, is the unavoidable consequence of exemption from being sued — of sovereignty. The interests of the United States are sometimes committed to subordinate agents. It was the case in Hoyt & Gelston,[17] in the case of Clarke and Edon,[18] and in many others. An independent foreign sovereign cannot be sued, and does not appear in court. But a friend of the court comes in, and, by suggestion, gives it to understand, that his interests are involved in the controversy. The interests of the sovereign in such a case, and in every other where he chuses to assert them under the name of the real party to the cause, are as well defended as if he were a party to the record. But his pretensions, where they are not well founded, cannot arrest the suit[19] of a party having a right to the thing for which he sues. Where the right is in the plaintiff and the possession in the defendant, the enquiry cannot be stopped by the meer assertion of title in a sovereign. The court must proceed to investigate the assertion & examine the title. In the case at bar, the tribunal established by the constitution for the purpose of deciding ultimately in all cases of this description had solemnly determined that a state law imposing a tax on the Bank of the United States was unconstitutional and void, before the wrong was committed for which this suit was brought.

We think then that there is no error in the decree of the circuit court   ¶139
for the district of Ohio so far as it directs ⟨r⟩estitution of the specific sum of $98000 which was taken out of the Bank unlawfully, and was in the possession of the defendant Samuel Sullivan when the injunction was awarded in September 1820 to restrain him from paying it away or in any manner using it, and so far as it directs the payment of the remaining sum of 2000$ by the defendants Ralph Osborne and John L Harper; but that the same is erroneous so far as respects the interest on the coin, part of the said $98000, it being the opinion of this court, that while the parties were restrained by the authority of the circuit court from using it, they ought not to be charged with intere[s]t.

The decree of the circuit court for the District of Ohio is affirmed as to   ¶140
the said sums of $98000 and $2000, and reversed as to the residue.

[Decree]

Osborne & al
    v
The President Directors & company of the Bank of the United States

This cause came on to be heard on the transcript of the record of the circuit court of the United States for the District of Ohio and was argued by counsel on consideration whereof this court is of opinion that there is no error in so much of the decree of the circuit court as directs the restitution of the specific sum of $98000 which was taken out of the bank of the United States by violence, and contrary to law, and was retained in his possession by the defendant Samuel Sullivan in the nature of a special deposit, which he was restrained by the writ of injunction awarded by the said circuit court from paying away or using in any manner whatever, nor in so much of the said decree as directs the payment of the remaining sum of $2000 as to the defendants Ralph Osborne and John L Harper, but that there is error in so much of the said decree as directs interest to be paid on part of the said sum of money, and as subjects the defendants   Currie and Samuel Sullivan to the payment of the said sum of $2000 which never came to their hands.

AD, Gilder Lehrman Collection, NNPM; printed, Henry Wheaton, *Reports of Cases Argued and Adjudged in the Supreme Court of the United States . . .* , IX (New York, 1824), 816–71. For JM's deletions and interlineations, see Textual Notes below.

1. Wheaton's text begins here.

2. *U.S. Statutes at Large,* III, 269.

3. Bank of the U.S. v. Deveaux, 5 Cranch 85 (1809); *PJM,* VII, 196–202.

4. *U.S. Statutes at Large,* I, 192.

5. Ibid., I, 194.

6. Wheaton's text omits "words which in their plain sense apply to a whole cause," an omission that obscures JM's meaning. The text as originally published in the *Daily National Intelligencer,* 22 Mar. 1824, includes these words.

7. Wheaton omits "or otherwise."

8. Bank of Columbia v. Patterson's Administrators, 7 Cranch 299 (1813). The unnamed case was Fleckner v. Bank of the U.S., 8 Wheat. 338 (1823), which counsel cited at 9 Wheat. 746, 801. Wheaton inserted "&c." in the space.

9. *U.S. Statutes at Large,* I, 91.

10. Corrected to "Osborn" in the newspaper and in Wheaton.

11. The newspaper and Wheaton omit "the interference of."

12. Henry Maddock, *A Treatise on the Principles and Practice of the High Court of Chancery* (3d Am. ed.; 2 vols.; Hartford, Conn., 1827), I, 154, 155.

13. Someone (Wheaton?) wrote "conceiving" above "supposing." The newspaper and Wheaton have "conceiving."

14. Someone here inserted "& rightfully." The newspaper and Wheaton have "and rightfully."

15. Wheaton has "local" before "property."

16. Corrected to "Osborne" in the newspaper and in Wheaton.

17. Gelston v. Hoyt, 3 Wheat. 246 (1818).

18. Wheaton styled this case as The Appollon, 9 Wheat. 362 (1824). The newspaper and Wheaton also cited the case of Doddridge's Lessee v. Thompson and Wright, 9 Wheat. 469 (1824).

19. The newspaper and Wheaton have "right" in place of "suit."

Textual Notes

¶	1 l. 1 beg.	In on the 2d. of ↑In↓ September 1819, a bill was ↑filed in↓ presented
	ll. 2–3	Ohio by ↑signed by↓ ↑in the name of the Bank of the U.S., signed by↓ gentlemen
	ll. 4–6	from levying on the property of the B ↑proceeding against complainants↓ under an act passed ↑the preceding February↓ by the state legislature of the state, ↑passed the preceding February↓ entitled
¶	2 l. 2	if, t ↑after↓ the
	l. 5	day of December ↑September,↓ the Auditor
	l. 13	chest &c [*erasure*] ↑in↓ search
¶	3 l. 1	The bill then ↑after reciting this act↓ states
	ll. 5–6	injunction, ↑on the execution of bond & security in the penalty of $100,000;↓ after
	ll. 6–7	on which was endorsed ↑the order that had been made for↓ the injunction
	l. 13	writ of subpœna ↑injunction↓ was

¶ 5 l. 2   injunction, ↑to wit↓ on the

 ll. 3–4   the tax ↑and well knew that an injunction had been allowed,↓ proceeded

 ll. 16–18   may be ~~decreed to restore~~ ↑enjoined from using or paying away↓ the coin and notes taken from the bank, ↑may be decreed to restore the same↓ and may be [*erasure*] ↑enjoined↓ from

¶ 6 l. 6   January [*erasure*] ↑or↓ February 1820

¶ 7 l. 1   answer ~~at~~ ↑an↓ attachment

¶ 8 l. 10   allowed ~~on an injunction~~ ↑by the circuit court on a↓ bill

 l. 15 $98000 was ~~collected~~ ↑levied↓ as a

¶ 9 l. 1   came on ↑to be heard↓ upon

 ll. 2–3   Harper; ~~when a decree was~~ ↑and the court↓ pronounced ↑a decree↓ directing

¶ 10 l. 3   is, ~~power of Congress to enable~~ the ↑Dright of↓ the Bank

 l. 5   deciding ↑on↓ the

¶ 11 l. 5   shall be ~~enabled~~ "made able

¶ 12 l. 3   "in ~~the~~ [*erasure*] ↑any↓ circuit court

 ll. 9–10   the ↑federal↓ courts. ~~of the United States.~~ The words of ↑the 3d sec. of↓ that act ~~were~~ ↑are↓ that the Bank ~~might~~ ↑ may↓ "sue and

 l. 12   general ~~right~~ ↑capacity↓ to sue,

 l. 15   Sec. ↑of the same act,↓ subjects

 l. 17   them [*erasure*] ↑.↓" The

 l. 18   courts in ~~one~~ ↑this↓ case

 l. 20   decision ~~was~~ ↑be↓ right

 ll. 21–22   to ~~this~~ ↑a declaration↓ that a general ~~power~~ ↑capacity↓ in the Bank

 l. 22   Union, ~~does~~ ↑may↓ not give

 l. 23   infer from ~~it~~ ↑this↓

¶ 14 ll. 1–2   of ~~this~~ ↑the↓ clause in the act ~~incorporating the Bank~~ ↑of incorporation↓ which

 l. 2   in the ~~circuit~~ ↑federal↓ courts. ~~of the United States~~

¶ 15 ll. 1–3   the ~~act being within the legislative powers of the~~ ↑Legislative, Executive and Judicial powers of every well constructed↓ government, ↑are↓ coextensive with ~~its legislative. That~~ each other.

 l. 3   coextensive. ~~As the~~ ↑The↓

 l. 5   make, ~~so~~ ↑and↓ the judicial

 ll. 6–7   law. ~~Every~~ ↑All governments which ~~is~~ are [*erasure*] not extremely defective in ~~its~~ their organization

 l. 10   great ↑political↓ principle

¶ 16 l. 3   them ↑shall↓ assume

 ll. 5–6   it ↑in the form prescribed,↓ by ~~parties~~ ↑a party↓ who ~~assert their respective~~ ↑asserts his↓ rights in the ~~form~~ ↑form↓ prescribed

¶ 19 l. 1   to ~~exclude~~ ↑withdraw a case from↓ the

 ll. 2–3   courts, ~~scarcely any case~~ ↑almost every case though involving the construction of a law ↓ would ll. 6–7   depends on ~~a law~~ ↑the constitution, laws, or treaties↓ of

l. 10   right [*erasure*] ↑is↓ barred,

l. 12   which ~~o~~ ↑may↓ occur

l. 14   constitution ~~and~~ laws,

¶ 20 l. 1   cases ~~to~~ ↑in↓ which ~~the~~ original jurisdiction ~~of~~ ↑is given to↓ the

l. 4   form ↑or both↓ as the

l. 6   is ~~no case~~ ↑none↓ to which

l. 9   power. [*erasure*] ↑We↓ find

l. 10   exercise ~~by this court, or by the inferior courts,~~ in

l. 12   form ↑only,↓ to

¶ 21 l. 2   It ~~de~~ enumerates

l. 3   defines ~~its~~ ↑that which is↓ appellate, ~~jurisdiction~~ but

l. 5   jurisdiction. ~~That~~ ↑It is not insinuated that↓ the

¶ 22 l. 2   that ~~the power of our~~ ↑Congress is incapable↓ of

¶ 23 l. 2   case ~~devolves~~ ↑involves↓ questions

l. 4   on ↑the construction of↓ a law

ll. 5–6   If ~~the circumstance~~ ↑it be a sufficient foundation for jurisdiction↓ that

l. 9   out, ~~be a sufficient foundation for jurisdiction~~ then

l. 10   to this ~~question~~ which gives

ll. 10–11   cannot ~~oust the jurisdiction~~ ~~suspend~~ arrest

l. 12   that ↑most↓ important

l. 19   from ~~enabling~~ ↑authorizing↓ the courts

ll. 19–20   jurisdiction [*erasure*] ↑of↓

ll. 20–21   congress from ~~enabling~~ ↑authorizing↓ those courts [*erasure*] ↑to↓ take

l. 22   a ↑whole↓ cause,

l. 23   in ~~a~~ ↑that↓ cause, ~~of securing~~ ↑to↓ ~~those who claim rights under the constitution, laws, and~~ ↑or↓ ~~treaties of the United States~~ and words

¶ 24 l. 2   Union ↑is↓ extended

¶ 25 l. 6   can ~~have~~ ↑acquire↓ no

l. 8   creature of ↑a↓ law,

¶ 27 l. 5   contract? ~~F~~ ↑If↓ this

l. 10   exercised [*erasure*] ↑antecedently↓ to ~~its~~ ↑the↓ first

ll. 14–15   particular ~~right~~ property, or to sue ~~for~~ ↑on account of↓ a particular injury, ~~may~~ belongs

ll. 16–17   forms an ~~ingredient~~ ~~ingredie~~ ↑original↓ ingredient

¶ 28 l. 9   action ↑still↓ originates

¶ 29 l. 2   with ~~suits~~ ↑the↓ acts

l. 5   under ~~those~~ ↑that↓ part

l. 13   a ~~suit~~ ↑case,↓ because ~~in~~ that suit too is ↑itself authorized, and is↓ brought

l. 15   moment ~~independent~~ ↑without↓ its authority.

¶ 30 l. 1   that ~~the cause~~ ↑a suit brought by the Bank↓ may

ll. 9–10   on ~~the~~ ↑that↓ construction of the constitution which ~~says~~ asserts the right of ~~congress~~ ↑the legislature↓ to give

¶ 31 l. 4   patent, ~~but~~ ↑or↓ make

¶ 32 l. 1   distinction [*erasure*] ↑exists↓ between
¶ 33 l. 2   more, ~~the distinction~~ ↑it↓ might
     l. 4   bestow [*erasure*] upon the ↑being it has made↓ all
     l. 5   which ~~it~~ ↑that being↓ possesses.
¶ 34 l. 4   standing, ~~under~~ ↑in the view of↓ the
¶ 36 l. 3   the ↑courts of the↓ United States
     l. 4   be ~~respected~~ ↑obeyed↓ in all ~~the~~ ↑courts.↓
¶ 38 ll. 1–2 erroneous, ~~because~~
¶ 48 l. 12   been ~~consider~~ ↑received↓ as
     ll. 15–16 in ~~the courts~~ ↑those↓ of any
¶ 49 l. 3   distinction. ~~The~~ ↑A↓ corporation,
     l. 6   the ~~person~~ ↑individual↓ professing
     l. 8   person. ~~If any distinction could be drawn between the cases, it would be founded on the suppo~~ The
     ll. 15–16 corporation ↑either as plaintiff or defendant,↓ by
     ll. 19–20 pronounced ↑in conformity with the general course of the court↓ in a
¶ 50 l. 2   the ~~want~~ ↑non↓ appearance
     ll. 3–4   may ~~be~~ very
     l. 4   in [*erasure*] ↑its↓ general
     l. 5   law. ~~in this respect~~ No reason is perceived [*erasure*] ↑why↓ the courts
¶ 51 l. 4   whether a ~~found~~ ↑fund↓ out
¶ 52 l. 2   will ~~consider~~ ↑look into↓ the
     l. 3   Sullivan. ~~as an~~ ↑In↓ objection
     ll. 5–6   another, [*erasure*] ↑so↓ that
     l. 8   his ~~heirs~~ ↑their,↓ or
     l. 10   him, ~~i~~ ↑might↓ be
     ll. 13–14 testimony ~~on which the decree was pronounced.~~ ↑taken against the vendor.↓
¶ 53 l. 2   Sullivan, [*erasure*] the
     l. 8   the ~~fact~~ ↑Bank,↓ the
¶ 54 l. 4   Bank ↑as a tax,↓ in
     l. 9   Sullivan ~~this~~ ↑the↓ gentleman
¶ 55 l. 5   is ~~strong and plain~~ ↑irresistible↓ that
     l. 10   by ↑the↓ law was
     l. 11   being ~~the~~ money ~~so~~ taken
     l. 13   Ohio, ~~for~~ ~~This money~~ if
     l. 14   person ~~have~~ doubted
     l. 15   hesitate ~~respecting~~ ↑in such a↓ case.
¶ 57 l. 1   transaction. ~~He~~ ↑That is, he↓ was
     l. 3   Bank, ~~and~~ ↑or↓ when
¶ 59 l. 1 $98000 ~~wh~~ ↑as↓ being
     l. 10   it. ~~Can~~ ↑Is↓ it
     l. 11   money? ~~3d. The next objection respects the decree against Osborne and Harper, against whom the bill was taken for confessed.~~
             ~~— The bill charges that the defendant Osborne employed the defendant Harper to collect the tax, who entered the~~

~~office of discount and deposit at chilicothe, and forcibly took therefrom $10000, though he knew at the time that an injunction had been allowed; which money was delivered either to Currie or Osborne.~~

¶ 60 ll. 1–2   his ~~own~~ liability

l. 4   that ~~the money was~~ ↑these $98000 were↓ delivered ↑to him↓ as

l. 5   it; ~~This d~~ for

¶ 61 l. 5   delivery. ~~The~~ ↑A↓ declaration

l. 8   Sullivan ~~is suff~~ then is,

l. 9   that ~~the sum of money~~ ↑these↓ $98000

¶ 62 ll. 1–2   Harper, ~~respecting~~ ↑as to↓ whom

¶ 66 l. 2   sum ~~which~~ ↑decreed to↓ the complainants. ~~claimed~~ Had

l. 7   party ↑in possession,↓ while

l. 9   person ~~wh~~ ↑in↓ whose

l. 12   into ~~his~~ ↑its↓ own

l. 14   had [*erasure*] ↑the↓ money

ll. 15–16   that [*erasure*] ↑the↓ injunction

¶ 68 ll. 2–3   The ~~injunction is prayed~~ ↑original bill prays for an injunction↓ against

ll. 9–10   statute ↑and whether a court of equity can decree ~~the~~ restitution if the act be performed.↓ In

l. 13   assumed ~~for the present~~ because

l. 16   We ~~dismiss~~ ↑suspend↓ also

ll. 17–18   state ~~of~~ ↑of↓ Ohio, as disclosed in the ~~bills~~ ↑bill↓ ↑shows a want of jurisdiction in the circuit court which↓ ought

l. 19   the ~~plain~~ appellants,

l. 20   The ~~present~~ ↑sole↓ enquiry ~~is,~~ ↑for the present, is,↓ whether,

l. 28   be ~~sustained~~ ↑affirmed↓ so

¶ 69 l. 8   state, ~~of Ohio~~ and

¶ 70 ll. 1–2   would ~~in the opinion of the court~~ be to disregard entirely ~~the~~ ↑its true character and↓ substantial merits. ~~of the case.~~

l. 3   was, ~~not~~ to

l. 5   but ~~from in the enjoyment~~ ↑from the total destruction↓ of

l. 6   privileges, ~~from total destruction~~ so

l. 8   must [*erasure*] be

l. 8   state. ~~of Ohio.~~ An

l. 9 $100000 [*erasure*] would ~~render the privilege~~ more

l. 10   would ~~completely~~ ↑consequently↓ annul it.

¶ 71 ll. 5–6   The ~~cases which have most frequently occurred are those in which an attempt has been made to violate~~ ↑interference of the court in this class of cases has ~~been~~ most frequently been to restrain a person from violating↓ an

ll. 9–10   strengthened ~~that~~ ↑than↓ weakened?

ll. 13–14   would ~~he~~ ↑such person or company↓ have been enjoined? ~~Because he does~~ ↑To prevent↓ a permanent injury ↑from being done↓ to

l. 18   respects ~~an~~ ↑the↓ estimate of

ll. 25–26   of [*erasure*] ↑its↓ franchise in the state of ~~ohio~~ ↑Ohio↓ is as ~~little~~

	ll. 27–28	act of ↑levying the tax in the↓ first
	l. 28	the f ↑cause↓ ⟨of⟩
	l. 33	trespass, ~~almost all~~ and in ↑many↓ cases
¶ 72	l. 3	the ~~proper~~ ↑real↓ party
	ll. 5–6	not ↑make a↓ decree unless all ~~the parties~~ ↑those↓ who
	l. 6	be ~~brought~~ ↑made↓ parties
¶ 73	l. 2	parties; ~~B~~ ↑but↓ if
	l. 11	being [*erasure*] ↑admitted↓ then
	ll. 14–16	him? ~~We put out of view~~ ↑Why may it not restrain him from the commission of a wrong which it would punish him for committing? We put out of view↓ the
	ll. 22–23	joint. ~~But will~~ ↑Without enquiring into the validity of this reason if true, we ask if it be true? Will↓ it
	l. 26	cannot: ~~there no~~ and
	ll. 26–27	no ~~possible~~ ↑plausible↓ reason
	l. 29	party. ~~But, could it even be maintained But, were it even to be admitted that the injunction was improperly awarded, and that the original bill could not be maintained that would not, we think materially affect the case. An amended and supplemental bill making new parties has been filed in the cause, and on that bill with the proceedings under it the decree has been pronounced. The question is whether upon that bill and the proceedings which have~~
¶ 74	l. 4	since ~~a~~ ↑this↓ principal
¶ 75	ll. 1–2	the ~~original~~ injunction ↑in the first instance↓ was
¶ 76	ll. 1–2	plaintiffs ↑in the circuit court,↓ have been
¶ 78	ll. 3–4	Thus ↑the holder of↓ negotiable securities indorsed ~~according to the~~ ↑in the usual manner,↓ if
	l. 6	Thus ↑too↓ a transfer
	l. 12	equity ~~to~~ in
	l. 13	complete ~~than~~ ↑than↓ the
¶ 79	l. 2	for ↑the interference of↓ a
¶ 80	l. 2	granted by ~~the laws~~ ↑a law↓ of the
	l. 3	asserts ~~its~~ ↑a↓ right
	ll. 7–8	court ↑though not directed against the state by name,↓ acts directly upon ~~its~~ ↑it↓ by
	l. 9	substantially ↑re↓ ~~against~~ though
¶ 81	ll. 2–3	state ↑in the suit as brought↓ is admitted,
	ll. 3–4	make ~~the state~~ ↑it↓ a party, ↑perhaps↓ no decree ~~could~~ ↑ought to↓ have
	ll. 5–7	Bank. ↑The 11th. amendment of the constitution has exempted a state from the suits of citizens of other states, or aliens,↓ and the very difficult question [*erasure*] ↑is↓ to
¶ 82	l. 1 beg.	[*erasure*] ↑Before↓ we
¶ 83	l. 7	shall ~~maintain~~ impose
	l. 11	from [*erasure*] ↑the↓ judicial
	l. 13	officer, ~~may~~ may
	l. 22	of ~~the~~ ↑its↓ defensive
	l. 23	agent ~~of~~ ↑or↓ executing

ll. 25–26   perpetrated, [*erasure*] ↑and↓ which must often be ineffectual.
↑, from the inability of the agents to make compensation.↓
¶ 84 l. 9   but, ~~the~~ in
ll. 10–11   one [*erasure*] as
¶ 85 l. 1 beg.   The ~~diff~~ distinction
¶ 86 l. 4   of ~~any~~ ↑a particular↓ state
¶ 87 l. 2   proceedings ↑whatever,↓ or
l. 4   agent, ~~can be sustained~~ because
¶ 88 l. 1   the ~~circuit~~ courts
¶ 90 l. 3   of ~~another~~ ↑another↓ state"
¶ 94 l. 3   but is ~~ap~~ ↑to↓ be
¶ 98 ll. 2–3   which ~~respect boundary~~ ↑decide on the extent↓ of
l. 4   controversies ~~, unless made~~ ↑if not plaintiff↓ or
l. 5   has ↑expressly↓ given
¶ 99 l. 7   take ~~jurisdiction over~~ ↑cognizance of↓ questions
l. 8   thought ~~necessarily~~ ↑necessary↓ expressly
¶100 l. 2   the ~~interest~~ ↑title↓ of the
¶103 l. 2   What ~~decree~~ ↑degree↓ of interest shall be ~~admitted~~
↑sufficient↓ to
ll. 11–12   and the ~~damages~~ ↑verdict and↓ judgement
l. 14   retain ↑the amount of the taxes↓ in
l. 15   may ~~defend himself by~~ ↑plead in bar↓ the
l. 18   the ~~interest~~ ↑revenue↓ of
l. 25   the ↑latter↓ action
¶104 l. 2   every ~~gentleman~~ ↑person↓ will
l. 3   to [*erasure*] ↑which↓ a
¶105 l. 14   intended, ↑for reasons which all comprehend,↓ to give the
~~federal~~ ↑national↓ courts
¶106 ll. 2–3   party, ~~the first in the enumeration is "controversies to which the United States shall be a party."~~ ↑the first in the enumeration he enumeration is "controversies to which the United States shall be a party. ["]↓
¶107 ll. 1–3   ~~Does this provision extend to cases where the United States are not named in the record, and may be concerned in interest? Let us examine this question.~~ ↑Does this provision extend to cases where the United States are not named in the record but claim and are actually entitled to the whole subject in controversy?↓
¶108 l. 1   ↑Let us examine this question.↓
¶109 ll. 1–7   ↑Suits brought by the Post master General are for money due to the United States. The nominal plaintiff has no interest in the controversy, and the United States are the only real party. Yet these suits could not be instituted in the courts of the Union under that clause which gives jurisdiction in all cases to which the United States are a party, and it was found necessary to give the Court jurisdiction over them as being cases arising under a law of the United States.↓
¶110 ll. 1–2   ~~It is admitted that the United States cannot at present be sued. As the law now stands no suit can be sustained against~~

the ~~United States we find it may be exercised in~~ ↑The judicial
power of the union is also extended to ~~controversies between~~
~~citizens of different States↓~~ controversies between

    l. 6   of ~~the~~ ↑this↓ testator

¶111 l. 2   court ~~would~~ ↑in a suit↓ against

¶113 ll. 1–2   the principle seems ~~to be~~ too well established ~~that we will not~~
~~devote more~~ ↑to require that more time should be↓ devoted

    l. 9   to ~~cases~~ suits brought ~~by~~ against

¶114 l. 1 beg. ~~The true question then,~~ The

    l. 3   but ~~is~~ whether

    ll. 4–5   defendants ↑: Whether they are to be considered as having a
real interest or as being only nominal parties.↓

¶115 l. 2   this ~~point~~ question

    ll. 10–11 it. ~~That~~ ↑The↓ judgement

    ll. 16–18 effective. ↑The parties must certainly have a real interest in
the case since their personal responsability is acknowledged,
and if denied, could be demonstrated.↓ ~~7th. If then the law~~
~~of the state of Ohio be repugnant to the constitution, or to a~~
~~law of the United States made in pursuance thereof,~~

¶116 l. 1 beg. It was ~~then~~ proper

    l. 3   or ↑to↓ a law

¶118 l. 1   this ~~state,~~ ↑court,↓ after

    l. 4   a ~~reconsideration~~ ↑review↓ of it.

¶120 l. 3   be ~~subjected~~ ↑subject↓ to

    l. 6   its ↑private business↓ from

    l. 7   exempt ↑the private business of↓ any

    ll. 9–10 is ~~private trade and private~~ ↑individual trade and individual↓
profit;

    l. 16   opinion ↑of the court↓ in

    l. 17   of [erasure] ↑Maryland↓ is

    l. 19   for ~~carr~~ ↑carrying↓ into

    l. 22   created ↑in the form in which it now appears,↓ for

    l. 24   great ~~ban~~ ↑instrument↓ by

¶121 l. 5   nation, [erasure] ↑if↓ it

¶123 ll. 10–11 It is ↑in that view of the subject,↓ the

    l. 12   preserve it ~~stands on the same ground~~ ↑originates in the
same principle↓ with

    l. 19   very [erasure] useless attribute.

¶125 l. 1   that ~~the~~ Congress

¶126 ll. 4–5 authority. ~~We maintain that if~~ ↑If↓ an

    ll. 13–14 as ~~an~~ ↑a national↓ instrument. ~~of the nation.~~ The

    l. 15   for the [erasure] ↑money↓ transactions

    l. 16   is ↑meerly↓ an

¶127 ll. 2–3 the ↑public↓ functions of ~~Banks~~ ↑the Bank↓

    l. 3   with ~~their~~ ↑its↓ faculties

    l. 5   as the ~~Banks~~ ↑Bank,↓

    l. 8   the ~~banking~~ ↑banking↓ business ~~which was essential to the~~
~~performance of his duties,~~ instead

    ll. 12–13 faculties ↑so↓ essential

¶128 ll. 5–6   without ~~this faculty,~~ ↑the employment of a banking capital,↓ those

    ll. 6–7   of ~~the~~ ↑these↓ faculties

¶129 l. 1 beg.   The ~~argument of th~~ appellants ~~insist that~~ ↑admit that, if↓ this

    ll. 1–2   the bank ~~an~~ a fit instrument

    l. 3   protect ~~it as to protect~~ the machine ~~itself in~~ ↑in this as in [*erasure*]↓ its

    l. 9   very ~~imperfect~~ ↑defective↓ instrument

¶130 ll. 1–2   Congress ~~to possess~~ to possess this power ~~it~~ ↑the exemption↓ ought

¶131 ll. 11–12   incidental to ↑and is implied in↓ the

¶134 ll. 2–3   were ~~the~~ ↑their↓ resemblance ~~of~~ to

    ll. 5–6   Can a ~~mail carrier be [erasure]~~ ↑contracter for supplying↓ a

    ll. 9–10   heard ↑these questions answered in↓ the affirmative.

¶135 l. 3   of ↑purchasing↓ or

¶136 l. 2   government, ~~that is~~ that

¶137 ll. 2–3   necessary ~~necessary~~ to make

    l. 9   that ~~such an~~ ↑a void↓ act

¶138 l. 2   act ~~of~~ ↑which↓ they

    l. 8   defendants ↑Oswold & Harper↓ are

    ll. 9–10   the ~~B~~ ↑bank;↓ that

    ll. 19–20   was ~~justifiable~~ ↑properly awarded↓ for

    l. 21   money ~~and the notes, they~~ having

    ll. 21–22   came ~~in violation~~ ↑with notice↓ of

    l. 23   deposit, ~~unmixed~~ ↑neither mixed↓

    l. 23   treasury, ~~and not~~ ↑nor↓ put

    l. 24   original ↑injunction↓ was

    l. 27   was ~~brou~~ filed

    ll. 28–29   the ~~defenants~~ ↑defendants,↓ and

    l. 38   the ~~was~~ ↑might be↓ as well ~~to be~~ sustained

    l. 43   Gelston, ~~it~~ ↑in↓ the

    ll. 44–45   sovereign ↑cannot be sued, and↓ does not ~~apear~~ ↑appear↓ in court.

    ll. 53–54   of ~~a~~ title in ~~the~~ ↑a↓ sovereign. ~~That~~ ↑The↓ court must proceed to investigate the ~~fact~~ ↑assertion↓ &

¶139 l. 2   directs ↑⟨r⟩estitution of↓ the

    ll. 6–8   it, ~~but that the decree is erroneous so far as respects~~ ↑and so far as it directs the payment of↓ the remaining sum of 2000$ ~~there not be sufficient proof~~ ↑in the record↓ ~~that that sum was taken from the bank;~~ ↑by the defendants Ralph Osborne and John L Harper;↓ but that the same is erroneous ~~and also~~ so far as respects the ~~coin~~ interest

    l. 10   the ↑circuit↓ court

¶140 l. 1 beg.   ~~It is therefore~~ The

    ll. 1–2   to [*erasure*] ↑the↓ said sums of $98000 ↑and $2000,↓ and

Bank of the United States v. Planters' Bank of Georgia
Opinion
U.S. Supreme Court, 22 March 1824

This case, like *Osborn* v. *Bank of the United States,* raised the issue of the right of the Second Bank of the United States to sue in the courts of the United States. The suit was the outcome of deteriorating relations between the Savannah branch of the Bank of the United States and a Georgia state bank, the Planters' Bank, also located in Savannah. As a depository of the federal treasury, the branch bank received notes issued by the state bank in payment of federal taxes. Attempts by the branch to obtain timely redemption of the notes in specie met increasingly stiff resistance from the state bank, which took offense at what it regarded as unwarranted federal interference with its expansionist credit policy. In June 1821 the Planters' Bank annulled an agreement whereby the branch would hold $100,000 in state bank notes without demanding redemption and the state bank would pay six percent interest on the balances in excess of that amount. Then it declared it would cash no more of its notes presented by the Bank of the United States. In December 1821 the Georgia legislature enacted a law providing that state bank notes held by the Bank of the United States should not be redeemable in specie except in extraordinary circumstances. As a result, the business of the Savannah branch rapidly declined. In the spring of 1823 the president and directors brought an action of assumpsit in the U.S. Circuit Court at Savannah, seeking damages for the failure of the state bank to redeem a set of its notes held by the Bank of the United States. The state bank entered a plea to the jurisdiction, to which the plaintiff demurred. Argument took place on 17 and 18 December 1823, the defendant contending that the state of Georgia was a stockholder in the bank and was therefore not suable; that the notes were originally payable to citizens of Georgia and assignment to the Bank of the United States could not give jurisdiction; and that the plaintiff could not sue either by the Constitution or by the Judiciary Act. The plaintiff maintained that Congress had the power to authorize suits by the Bank of the United States in federal courts and had in fact exercised that power by granting the charter. On 22 December Judges William Johnson and Jeremiah Cuyler agreed to a *pro forma* division in order to certify the case to the Supreme Court, where "it might undergo the fullest investigation." On 10 and 11 March counsel in this case and in *Osborn* argued the question of the right of the Bank of the United States to sue in federal courts. Ethan A. Brown and John C. Wright represented Osborn; John Sergeant and Daniel Webster spoke for the Bank of the United States; and Robert G. Harper appeared on behalf of the Planters' Bank. On 12 March Harper and Henry Clay (for the Bank of the United States) took up the remaining questions in the suit against the Planters' Bank. Marshall delivered the opinion of the Court on 22 March (Ralph C. H. Catterall, *The Second Bank of the United States* [Chicago, 1903], 84–89; Bank of the U.S. v. Planters' Bank of Georgia, App. Cas. No. 1270; *Niles' Weekly Register* [Baltimore], XXV [1824],

328; 9 Wheat. 910; U.S. Sup. Ct. Minutes, 10, 11, 12 Mar. 1824; *Daily National Intelligencer,* 11, 12, 13, 23 Mar. 1824).

In this case, the petition of the plaintiffs, which, according to the practice of the State of Georgia, is substituted for a declaration, is founded on promissory notes, payable to a person named in the note, "*or bearer,*" and states, that the notes were "duly transferred, assigned and delivered" to the plaintiffs, "who thereby became the lawful bearer thereof, and entitled to payment of the sums therein specified; and that the defendants, in consideration of their liability, assumed," &c.

The Planters' Bank pleads to the jurisdiction of the Court, and alleges, that it is a corporation, of which the State of Georgia, and certain individuals, who are citizens of the same State with some of the plaintiffs, are members. The plea also alleges, that the persons to whom the notes mentioned in the petition were made payable, were citizens of the State of Georgia, and, therefore, incapable of suing the said Bank in a Circuit Court of the United States; and being so incapable, could not, by transferring the notes to the plaintiffs, enable them to sue in that Court.

To this plea the plaintiffs demurred, and the defendants joined in demurrer.

On the argument of the demurrer, the Judges were divided on two questions:

1. Whether the averments in the declaration be sufficient in law to give this Court jurisdiction of the cause?[1]

2. Whether, on the pleadings in the same, the plaintiffs be entitled to judgment?

The first question was fully considered by the Court in the case of *Osborne* v. *The Bank of the United States,* and it is unnecessary to repeat the reasoning used in that case. We are of opinion, that the averments in the declaration are sufficient to give the Court jurisdiction of the cause.

2d. The second point is understood to involve two questions:

1. Does the circumstance that the State is a corporator, bring this cause within the clause in the constitution which gives jurisdiction to the Supreme Court where a State is a party, or bring it within the 11th amendment?

2. Does the fact that the note is made payable to a citizen of the State of Georgia, or bearer, oust the jurisdiction of the Court?

1. Is the State of Georgia a party defendant in this case? If it is, then the suit, had the 11th amendment never been adopted, must have been brought in the Supreme Court of the United States. Could this Court have entertained jurisdiction in the case?

We think it could not. To have given the Supreme Court original jurisdiction, the State must be plaintiff or defendant as a State, and must, as a State, be a party on the record. A suit against the Planters' Bank of Georgia, is no more a suit against the State of Georgia, than against any other individual corporator. The State is not a party, that is, an entire party, in the cause.

If this suit could not have been brought originally in the Supreme Court, it would be difficult to show, that it is within the 11th amendment. That amendment does not purport to do more than to restrain the construction which might otherwise be given to the constitution; and if this case be not one of which the Supreme Court could have taken original jurisdiction, it is not within the amendment. This is not, we think, a case in which the character of the defendant gives jurisdiction to the Court. If it did, the suit could be instituted only in the Supreme Court. This suit is not to be sustained because the Planters' Bank is suable in the federal Courts, but because the plaintiff has a right to sue any defendant in that Court, who is not withdrawn from its jurisdiction by the constitution, or by law. The suit is against a corporation, and the judgment is to be satisfied by the property of the corporation, not by that of the individual corporators. The State does not, by becoming a corporator, identify itself with the corporation. The Planters' Bank of Georgia is not the State of Georgia, although the State holds an interest in it.

It is, we think, a sound principle, that when a government becomes a partner in any trading company, it devests itself, so far as concerns the transactions of that company, of its sovereign character, and takes that of a private citizen. Instead of communicating to the company its privileges and its prerogatives, it descends to a level with those with whom it associates itself, and takes the character which belongs to its associates, and to the business which is to be transacted. Thus, many States of this Union who have an interest in Banks, are not suable even in their own Courts; yet they never exempt the corporation from being sued. The State of Georgia, by giving to the Bank the capacity to sue and be sued, voluntarily strips itself of its sovereign character, so far as respects the transactions of the Bank, and waives all the privileges of that character. As a member of a corporation, a government never exercises its sovereignty. It acts merely as a corporator, and exercises no other power in the management of the affairs of the corporation, than are expressly given by the incorporating act.

The government of the Union held shares in the old Bank of the United States; but the privileges of the government were not imparted by that circumstance to the Bank. The United States was not a party to suits brought by or against the Bank in the sense of the constitution. So with respect to the present Bank. Suits brought by or against it are not understood to be brought by or against the United States. The government, by becoming a corporator, lays down its sovereignty, so far as respects the transactions of the corporation, and exercises no power or privilege which is not derived from the charter.

We think, then, that the Planters' Bank of Georgia is not exempted from being sued in the federal Courts, by the circumstance that the State is a corporator.

2. We proceed next to inquire, whether the jurisdiction of the Court is ousted by the circumstance, that the notes on which the suit was instituted, were made payable to citizens of the State of Georgia.

3. Without examining whether, in this case, the original promise is not to the bearer, the Court will proceed to the more general question, whether the Bank, as endorsee, may maintain a suit against the maker of a note payable to a citizen of the State. The words of the Judiciary Act, section 11. are, "nor shall any District or Circuit Court have cognizance of any suit, to recover the contents of any promissory note, or other chose in action, in favour of an assignee, unless a suit might have been prosecuted in such Court to recover the said contents, if no assignment had been made, except in cases of foreign bills of exchange."[2]

This is a limitation on the jurisdiction conferred by the Judiciary Act. It was apprehended that bonds and notes, given in the usual course of business, by citizens of the same State, to each other, might be assigned to the citizens of another State, and thus render the maker liable to a suit in the federal Courts. To remove this inconvenience, the act which gives jurisdiction to the Courts of the Union over suits brought by the citizen of one State against the citizen of another, restrains that jurisdiction, where the suit is brought by an assignee to cases where the suit might have been sustained, had no assignment been made. But the Bank does not sue in virtue of any right conferred by the Judiciary Act, but in virtue of the right conferred by its charter. It does not sue because the defendant is a citizen of a different State from any of its members, but because its charter confers upon it the right of suing its debtors in a Circuit Court of the United States.

If the Bank could not sue a person who was a citizen of the same State with any one of its members, in the Circuit Court, this disability would defeat the power. There is, probably, not a commercial State in the Union, some of whose citizens are not members of the Bank of the United States. There is, consequently, scarcely a debt due to the Bank, for which a suit could be maintained in a federal Court, did the jurisdiction of the Court depend on citizenship. A general power to sue in any Circuit Court of the United States, expressed in terms obviously intended to comprehend every case, would thus be construed to comprehend no case. Such a construction cannot be the correct one.

We think, then, that the charter gives to the Bank a right to sue in the Circuit Courts of the United States, without regard to citizenship; and that the certificate on both questions must be in favour of the plaintiff.[3]

Printed, Henry Wheaton, *Reports of Cases Argued and Adjudged in the Supreme Court of the United States . . .*, IX (New York, 1824), 904–10.

1. After reciting twenty-one counts on the bank notes, the plaintiff's declaration (or petition, in this case) concluded by averring that the Bank of the United States was incorporated by an act of Congress of Apr. 1816 by which the bank was made able and capable to

sue in any U.S. Circuit Court (Bank of the U.S. v. Planters' Bank of Georgia, App. Cas. No. 1270).

2. *U.S. Statutes at Large*, I, 79.

3. Justice Johnson delivered a dissenting opinion, citing Bank of the U.S. v. Deveaux (1809) as controlling precedent. In that case the Court decided that a corporation's capacity to sue in the federal courts depended on the character of the individual persons composing the corporation and that the act incorporating the first Bank of the United States did not confer such jurisdiction. Johnson contended that on the principle of this case, the federal court had no jurisdiction either on the ground that the suit was between citizens of the same state or that the state of Georgia was a defendant (9 Wheat. 910–14; 5 Cranch 84–92; *PJM*, VII, 196–202).

The Supreme Court's mandate was entered in the minutes of the circuit court on 6 May 1824 (U.S. Cir. Ct., Ga., Minutes, VI, 1823–1834, 65–66, RG 21, GEpFRC).

To Mary W. Marshall

My dearest Polly   Washington March 23d. [1824]

The time now approaches when I shall again see my beloved wife whom I hope to meet in tolerable health and spirits. I shall reach Richmond in the steamboat which comes up on friday night but suppose I shall not be at home till saturday morning. I imagine the boat will not be up before nine Oclock at night in which case I shall remain in it all night. If I do not come up till it is too late to come home I wish you would direct Oby to come down to Rockets very early in order to carry home my portmanteau.

I have not the use of my arm sufficiently to put it into the sleeves of my coat, but I am entirely free from pain.

I was very much surprized at the arrival of John and Elizabeth last tuesday evening. They came by this place in their way to Baltimore, in consequence of the Baltimore boat being stopped for repairs.[1] They proceeded on wednesday in the stage & on thursday John returned on his way to Fauquier. All was well.

I am just called in to conference. Heaven bless you my dearest Polly, I am your ever affectionate

J MARSHALL

ALS, Marshall Papers, ViW. Addressed to Mrs. Marshall in Richmond; postmarked Washington, 23 Mar. Year based on internal evidence.

1. JM's visitors were John Marshall, Jr., and his wife, the former Elizabeth M. Alexander (1802–1847) of Baltimore (Paxton, *Marshall Family*, 101).

To Martha Jackson

Dear Madam   Richmond May 7th. 1824

I received a few days past your letter of the 15th. of April, & immediately searched the office of every court in which your Uncles will could have been recorded.[1] I am sorry to inform you that no trace of it can be found, nor do any of his connexions here recollect to have heard it spoken of. If he ever made a will, it has not been recorded, and is now lost. It is however probable that what related to you might be some verbal declaration made to your Father with which he intended to comply, but which he has been induced, by the unfortunate course of his affairs, to neglect.

Unless a will could be found I fear that nothing said by your Father can avail you. His declarations might operate against a legatee but not against a creditor. His long possession & ostensible ownership of the property will give a strength to the claim of a creditor which would be irresistable.

Your acquaintances here, and especially Mrs. Marshall, remember you with affectionate regard, & are thankful for your enquiries after them. They desire me to tender you their best wishes for your happiness. Mrs. Marshalls health which was you know always delicate, has long been so wretchedly bad as to make life almost a burthen to her.

I regret very sincerely that my enquiries have terminated so unfavorably, and beg you to beleive that I am with true and respectful regards, Your Obedt. Servt

J Marshal⟨l⟩

ALS (owned by Mrs. Henry E. Colton, Asheville, N.C., 1970). Addressed to Mrs. Jackson in Athens, Ga.; postmarked Richmond, 7 May. Endorsed.

1. Letter not found. The uncle was a brother of Thomas Reade Rootes (see JM to Henry Jackson, Feb. 1824 and n. 2).

To Henry Lee

Dear Sir   Richmond May 7th 1824

A few days past, on my return from a visit to Fauquier, I received your "Campaign of 1781 in the Carolinas."[1] You have I think succeeded in demonstrating that public opinion has not erred in the estimate it has made of the military talents & services of your Father; and that he stood deservedly high with the commander in chief, and the best officers of the southern Army.

I have read this work with deep interest, and entreat you to receive my thanks for this mark of your polite attention, in forwarding it ⟨to⟩ me. With great respect, I am dear Sir your obedt

J Marshall

ALS, ViHi. Addressed to Lee at Stratford, Westmoreland County. Readdressed in another hand to Fredericksburg; postmarked Richmond, 7 May. Endorsed: "Missent to Westmd. C.H. & forwd. / to Fredericksbg. June 29."

1. Henry Lee (1787–1837), the son of Gen. Henry "Light-Horse Harry" Lee, was a politician, soldier, and author. His first book was *The Campaign of 1781 in the Carolinas; with Remarks Historical and Critical on Johnson's Life of Greene* (Philadelphia, 1824).

To Bushrod Washington

My dear Sir   Richmond May 24th. 1824

I presume you are now at Mount Vernon & I hope in better health than when I heard from you in Philadelphia.

I have been endeavouring to arrange the correspondence for publication & find to my great surprize that I have not a single letter for the year 1787. There is a chasm from Decr. 1786 to Feby. 1888 [*sic*]. How this has happened I cannot imagine. Perhaps it may have been copied & not sent to me. As the correspondence of this period is of deep interest I think it necessary that it should appear with that which precedes and follows it. Such a hiatus as its omission would create would surprize every body. As I have no doubt of your concurring in the opinion I must ask the favor of you to have the letters of 1787 copied & sent to me by some opportunity. The steam boat I presume will always afford one.

I find the letters more numerous than I had expected & think it advisable to omit those which were written during Braddocks war. They are filled with the distresses of the people & the incursions of the Indians & the misconduct of the militia. These subjects were very interesting at the period but have long ceased to be so. I think the volumes will be better received if they begin with the war of our revolution. The letters will then make three large volumes. I submit this matter to your consideration. My own opinion is decided in it. At any rate, as there is no connexion between the subjects I would suggest that the correspondence beginning in 1755 be postponed for subsequent consideration after trying the success of that which begins in 1775. I am my dear Sir your,

J MARSHALL

ALS, Marshall Papers, DLC. Addressed to Washington at Mount Vernon; postmarked Richmond, 24 May. Endorsed by Washington.

To Timothy Pickering

Dear Sir   Richmond May 31st. 1824

I received a few days past your review of the unfortunate correspondence with Cuningham, which I have read with deep interest.[1] I take it for granted that I am indebted to you for this additional mark of your polite attention, & friendly recollection. While I may be allowed to feel & to express my sincere regret at this whole unpleasant affair—both cause & effect—I should do injustice to my real sentiments if I did not acknowledge my gratification at the terms in which you have uniformly expressed yourself as regards me personally.

You may beleive me when I say that my esteem for you never has, & never can be, changed. I succeeded to you in office without knowing or enquiring into the causes of your removal, and without any diminution of that high opinion and regard which I had always entertained for you. It gave me no small satisfaction to perceive that you did not consider your successor as your enemy. I never supposed that my real veneration & respect for Mr. Adams required that I should change my opinion of men, or that my real gratitude for his favorable notice of me, while it attached me truely to him, ought to detach me from others whom I beleived to deserve much from their country. With very much respect & esteem, I am dear Sir your obedt

J MARSHALL

ALS, Pickering Papers, MHi. Addressed to Pickering in Salem, Mass.; postmarked Richmond, 31 May. Endorsed by Pickering as received 7 June.

1. Timothy Pickering, *A Review of the Correspondence between the Hon. John Adams, Late President of the United States, and the Late Wm. Cunningham, Esq., Beginning in 1803 and Ending in 1812* (Salem, Mass., 1824). For background and context, see Gerard H. Clarfield, *Timothy Pickering and the American Republic* (Pittsburgh, Pa., 1980), 265–67.

To Bushrod Washington

My dear Sir   Richmond May 31st. 1824

I have not heard from you since your letter informing me that you had discharged your juries in Philadelphia, & cannot help being a little apprehensive that your health is not so firm as I could wish it to be. I hope my fears will soon be removed.

I have finished the perusal of the letters in my possession & wait only for those of 1787 to arrange the whole in volumes for publication. They will then be transmitted to you for ultimate revisal. I find very few letters after 1791, and scarcely any after General Washington retired from the Presidency.

I am now employed in the court at this place, but it is a lazy term & seldom furnishes much employment for the Judge. Other courts in which the lawyers feel more interest are in session, & they neglect me. A question which is to me new if not difficult was made on saturday, & I should like to know whether it has ever been raised before you. In a suit against a surety of one of the persons who had received public money, an objection was made to the admissibility of the copies from the books of the treasury department—it being alleged that the law applied to the principal only.[1] Its terms give some countenance to the objection, but I did not think there was much in it. I should however like to hear whether the same objection has been taken elsewhere. With the best wishes for your health & with affectionate esteem, I am dear Sir your

J MARSHALL

ALS, ICHi. Addressed to Washington at Mount Vernon; postmarked Richmond, 31 May. Endorsed by Washington.

1. JM was possibly referring to the unreported cases of U.S. v. James P. Preston, U.S. v. John Preston, and U.S. v. John Bowyer (U.S. Cir. Ct., Va., Ord. Bk. XI, 449; XII, 13, 14, 15, 16–17, 18–19, 42–46, 176–77).

United States v. Belew
Opinion
U.S. Circuit Court, Virginia, 2 June 1824

Solomon Belew (also spelled Ballew or Balew), a mail carrier on the route between Richmond and Charlottesville, was charged with secreting and embezzling letters containing bank notes. The trial took place on 25 May, with U.S. Attorney Robert Stanard prosecuting and Robert G. Scott representing Belew. The evidence against Belew was virtually conclusive, "though the situation of the prisoner, burdened with the support of a numerous family, and his irreproachable character as a mail-carrier for nearly 20 years, inspired universal sympathy." The jury after deliberating a few minutes returned a verdict of guilty. On 31 May Scott moved to arrest judgment on the ground that the act under which Belew was indicted did not embrace mail carriers. JM ruled on this motion on 2 June (U.S. v. Belew, indictment [22 May 1824], U.S. Cir. Ct., Va., Ended Cases [Unrestored], 1824, Vi; U.S. Cir. Ct., Va., Ord. Bk. XI, 438, 443; U.S. v. Ballew, Notes of Arguments, 31 May 1824, Tucker-Coleman Papers, ViW; Richmond *Enquirer,* 28 May, 8 June 1824).

The United States
v
Bellew

The prisoner is convicted under the 18th. Sec. of the "act regulating   ¶1
the post office establishment," and the question submitted to the consid-

eration of the court is whether a carrier of the mail be "a person employed in any of the departments of the General Post Office"?[1]

¶2   To answer this question, it becomes necessary to settle the meaning of the word "department" as used in the act of Congress. One of its significations, as our Lexicons inform us, is "a province, or business, assigned to a particular person." The business assigned to a particular person is, according to this definition, in his department. The business belonging to the post office is in a department of the post office. A person employed in that business, is a person employed in a department of the post office. If then the carrying of the mail be a part of the business of the post office, it would seem that the person who carries it, is a person employed in a department of the general post office.

¶3   The first section of the act makes it the duty of the post master general to "provide for the carriage of the mail on all post roads that are or may be established by law." The carriage of the mail then is a part of the business of the Post Master General; it is within his department, and a person employed in it is "employed in a department of the General Post office.["] There are several other sections of the act which obviously contemplate the carrier of the mail as a person who is particularly within the purview of the statute. The 2d sec. enacts that ["]the Post Master General and all other persons employed in the general post office, or in the care custody or *conveyance* of the mail" shall take an oath prescribed by the law. But "every person who shall be in any manner employed in the care custody conveyance or management of the mail shall be subject to all pains penalties and forfeitures for violating the injunctions or neglecting the duties required of him by the laws relating to the establishment of the post office & post roads whether such person shall have taken the oath above prescribed or not.["][2]

¶4   It is apparent from this sec. that the framers of the act designed to provide particularly for the punishment of offences committed by persons carrying the mail. They are supposed to be subjected to particular "pains, penalties, and forfeitures." Yet it is by the 18th. Sec. only that these pains & penalties are inflicted, and they are described only as "persons employed in a department of the General post office." We say it is by this sec. & by this description only that pains & penalties are inflicted on the carriers of the mail for stealing a letter out of the mail, because we beleive that the 19th. Sec. is not intended to be applicable to them.[3]

¶5   The counsel for the prisoner supposes that no person can be the object of the 18th. Sec. who is not appointed directly by the Post Master General, or for whose appointment a special provision is not made by the act. He must be an officer. But this is not the language of the law. The terms of the enactment do not require an officer; they are satisfied with an agent, or any person employed in any of the departments, or in other words in the business allotted to the general post office: Nor do they require that he shall be employed by the Post master General or by authority expressly delegated by him. It is enough to satisfy the law that they are so employed. The contracter cannot himself carry the mail through the whole extent of his contract; & the law contemplates his employing other persons. The 4th. sec. provides that these shall be free white persons, & subjects the contracter to a penalty for employing others. The mail carrier then is in this section also specially the object of the act.

The reason as well as the language of the law leads to the opinion that ¶6 all persons entrusted with the mail should be alike subjected to the penalties of the law for a fraudulent violation of the trust reposed in them. The carrier of the mail is as much entrusted with it, as the person who makes it up & places it in his custody, & there are the same motives for subjecting him to the penalties inflicted on the violaters of that trust. If then as we think, the words employed do in their natural import comprehend him, the court would not be justified in a strained construction to exclude him from their operation.

The counsel for the prisoner maintains that the act does in its language ¶7 distinguish between a mail carrier, & persons to whom the 18th. section applies. He supposes that the concluding sentences of the 18th. Section exhibit this distinction. We do not think so. The preceding part of that section enumerates offences which may be committed by any person entrusted with the mail or with the letters to be carried by the post, and in that part the offenders are described in general terms. The concluding sentences enumerate offences which can be committed only by the person carrying the mail, & in those sentences he is mentioned particularly.

The 19th. Section too enumerates particularly the offences which may ¶8 be committed & in the recital mentions both the mail carrier and the post office. This distinguishes them from each other but does not indicate that either is not comprehended in the general terms of the 18th. section. Those general terms are not introduced into the 19th. Sec. nor was it necessary that they should. Their absence no more proves that a mail carrier is not employed in any of the departments of the general post office, than that the person who receives the mail or delivers out the letters is not so employed.

The counsel also supposes that the 2d. sec. distinguishes between a ¶9 person employed in the departments of the general post office, & a mail carrier. But we can not concur in this opinion. The language is "That the post master general and all other persons employed in the general post office, or in the care, custody or conveyance of the mail, shall" &c.

It is obvious that this section in using the terms "persons employed in ¶10 the general post office" designates the general post office itself, & uses a phrase more limited & intended to be more limited than the phrase "any person employed in *any department* of the general post office.["] It excludes persons employed in the particular post offices established in the several states. These are comprehended by the words "care or custody" of the mail. These words comprehend all persons who have the care or custody of the mail & who are not comprehended by the words "other person employed in the general post office.["] But the separate enumeration of individuals in this section no more proves that the one than that the other is not comprehended in the general term which designates them all. It no more proves that the person carrying the mail is not employed in any of the departments of the general post office, than it proves that a person having the care or custody of the mail in a particular post office, is not within any of those departments.

¶11   The decisions of the English courts showing the strict construction which has been given to the law,[4] will not apply to this case because we think a mail carrier is within the very words of the 18th. Sec. of the act of Congress.[5]

AD, Marshall Judicial Opinions, PPAmP; printed, John W. Brockenbrough, *Reports of Cases Decided by the Honourable John Marshall . . .* , II (Philadelphia, 1837), 280–84 (erroneously placed at the May 1826 term). For JM's deletions and interlineations, see Textual Notes below.

1. This was the act of 1810 (*U.S. Statutes at Large*, II, 592, 597).

2. Ibid., II, 593, 594.

3. This section provided for the punishment of any person who robbed a mail carrier or any other person entrusted with the mail (ibid., II, 598).

4. As reported by Tucker, Scott, for the prisoner, cited Rex v. Shaw, 1 Leach 79, 168 Eng. Rep. 142 (Crown, 1771); Rex v. Skutt, 1 Leach 106, 168 Eng. Rep. 155 (Crown, 1774); Rex v. Sloper, 1 Leach 81, 168 Eng. Rep. 143 (Crown, 1772); (U.S. v. Ballew, Notes of Arguments, 31 May 1824, Tucker-Coleman Papers, ViW).

5. The court on 26 June sentenced Belew to serve seven years in prison. In Feb. 1826 a group of citizens of Charlottesville and Albemarle County, whose "respectability" was vouchsafed by Thomas Jefferson, petitioned President Adams to release Belew from the remainder of his sentence. The petition recited the prisoner's "fair and reputable character for honesty, and integrity" while employed as a mail carrier during the twenty years preceding his conviction, the indigent circumstances of his wife and "five helpless children," and the likely prospect that he would devote "his best efforts" to support them (U.S. Cir. Ct., Va., Ord. Bk. XI, 478; petition on behalf of Solomon P. Balew, [8 Feb. 1826], Adams Family Papers, MHi).

Textual Notes

¶ 2	l. 3	"a ↑province, or↓ business,
¶ 3	l. 2	for the ~~carrying~~ carriage of
	ll. 6–7	obviously ~~contemplates~~ ↑contemplate↓
	ll. 10–11	prescribed ~~in~~ ↑by↓ the law.
¶ 4	ll. 2–3	punishment of ↑offences committed by↓ persons
	l. 6	office." ~~I~~ ↑We↓ say
	l. 8	the mail ↑for stealing a letter out of the mail,↓ because
¶ 5	l. 2	is not ~~employed~~ ↑appointed↓ directly
	l. 3	provision is ↑not↓ made
	l. 7	to the ↑general↓ post office:
	l. 8	or by ~~express~~ authority
	l. 10	The ~~4th. sec.~~ ↑contracter↓ cannot

l. 14   section also ~~contemplated~~ specially
¶ 6 l. 8   for a ↑fraudulent↓ violation
  ll. 5–6   motives for ~~bringing~~ ↑subjecting↓ him
  ll. 6–7   then ↑as we think,↓ the words
¶ 7 l. 2   carrier, & ~~other~~ persons to
¶ 8 l. 2   committed & ~~distinguishes between taking a~~
                 ~~mail or a letter fro~~ ↑in the recital↓ mentions
¶ 9 l. 3   opinion. ↑The language is↓ "That
¶10 l. 6   the words ~~"in the~~ "care or custody"
  ll. 9–10   separate ↑enumera↓tion of individuals
¶11 l. 1 beg.   The [*erasure*] decisions

From Timothy Pickering

Dear Sir,   Salem June 7. 1824.
   I have this day had the pleasure of receiving your letter of the 31st ulto. acknowledging the receipt of my Review of the Adams & Cunningham Correspondence. You are correct in believing that I sent it to you. But I purposely avoided accompanying it with a letter; lest it should seem to intimate a desire of an answer; when it might be your choice to be silent on the subject. I am the more gratified with your letter.
   Nothing could have been more unexpected to me than such a Correspondence as that between Mr. Adams & his friend Cunningham. I had no unkind feelings towards Mr. Adams; and was willing that "his hoar head should descend to the grave in peace." The style of my letter to him, of the 2d. of August 1822, expressing my opinion that the history of the declaration of independence should be ascertained, and that he alone could give it, was respectful. His answer in four days was in the same spirit of amity.[1] In the next year appeared his Correspondence with Cunningham. At that time tho' making Salem my home, I retained my little farm in the country, & was then labouring upon it, as I had been for years, with my own hands; and I continued my labours until the farming season ended. But I never hesitated a moment on the course proper for me to take, for my own reputation, and the satisfaction of my children and friends. The result you have seen.
   Mr. Walsh, in his National Gazette, has come out in a manner which, from my acquaintance with him, I had not looked for; although I had for a good while witnessed his uncommon zeal to advance J. Q. Adams's pretensions to the Presidency; as exemplified in every gazette. His sympathy was perfectly natural; he like Adams, having apostatized from better principles. He affects to consider my pamphlet as an *electioneering business,* veiled in the form of a vindication.[2] But the A. & C. Correspondence, was alike unknown to me & to him, until it was published. Of such a man as

Cunningham I had once heard, several years ago; but never saw him; and know not whether he was living or dead; nor did I know that a son of his was in existence. Mr. Jefferson, in his letter of Oct. 12th. says he had seen, in the news-papers, intimations that such a Correspondence was to be published.[3] But I had seen none of them, nor even heard the breath of rumour on the subject. In truth, I had little leisure or inclination to attend to many Newspapers. I rarely read a paper except the Salem Gazette & Walsh's National Gazette; the latter comprehending general politics, American & European; and often giving me the first information of what was passing in Boston, within 14 miles of me. I had particularly abstained from publicly expressing my opinion as to the numerous candidates for the Presidency; not expecting, whoever might succeed, any change that would do justice to federalists. In this course I had concluded to persevere. I hoped, however, that John Q. Adams might not obtain the chair of state. With much talent and a great deal of learning, I believed him to possess the malignity of a monk; and by his public acts, & final open apostacy, he had shown that, like his father, to affect the object of his ambition, he was capable of making sacrifices utterly repugnant to the character of an honest statesman. My friend the late eminent chief justice Parsons, when I was conversing with him, some ten or twelve years ago, made this remark, concerning Mr. Adams & his son John Q. Adams — "They are both men of strong passions; but there is this difference between them — the father is placable — the son implacable." Mr. Parsons knew them very well. J. Q. A. read law in his office. And notwithstanding the father's virulent calumnies in the Correspondence, I still believe Judge Parsons's distinction to be substantially correct. The review of the works of Fisher Ames by the son, is marked with rancour; and the style, sentiments & spirit of his Washington 4th of July oration are of a character to disgrace him as well as a scholar as a man — especially of a man holding the high office in our govt. which embraces our foreign relations.[4] He expected by it to advance his interest in the southern, western & other states, where the haters of England were supposed to be most numerous: but I believed that with every man of sense & honour it would be read with disgust, & by many with abhorrence.

As to Mr. Walsh, I have much to say; so much that I will here only remark, that his notices of the Review are written with virulence, & with such palpable misrepresentations of my remarks, as to justify me in saying, that he has written *for the purpose of Deception.* His object cannot be mistaken. An able writer under the signature of Servius Sulpitius, of Baltimore I suppose, for the pamphlet was printed there in 1821 — criticised, with just & pointed sarcasm John Q Adams's Washington oration. In the pamphlet is this passage: "Should southern eulogies be as desirable to the secretary as southern votes, the promise of an embassy or a clerkship, may perhaps fix even the *varying politics* of Mr. Walsh."[5] From pecuniary considerations, and with his large family of children, I presume an embassy would not now be desirable to Walsh but the office of Secretary of State with that of President in expectancy according to usage, would gratify the wishes of his heart. He deserves chastisement from the hand of *Truth.* With sincere respect & esteem I remain, dear Sir, Your obedt servt.

T. PICKERING

ALS (draft), Pickering Papers, MHi.

1. Adams's reply to Pickering recounted the circumstances of the drafting of the Declaration of Independence in a way that seemed to diminish Jefferson's role. Pickering later quoted extensively from this letter in his address at Salem on 4 July 1823. After seeing Pickering's address, Jefferson wrote privately to James Madison complaining of Adams's faulty memory (Charles Francis Adams, ed., *The Works of John Adams* [10 vols.; Boston, 1850–56], II, 512–15 n.; Octavius Pickering and Charles W. Upham, *The Life of Timothy Pickering* [4 vols.; Boston, 1867–73], IV, 466–69; Dumas Malone, *Jefferson and His Time,* VI: *The Sage of Monticello* [Boston, 1981], 432–34).

2. Robert Walsh (1784–1859), a journalist and literary editor, was then editor of the *National Gazette and Literary Register,* published in Philadelphia. The 24 May 1824 issue of that newspaper contained an article by Walsh attacking Pickering's *Review.*

3. Pickering referred to Jefferson's letter to John Adams of 12 Oct. 1823, which was published in a Boston newspaper in Dec. 1823 and reprinted in Walsh's *National Gazette* (Malone, *Sage of Monticello,* 434–35; *National Gazette* [Philadelphia], 29 Dec. 1823).

4. Pickering referred to two publications by John Quincy Adams: *American Principles, a Review of the Works of Fisher Ames, Compiled by a Number of His Friends* (Boston, 1809), and *An Address Delivered at the Request of a Committee of the Citizens of Washington; on the Occasion of Reading the Declaration of Independence, on the Fourth of July, 1821* (Washington, D.C., 1821).

5. Servius Sulpitius, *Remarks on an Address Delivered at Washington, July 4, 1821; by John Quincy Adams, Secretary of State* (Baltimore, 1821), 8.

Hopkirk v. Randolph
Opinion and Decree
U.S. Circuit Court, Virginia, ca. 22 June 1824

This was another of the numerous suits brought by James Hopkirk as surviving partner of the Glasgow firm of Speirs, Bowman & Company in the U.S. Circuit Court for Virginia. The plaintiff sought recovery of a debt incurred before the Revolution by Thomas Isham Randolph (1736–ca. 1800) of Goochland County. Randolph confessed judgment on this debt in the federal court in 1796, but a writ of execution levied upon the debtor's estate in June 1800 failed to produce any goods or effects. After Randolph's death Hopkirk turned to the chancery side, filing his bill in 1803 against Archibald C. Randolph, Isham Randolph, Thomas Randolph, sons of the decedent, and Randolph Harrison and his wife Mary, daughter of the decedent. The defendants filed answers in 1804 and 1805, and in June 1808 the court ordered accounts to be taken before the chancery commissioner. After the taking of depositions and affidavits, the preparation of the commissioner's reports, the filing of an amended answer by Randolph Harrison and his wife Mary, and several interlocutory decrees, the suit finally came up for hearing at the May 1824 term. By this time the sons Archibald C. Randolph and Thomas Randolph had died insolvent, and the surviving son Isham Randolph was also insolvent. The issue before the court was the extent to which Randolph Harrison was liable for this debt. Marshall delivered the first of two opinions in this suit at this term sometime between the filing of an amended bill and answer on 19 June and the second opinion on 28 June (Gerald S. Cowden, "The Randolphs of Turkey Island: A Prosopography of the First Three Generations, 1650–1806" [2 vols.; Ph.D. diss., College of William and Mary, 1977], I, 379–82; U.S. Cir. Ct., Va., Ord. Bk. VII, 89; IX, 64–65, 470; XI, 469, 487–88; Hopkirk v. Randolph, U.S. Cir. Ct., Va., Ended Cases [Unrestored], 1824, Vi).

Hopkirk surviving partner &c

v

Randolph & al.

¶1   In the year 1790 the defendant R. Harrison intermarried with the defendant Mary daughter of Thomas Randolph deceased who was then in possession of a maid servant, a negroe girl & a riding horse which had been given her some years before by her Father who was at the time of the gift & of the intermarriage possessed of a considerable estate.[1] This property was, upon the intermarriage retained by the donee, and has ever since remained in possession of R. H. In the autumn of the year 1793 Thomas Randolph & his three sons Archibald Cary, Isham, & Thomas, agreed on a division of his estate, and property to a large amount was conveyed to each of the sons in consideration of love & natural affection, of certain specific debts & also of bonds for £250 payable by each of them to their sister Mary Harrison.

¶2   In the year 1795 John Bowman styling himself surviving partner of Spiers Bowman & Co. instituted a suit in this court against T. R. & in May 1796 obtained a judgement by confession for the debt in the declaration mentioned to be discharged by the payment of $1532.46 with int. at the rate of 5 per cent. per an. from the 1st. day of Septr. 1775 till paid & costs. Execution on this judgement was stayed & the judgement was to be discharged in equal instalments of one two & three years.[2] A. C. R. who transacted his Fathers business made the agreement for the confession in his Fathers name, & engaged to pay the judgement according to its terms. To obtain his undertaking for the payment of the judgement appears to have been the principal motive with the plfs agent for suspending execution.

¶3   On the 25th. of June 1800 a fi. fa.[3] was issued which was returned "no effects." A. C. R. had wasted & misapplied the estate & crops of his father.

¶4   In 180   T. R. departed this life intestate & in the year 1803 James Hopkirk stating himself to be the surviving partner of Spiers Bowman & Co. filed his bill in this court making A C. R admr. of T. R. deceased & the said A. C. R., I. R, & T. R. & R. H., & M H. his wife children & distributees of T. R. deceased defendants thereto. The bill alleges that the estate of

T. R. was considerable, that the deeds to his sons are fraudulent, that his children are in possession of property which ought to satisfy his debt, and prays a decree against them in such proportions as the court may direct, or such other decree as may be adapted to his case.[4]

Several accounts have been taken, & in the progress of the cause it appears that the estate of T. R. is wasted & that all his sons are notoriously insolvent. The plf. claims the whole debt from R. H. or so much thereof as can be satisfied out of the property he has received with his wife. ¶5

On the hearing the court was of opinion that the personal representative of John Bowman ought to be a party; whereupon the bill was amended and   John Williams admr. &c of John Bowman deceased was made a defendant & his answer was filed admitting the right of the plf to the debt.[5] ¶6

The defendant resists the claim on two grounds. ¶7
1st. He contends that receiving a judgement with a stay of execution with a stipulation that A. C. R. would pay the debt changes its character & amounts to a waiver of his claim upon the property in the hands of R. H.
2d. That the gifts to R. H. are not within the statute of frauds. ¶8
1st. The judgement is against T. R. and appears by the record to have been confessed by his attorney. This was probably under the instructions of A. C. R., but A. C. R. acted as his agent, and it is to be presumed from all the circumstances, with full power. The judgement could not merge in the agreement with A. C. R. and was indeed a part of that agreement. It was not understood that T. R. was to be discharged, & A. C. R substituted in his place; but that time was to be given to T. R. in consideration of the collateral security furnished by the undertaking of A. C. R. to pay the debt. ¶9

But the defendant insists that the plf. by disabling himself from proceeding against T. R. has discharged R. H upon the principle that the same act would have discharged a security of T. R. ¶10

The two cases do not, in the opinion of the court, stand on the same reason. The creditor who gives time to his debtor, hinders the security from proceeding himself against the debtor to recover the money he may have paid. But had Mr. Harrison paid this debt he could not have recovered it from T. R. A voluntier who loses the property given him from defect of title has no legal recourse against the Donor at any rate unless there be an express warranty. I am then of opinion that the stay of execution & the transaction with A. C. R., although the debt might certainly have been satisfied had the creditor proceeded in the usual manner, constitute no bar to the present suit. They aggravate the hardship of the defendants case, but do not constitute a defence at law or in this court. ¶11
2d. I proceed then to the enquiry, how far the property which came to the possession of R. H. is liable to the creditors of T. R. ¶12

The words of the statute are, "Every gift &c had or made and contrived of malice, fraud, covin, collusion, or guile: to the intent or purpose to ¶13 delay hinder or defraud creditors of their just & lawful actions &c shall be from henceforth deemed & taken (only &c) to be clearly & utterly void &c."[6]

¶14   Were this statute now, for the first time, to be expounded, the court would find much difficulty in construing it as directed against voluntary gifts or conveyances meerly because they were voluntary. The language of the act comprehends such as are made of malice, fraud, covin, collusion, or guile with intent or purpose to delay hinder or defraud creditors. This intent or purpose would be supposed to constitute the contaminating principle which could infect & vitiate the gift or conveyance, & would be required to bring the particular case within the act.

¶15   But as this intent is concealed within the bosoms of the actors, it would be the duty of the court to infer it from the character of the transaction; and as the equity of creditors is generally stronger than that of meer voluntiers, the court ought to lean to the side of the creditor, and to consider every gift or voluntary conveyance as coming within the statute, the fairness of which was not conclusively proved. Even independent of the statute, gifts or voluntary conveyances which obviously defeated the claim of a creditor would be considered as fraudulent so far as regarded him. The donee therefore would always be required to prove the fairness of his title. If he be not a purchaser for a valuable consideration, it would be incumbent on him to show a case not only without taint, but free from suspicion. If the circumstances of the gift be such that according to any reasonable probability it might originate in an impure motive, or might in fact prove injurious to creditors by withdrawing a subject to which they had just pretensions, the fair construction of the act would comprehend it. But a construction which should under all circumstances comprehend every gift meerly because it was voluntary might derange the ordinary course of society, and produce much greater injustice than it would prevent. A man, for example of great opulence, owing some debts, feels himself bound to advance his children when they leave him to act for themselves, and to perform their own parts on the great theatre of the world. His own feelings & public opinion would equally reproach him should he withhold from them those aids which his circumstances & their education & station in life would seem to require. A reasonable advancement under such circumstances, so far from being considered as collusive, or made with an intent to defraud creditors, would be obviously a provision required by justice & the common sense of mankind. If, after a long lapse of time, the child having acquired credit in virtue of the estate in his possession & apparently his own, should as well as his parent become insolvent, all would admit that the equity of his creditors would be stronger than that of the creditors of his father. But should he not become insolvent, but should settle in life, marry in the visible possession of property given to him in good faith as a reasonable provision made by an opulent parent, whose circumstances were not only unsuspected, but were in truth perfectly sound, the subsequent failure of that parent, at a distant period of time, could not reasonably be connected with that advancement so as to impress upon it the stamp of fraud. No fraudulent intent, no intent to delay or in any manner to injure creditors could be inferred. The consequence could not be apprehended from the act, and therefore the act could not be considered as constructively fraudulent. It would seem to be a fair disposition of property, a fair exercise of the power of ownership, and not, I think within the statute of frauds, were that statute now first to be applied to such a case.

But the statute has been long in force, and numerous decisions have ¶16 been made upon it both in England, and in this country. Those decisions are admitted to bind this court. They determine that a voluntary gift is void as to creditors whose debts existed at the time the gift was made. This is the general principle; and as a general principle it is beleived to be unquestionably a sound one. Untrammelled by precedents, this court would, at this time and in this case establish it. But the difference between a general principle and one which is universal in its application, which is so inflexible as to permit no case to be withdrawn from it by any circumstances however strong, which would make this act equivalent to an act expressly annulling all gifts or voluntary conveyances made by a person indebted at the time, however large his fortune, & however inconsiderable his debts or his gift, must be admitted by all. The extent of the principle then, established by these decisions, must be ascertained by a review of the decisions themselves, of the terms in which they have been expressed, and of the circumstances to which those terms have been applied.

It has been truely observed that some shades of difference appear in ¶17 the cases on this subject. Some Judges have shown a disposition to press the principle farther than others & have expressed themselves in terms more or less favorable to the creditor or donee.

Questions on these acts have been most common in chancery, but as ¶18 courts of law have concurrent jurisdiction, & as they have received the same construction in both courts, it may be proper to notice the opinions which have been expressed by an eminent Judge in a court of common law. In the case of Cadogan v Kennet Cowper 434 Lord Mansfield said "These statutes (the stat. of the 13th. & 27th. of El) cannot receive too liberal a construction, or be too much extended in the suppression of fraud.["]

["]The statute of the 13th. El. ch 5th., which relates to frauds against ¶19 creditors directs that no act whatever done to defraud a creditor shall be of any effect against such creditor or creditors, but then such a construction is not to be made in support of creditors as will make third persons sufferers. Therefore the statute does not militate against any transaction *bona fide,* and where there is no imagination of fraud. And so is the common law."[7]

¶20   In the case of Doe v Routledge, Cowper 710 the same Judge says "A custom has prevailed & leant extremely, to consider voluntary settlements fraudulent against creditors. But if the circumstances of the transaction show it was not fraudulent at the time, it is not within the meaning of the statutes though no money was paid."[8]

¶21   In the same case he afterwards says "One great circumstance which should always be attended to in these transactions is, whether the person was indebted at the time he made the settlement. If he was, it is a strong badge of fraud."[9]

¶22   The impression made by these declarations of Lord Mansfield is that every gift made by a person indebted at the time is liable to great & serious objection, and is, to use his own expression a strong badge of fraud; but is not necessarily, & under all possible circumstances, absolutely fraudulent. They were made too in cases where a considerable amount of property was settled.

¶23   No English Chancellor has leaned more to the creditor in questions arising on these statutes than Lord Hardwicke.

¶24   In the case of Russel & al. v Hammond & al 1st Adk 13. Lord Hardwicke said "A great deal has been said on this head, but it depends upon circumstances, and every case varies in that respect.["]

¶25   ["]There are many opinions that every voluntary settlement is not fraudulent; what the Judges mean is, that a settlement being voluntary is not for that reason fraudulent, but an evidence of fraud only. Though I have hardly known one case where the person conveying was indebted at the time of the conveyance, that has not been deemed fraudulent."[10]

¶26   This strong expression of opinion against voluntary settlements made by a person indebted at the time was used in a case where the relative value of the subject settled to the estate & debts of the settler is not indeed stated, but where there is reason to beleive it was considerable. It was made too in a case where the settlement was in part supported because it was made on a valuable consideration, & in part declared void because made for the benefit of the settler himself. Trivial gifts made without any view to creditors, with intentions obviously fair & proper, do not seem from his language, to have been in the mind of the Judge. It is observable too that he does not lay down the principle as being universal, but says "he has hardly known one case where the person conveying was indebted at the time that the conveyance has not been deemed fraudulent."

¶27   In Taylor v Jones 2 Adk. 600 The master of the Rolls said "I look upon it to be a standing rule as to creditors for a valuable consideration that it (a voluntary settlement after marriage) is always looked upon as fraudulent & within the 13th. of El. ch 5."[11] This expression is certainly a very comprehensive one. But it is applied expressly to a family settlement, not to an inconsiderable gift, and is used in a case in which the settler reserved to himself an interest for his life.

In the case of Lord Townshend v Wyndham 2 Vez. 1. the Chancellor ¶28
said "But I know no case on the 13th. of El. where a man indebted at the
time makes a mere voluntary conveyance to a child without consideration & dies indebted but that it shall be considered as part of his estate
for benefit of his creditors."[12]

This language is undoubtedly very strong, but it is used in a case in ¶29
which the Father had by deed in pursuance of a general power appointed
money to be raised for the benefit of his daughter. The case was in
substance this. Mr. Wyndham being seized for life of a large estate remainder to his Nephew in tail, covenanted that his nephew should take
the profits during his life on his permitting any person whom Mr. Wyndham should appoint by deed or will, to take the profits for the same
length of time after the estate should come to the Nephew. The testator
by deed appointed that his daughter Catharine should take these profits,
and it being determined that they were part of the general assetts, the
chancellor declared them liable to the claims of creditors. This language
therefore is applied to a conveyance which is to take effect after the death
of the testator. It may well be doubted whether the nephew could have
been compelled to refund the profits received had the conveyance to
him been purely voluntary.

In the case of Kidney v Cousmaker 12 Vez. the general doctrine that a ¶30
voluntary settlement is void as to creditors is again recognized, but that
too was a settlement affecting a considerable portion of the property of
the settler.[13]

The books are full of cases in which the principle is acted on as one ¶31
perfectly settled but in all of them, so far as my researches have gone,
there has been a conveyance of property to a considerable amount; some
settlement of a thing still existing, or some bond or contract to be complied with in future. The case of Partridge & wife against Gop & others
Ambler 596. cited by the defendant is a case of a gift of money; but that
case is obviously founded on the actual fraudulent intent of the giver.[14]

The suit was brought by the legatees of Edward Godfrey against his exrs. ¶32
for an account of the personal estate of the testator & to have a legacy of
£6000 secured. An account was directed in 1736, and Joseph Sewell one
of exrs. was reported to be largely indebted. He was, in 1745 committed to
the Fleet prison for not complying with an order of court directing him to
pay into the bank £3000 part of the money in his hands, where he remained till 1750 when he died insolvent. The plfs. brought a supplemental bill against his children four daughters who had been advanced by
Sewell in his lifetime. Two of the daughters were married & the bill was dismissed at the hearing as to them, because the money they had received
was given as marriage portions. The two remaining daughters were single
& stated in their answers, each of them, that she had received £500 in December 1743 as a free gift for her maintenance & subsistence in the world.

¶33   The chancellor took time to consider the question whether this money should be refunded. He says "It struck me at first as a hardship to make the children refund especially as such a gift could not be considered as a trust for the giver; but on consideration I think no man has such a power over his own property to dispose of it so as to defeat his creditors unless for consideration. It is the motive of the giver, not the knowledge of the acceptor that is to weigh. The statute extends to all cases except where there is good consideration and *bona fide;* blood has been held not to be a good consideration. I have no doubt but that this voluntary gift proceeded from affection getting the better of justice." "It was done secretly & *pendente lite.*["] His Lordship was asked for the information of the bar who thought he had laid down the position too large, whether he did not mean to confine it to the circumstances of the case? That otherwise a parent could not make any present whatever of ever so small value to his child without its being liable to be taken away in favor of creditors. To which he said "that the fraudulent intent is to be collected from the magnitude and value of the gift."[15]

¶34   The idea of the bar that the Chancellor had laid down the position too large must have been founded on the words "I think no man has such a power over his own property to dispose of it so as to defeat his creditors unless for consideration." "The statute extends to all cases except where there is good consideration and *bona fide.*" These words, it was supposed by the gentlemen of the bar would extend to any present whatever, of ever so small a value, a parent might make to his child. His Lordship confines their application to gifts of magnitude & value. In the case itself the gifts were of very great value compared with the property of the giver, and were made under circumstances which exposed them in an eminent degree to the charge of being made for the purpose of defrauding creditors.

¶35   The case of Chamberlayne v Temple, decided in the court of appeals is a case where a parent much embarassed at the time disposed of a considerable portion of his property among his children & afterwards died insolvent.[16] It is true that he retained enough to pay his debts, and that his insolvency was produced by misfortune & accident, but the property conveyed away was very considerable, and the most valuable part of that which he retained consisted of vessels & of the slaves who worked them. A circumstance too which is I think entitled to great consideration in that case is that the children were infants residing with their Father so that the slaves given still remained in his possession. The gifts were not made to advance his children in the world, and it is difficult to conceive any motive for making them at the time, other than a desire to reserve them for his children from the claims of his creditors. That case is a construction by the highest tribunal of our country of a statute of this state & is undoubtedly complete authority as far as it goes; but it does not, I think go at all beyond the English decisions. I should not I think have hesitated, even before the case of Temple & Chamberlayne, to have determined such a conveyance to be fraudulent under our statute. It was a voluntary conveyance of a very large portion of the donors estate, made by a person in embarassed circumstances, to infants who were not at the time in need of any immediate provision, and who were not in a situation to take the property out of his possession.

In the case of Sexton v Wheaton the Supreme court of the United States has said that "in construing the statute of the 13th. of El. the courts have considered every conveyance not made on consideration deemed valuable in law, as void against previous creditors."[17] This is a general proposition respecting the extent of the English decisions, not a decision of the court itself declaring that every gift, however trivial is at any distance of time & under any circumstances, to be avoided by a creditor. The term "conveyance" indicates property of considerable value as respects the situation of the parties, since it is chiefly in such cases that voluntary donations of chattels personal assume the form of conveyance. The general proposition was all which could be in the mind of the court, as the case was one of a subsequent creditor, and did not lead to any minute investigation of distinctions which might possibly exist in cases of gifts made by a person indebted at the time. As a general proposition it is unquestionably true. No voluntary conveyance of property has been sustained against creditors existing at the time; but no gift, of such inconsiderable value as to come under the denomination of a present, made under circumstances entirely free from suspicion, has ever, so far as I am informed, been hunted up by a creditor, and claimed as a part of the donors estate. ¶36

I will now proceed to a consideration of the particular items which constitute the subject of the present controversy. ¶37

The first is the gifts made by T. R. to his daughter which, on the marriage in 1790 were taken into the possession of her husband as her property. There were two negroe girls, one of them an attendant on her person, & a riding horse. ¶38

T. R was a gentleman of ample fortune, not embarassed in his circumstances, nor so much indebted as to create any suspicion of difficulty in the payment of his debts. The idea cannot be admitted for a moment that any apprehension concerning his creditors was in any manner connected with the motives to this gift. That of the waiting maid, and that of the riding horse, especially, are usual in this country, & come strictly, when made by a parent of unquestionable solidity, within that class of gifts which are denominated presents. They do not much differ from wedding clothes, if rather more expensive than usual, from jewels, or an instrument of music given by a man whose circumstances justified the gift. I have never known a case in which such gifts, so made have been called into question. These gifts come I think completely within that class of presents which according to the case reported by Ambler, ought to be excepted from the general rule in favor of creditors. The gift of the other ¶39 girl is not I think so perfectly clear, but I find great difficulty in separating it from the waiting maid, both having been given with intentions perfectly fair & both having passed together to the husband at the time of the marriage & having remained in his possession ever since.[18]

¶40   This case bears no resemblance to that of Temple v Chamberlayne. If it did, I should not hesitate to follow the opinion of the court of appeals. But the distinction between them is too obvious to require that I should contrast them.

¶41   In the case of Jacks v Tunno & al, decided in South Carolina, a trader supposed to be in good circumstances at the time, though considerably in debt, purchased a house & lott which was conveyed to the plaintiffs his infant daughters. A few years afterwards he became bankrupt, and this bill was brought by the donees to restrain the defendants, who are not stated to be, but I presume were, the assignees of the bankrupt, from selling the property. The injunction was made perpetual; and, in giving his opinion Chancellor Rutledge said, "Suppose a person in this state being indebted, though to a considerable amount, is possessed of a large estate in houses in the city, gives a small part of that property to his child or children; or one similarly circumstanced & indebted, possessed of a considerable estate in land & negroes, gives a few negroes & some land to his children, and either the accident of fire in the city or the death of the negroes, should reduce his estate so considerably as to occasion his insolvency would this court under such circumstances, meerly because the person was largely indebted at the time of the gift, consider such gift as fraudulent & set them aside because creditors were interested? I should apprehend not."[19]

¶42   In the case of Salmon v Bennet 1st. Connecticut reports 525, the court says "Where there is no actual fraudulent intent and a voluntary conveyance is made to a child in consideration of love and affection, if the grantor is in prosperous circumstances, unembarassed, and not considerably indebted, and the gift is a reasonable provision for the child according to his estate & condition in life, comprehending but a small portion of his estate leaving ample funds unincumbered for the payment of the grantors debts, then such conveyance will be valid against creditors existing at the time.["][20]

¶43   These cases are not cited as having the authority which the decisions of our court of appeals would have in this court; but as containing a great deal of good sense, & being entitled to great respect.

¶44   If these two girls & this riding horse are to be considered as given before the marriage, so as to have become ostensibly the property of the young lady to whom they were given, there would be some difficulty, the perfect fairness of the gift being shown, to set aside the rights of the husband. In the East India company agt. Clavel Pres. in chy. 377 Sir Edward Lyttleton being appointed by the East India Company President at Bengal entered into Articles of agreement on the 16th. of Jany. 1698 for the faithful execution of the trust, & also gave his bond binding his heirs in the penalty of £2000 conditioned for the performance of the covenant. Afterwards on the 21st. of the same month he made a settlement on his daughter of £5000 to be raised out of land, & sailed for the East Indias. Some time after the departure of Sir Edward, Mr. Clavel made an application to the young lady in the way of marriage, & she placed the settlement in his hands. Being advised that it was valid the marriage took effect, some time after which Mrs. Clavel died without issue. Mr. Clavil administered on her estate & brought his bill to have the money raised as directed by the settlement. Sir Edward Lyttleton had embezzled the effects of the company to the amount of 26000£ & they claimed this money, the settlement being voluntary.

The counsel for Mr. Clavel contended that if the settlement was voluntary in its creation, yet being the motive & inducement to Mr. Clavil to marry her, this had now made it valuable.   ¶45

The Lord Chancellor thought the settlement a reasonable provision without colour of fraud. The articles did not bind the real estate, & the bond bound it only to the extent of the penalty. He directed the amount of the settlement except as to the £2000 the penalty of the bond to be paid to Mr. Clavil.[21]   ¶46

There is some difficulty in ascertaining the principle of this case. Most probably the decision turned upon the point that the debt to the East India company could not affect the subject out of which the £5000 were to be raised. Yet in argument the circumstance that the settlement might have influenced her marriage was considered important. I cite it because it was mentioned in a subsequent case as deserving consideration on that account.   ¶47

In George v Milbank 9th. Vez. 190 the case was this. In July 1697 Sir Ralph Milbank directed by deed poll that £500 should be raised immediately after his decease out of certain trust premises for his natural son George Milbank, & died in January 1798.[22] In February 1798 George Milbank in consideration of £400 assigned this money to Frederick Glenton & Thomas Peacock, subject to redemption on the payment of £400 with interest. The bill was brought by a specialty creditor of Sir Ralph Milbank to subject this fund to his debt. The case was decided so far as respected the £400 in favor of Glenton & Peacock because their equity being to the specific article was superior to that of the general creditors. In the argument of the cause the case of the East India company & Clavil was cited from Bacons abr. The Lord chancellor said ["]if the doctrine is rightly collected from the authorities, it imports all this; that if a man is indebted, and makes a provision for his child by a pure voluntary settlement, and that child afterwards marries, the circumstance of its leading to the marriage, makes the settlement good against creditors; though it would have been bad if no marriage had taken place. I doubt whether it will not be found in the circumstances of that case that the child was not a ¶48 pure voluntier. If it can be supported as here stated, it goes a great way to decide this case; for though this is the case of a stranger there is no difference between a voluntary settlement, made good by a subsequent marriage, and one made good by a subsequent advance of money."[23]

¶49   Undoubtedly neither of these cases establishes the principle that a subsequent marriage will make a voluntary settlement good, and yet the chancellor treats that point as if such subsequent marriage was not without its weight.

¶50   If the gift was made at the time of the marriage the claim of the husband will not be weakened by that circumstance. A reasonable gift made contemporaneously with a marriage & accompanied with a delivery of possession, has strong claims to being considered as a gift in consideration of the marriage. Where the circumstances of the parties exclude the idea of any interference on the part of creditors, it is not usual to convey by deed property which passes by delivery, nor to use the solemnity of delivering expressly in consideration of marriage although that may be the real consideration. I do not however place this case on that ground. I think a customary & inconsiderable gift by a parent to a child, which may properly be denominated a present, and which is free from all suspicion of an intention to defraud or injure creditors, cannot, if by subsequent mismanagement the estate of the parent be wasted, be considered as a fraudulent gift at common law or under our statute.

¶51   There was also a negroe girl sent on the birth of Mrs. Harrisons first child. But this girl was sent as a present to the child.

¶52   In 1793 T. R. divided the greater part of his estate among his sons stipulating that each of them should pay certain debts & should execute a bond to R. H. for £250. R. H. took no part in this arrangement but afterwards parted with the bonds to persons & for a sum not mentioned in the proceedings.

¶53   The estates given by T. R. to his children were of much greater value than the debts or money they were directed to pay, & no provision was made for the debt due to Spiers Bowman & Co. Where a conveyance is made to children of property to a large amount charged with debts bearing no proportion to its value, the children cannot be considered as purchasers of the whole, but must take the clear surplus value of the property as volunties. With respect to this debt, for which no provision was made, such voluntary conveyance, according to all the cases, must be considered as fraudulent. But the property thus conveyed is wasted, & is now beyond the reach of the creditor. How are the bonds given by the sons to be considered?

¶54   This question is not without its difficulties. They were given by the sons in part payment for the property conveyed to them by their Father, not to their Father, but directly to R. H. I have felt some doubt whether such bonds were within the statute, but, upon the best consideration I can give the subject the opinion I have formed is that as they are in fact the gift of the Father to his daughter they are in substance equivalent to a charge upon the property conveyed to the sons, which charge would be as liable to creditors as the property itself. I therefore consider Mr. Harrison as liable for these bonds, but liable only for the amount actually received on them. Had they never been paid, it cannot be pretended that he would be accountable for their amount to the creditors. If it cannot, then he will I think be at liberty to show what was the amount actually received.

The subject which remains to be considered is the bond given to Mr. Harrison by Mr. Randolph himself. ¶55

Supposing this to be an obligation which bound Mr. Randolph to the payment of money, the question is whether R. H. is liable for the money actually received upon it. I think the cases of Stiles v The Attorney General 2 Atk 152. Gilham v Locke 9. Vez. 612 & Berry ex parte, 19th. Vez. 218 decide this question in the negative.[24] They decide that satisfaction by bond, & I think by payment, of what is due on a voluntary bond or conveyance is not to be considered as a voluntary act within the statute. ¶56

If then this bond is to be considered as binding in its terms I do not think R. H. accountable for the amount received upon it. If it is not binding it is nothing & R. H. can only be chargeable with the amount actually paid by T. R. of which there is no evidence before the court. It is however a subject into which an enquiry would be useless, because the bonds given by the three sons would, on any probable estimate of their value, exceed the amount of the debt due the plaintiff. ¶57

According to the former course of this court, founded on what was supposed to be the course of the state courts, R. H. would be accountable only for such proportion of the debts of T. R. as the property received by him bore to that received by the sons. But that principle is completely overturned by the case of Temple & Chamberlayne & I consider it as now settled that the whole sum is liable to creditors. If it be, then the decree must be that R. H. the defendant pay to the plf. the sum $3064.92 that being the amount of the judgement rendered in this court against T. R. in favor of John Bowman as surviving partner of Spiers Bowman & Co. in May 1796. ¶58

[Decree]

Hopkirk surviving partner &c
v
Randolph & al

This cause came on to be heard on the bills answers exhibits & depositions & on the report of the commissioner and was argued by Counsel; on consideration whereof it being admitted by the counsel for the parties that Archibald C. Randolph & Thomas Randolph the sons of Thomas Randolph the elder deceased are dead insolvent without any known personal representative, and that the defendant Isham Randolph is also insolvent, it is the opinion of the court that the defendant Randolph Harrison is responsible to the plaintiff for the amount of the debt in the bill mentioned whereupon this court doth decree & order that the defendants Isham Randolph and Randolph Harrison do pay to the plaintiff the sum of three thousand and sixty four dolls, ninety three cents, that being the amount of the judgement rendered by this court sitting as a court of law on the 24th day of May 1796 against Thomas Randolph decd. in favor of John Bowman then alleged to be the surviving partner of Speirs Bowman & Co.

AD, Marshall Judicial Opinions, PPAmP; printed, John W. Brockenbrough, *Reports of Cases Decided by the Honourable John Marshall* . . . , II (Philadelphia, 1837), 133–51. Decree, AD, Hopkirk v. Randolph, U.S. Cir. Ct., Va., Ended Cases (Unrestored), 1824, Vi. For JM's deletions and interlineations, see Textual Notes below.

1. Answer of Randolph Harrison and Mary Harrison, 10 Nov. 1804, Hopkirk v. Randolph. The Harrisons, along with Archibald C. Randolph, had testified at the 1793 hearing of the infanticide case involving the Randolph family, as shown by JM's notes of evidence (*PJM*, II, 170–72, 173–74).

2. Judgment, 24 May 1796, U.S. Cir. Ct., Va., Ord. Bk. II, 108.

3. An abbreviation for the writ of fieri facias.

4. Bill in chancery, (filed Sept. 1803), Hopkirk v. Randolph.

5. The original law judgment against Randolph in 1796 was obtained by John Bowman as the surviving partner of the Glasgow company. In his amended bill filed in court on 19 June 1824, Hopkirk averred that he was a surviving partner at the time of the law judgment and that he was the sole surviving partner at the time of exhibiting his bill in chancery in 1803. On the same day John G. Williams, administrator of John Bowman, filed his answer admitting these allegations and Hopkirk's right to collect the debts of the company (Hopkirk v. Randolph).

6. For Virginia's act "to prevent frauds and perjuries," enacted in 1785 and derived from the English statutes of 13 Eliz. I, c. 5 and of 27 Eliz. I, c. 4, see *Revised Code of Va.*, I, 372.

7. Cadogan v. Kennett, 2 Cowp. 432, 434, 98 Eng. Rep. 1171, 1172 (K.B., 1776).

8. Doe v. Routledge, 2 Cowp. 705, 710, 98 Eng. Rep. 1318, 1321 (K.B., 1777).

9. 2 Cowp. 711, 98 Eng. Rep. 1321.

10. Russel v. Hammond, 1 Atk. 13, 15, 26 Eng. Rep. 9, 11 (Ch., 1738).

11. Taylor v. Jones, 2 Atk. 600, 26 Eng. Rep. 758, 759 (Ch., 1743).

12. Townshend v. Windham, 2 Ves. sen. 1, 11, 28 Eng. Rep. 1, 7 (Ch., 1750).

13. Kidney v. Coussmaker, 12 Ves. 136, 33 Eng. Rep. 53 (Ch., 1806).

14. Partridge v. Gopp, Amb. 596, 27 Eng. Rep. 388 (Ch., 1758).

15. Amb. 598–99, 27 Eng. Rep. 389–90.

16. Chamberlayne v. Temple, 2 Rand. 384 (Va. Ct. App., 1824).

17. Sexton v. Wheaton, 8 Wheat. 229, 243 (1823). JM quoted from his opinion in that case.

18. Here JM wrote "**A** see in Sep. pa. **A.**" On a separate sheet headed "**A** To be inserted at **A** in the last page of the 3d. sheet," he wrote four paragraphs that were to be inserted at this point in the text.

19. Jacks v. Tunno, 3 Desaus. 1, 5 (S.C. Eq., 1809).

20. Salmon v. Bennett, 1 Conn. 525, 547–50 (Conn. Sup. Ct., 1816).

21. East-India Co. v. Clavel, Prec. Ch. 377, 24 Eng. Rep. 170 (Ch., 1714).

22. George v. Milbanke, 9 Ves. 190, 32 Eng. Rep. 575 (Ch., 1803). According to the report the date of the deed poll was July 1727, though the circumstances suggest that the date should be July 1797.

23. 9 Ves. 193, 32 Eng. Rep. 576. For Bacon's report of East India Co. v. Clavel, see Bacon, *Abridgment*, III, 315–16.

24. Stiles v. Attorney General, 2 Atk. 152, 26 Eng. Rep. 496 (Ch., 1740); Gilham v. Locke, 9 Ves. 612, 32 Eng. Rep. 741 (Ch., 1804); Berry, Ex parte, 19 Ves. 218, 34 Eng. Rep. 499 (Ch., 1812).

Textual Notes

¶ 1	l. 1	year [*erasure*] ↑1790↓
	ll. 10–11	sons ~~charged with~~ ↑in consideration of love & natural affection, of↓ certain specific debts & ~~charged~~ also ~~with~~ ↑of bonds for↓ £250
¶ 2	l. 10	his [*erasure*] undertaking
¶ 3	l. 1	25th. of ~~Jany.~~ ↑June↓ 1800
¶ 4	l. 1	life ↑intestate↓ & in the
	l. 3	bill ~~on~~ in this
	l. 5	thereto. ~~and praying~~ The
¶ 5	l. 4	can be [*erasure*] satisfied
¶ 6	l. 2	to be ~~made~~ a party;
¶ 7	l. 2	He [*erasure*] contends
¶ 9	l. 2	confessed ~~by himself or~~ by his
	l. 6	A. C. R [*erasure*] substituted
¶11	l. 1	cases do [*erasure*] not,
	l. 3	from ~~paying the money &~~ proceeding
	ll. 3–4	recover the ↑money he may have paid.↓ But
	ll. 6–7	the Donor ↑at any rate unless there be an express warranty.↓ I
¶14	l. 1	to be ex↑pounded,↓ the court
	l. 2	in ~~considering~~ construing it
	l. 3	gifts ↑or conveyances↓ meerly
	l. 4	made of ↑malice, fraud,↓ covin,
	l. 5	with intent ~~to~~ or purpose
¶15	l. 4	side ↑of the creditor,↓ and
	l. 7	gifts or ↑voluntary↓ conveyances
	l. 10	valuable [*erasure*] consideration,
	l. 13	probability ~~creditors might be~~ it
	ll. 15–16	comprehend ~~the~~ it. But
	l. 17	gift ~~under all~~ ↑meerly because↓ it was voluntary ~~would~~ ↑might↓ derange the
	l. 24	require. ~~a~~ A reasonable
	ll. 29–30	should ↑as well as his parent↓ become
	l. 31	But should ~~the~~ he not
	l. 35	sound, [*erasure*] the subsequent
	l. 39	inferred. ~~the~~ The consequence
	l. 40	considered as [*erasure*] constructively
¶16	l. 4	creditors ~~existing existed~~ ↑whose debts existed↓ at the
	l. 15	they ~~opinions of the court has~~ ↑have↓ been
¶17	l. 3	have ~~shown~~ expressed
¶18	ll. 1–3	on ↑these acts have been most common in chancery, but↓ as

               courts of law ~~and equity~~ have concurrent jurisdiction, ~~,on this~~
               ~~subject~~ ↑& as they have received the same construction in both
               courts,↓ it may

	l. 4	Judge ~~of~~ in a court
¶21	l. 2	attended to ~~at the~~ in these
¶24	l. 1	Lord [*erasure*] Hardwicke
¶26	ll. 2–3	value ~~where the relative value~~ of the
	ll. 3–4	indeed [*erasure*] stated, but
	ll. 5–6	because ↑it↓ was made
¶27	l. 5	But ~~if it be considered in relation to the case in which it~~ it is
	l. 6	the ~~donor~~ settler
¶29	l. 2	deed ↑in pursuance of a general power↓ appointed
¶30	l. 1	Cousmaker ↑12 Vez.↓ the general
¶31	l. 2	perfectly ↑settled↓ but
	l. 3	amount; ~~and generally a settlement by deed of property which would not pass by delivery in the precise manner of the conveyance or some bond or other continuing obligation not discharged when its validity was questioned . . .~~ some
¶32	l. 1	legatees of ~~Sarah Clarkes~~ ↑Edward↓ ~~& he has~~ Godfrey
	l. 2	testator & ~~for the payment of 6000£ Joseph An~~ ~~security~~ to have
	l. 5	for not [*erasure*] complying
	l. 7	The ~~suit was a~~ plfs. brought
	l. 8	children ↑four daughters↓ who had
	l. 10	because the ~~fortunes~~ ↑money↓
	l. 12	answers, [*erasure*] each of
	l. 13	the world. ~~The Chanc~~
¶33	l. 7	weigh. " ~~"I have no doubt but~~ The
	l. 7	except ~~except~~ where
¶34	l. 3	power over his ↑own↓ property
¶35	l. 2	parent [*erasure*] much
	l. 12	them ↑at the time,↓ other ~~that~~ ↑than↓ a
	l. 14	highest ~~authority~~ ↑tribunal of our country↓ of a
	l. 16	should not ↑I think↓ have
	l. 20	who [*erasure*] were not
¶36	l. 10	donations ↑of chattels personal↓ assume
	l. 12	case ~~did~~ was one of
	l. 15	No ↑voluntary↓ conveyance of property [*erasure*] has
	l. 16	but no ~~present~~ gift,
	ll. 17–18	present, ↑made under circumstances entirely free from suspicion,↓ has ever,
¶37	l. 2	present ~~claim~~ controversy.
¶39	l. 9	if ~~beyo~~ rather more
	l. 12	question. ~~The case of the other girl~~ These
	l. 17	having [*erasure*] passed
¶40	l. 2	hesitate [*erasure*] to follow
¶41	l. 1	Tunno ↑& al,↓ decided in South Carolina, a ~~person in go~~ ↑trader↓
	l. 5	brought ↑by the donees↓ to
	l. 6	bankrupt, ~~to~~ from

	ll. 7–8	in [*erasure*] giving his
¶44	l. 1 beg.	If ~~this property is~~ ↑these two girls & this riding horse are↓ to be
	l. 2	have become ↑ostensibly↓ the property
	l. 10	Afterwards [*erasure*] on the
	l. 11	£5000 ↑to be raised out of land,↓ &
	l. 17	settlement. [*erasure*] Sir Edward
¶45	ll. 2–3	Clavil [*erasure*] to marry
¶46	l. 3	the bond ↑bound it↓ only
¶47	l. 2	debt ~~of~~ ↑to↓ the East
	l. 5	I ~~men~~ cite it
¶48	l. 5	Milbank ↑in consideration of £400↓ assigned
	ll. 8–9	decided ↑so far as respected the £400↓ in
¶51	l. 2	child. ~~Whatever opinion might be formed respecting this girl if given to Mr. Harrison~~
¶53	l. 1	given ↑by T. R.↓ to his
	l. 2	than the ↑debts or↓ money they
	l. 3	for ~~that~~ the debt due
	l. 4	charged with [*erasure*] debts
	l. 5	proportion to ~~the~~ ↑its↓ value, ~~of the property~~ the
	l. 6	must ~~make~~ take the
¶54	l. 1	~~The money was~~ They were given
	ll. 2–3	Father, ↑not to their Father,↓ but directly to R. H. ~~I have~~ I have
	l. 7	upon the ~~bond~~ property
¶58	l. 2	R. H. [*erasure*] would be
	l. 6	to creditors. ~~Does it bear interest~~ If it be
	l. 7	be that ~~R. and~~ R. H.
	ll. 7–8	plf. ↑the sum $3064.92 that being↓ the amount
	l. 9	partner of [*erasure*] Spiers

Hopkirk v. Randolph

Opinion

U.S. Circuit Court, Virginia, 28 June 1824

Hopkirk surviving partner &c

v

Randolph & al.

A reargument of this cause having been granted at the request of the ¶1 counsel for R. H. it has been reconsidered by the court.[1]

The argument has turned chiefly on two points. ¶2

1st.   That the estate conveyed to the sons is chargeable with this debt.

2d.   That a gift of money by a parent to a child, not really made with a fraudulent intent, is not constructively fraudulent under the statute.

¶3   1st. That the whole debt should be paid by the sons, were they now solvent & before the court, will be readily admitted. But two of them are dead insolvent, and the third, who is now alive, is admitted to be insolvent. The creditor can obtain nothing from that source.

¶4   It is insisted that the land is liable in the hands of the purchasers.

¶5   Of this I am not confident. But were it to be admitted that a person who holds by purchase from a voluntier, takes the property subject to the creditors of the original donor, I should still be of opinion that the creditor would not be compellable to proceed against such purchaser, & I should also think that no decree could be made against him, in aid of a voluntier who were able to pay the debt.

¶6   2d. It is true that few cases are to be found in the books in which a child has been decreed to refund money actually received from a parent. From the nature of the transaction, such gifts would not frequently be the subject of enquiry. Where they are inconsiderable in amount they are seldom made the subject of enquiry, and, were they even looked into would perhaps not be deemed fraudulent; and where large advances are made, they most generally consist of money in the funds, or charged on lands. But in the case of Partridge v Gop reported in Ambler, a gift of money to a child was declared to be fraudulent as against creditors and the chancellor founded his opinion on the magnitude & value of the gift.[2] That case was it is true tainted with circumstances leading strongly to the opinion that the gift was made for the purpose of providing for his family at the expence of a creditor, but the chancellor places his decree chiefly on the magnitude of the gift. The fraud was inferred in a great degree from that circumstance. In the case at bar, the gift to R. H. forms a part of a more considerable transaction & cannot easily be separated from it. That transaction was the division of the estate of T. R. among all his children. Though only a small part was allotted to R. H., that small part must I think partake of the character of the whole transaction. It would be very difficult to releive this whole family arrangement entirely from the taint of being made, at any rate, without sufficient regard to the claim of a creditor not provided for. It has been said at the bar that there was a general promise on the part of the sons to pay any debts which might appear; but there is no proof of such promise, & had any debt not mentioned in the conveyances formed a part of the consideration a stipulation to that effect ought to have been inserted. It has been said with some probability that this debt was forgotten; but, however satisfactory this excuse may be in an enquiry into the morality of the arrangement, it would be dangerous to admit it in an enquiry concerning its legality.

¶7   The cases of Gilham v Locke 9th. Vez. 612 & Berry ex parte 19th. Vez. 218, from which it is inferred that money paid in discharge of a voluntary bond is not within the statute, rather support the opinion; I think that money given in the first instance, not under the obligation of such bond, would be within the statute.[3] The validity of such payment would not I think have been placed on the obligation which a voluntary bond creates between the parties, if the advance of the money, independent of such prior obligation, had been considered as beyond the reach of the statute.

This case is one of extreme hardship, which ought not to be carried ¶8 beyond express authority. But I think myself bound to adhere to the decree in favor of the plaintiff.[4]

AD, Marshall Judicial Opinions, PPAmP; printed, John W. Brockenbrough, *Reports of Cases Decided by the Honourable John Marshall . . .* , II (Philadelphia, 1837), 152–55. For JM's deletions and interlineations, see Textual Notes below.

1. According to Brockenbrough, the reargument took place at the same term. JM evidently delivered his second opinion on 28 June, the date the decree was entered in the order book (U.S. Cir. Ct., Va., Ord. Bk. XI, 487–88).

2. Partridge v. Gopp, Amb. 596, 27 Eng. Rep. 388 (Ch., 1758).

3. Gilham v. Locke, 9 Ves. 612, 32 Eng. Rep. 741 (Ch., 1804); Berry, Ex parte, 19 Ves. 218, 34 Eng. Rep. 499 (Ch., 1812).

4. Randolph Harrison took an appeal to the Supreme Court, which in Jan. 1828 dismissed the case on receiving notice that the parties had compromised and settled all matters in controversy (Harrison v. Randolph, App. Cas. No. 1337; U.S. Sup. Ct. Minutes, 17 Jan. 1828).

Textual Notes

¶1	l. 1 beg.	~~The counsel for R. H. having requested~~
¶3	l. 1	That ~~this court would decree~~ ↑that↓ the
¶5	l. 3	original ~~donors~~ ↑donor,↓
	ll. 5–6	against ~~them while~~ him, in aid of ↑a↓ voluntier
¶6	ll. 1–2	which a ~~person~~ ↑child↓ has
	ll. 8–9	Gop ↑reported in Ambler,↓ a gift of money ~~was declared~~ to a child
	ll. 14–15	gift. ↑The fraud was inferred in a great degree from that circumstance.↓ In
	ll. 24–25	debt not ~~inserted~~ ↑mentioned↓ in
	ll. 25–26	consideration ~~it~~ a stipulation
	ll. 27–28	however ~~fully~~ ↑satisfactory↓ this excuse may ~~satisfy~~ ↑be↓ in an
¶7	l. 4	of ~~a~~ ↑such↓ bond,

To Henry Lee

Dear Sir   Richmond July 6th. 1824

I received a few days past your letter of the 28th of June.[1] As I do not possess Colo. Tarltons work I enquired for it, but it is I beleive in a book store in town. As well as I recollect the difference between his account of Bufords defeat & that given by Genl. Lee & other American writers consists chiefly in the circumstances which led to the bloody charge made by the British dragoons on the American party. As I was not myself in the southern army, I have that knowledge only which is to be collected from occasional conversations with those who survived that massacre. There were I beleive a few guns fixed by the Americans; but those with whom I have conversed assert that they were fired after the movements of the British horse were actually hostile, or such indications of hostility were given as could not be mistaken. My own impression has been that the British, with or without the orders of their commanding officer, were the aggressors. It is however a subject on which positive certainty is I beleive now unattainable.[2]

Your letter enclosing the errata was received after my first letter acknowledging the receipt of the Campaign in the Carolinas.[3]

I am glad to hear that you are about to publish a second edition of the m⟨e⟩moirs.[4] With respect & esteem, I am dear Sir your obedt.

J MARSHALL

ALS, Tucker Family Papers, Southern Historical Collection, NcU. Addressed to Lee in Fredericksburg; postmarked Richmond, 6 July. Endorsed by Lee.

1. Letter not found.
2. On 29 May 1780, Lt. Col. Banastre Tarleton's Tory Legion routed a detachment of 350 Virginia Continentals under Col. Abraham Buford at Waxhaws, South Carolina. Tarleton claimed that he asked for Buford's surrender but that Buford refused, while Col. Henry Lee maintained that Tarleton refused Buford's offer to surrender. The slaughter of the American line gave Tarleton his reputation for brutality (Don Higginbotham, *The War for American Independence: Military Attitudes, Policies, and Practice, 1763–1789* [New York, 1971], 361; Banastre Tarleton, *A History of the Campaigns of 1780 and 1781, in the Southern Provinces of North America* [London, 1787], 29–32; Henry Lee, *Memoirs of the War in the Southern Department of the United States* [2 vols.; Philadelphia, 1812], I, 148–49).
3. See JM to Lee, 7 May 1824.
4. Lee published a second edition of his father's *Memoirs* in 1827.

Preface to *A History of the Colonies*

[ca. 7 July 1824][1]

So large a portion of the life of General Washington was devoted to the public, so elevated and important were the stations which he filled, that the history of his life is, at the same time, the history of his nation.

The part he took, while commander in chief, in the civil as well as military affairs of the United States, was so considerable, that few events of general interest occurred, which were not, in some degree, influenced by him. A detail of the transactions in which he was either immediately or remotely concerned, would comprehend so great a part of those which belong to general history, that the entire exclusion of the few in which he bore no part, while it would scarcely give to the work more of the peculiar character of biography, would expose it to the charge of being an incomplete history of the times.

His administration of the government while President of the United States, cannot be well understood without a full knowledge of the political measures of the day, and of the motives by which his own conduct was regulated.

These considerations appeared to require that his biography should present a general historical view of the transactions of the time, as well as a particular narrative of the part performed by himself.

Our ideas of America, of the character of our revolution, of those who engaged in it, and of the struggles by which it was accomplished, would be imperfect without some knowledge of our colonial history. No work had been published when this was undertaken, from which that knowledge could be collected. To have taken up the history of the United States when the command of the army was conferred on General Washington, would have been to introduce the reader abruptly into the midst of scenes and transactions, with the causes of which, and with the actors in them, he would naturally wish to be intimately acquainted. This was the apology of the author for the introductory volume to the Life of General Washington. Had the essays since written towards a general history of the English colonies been then in possession of the public, this volume would not have appeared. But, although they might have prevented its appearance, they ought not to prevent its being corrected and offered to the public in a form less exceptionable than that which it originally bore. From the extreme, I may add unpardonable, precipitation with which it was hurried to the press, many errors were overlooked which, on a perusal of the book, were as apparent to the author as to others. He was desirous of correcting these errors, and of making the work more worthy of the public to which it was offered, as well as more satisfactory to himself. For this purpose he has given it, since the impressions under which it was compiled have worn off, more than one attentive reading; has made several alterations in the language; and has expunged much of the less essential matter with which the narrative was burthened. He dares not flatter himself that he has succeeded completely in his attempt to entitle this work to the approbation of the literary public of America; but hopes that its claims to that approbation are stronger than in its original form.

Believing that motives no longer exist for connecting the History of the English Colonies in North America with the Life of Washington, the author has obtained the permission of the proprietor of the copy-right to separate the Introduction from the other volumes, and to publish it as a distinct work.[2]

Printed, *History of the Colonies Planted by the English on the Continent of North America . . .* (Philadelphia, 1824), v–viii.

1. JM filed the copyright to this work in the U.S. District Court at Richmond on 7 July 1824 (ibid., ii).

2. During the past several years JM had worked steadily on revising the *Life of Washington* and by the spring of 1823 was ready to publish a second edition in four volumes. He subsequently decided to publish the "introduction" separately in a small edition (*PJM*, IX, 195–96, 303, 322, 329, 333–34, 336, 339, 340–41). A second edition of the *Life of Washington* in two volumes was eventually published in 1832.

To [Joseph Story?]

Dear Sir   Richmond July 14th 1824
    The bearer Mr. Peyton is my friend & neighbor & a Merchant of reputation in Richmond.[1] He goes to Salem on commercial business & may probably apply to some of your friends or connexions in the line of his profession. I introduce him to them through you.[2] I am dear Sir with much esteem, Your

                                        J MARSHALL

ALS, PHi.

    1. Bernard Peyton (1792–1854), was a Richmond merchant who served as adjutant general of the Virginia militia, as a director of the Farmers' Bank of Virginia, and as Richmond factor for Thomas Jefferson Randolph and Thomas Jefferson. Jefferson recommended Peyton as postmaster for Richmond in 1824 (*The Richmond Directory, Register and Almanac for the Year 1819* [Richmond, Va., 1819], 19, 62; Dumas Malone, *Jefferson and His Time*, VI: *The Sage of Monticello* [Boston, 1981], 311, 392, 430; The Peyton Society of Virginia, *The Peytons of Virginia: Being an Account of the Ancient and Knightly Family* . . . [Stafford, Va., 1976], 29–30).
    2. Another possible addressee of this letter is Salem resident Timothy Pickering.

To Thomas G. Marshall

My dear Nephew   Richmond July 15th 1824
    I presume the cloudiness of the day prevented my seeing you at Hanover court house on monday.[1] I have determined to be there in the hope of meeting you on the court day for this month as I suppose that day will suit you as well & perhaps better than any other.[2] Should anything make that day inconvenient to you I will thank you to let me know it immediately & to appoint some other. If I do not hear from you I shall be there by about 12 o clock on the first day of the court. I am my dear Nephew, Your affectionate

                                        J MARSHALL

ALS, Collection of the Association for the Preservation of Virginia Antiquities, ViHi. Addressed to Marshall in Taylorsville, Hanover County; postmarked Richmond, 15 July.

1. Thomas G. Marshall (1800–1880) was the son of JM's brother William (Paxton, *Marshall Family*, 145).

2. Hanover Court met on the fourth Wednesday of the month — in this instance on 28 July (*Revised Code of Va.*, I, 249).

To Martin P. Marshall

My dear Nephew   Richmond July 16th. 1824

I received your letter in Jany. last[1] transmitting a statement of the land account with Mr. Marshall but as this statement does not comprehend his commission or his premium on remittances, nor his liability for money received from Colo. Daviess I am unable to form any estimate of the true state of our accounts. You will take & have taken a good deal of trouble in this affair for which I must certainly make you compensation & as it is not probable that you will receive what I supposed you would from Mr. Marshall I will either settle it with my sister or remit to you as you may prefer.[2]

I regretted very much that I did not see you while you were in Richmond. Mr. Call paid me the $480 for my sister which I have settled with her & after some time he gave her your letter mentioning the twenty three dollars which I have also accounted for to my sister.

I received a few days past a letter from Mr. Pollard informing me that he is desirous of purchasing some land belonging to the estate of Colo. Daviess which adjoins him & that the debt due to me will be a very convenient addition in this operation to that which is due to my sister. He offers ample security for the repayment of the money in 1⟨8?⟩ months or two years. I have written to him that the business is under your management & that I am ignorant of its situation, but that I am perfectly willing he should make any use of the claim which does not delay its final decision or embarass it on his giving you sufficient security for its repayment. He offers security on land or slaves.[3]

I shall be very glad to hear as soon as possible how my accounts with Mr. Marshall are ultimately adjusted. I am much grieved at the informati⟨on⟩ given me by Mr. Pollard that m⟨y⟩ sister Marshall is seriously indi⟨sposed.⟩[4]

Your Aunt sends her lo⟨ve⟩ &c. I am my dear Nephew, Your affectionate

J MARSHALL

ALS (owned by Brooke Alexander, New York, N.Y., 1967). Addressed to Marshall in Washington, Mason County, Ky.; postmarked Richmond, 20 July.

1. Letter not found.

2. For some years JM had been communicating with Martin Marshall and other Kentucky relatives about the affairs of his sister, Jane Marshall Taylor, who was trying to recover money from Humphrey Marshall, and concerning his own account with the estate of the late Joseph Hamilton Daveiss. See *PJM*, VIII, 315–16, 364; IX, 61–62, 241–42.

3. JM's correspondence (not found) was presumably with William Pollard. He was the second husband of JM's sister Nancy, Daveiss's widow (Paxton, *Marshall Family*, 78).

4. JM was possibly referring to his sister Mary, wife of his cousin Humphrey Marshall (ibid., 80).

To Peter S. Du Ponceau

Dear Sir   Richmond July 17th. 1824

I have deferred my acknowledgements for your polite attention in sending me a copy of your "Dissertation on the nature and extent of the jurisdiction of the courts of the United States," til I should finish its perusal.[1] I have now read it with attention & pleasure. That part of it particularly which respects the criminal jurisdiction of the court in some cases where the punishment is not prescribed by any act of Congress connected with Chief Justice Tilghmans opinion in the case of Kosloff, deserves the most serious consideration.[2]

I thank you for the flattering manner in which you have noticed some opinions of mine which were expressed in such general terms as to extend farther than was required by the particular case to be decided.[3] With great respect, I am Sir your Obedt Servt.

J MARSHALL

ALS, PP. Addressed to Du Ponceau in Philadelphia; postmarked Richmond, 17 July. Endorsed by Du Ponceau.

1. Peter S. Du Ponceau (1760–1844), a native of France, came to America in 1777, took a commission in the Continental army, and served as Baron von Steuben's aide-de-camp. He settled in Philadelphia after the war and rose to prominence in the legal profession. He founded the Law Academy of Philadelphia in 1821, later serving as its provost and president. His *Dissertation on the Nature and Extent of the Jurisdiction of the Courts of the United States* (Philadelphia, 1824) was originally delivered as an address to the students of the law academy in Apr. 1824. In addition to his writings on law, Du Ponceau was the author of numerous studies in the field of philology.

2. Du Ponceau argued that where jurisdiction was vested in the federal courts, such as in cases affecting consuls, those tribunals could prescribe punishment of common law crimes in the absence of a federal statute on the subject. In 1816 Pennsylvania Chief Justice William Tilghman quashed an indictment for rape against Russian consul general Nicholas Kosloff on the ground that state courts had no jurisdiction in cases involving foreign consuls. Du Ponceau contended that Kosloff could have been tried in federal court and punished according to the law of Pennsylvania, either common law or statute. In support of this conclusion he cited section 34 of the Judiciary Act of 1789, which provided "that the laws of the several States, except where the Constitution, treaties or statutes of the United States shall otherwise require or provide, shall be regarded as the rules of decision in trials at common law, in the Courts of the United States, in cases where they apply" (*Dissertation*, 32–45, 249–54; Commonwealth of Pa. v. Kosloff, 5 S & R 545 [Pa. Sup. Ct., 1816]).

3. Du Ponceau gave particular notice to a passage in JM's opinion in U.S. v. Burr, 3 Sept. 1807, which appeared to read section 34 of the Judiciary Act as applying to civil cases, not to criminal cases. In deferential and respectful language the author maintained that this passage was *obiter dictum*, not essential to deciding the particular point before the court (*Dissertation*, 37–43; U.S. v. Burr, Opinion [3 Sept. 1807], *PJM*, VII, 119–20).

To Bushrod Washington

My dear Sir   Richmond Oct. 6th. 1824

I have expected to hear from you since you have had an opportunity to look into the trunks and chests last sent up for the volume of letters containing those which have not been copied, and am uneasy at not receiving a letter from you. I have been apprehensive that you have been prevented by indisposition. Still, as I have not heard of your being sick I will flatter my self that some accident has prevented your looking into the trunks, or has prevented your writing. I am confident the volume is in one of them.

Will you have the goodness to obtain from Mr Small on my account five copies of my history of the colonies & retain one for yourself. Present one to my friend Mr. Hopkinson & one to Mr. Sergeant with my compliments & a request that they will receive them as a testimonial of my esteem & regard.[1] One with my compliments to Mr. Duponceau. It is in return for the book he sent me. You need not however tell him this. One to Mr Wayne. It is a compliment on account of his great attention to the publication of the Life of Washington. Tell him I have taken the precaution to take out a copy right for this volume at the instance of Mr Small to prevent the interference of others — not to affect him. Should he ever, which is not likely, wish to publish an edition as amended I will most cheerfully assent & aid him by correcting the few — very few typographical errors which have escaped the vigilance of Mr. Small & making any trifling corrections which I may hereafter suppose necessary.

I have requested a copy to be presented with my compliments to Judge Peters. I hope it is done. Should it be otherwise I must ask the favor of you to superintend this little affair also.

Wishing you a pleasant session & of course good health for it. I am dear Sir yours truely

J MARSHALL

Ask Mr. Small to furnish me with eight copies of the history this February in Washington

ALS, Miscellaneous Manuscripts, NHi. Addressed to Washington in Philadelphia; postmarked Richmond, 6 Oct. Endorsed by Washington.

1. Joseph Hopkinson (1770–1842) and John Sergeant (1779–1852) were distinguished Philadelphia lawyers who had lately been members of the House of Representatives. As congressmen they also regularly argued cases in the Supreme Court. Hopkinson was appointed U.S. district judge for eastern Pennsylvania in 1828, serving until his death. Sergeant again served in the House from 1827 to 1829 and from 1837 to 1841.

Speech
Richmond, Virginia
27 October 1824

Lafayette's "Triumphal Tour" of the United States brought him to Virginia in October 1824. He arrived by steamboat on the lower Peninsula on 18 October, and during the following week he and his party progressed with great pomp and ceremony from Yorktown to Williamsburg and Norfolk. The next stop was Richmond, where he arrived on the afternoon of 26 October. The main event occurred on 27 October and included a procession to City Hall, a speech by Mayor John Adams, Lafayette's reply, and a further procession to Capitol Square. In compliance with a formal request made two months earlier by city officials, Marshall prepared "an appropriate address" for the occasion (Robert D. Ward, *An Account of General La Fayette's Visit to Virginia, in the Years 1824–25* [Richmond, Va., 1881], 18–19, 51–59; Edgar Ewing Brandon, ed., *Lafayette Guest of the Nation: A Contemporary Account of the "Triumphal Tour" of General Lafayette* [3 vols.; Oxford, Ohio, 1957], III, 95–102).

GENERAL:

The surviving officers of our Revolutionary Army, who are inhabitants of the state of Virginia, Welcome you to her Metropolis with feelings which your own heart will best tell you how to estimate. We have been the more gratified by the offering of respect and affection from a whole people, spontaneously flowing from sincere gratitude for inestimable services, and a deep sense of your worth, because we believe that to a mind like yours, they will compensate for the privations you sustain, and the hazards and fatigues you have encountered in re-visiting our country. So long as Americans remember that noble struggle which drew you first to their shores, that deep gloom which overshadowed their cause when you embraced it, they cannot forget the prompt, the generous, the gallant, and the important part you took in the conflict.

The history of your eventful life attests the sublime motive which enlisted you on the side of a people contending for liberty; but we love to believe that feelings of a softer and more endearing character were soon mingled with that exalted principle. We delight to consider this visit as furnishing additional evidence that the sentiments we felt and manifested towards you, sunk deep into your heart, and were greeted by kindred feelings; that as America has always regarded you as one of the best and bravest of her sons, so you have never ceased to regard her as a second country, ranking in your affections next to that which gave you birth.

In common with our fellow-citizens throughout the United States, we rejoice to see you. With them we review your various and valuable services to our infant republics, and your unceasing devotion to liberty; and find in the retrospect the same reasons to excite our gratitude and esteem which excite those sentiments in them; but in one part of your life we claim an interest peculiar to ourselves.

We look back with mingled gratitude and applause to the period of our revolutionary War, when the supreme command in Virginia was conferred on you. We retrace your conduct through those trying scenes. We recollect the difficulties you encountered, and the dangers which threatened us. We remember the skill, the patient fortitude, the persevering courage, with which you conducted us through those difficulties, and extricated yourself and us from those dangers.

At the head of an undisciplined and ill-armed militia, supported by only a small band of Regulars, you kept the open field in the face of a numerous, well appointed and high spirited army, protected our scanty magazines, covered a great portion of our country, sustained the hopes and the confidence of our people, and, without sustaining any serious disaster, pressed the rear of the hostile army in its retreat to the ground on which its expiring effort was made.

It is your praise, during this arduous and trying conduct for Virginia, to have so happily tempered the enterprizing courage of youth with the caution and prudence which belong to riper years, that you performed every practicable service without sustaining any serious disaster, and preserved your army entire for the great achievement which not only liberated Virginia, but accomplished the independence of the United States.

The distinguished part you bore in the last and glorious scene, is indelibly impressed in the memory of all Virginians. In the bosoms of none is it more deeply engraved than in those of the men who stand before you. Some of us served under you in that memorable campaign; many in the course of the war. While duty required obedience, your conduct inspired confidence and love. Time, which has thinned our ranks, and enfeebled our bodies, has not impaired these feelings. They retain their original vigour.

These expressions flow from hearts replete with sentiments of affection for your person, esteem for your character, and gratitude for your services. They will continue to animate us long after we shall have parted with you; we are unwilling to add — for ever! Under their influence, we supplicate the supreme author of all good to extend to you his protection, and to make the evening of your life as serene, tranquil, and happy, as its morning was glorious.[1]

Printed, *The Enquirer* (Richmond, Va.), 29 Oct. 1824.

1. Lafayette made a brief reply, in which he referred to JM as "the Eloquent Historian of the Revolution, and of its matchless military chief." JM's other activities in connection with Lafayette's Richmond visit included offering toasts at dinners, presiding at a Masonic dinner, and hosting a dinner for the general at his home (Toast, 26 Oct. 1824; Toast, 28 Oct 1824 [App. II., Cal.]; Brandon, ed., *Lafayette Guest of the Nation*, III, 116–17; *Enquirer* [Richmond, Va.], 29 Oct., 2 Nov. 1824).

To Bushrod Washington

My dear Sir   Richmond Novr. 4th. 1824

 I have found the missing book. It had been brought out of my office into the house & placed on a settee where it was covered with a pile of newspapers. I had put some other book into one of the trunks & supposed it must be this.

 I have directed the letters to be copied & will bring them with me to the Supreme court should I not have an earlier opportunity of sending them to you. It will be difficult to comprise them in three volumes.

 Did the act pass last congress for fixing the commencement of our term at an earlier day.[1] If it did, what day is named? Yours truely

                 J MARSHALL

ALS, Miscellaneous Manuscripts, NHi. Addressed to Washington at Mount Vernon; postmarked Richmond, 4 Nov. Endorsed by Washington.

 1. An act to change the day of the commencement of the Supreme Court term was not adopted by Congress until May 1826. It changed the day from the first Monday in February to the second Monday in January (*U.S. Statutes at Large,* IV, 160).

To Thomas W. White

Sir[1]   Richmond Novr. 29th. 1824

 I have received the volume of Mr. Garnetts lectures with which you favored me, and have devoted the first liesure time I could well spare to its perusal. I had read this little work when first published, and was so well pleased with it as to place it in the hands of several of my young friends for whose improvement I was particularly sollicitous.[2]

 The subject is, in my opinion of the deepest interest. I have always believed that national character, as well as happiness, depends more on the female part of society than is generally imagined. Precepts from the lips of a beloved mother, inculcated in the amiable, graceful, and affectionate manner which belongs to the parent and the sex, sink deep in the heart, and make an impression which is seldom entirely effaced. These impressions have an influence on character which may contribute greatly to the happiness or misery, the eminence or insignificancy of the individual.

 If the agency of the mother in forming the character of her children is, in truth, so considerable as I think it, if she does so much towards making her son what she would wish him to be, and her daughter to resemble herself, how essential is it that she should be fitted for the beneficial performance of these essential duties.

 To accomplish this beneficial purpose is the object of Mr. Garnetts lectures; and he has done much towards its attainment. His precepts appear to be drawn from deep and accurate observation of human life and manners, and to be admirably well calculated to improve the understanding, and the heart. They form a sure and safe foundation for female character, and contain rules of conduct which cannot be too well considered or too generally applied. They are communicated too with a sprightliness of style and agreeableness of manner which cannot fail to ensure a favorable reception to the instruction they convey.[3] I am Sir very respectfully, Your obedt

J MARSHALL

ALS, Emmet Collection, NN. Inside address to White.

1. Thomas W. White (1788–1843) was a Richmond printer who founded the *Southern Literary Messenger* in 1834.

2. White published James Mercer Garnett's *Seven Lectures on Female Education, Inscribed to Mrs. Garnett's Pupils, at Elm-Wood, Essex County, Virginia* (Richmond, Va., 1824). Garnett (1770–1843), a former state legislator and congressman, was a noted agricultural writer and reformer. In the early 1820s he opened a school for young ladies, in which he and his wife and daughters served as instructors. His book was a collection of his lectures delivered to the students. The first edition had appeared earlier in 1824. White sent JM the revised and expanded second edition and in later editions (published as *Lectures on Female Education*) printed JM's letter along with other commendatory letters.

3. White provided a copy of this letter to the Richmond *Enquirer,* which published it on 2 Dec. 1824 preceded by an editorial introduction praising the progress of female education.

Lidderdale's Executors v. Robinson
Opinion
U.S. Circuit Court, Virginia, 30 November 1824

The original plaintiffs in this suit were representatives of British merchant John Lidderdale. They sought recovery of claims against the estate of John Robinson, the powerful speaker of the House of Burgesses and treasurer of Virginia from 1738 to his death in 1766. The defendants were representatives of Edmund Pendleton and Peter Lyons, the original administrators of Robinson's complicated estate. In 1820 Lidderdale's representatives filed their bill stating the circumstances of an earlier suit brought by Lidderdale's executor on the chancery side of the federal circuit court for the recovery of the amount on four protested bills of exchange drawn by Robinson in the 1760s. In 1797 the executor had obtained a decree for this amount, to be paid when assets should come into the hands of the administrators. The bill alleged that assets to a great amount had recently come into the hands of the present administrator and requested that he be ordered to render an account. The court issued an interlocutory decree on 12 June 1822 directing the commissioner to make a report of the administration account and of the various debts due from Robinson's estate and of assets now outstanding and not collected. At the same time the representatives of the surviving partner of the British firm of Capel and Osgood Hanbury were made parties to this account and permitted to exhibit their claims before the commissioner. The commissioner reported in December 1822, at which time the court ordered the report to be recommitted with additional instructions and allowing any other creditors of Robinson's estate to exhibit their claims. The commissioner made another report in March 1824, to which the plaintiffs filed exceptions. Marshall delivered his opinion on this report and the exceptions on 30 November 1824 (David J. Mays, *Edmund Pendleton, 1721–1803: A Biography* [2 vols.; Cambridge, Mass., 1952], I, 174–86; U.S. Cir. Ct., Va., Rec. Bk. XX, 274–376).

OPINION

The counsel for the plaintiffs, Lidderdale and Hanberry, have filed several exceptions to this report, the most important and difficult of which, respects a sum alleged by the administrator *de bonis non* of John Robinson, to be due to Peter Lyons, the surviving administrator of John Robinson, whose executor the said James Lyons is. The commissioner has stated this claim in different ways.[1]

The counsel for the plaintiffs objects to this account altogether, because he alleges:[2]

1. That it is not supported by vouchers.

2. That Peter Lyons is responsible for his co-administrator, Edmund Pendleton, they having given a joint bond, and Edmund Pendleton appearing to be largely indebted to Robinson's estate.

3. That balances are stated to be due from George Brooke and others, the agents of the administrators, for which the said Peter Lyons is responsible.

1. The commissioner states that this account, from 1766 to 1784, inclusive, was collected from the books of Peter Lyons, and from 1799 to the date of the report, is supported by vouchers, and this Court must presume that his statement is correct, unless the contrary is shown. The account from the year 1784, to January, 1799, is taken from a report made by Commissioner Hay, in pursuance of an order of the high court of chancery, in which   were plaintiffs, and the administrators of John Robinson, deceased, were defendants. This part of the account does not show the particular items, but the annual amount of receipts and disbursements. Commissioner Hay's report was made in the year 1799, while the administrators were alive, but does not appear ever to have been acted on by the court.[3] If the transactions were recent, vouchers to sustain the account would of course be required. But in a case of such long standing, where the parties are all dead, strict proof is not to be looked for. It is the less to be expected in this case, as it is known that the office of Peter Lyons was consumed by fire, and that very many of his papers were destroyed with it. In such a state of things, the Court is much inclined to the opinion that the books of the administrator, if they appear

to have been fairly kept, and the account of Commissioner Hay, founded on those books, ought to be received as *prima facie* evidence, subject to be disproved, as far as either party may disprove them, or to such exception as either party may make, or be able to sustain. If this course be not pursued, and the books and account be discarded, it would be necessary to remodel the account on such vouchers as either party may be able to adduce. The result of such an account could not be as satisfactory, and probably would not approach the truth as nearly as that which is now before the Court.

2. The responsibility of Peter Lyons for his co-administrator must be admitted, but the amount due from that co-administrator cannot be assumed, unless his representative were before the Court. It is the duty of the administrator *de bonis non* of John Robinson, to bring him to an account before that forum which can take cognizance of the case, and he is chargeable with great neglect of duty in this respect, as Edmund Pendleton has been dead twenty years. The Court will not, for the present, decide positively on this subject, but must resume the consideration of it, should this unjustifiable delay be continued.

3. The surviving administrator ought to have brought the agents of the administrators to a settlement of their accounts, and this duty, on the death of Peter Lyons, devolved on the administrator *de bonis non,* who is also executor of the surviving administrator. It appears to me to be reasonable that the whole balances due from these agents should be chargeable to him, unless he can free himself from the charge of gross negligence for having failed to call them to a settlement.

The debt due to Peter Lyons, whatever may be its amount, is admitted to be a debt of the first dignity. It is next to be inquired how the remaining creditors rank.

There being many judgments rendered, to be discharged when assets shall come to the hands of the administrators, the first question was, whether these judgments should rank according to their date, and should take rank of other debts on which no judgment had been rendered, or should retain the same rank which would belong to the particular instruments on which they were rendered. This Court is of opinion that they retain their original rank, because every creditor is supposed to be entitled to a judgment when assets, and it is not reasonable that such a judgment should disturb the order in which debts are payable by law, or should have any other effect than to establish the amount, and to give priority to other debts of equal dignity on which either no judgment, or a subsequent judgment, may have been rendered.

Money due to the estate of a deceased person, committed by a court to the said John Robinson, (1 R. C., 1819, p. 389, sec. 60,) or on judgments against the said intestate in his lifetime, are first in rank.[4] Next, are protested bills of exchange, and then specialties. Among these, judgments on bills of exchange first rank according to their date; and next, protested bills on which no judgments have been obtained, if the requisites of the law have been complied with.[5]

Next in order, are debts due on bills which have been paid by securities; on this subject, a question of difficulty has been made. John Smith and John Robinson, were co-sureties on bills of exchange and specialties to a very great amount, on which John Smith paid more than his proportion, and his representatives now claim contribution from the estate of John Robinson.[6] This claim is admitted, but it is contended that it is to be considered merely as a debt on simple contract. The question submitted to the Court is, whether a co-surety who has paid a debt, has a right to stand in the place of the creditor, and to be clothed with all the rights and privileges of the creditor, so far as his equity extends, or can resort only to the implied contract which the law raises in such a case. This is a question which depends on the authority of decided cases; it has occurred most frequently in controversies between a surety and the principal debtor.

In the case of Eppes et al., Executors of Wayles v. Randolph, a bond was executed by Randolph to Bevins, with Wayles as his surety. Randolph afterwards conveyed his estate to his sons, and the creditor obtained a decree against the executors of Wayles for the amount of the bond. A suit was brought by the executors of Wayles against the representatives and heirs of Randolph, alleging the insufficiency of the personal estate, and praying that the estates conveyed to the children might be subjected to the claims of creditors. Other creditors also filed their claims, and insisted that the debt to the executors of Wayles had only the dignity of a simple contract. In delivering his opinion the chancellor said: "That if Wayles's executors had taken an assignment to their trustees of Bevins's bond, they would, in his name, have been entitled to the same relief that Bevins himself would, and that a court of equity would have enjoined the heir of Richard Randolph, deceased, from pleading payment by the sureties' executors: that they ought to have the same remedy as if such assignment had been made." In affirming this part of the chancellor's decree, the president of the court of appeals said: "that the appellees, executors of John Wayles, ought to stand in the place of John Bevins, and be considered as bond creditors, so far as may effect the distribution of remaining assets, but not so as to charge the executors with a devastavit on account of payments or judgments to simple contract creditors."[7]

In the case of Tinsley v. Anderson, 3 Call, 329, where the proceeds of the real estate of a living debtor were to be distributed according to the priority of the several liens upon it, the court said: "that all the creditors by judgments or decrees, ought to be paid out of the general fund, according to the priority of recovery, with this reservation, that when a prior creditor shall not have received his money of sureties, or sued out execution on his judgment within a year, he shall yield priority to subsequent judgments on which executions shall have been so issued, or the money received of sureties. In both instances of the money paid by sureties, as well as in all other instances, sureties ought to be placed in the situation of the creditors they shall have paid, or be bound to pay."[8]

These two cases establish the principle incontrovertibly in Virginia, that the surety who has paid a debt stands, as respects his claim on the principal or his estate, to every purpose in the place of the creditor.

The same principle is recognised in New York, as appears by 4 Johns. Ch. Rep. 123 and 530. In Lawrence v. Cornell et al., 4 Johns. Ch. Rep. 545, it was enforced against a junior mortgagee.[9]

This principle is also recognised in South Carolina, 4 Desaussure, 44.[10]

The principle that a person who has paid money as surety, or on account of another, shall be substituted in the place of the creditor, seems to be familiar in England. In 3 P. Wms. 400, it is laid down by the chancellor, that an executor who has paid beyond the assets which have come to his hands, shall rank as the creditor whose debt he has paid;[11] and in 1 Atk. 134, the chancellor says: "Indeed, where there is a principal and surety, and the surety pays off the debt, he is entitled to have an assignment of the security in order to enable him to obtain satisfaction for what he has paid over and above his own share."[12] The principle is also laid down in 2 Ves., Sen., 302, and 11 Ves., Jr., 22.[13] Indeed it seems to be too well settled to be controverted, and we find it generally laid down as an acknowledged rule rather than decided in a contested case.

But it has been supposed that, though this rule must be admitted as applicable to cases between a surety and his principal, it will not apply between co-sureties.

I can perceive no reason for this distinction. The principle which the cases decide is this: Where a person has paid money for which others were responsible, the equitable claim which such payment gives him on those who were so responsible, shall be clothed with the legal garb with which the contract he has discharged was invested, and he shall be substituted, to every equitable intent and purpose, in the place of the creditor whose claim he has discharged. This principle of substitution is completely established in the books, and being established, it must apply to all persons who are parties to the security, so far as is equitable. The cases suppose the surety to stand in the place of the creditor, as completely as if the instrument had been transferred to him, or to a trustee for his use. Under this supposition, he would be at full liberty to proceed against every person bound by the instrument. Equity would undoubtedly restrain him from obtaining more from any individual than the just proportion of that individual; but to that extent, his claim upon his co-surety is precisely as valid as upon his principal.

In reason, I can draw no distinction between the cases, and none, I think, has been drawn by the courts. In Parsons and Cole v. Dr. Briddock et al., 2 Vernon, 608, the sureties who had paid a bond debt, on which a judgment was obtained against Dr. Briddock, were substituted in the place of the creditor, as against the bail to the action in which the judgment against Briddock had been rendered, and the bail was compelled to pay them the money they had paid to the creditor. In this case, the principle of substitution was applied against a surety.[14]

The liability of co-sureties, and the dignity of a debt in a case where judgment had been discharged by a co-surety, who was entitled to contribution, was decided, on great deliberation, after very solemn argument, in the case of Burrows & Brown *v.* The Administrators of Patrick Carnes, 1 Desaussure, 409.[15]

I was originally strongly inclined to the opinion that, in a case where a party could sue at law, and would be, in a court of law, a simple contract creditor only, he would retain the same rank in a court of equity also, and would not be substituted in the place of the original creditor. But I am satisfied, on examining the subject, that the decisions are otherwise, and I must acquiesce in those decisions.

The representatives of John Smith, then, will rank according to the dignity of the claims on which they have paid more than their equal proportion.

All other sureties will, in like manner, be substituted for the creditor whose debt they have discharged, and will rank as he would have ranked were he before the Court.[16]

Printed, John W. Brockenbrough, *Reports of Cases Decided by the Honourable John Marshall . . .* , II (Philadelphia, 1837), 162–69.

1. An administrator *de bonis non* (an abbreviation for "of the goods not administered") is one who succeeds to the administration of an estate not yet fully settled. In this case James Lyons, son of Peter Lyons, was administrator de bonis non of Robinson's estate and executor of Peter Lyons. For Commissioner Ladd's report, 31 Mar. 1824, see U.S. Cir. Ct., Va., Rec. Bk. XX, 287–368.

2. U.S. Cir. Ct., Va., Rec. Bk. XX, 374–75.

3. JM referred to the commissioner's introductory remarks that preceded his statement of the account (ibid., XX, 288).

4. *Revised Code of Va.,* I, 389.

5. By a 1748 law that governed in this case protested bills of exchange, after the death of the drawer or indorser, were to be considered as of equal dignity with a judgment (Hening, *Statutes,* VI, 86). On the priority of debts to be followed by executors and administrators, see Tucker, *Blackstone's Commentaries,* II, 511 and nn.

6. On John Smith's claim, see U.S. Cir. Ct., Va., Rec. Bk. XX, 285–86, 354–55, 354, 370.

7. Wayles's Executors v. Randolph et al., 2 Call 125, 136–37, 188–89 (Va. Ct. App., 1799). JM served as counsel for the defendants in this case (*PJM,* V, 117–60).

8. Tinsley v. Anderson, 3 Call 329, 333 (Va. Ct. App., 1802).

9. Hayes v. Ward, 4 Johns. Ch. 123 (N.Y. Ch., 1819); Scribner v. Hickok, 4 Johns. Ch. 530 (N.Y. Ch., 1820); Lawrence v. Cornell, 4 Johns. Ch. 545 (N.Y. Ch., 1820).

10. Tankersley v. Anderson, 4 Desaus. 44 (S.C. Eq., 1809).

11. Robinson v. Tonge, 3 P. Wms. 398, 400, 24 Eng. Rep. 1117, 1118 (Ch., 1735).

12. Ex parte Crisp, 1 Atk. 133, 135, 26 Eng. Rep. 87, 88 (Ch., 1744).

13. Ex parte Mills, 2 Ves. jun. 295, 302, 28 Eng. Rep. 640, 643–44 (Ch., 1793); Wright v. Morley, 11 Ves. 12, 22, 32 Eng. Rep. 992, 995 (Ch., 1804). JM mistakenly cited Vesey senior in the first case.

14. Parsons and Cole v. Briddock, 2 Vern. 608, 23 Eng. Rep. 997 (Ch., 1708).

15. Burrows and Brown v. Carnes's Administrators, 1 Desaus. 409 (S.C. Eq., 1794).

16. Judge Tucker, who was absent most of this term, sat in this case, presumably for the purpose of dividing on the question of whether John Smith's representatives could claim according to the dignity of the original creditor (having the rank of judgment creditor) or only that of simple contract creditor. The case was accordingly certified to the Supreme Court, which speaking through Justice Johnson decided the question at the 1827 term in conformity with JM's circuit opinion. The case then went back to the circuit court, where it remained on the docket until 1832, when JM decreed a large balance in favor of Lyons's estate and against Pendleton's representative (U.S. Cir. Ct., Va., Ord. Bk. XI, 503–4; 12 Wheat. 594–98; Mays, *Edmund Pendleton*, I, 338–40 n. 93).

Hoffman v. Porter
Opinion
U.S. Circuit Court, Virginia, 10 December 1824

John Hoffman (1796–1846), the plaintiff, was a member of a prominent merchant family of Baltimore. His brother, David Hoffman (1784–1854), earned a notable reputation as a writer on legal education and as a teacher at the University of Maryland. As surviving partner of Peter Hoffman & Son, John Hoffman brought an action of covenant against William Porter, Jr., of Fredericksburg in December 1816. Porter had sold two tracts of land in Spotsylvania County to the Baltimore firm in April 1800. The declaration alleged breach of covenant for conveying a defective title. The defendant entered two pleas and a demurrer to the declaration in May 1817. The case was continued on the rule docket and the court docket until December 1824, when further pleadings were filed, including the plaintiff's demurrer to the plaintiff's first plea. Marshall's opinion of 10 December 1824 dealt with the issues arising on the demurrers (J. Thomas Scharf, *History of Western Maryland: Being a History of Frederick, Montgomery, Carroll, Washington, Allegany, and Garrett Counties* [2 vols.; Baltimore, 1968], I, 459; "The Diary of Robert Gilmor," *Maryland Historical Magazine*, XVII [1922], 238–40, 254; Thomas L. Hollowak, comp., *Index to the Marriages and Deaths in the Baltimore Sun, 1837–1850* [Baltimore, 1978], 279; U.S. Cir. Ct., Va., Ord. Bk. XI, 510, 514; declaration [Dec. 1816]; copy of deed, 10 Apr. 1800, Hoffman v. Porter, U.S. Cir. Ct., Va., Ended Cases [Unrestored], 1837, Vi).

This suit is brought by John Hoffman, surviving partner of "Peter Hoffman & Son," against William Porter, to recover damages for the breach of covenants contained in a deed conveying land to "Peter Hoffman & Son."

The declaration states, that by a certain indenture, made the 10th day of April, in the year 1800, between William Porter the younger, and Polly his wife, of the one part, and Peter Hoffman & Son of the other part, which son is the said John, the plaintiff, they, the said William Porter the younger, and Polly his wife, in consideration of the sum of £1002 10s. current money of Virginia, conveyed to the said Peter Hoffman & Son, merchants and partners, a certain tract of land in the deed mentioned; and the said William Porter the younger, for himself and his heirs, covenanted to and with the said Peter Hoffman & Son, that they, the said William Porter the younger, and Polly his wife, had a good title to the premises, and that the said Peter Hoffman & Son might quietly enjoy the same; that the said Peter Hoffman had departed this life, and all his rights in the land and covenant survived to the plaintiff. The averment is, that the said William Porter, and Polly his wife, were not, at the date of the said deed, possessed of a good title to the said land, nor did the said Peter Hoffman & Son, in the lifetime of the said Peter, nor had the plaintiff since his death, enjoyed the same quietly; but in consequence of the defective title of the said William Porter the younger, and Polly his wife, the plaintiff has been molested, &c. in the enjoyment thereof.

The defendant craved oyer of the deed, which is spread on the record, and appears to be a conveyance from William Porter, senior, and Margaret his wife, and William Porter, junior, and Polly his wife, of the land in the declaration mentioned, to Peter Hoffman & Son, of Baltimore. The covenants for good title and quiet enjoyment are, that the said William Porter, senior, and Margaret his wife, and William Porter, junior, and Polly his wife, have good title, and that the said Peter Hoffman & Son may quietly enjoy the premises.

The defendant pleads,

1st. That he was formerly impleaded for the same cause of action, which suit, by the judgment of the Court, the same being agreed by the parties, was dismissed.[1]

2d. That the covenants stated by the plaintiff in his declaration, were none of them made with the plaintiff.

He also demurs to the declaration.

The plaintiff demurs to the plaintiff's[2] first plea, and the defendant joins in demurrer.

The validity of the plea depends on the question, whether the judgment rendered in the former action is a bar to a new suit?

The practice in the English courts furnishes no exact precedent for the case. The books mention a retraxit, a judgment of nonsuit, or a discontinuance. A retraxit only is a bar to a new action. This, I think, is not a retraxit. In a retraxit, the plaintiff openly renounces his action.[3] In this case, some agreement is made between the parties for the termination of the existing suit, and the entry is made by the clerk without any exercise of judgment on the part of the Court. It is the mere act of this party, and, I believe, is not, in the common practice, considered as more than a dismission of his suit by the plaintiff.

But this demurrer to the plea, as well as the demurrer to the declaration, brings before the Court the validity of the declaration, and, consequently, of the conveyance which it sets forth.

The conveyance is to Peter Hoffman & Son, and this action is brought by John Hoffman, who states himself to have been the partner in trade of Peter Hoffman, and to have been the son intended in the conveyance.

The question is, whether John Hoffman can take as a purchaser by this description?

That the word "son," connected with other words which ascertain the son intended, is a word of purchase, has been very well settled. In all the conveyances in what is termed "strict settlement," a conveyance to A., remainder to the first, second, third, and fourth sons of B., has been considered as unquestionably valid. If these words are good to pass a remainder, I can perceive no reason why they might not pass a present estate. If, then, this conveyance had been to the first son of Peter Hoffman, the estate might have passed to the first son. So, if he had been an only son.

But it is admitted that a conveyance to the son of A., he having several sons, would be void for uncertainty, and that no averment could make it good.

The question then is, whether there is any thing in this deed to ascertain the son who is the purchaser?

Peter Hoffman was in partnership with his son John, and the firm was known by the name of "Peter Hoffman & Son," I am disposed to think that this circumstance may designate the son intended in the deed.

I will not pretend that this question is free from doubt. But the justice of the case is clearly with the plaintiff, is clearly in favour of giving validity to the conveyance, and, I do not think that law ought to be separated from justice, where it is at most doubtful.

The demurrer to the plea is sustained, and that to the declaration is overruled.[4]

Printed, John W. Brockenbrough, *Reports of Cases Decided by the Honourable John Marshall* . . . , II (Philadelphia, 1837), 156–59.

1. A case between these parties was originally brought in the state district court at Fredericksburg (copy of record, 7 Oct. 1807, Hoffman v. Porter).

2. Should be "defendant's."

3. JM may have consulted the discussion in Blackstone, *Commentaries*, III, 295–96.

4. The defendant entered additional pleas in 1825, to which the plaintiff filed replications and demurrers in 1829. The case continued on the docket until Nov. 1837 (U.S. Cir. Ct., Va., Ord. Bk. XII, 310, 377, 400, 401; U.S. Cir. Ct., Va., Index to Ended Causes, 1790–1861, Vi).

To Bushrod Washington

My dear Sir   Richmond Decr. 11th. 1824

In conformity with your wish expressed in your last letter I have deposited the boxes in the steam boat addressed to You to the care of Mr

Herbert.[1] The captain received them from me & assured me that he would put them in his room & deliver them safely at Alexandria.

I shall be much gratified if you can give the letters a reading. There is a letter written to General Greene while Quarter Master General in Decr. 1779 or Jany. 1780, I forget which, complaining of delay in furnishing him with quarters at Morristown. I have thought that letter should be omitted but believe I deferred st⟨ri⟩king it out till you should see it, or neglected it from forgetfulness.[2] If you read the letters I ask your attention to it, and if you should not read them nor open the boxes but send them on to Mr. Small I wish you would, if you concur with me, request him to omit it. There is also a letter written I think to Mr Madison, while the constitution was depending before the conventions in which he mentions Colo. G. Mason & Colo. R. H. Lee rather in terms of reprobation. I thought that the passage should be omitted or the names left blank. I have not however executed this intention & suggest it to you for your consideration.[3] I am dear Sir yours truely

J Marshall

ALS, NHi. Addressed to Washington at Mount Vernon; postmarked Richmond, 11 Dec. Endorsed by Washington.

1. Probably Maurice Herbert.

2. Washington to Nathanael Greene, 22 Jan. 1780 (Richard K. Showman et al., eds., *The Papers of Nathanael Greene*, V [Chapel Hill, N.C., 1989], 302–3). Jared Sparks printed the letter in *The Writings of George Washington* . . . (12 vols.; Boston, 1834–39), VI, 449–50.

3. Washington to James Madison, 10 Oct. 1787 (Robert A. Rutland et al., eds., *The Papers of James Madison*, X [Chicago, 1977], 189–90). Sparks omitted the offending passage in his edition (*Writings of Washington*, IX, 267–69).

To James Monroe

Sir   Richmond Decr. 13th. 1824

I am indebted to your polite attention for a copy of your message to Congress and am much gratified by this mark of your recollection.[1]

While I take the liberty to express my personal regrets that your retirement approaches so nearly, and that circumstances are supposed to forbid your continuing to afford your services to your country, I may be permitted to congratulate you on the auspicious circumstances which have attended your course as chief Magistrate of the United States, and which crown its termination. You may look back with pleasure to several very interesting events which have taken place during your administration, and have the rare felicity not to find the retrospect darkened by a single spot the review of which ought to pain yourself or your fellow citizens. With great & respectful esteem, I remain your Obedt.

J Marshall

ALS, Monroe Papers, DLC. Addressed to the president and franked; postmarked Richmond, 13 Dec. Endorsed by Monroe "private message."

1. President Monroe sent his final annual message to Congress on 7 Dec. (James D. Richardson, ed., *A Compilation of the Messages and Papers of the Presidents, 1789–1897* [11 vols.; Washington, D.C., 1896–99], II, 248–64).

Byrd v. Byrd's Executor
Opinion and Decree
U.S. Circuit Court, Virginia, 16 December 1824

This was a friendly suit for the distribution of the estate of the late William Byrd III of Westover, who had died in 1777. His wife Mary served as executrix of her husband's heavily encumbered estate until her death in 1814. At the time he filed his bill in chancery in December 1822, Charles Willing Byrd (1770–1828), who had been U.S. District Judge for Ohio since 1803, was the only surviving son of the testator. He contended that the estate had a large surplus beyond any possible claim against it that should now be divided among the legatees. William Byrd Page, executor of Mary Byrd and a defendant in this suit, stated that he wished to retain a sufficient fund to meet outstanding claims and that he did not feel safe in disposing of this fund without directions from the court. The other defendants were a surviving daughter and the representatives of the deceased children of William Byrd. After the filing of the bill and answers, the court directed the commissioner to make a report of the administration account of Byrd's estate. Marshall's opinion was based on the commissioner's report of 12 December 1823 and accompanied the court's interlocutory decree of 16 December 1824 (U.S. Cir. Ct., Va., Ord. Bk. XI, 318–19, 525–26; bill in chancery [filed 28 Dec. 1822]; answer of William Byrd Page, 31 Dec. 1822; commissioner's report, 12 Dec. 1823, Byrd v. Byrd, U.S. Cir. Ct., Va., Ended Cases [Restored], 1838, Vi; W. H. Burtner, Jr., "Charles Willing Byrd," *Ohio Archaeological and Historical Quarterly*, XLI [1932], 237–40).

Byrd
v
Byrds representatives

This suit is brought for the distribution of the estate of William Byrd ¶1
decd. among his legatees.

The testator, by his last will, created, in the first instance, a fund consist- ¶2
ing of a tract of land, one hundred negroes, and other personal property,
for the payment of his debts. He then gives to his wife for life, the planta-
tions of *Westover* and *Buckland* with all the remaining negroes and stock of
all sorts; and adds "It is my will and desire that at the death of my dearest
wife all my estates whatsoever, consisting of land, negroes, stocks of all
sorts, plate, books, and furniture be sold as soon as convenient, and the

money arising from the sale thereof be equally divided among all my children that are alive at the time of my dear wife's death, deducting therefrom such sums as they may claim under the wills of" his mother & son William. The testator then enumerates advances he had made to several of his children, which are to be deducted from the amount of their respective portions, and also states contingencies on which the legacies of individuals are to be forfeited; after which he adds "should any of my children die before my wife and leave lawful issue, the share of my deceased child shall go to them, and be equally divided." "I give to my son John, over and above what he will share of the money aforesaid all my right to the mines in Fincastle known by the name of Chiswells mines and two thousand acres of the land I claim under his Majesty's proclamation of 1763. I likewise give to him his choice of ten negroes, after my wife has chose such as she pleases."[1]

¶3   The testator then devises to several sons certain portions of the land surveyed for him, under the proclamation of 1763, over and above their several shares of the fund directed to be distributed among them all, and to his daughters, in like manner, certain slaves by name.

¶4   The whole estate including the specific legacies of slaves has been sold and the debts paid; and there remains the sum of $28645.45. to be distributed among the legatees.[2] The specific legatees claim their legacies as a charge upon this joint fund, to be paid before the distribution directed by the will. This claim is resisted by the other legatees.

¶5   It has been placed on two grounds.
1st. The will of the testator.
2d. On the principle of Marshalling assets.
1st. The will of the testator.

¶6   In its construction, the whole is to be taken together, and the intent is to be collected from the entire instrument without paying too much regard to the arrangement of the clauses. It is not denied that the testator intended the specific legacies as additional to the distributive share of each child in the aggregate fund. He says so in express words; and there is no contrary opinion advanced in any part of the will. He supposed that the fund assigned for the payment of debts would be sufficient; and makes his will under that impression. Had the fact conformed to this opinion, and the whole estate except that fund had remained together, untouched by debts, it is not probable that this controversy ever could have arisen. It would scarcely be denied that a bequest to his son John of ten slaves over and above his equal share of his estate, was what it purported to be; and that those ten slaves were to be taken by John, in addition to his equal distributive share of the general fund. The mistake of the testator respecting the adequacy of the fund for the payment of debts, cannot change the construction of his will in this particular. His intention respecting his specific bequests remains the same; and though we may conjecture that he would have made some change in this respect had he understood the true state of his affairs, no court can undertake to make the change for him. In adjusting the rights of the parties then, this intent must be kept in view, and the enquiry is, how does it affect the fund now to be distributed?

After setting apart one hundred slaves for the payment of his debts, the ¶7 testator gives to his wife Westover & Buckland, & all the remaining negroes, stock &c for her life, and directs that, at her death, his whole estate of every description shall be sold, and the money arising from the sale be equally divided among his children.

This clause certainly requires an equal distribution of all the money ¶8 arising from the property to be sold under it; and it becomes material to enquire what property it comprehends. The language is that it comprehends his whole estate; and if these words are not clearly restrained by other parts of the will, the direction must be considered as extending to the whole.

I think it perfectly clear that they are so restrained. The testator directs ¶9 his whole estate to be sold at the death of his wife. This direction can operate only on property which shall at that time form a part of his estate. Property previously disposed of cannot be the subject of this clause. Thus he devises two thousand acres of his military land to his son John. The devise operates as a conveyance, and, on the death of the devisor, vests the land in the devisee. It ceased to be a part of the estate of the testator when that estate is to be sold, and consequently, cannot be acted on by that clause under consideration. In like manner the testator devises separate tracts of land to his sons Thomas, Otway, and Charles. Upon his death, these lands cease to be a part of his estate, and vest in the devisees. To construe the clause directing the sale of his estate at the death of his wife, as extending to them, would be to annul these devises, and to set aside a large portion of the will.

The same principle applies with equal force to the specific legacies. ¶10 After the devise to his son Charles of 1000 acres of land in the county of Fincastle the testator adds "I likewise give him his man Tom & little Jack White, and his choice of two negroe girls, over and above his share of the money aforesaid."

This bequest was obviously intended to take effect immediately. From ¶11 the language of the will Tom was probably at the time in possession of the legatee. It is impossible to reconcile this bequest with an intention to sell these negroes and to place the money in a common fund out of which the legatee was afterwards to draw it. It is not their proceeds which he is to draw from the fund over & above his equal share in it, but he is to have the negroes themselves over and above that equal share. So with respect to the other specific legacies. It is perfectly clear that they are not to be sold, but are to pass specifically to the several legatees.

Between those legacies which express the names of the slaves which are ¶12 given, and those which express only their number, leaving the choice to the legatee, there can be no difference so far as respects this point. The intention of the testator to exempt them from the clause directing the sale of his estate is equally clear. Indeed in the expressions of the clause giving ten slaves to his son John, there are some additional evidences of this intent. He shows that the selection is to be made by his son during the continuance of his wife's life estate, and consequently anterior to the sale of his estate, since he restrains his sons right of choice, so far as to prevent its interfering with the choice of his wife. He gives to his wife "all the remaining negroes," for life, and yet he gives his son John his choice of ten slaves out of these remaining negroes; but, in selecting them, he is not to interfere with the choice of his wife. The plain meaning is, that after setting apart the fund for the payment of debts, his son is to chuse ten slaves; but if in exercising this right, he should take any which his wife might be particularly anxious to retain, her choice should, in such case be respected. It is perfectly clear that the will is to be construed as if the clause giving all the remaining negroes to his wife for life had been postponed to those which give specific legacies. The word "remaining" refers to all the clauses giving specific legacies, as well as to that which constitutes the fund for the payment of debts. This avoids the manifest re-pugnancy which would otherwise exist in these different bequests. Upon this construction, which gives effect to what I think the obvious intent of the testator, the specific legacies are neither comprized in the bequest to his wife nor in the clause directing the sale of his estate; and consequently they compose no part of the fund which is to be equally divided among his children.

¶13   So far as the intent of the testator can be carried into effect, the lega-tees were entitled, during the life of Mrs. Byrd to their specific legacies; but the law interposes, and casts the whole personal estate upon the exx. for the benefit of creditors. Their claims must be satisfied, before any interest can vest in the legatees; but after the satisfaction of their claims, should any of the slaves specifically bequeathed, or their descendants remain unsold, the legatees are unquestionably entitled to them. If they have been sold ⟨by⟩ the exx. not[3] for the payment of debts, but under that clause of the will which directs the sale of the whole estate, the money must represent them, and remain the property of the person who was entitled to the slaves themselves. If it has been carried into the aggregate fund, it has been improperly placed there, and must be taken from it. If the slaves have been sold for the payment of debts, the rights of the parties must be governed by those principles which regulate courts in marshalling assetts.[4]

¶14   2d. Have the legatees, whose specific legacies have been sold and the money applied to the payment of debts, a right to demand satisfaction from the general fund?

¶15   Had this fund been derived from the personal estate alone, as that estate was chargeable with debts in the first instance, and ought to have been exhausted before recourse was had to the specific legacies, the fund would, unquestionably be liable, in the first instance, to compensate the specific legatees for such of their legacies as had been sold for an object with which it was first chargeable.

Had the fund been derived entirely from real estate, and that had been charged with the payment of debts, the same principle would have governed the case. But had the real estate not been subjected to the payment of debts either by the will of the testator, or by the law of the land, I know of no case which has gone so far as to subject it to the claims of legatees whose legacies have been taken by creditors. In this case the testator has not subjected his real estate to the payment of debts. It is therefore liable no farther than for specialty debts which bind the heir, and can be charged with legacies so far only as the personal estate has been applied in payment of debts for which the real was liable. ¶16

Being a mixed fund, composed of the proceeds partly of personal, and partly of real estate, that portion of it which comes from the personal is liable in the first instance, to make good such specific legacies as may have been sold for debts; and if that be insufficient the money arising from the sale of real estate must be applied to the same object, so far as debts by which the land was bound have been satisfied from the personal estate. ¶17

A difficulty arises in adjusting the amount between the real and personal estate; from the fact which is alleged at the bar, that many of the specialty debts which have been discharged by the personal estate, have been paid off in paper money; and it is contended that these as between those parties, are advances made at the time of payment, which must be subjected to the scale of depreciation established by law.[5] ¶18

It is certainly true that the legatees have no legal claim on the real estate, to be reimbursed monies paid by the personal property, in discharge of debts for which both were bound; and there is great reason in the position that their title to the aid of a court of equity can be coextensive only with their equity. But how far does their equity extend. The real estate is undoubtedly relieved to the extent of the debt from which it is discharged; and can make no just objection to retributing the personal estate to the extent of the injury that estate has sustained; but I am not satisfied that a principle which courts of equity have taken up solely for the protection of simple contract creditors & legatees, can be justifiably so applied as to enable those persons to make large profits out of the real estate. Admitting the real estate to be relieved to the amount of one thousand dollars, by the advance of five dollars from the personal, a court of equity might not interpose to restrain those entitled to the personal estate from asserting their legal claim to its extent; but I am not satisfied that a court of equity ought to interpose in aid of those persons beyond the sum actually advanced. But there is much difficulty in ascertaining what this sum is. The value of the money, on the day of its payment, is not, ¶19 necessarily, the real amount of loss sustained by the person making the payment. The depreciation was continual; and as the gain of the real estate is the whole nominal sum, the reimbursement ought to be the whole actual loss of the personal estate.

¶20   It will be extremely difficult to adjust this subject with any degree of certainty. If the parties can make any arrangement satisfactory to themselves or state any account by which the necessary information can be given to the court, I shall be much disposed to apply the principle which has been stated to this part of the case.

¶21   Having determined that the legatees who claim under the will of the testator a certain number of slaves not named by him, but to be chosen by themselves, and it being stated that these legacies are unsatisfied, it remains to determine how they are now to be satisfied.

¶22   If after the payment of debts there were negroes remaining in the estate not given by name, they would be liable to these legacies, if the legatees chose to take them. If there were no such slaves remaining then the value of the legacies must be determined on some equitable principle.

[Decree]

Byrds legatees
v
Byrds representative

This cause came on to be heard on the papers formerly read and on the report of commissioner Ladd and was argued by counsel on consideration whereof this court is of opinion that the specific legacies given in the will of the late William Byrd are not comprehended in the clause which gives the remainder of his slaves to his wife for life, nor in that which directs the sale of all his estate at her death, but were intended to pass immediately to the legatees, and might be claimed by them as soon as the condition of the estate with respect to creditors would justify the exx. in paying legacies. If, therefore, after the payment of debts any slaves bequeathed by name in the will, or their descendants, remained in the possession of the personal representative of William Byrd, the person to whom the same were bequeathed, or his or her representative would be entitled to demand them; and if they have been sold, and the proceeds are not required for the payment of debts, such person is entitled to the money arising from the sale.

And this court is farther of opinion that the representative of John Byrd to whom ten slaves were given, to be chosen by himself, and of Charles Byrd, to whom two girls were given to be chosen by himself, those legatees or their representatives might exercise the right of choice given in the will, if the condition of the estate after the payment of debts would admit of it; and if such slaves have been sold then they are entitled to the money arising from the number which they respectively claim with interest from the expiration of the credit given at the sale. But if the number to be chosen did not remain unsold when the debts were discharged, so that these legacies cannot be satisfied by receiving the slaves themselves, then they ought to be satisfied out of the residuary fund, so far as the principles hereinafter stated will allow them to resort to it.

That portion of the fund which arises from the personal estate is liable in the first instance to the payment of the specific legacies which have been sold for the payment of debts; and if this shall prove insufficient, an account must be taken of the personal estate which has been applied to the payment of debts that bound the land, and the fund arising from the real estate must be charged to the amount so paid by the personal[6] estate. If in taking this account it shall appear that specialties binding the land have been paid by the personal estate in paper money, and it can be shown what the real value of such paper money was to the personal estate, the real estate ought to be charged only to the extent of that value.[7]

AD, Marshall Judicial Opinions, PPAmP; printed, John W. Brockenbrough, *Reports of Cases Decided by the Honourable John Marshall . . .*, II (Philadelphia, 1837), 171–78. Decree, AD, Byrd v. Byrd, U.S. Cir. Ct., Va., Ended Cases (Restored), 1838, Vi. For JM's deletions and interlineations, see Textual Notes below.

1. Will of William Byrd III (copy), 5 Feb. 1777, Byrd v. Byrd. The Proclamation of 1763 provided land bounties for officers and soldiers residing in America who had served in the French and Indian War (Hening, *Statutes*, VII, 666).

2. Commissioner's report, 12 Dec. 1823, Byrd v. Byrd. The commissioner found a surplus of real assets amounting to $1,786.29 and of personal assets amounting to $26,859.16, which together totaled $28,645.45.

3. Brockenbrough crossed through "exx. not" and inserted "executor not."

4. A creditor by bond in which the heir was bound could choose from the personal or real estate to satisfy his claim. If such creditors exhausted the personal estate, a court of equity by the principle of marshaling assets would allow simple contract creditors to stand in place of the bond creditors and recover from the real estate the amount charged on the personal estate (*PJM*, V, 148–49, 156 n. 3).

5. By a law enacted at the Nov. 1781 session the Virginia legislature established a scale of depreciation for reducing contracts made during the time paper money passed current (1777–1781) to their actual specie value (Hening, *Statutes*, X, 471–74).

6. JM wrote "real," which someone else crossed through and corrected to "personal."

7. See the further opinion in this case at 9 June 1825.

Textual Notes

Title	l. 1	~~Bird~~ Byrd
¶ 2	l. 1	instance, [*erasure*] a fund
	ll. 1–2	consisting of ↑a tract of land,↓ one hundred negroes, ~~a tract of land,~~ and
¶ 3	l. 2	him, ~~as an officer,~~ under the
	l. 4	daughters, ↑in like manner,↓ certain slaves by name. ~~To his son charles~~
¶ 4	l. 1	the ↑specific↓ legacies of slaves
¶ 5	l. 2	The ~~intent~~ ↑will↓ of the

¶ 6   l. 1 beg.   In ~~construing this instrument,~~ ↑its construction,↓ the
　　　 l. 3   It ~~is apparent~~ is not
　　　 ll. 4–5   share of ↑each [*erasure*] child in↓ the
　　　 l. 8   will ~~on~~ ↑under↓ ~~this~~ that impression
　　　 l. 20   him. ↑In adjusting↓ ~~The~~ the rights
¶ 7   l. 2   his wife ↑Westover & Buckland, &↓ all
¶ 8   ll. 5–6   extending to ~~his~~ ↑the↓ whole ~~estate~~.
¶ 9   ll. 7–8   the testator ↑when that estate is to be sold, and consequently,↓
　　　　　　　　 ~~and~~ cannot
¶11   l. 2   probably ↑at the time↓ in possession of
　　　 l. 6   share ↑in it,↓ but he
　　　 l. 7   above ~~his~~ ↑that↓ equal share ~~of the common fund~~. So
　　　 l. 9   to the ↑several↓ legatees.
¶12   l. 1 beg.   Between those ~~slaves which are given by~~ ↑legacies which
　　　　　　　　 express the↓ names
　　　 l. 2   express ~~a certain~~ ↑only their↓ number,
　　　 l. 11   negroes," [*erasure*] ↑for life, and↓ yet
¶13   ll. 12–13   If ~~they~~ ↑the slaves↓ have been
　　　 l. 14   must be ~~regulated~~ ↑governed↓ by those
¶15   ll. 1–2   as ~~that fund would be~~ ↑that estate was↓ chargeable
　　　 ll. 2–3   and ought to ~~be~~ ↑have been↓ exhausted
　　　 ll. 3–4   legacies, ~~it . . . .~~ ↑the fund would,↓
　　　 l. 6   first chargeable. ~~H~~
¶16   l. 5   it to ↑the claims of↓ legatees
　　　 l. 6   taken ~~for the p~~ by creditors.
　　　 l. 9   charged with ↑these↓ legacies ~~no farther~~ so far
¶17   l. 1   composed ↑of the proceeds↓ partly of
　　　 l. 2   which ~~is~~ ↑comes from the↓ personal
¶18   ll. 4–5   that these ↑as between those parties,↓ are
¶19   l. 2   estate, ~~for it~~ to be reimbursed
　　　 ll. 2–3   property, [*erasure*] in discharge
　　　 l. 3   bound; and ~~their title to~~ there
　　　 ll. 6–7   from which it [*erasure*] is discharged;
　　　 l. 22   the whole ↑actual↓ loss
¶20   l. 2   If ~~gentlemen~~ ↑the parties↓ can make
　　　 ll. 2–3   arrangement ↑satisfactory to themselves↓ or
¶22   l. 1 beg.   If ~~on the death of Mr. Byrd~~ ↑after the payment of debts↓ there

To [Thomas L. Winthrop]

Sir   Richmond Decr. 30th. 1824

   I have received your favor of the 30th. of Novr., and beg you to beleive
that I estimate as I ought, the kindness expressed towards me for which I
am indebted to your goodness.[1]

   I regret very much that I am not in possession of the papers you mention, or of any others which could be useful to Mr. Savage.[2] If Mr. Win-

throp ever tran⟨s⟩mitted papers of any description for me, they have never reached me.[3] With great respect and esteem, I am, Sir your Obedt. Servt

J MARSHALL

ALS, MeB. Endorsed (by Winthrop?). Identity of recipient based on repository information and on internal evidence.

1. Letter not found. Thomas L. Winthrop (1760–1841) graduated from Harvard in 1780 and followed a mercantile career. He served as lieutenant governor of Massachusetts from 1826 to 1832 and later as president of both the Massachusetts Historical Society and the American Antiquarian Society. He was a descendant of John Winthrop, the first governor of the Massachusetts Bay Colony (William Jenks, "Memoir of the Late Thomas L. Winthrop," *Collections of the Massachusetts Historical Society*, ser. 4, vol. 2 [Boston, 1854], 202–14).

2. James Savage (1784–1873), a Boston native and graduate of Harvard College (1803), was a noted New England antiquarian. He was then engaged in preparing an annotated edition of John Winthrop's history of New England. See *The History of New England from 1630 to 1649 by John Winthrop* (2 vols.; Boston, 1825–26).

3. The reference is possibly to James Bowdoin Winthrop (d. 1833) or to John Temple Winthrop (d. 1843), sons of Thomas L. Winthrop (Jenks, "Memoir of the Late Thomas L. Winthrop," *Collections of the Massachusetts Historical Society*, ser. 4, vol. 2 [1854], 211).

To [John C. Calhoun]

Dear Sir   Richmond Jany. 19. 25

This will be presented to you by Mr. Dixon a young gentleman who is desirous of entering into the army or navy of the United States. I am not particularly acquainted with him, though I know him well enough to beleive that he will perform the duties of either situation with propriety. I write to say that his Father was a most respectable gentleman, connected with many of the best families of our country, and very generally esteemed.

With my congratulations both to yourself and our country on the late election of Vice President I remain dear Sir, Your Obedt. Servt

J MARSHALL

ALS (owned by Independence Hall of Chicago, 1967). Addressee identified by internal evidence.

From DeWitt Clinton

Sir   Albany 4 february 1825[1]

Mr Littell an enterprising, intelligent and respectable Citizen of Philadelphia will communicate to you a plan which he has projected for the promotion of education, literature and sciences on an extensive scale. He has conferred with me on this subject. Approving its outlines and viewing you as a sincere and distinguished friend of these great interests, I have taken the liberty of recommending him and his plan to your favorable consideration.[2] I have the honor to be, With great respect, Your most Obdt Sevt

AL (letterbook copy), DeWitt Clinton Papers, NNC.

1. DeWitt Clinton (1769–1828), best known for his role in promoting the Erie Canal, served as governor of New York from 1817 to 1823 and again from 1825 to 1828. JM was one of six designated persons to whom this letter was to be sent and whose names were listed below the body of the letter. The others were Thomas Jefferson, James Kent, William Wirt, John Quincy Adams, and John C. Calhoun.

2. Eliakim Littell (1797–1870) edited and published literary periodicals in Philadelphia during the 1820s and 1830s. He moved to Boston in 1844 and began publishing *Littell's Living Age*. As he explained to Jefferson, Littell proposed a scheme to publish books for educational curricula. He intended to petition the Pennsylvania legislature to grant a lottery for the sale of the books and then apply to each of the other states for permission to sell tickets or perhaps obtain authority for a general sale from Congress (Littell to Jefferson, 17 Feb. 1825, Jefferson Papers, DLC).

To Mary W. Marshall

My dearest Polly   Washington Feby. 8th. 1825

I reached this place yesterday & paid our accustomed visit to the President whom I found in good health & looking quite chearful. I am now sitting by a good fire in an excellent room, the same I occupied last year, scribling to my beloved wife. Neither Judge Johnson nor Story has arrived, and our brother Todd I am told is so very unwell that we have reason to fear we shall never see him again. Story too has been sick, but is on the way and we look for him today.

I have never found the roads so good before in the winter season. I reached Alexandria on saturday evening before five, and have never before got in by daylight, seldom earlier than nine, and once or twice as late as eleven. I rejoiced that I had not taken the steamboat.

I have seldom gone counter to your advice without repenting it; but as I came on friday & saturday, hugging myself up in my warm cloak, I could not help congratulating myself on the comfort I enjoyed compared to the suffering I should have felt had I come without it.

I rode from Hanover court house to Fredericksburg with a Mrs. Stone, formerly Miss Booth, a niece of Mrs. Dandridge. She told me that the first ball at which she had ever been was in Richmond when she accompanied her aunt in Mrs. Amblers coach, and that both you and myself were in the same carriage, then unmarried. She said she had never seen me since, and that when I got into the stage she remembered the evening and all she saw as perfectly as if it had been yesterday.

I dined on sunday with my Aunt Keith.[1] She was at first very much affected, but became chearful in a few minutes. I was visited on Saturday night by my nephew William Marshall, son of my brother Lewis, who is studying divinity at the Theological school in Alexandria.[2] He is a very promising and a remarkably fine looking young man. He dined at my Aunt Keiths on sunday, & I was very much pleased with him.

I cannot help hoping that Mr. Picket has been able to fill the ice house on friday & saturday. If those two days have passed away without accomplishing the object I fear all the ⟨chance?⟩ is over & that we must look else wher⟨e for ice?⟩ unless he should fill it with a cargo ⟨from the?⟩ north. He spoke of this bef⟨ore . . . ⟩. Farewell my d⟨earest Polly⟩

⟨J Marshall⟩

AL[S], Marshall Papers, ViW. Addressed to Mrs. Marshall in Richmond. Bottom portion of second sheet torn off.

1. Elizabeth Contee Keith.
2. William Louis Marshall (1803–1869) studied at his father's school in Kentucky before attending the Virginia Theological Seminary in Alexandria. In 1825 he married Ann Lee, daughter of the late Henry "Light-Horse Harry" Lee. He later moved to Baltimore, where he served as a clergyman and then as a lawyer. After the Civil War he settled in Missouri and spent his last years in California (Paxton, *Marshall Family,* 167).

To James M. Marshall

My dear brother   Washington Feb. 14. 1825

You were probably as much surprized as I was to find that the President was elected on the first ballot. It is believed by many that this effect is in some measure to be ascribed to Kremers letter.[1] That was and is thought a sheer calumny; and the resentment of Clays friends probably determined some of the western members who were hesitating. It is supposed to have had some influence elsewhere. The vote of New York was not decided five minutes before the ballots were taken. Mr. Vanraensaeller, I am assured did not consent to vote for Mr. Adams till it was ascertained that his vote determined the election, and did it then with much reluctance.[2]

There is a good deal of speculation respecting the cabinet. Mr. Crawford has been offered the treasury & has refused it. This is certain. It is said, I know not on what authority, that the department of state is offered to Mr. Clay and that he has agreed to accept it. This is asserted with some confidence, but it is mccr common rumor. Mr. Adams will undoubtedly wish to strengthen himself in the west, and Mr. Clay, if his vote has not impaired his influence, is strong in that quarter. Yet Kremers letter was supposed to interpose considerable obstacles to this arrangement. I at first thought them insuperable; but on reflection I doubt whether his rejection or acceptance of the department will make any difference in that respect. His enemies will say that the disclosure made by Kremer has prevented the execution of the contract; and his friends that he ought not to be driven out of his course by an atrocious falsehood.

Some suspicions are whispered that Cheves or Serjeant will be called to the treasury.[3] Not a conjecture has been ⟨ . . . ⟩. The conduct of Genl. J⟨ackson . . . ⟩ approved. He appea⟨rs . . . ⟩ the usual party at ⟨ . . . ⟩ chearfulness; and ⟨ . . . ⟩ on his election. His ⟨ . . . ⟩ friends to a public ⟨ . . . ⟩ment and discret⟨ion . . . ⟩.

I saw ⟨ . . . ⟩ some enquiries re⟨ . . . ⟩ has prevailed upon ⟨ . . . ⟩ to argue a very gr⟨ . . . ⟩ of appeals in which ⟨ . . . ⟩ credit.

I cannot lea⟨ . . . ⟩ ⟨ex⟩amination. As I hea⟨ . . . ⟩ entertained no do⟨ubt⟩ ⟨ . . . ⟩ told that he ⟨was⟩ ⟨ . . . ⟩ I feel a good dea⟨ . . . ⟩

⟨J MARSHALL⟩

AL[S], William Keeney Bixby Collection, MoSW. Part of second sheet (including signature) missing, having been clipped along vertical axis.

1. George Kremer (1775–1854) of Pennsylvania sat in the House of Representatives from 1823 to 1829. A rabid supporter of Andrew Jackson, Kremer had recently identified himself as the author of a letter first published in the Philadelphia *Columbian Observer* on 28 Jan. 1825 that stated Adams had offered Clay the secretaryship of state in exchange for Clay's support (Philip Shriver Klein, *Pennsylvania Politics, 1817–1832: A Game without Rules* [Philadelphia, 1940], 183–84; James F. Hopkins and Mary W. M. Hargreaves, eds., *The Papers of Henry Clay,* IV [Lexington, Ky., 1972], 48, 52–53).

2. Stephen Van Rensselaer (1764–1839) represented New York in the House of Representatives from 1822 to 1829. He cast the deciding vote of the divided New York delegation for Adams on 9 Feb. (George Dangerfield, *The Awakening of American Nationalism, 1815–1828* [New York, 1965], 226–28).

3. Langdon Cheves (1776–1857) of South Carolina had served as a member of the House of Representatives from 1810 to 1815, as justice of the South Carolina Court of Appeals from 1816 to 1819, and as president of the Second Bank of the United States from 1819 to 1822.

To [William Wirt]

Dear Sir   [ca. 20 February 1825]

We are truely sorry for the continuance of your indisposition on your own account and shall be happy when the state of your health may permit you to revisit the courtroom. I write for the purpose of giving you notice of the state of the docket that you may come prepared for a cause of yours which will be called as soon as you arrive. It is that which respects the African negroes.[1] Should you be ready it is probable that it may be the first for argument.

With the best wishes for the restoration of your health, I am dear Sir your obedt

J MARSHALL

The court is at present sufficiently employed so that there is no reason for your exposing yourself on that account in bad weather.

ALS, PHi. Identity of recipient and date based on internal evidence (see n. 1).

1. Wirt argued cases on 11 Feb. and 16 Feb. His next appearance was on 25 Feb. He was present for the opening of the argument of The Antelope on 26 Feb. (U.S. Sup. Ct. Minutes, 11, 16, 25 Feb. 1825; 10 Wheat. 69).

To Gales & Seaton

GENTLEMEN: RICHMOND, FEBRUARY 22, 1825.[1]

I have just received your letter of the 19th, and much obliged by the inquiry it makes.[2] I know not from what quarter the intimation is given that I am engaged in writing a history of our country, but know that it is entirely without foundation. I have always considered the *Life of Washington* as being substantially a history of his country while he was at the head of her armies or of her counsels, nor could it be otherwise. It was composed with too much precipitation, and I have been engaged in correcting its language where it has been negligently written, and in pruning a minuteness of detail which gives a wearisome tediousness to the narrative now, though the facts were at the time of immense importance. I have occasionally mentioned among my friends my determination to make the Biography of Washington at least satisfactory to myself, and this has probably given rise to the report you mention.[3] With great regard and respect, I am, gentlemen, your obedient servant,

J. MARSHALL.

Printed, *Daily National Intelligencer* (Washington, D.C.), 22 Feb. 1854. Possibly misdated by Gales (see n. 1).

1. JM was in Washington, not Richmond, on this date. Gales may have inadvertently dated the letter 22 Feb. (George Washington's birthday), which was the day and month he published it in 1854. If Gales misdated the letter, the correct date might be July 1825 (see n. 3).

2. Letter not found. As Gales explained in a headnote to his 1854 printing of this letter, JM's letter "came to light in a bundle of old manuscripts" that he happened to open at this time.

3. *Niles' Weekly Register,* 9 July 1825, reprinted an item from the *New York Evening Post* stating that JM was "engaged in writing, and, indeed, is far advanced towards completing, a history of the American government, from the adoption of the constitution to the termination of Washington's presidency" (*Niles' Weekly Register* [Baltimore], XVIII [1825], 292).

To Mary W. Marshall

My dearest Polly   Washington Feb. 27th. 1825

I have been feasted within a few days by two letters from Richmond, the one from our Nephew George & the other from our son.[1] They both afford me the pleasure of hearing from you. I am happy that the 22d. has passed off with so little inconvenience to you.[2]

Both these letters give me a piece of intelligence which surprizes me very much. Our Nephew Edward Colston has I am told over come all his prejudices against the Richmond ladies, and is about to carry one of them to Honeywood. He has at least this consolation — she is young enough for him.[3]

Tell Mr. Call that last night the taylors boy brought home my new suit of black. I have not yet tried it on, but take it for granted it will fit me. You know I always expect the best. I have his piece of cloth and shall bring it with me. Tell him also that Kremer is coming out as I am told with a most scurrilous piece of abuse against Mr. Clay. This was to be expected. Kremer will probably keep himself up by it in the district whatever may be thought of him elsewhere.[4]

I received a letter to day from your cousin Mrs. Walker thanking me for my check & telling me that she had received a subscription raised by Mr. Tucker among the members of Congress which would enable her to subsist for some time.[5] She says nothing about the office concerning which she had written to me ⟨ . . . ⟩ made to me. ⟨ . . . ⟩ suggestion of the ⟨ . . . ⟩ occasion.

I have ⟨ . . . ⟩ your cousin Ro⟨ . . . ⟩choly and ful⟨ . . . ⟩ money wasted on ⟨ . . . ⟩ her tomorrow. Farewel⟨ . . . ⟩ I am y⟨ . . . ⟩

⟨J MARSHALL⟩

AL[S], Marshall Papers, ViW. Half of second sheet (including signature) missing, having been clipped along vertical axis.

1. Letters not found. The nephew was probably George Daniel Fisher (1804–1891), son of George Fisher and Ann Ambler Fisher, Mary Marshall's younger sister (Louise Pecquet du Bellet, *Some Prominent Virginia Families* [1907; 4 vols. in 2; Baltimore, 1976 reprint], I, 50–51).

2. JM alluded to Richmond's celebration of George Washington's birthday. Mary Marshall had probably gone to the Chickahominy farm to escape the "noisy rejoicings" (*PJM*, IX, 104).

3. Edward Colston, a widower of thirty-eight, married as his second wife Sarah Jane Brockenbrough (b. 1805) of Richmond on 2 May 1825. Honeywood was the Colston estate near Martinsburg in Berkeley County (Paxton, *Marshall Family*, 105).

4. Kremer's address "To the Electors of the Ninth Congressional District of the State of Pennsylvania" was published in the *Washington Gazette*, 28 Feb. 1825. Gales & Seaton refused to publish this piece, commenting that it "appears in the Washington City Gazette of last evening, with some alterations, which it is, perhaps, not necessary to particularize, but which, so far as they go, render it less exceptionable than in its original form it appeared to

us to be" (James F. Hopkins and Mary W. M. Hargreaves, eds., *The Papers of Henry Clay,* IV [Lexington, Ky., 1972], 113–14; *Daily National Intelligencer,* 1 Mar. 1825).

5. Letter not found. Mrs. Walker was apparently the widow of George Walker (1763–1819), who served in the U.S. Senate from Kentucky from 1814 to 1819. In a letter written about this time, Andrew Jackson recommended Joseph W. Walker, son of George Walker, for appointment to the U.S. Military Academy, adding that the late Senator Walker, a veteran of the War of 1812, had left about thirteen children with no means of support (Jackson to John C. Calhoun, 4 Jan. 1825 [calendar summary], W. Edwin Hemphill, ed., *The Papers of John C. Calhoun,* IX [Columbia, S.C., 1976], 474). George Tucker (1775–1861) was then completing his service as a Virginia member of the U.S. House of Representatives. He subsequently became the first professor of moral philosophy at the University of Virginia.

From John Quincy Adams

Sir   Washington 2 March 1825.
I have to request of you the favor to administer to me the Official Oath, prescribed by the Constitution to the President of the United States on the 4th. instt. at twelve o'clock in the Hall of the House of Representatives; & to invite the attendance on that occasion of the Associate Justices of the Supreme Court of the United States. I have the honor to be with great respect, Sir, Your very humble & obedt. Servt.

AL (letterbook copy), MHi.

To John Quincy Adams

Sir   Washington March 3d. 1825
I have the honour to acknowledge your polite letter of yesterday, and will certainly do myself the pleasure to attend at the time and place you mention for the purpose of administering the oath prescribed in the constitution for the President of the United States.[1] With very great respect I am Sir, your Obedt. Servt

J MARSHALL

ALS, Adams Family Papers, MHi.

1. A portion of Adams's diary entry for 4 Mar. 1825 reads: "I repaired to the hall of the House of Representatives, and, after delivering from the Speaker's chair my inaugural address to a crowded auditory, I pronounced from a volume of the laws held up to me by John Marshall, Chief Justice of the United States, the oath faithfully to execute the office of President of the United States, and, to the best of my ability, to preserve, protect, and defend the Constitution of the United States" (Charles Francis Adams, ed., *Memoirs of John Quincy Adams,* VI [Philadelphia, 1875], 519).

A HISTORY

OF THE

COLONIES PLANTED BY THE ENGLISH

ON

THE CONTINENT OF

NORTH AMERICA,

FROM THEIR

SETTLEMENT, TO THE COMMENCEMENT OF THAT WAR WHICH
TERMINATED IN THEIR

INDEPENDENCE.

BY JOHN MARSHALL.

PHILADELPHIA:
PUBLISHED BY ABRAHAM SMALL.

1824.

TITLE PAGE TO *A HISTORY OF THE COLONIES*

Marshall's revised introduction to the *Life of George Washington* published
in Philadelphia, 1824. *Courtesy of the Department of Manuscripts and Rarebooks, Earl Gregg Swem Library, College of William and Mary.*

To James Monroe

Dear Sir   Washington March 7th. 1825

Permit me to ask your acceptance of our colonial history which is offered as a mark of the affectionate recollections excited in the bosom of the author when he looks back to times long since gone by.[1]

In the momentous and then unlooked for events which have since taken place, you have filled a large space in the public mind, and have been conspicuously instrumental in effecting objects of great interest to our common country. Believe me when I congratulate you on the circumstances under which your political course terminates, and that I feel sincere pleasure in the persuasion that your administration may be reviewed with real approbation by our wisest statesmen. With great respect and esteem, I am dear Sir, Your obedt

J MARSHALL

ALS, Monroe Papers, DLC. Addressed to Monroe and endorsed by him.

1. The enclosed book was JM's *History of the Colonies Planted by the English on the Continent of North America . . .* (Philadelphia, 1824).

To James Barbour

Dear Sir   Washington March 8th. 1825

The bearer wishes to be engaged in some of the measures about to be taken by the government as preliminary to the improvements which are in contemplation. He says that he was employed by you while Governour of Virginia during the late war; but as you may have forgotten him he requests me to mention him. He has been employed very extensively in Richmond and its vicinity as a surveyor & has always been thought an accurate surveyor and respectable man. I am Sir very respectfully, Your Obedt. Servt

J MARSHALL

ALS, RG 77, DNA. Addressed to the secretary of war. Endorsed.

To Henry Lee

Dear Sir   Washington March 9th. 1825

I received yesterday morning your letter of the 6th. inclosing an essay on the election of the President by the House of Representatives for which I thank you & expressing your wish to enter the department of state as first Clerk.[1] I feel it absolutely impossible to go farther in any recommendation than to state my opinion of the capacity of the applicant by way of information to the person who can bestow the office, and I could not go so far generally. In this particular case however I will at your request state to Mr. Clay my high opinion of your abilities provided the place you wish is vacant. I have an invincible repugnance to doing an act which might look like an effort to remove a worthy man from office in any case, and that general repugnance would be increased in this because Mr. Brent was appointed by my s⟨e⟩lf while Secretary of State a clerk in that department. Should he have resigned I will mention to Mr. Clay the high opinion I entertain of your talents, if you wish me to do so.[2]

I wrote yesterday to you in the apprehension that there was some doubt respecting the confirmation of the nominations made by the President, and as I understood before the rising of the court that the senate had confirmed them, I brought back the letter.[3] With respect & esteem, I am dear Sir your Obedt

J MARSHALL

ALS, Charles Carter Lee Papers, Vi. Addressed to Lee at the Union Hotel in Georgetown. Endorsed by Lee. Cover torn; Lee's summary of answer on verso (see n. 2).

1. Letter not found.
2. Lee then held a minor position in the Post Office Department. Daniel Brent (1774–1841), who had been employed by the State Department since 1800, became chief clerk during the secretaryship of John Quincy Adams (Leonard D. White, *The Jeffersonians: A Study in Administrative History, 1801–1829* [New York, 1956], 189–90, 372; Chester Horton Brent, *The Descendants of Collo. Giles Brent, Capt. George Brent and Robert Brent . . .* [Rutland, Vt., 1946], 136–37). According to his summary of a reply (partly mutilated), Lee told JM he would not have applied for the clerkship had he "known Mr. M's relation to" Brent.
3. Clay was nominated secretary of state on 5 Mar. On 8 Mar. the Senate voted to remove the injunction of secrecy from proceedings on his nomination (*Journal of the Executive Proceedings of the Senate . . .* , III [Washington, D.C., 1828], 436, 443).

To Mary W. Marshall

[Washington, 9 March 1825]

I administered the oath to the President in the presence of an immense concourse of people, in my new suit of domestic manufacture. He, too, was dressed in the same manner, 'though his cloth was made at a different establishment. The cloth is very fine and smooth.

Printed, Marion Harland, *Some Colonial Homesteads and Their Stories* (New York, 1897), 98. This is undoubtedly an extract of a longer letter, the original of which was in the possession of JM's granddaughter, Margaret Lewis Marshall Smith, in the late nineteenth century. James Bradley Thayer, who quoted the above text in his 1901 biography of Marshall, used as his source a "Mem. Of letters of Marshall / to his wife / furnished by Mrs. Smith / his granddaughter." The memorandum also included extracts of JM's letter to Mary W. Marshall, 23 Feb. 1824. Thayer noted that the memorandum was originally published in the Baltimore *Sun,* from which it was extracted and then lent to him by Mrs. Smith's son (typescript memorandum, Thayer Papers, MH-L). Marion Harland presumably used the text published in the Baltimore *Sun.*

From James Monroe

Dear sir   Washington March 10. 1825
    I have received with great interest your letter of the 7th. with the Vol: of your history of our Colonial State, which I shall retain as a testimonial of your regard.
    The favorable opinion which you have expressed of my Conduct in discharge of the arduous duties, of the very important office, from which I have just retired, affords me the highest gratification. We began our Career together in early youth, and the whole Course of my Public conduct has been under your observation. Your approbation therefore of my administration of the affairs of our Country, deserves to be held & will be held by me in the highest estimation. For your own welfare & happiness be assur'd of my best wishes.

ADf, Monroe Papers, DLC. Endorsed by Monroe on verso.

The Antelope
Opinion
U.S. Supreme Court, 15 March 1825

EDITORIAL NOTE

The Antelope was actually two cases brought by the United States as "claimants of certain African Negroes part of the Cargo of the Vessel called the Antelope otherwise called the General Ramirez." The defendants were Charles Mulvey, vice-consul of Spain, and Francis Sorrell, vice-consul of Portugal, who acted on "behalf of certain claimants of Sundry African Negroes part of the Cargo of the Antelope or Ramirez."[1] The fate of some two hundred Africans, survivors of a group of nearly three hundred who had been captured for the purpose of being sold into slavery, hinged on the Supreme Court's decision. A central question in the case was whether international law prohibited the slave trade. A negative answer, however, did not preclude the Court from finding that the Africans were entitled to freedom in the absence of clear proof that they belonged to persons who could legitimately claim them as slave property. Although the United States had outlawed the slave trade, it was a notorious fact that American citizens continued to engage in the traffic under cover of foreign flags. *The Antelope* posed the question whether the claimants, ostensibly subjects of Spain and Portugal, had a greater burden of proof to establish title than was required in ordinary cases of restoring goods and merchandise.

The ordeal of the captured Africans, both as prisoners and as wards of the American federal judicial system, had begun in 1820 and continued for seven years.[2] The privateer *Arraganta,* formerly the *Columbia,* sailed from Baltimore in December 1819 manned by a largely American crew. The vessel carried a commission signed by José Artigas, leader of a revolutionary South American republic, authorizing it to make war on Spanish and Portuguese shipping. After reaching the west coast of Africa, the *Arraganta* seized an American vessel and several ships flying Portuguese colors, taking on board a number of Africans. In March 1820 the privateer captured the *Antelope,* a slave vessel flying the Spanish flag and carrying a large number of Africans. The *Arraganta* and the *Antelope* (renamed the *General Ramirez*) subsequently sailed in tandem towards South America. Off the coast of Brazil the *Arraganta* wrecked, the survivors climbing on board the *Antelope.* This vessel, now carrying all the Africans taken by the *Arraganta,* sailed north towards Florida. In late June an American revenue cutter seized the *Antelope* on suspicion of being engaged in the slave trade in violation of American laws. The vessel and its human cargo were eventually brought into Savannah for adjudication.

In August 1820 the vice-consuls of Spain and Portugal filed libels in the U.S. District Court, each claiming a portion of the Africans as belonging, respectively, to Spanish and Portuguese subjects. U.S. Attorney Richard W. Habersham filed a libel on behalf of the United States, claiming the Africans as being illegally transported from foreign parts by American citizens and as entitled to freedom by American laws and by the law of nations. Throughout the protracted legal proceedings in this case the Africans remained in custody of the federal marshal in a state of virtual slavery. The marshal sent fifty of them to work for the city of Savannah, hired out others to local residents, and placed more than a hundred on his own plantation. Over the years death steadily reduced the number originally found on board the *Antelope.*

In February 1821 U.S. District Judge William Davies upheld both the Spanish and the Portuguese claims—the latter despite the fact that counsel offered no evidence other than testimony of the *Arraganta's* crew that the privateer had attacked Portuguese ships and acquired slaves from them. During the several hearings of this case, no one ever appeared in court to identify himself as owner of the Africans taken from the Portuguese vessels. Judge Davies distributed the Africans among the several claimants according to the number originally taken from the Spanish, Portuguese, and American ships, calculating "average losses." Habersham took an appeal to the U.S. Circuit Court, which heard the case in May and December 1821. That court, consisting of Justice William Johnson and District Judge Jeremiah Cuyler (who had succeeded Davies) confirmed, with some modifications, the lower court's decree. It distributed most of the Africans between the Spanish and Portuguese claimants, awarding sixteen to the United States, who by law were to be set free and transported back to Africa. Because there was no way to identify those Africans who were originally taken from the American ship, the court ordered that the names of sixteen of the whole number were to be drawn by lot.

Dissatisfied with this decree, particularly in upholding the Portuguese claim,

U.S. Attorney Habersham appealed the case of the Africans to the Supreme Court, where it was placed on the docket in February 1822. The Monroe administration was in no hurry to prosecute the appeal, however, evidently concerned about the case's potential for interfering with pending diplomatic efforts to suppress the international slave trade and for arousing domestic political passions. Not until 1825, when these concerns were less urgent, was the government ready to proceed. Arguments commenced on 26 February and continued for five days. Francis Scott Key and Attorney General Wirt appeared for the government on behalf of the Africans; John M. Berrien (1781–1856), recently elected U.S. Senator from Georgia, and Charles J. Ingersoll represented the Spanish and Portuguese claimants.

The purpose of the appeal was to liberate the Africans found on the *Antelope* and transport them back to Africa, as provided by a law enacted by Congress in 1819. The "Act in addition to the Acts prohibiting the slave trade" authorized the president to employ public armed vessels to seize American ships unlawfully engaged in the slave trade. It further authorized him to provide for the safekeeping, support, and removal of all blacks brought into the United States as a result of the seizure of slaving vessels and to appoint an agent residing in Africa to receive them.[3] This act, as President Monroe interpreted it, meshed with the purposes of the American Colonization Society, which in 1821 purchased land on the west coast of Africa and established the colony that came to be known as Liberia. By 1824 the Society was seeking to increase the colony's population and regarded the *Antelope* Africans as a source of fresh recruits. Lobbying from the Society probably contributed to the government's decision to revive the case in 1825. On 19 February, a week before arguments began, the Society held its annual meeting in the Supreme Court room. Chief Justice Marshall, a member of the Society, was one of several justices who attended the meeting and heard two stirring addresses denouncing the slave trade.

Key, an active member of the Colonization Society, presented a broadly based argument for the freedom of the *Antelope* Africans. If they were not free by United States laws prohibiting the importation of blacks, yet the burden of proof lay upon the Spanish and Portuguese claimants to show that they had rightfully acquired the Africans as slaves. Mere possession was insufficient, Key insisted; the claimants had to demonstrate that the law of nations compelled an American court to restore the Africans to their purported owners. Key submitted abundant testimony in the form of treaties, statutes, public acts, and legal decisions to show that the slave trade was now condemned by the general consent of civilized nations and that the claimants could derive no support from this source to demand restitution. Wirt also emphasized the point that the burden of proof fell to the claimants, for the Africans having come under the custody of the United States were by its laws "*prima facie,* free." The true question, he said, was whether naked possession was "sufficient evidence of title, not as against the United States, but as against these Africans." Neither the municipal laws of various European nations nor the law of nations supported the presumption that possession was "*prima facie* evidence of property." Moreover, to presume that the Africans were " 'effects' " or " 'merchandise' " taken by pirates and thus liable to restitution under the 1795 treaty with Spain, was "to beg the whole question in controversy."[4]

For the claimants Berrien replied that the United States could not by its own laws refuse restitution of the Africans, who were lawfully acquired property that had been forcibly taken from their Spanish and Portuguese owners. The applicable law was the treaty of 1795, which required restitution of those Africans originally taken from the *Antelope*. Restitution could not be refused on the ground that the slave trade was contrary to the law of nations, he said. Since that law demonstrably did not abolish slavery, it could not reasonably apply to the traffic in slaves, which was "but an *incident* to the original sin of slavery."[5] Ingersoll, too, urged the imperative under the treaty with Spain to restore the Africans, who having been acquired south of the equator (where Spanish and Portuguese law permitted the slave trade) were to be presumed to be legitimately held as slaves. He pointed to the absence of any positive law of nations or of any treaty by which the United States was to cooperate with other nations in prohibiting the slave trade. It was not for the Supreme Court, he said, "to anticipate, by judicial legislation, the exercise of the treaty making power."[6]

On 15 March, twelve days after the close of arguments, Marshall delivered the Court's opinion. At the outset the chief justice stated the Court's duty to adhere to "the mandate of the law" and not to be swayed by "feelings" excited by a case involving a conflict between "the sacred rights of liberty and of property." Further into the opinion he observed that "public feeling" on the subject of the slave trade was "somewhat in advance of strict law." Taking up the question of whether the slave trade was sanctioned by international law, Marshall declined to act as a "moralist" and asserted that a "jurist" must find a "legal" answer.[7]

The Court's cautious, legalistic approach was consistent with its disposition of the relatively few slave freedom suits it heard. In these cases, too, Marshall employed the contrast between feelings and the law.[8] Although the manifest iniquity of the slave trade and the desire to punish fraudulent evasions of American laws prohibiting the trade no doubt weighed heavily on the minds of the justices, the chief justice probably had little difficulty in persuading a majority of his brethren to subordinate these considerations based on feelings. In taking refuge behind the law in *The Antelope*, the Court was adhering to its traditional deference to the political branches in cases that implicated questions of foreign policy and diplomacy. A pronouncement that the slave trade was contrary to the law of nations would have been tantamount to legislating a reciprocal right of visitation and search during peacetime. The appropriate means of making so vital a concession of national sovereignty, however, was by diplomatic negotiation and adoption of a treaty. The Court was not unmindful that the Senate had recently rejected a treaty with Great Britain that contained such a provision.[9]

The case's implications for domestic politics also counseled caution. Acutely sensitive to its vulnerable political position, the Marshall Court was anxious to avoid any appearance of intermeddling with the institution of slavery. A judicial fiat that the slave trade was illegal under international law might be regarded as an attack on the right to hold property in persons. Berrien made certain the justices got the hint by denying there was any solid distinction between the slave trade and slavery. An indication of the case's explosive potential may be seen in the testy response it provoked from Georgia Governor George M. Troup. Addressing the state legislature shortly after the decision, the governor complained that Wirt in his argument had denied the legitimacy of slavery and that his views reflected the government's hostility towards the institution. The attorney general publicly denied that he had advanced such a proposition and offered supporting testimony from the Supreme Court justices. Marshall's recollection was that Wirt "denounced the slave trade, not slavery," adding: "I think it impossible that you can have hinted at any interference of the government of the Union with slavery in the respective States; because I think such a hint, however remote, would have excited my attention too strongly to be entirely forgotten."[10]

Although it shied away from a general condemnation of the slave trade on the basis of international law, the Supreme Court could still aid the cause of the *Antelope* Africans by its interpretation of "strict law." For example, the Court took the view that it could inquire into the claimants' title and that something more than mere possession was needed to prove title under the peculiar circumstances of this case. The Spanish claimant had presented some supporting documentation: ownership of the *Antelope* by a merchant firm of Cádiz, its registry with Spain's Department of Marine, and a license from the royal governor of Cuba to trade for "new Negroes."[11] Was this sufficient? Opposing counsel insisted that the Africans claimed as slaves must be identified individually. The six sitting justices — Marshall, Washington, Johnson, Story, Duvall, and Thompson — split on this question, leaving intact the lower court's decree of restitution to the Spanish claimant.[12] Still, as in any ordinary case for the restitution of property, the claimant did have the burden of proving the number of Africans on board the *Antelope* at the time of its capture. Here the Court found that the proof was insufficient beyond a number that was considerably smaller than that decreed by the circuit court. Finally, the Court completely reversed the lower court by dismissing the Portuguese claim, the chief justice stating that the long continued omission of a Portuguese subject to assert title was "irresistible testimony, that no such claimant exists."[13] The burden of proof lay with the claimant, who refused to identify himself. The operative laws in this instance were those of the United States for suppressing the slave trade.

Strict law, then, did not liberate all the Africans but did substantially increase the number awarded to the United States for transportation to the colony of Liberia. Unhappily, subsequent judicial proceedings concerning the proper mode of implementing the Supreme Court's mandate extended the Africans' ordeal another two years. After the case was remanded to the circuit court, the Spanish claimant insisted that the Africans to be delivered to him should be determined by lot. In December 1825 the circuit court divided on the question whether the designation should be by lot or "upon proof on the part of the Spanish claimant."[14] Marshall, as yet unaware of this delay, wrote to Secretary of the Navy Samuel Southard on 1 January 1826 to inquire if the Africans had been delivered over to the United States "in conformity" with the Supreme Court's decree. He inquired not in his official capacity but as president of the local branch of the American Colonization Society, which was soon to meet in Richmond. He hoped to communicate news of the delivery and resulting "augmentation of the colony."[15]

Like a bouncing ball, the case reappeared on the Supreme Court's 1826 docket on the certificate of division. Without argument, the Court issued a tersely worded order that the Africans to be delivered to the Spanish claimant "must be designated by proof made to the satisfaction" of the circuit court.[16] At length that court identified thirty-nine individuals to be turned over to the Spanish claimant, including at least one who had been certified free by the lottery employed in the original circuit court decree. Habersham once again appealed to the Supreme Court on the ground that the evidence was insufficient to identify any of the Africans as belonging to the Spanish claimants. On 15 March 1827 the Court, speaking through Justice Robert Trimble, affirmed the decree.[17] In July 1827 some 130 Africans adjudicated to the United States sailed from Savannah for Liberia. Those decreed to be Spanish property were eventually sold to Richard Henry Wilde, a Georgia lawyer and member of Congress who had argued the case in the circuit court in 1826 and also the 1827 appeal to the Supreme Court. A private letter written by Wilde concerning this sale appears to confirm the likelihood that the Spanish claim, like that of the Portuguese, was a cover for American interests.[18]

1. U.S. Sup. Ct. Minutes, 15 Mar. 1825.
2. The narrative of this case is drawn from John T. Noonan, Jr., *The Antelope: The Ordeal of the Recaptured Africans in the Administrations of James Monroe and John Quincy Adams* (Berkeley, Calif., 1977).
3. *U.S. Statutes at Large*, III, 532–34.
4. 10 Wheat., 107, 110, 111, 113.
5. 10 Wheat. 89.
6. 10 Wheat. 105.
7. Opinion, 15 Mar. 1825 (158–59, 162, below).
8. See Mima Queen v. Hepburn, 7 Cranch 290, 295 (1813); *PJM*, VII, 383. See also Brig Caroline v. U.S., 7 Cranch 496–500 (1813); *PJM*, VIII, 404.
9. Hugh G. Soulsby, *The Right of Search and the Slave Trade in Anglo-American Relations, 1814–1862* (Baltimore, 1933), 27–38.
10. Wirt to JM, 2 July 1825 and nn.; JM to Wirt, 6 July 1825.
11. Noonan, *The Antelope*, 13–14.
12. A close student of this case conjectures that Story, Thompson, and Duvall voted against restitution on this proof. The placing of JM and Duvall on opposing sides is based on the opinion and dissent in the 1813 case of Mima Queen v. Hepburn (Noonan, *The Antelope*, 114–16; 7 Cranch 290, 293–99; *PJM*, VII, 382–86).
13. Opinion, 15 March 1825 (166, below).
14. The Antelope, 11 Wheat. 413–14 (1826).
15. JM to Samuel Southard, 1 Jan. 1826.
16. 11 Wheat. 414.
17. 12 Wheat. 546, 552–54.
18. Noonan, *The Antelope*, 133–48.

OPINION

In prosecuting this appeal, the United States assert no property in themselves. They appear in the character of guardians, or next friends, of these Africans, who are brought, without any act of their own, into the bosom of our country, insist on their right to freedom, and submit their claim to the laws of the land, and to the tribunals of the nation.

The Consuls of Spain and Portugal, respectively, demand these Africans as slaves, who have, in the regular course of legitimate commerce, been acquired as property by the subjects of their respective sovereigns, and claim their restitution under the laws of the United States.

In examining claims of this momentous importance; claims in which the sacred rights of liberty and of property come in conflict with each other; which have drawn from the bar a degree of talent and of eloquence, worthy of the questions that have been discussed; this Court must not yield to feelings which might seduce it from the path of duty, and must obey the mandate of the law.

That the course of opinion on the slave trade should be unsettled, ought to excite no surprise. The Christian and civilized nations of the world, with whom we have most intercourse, have all been engaged in it. However abhorrent this traffic may be to a mind whose original feelings are not blunted by familiarity with the practice, it has been sanctioned in modern times by the laws of all nations who possess distant colonies, each of whom has engaged in it as a common commercial business which no other could rightfully interrupt. It has claimed all the sanction which could be derived from long usage, and general acquiescence. That trade could not be considered as contrary to the law of nations which was authorized and protected by the laws of all commercial nations; the right to carry on which was claimed by each, and allowed by each.

The course of unexamined opinion, which was founded on this inveterate usage, received its first check in America; and, as soon as these States acquired the right of self-government, the traffic was forbidden by most of them. In the beginning of this century, several humane and enlightened individuals of Great Britain devoted themselves to the cause of the Africans; and, by frequent appeals to the nation, in which the enormity of this commerce was unveiled, and exposed to the public eye, the general sentiment was at length roused against it, and the feelings of justice and humanity, regaining their long lost ascendency, prevailed so far in the British parliament as to obtain an act for its abolition. The utmost efforts of the British government, as well as of that of the United States, have since been assiduously employed in its suppression. It has been denounced by both in terms of great severity, and those concerned in it are subjected to the heaviest penalties which law can inflict. In addition to these measures operating on their own people, they have used all their influence to bring other nations into the same system, and to interdict this trade by the consent of all.

Public sentiment has, in both countries, kept pace with the measures of government; and the opinion is extensively, if not universally entertained, that this unnatural traffic ought to be suppressed. While its illegality is asserted by some governments, but not admitted by all; while the detestation in which it is held is growing daily, and even those nations who tolerate it in fact, almost disavow their own conduct, and rather connive at, than legalize, the acts of their subjects; it is not wonderful that public feeling should march somewhat in advance of strict law, and that opposite opinions should be entertained on the precise cases in which our own laws may control and limit the practice of others. Indeed, we ought not to be surprised, if, on this novel series of cases, even Courts of justice should, in some instances, have carried the principle of suppression farther than a more deliberate consideration of the subject would justify.

The *Amedie*, (1 *Acton's Rep.* 240.) which was an American vessel employed in the African trade, was captured by a British cruiser, and condemned in the Vice Admiralty Court of Tortola.[1] An appeal was prayed; and Sir William Grant, in delivering the opinion of the Court, said, that the trade being then declared unjust and unlawful by Great Britain, "a claimant could have no right, upon principles of universal law, to claim restitution in a prize Court, of human beings carried as his slaves. He must show some right that has been violated by the capture, some property of which he has been dispossessed, and to which he ought to be restored. In this case, the laws of the claimant's country allow of no right of property such as he claims. There can, therefore, be no right of restitution. The consequence is, that the judgment must be affirmed."[2]

The *Fortuna* (1 *Dodson's Rep.* 81.) was condemned on the authority of the *Amedie*, and the same principle was again affirmed.[3]

The *Diana* (1 *Dodson's Rep.* 95.) was a Swedish vessel, captured with a cargo of slaves, by a British cruiser, and condemned in the Court of Vice Admiralty at Sierra Leone.[4] This sentence was reversed on appeal, and Sir William Scott, in pronouncing the sentence of reversal, said, "the condemnation also took place on a principle which this Court cannot in any manner recognise, inasmuch as the sentence affirms, 'that the slave trade, from motives of humanity, hath been abolished by most civilized nations, *and is not, at the present time, legally authorized by any.*' This appears to me to be an assertion by no means sustainable."[5] The ship and cargo were restored, on the principle that the trade was allowed by the laws of Sweden.

The principle common to these cases is, that the legality of the capture of a vessel engaged in the slave trade, depends on the law of the country to which the vessel belongs. If that law gives its sanction to the trade, restitution will be decreed; if that law prohibits it, the vessel and cargo will be condemned as good prize.

This whole subject came on afterwards to be considered in the *Louis*, (2 *Dodson's Rep.* 238.).[6] The opinion of Sir William Scott, in that case, demonstrates the attention he had bestowed upon it, and gives full assurance that it may be considered as settling the law in the British Courts of Admiralty as far as it goes.

The *Louis* was a French vessel, captured on a slaving voyage, before she had purchased any slaves, brought into Sierra Leone, and condemned by the Vice Admiralty Court at that place. On an appeal to the Court of Admiralty in England, the sentence was reversed.

In the very full and elaborate opinion given on this case, Sir William Scott, in explicit terms, lays down the broad principle, that the right of search is confined to a state of war. It is a right strictly belligerent in its character, which can never be exercised by a nation at peace, except against professed pirates, who are the enemies of the human race. The act of trading in slaves, however detestable, was not, he said, "the act of freebooters, enemies of the human race, renouncing every country, and ravaging every country, in its coasts and vessels, indiscriminately."[7] It was not piracy.

He also said, that this trade could not be pronounced contrary to the law of nations. "A Court, in the administration of law, cannot attribute criminality to an act where the law imputes none. It must look to the legal standard of morality; and, upon a question of this nature, that standard must be found in the law of nations, as fixed and evidenced by general, and ancient, and admitted practice, by treaties, and by the general tenor of the laws and ordinances, and the formal transactions of civilized states; and, looking to those authorities, he found a difficulty in maintaining that the transaction was legally criminal."[8]

The right of visitation and search being strictly a belligerent right, and the slave trade being neither piratical, nor contrary to the law of nations, the principle is asserted and maintained with great strength of reasoning, that it cannot be exercised on the vessels of a foreign power, unless permitted by treaty. France had refused to assent to the insertion of such an article in her treaty with Great Britain, and, consequently, the right could not be exercised on the high seas by a British cruiser on a French vessel.

"It is pressed as a difficulty," says the Judge, "what is to be done, if a French ship, laden with slaves, is brought in? I answer, without hesitation, restore the possession which has been unlawfully devested; rescind the illegal act done by your own subject, and leave the foreigner to the justice of his own country."[9]

This reasoning goes far in support of the proposition, that, in the British Courts of admiralty, the vessel even of a nation which had forbidden the slave trade, but had not conceded the right of search, must, if wrongfully brought in, be restored to the original owner. But the Judge goes farther, and shows, that no evidence existed to prove that France had, by law, forbidden that trade. Consequently, for this reason, as well as for that previously assigned, the sentence of condemnation was reversed, and restitution awarded.

In the United States, different opinions have been entertained in the different Circuits and Districts; and the subject is now, for the first time, before this Court.[10]

The question, whether the slave trade is prohibited by the law of nations has been seriously propounded, and both the affirmative and negative of the proposition have been maintained with equal earnestness.

That it is contrary to the law of nature will scarcely be denied. That every man has a natural right to the fruits of his own labour, is generally admitted; and that no other person can rightfully deprive him of those fruits, and appropriate them against his will, seems to be the necessary result of this admission. But from the earliest times war has existed, and war confers rights in which all have acquiesced. Among the most enlightened nations of antiquity, one of these was, that the victor might enslave the vanquished. This, which was the usage of all, could not be pronounced repugnant to the law of nations, which is certainly to be tried by the test of [ge]neral usage. That which has received the assent of all, must be the law of all.

Slavery, then, has its origin in force; but as the world has agreed that it is a legitimate result of force, the state of things which is thus produced by general consent, cannot be pronounced unlawful.

Throughout Christendom, this harsh rule has been exploded, and war is no longer considered as giving a right to enslave captives. But this triumph of humanity has not been universal. The parties to the modern law of nations do not propagate their principles by force; and Africa has not yet adopted them. Throughout the whole extent of that immense continent, so far as we know its history, it is still the law of nations that prisoners are slaves. Can those who have themselves renounced this law, be permitted to participate in its effects by purchasing the beings who are its victims?

Whatever might be the answer of a moralist to this question, a jurist must search for its legal solution, in those principles of action which are sanctioned by the usages, the national acts, and the general assent, of that portion of the world of which he considers himself as a part, and to whose law the appeal is made. If we resort to this standard as the test of international law, the question, as has already been observed, is decided in favour of the legality of the trade. Both Europe and America embarked in it; and for nearly two centuries, it was carried on without opposition, and without censure. A jurist could not say, that a practice thus supported was illegal, and that those engaged in it might be punished, either personally, or by deprivation of property.

In this commerce, thus sanctioned by universal assent, every nation had an equal right to engage. How is this right to be lost? Each may renounce it for its own people; but can this renunciation affect others?

No principle of general law is more universally acknowledged, than the perfect equality of nations. Russia and Geneva have equal rights. It results from this equality, that no one can rightfully impose a rule on another. Each legislates for itself, but its legislation can operate on itself alone. A right, then, which is vested in all by the consent of all, can be devested only by consent; and this trade, in which all have participated, must remain lawful to those who cannot be induced to relinquish it. As no nation can prescribe a rule for others, none can make a law of nations; and this traffic remains lawful to those whose governments have not forbidden it.

If it is consistent with the law of nations, it cannot in itself be piracy. It can be made so only by statute; and the obligation of the statute cannot transcend the legislative power of the state which may enact it.

If it be neither repugnant to the law of nations, nor piracy, it is almost superfluous to say in this Court, that the right of bringing in for adjudication in time of peace, even where the vessel belongs to a nation which has prohibited the trade, cannot exist. The Courts of no country execute the penal laws of another; and the course of the American government on the subject of visitation and search, would decide any case in which that right had been exercised by an American cruiser, on the vessel of a foreign nation, not violating our municipal laws, against the captors.

It follows, that a foreign vessel engaged in the African slave trade, captured on the high seas in time of peace, by an American cruiser, and brought in for adjudication, would be restored.

The general question being disposed of, it remains to examine the circumstances of the particular case.

The Antelope, a vessel unquestionably belonging to Spanish subjects, was captured while receiving a cargo of Africans on the coast of Africa, by the Arraganta, a privateer which was manned in Baltimore, and is said to have been then under the flag of the Oriental republic. Some other vessels, said to be Portuguese, engaged in the same traffic, were previously plundered, and the slaves taken from them, as well as from another vessel then in the same port, were put on board the Antelope, of which vessel the Arraganta took possession, landed her crew, and put on board a prize master and prize crew. Both vessels proceeded to the Coast of Brazil, where the Arraganta was wrecked, and her captain and crew either lost or made prisoners.

The Antelope, whose name was changed to the General Ramirez, after an ineffectual attempt to sell the Africans on board at Surinam, arrived off the coast of Florida, and was hovering on that coast, near that of the United States, for several days. Supposing her to be a pirate, or a vessel wishing to smuggle slaves into the United States, Captain Jackson, of the revenue cutter Dallas, went in quest of her, and finding her laden with slaves, commanded by officers who were citizens of the United States, with a crew who spoke English, brought her in for adjudication.

She was libelled by the Vice Consuls of Spain and Portugal, each of whom claim that portion of the slaves which were conjectured to belong to the subjects of their respective sovereigns; which claims are opposed by the United States on behalf of the Africans.

In the argument, the question on whom the *onus probandi* is imposed, has been considered as of great importance, and the testimony adduced by the parties has been critically examined. It is contended, that the Antelope, having been wrongfully dispossessed of her slaves by American citizens, and being now, together with her cargo, in the power of the United States, ought to be restored, without farther inquiry, to those out of whose possession she was thus wrongfully taken. No proof of property, it is said, ought to be required. Possession is in such a case evidence of property.

Conceding this as a general proposition, the counsel for the United States deny its application to this case. A distinction is taken between *men,* who are generally free, and *goods,* which are always property. Although, with respect to the last, possession may constitute the only proof of property which is demandable, something more is necessary where men are claimed. Some proof should be exhibited that the possession was legally acquired. A distinction has been also drawn between Africans unlawfully taken from the subjects of a foreign power by persons acting under the authority of the United States, and Africans first captured by a belligerent privateer, or by a pirate, and then brought rightfully into the United States, under a reasonable apprehension that a violation of their laws was intended. Being rightfully in the possession of an American Court, that Court, it is contended, must be governed by the laws of its own country; and the condition of these Africans must depend on the laws of the United States, not on the laws of Spain and Portugal.

Had the Arraganta been a regularly commissioned cruiser, which had committed no infraction of the neutrality of the United States, her capture of the Antelope must have been considered as lawful, and no question could have arisen respecting the rights of the original claimants. The question of prize or no prize belongs solely to the Courts of the captor. But, having violated the neutrality of the United States, and having entered our ports, not voluntarily, but under coercion, some difficulty exists respecting the extent of the obligation to restore, on the mere proof of former possession, which is imposed on this government.

If, as is charged in the libels of both the Consuls, as well as of the United States, she was a pirate, hovering on the coast with intent to introduce slaves in violation of the laws of the United States, our treaty requires that property rescued from pirates shall be restored to the Spanish owner on his making proof of his property.

Whether the General Ramirez, originally the Antelope, is to be considered as the prize of a commissioned belligerent ship of war unlawfully equipped in the United States, or as a pirate, it seems proper to make some inquiry into the title of the claimants.

In support of the Spanish claim, testimony is produced, showing the documents under which the Antelope sailed from the Havana on the voyage on which she was captured; that she was owned by a Spanish house of trade in that place; that she was employed in the business of purchasing slaves, and had purchased and taken on board a considerable number, when she was seized as prize by the Arraganta.

Whether, on this proof, Africans brought into the United States, under the various circumstances belonging to this case, ought to be restored or not, is a question on which much difficulty has been felt. It is unnecessary to state the reasons in support of the affirmative or negative answer to it, because the Court is divided on it, and, consequently, no principle is settled. So much of the decree of the Circuit Court as directs restitution to the Spanish claimant of the Africans found on board the Antelope when she was captured by the Arraganta, is affirmed.

There is some difficulty in ascertaining their number. The libel claims one hundred and fifty as belonging to Spanish subjects, and charges that one hundred or more of these were on board the Antelope. Grondona and Ximenes, Spanish officers of the Antelope before her capture, both depose positively to the number of one hundred and sixty-six. Some deduction, however, is to be made from the weight of Grondona's testimony, because, he says, in one of his depositions, that he did not count the slaves on the last day when some were brought on board, and adds, that he had lost his papers, and spoke from memory, and from the information he had received from others of the crew, after his arrival in the Havana. Such of the crew as were examined, concur with Grondona and Ximenes as to numbers.[11]

The depositions of the Spanish witnesses on this point, are opposed by those of John Smith, the Captain of the General Ramirez, and William Brunton, one of the crew of the Arraganta, who was transferred to the Antelope.

John Smith deposes, that ninety-three Africans were found on board the Antelope when captured, which he believes to have been Spanish property. He also says, that one hundred and eighty-three were taken out of Portuguese vessels.[12]

William Brunton deposes, that more slaves were taken out of the Portuguese ship than were in any other, and that ninety odd were represented by the crew to have been on board the Antelope when she was captured.[13]

If, to the positive testimony of these witnesses, we add the inference to be drawn from the statement of the libel, and the improbability that so large a number of Africans as are claimed could have been procured, under the circumstances in which the Antelope was placed, between the 13th, when she was liberated by the first pirate who seized her, and the 23d, when she was finally captured, we are rather disposed to think the weight of testimony is in favour of the smaller number.[14] But supposing perfect equality in this respect, the decision ought, we think, to be against the claimant.

Whatever doubts may attend the question whether the Spanish claimants are entitled to restitution of all the Africans taken out of their possession with the Antelope, we cannot doubt the propriety of demanding ample proof of the extent of that possession. Every legal principle which requires the plaintiff to prove his claim in any case, applies with full force to this point; and no countervailing consideration exists. The *onus probandi,* as to the number of Africans which were on board when the vessel was captured, unquestionably lies on the Spanish libellants. Their proof is not satisfactory beyond ninety-three. The individuals who compose this number must be designated to the satisfaction of the Circuit Court.

We proceed next to consider the libel of the Vice-Consul of Portugal. It claims one hundred and thirty slaves, or more, "all of whom, as the libellant is informed and believes," are the property of a subject, or subjects of his Most Faithful Majesty; and although "the rightful owners of such slaves be not at this time individually and certainly known to the libellant, he hopes and expects soon to discover them."[15]

John Smith, and William Brunton, whose depositions have already been noticed, both state, that several Africans were taken out of Portuguese vessels; but neither of them state the means by which they ascertained the national character of the vessels they had plundered. It does not appear that their opinions were founded on any other fact than the flag under which the vessels sailed. Grondona, also, states the plunder of a Portuguese vessel, lying in the same port, and engaged in the same traffic with the Antelope when she was captured; but his testimony is entirely destitute of all those circumstances which would enable us to say, that he had any knowledge of the real character of the vessel, other than was derived from her flag. The cause furnishes no testimony of any description, other than these general declarations, that the proprietors of the Africans now claimed by the Vice-Consul of Portugal, were the subjects of his king; nor is there any allusion to the individuals to whom they belong. These vessels were plundered in March, 1820, and the libel was filed in August of the same year. From that time to this, a period of more than five years, no subject of the crown of Portugal has appeared to assert his title to this property, no individual has been designated as its probable owner. This inattention to a subject of so much real interest, this total disregard of a valuable property, is so contrary to the common course of human action, as to justify serious suspicion that the real owner dares not avow himself.

That Americans, and others, who cannot use the flag of their own nation, carry on this criminal and inhuman traffic under the flags of other countries, is a fact of such general notoriety, that Courts of admiralty may act upon it. It cannot be necessary to take particular depositions, to prove a fact which is matter of general and public history. This long, and otherwise unaccountable absence, of any Portuguese claimant, furnishes irresistible testimony, that no such claimant exists, and that the real owner belongs to some other nation, and feels the necessity of concealment.

An attempt has been made to supply this defect of testimony, by adducing a letter from the secretary to whose department the foreign relations of Portugal are supposed to be intrusted, suggesting the means of transporting to Portugal those slaves which may be in the possession of the Vice-Consul, as the property of his fellow subjects. Allow to this document all the effect which can be claimed for it, and it can do no more than supply the want of an express power from the owners of the slaves to receive them. It cannot be considered as ascertaining the owners, or as proving their property.

The difficulty, then, is not diminished by this paper. These Africans still remain unclaimed by the owner, or by any person professing to know the owner. They are rightfully taken from American citizens, and placed in possession of the law. No property whatever in them is shown. It is said, that possession, in a case of this description, is equivalent to property. Could this be conceded, who had the possession? From whom were they taken by the Arraganta? It is not alleged that they are the property of the crown, but of some individual. Who is that individual? No such person is shown to exist, and his existence, after such a lapse of time, cannot be presumed.

The libel, which claims them for persons entirely unknown, alleges a state of things which is *prima facie* evidence of an intent to violate the laws of the United States, by the commission of an act which, according to those laws, entitles these men to freedom. Nothing whatever can interpose to arrest the course of the law, but the title of the real proprietor. No such title appears, and every presumption is against its existence.

We think, then, that all the Africans, now in possession of the Marshal for the District of Georgia, and under the control of the Circuit Court of the United States for that District, which were brought in with the Antelope, otherwise called the General Ramirez, except those which may be designated as the property of the Spanish claimants, ought to be delivered up to the United States, to be disposed of according to law. So much of the sentence of the Circuit Court as is contrary to this opinion, is to be reversed, and the residue affirmed.

Printed, Henry Wheaton, *Reports of Cases Argued and Adjudged in the Supreme Court of the United States . . .* , X (New York, 1825), 114–32.

1. The Amedie, 1 Acton 240, 12 Eng. Rep. 92 (P.C., 1810).

2. 1 Acton 251, 12 Eng. Rep. 96–97. JM's quotation was not from Acton's report but from a slightly different version of Grant's judgment contained in a note to The Fortuna, 1 Dods. 84 n., 165 Eng. Rep. 1241 (Adm., 1811).

3. The Fortuna, 1 Dods. 81, 165 Eng. Rep. 1240 (Adm., 1811).

4. The Diana, 1 Dods. 95, 165 Eng. Rep. 1245 (Adm., 1813).

5. 1 Dods. 97, 165 Eng. Rep. 1246.

6. Le Louis, 2 Dods. 210, 238, 165 Eng. Rep. 1464, 1473 (Adm., 1817).

7. 2 Dods. 247, 165 Eng. Rep. 1476.

8. 2 Dods. 249–50, 165 Eng. Rep. 1477.

9. 2 Dods. 255, 165 Eng. Rep. 1479.

10. Although he did not cite it by name, JM surely had in mind La Jeune Eugénie, decided by Justice Story on circuit in 1822. In this case an American naval vessel captured an empty slaver, American-built but flying the French flag. His decree upheld the seizure, though at the request of the executive he ultimately agreed to turn the vessel over to the French government. In the course of his opinion Story stated that an American court could consider the slave trade to be an offense against the law of nations (26 Fed. Cas. 846–47). According to Story, JM at the time was in agreement with his opinion: "He thinks I am right, but the questions are new to his mind." Three years later the Court majority (presumably including JM) declined to adopt this view. Story kept silent, but privately he maintained that he had been overruled in The Antelope. "I always thought that I was right," he wrote in 1842, and "continue to think so" (Story to Jeremiah Mason, 21 Feb. 1822, in G. J. Clark, ed., *Memoir, Autobiography and Correspondence of Jeremiah Mason* [Kansas City, Mo., 1917], 256; Story to Ezekiel Bacon, 19 Nov. 1842, Story, *Life and Letters*, II, 431).

11. Depositions of Domingo Grondona, 29 Dec. 1820, 13 Feb. 1821; deposition of Tomás Ximenes, 13 Feb. 1821, The Antelope, record on appeal (second case, Spanish claim), 40, 56, App. Cas. Nos. 1161–62.

12. Deposition of John Smith, 14 Feb. 1821, ibid., 58.

13. Deposition of William Brunton, 18 Jan. 1821, ibid., 48–49.

14. Two weeks before the *Arraganta* captured the *Antelope*, the Spanish vessel was raided by a vessel flying the flag of a revolutionary South American republic. It carried off most of the Africans then on board. The *Antelope* then began to replenish its supply (Noonan, *The Antelope*, 28–29, citing "Declaration" of the captain of the *Antelope*, 30 Mar. 1820; The Antelope, record on appeal [second case, Spanish claim], 16–17).

15. Libel of Portuguese consul, Francis Sorrell, filed 12 Aug. 1820, The Antelope, record on appeal (first case, Portuguese claim), 3–4.

To John Adams

Sir   Washington March 19th. 1825

To the frequent inquiries which I make respecting your health I have the satisfaction to receive the general answer that you enjoy a larger share of that blessing than usually belongs to a person who is so nearly approaching the beginning of his second century. You have my best wishes for its continuance.

A desire to leave behind me a less objectionable impression of the only work I ever published than the first edition has induced me to revise and correct it; and I now ask you to accept a copy of my history of the colonies; originally the Introduction to the Life of Washington; as a testimonial of my grateful recollection of former personal kindness, and of the profound respect with which I remain Your Obedt. Servt

J MARSHALL

ALS, Adams Family Papers, MHi. Addressed to Adams in Massachusetts and noted by JM as delivered by Joseph Story. Endorsed by Adams.

To Timothy Pickering

My dear Sir   Washington March 19th 1825

You are among the very few of those statesmen of the last century who are still in being, and who remain the same. Be assured it is with no little gratification I hear of the uncommon share of good health and spirits with which you are blessed.

I have revised my Introduction to the life of Washington, and have published it as a sketch of our colonial history. I ask you to accept it as a mark of the sincere respect and esteem of dear Sir, Your Obedt. Servt

J MARSHALL

ALS, Pickering Papers, MHi. Addressed to Pickering in Salem, Mass.; noted as carried by "The Honble Mr. Story." Endorsed by Pickering as received 30 Mar.

To James Barbour

Dear Sir   Richmond March 27th. 1825

    I had yesterday the pleasure of receiving your letter enclosing a warrant for the admission of Young Mr. Brown as a student in the Academy at West Point, should he, on examination be found worthy of Admission.[1] Be pleased to receive my acknowledgements for this favor & be assured that I shall not be unmindful of it. With great respect & esteem, I am your Obedt

                                   J MARSHALL

ALS, RG 94, DNA. Addressed to Barbour in Washington and franked; postmarked Richmond, 27 Mar. Endorsed "acknowledges the rect of the appt of J Brown Jr for 1826."

1. Letter not found. James Brown was the son of James Brown, Jr., one of Virginia's auditors of public accounts. He was presumably the James D. Brown of Virginia who was admitted to the academy in 1827 (file of James Brown, U.S. Military Academy Application Papers, RG 94, DNA; *List of Cadets Admitted into the United States Military Academy* [West Point, N.Y., 1912], 14).

To Benjamin W. Leigh

Dear Sir   [ca. 30 March 1825]

    I will not be so unreasonable as to request that you will read the volume which this note accompanies. But I may ask you to accept it as a mark of the true esteem with which I remain your Obedt

                                   J MARSHALL

ALS, ViU. Addressed to Leigh. Endorsed by Leigh. Undated (see n. 1).

1. JM at this time was sending out copies of his *History of the Colonies*. He probably sent a copy to Leigh, his Richmond neighbor, after returning from the Supreme Court term.

To Henry Clay

Dear Sir   Richmond April 4th. 1825

    I have received your address to your former constituents; and, as it was franked by you, I presume I am indebted to you for it.[1] I have read it with great pleasure as well as attention, and am gratified at the full and complete view you have given of some matters which the busy world has been employing itself upon. I required no evidence respecting the charge made by Mr. Kremer, nor should I have required any had I been unacquainted with you or with the transaction, because I have long since ceased to credit charges destitute of proof, & to consider them as meer aspersions. The minuteness of detail however will enable your friends to encounter any insinuations on that subject which may be thrown out in their hearing. More of this may be looked for than any hostility to you would produce. There is unquestionably a party determined to oppose Mr. Adams at the next election, and this party will attack him through you. It is an old and has been a successful Stratagem. No part of your letter was more necessary than that which respects your former relatio⟨ns⟩ with that Gentleman. I am dear Sir with respect & esteem, Your Obedt Servt

J MARSHALL

ALS, Clay Papers, DLC. Addressed to Clay in Washington and franked; postmarked Richmond, 4 Apr. Endorsed by Clay.

1. Henry Clay, *Address to the People of the Congressional District Composed of the Counties of Fayette, Woodford, and Clarke in Kentucky* (Washington, D.C., 1825). It is reprinted in James F. Hopkins and Mary W. M. Hargreaves, eds., *The Papers of Henry Clay,* IV (Lexington, Ky., 1972), 143–65.

To Bushrod Washington

Dear Sir   Richmond Apl. 9th. 1825

I am closely engaged in preparing my corrections of the life, and have no doubt they will be in perfect readiness by the winter, should any printer be disposed to engage in the publication. This however is a business which we cannot press. My present employment has brought to my recollection a letter which I think ought to be suppressed but which I forgot to mention to you in Washington. It is a letter written at Morristown to General Greene about the last of December 1779 or beginning of January 1780, in which General Washington expresses a good deal of dissatisfaction with General Greene about his quarters.[1] I wish you would look at it & do what you think right. Yours truely

J MARSHALL

ALS, Marshall Papers, DLC. Addressed to Washington in Philadelphia; postmarked Richmond, 8 Apr. Endorsed by Washington.

1. See JM to Washington, 11 Dec. 1824 and n. 2.

To Bushrod Washington

My dear Sir   Richmond April 13th. 1825

I have received your letter and am very happy to be informed that you will devote a part of this summer to a perusal of the letters.[1] I believe it will be proper to make some deductions for the purpose of avoiding repetition but several letters may be withdrawn or abridged without affecting the number of volumes. I could not estimate accurately the number of printed pages which would be required to comprehend the manuscript, but my conjecture was that the volumes would be rather larger than is to be wished.

If Mr. Small is broke, for which I shall be truely sorry, you will much oblige me if you can enquire what arrangement is made respecting my history.[2] I suppose the unsold volumes will be transferred to some other bookseller; but I shall be glad to hear something farther on the subject. I am just setting out for Fauquier. Yours truely

J MARSHALL

ALS, Miscellaneous Manuscripts, NHi. Addressed to Washington in Philadelphia; postmarked Richmond, 13 Apr. Endorsed by Washington.

1. Letter not found.
2. Abraham Small was the Philadelphia publisher of JM's *History of the Colonies.*

To Edward Everett

Sir   Richmond May 3d. 1825

A temporary absence from Richmond prevented my receiving your letter of the 29th. of March until a day or two past, and will be my apology for not answering it sooner.[1] I am much honoured by being elected a member of the Bunker hill monument Association and beg you to make my profound acknowledgements to the institution.[2] As I am entirely uninformed of what it may be proper for me to do, I ask the favour of you to make me such communications as will enable me to do whatever is requisite. With very great respect I am Sir, Your Obedt. Servt

J MARSHALL

ALS, KHi. Addressed to Everett in Boston; postmarked Richmond, 4 May. Endorsed by Everett.

1. Letter not found. Everett (1794–1865), the noted orator, statesman, and man of letters, was then serving the first of five terms in Congress. Among his many pursuits was the editorship of the *North American Review.* He was later governor of Massachusetts, minister to Great Britain, secretary of state, and U.S. senator.
2. Everett was one of the founders of the Bunker Hill Monument Association and served

as director from 1823 to 1825 (George Washington Warren, *The History of the Bunker Hill Monument Association during the First Century of the United States of America* [Boston, 1877], 36–39, 417).

United States v. Cochran
Opinion
U.S. Circuit Court, North Carolina, 13 May 1825

This equity suit proceeded by way of information rather than by bill, the difference between the two being mainly one of form. Where the rights of the sovereign were concerned, the subject matter was presented as the information of the government officer — in this case the U.S. attorney for North Carolina — and stated the acts of the defendant that were injurious to the sovereign. U.S. Attorney Thomas Devereux filed an information against Robert Cochran, collector of the port of Wilmington, and others in August 1823. Prior to this suit the United States had obtained a law judgment against Cochran for $145,000 and another judgment against his sureties for $10,000, the penalty of his performance bond. The execution against Cochran failed to produce any property on which to recover the judgment against him. The sureties paid the $10,000 judgment against them. According to the information, Cochran in 1820 had conveyed all his visible property to trustees, one of whom was one of his sureties. In addition, the information stated, Cochran secretly set aside $10,000 to indemnify his sureties, which the sureties later paid to the U.S. Treasury in satisfaction of the judgment against them. The information charged that Cochran's actions were taken with an intent to defraud the United States and that the sureties' payment of $10,000 out of Cochran's funds did not discharge them from their original liability for that amount. Marshall's opinion of 13 May 1825 accompanied a partial decree dealing with the question of the sureties' liability (John Mitford [Lord Redesdale], *A Treatise on the Pleadings in Suits in the Court of Chancery* [3d Am. ed., New York, 1833], 7, 99–100; U.S. Cir. Ct., N.C., Min. Bk., 13 May 1824, 13 Nov. 1824, 13 May 1825; information [filed 25 Aug. 1823], U.S. v. Cochran, 1823, Records of U.S. Cir. Ct., N.C., RG 21, GEpFRC).

In this case Robert Cochran, collector at the port of Wilmington, being very largely indebted to the United States, made a deed of his property for their benefit. Previous to the execution of this deed, he deposited $10,000, the amount of the bond executed to the United States, for the faithful performance of his duty, in a trunk which was placed in the bank, and absconded. From Baltimore he addressed a letter to his sureties, requesting the trunk to be taken out of the bank, and the money to be applied to their exoneration.[1]

The money was received at the treasury and the bond given up. It being afterwards discovered that this was the money of the collector and not of the securities, this suit is brought to compel the securities to pay the amount of the bond, considering the money received as constituting no equitable discharge to them.

It is contended on the part of the United States, that the insolvency of Cochran, vested all his property, including this $10,000, in the United States, and that this sum being theirs could not be applied in exoneration of his securities.

The act of Congress declares, that where any revenue officer, &c., indebted to the United States, shall become insolvent, the debt due to the United States shall be first satisfied, and that this priority shall extend to cases where a debtor not having sufficient property to pay all his debts, shall make a voluntary assignment thereof.[2]

This act does not transfer the property itself to the United States, but subjects it to their debt in the first instance.

The assignee holds it as the debtor would hold it, liable to the claim of the United States, and if he converts it to his own use, or puts it out of reach of the United States, he is undoubtedly responsible for its value.

But the property thus liable to the United States, is liable for the whole debt; for one part of it as much as for the other. It is as applicable to the bond in which the sureties are bound, as to that part of the debt for which the principal alone is responsible. No person will doubt the legal capacity of the United States to apply any sum of $10,000, to the discharge of the bond-debt, leaving the residue unpaid. Such an application of a payment would undoubtedly never be presumed from any equivocal act; but a plain and positive appropriation of a payment to the bond, could not afterwards be set aside.

But the power of the debtor to apply his payments, is co-extensive with that of the creditor, and is to be exercised in the first instance. This principle has, it is believed, never been denied. If it be correct, then the power of Mr. Cochran to apply this sum of money in discharge of the bond, and in exoneration of the sureties to it, is co-extensive with that of the United States to make the same application of it. If, then, Mr. Cochran had, without any assignment of his property, paid this money into the treasury, with a direction that it should be applied to the bond, he would have exercised a right which the law gives to every debtor.

If the money should be received under this direction, no doubt can be entertained of the obligation to apply the payment as directed. If it should be rejected, it might be tendered in due form, and to suits brought on the bond, and on the open account a tender might be pleaded to the suit on the bond, unless some distinction can be taken between this bond, and the common case of a bond given for part of a debt. The Court has reflected on this distinction, and cannot perceive any legal difference between the cases.

Does the transfer of this money to the sureties change the law of the case? We think not.

The sureties have paid it into the treasury in discharge of their bond, which has been delivered up. Had this transaction taken place, with the full knowledge of the treasury department, that the money had been received by the sureties from Mr. Cochran, no question could have arisen respecting it. Is the payment the less valid because it was made without communicating this circumstance?

If the United States have sustained any injury by the concealment, equity will relieve against that injury, and place them in the situation in which they stood before the payment was made. If, with full knowledge of the circumstance, the money might still have been legally applied in discharge of the bond, then, the fact that it was not communicated cannot change the law.

It has been very properly argued, that the act of Congress gives to the debt due to the United States priority over debts due to individuals, but not to one part of the debt due to the United States over any other part of it; nor does it vest the property absolutely in the United States, though it gives them a right to pursue it for the purpose of appropriating it in payment. It would seem to follow, that the right to apply payments while the money is in the hands of the debtors, is not affected by the act of Congress, but remains as it would stand, independent of that act.

If, then, the sureties had declared to the treasury department that the money was received from Mr. Cochran, to be paid in discharge of their bond, and had tendered it in payment thereof, we think the tender would have been valid, and might have been pleaded to a suit on the bond.

We are of opinion, therefore, that this suit must be dismissed as against the sureties.[3]

Printed, John W. Brockenbrough, *Reports of Cases Decided by the Honourable John Marshall...*, II (Philadelphia, 1837), 277–79.

1. In his answer Cochran recited previous attempts to indemnify his sureties long before he contemplated any act of insolvency. The sureties refused any security, however, stating their full confidence in him. Finally, in Aug. 1820, more than a month before assigning his property in trust for the benefit of the U.S., he put the sum of $10,000 in two packages of $5,000 each, which were sealed up and addressed to the two sureties. Cochran placed the packages in a trunk, which he later deposited in a Fayetteville bank. Embarrassed by his desperate circumstances, he left the state and resigned as collector. From Baltimore in Oct. 1820 he addressed a letter to one of his sureties, informing him of the money set aside for him and his co-surety. Cochran insisted that his action had completely divested him of all right and title to the $10,000 (answer of Robert Cochran, 10 Nov. 1824, U.S. v. Cochran).

2. JM referred to the 1797 act concerning the settlement of accounts with receivers of public money (*U.S. Statutes at Large*, I, 515).

3. According to one of the sureties, the U.S. treasury was grossly negligent in not detecting Cochran's defalcations, which began from the time he became collector in 1807 and continued until his resignation in 1820. Cochran regularly diverted public money to his own use, concealing this fraud in his reports under the heading of "Bonds outstanding & unpaid," a category that reflected a steadily increasing sum throughout his tenure. The suit proceeded against Cochran's trustee, against whom a decree was pronounced on 14 May 1828 (answer of John Huske, executor of John Winslow, 11 Nov. 1824, U.S. v. Cochran; U.S. Cir. Ct., N.C., Min. Bk., 14 May 1828).

From Elias B. Caldwell

Washington May 23. 1825

To the Honorable Chief Justice and the associate Justices of the Supreme Court of the United States

When this shall be handed you, I shall be in the eternal world. I thank you for all your kindness to me personally & officially.[1]

I leave a large and helpless family. I believe my son James fully able to discharge the duties of Clerk. If you should see fit to appoint him, it would be an entire relief to my family. I have the Honor to be, with great respect, your obt. sert.

(SIGNED) E. B. CALDWELL

Copy, RG 267, DNA.

1. Caldwell (1776–1825), chief clerk of the Supreme Court since 1800, died in June after a lengthy illness (Hallie L. Wright, "Sketch of Elias Boudinot Caldwell," *Records of the Columbia Historical Society*, XXIV [1922], 204–13; P. J. Staudenraus, *The African Colonization Movement, 1816–1865* [New York, 1961], 24–25, 74, 97).

Byrd v. Byrd's Executor
Opinion
U.S. Circuit Court, Virginia, 9 June 1825

In accordance with the earlier decree in this case of 16 December 1824, the chancery commissioner made a further report to the court in May 1825. This report stated an account of the personal estate that had been applied to debts that bound the real estate. It showed both the amount in specie according to the scale of depreciation and the amount in paper money. The commissioner also reported the amount of specialty debts — debts that bound the land — paid by the estate in slaves purchased at the sale of the estate. This account contained three columns: the specie value of slaves based on the average price per slave in sales preceding the issuance of paper money; the specie value according to the scale of depreciation; and the value in paper money. Marshall discussed the issues arising from this report in his opinion accompanying the court's decree of 9 June 1825 (Byrd v. Byrd's Executor, Opinion, 16 Dec. 1824; commissioner's report, 30 May 1825, Byrd v. Byrd, U.S. Cir. Ct., Va., Ended Cases [Restored], 1838, Vi; U.S. Cir. Ct., Va., Ord. Bk. XII, 23–25).

Bird & al
   v
Birds admr.

The principal question now to be determined is, What rule shall govern in ascertaining the value of the paper money paid by the personal estate in discharge of debts which bound the land? ¶1

¶2   It was decided at the last term, that the claim of the personal estate did not extend to the full relief which the real estate obtained, but to the actual burthen borne by itself. That opinion is still retained.

¶3   The parties have suggested three rules by one of which it has been supposed that the value of these payments must be ascertained.

1st. The first is the value of slaves according to sales made in specie some short time before the emission of paper.

———

2d. The value of the money according to the scale of depreciation for which the slaves and personal estate actually sold.

———

3d. The third is the value of the money by the scale at the time each debt was discharged.

¶4   1st. If the actual value of the particular slaves and other property constituting the subject of the present enquiry was totally unknown it would be necessary to resort to other extraneous evidence for the purpose of fixing this value, and on the failure of any estimate made of the property itself, other less certain evidence would be received. In looking for this other testimony, that to which the counsel for the specific legatees have resorted, the actual sales of property of the same description, and probably of nearly the same value would not be disregarded.[1] But when the property itself has been actually sold, fairly and legally sold, its value is ascertained by that standard which determines the worth of everything. We cannot desert this certain standard for one which is conjectural. Had this sale been made for specie instead of paper money, no person would have resorted to other sales in order to ascertain the value of the property sold. That the sales were made for paper can make no other difference than arises from a supposed misapprehension in the bidders at the sale of the real value of the medium in which it was made. This value was afterwards established by the legislature who must be supposed to have been regulated by their knowledge of the actual state of the currency. The rule probably works unjustly in many cases; but it is a general rule, it has governed all the transactions of the day, and we cannot be sure that a departure from it would not work more injustice than an adherence to it.

¶5   There were many circumstances to reduce the price of slaves and other property at the time this sale was made. Our ports were blocked up, the produce of labour was unsaleable, and the nation was engaged in a war which would probably render this gloomy state of things of incalculable continuance. These circumstances might have great influence on the intrinsic value of property. Within our own recollection changes almost equally great have taken place. Who would ascertain the value of property in 1787 by sales made in 1784? or the value of property at this day by sales made in 1817? It is not unreasonable to suppose that the sales of 1768 or of 1772 may afford as inaccurate a standard for the value in 1777. It is true that just ideas of depreciation may not have prevailed at the time and had these sales been occasioned by the illegal or iniquitou⟨s⟩ conduct of the heirs, there might be justice in throwing the loss on them. But the sale was inevitable. The law required it; and the exx. whose duty it was to sell the personal estate had no power to sell the lands. There is then no blame attached to any person. No person could have brought the real estate to the aid of the personal or have prevented its sale. The loss produced by that sale is one of those calamities which grew out of the state of things, and which human wisdom could not avoid. Equity when it interposes in such a case, must consider all its circumstances, and the situation of all parties. In doing so, no reason is perceived which will justify a departure from the sales themselves in search of any other standard to ascertain the value of the property sold, nor a departure from the scale of depreciation to ascertain the value of the money given for it.

But supposing the scale of depreciation to furnish the rule, the parties ¶6 still differ as to its application. The specific legatees claim the date of the sale and the residuary legatees, the time when the money was applied in discharge of the debts.

That the time of payment does not furnish the true rate of reimburse- ¶7 ment to the personal estate was, I think substantially decided at the last term, and I still retain that opinion. It is true, as has been urged by counsel, that if we personify the personal and real estate; and suppose one to have advanced a given sum for the other on a given day, the value of the sum on that day by the scale of depreciation would have constituted the demand both in law and equity of the person making the advance. It would have been a legal demand, regulated by the law. But this case stands on distinct principles. The claim of the personal estate is not given or measured by the act of assembly. It originates in equity, and is coextensive with its equity. This equity regards the gain of the real estate and the loss of the personal. There is no exact standard by which these are to be measured in the case which has actually occurred, but certainly the value of money which in fact depreciated daily, at the time of its payment to the creditor, does not approach the actual loss sustained by the person making the payment so nearly as its value when the property was sold to raise it.

I felt some doubts whether, as the sales were probably made on credit, ¶8 the scale at the day of sale or at the day of payment ought to be applied. I have supposed that the scale at the day of sale furnishes the true standard, because, at that early stage of depreciation, it is not probable that the future rapid decline of the money was foreseen, and because the legislature has fixed the value of all contracts payable in future at their date.

I am therefore of opinion that the value of the money advanced by the ¶9 personal for the real estate is to be ascertained by the scale of depreciation on the day the personal property was sold.

The next question is to what sum the specific legatees are entitled from ¶10 the general fund.

¶11   This question has been already decided so far as respects slaves given by name. Where they have been given by number to be selected by the legatee, it remains to be decided by what rule their value, or price, shall be estimated.

¶12   The testator constituted a fund for the payment of his debts, to consist in part of one hundred slaves. He then gave, to his son John, a choice of ten slaves, not to interfere with those which his wife might chuse to keep.

¶13   It appears that the testator left 125 slaves at his death. Of these 100 were withdrawn by his will for the payment of debts. It could not be intended by the testator that his sons choice should interfere with this fund. It must be made from the residue. Ninety two slaves were sold in April 1777 & the residue in November of the same year. The first sale must be presumed to have been made in pursuance of the will; and as the debts exceeded the fund it would have been the duty of the exx., had she been limited to the number prescribed in the will, to have selected the most valuable for sale. It follows that eight of the highest priced slaves sold in Novr. 1777 must be considered as part of the hundred directed to be sold by the will and John Bird is at liberty to select ten from those which remain. He will be entitled to twenty years interest on this sum.

¶14   If his legacy were to be satisfied out of the jointure slaves sold after the death of Mrs. Bird he would be entitled to interest only from that sale.

¶15   It has been also made a question what interest shall be allowed the personal estate on the sums it has advanced for debts with which the real estate was chargeable?

¶16   I think it most consistent with the general course of the court, and with the justice of this particular case to limit the interest to twenty years.[2]

AD, Marshall Judicial Opinions, PPAmP; printed, John W. Brockenbrough, *Reports of Cases Decided by the Honourable John Marshall . . .* , II (Philadelphia, 1837), 180–84. For JM's deletions and interlineations, see Textual Notes below.

1. The commissioner settled on a value of £60 per slave, based on the average price of mortgaged slaves sold in 1768 and 1772 (commissioner's report, 30 May 1825, Byrd v. Byrd).

2. For the detailed decree, see U.S. Cir. Ct., Va., Ord. Bk. XII, 23–25. Further decrees and reports occurred in 1826 and 1827. After the deaths of Charles W. Byrd and William Byrd Page in 1828, the suit was revived in the names of their executors and administrators. It remained on the docket until 1838 (U.S. Cir. Ct., Va., Ord. Bk. XII, 62, 70–71, 105, 160, 295, 319; U.S. Cir. Ct., Va., Index to Ended Causes, 1790–1861, Vi).

Textual Notes

¶ 2 l. 2   estate ~~gained~~ ↑obtained,↓ but
¶ 3 l. 1 beg.   ~~In~~ The parties have
    l. 3   sales made ~~for~~ ↑in↓ specie
¶ 4 ll. 7–8   probably of ↑nearly↓ the same
    l. 9   sold, [*erasure*] fairly and legally ↑sold,↓ its
    l. 21   would not ~~be~~ ↑work↓ more

¶ 5 ll. 7–8	property ~~made~~ in 1787	
l. 10	afford as ~~untrue~~ ↑inaccurate↓ a standard	
l. 16	attached to ~~those who claim the personal estate. Neither they, nor the person who acted for them,~~ ↑any person. No person↓ could	
l. 17	aid ↑of the personal↓ or have	
l. 20	must consider ↑all its circumstances, and↓ the	
l. 21	perceived [*erasure*] which	
l. 23	sold, nor ~~of~~ ↑a↓ departure from	
¶ 7 ll. 4–5	suppose ~~the personal~~ ↑one↓ to have	
l. 6	that day ↑by the scale of depreciation↓ would	
l. 14	money which ↑in fact↓ depreciated	
¶ 8 l. 1 beg.	I ~~had~~ ↑felt↓ some	
¶ 9 l. 3	the day ~~of sale~~ the personal	
¶11 l. 1 beg.	~~It~~ ↑This question↓ has	
¶13 l. 1 beg.	~~Ninety~~ It appears	
ll. 10–11	hundred ↑directed to be↓ sold	
¶15 ll. 2–3	which the ~~person~~ real estate	

To Bushrod Washington

My dear Sir   Richmond June 12th. 1825

I received your letter a few days past[1] & ought immediately to have answered it, but when you reach my age you will find that when a man is engaged as I am at present, a thing postponed is very apt to slip the memory & to be longer neglected than it ought to be. I concur with you in the opinion that the Clerk can be appointed only when the court is in session, & I suppose there would be an impropriety if indeed there would be a power to make the appointment at the August term. I wish most devoutly that the business was over. I receive continual applications which are extremely painful to me because most of them are from gentlemen I should feel great pleasure in serving. I hope never again to have any voice in an appointment.

I received the other day a letter from Mr. Griffith.[2] I write to him that you had mentioned him to me in such terms as to co[n]vince that no gentleman could be proposed whose pretensions were superior to his, but that I had pledged myself to a very respectable young man the son of a particular friend. That I did not believe this young gentleman could succeed; and that as soon as his failure should be ascertained I would most unquestionably support Mr. Griffith. I still believe that Mr. Randolph has no chance, and that I shall be at liberty to promote your wishes as to Mr. Griffith.[3]

I have some long & troublesome suits in chancery which occupy me very closely one of which is particular[ly] unpleasant because between old friends, and one of those unfortunate cases that the ruin or nearly the ruin of one or the other must be the consequence.[4] I have just made up an opinion in one for the division of a man's estate who was married at the same time to two women the first of whom had two husbands. The case depended on the legitimacy of children born in wedlock & I have determined that the conclusion of the law in favour of legitimacy may be rebutted by strong circumstances although access of the husband to the wife was not impossible.[5] I am my dear Sir Your affectionate

J MARSHALL

ALS, Marshall Papers, DLC. Addressed to Washington at Mount Vernon; postmarked Richmond, 13 June. Endorsed by Washington.

1. Letter not found.

2. Letter not found. William Griffith (1766–1826) was a prominent New Jersey lawyer and legal writer. From 1820 to 1824 he published the *Annual Law Register,* a compilation of state government officials, laws, and regulations. He was eventually appointed clerk of the Supreme Court but died before assuming his duties.

3. JM's candidate was possibly Thomas Mann Randolph II (1792-1848) of the Tuckahoe branch of the Randolph family. Randolph's stepfather was JM's friend John Brockenbrough (Jonathan Daniels, *The Randolphs of Virginia* [Garden City, N.Y., 1972], xii, 273).

4. Probably Garnett, Brooke's Executor v. Macon (see Opinion, 25 Nov. 1825).

5. Stegall v. Stegall's Administrator, Opinion, 22 June 1825.

To Bushrod Washington

My dear Sir   Richmond June 20th. 1825

I have just received a letter from Colonel Troup of New York which surprised me a good deal.[1] It seems that a correspondence took place between General Washington and General Hamilton respecting the Farewell address which shows perhaps, for the letter to me does not state the fact positively, that it was written by General Hamilton. This correspondence was placed by Mr. Pendleton one of the exrs. of General Hamilton, confidentially in the hands of Mr. King. When Mr. King was preparing to sail for Europe young Mr. Hamilton demanded these papers from him, and he refused to surrender them; upon which a bill was filed in the name of Mrs. Hamilton to compel the restoration of them. Colo. Fish the surviving representative of General Hamilton is made a defendant to this bill and the object of Colonel Troups letter to me is to request that I would write to Colo. Fish advising him to resist the claim set up in the bill.[2] I write to Colonel Troup that I cannot take the liberty to obtrude my advice, unasked, on Colo. Fish; and that I do not know enough of the case to say what I think most advisable.[3] The existence of the correspondence cannot now be concealed, did the wish to conceal it exist; and should it go no farther than to show that General Hamilton retouched what was written by General Washington, or put in his own language sentiments expressed by both, it will still be supposed, should the correspondence be suppressed by the interference of those supposed to be most attached to the fame of General Washington, that the address is the entire production of General Hamiltons pen. It may also be thought that this correspondence was among the General's papers, and was concealed by you and myself. The fact undoubtedly is that we have never seen it. I am my dear Sir with esteem & affection, Your Obedt

J MARSHALL

ALS, Marshall Papers, DLC. Addressed to Washington at Mount Vernon; postmarked Richmond, 20 June. Endorsed by Washington.

1. Letter not found. Robert Troup (1757–1832) was a New York lawyer and a close friend of Alexander Hamilton.

2. For some years a controversy had been brewing over the authorship of President Washington's Farewell Address. In 1810 Nathaniel Pendleton, one of Hamilton's executors, found among the late statesman's papers Hamilton's major draft and "Abstract of Points for a Farewell Address" and correspondence from Washington about the address. Apparently out of concern that Hamilton's family would use the papers to show that Hamilton was the real author of the Farewell Address, Pendleton had the documents bundled and sealed and turned over to Rufus King. In May 1825 Hamilton's sons and his surviving executor, Nicholas Fish, visited King and asked for the papers. King, about to sail to London to assume his post as minister to Great Britain, refused to surrender the bundle, which gave rise to the suit in chancery. After his return from London, King in Oct. 1826 delivered the papers to the Hamilton family, which dropped the suit (Victor Hugo Paltsits, ed., *Washington's Farewell Address* [New York, 1935], 75–89).

3. Letter not found.

Stegall v. Stegall's Administrator
Opinion
U.S. Circuit Court, Virginia, 22 June 1825

The plaintiffs in this chancery suit claimed to be the widow and children of the late John Potter Stegall of Halifax County, Virginia. Catharine Stegall and her children, Martha Wright (wife of James Wright) and Jordan Sherrod (who had legally changed his surname), were residents of Franklin County, North Carolina. The former Catharine Newby and John Potter Stegall were married in Franklin County in December 1789. Catharine and her husband never lived together, she continuing to reside in North Carolina, while he resided some sixty or seventy miles away in Halifax County, Virginia. According to the bill in chancery, Stegall made regular visits to Catharine during the early years of their marriage and fathered two children, Martha and Jordan. Stegall eventually ceased his visits and married Susannah Portwood, with whom he lived in Halifax County until his death around 1819. Catharine and her children now claimed to be entitled to their legal portion of Stegall's real and personal estate. The defendants, in addition to Stegall's administrator, were the children Stegall fathered by

Susannah Portwood. After the filing of answers in 1823 and 1824 and taking of depositions, Marshall delivered his opinion accompanying an interlocutory decree of 22 June 1825 (bill in chancery [ca. 1822], Stegall v. Stegall's Administrator, U.S. Cir. Ct., Va., Ended Cases [Unrestored], 1832, Vi; U.S. Cir. Ct., Va., Ord. Bk. XII, 38–39).

This suit is brought by Catharine Stegall, widow of John Potter Stegall, deceased, and by James Wright, and Martha his wife, and Jordan R. Sherwood,[1] which said Martha and Jordan, are the children of the plaintiff, Catharine, and claim to be the children of the said John Potter Stegall, deceased, against Beverly Borum, administrator of the said John Potter Stegall, and John Jennett, and Elizabeth his wife, and William Smith, and Nancy his wife, and Elisha Hodge, which said Elizabeth and Nancy claim to be the children of the said John Potter Stegall, by a subsequent marriage, and which said Hodge is the purchaser of Nancy Smith's portion of the real estate.

The object of the suit on the part of Catharine Stegall is to recover her dower and distributive share of the personal estate of the said John Potter Stegall, and on the part of the other plaintiffs, to recover their just share of his lands and personal estate.

The bill states the intermarriage of the plaintiff, Catharine, with the said John Potter Stegall, and their intercourse with each other, which, though they did not live together, was continued for some years, during which the plaintiffs Jordan and Martha, who are his children, were born, and that this intercourse was continued until it was broken off by his marriage with Susannah Portwood, the mother of the other defendants; that he continued to reside with the said Susannah until his death, which happened in the year 1818 or 1819; that Elizabeth was born before marriage, and is, consequently, illegitimate, not having been recognised, or if recognised, still illegitimate.[2]

The answers of the children of the second marriage, assert their legitimacy, and controvert the marriage of the plaintiff, Catharine, who, about the year 1800, intermarried with Henry Hill by whom she has several children. They also deny that the plaintiffs, Martha and Jordan, are the children of John Potter Stegall.[3]

The answer of the administrator states, that he has, in obedience to a decree of the county court, delivered over the slaves to the persons who were supposed to be the distributees.[4]

As the claims of the several parties in this suit stand on distinct principles of law and fact, they will be separately considered; and, first, that of the plaintiff Catharine, who claims her dower in the land, and her distributive share of the personal estate of the deceased.

The facts that the plaintiff, Catharine Stegall, was the lawful wife of John Potter Stegall; that she lived separate from him in adultery with another man, to whom she was probably married, are satisfactorily proved.[5]

Her counsel, however, insist, that separation from her husband and her subsequent connexion with another man, are to be justified by the circumstances of the case. Her husband, it is said, was supposed to be married to another woman, and her parents would not permit her to accompany him. The words of the act of assembly are: "But if a wife willingly leave her husband, and go away and continue with her adulterer, she shall be barred forever of action to demand her dower, that she ought to have of her husband's lands, if she be convicted thereupon, except &c." 1 Rev. Code of 1819, ch. 107, sec. 10, p. 404.[6]

So far as respects that part of the provision which relates to the wife's willingly leaving her husband, I think it is satisfied by any separation which is voluntary on her part; and I think any separation voluntary, which is not brought about by his act or by any restraint on her person. In this case, it does not appear that her person was restrained, and the authority of her parents ceased on her marriage. Her husband wished her to accompany him, and she refused. The separation must therefore be considered as voluntary on her part. The report that he was married with another woman does not justify her refusal to accompany him, because it was not true, in fact, and she ought not to have acted upon it. But if his real situation was such as to justify separation, it could not justify her subsequent conduct. That was incompatible with the continuance of her claims on him as a husband.

The words, "and go away and continue with her adulterer," would, I am much inclined to think, be satisfied by an open state of adultery, whether the woman resided in the same house with her adulterer, or in separate houses; whether in her own or a friend's house, or in his; whether with or without the ceremony of marriage, which, in this case, is absolutely void, and which, if performed in the belief that her marriage with Stegall was a nullity, may justify that act to her own conscience, but cannot justify her claim to dower in Stegall's estate. I think it perfectly clear that she is not entitled to dower in his lands.

Her claim to a distributive share of his personal estate stands upon different ground. The act of assembly, 1 R. C. ch. 104, sec. 29, p. 382, gives a lawful wife an absolute right to a portion of her husband's personal estate, and she does not forfeit that right by her conduct, however unworthy it may be.[7] This Court is, I think, as much bound by that act, as a court of common law would be. The principle, that a court of equity will not interfere in aid of a person whose conduct has been reprehensible in the particular case in which its aid is asked, applies, I think, to cases in which the party has a remedy at law; and if ever applied to one in which no remedy at law exists, it must be a right which originates merely in equity, and may therefore be withheld or granted according to circumstances; but a right given by a statute cannot, I think, be denied by a court of chancery, if it can be asserted in no other court. In such a case, a court of chancery can exercise no more discretion than a court of common law.

The plaintiff, Catharine, is therefore entitled to her distributive share in John Potter Stegall's personal estate.

The next claim to be considered, is that of Jordan R. Sherwood, formerly Jordan R. Stegall, her eldest son, who was born six months after the marriage took effect.

Being born in wedlock, he is legitimate, unless the conclusion of law can be met by such testimony, as according to principles settled in adjudged cases, is sufficient to repel it.

There is no positive testimony showing the first acquaintance between the parties. Joseph Gill was well acquainted with Stegall, lived within three miles of Colonel Sherwood, the stepfather of Catharine, the plaintiff, with whom she resided, and does not recollect seeing Stegall in the neighbourhood before his marriage.[8]

Penelope Sherwood, her half-sister, was about three years old when the marriage took effect; and her recollection as to the length of time Stegall was at her father's house, cannot be accurate. Her present impressions, must depend more on the statements she has heard in the family, than on her positive memory. She would represent the first appearance of Stegall at the house, to have preceded the birth of Jordan about eight months.[9]

Polly Pinny represents the first visit of Stegall to have preceded the marriage five or six weeks, and the birth to have followed it seven or eight months.[10] But the proof is satisfactory, that the marriage did not precede the birth more than six months, so that the first visit of Stegall to the family cannot have taken place more than seven, or at most, eight months before the birth of the plaintiff, Jordan, and there was no reason to suppose that the birth was premature. There is, however, no testimony that the acquaintance between the parties commenced with this first visit, and although Stegall lived in Halifax county, in Virginia, about sixty or seventy miles from the residence of Catharine Newby, in Franklin county, in North Carolina, yet the presumption that he had no access to her before this visit, is not so violent as to contradict the conclusion which the law draws from the marriage, unaided by other circumstances.

This presumption, however, is supposed to derive considerable strength from the testimony, that according to the reputation of the neighbourhood, Jordan was the son of William Bowers; that Bowers claimed him, and that Catharine herself said that he was the son of Bowers.[11]

If the declaration of the mother is admissible testimony, it would be entitled to great weight, if it should not be conclusive; but the counsel for the plaintiff contends, that these declarations are inadmissible. In arguing this point, the admissibility of the mother, as a witness, has been affirmed by the defendants and denied by the plaintiffs; but I think it unnecessary to decide this point, because the question before the Court does not, I think, depend upon it. If the mother could not be received as a witness, it follows that her declaration cannot be received as testimony against her son; and if she could be received as a witness, then her deposition ought to have been taken.

. It is said, that hearsay is good evidence in cases of pedigree, and in cases of legitimacy; but it is the hearsay of persons who are dead, or whose testimony is unattainable. There is, I think, no case in which the declaration of one person can be admitted as evidence against another, when that person may be examined as a witness. I am compelled, therefore, to reject the declarations of the mother, whatever may be my private confidence in their truth.

The same principle applies to the declaration of Bowers, who is not proved to be dead, and who could, perhaps, go no further than to state his chance of being the father of the boy.

The general report of the neighbourhood, cannot be entirely disregarded; but the weight to which this, and all other hearsay testimony is entitled, depends on the circumstances of the case. Hearsay is admitted only from necessity; and its weight must depend on the circumstances of the case, and much on the remoteness of the time when the fact occurred, and the difficulty of producing any positive testimony respecting it. The supreme court has said, in the case of Mima Queen and Child *v.* Hepburn, 7 Cranch, that it will not extend the exceptions to the rule that hearsay is inadmissible further than they have been already carried.[12]

The result of the whole testimony is, that the presumption that Jordan is not the son of John Potter Stegall, is strong; but not so strong as to approach impossibility. It becomes, necessary, therefore, to inquire what degree of improbability has been considered by courts, as sufficient to overrule the conclusion of law.

The plaintiffs contend that the rule must prevail, unless there be a physical impossibility, that the husband can be the father. The defendants insist that the ancient rule is relaxed, and that the facts, like most others determinable by human tribunals, must depend on probabilities, and on the comparative weight of testimony.

Mr. Blackstone, in his Commentaries, Vol. I. p. 457, says: "That children born during wedlock, may, under some circumstances, be deemed illegitimate; as if the husband be out of the kingdom." "But, generally, during the coverture, access of the husband shall be presumed, unless the contrary be shown, which is such a negative as can only be proved by showing him to be elsewhere; for the general rule is *presumitur pro legitimatione.*["]

"After a divorce, *a mensa et thoro,* the children are bastards; but in a voluntary separation by agreement, the law will suppose access, unless the negative be shown."[13]

Mr. Blackstone goes no further than to state the general presumption of law, and, consequently, that the *onus probandi* is thrown on him who would establish illegitimacy; but does not intimate that stronger testimony would be required to prove non-access, than in any other case of an *alibi;* in all which cases the degree of negative proof which is required, must depend, in some degree, upon the strength of the positive testimony. The fact of marriage, is the fact on which the plaintiffs rely as the positive testimony in this case; and it is the testimony on which the law erects the presumption of legitimacy; but it cannot be denied that a marriage, so early after conception, that the husband might not have discovered the pregnancy, does not afford so strong an inference in favour of his belief that he was the father of the child, as a marriage after the fact of pregnancy had become notorious.

In Pendrell v. Pendrell, 2 Strange, 925, the husband and wife parted after living together some months, she staying in London, and he going to Staffordshire. After a separation of three years, the plaintiff was born, and it being uncertain whether the husband had visited London within the year, an issue at law was directed; and upon strong evidence of no access, the legal presumption in favour of legitimacy was overruled, and the law left to the jury, whose verdict was against the plaintiff.[14]

The case informs us that the evidence of no access was strong, but does not say what that evidence was. There is, however, no hint that it was such as to make access impossible. It is also observable that there was, probably, some doubt whether the husband had not been in London within the year. The circumstances are not fully stated in the case; but, so far as they are stated, there is no reason to suppose that there was any other proof of an *alibi*, than is afforded by the general residence of the husband in Staffordshire, and of the wife in London, without any testimony that he had visited London, or she Staffordshire.

It is worthy of observation that evidence was admitted that the mother was of ill fame.

The case of Goodright, lessee v. Saul et al., 4 D. & E., 356, turns upon the legitimacy of John T. Hales, whose title was set up by the defendant.[15]

Elizabeth Tilyard, the great-grandmother of John T. Hales, had intermarried with Simon Kilburn, with whom she lived in Norwich some time without having any children. The husband then went away, after which, Elizabeth lived publicly with Joseph Hales, during which time a son, Joseph, was born, (from whom John T. Hales descended), who was always considered in the family as a bastard. It did not clearly appear where the husband was during this time, but one very old witness proved that he went to London, where it was supposed he remained, and returned to Norwich after the death of his wife. The son, Joseph, went by the name of Hales. The counsel for the defendant insisted on the presumption of law, in favour of legitimacy; and the judge instructed the jury, that though it was not absolutely necessary to prove the husband out of the realm in order to bastardize the issue, yet it was incumbent on the party insisting on that fact, to prove that the husband could not by any probability have had access to the wife at the time, which, he conceived, had not been shown in the present instance. The jury found for the defendant, and on a rule to show cause, a new trial was granted. Ashurst, J., said he was convinced he had laid too much stress on the necessity of proving non-access, when the husband was within the realm, by witnesses who could prove him constantly resident at a distance from his wife. That the husband in this case left the wife and went to reside at another place, as it was believed, in London, and that there was no direct evidence of his access: there was other evidence which went strongly to rebut the presumption of access; a very forcible circumstance was, that himself and his family had taken the name of his putative father.

The instruction given to the jury in this case was, that it was necessary to prove that the husband could not, by any *probability*, have had access to the wife, and that the testimony did not amount to such proof. This instruction was declared to be erroneous, and must have been so either in its general principle, or in the particular application of the principle. The general principle was, that it was necessary to show that the husband could not, by any *probability*, not *possibility*, have had access to the wife; and the particular application of the principle was, to the case of living openly with another man, and having a son at the time, who was considered in the family as the child of that other man, and who took the name of the putative father. This case shows clearly, that without positive proof of non-access, circumstances may rebut the presumption arising from marriage.

The case of The King *v.* Luffe, 8 East, 193, turned on the legitimacy of a child born in wedlock, where the proof of the non-access of the husband until within a fortnight of the birth, was positive. In the course of the trial, Lord Ellenborough said: "Where the thing cannot certainly be known, we must call in aid such probable evidence as can be resorted to, and the intervention of a jury must, in all cases in which it is practicable, be had to decide thereupon; but where the question arises, as it does here, and where it may certainly be known from the invariable course of nature, as in this case it may, that no birth could be occasioned and produced within those limits of time, we may venture to lay down the rule plainly and broadly, without any danger arising from the precedent."[16]

In giving his final opinion in the cause, the language of his lordship is much more positive. After stating cases which show that a natural incapacity of the husband to be the father, constitutes an exception to the rule of law, he adds: "And, therefore, if we may resort at all to such impediments arising from the natural causes adverted to, we may adopt other causes equally potent and conclusive, to show the absolute physical impossibility of the husband being the father; I will not say the improbability of his being such, for upon the ground of improbability, however strong, I should not venture to proceed." "The general presumption," he also said, "will prevail, except a case of plain natural impossibility is shown."[17]

Justice Grose said: "In every case, we will take care, before we bastardize the issue of a married woman, that it shall be proved that there was no such access as could enable the husband to be the father of the child."[18]

Justice Lawrence said: "It had been shown that imbecility from age, and natural infirmity from other causes, have always been deemed sufficient to bastardize the issue, all which evidence proceeds upon the ground of a natural impossibility that the husband should be the father of the child. Then why not give effect to any other matter which proves the same natural impossibility?"[19]

Le Blanc lays down the old rule and says: "Afterwards, the rule was brought to this, that where there was an impossibility that the husband could have had access to the wife, and have been the father of the child, there it should be deemed illegitimate; and in Goodright v. Saul, the court held that there was no necessity to prove the impossibility of access, if the other circumstances of the case went strongly to rebut the presumption of access. If it do not appear, but that he might be the father, the presumption of law still holds in favour of the legitimacy."[20]

This is certainly a very strong case in favour of the opinion that positive proof of non-access is required to bastardize a child born in wedlock. The force of the decision, however, is in some degree diminished by two considerations; the first is, that access was clearly impossible. The question, therefore, was not whether illegitimacy might be proved where access was possible, but whether it was the legal consequence of the impossibility of access. When the judges proceeded to recognise the rule that legitimacy must be presumed where access was possible, they undoubtedly travelled out of the case before them; and although these *obiter* opinions are entitled to great respect, they do not stand on the same ground with opinions given on the very point which is decided.

The second consideration is, that the case of The King v. Luffe, was not a jury cause, but a case to be decided entirely by the court; and unless we suppose Lord Ellenborough to have changed his view of the case on hearing the whole argument, this circumstance was not without its weight; his language during the trial certainly countenances this idea.

It is not entirely unworthy of remark, that though the Chief Justice and Grose, Justice, lay down the rule positively, Lawrence, Justice, avoids it, and Le Blanc, Justice, is not so explicit as the two whose opinions were first given.

This question is said in Phillips's Law of Evidence, p. 118, to have been afterwards considered by the judges in the case of the Banbury claim of Peerage, in which, Phillips says: "The principle laid down in the case of Goodright v. Saul, was affirmed." "It was held that where the husband and wife are not proved to be impotent, and have had opportunity of access to each other during the period in which a child could be begotten and born in the course of nature, the presumption of legitimacy arising from the birth of the child during wedlock, may be rebutted by circumstances inducing a contrary presumption; and the fact of non-access, (that is, the non-existence of sexual intercourse,) as well as the fact of impotency, may always be proved by means of such legal evidence, as is strictly admissible in every other case where a physical fact is to be proved."[21]

I have searched in vain for a report of this case, and must, therefore, be content with the statement Phillips makes of it.[22]

The case of Bowles v. Bingham, 3 Munf. 599, is also a very strong case in favour of the presumption of law in favour of legitimacy, and the judge who delivered the opinion, unquestionably admits the law to be, that legitimacy must be presumed unless its impossibility be shown; but the same opinion shows that in the actual case, intercourse between the husband and wife at the time of conception, was probable, and the decision was in favour of the injured party.[23]

The conclusion to which I am brought by a comparison of the cases I have had an opportunity of examining, is, that the presumption of law is in favour of the legitimacy of a child born in wedlock, but that this presumption may be rebutted by other testimony, which does not go to the full extent of absolute impossibility. I will not say that mere probability is enough; I think it is not enough; the known connexion of a woman with another man while she cohabited with her husband, or might, upon any reasonable calculation, be supposed to have intercourse with him, would weigh as nothing. In such case as this, if the marriage had taken place in such an advanced state of pregnancy, that the situation of the wife must have been known to the husband, I should be disposed to consider it as a recognition of the child afterwards born. Any conduct of the husband after the birth, indicating a belief that the child was his, would have been entitled to great weight, and would probably have been decisive; but in this case, the marriage took place when the pregnancy was probably unknown. The acquaintance between the parties, most probably commenced too late for the husband, according the law of gestation, to be the father of the child afterwards born; the common opinion of the neighbourhood gave the child to another man; the boy grew up, not in the household of Stegall, not looking upon him as a father, not being considered as a son, and the presumption of law derives no aid from the reputation of the woman. Under all these circumstances, the Court would be restrained from directing an issue, only by the opinion that the presumption of law must prevail, unless it be clearly impossible that the husband can be the father of the child. As I am not of that opinion, but think that this presumption of law may be rebutted by testimony which places the negative beyond all reasonable doubt, I shall direct an issue to try the legitimacy of the plaintiff, Jordan R. Sherwood.

It will be unnecessary again to go through the law of the case in relation to the claim of Martha Wright. The probability that she is legitimate, is not stronger than that in favour of her brother, and I shall direct an issue as to her likewise.

It will be unnecessary to discuss the rights of the defendants, until this issue shall be tried.[24]

Printed, John W. Brockenbrough, *Reports of Cases Decided by the Honourable John Marshall . . .* , II (Philadelphia, 1837), 258–71.

1. Here and elsewhere in the opinion the name "Sherwood" should be "Sherrod."

2. Bill in chancery [ca. 1822], Stegall v. Stegall's Administrator.

3. Answer of John Jennett and Elizabeth his wife, 6 Nov. 1823; answer of Nancy Smith, 30 Jan. 1824, ibid.

4. Answer of Beverly Borum, 6 Nov. 1823, ibid.

5. Among the papers in this suit is a certified copy of a marriage bond between John P. Stegall and Catharine Newby, 20 Dec. 1789, Franklin County, N.C. Several witnesses deposed that Catharine Stegall later lived with Henry Hill and had presumably married him (depositions of Reuben Huff and Penelope Sherrod, 11 Sept. 1823; deposition of Polly Perry, 24 Oct. 1823; depositions of Penelope Sherrod, John Pulliam, and Mark White, 22 Apr. 1824, ibid.).

6. *Revised Code of Va.,* I, 404.

7. Ibid., I, 382.

8. Deposition of Joseph Gill, 11 Sept. 1823, Stegall v. Stegall's Administrator. Catharine Newby Stegall's mother, Elizabeth, married Col. Thomas Sherrod after her first husband's death. In her will of Mar. 1819 Elizabeth Sherrod left to her daughter, Catharine Hill, "all the property that I may die holding under the will of my dec'd husband Thomas Sherrod." Thomas Sherrod's will of July 1818 left property to his wife, children, grandchildren, and to "Jordan R. Sherrod formerly Jordan R. Stegall" (Stephen E. Bradley, Jr., *Franklin County North Carolina Original Wills. Volume 1: 1780–1861* [Virginia Beach, Va., 1996], 79, 80–81).

9. Deposition of Penelope Sherrod, 11 Sept. 1823, Stegall v. Stegall's Administrator.

10. Deposition of Polly Perry, 24 Oct. 1823, ibid.

11. Penelope Sherrod testified that she heard Catharine Stegall say that her son Jordan Sherrod was the child of William Bowers, that Jordan was always considered to be Bowers's son, and that Bowers claimed him (deposition of Penelope Sherrod, 11 Sept. 1823, ibid.).

12. Mima Queen v. Hepburn, 7 Cranch 290 (1813); *PJM,* VII, 382–86.

13. Blackstone, *Commentaries,* I, 457. The quoted passage is more of a paraphrase than a direct quotation.

14. Pendrell v. Pendrell, 2 Str. 925, 93 Eng. Rep. 945 (K.B., 1732).

15. Goodright v. Saul, 4 T.R. 356, 100 Eng. Rep. 1062 (K.B., 1791).

16. The King v. Luffe, 8 East 193, 201–2, 103 Eng. Rep. 316, 319 (K.B., 1807).

17. 8 East 207, 103 Eng. Rep. 321.

18. 8 East 208, 103 Eng. Rep. 322.

19. 8 East 210, 103 Eng. Rep. 322.

20. 8 East 212–13, 103 Eng. Rep. 323.

21. S[amuel] M. Phillipps, *A Treatise on the Law of Evidence* (1st Am. ed.; New York, 1816), 113.

22. Phillipps cites Banbury's Case as "2 Selw. N.P. 681 (MS)." Elsewhere, he says the case was decided in 1809 (ibid., 178). The case is discussed in William Selwyn, *An Abridgment of the Law of Nisi Prius* (2 vols.; 7th Am. ed.; Philadelphia, 1857), II, 759–60. Selwyn cites opinions of the judges in 1811 and 1813, when Banbury's claim was disallowed.

23. Bowles v. Bingham, 3 Munf. 599 (Va. Ct. App., 1811).

24. The accompanying decree directed a jury to try the issues of the legitimacy of Jordan Sherrod and Martha Wright, plaintiffs and children of the plaintiff Catharine Stegall. A jury was empaneled at the May 1826 term and again at the Dec. 1826 term, but could not agree on a verdict. On 6 June 1827 the court, after setting aside the 1825 decree, issued a decree stating that Catharine Stegall was barred from her claim to dower of the real estate of John

P. Stegall but not precluded from a share of his personal estate. The decree further stated that Jordan Sherrod and Martha Wright were to be "deemed the legitimate children" of John P. Stegall by his wife Catharine; that the marriage of Stegall with Susannah Portwood was null and void and that she was not entitled either to dower or to a share of his personal estate; and that Susannah Portwood's children by Stegall, Nancy Smith and Elizabeth Jennett, were also to be "deemed the legitimate children" of John P. Stegall. Stegall's four children by the two wives were accordingly entitled to an equal share of his real and personal estate (U.S. Cir. Ct., Va., Ord. Bk. XII, 38–39, 161–63).

To James Barbour

Dear Sir   Richmond June 24th. 1825

Mr. John Dandridge, a young gentleman who has been educated for the bar, with whose family you are acquainted, is a candidate for the office of Pay Master of the army, and wishes me to state my opinion of him.

I have known Mr. Dandridge from his boyhood, and have the most entire confidence in his honour and integrity. I have equal confidence in his capacity for the duties of the office.

I know very well that those who have appointments to make are pressed much by the friends of various applicants, who cannot generally succeed. I will however venture to express my belief that the success of Mr. Dandridge will give general satisfaction in this part of Virginia. With great respect & esteem, I am dear Sir Your Obedt

J MARSHALL

ALS, NjP. Addressed to Barbour in Washington.

From Walter Jones and Others

[Washington 27 June 1825]

To the Chief Justice and the Associate Justices of the Supreme Court

The melancholy fact being now ascertained that the dissolution of Elias B. Caldwell the present Clerk of your Court may speedily ensue; and feeling the deepest sympathy for the distressed condition in which the family of that lamented individual is likely to be left; and the very inadequate provision that it is in his power to make for them; we have voluntarily and from a provident regard to their welfare; prompted by our sincere esteem and sympathy, determined to anticipate the event by recommending to your consideration the expediency of appointing his son James Caldwell as his successor; who has for some time served as his father's deputy; and of whose excellent character and entire competency to discharge the duties of the office, we have good opportunity from our own situation as members of the bar, to be satisfied; and in such capacity beg leave to recommend him.

SIGNED   W. JONES

F. S. KEY

WM WIRT

DAVID HOFFMAN

CHARLES F. MAYER

Confiding in the knowledge and statements of Gentlemen who are well acquainted with Mr. Caldwell's son We willingly join in the foregoing recommendation

SIGNED   R. B. TANEY

J MEREDITH

J. GLENN

WM GWYNN

D. RAYMOND

Copy, RG 267, DNA. In the hand of James Caldwell and embodied in his letter to Gabriel Duvall, 27 June 1825.

1. Caldwell's letter to Duvall follows immediately below the signatures.

From William Wirt

SIR: WASHINGTON JULY 2 1825.,

In a late official communication by Gov. Troup to the Legislature of Georgia, I find myself charged with having maintained before the Supreme Court of the United States, at the last term, the proposition "that slavery, being inconsistent with the laws of God and nature, cannot exist."[1] Will you do me the justice to say, in reply, whether either your notes of argument or your recollection impute that proposition to me, or any sentiment or opinion that slavery, as it now exists in the several States, could be or ought to be abolished, or be attempted to be abolished, or interfered with at all, by the authority of the government of the United States.[2] I have the honor to remain, &c.

W. WIRT.

Printed, *Daily National Journal* (Washington, D.C.), 25 July 1825.

1. George M. Troup (1780–1856), elected governor of Georgia in 1823 and reelected in 1825, had formerly served in the U.S. House of Representatives (1807–15) and Senate (1816–18). A conspicuous exponent of states' rights, Troup was then embroiled in a dispute with the Adams administration over the state's treatment of the Creek Indians. In messages to the state legislature in the spring of 1825, Troup denounced the federal government's "officious and impertinent intermeddlings" with Georgia's domestic con-

cerns. He singled out Attorney General Wirt's argument in the case of The Antelope as reflecting the administration's hostile policy toward slavery (messages of 23 May and 7 June 1825, *Niles' Weekly Register* [Baltimore], XVIII [1825], 240, 277).

2. Wirt wrote the same letter to the other justices and to others who had heard his argument. After receiving the replies, he published this correspondence in the Washington *Daily National Journal,* from which it was reprinted in other newspapers. See *Niles' Weekly Register* (Baltimore), XVIII (1825), 347–49.

To William Wirt

SIR: RICHMOND JULY 6 1825.,

I received yesterday evening your letter of the 2d, stating that Governor Troup, in an official report to the Legislature of Georgia, had charged you with having maintained before the Supreme Court, at the last term, the proposition "that slavery, being inconsistent with the laws of God and nature, cannot exist"; and requesting me to say "whether my notes of the argument or recollection impute that proposition to you, or any sentiment or opinion, that slavery, as it now exists in the several States, could be, or ought to be, abolished, or attempted to be abolished, or interfered with at all, by the government of the United States."

It is not in my power to refer to my notes, because they were, as is my custom, delivered to Mr. Wheaton at the close of the term, who supposes they may be of some use to him in drawing out the arguments of counsel. I can, therefore, appeal only to memory.

I have no recollection of your having uttered, in any form, the sentiment imputed to you. The impression on my mind is, that you denounced the slave trade, not slavery; the practice of making freemen slaves; not that of holding in slavery those who were born slaves. I think it impossible that you can have hinted at any interference of the government of the Union with slavery in the respective States; because I think such a hint, however remote, would have excited my attention too strongly to be entirely forgotten. I recollect distinctly that in some argument—I think in the case of the Africans claimed by the consuls of Spain and Portugal—you stated in terms that you had no authority to speak the sentiments of the government; and that the arguments you should use were to be considered as entirely your own.[1] I am, very respectfully, your obe't servant,

J. MARSHALL.

Printed, *Daily National Journal* (Washington, D.C.), 25 July 1825.

1. The replies of Justices Washington, Duvall, and Thompson were to like effect, as were those of Thomas A. Emmet and Henry Wheaton (ibid.). For Wirt's reported argument in The Antelope, see 10 Wheat. 105–14.

To Bushrod Washington

My dear Sir   Richmond July 7th. 1825

I received a few days past your letter of the 29th. of June and am much gratified at its contents.[1] It is extremely fortunate that Mr. Jay was privy to the whole transaction and that he has lived long enough to explain it.[2]

I cannot pretend to advise what may be proper in the actual state of things but am disposed to think that, should the chancellor refuse to decree a delivery of the papers, Mr. Jays statement ought to be published. Till then no publication can be made without his consent. Should the papers be delivered they will I presume be made public, & I suppose will coincide with Mr. Jays representation. His representation may still be useful to connect the parts of the correspondence.

Having had no suspicion that any claim would be put in for the Authorship of the Farewell Address when the Life of General Washington was written, I do not recollect the condition of the manuscript. It is very possible that the original in the hand writing of General Washington or of his clerk, which was transmitted to General Hamilton and returned by him, may be among the papers. That would show the extent of alterations made by others. I am very certain there is nothing in the correspondence which can allude to the subject, unless it be one short letter from General Hamilton which speaks of the transmission of some paper not described, and which may possibly be the Farewell Address. It is however extremely probable that the original may be found. It is certainly worth a search among the papers of the time.

I am unwilling to believe that General Hamilton can have preserved these papers for the purpose to which his family now wish to apply them. Mrs. Hamilton and his son appear to be more to blame than I had supposed, since they must know that the address was written by General Washington and revised by his friends. I am my dear Sir yours truely

J Marshal⟨l⟩

ALS, Farewell Address Papers, NN. Addressed to Washington at Mount Vernon; postmarked Richmond, 8 July. Endorsed by Washington.

1. Letter not found.

2. The reference is to a letter from John Jay to Richard Peters, 29 Mar. 1811, in which Jay defended General Washington's authorship of the Farewell Address. Bushrod Washington made a copy of this letter in 1819, with a memorandum that he intended " 'never to use or to authorise its being publickly used unless it should become necessary to rescue the General's character from the charge, now slyly propagating, but which may be more publickly avowed, that Genl Washington was not, & that Genl Hamilton was the writer of that address.' " Bushrod Washington also made an extract of another letter from Jay to Peters, 25 Jan. 1819, concerning the drafting and revising of the address (Victor Hugo Paltsits, ed., *Washington's Farewell Address* [New York, 1935], 80, 264–72, 281–82).

To James Monroe

Dear Sir   Richmond July 13th. 1825

I am greatly flattered by your letter of the 29th. of June accompanying the documents stating your claims on the United States.[1]

There was undoubtedly great reason for your requesting such a final settlement of all your accounts as would releive you from future disquiet; and in making that settlement you have I think a right to expect that the justice of your country will not be stinted by any implied concession made under circumstances when it could not be withheld. I can perceive no reason why you should not receive as much as has ever been allowed to others for similar services; and I trust this reasonable expectation will not be disappointed.[2]

With the sincerest wishes for your health and happiness and with high and respectful esteem, I am dear Sir Your Obedt

J MARSHALL

ALS, Monroe Papers, DLC. Addressed to Monroe at "Oakhill / Loudoun"; postmarked Richmond, 14 July. Endorsed by Monroe. Endorsed by postal clerk "ford. from Oak Hill Fauqr. Cty" and redirected to "Aldie."

1. Letter not found.

2. Monroe's claims against the government for services dating back to 1794 had long remained unsettled. Faced with mounting debt, Monroe in Jan. 1825 sought a reimbursement totaling $53,000. Congress finally approved a settlement of $29,500 for the former president in May 1826 (Harry Ammon, *James Monroe: The Quest for National Identity* [New York, 1971], 553–56).

From Richard Bland Lee

Dear Sir,   Washington July 28h. 1825

I trust you will find in the inclosed letter & the accompanying paper sufficient facts & motives to justify this address. I cannot doubt that you will give to them an attentive perusal & deliberate consideration. And if it shall be deemed proper to open again in full court the subject, which seems to have been prematurely taken up & suddenly & informally decided, without affording an opportunity to the numerous meritorious & qualified citizens of the U. States to present their fair & just pretensions for examination, is it too late to hope that mine will be fully & dispassionately weighed? I have only asked the office — first on the ground of personal fitness: second on account of services rendered at a critical period of our national existence in supporting measures which in their consequences saved the Union, preserved the Peace & permanently established the prosperity and liberty of the whole poeple of the U. States;[1] and third, because of my present unexpected & undeserved poverty.

In the extract from my letter to Judge Duvall & other members of the Court, I find that I have not specially copied the reference to one prominent act of the first Congress — that — establishing the Judiciary system of the U. States.

Here too the journals of Congress will shew that I aided in and supported this important measure; (as well as every other organic measure on which the Executive Administration has since depended for its order & symmetry;) from which the Supreme Court of the U. States derive their power, of now decidin⟨g⟩ on my present application.

The extract alluded to, being taken from an hasty sketch may not in every expression be an accurate transcript, tho it is in every idea. It contains however a sufficient detail of my public conduct.

I do not ask you to give any opinion at this time on the subject of this commun⟨ic⟩ation, but only to acknowledge its receipt, & that you will at the proper time lay the whole before the honorable court, over which you preside with so much personal dignity & general satisfaction to the Nati⟨on.⟩

One thing before I conclude, tho' fully stated in the extract refered to permit me here to repeat: if the Judges shall be inclined — and shall feel themselves justified on public grounds to appoint the son of the late estimab⟨le⟩ Incumbent their Clerk, that I do not interfere to prevent it. But if they sha⟨ll⟩ deem it right to cast their eyes over the whole community to select that officer, I have only to ask, that they will include my pretensions in the Scope of their view; especially as I am disposed to employ as an Assistant Young Mr. Caldwell, allowing a just & liberal reward for his services.

It cannot be unknown to you, that the whole bar of Washington have united in recommending him to the court on account of their just esteem of his Father and of the deranged state in which that gentleman is supposed to have left his affairs, to enable him to provide for the numerous family of the deceased.

I am as sensible as you can be, that in bestowing the office the court cannot make any formal conditions, which can be obligatory in law; and that whatever be the understanding & intention, the execution must depend on the honor of the Individual appointed.

Mr. Madison, one of the Ex-presidents with whom I had long acted in most important public scenes, often in conjunction & sometimes in opposition, would if asked bear ample testimony to my public deserts. To such as have doubts I have no hesitation in refering them to him & am ready to stand or fall by his opinion. I again subscribe myself your friend & servant

RICHARD BLAND LEE

ALS (Df), Gray-Glines Collection, Ct. Inside address to JM above salutation.

1. Lee served as a Federalist member of the House of Representatives from 1789 to 1795, earning a footnote to the history of that period for his role in the "Compromise of 1790." He was one of two Virginia congressmen to switch their votes to support Hamilton's assumption bill in exchange for the placement of the national capital on the Potomac. In soliciting the office of collector of customs at Alexandria in 1820, Lee recounted this incident to John Quincy Adams (Charles Francis Adams, ed., *Memoirs of John Quincy Adams*, V [Philadelphia, 1875], 27–28).

From John Adams

Dear Sir   Quincy August 17th. 1825

The extreme imbecility of old age must be my apology for neglecting to write, and thank you for your valuable Book. It has not been for want of esteeme or respect, or admiration that I have not written frequently to you. There is no part of my Life that I look back upon with more pleasure, than the short time I spent with you. And it is the pride of my life that I have given to this nation a Chief Justice equal to Coke or Hale, Holt or Mansfield.

I am unalterably your friend, and well wisher though on the point of departure.

JOHN ADAMS

LS, Gray-Glines Collection, Ct. Text and signature in hand of secretary. Addressed to JM in Virginia and franked by Adams in his own hand.

Speech
Warrenton, Virginia
23 August 1825

Lafayette's visit to Fauquier County occurred on the return trip to Washington from a second visit to Jefferson at Monticello in August 1825. From Charlottesville Lafayette proceeded to Montpelier, home of James Madison, near Orange. On 22 August he was in Culpeper for a reception, dinner, and ball. The next day he departed for Warrenton, where he arrived shortly before noon. After replying to a welcoming speech at the portico of the courthouse, Lafayette adjourned to his quarters at Mrs. Norris's Tavern for a reception with Revolutionary war veterans. This was followed by a "sumptuous and elegant dinner prepared by Mrs. Norris under a handsome arbour in the beautiful green in front of the Tavern." A series of twelve "patriotic toasts" were drunk, the last to "*John Marshall:* The Soldier: The statesman: The jurist: Our Country with exultation points to her son." The newspaper account proceeds: "After the cheering (which was loud and repeated) had ceased—

Gen. Marshall rose and addressed the company as follows" (Robert D. Ward, *An Account of General La Fayette's Visit to Virginia, in the Years 1824–25* [Richmond, Va., 1881], 110–15; *Enquirer* [Richmond, Va.], 6 Sept. 1825).

It would not be easy, Gentlemen, to express my thanks for the kindness I have experienced today in terms which would do justice to the emotions it has excited. To be associated in any manner with the illustrious Guests among whom I am placed, cannot fail to be highly gratifying to my feelings. Among them I see the oldest surviving officer of our revolutionary army; one who relinquished all the pleasures and enjoyments which Europe could furnish to encounter the dangers, and share the toils and privations which were the lot of all those who engaged in our struggle for independence, who has since devoted himself to that glorious cause which brought him to our country, and who through all the vicissitudes of his eventful life has been its steadfast champion — neither subdued by adversity, nor too much elevated by prosperity.

I perceive also, a person on whom his fellow citizens have bestowed the highest office in their gift, the arduous duties of which he has discharged in such a manner as to secure the continuance of their confidence and esteem. In him I am proud to recognize one of my earliest associates, one with whom I have frequently acted in the most trying scenes, for whom I have felt and still retain the most affectionate and respectful esteem, without a taint of that bitter spirit which has been too long the scourge of our Country.

To be connected with these gentlemen in any place on any occasion, would be my pride and my pleasure, but to be associated with them by your kindness, Gentlemen, and in this place, brings up recollections which must ever be most dear to my heart. I can never forget that this County was the residence of the revered author of my being, who continued to be your representative until his military character first, and his removal afterwards, rendered him ineligible, that in this County I first breathed the vital air, that in it my infancy was cradled, and my youth reared up and encouraged; that in the first dawn of manhood I marched from it with the gallant young men of the day to that glorious conflict which gave Independence to these States, and birth to this mighty Nation, that immediately on my return I was chosen almost unanimously to represent them in the Legislature, and that they did not cease to support me till I ceased to reside among them. Here my affections as well as my interest still remain, and all my sons are planted among you. With so many motives for receiving the kindness of today with peculiar gratitude allow me, gentlemen, to indulge the feelings it excites by giving as a toast

The People of Fauquier: Brave soldiers in time of war, good citizens in time of peace, and inteligent patriots at all times.[1]

Printed, *Enquirer* (Richmond, Va.), 6 Sept. 1825.

1. The festivities continued until ten that evening. The next day JM accompanied Lafayette at least part of the way to Monroe's home near Leesburg in Loudoun County (Ward, *An Account of General La Fayette's Visit to Virginia*, 116–17).

To Lafayette

Dear Sir   Oak hill Aug. 26th. 1825

I have devoted my first leisure after returning to this place to the perusal of the "plan for the gradual abolition of slavery in the United States" which your goodness placed in my hands when I had last the pleasure of seeing you.[1] The object is of the deepest interest, and must be dear to the heart of every philantropist, and of every well wisher to the United States; but its attainment is attended with such difficulties as to impress despair rather than hope on the minds of those who take a near view of the subject.

The basis on which all the calculations of the plan are founded is the immense value of slave labour employed in the manner which this scheme proposes. Should the foundation be unsound the fabric reared upon it will fall to the ground. The estimate is that any given number of persons between nine and fifty will by the net produce of their labour replace the purchase money given for them with interest in five years.[2] If this proposition be true, the result may be as favourable as is anticipated by the philantropist who has devised the plan; but if it be untrue the progress of the scheme must be retarded in the proportion which the actual bear to the estimated profits. The annual increase of slaves in the United States is probably about six thousand; and you will perceive that no plan can be successful which will not operate with sufficient activity to meet this increase.

If the profits of slave labour would in fact double a given capital in five years, their owners ought to grow rich with a rapidity of which we have no example. The general fact is known to be that it requires a combination of industry skill and economy in a proprietor of slaves to accumulate even a moderate fortune in the course of a long life. In truth, the profits of their labour, in the general, will barely support a family and rear up the young slaves. The increase constitutes nearly the whole profit which is added to the support of a family. Those who know this fact will doubt the accuracy of calculations which give a result so much more flattering than their experience will justify.

The treatise itself supposes slave labour to be unprofitable in Maryland and Virginia, and to be incapable of sustaining a fair competition with that which is free.[3] Yet free men who labour do not immediately become opulent, which they would do if the profits of labour were so immense. Were the plan to be attempted in those states, A man and woman slave, unincumbered with a family, would require, at a favourable calculation, ten years to replace the money they would cost with interest. But this man and woman would have children, the expense of rearing whom to the age of eleven or twelve years, must be charged on the labour of their parents. Old negroes too who have humane masters, continue for many years a burthen on their owners. They sometimes nurse their descendants but seldom produce any profit. The slaves too must be employed on land, which must be fertile to make their labour profitable, and, if fertile, will cost a great deal of money. The effect of these and other causes is such that, in point of fact, the increase of slaves, whom a man divides among his children, and the support of his family, constitute their chief profit. In Maryland and Virginia the net profits of their labour would probably not liberate them as fast as they multiply.

But the plan is to operate in the more southern states where a more valuable staple is cultivated.

There is in the more southern states such a jealousy on this subject as would prove a great impediment to an experiment. I am much inclined to think that any plan for ⟨e⟩mancipation must make a considerable progress in the most northern of the slave holding states before it can be introduced into those of the south. I am much disposed too to think that the profits of labour in the south are estimated higher than reality will justify. This however is a subject on which I have too little knowledge to speak with any confidence. But the expence of lands in the states of South Carolina & Georgia, perhaps in Alabama & Louisiana likewise, would constitute a much more considerable item in the account than is allowed to it in the plan.

Were the experiment to be made in Maryland or Virginia, the most sanguine could scarcely hope for success. But the plan seems to contemplate the transfer of slaves purchased in these states to the territories in the south where lands are cheap and labour profitable.

Sufficient allowance is not I think made for the expences of removal and of maintaining the slaves till the lands can be cleared and put in a state for profitable culture. These must be considerable. But the great objection to executing the plan in this mode consists in the invariable fact that distant estates are not profitable to the Proprietor. The managers keep all that is gained, the employers get nothing; consequently there would be nothing to apply towards the liberation of the labourers.

Although this is the result of all our experience the philantropic author of the plan perceives a remedy for it in the "advantages of united over individual labour."[4] Advantages supposed to be demonstrated by the experience of certain societies whose exertions have been crowned with success.

The success of these societies is probably to be ascribed to causes which can operate only in limited circles. It is I think not less true in reason than experience that the surest stimulus to labor is the certainty of enjoying its profit. Enthusiasm, or other motives, may work wonders in small societies for a limited time, but they will not animate so large a mass as must be acted upon to effect the abolition of slavery in the United States by the labour of the slaves. In all the settlements made by the English on our coast, the settlers in the first instance laboured in common, and brought the fruits of their labour into a common stock. The result was idleness & famine; nor could industry & plenty be procured but by a division of property & of labour.[5]

I cannot avoid thinking that the plan with a view of which you have favoured me must fail in its execution because the profits of labour, modified as it proposes, can never bear any proportion to the multiplication of slaves, and can consequently never reduce their numbers. The plan submitted by Mr. King to the Senate at its last session seems to me to be the only one which promises to be in any degree adequate to its object.[6]

I wish you and M. Lafayette, a happy restoration to your friends. You carry with you the prayers and good wishes of all Americans, and of no one more sincerely than of him who remains, with respectful and ardent esteem Your Obedt

J MARSHALL

ALS, Dean Lafayette Collection, Division of Rare and Manuscript Collections, NIC. Notation in top left corner "No. 7."

1. Benjamin Lundy, *A Plan for the Gradual Abolition of Slavery in the United States, without Danger or Loss to the Citizens of the South* (Baltimore, 1825). Lundy (1789–1839), a Quaker from New Jersey, settled in Ohio in 1815 and entered upon his lifelong calling as an antislavery crusader. In 1821 he began publication of an antislavery paper, *Genius of Universal Emancipation*, which he continued to edit until his death. Lundy and his paper moved to Baltimore in 1824.

2. Lundy, *Plan for the Gradual Abolition of Slavery*, 6.

3. Lundy argued that slave labor was unprofitable when in direct competition with free labor, as with the agricultural produce of Maryland and Virginia. Slave labor was profitable only in the production of such staples as cotton, rice, and sugar (ibid., 4).

4. "The great advantages of united, over individual labor, have been evinced by the practice of several religious communities — Moravians, Shaking Quakers, and Harmonites" (ibid., 4).

5. In his *History of the Colonies*, JM wrote of the effect of the policy of holding property in common: "Industry, deprived of its due reward, exclusive property in the produce of its toil, felt no sufficient stimulus to exertion, and the public supplies were generally inadequate to the public necessities." Plymouth Colony "fell into the same error" as Virginia, with the result that the colonists "were often in danger of starving; and severe whipping, administered to promote labour, only increased discontent" (John Marshall, *A History of the Colonies Planted by the English on the Continent of North America* . . . [Philadelphia, 1824], 49, 81).

6. In Feb. 1825 Sen. Rufus King submitted "as a matter for the future consideration of the Senate" a resolution calling for the establishment of a fund from the sale of public lands to be used to aid the emancipation and the removal of slaves and "free persons of color" to any territory or country beyond the limits of the U.S. (Charles R. King, ed., *The Life and Correspondence of Rufus King*, VI [New York, 1900], 594).

To Bushrod Washington

My dear Sir   Richmond October 3d 1825

I received this morning your favour of the 29th of Septr. and concur with you perfectly in the course which ought to be pursued in the very unpleasant affair which Mrs. Hamilton has so unwisely brought before a court of chancery.[1] I do not think the most remote opposition ought to be made by the friends of General Washington to the publication of any correspondence respecting his farewell letter. I firmly believe Mr. Jays statement to be correct. Should he have received it from General Hamilton for the purpose of concealing even from him the fact that the paper was written solely by Genl. Hamilton, I can have no doubt that it was published in the name of Washington from a perfect conviction that the valuable sentiments it contains would do more good if proceeding from him than from any other person. The public opinion of General Washington will remain unaltered, but their respect for the address will be changed. Whatever the letters may disclose I do not think their publication ought to be resisted.

One thing requires your attention. It is said that Mrs. H. has demanded these letters and that you have withheld them. It is material to let the fact be known that no such letters were retained by Genl. Washington. I can aver that I never saw them.[2] Yours affectionately

J MARSHALL

ALS, Farewell Address Papers, NN. Addressed to Washington in Philadelphia; postmarked Richmond, 3 Oct. Endorsed by Washington.

1. Letter not found.

2. In his letter to JM, Bushrod discussed a letter he had recently received from Charles King, son of Rufus King, which stated that Mrs. Hamilton had requested Bushrod to deliver her the letters Hamilton had written to President Washington about the Farewell Address. After receiving JM's reply, Bushrod on 6 Oct. wrote to Charles King to correct this impression. He stated that Mrs. Hamilton had visited him at Mount Vernon some years earlier and that he gave her certain specified letters to have copied and returned. None of these letters concerned the Farewell Address, said Bushrod, nor did this subject come up in conversation. He had never seen any letter in Washington's papers that "could warrant the conclusion that Genl H wrote the farewell address," adding that he was "authorised by Chief Justice Marshall, who had possession of all the papers for some years, whilst writing the life of Washington, to aver that he never met with any such letter" (Victor Hugo Paltsits, ed., *Washington's Farewell Address* [New York, 1935], 80–81, 284, 286–87).

To Bushrod Washington

My dear Sir   Oct. 17th. 1825

I have the pleasure of receiving your favour of the 14th. & thank you for your attention to my request.[1] The mode of conveyance you propose suits me precisely as I shall want the books in Washington next February. Yours truely & affectionately

J MARSHALL

ALS, Aldrich Collection, Ia-HA. Addressed to Washington in Philadelphia; postmarked Richmond, 17 Oct. Endorsed by Washington.

1. Letter not found; written in response to JM's letter of 11 Oct. requesting copies of his *History of the Colonies* (App. II, Cal.).

To Susan Ledyard

Dear Madam   Richmond November 6th. .25
    I was much gratified and flattered by your letter of the 29th. of October which reached me yesterday.[1] The amiable motive which has induced your recommendation of young Mr. Caldwell, far from requiring an apology, is an additional evidence of your goodness, and serves to increase that respect and high opinion with which you inspired me during your transient residence under the same roof at Washington, under most afflicting circumstances. The truely filial piety, the entire self devotion, with which you attended the sick bed, and watched the last moments of your expiring Father, my very estimable and ever to be lamented friend, could not fail to make a deep impression on the heart of every lover of the domestic virtues; and, be assured madam, were not lost on mine. It would give me pleasure at any time to manifest by more than words, my real desire to comply with any request with which you may honour me; and my wish that it was in my power to give my voice in favour of young Mr. Caldwell, which was not weak before, is much strengthened by the interest you take in his behalf. But before I had even heard him mentioned as a candidate for the office, and before I suspected the dependent state of his mother and family, I had pledged myself in favour of another of whose fitness I have the most entire conviction; and, however I may regret the pledge, I must redeem it. Should any circumstance in the progress of things put this gentleman out of the question, be assured madam that neither Mr. Caldwells situation, nor your recommendation of him will be forgotten.
    For your kind expressions respecting myself I pray you to accept my sincere thanks. The sentiments contained in your letter are not the less grateful to me from a consciousness that they are founded on no proof of my deserving them, and that they flow[2] entirely from the goodness of your own heart.[3] With the most respectful esteem, I remain Madam your Obedt Servt

J MARSHALL

JOHN MARSHALL
Oil on canvas by John Wesley Jarvis, ca. 1823. *Courtesy of the Firm of Carter, Ledyard, & Milburn, New York*

ALS (draft copy?), Marshall Papers, ViW. Addressed to Mrs. Ledyard in New York.

1. Letter not found. Susan Livingston Ledyard (1789–1864), daughter of the late Supreme Court Justice Brockholst Livingston, was the widow of Benjamin Ledyard, Jr. (1779–1812), a New York lawyer (Cass Ledyard Shaw, *The Ledyard Family in America* [West Kennebunk, Me., 1993], 74–75).

2. JM interlined "proceed" immediately above "flow," which he did not delete.

3. In May 1823 Mrs. Ledyard wrote a letter to Story that casts light on one of the John Wesley Jarvis likenesses of JM: "Jarvis has an admirable likeness of the Chief Justice, which he has just informed me was painted for my Father; I have of course ordered him to send it to my House. . . . My Father valued & loved the original" (Susan Ledyard to Joseph Story, 30 May 1823, Story Papers, MiU-C). This is the portrait the Ledyard family bequeathed to the New York law firm of Carter, Ledyard, and Milburn. Jarvis evidently painted his original life portrait of the chief justice before his Virginia sojourn of 1825–27. See Andrew Oliver, *The Portraits of John Marshall* (Charlottesville, Va., 1977), 54–63.

Garnett, Brooke's Executor v. Macon
Opinion
U.S. Circuit Court, Virginia, 25 November 1825

The subject of this complicated equity suit was the estate known as Mantapike, which was situated on the banks of the Mattaponi River in King and Queen County and had long been in possession of the Brooke family. George Brooke (1728–1782) purchased the estate in 1764 and resided there until his death. He bequeathed it to his son Richard Brooke, who died in 1817 having directed his executors to sell his real estate. In 1818 William Garnett (1786–1866), Richard Brooke's son-in-law and executor, sold Mantapike to William H. Macon (1760–1848) of New Kent County. After paying part of the purchase money, Macon was informed that George Brooke had been security for a large debt incurred fifty years earlier by Carter Braxton to Robert Campbell. Apprehensive that Mantapike was liable for this debt, Macon refused to complete the purchase and requested return of the money he had already paid. In December 1818 Garnett brought suit in the state superior court of chancery at Richmond seeking specific performance of the Mantapike sale contract on the ground that George Brooke's estate was not liable for Braxton's debt.

Besides Macon, other parties named as defendants in this suit were John Campbell, Robert Campbell's representative, and John W. Page, administrator of Robert Page, who was also a security for Braxton's debt. Campbell, a British subject, had no knowledge of the suit and did not appear. In June 1821 the chancery court issued an interlocutory decree stating its opinion that George Brooke had been discharged of his obligation as surety for Braxton, that Brooke's heirs and devisees were not precluded from insisting on that discharge as to them, and that the contract for the sale of Mantapike ought to be performed. On information being received of Campbell's death, the suit was revived in 1823 against William Keith, a resident and subject of Great Britain, who represented himself as assignee of Campbell's claim. Keith in February 1824 petitioned for removal of the suit to the U.S. Circuit

Court, where it was placed on the docket at the May 1824 term. In December 1824 Keith put in his answer and shortly thereafter filed his own bill against Brooke's heirs and devisees and Macon to subject Mantapike to the payment of Campbell's debt. The case was argued at the May 1825 term by Robert Stanard and Benjamin W. Leigh for the plaintiff and Daniel Call, John Wickham, and William Hay for the defendants. Marshall delivered his opinion on 25 November 1825 (Alfred Bagby, *King and Queen County, Virginia* [New York, 1908], 75, 303, 326; Malcolm Hart Harris, *Old New Kent County* [2 vols.; West Point, Va., 1977], I, 136–38, 414–18; James Mercer Garnett, *Genealogy of the Mercer-Garnett Family of Essex County, Virginia* [Richmond, Va., ca. 1910], 35; U.S. Cir. Ct., Va., Rec. Bk. XVII, 1–301; 6 Call 308–30).

Richard Brooke, by his last will, empowered his ex'rs. to sell his whole estate, and William Garnett, the plaintiff, alone proved the will, and took the Executorship upon himself.

On the 10th of June, 1818, William Garnett, sold the estate called Mantipike, to William H. Macon, the Defendant, "for the sum of twenty-two dollars per acre; $6000 of which are to be paid on the first day of January next, when possession will be given, and the balance in two equal annual payments from that date, which said two last payments, are to be secured by mortgage on the said land. The said William Garnett farther agrees to put the present corn-field land, in wheat, the said William H. Macon furnishing the seed. And it is farther agreed, that the said William H. Macon is to have power to make this agreement valid in one month from the date hereof, or to make the same null, and of no effect, by giving due notice to the said William Garnett, to that purport, within the time aforesaid."[1]

On the 22d of August, William H. Macon, paid William Garnett, four thousand dollars in part of the first payment;[2] but having received notice afterward, that George Brooke, who devised Mantipike to Richard, had by his last will, charged his whole estate with the payment of his debts; and had in his life-time, become surety for Carter Braxton, in a large sum, to Robert Campbell, for which a Decree had been pronounced in the Court of Chancery against Carter Braxton, Robert Price, ex'r. of George Brooke, and against the representatives of Robert Page, who was also surety for Carter Braxton, which Decree was affirmed in the Court of Appeals, in October, 1799, and remains unsatisfied;[3] and being advised by Counsel, that he, having notice thereof, the estate called Mantipike, would be charged with the said debt in his hands; he, on the 16th of December, addressed the following letter to the plaintiff:

"Sir

I am informed that Colonel George Brooke, the former owner of the Mantipike tract of land, became Carter Braxton's security for a large debt to Robert Campbell, and by his will, charged his lands with the payment of his debts; that the debt to Campbell is still due, and that the Mantipike lands are liable to be sold for the payment thereof. I, therefore, think proper to inform you, that I consider the contract, which I made with you, for the purchase of the said tract of land, as void; and request you, to return me the four thousand dollars, which I paid you, in part of the purchase money, with interest.

I am Sir, very respectfully,

W. H. MACON.''[4]

On the 26th of the same month, William Garnett, instituted his suit, in the Court of Chancery, of the State, against William H. Macon, and against the representatives of Robert Campbell, praying for a specific performance of the contract, and insists in his Bill, that the estate called Mantipike, would not be chargeable with the debts of George Brooke, in the hands of a purchaser; and insists also, for several reasons, which are dilated[5] at length, that George Brooke was not liable for the debts to Campbell, and that his devisees were not bound by the Decree against his Ex'r. or estopped from contesting the claim.[6]

The Chancellor was of opinion, that Brooke had been released by the conduct of Campbell, and that a specific performance of the contract ought to be Decreed, and directed an account of the rents and profits of the estate received by the Plaintiff, since the sale;[7] but, information was received of Campbell's death, on which the suit abated, as to him, and was revived against William Keith, his representative, who appeared, and petitioned that the cause should be removed into this Court; which was ordered accordingly.[8] Keith, as the representative of Campbell, has also filed a Bill against the representatives, heirs and devisees of George Brooke, praying that his debt may be paid; and to this Bill, William H. Macon, is made a Defendant; but this suit is not ready for trial.[9]

In May, 1820, William H. Macon filed his answer, in which he insists that he ought to stand discharged from his contract, on account of the lands being incumbered with Campbell's debt, of which he had no notice, and that he purchased, "supposing the said Mantipike tract of land was free from incumbrances and charges of all kinds, except a mortgage by Richard Brooke to General Young, which was represented as of no great moment,[10] and which the complainant was to pay off, before he made a deed for the land to this Defendant, but has failed to do so, as this Defendant understands."

He says, that on examining the records, which he did, in consequence of receiving notice of Campbell's debt, he found the question to be so perplexed and intricate, that the controversy would probably not be determined during his life, in consequence of which, he resolved to abandon the contract, and addressed a letter to the Plaintiff giving notice of his resolution. That in consequence thereof, as he presumes, the complainant kept possession of the tract of land, failed to tender a deed to the Defendant for it, or to demand the instalment in January, 1819; and paid for the seed wheat which Macon had purchased to seed the corn-field, according to the written contract; thus exhibiting every mark of a reciprocal abandonment of the contract on his part; and he gave no indication to the contrary till the institution of this suit, several months afterwards.[11]

In argument, the first point which has been made by the Defendant Macon, is, that the contract was abandoned by both parties.

It is not pretended that there has been any express or formal abandonment on the part of the Plaintiff. The allegation is, that it is to be implied from his conduct. To sustain this implication, the conduct of the vendor, ought to be such, as to justify a reasonable man, in believing that he acquiesced in the decision of the vendee, to abandon the contract; it ought to be such as might reasonably influence the conduct of the vendee, and induce him to regulate his own affairs on the presumption that he was no longer incumbered by his contract. The attempt of the vendor to re-sell the estate, or the unequivocal exercise of ownership over it, unaccompanied with any explanation showing that he still considered the contract as binding, might be such an act; but there has been no attempt to re-sell the estate, nor any unexplained act of ownership over it. On the contrary, a subpœna was taken out within ten days after the date of the letter of abandonment, and the Bill, since filed in consequence of this subpœna, claims a specific performance.

Had the Bill been immediately filed, and the subpœna executed, this point, it is presumed, would not have been made; but the Bill was not filed until June, 1819, and the subpœna was not returned executed, until January, 1820.

From these circumstances, the counsel for the Defendant, claim the same advantages to their client, as if the Plaintiff had acquiesced silently in his letter of the 16th December, 1818, until the service of the subpœna, informed him, that a suit was depending. But I do not think this claim can be supported.

No laches[12] are imputable to the Plaintiff. His determination to insist on the contract, seems to have been immediate; and the measures taken by him in pursuance of that determination were sufficiently prompt. A subpœna was issued, on the 10th day after the date of Colonel Macon's letter, but there was not time to execute it. New process was directed, and the law makes it the duty of the officers of the Court, to attend to that process. I do not think the delay which took place in executing it, can be justly imputed to Colonel Garnett, nor ought any forfeiture of right to be the consequence of that delay, unless some injury to Colonel Macon, had resulted from it. No injury is shewn or alledged, nor is it probable that any can have arisen. From the vicinity of the two gentlemen to each other, their rank in life, the common conversations which grow out of such controversies, the interest which the parties took in it, and the enquiries they would naturally make, it is not reasonable to suppose, that while the vendor was in fact actively pressing his suit, and continually issuing new process, the vendee could act upon the presumption that he had abandoned his contract. But if these circumstances, which generally accompany transactions of this character, cannot be considered as belonging to this cause, the record, I think, furnishes satisfactory evidence, that Colonel Macon, was apprized of the determination of Colonel Garnett, to insist on the specific performance of the contract. Thomas G. Smith, deposes to a conversation with Colonel Macon, in which that gentleman said, that though, the counsel consulted by him had been of opinion that Mantipike was bound for Campbell's debt, the counsel consulted by William Garnett had advised otherwise, and that William Garnett said, he did not think himself at liberty, as a representative, to cancel the bargain.[13]

The deposition of James M. Garnett too, though less explicit, bears on the same point. The very fact, that the vendee did not repeat his demand for re-payment of the four thousand dollars, he had advanced, shews, that he did not suppose the vendor had relinquished the contract.[14]

Since then, the vendor did never in fact, relinquish the contract, but took early measures to enforce its specific performance; since the delay which took place in the service of process, did not proceed from him, and did not produce any real mischief to the vendee, I cannot think that the right to enforce a specific performance is in any degree affected by that delay.

It has been also argued, that the vendor ought to have done all that was required from him by the contract. He ought to have tendered possession and a conveyance, on the first of January, 1819.

He certainly might have done so. But when it is recollected that previous to the first of January, 1819, he had received a letter from the vendee, announcing his determination not to receive possession, or a conveyance, and had himself resorted to the laws for that remedy, which they afforded for a broken contract, I cannot think that the omission, if it may be so termed, ought to vary that remedy, so far as respects a specific performance, whatever might be its influence on other questions which would arise in the cause, should the contract be carried into execution.

I come now to consider the validity of the objections made by the vendee, to a specific performance of the contract, supposing it not to be abandoned. He complains, that the title is incumbered and embarrassed with liens, of which he had no knowledge when the contract was made; and which would certainly have deterred him from making it, had they been communicated to him.

A Court of Equity compels the specific performance of contracts, because it is the intention of the parties that they shall be performed. But the person who demands it, must be in a capacity to do, substantially, all that he has promised, before he can entitle himself to the aid of this Court. At what time this capacity must exist, whether it must be at the date of the contract, at the time it is to be executed, or at the time of the Decree, depends, I think, upon circumstances, which may vary with every case. There is no subject which more requires the exercise of a sound discretion. The enquiry in every case of the kind, must be, whether the vendor could at the time, have conveyed such a title, as the vendee had a right to demand? If he could not *then*, whether he can *now*? And if he can, whether there has been such a change of circumstances, that a Court of Equity, ought not to compel the vendee to receive it? The first and great objection to the title, is the lien supposed to be imposed on the Mantipike estate, by the Will of George Brooke, for the payment of his debts.

In the year 1781, George Brooke, made his last will in writing, in which he devised as follows: "After my just debts are paid, I give and dispose of the remainder of my estate, in the manner following" &c.[15] The testator was then seised and possessed of Mantipike, which he devised to his son Richard. Richard Brooke, entered upon the property devised to him, and remained in possession of it, until his death, which happened in the year 1816. By his last will, he empowered his Executors, or such of them as might act, to sell his land. William Garnett, the Plaintiff, alone qualified as Executor to the will, and sold the land to the defendant William H. Macon, without any intimation of the existence of Campbell's claim, or that George Brooke had charged his land with the payment of his debts.

He, now contends, that this claim constitutes no obstacle to a specific performance, of the contract, because: *First,* It was not one of George Brooke's just debts, at the date of his Will, or at the time of his death. *Second,* If it was a just debt, it does not charge the estate in the hands of William H. Macon.

First. Is the claim now made by Keith, on the part of Campbell, for a debt, legally due from the estate of George Brooke, deceased?

As the suit for that claim is now depending, and is not yet ready for hearing, any positive decision respecting it, would, perhaps, be premature. It is, however, in the power of the Court, to form opinions on some points of that case, subject, indeed, to future revision; because the facts on which those points must certainly depend, are in the record; and it may be proper to do so, because, if the claim be obviously unfounded, the course of the Court would be different from what it ought to be, if any strong presumptions exist in its favour.

The Defendants insist, that the Decree against the personal representatives of George Brooke, is conclusive evidence against his devisee, of the existence of the debt.[16]

The cases cited by counsel, in support of this proposition, do not decide the very point. Not one of them brings directly into question, the conclusiveness of a judgment against the Executor, in a suit against the heir or devisee. They undoubtedly, show that the Executor completely represents the testator, as the legal owner of his personal property, for the payment of his debts in the first instance, and is, consequently, the proper person to contest the claims of his creditors. Yet, there are strong reasons for denying the conclusiveness of a judgment against an Executor in an action against the heir. He is not a party to the suit, cannot controvert the testimony, adduce evidence in opposition to the claim, or appeal from the judgment. In case of a deficiency of assets, the Executor may feel no interest in defending the suit, and may not choose to incur the trouble or expense attendant on a laborious investigation of the claim. It would seem unreasonable that the heir, who does not claim under the Executor, should be estopped by a judgment against him.

In the case against Munford's heirs, in this Court, the question was decided against the conclusiveness of such a judgment, and I am not satisfied that the decision was erroneous.[17]

This case, however, varies from that, in a material circumstance. In that case, the heir was bound by the obligation of his ancestor, and was liable to the creditor directly. In this case, the creditor is bound to proceed against the Executor and to exhaust the personal estate, before the lands become liable to his claim. The heir, or devisee, may indeed, in a Court of Chancery, be united with the Executor in the same action, but the Decree against him, would be dependant on the insufficiency of the personal estate. Since, then, the proceeding against the Executor, is, in substance, the foundation of the proceeding against the heir, or devisee, the argument for considering it as *prima facie* evidence, may be irresistable, but I cannot consider it as an estoppel. The judgment not being against a person representing the land, ought, I think, on the general principle, which applies to giving records in evidence, to be re-examinable when brought to bear upon the proprietor of the land.

It was said, but not pressed, by the counsel for the Plaintiff, that the Decree of the Court of Chancery, was not even *prima facie* evidence against the representatives of George Brooke. I do not concur with him in this proposition; but if I did, it would not, I think, materially affect this case. The Decree was against Braxton, as well as against the representatives of Brooke and Page; and is admitted to be conclusive against Braxton and his representatives. They could never be permitted to deny that Braxton owed Campbell the money specified in that Decree.

The undertaking, on which the Decree was pronounced against Brooke's ex'r. is dated in 1775, and promises, under seal, to stand security for Braxton to Campbell, for the sum then due. This sum is fixed by the Decree against Braxton; and the defence now set up for Brooke, does not controvert that Decree, as to Braxton, but insists on several circumstances which, as they contend, discharge Brooke from the liability incurred by his undertaking, as Braxton's surety.

The first of these is, the release of Broad-neck, which had been mortgaged for the debt, in 1769, when the Bills drawn by Braxton and sold to Campbell, came back protested.[18] William Aylett and George Brooke, became sureties to Campbell for this debt.

On the 21st day of May, in the year 1773, Campbell joined Braxton in a conveyance of the mortgaged premises to John Shermer, which is recorded in September, of the same year.[19] On the 15th of December, 1775, Aylett and Brooke transmit to Campbell an instrument of writing under seal, which, after reciting a former undertaking as sureties for Braxton, contains these words: "We therefore, in consideration of our former agreement, do promise and oblige ourselves to stand security for the said Braxton to the said Campbell, his heirs, ex'rs. adm'rs. and assigns, for the sum of money now due from the said Braxton, to the said Campbell."[20]

It is contended for the Plaintiff, that this suretyship was probably undertaken, in the confidence that the mortgaged property was amply sufficient to discharge the debt, and that Campbell, by releasing this property without the consent of the sureties, discharged them.

There would be great force in this objection, had the release of the mortgaged premises been dated subsequent to the engagement made by Aylett and Brooke. But that engagement was dated in December, 1775, and the deed of conveyance by Braxton and Campbell to Shermer, was recorded in September, 1773. No evidence exists, that either the mortgage or its release, was communicated to Aylett or Brooke, other than the presumption arising from the notoriety of such transactions, and from the fact that both deeds were recorded. These circumstances are precisely as strong to prove a knowledge of the deed to Shermer, as of the deed to Campbell, were it even proved, that the first bond of Aylett and Brooke, anteceded the deed to Shermer. The undertaking made in December, 1775, cannot be presumed to have been induced by a deed of mortgage which had been released more than two years, and although it is expressed to be made in consideration of the prior undertaking, yet that prior undertaking would not have been renewed, under circumstances, which, in the opinion of the parties themselves, absolved them from it, both in law and conscience. The fair inference from this renewal is, that the parties being mutual friends, the conveyance to Shermer was with the knowledge and assent of all.

The second objection arises from a fact, which is considered as an implied release of Aylett from his joint obligation with Brooke.

On that instrument, is this indorsement: "Aug. 6th, 1777, I do oblige myself to perform every engagement that Colonel William Aylett, was bound by the within, to perform, and to be considered as one of the securities of Wm. Braxton, in the room of Col. Aylett. Witness my hand, this 6th day of Aug. 1777.

ROBERT PAGE."[21]

It is contended, that this indorsement must be considered as made with the consent of Campbell, who, from its terms, and from suing the representatives of Brooke and not of Aylett, must be considered as having agreed to discharge Aylett.

The inference is, I think, a fair one. The instrument always remained in possession of Campbell, who must be presumed to have been privy and assenting to the indorsement; and who has avowed it, by his suit.

It is insisted, that the legal effect of this agreement is to discharge Brooke as well as Aylett, because the release of one joint obligor, releases the other.

It is obvious that the release of Brooke was not contemplated by the parties. If such be the effect of the instrument; an operation is given to the words, which they do not naturally import, and which the parties could never have foreseen or intended. If a positive rule of law require such a construction, the Court must make it; but the construction can be justified only by a positive and well settled rule. The common rule of law, and it seems also, to be the rule of reason, is, that words shall subserve the intent; but when the reverse of this rule is to be adopted, and both the words and the intent of an agreement are to yield to a technical principle, that principle ought to be sustained by decisions of unquestionable authority, the application of which, cannot be doubted.

The principle is, that a covenant never to put a bond in suit, is a release; and, it is also settled, that a release to one of several obligors, is a release to his co-obligors.

Both these points, have been frequently decided; and the Plaintiff is certainly entitled to the benefit of those decisions, as far as they apply to his case.

The principle will be found in any abridgement, or general treatise on the subject, with a reference to the cases, which establish it.[22] In no one of them, does the obligation contain any other party than him with whom the covenant is made. In all of them, the covenant, if broken, gives a right of action to the parties bound in the obligation, and the measure of their damages is given by the recovery of the obligee in his suit against them. If A. is bound to B. in an obligation, and they enter into a covenant, stipulating that it shall never be put in suit, notwithstanding which B. puts it in suit, this breach of covenant gives A. an action against B. in which he must recover in damages, precisely the sum to which the judgment obtained by B. may amount. To avoid circuity of action, this covenant may be pleaded as a release.

Thus far the cases go; and if there be one which goes farther, I have not found it. To bring himself within their letter, Brooke, ought to show a covenant, in which Campbell stipulates with Aylett and himself, never to put their bond in suit. To bring himself within their spirit, he ought to show some agreement giving him an action against Campbell, in which his right would be commensurate with any judgment Campbell might obtain against him. In such a case and in such a case only, would the principle of the decisions relied on apply; because, in such a case only, the sole effect of leaving the instrument to operate according to its language, would be to produce circuity of action. In such a case, too, the parties can have no other intention than to defeat the obligation. It is the sole object and effect of their covenant. To construe such an instrument, then, as a release, is to give it the effect intended by the parties.

I think the proposition may be stated, without fear of its being disproved by the books, that a covenant containing no words of release, has never been construed as a release, unless it gave to the party claiming that construction, a right of action, which would precisely countervail that to which he was liable; and unless also, it was the intention of the parties, that the last instrument, should defeat the first.

This general view of the precedents on which the Plaintiff relies, would be sufficient to satisfy my mind, that they do not apply to the case under consideration, had not the contrary opinion been urged at bar, with all the earnestness of conviction, and been supported by an authority, given on the case itself, which is entitled to the utmost respect. I shall, therefore, look farther into the question, and examine some cases and principles, which are adverse to the construction claimed by the Plaintiff's counsel.

Lacy v. *Kynaston,* (2 Salk. 575, 12 Mod. 551,) [2 Ld. Raym. 688,] was in substance this, — Articles were entered into by the members of a company of commedians, binding themselves, to pay one hundred pounds, to the representative of the Plaintiff's intestate, who was a member of the company, within three months after his death, should he continue to act during his life. The action was brought against Kynaston, who was also a member of the company, and the declaration avers, that Plaintiff's intestate, did continue to act during his life. The Defendant pleads in bar, articles subsequently entered into, by the same parties, including the Plaintiff's intestate, stipulating jointly and severally, that if the Defendant, Kynaston, should give notice of his intent to give over acting in said companies he should be free and discharged of and from all debts, &c. entered into by him, on account of the company, and that the Plaintiff's intestate, and the rest, should save harmless and indemnify the Defendant, from all such debts, &c. or any matter or thing relating to the company. To this plea, the Plaintiff demurred, and the only question was, whether the articles amounted in law to a defeasance or release, or were to be construed only as a covenant.[23] The Court was of opinion, that it was only a covenant, for several reasons, which are assigned in the opinion. In discussing the question, the principle, that a perpetual covenant amounts to a release, was particularly considered, and the reason given for construing such a covenant as a release, is to avoid circuity of action, "Because" says the Court, "there, one should precisely recover the same damage that he had suffered by the others suing the bond. A. is bound to B. and B. covenants never to put the bond in suit against A., if after B. will sue A. upon the bond, he may plead the covenant, by way of release. But if A. and B. be jointly and severally bound to C. in a sum certain; and C. covenants with A. not to sue him, that shall not be a release, but a covenant only; because he covenants only, not to sue A. but does not covenant not to sue B. for the covenant is not a release in its nature, but only by construction, to avoid circuity of action; for when he covenants not to sue one, he still has a remedy, and then it shall be construed as a covenant, and no more."[24] The same point was determined in *Dean* v. *Newhall,* (8 T. R. 168,) in which the authorities were reviewed at length, and a distinction of great importance taken, between an actual and a constructive release.[25]

It has been insisted by the Plaintiff's counsel, that these cases do not apply, because they relate to obligations which were joint and several, whereas the obligation of Aylett and Brooke was joint.

This objection merits consideration.

It is admitted to be law, that a release to one of several obligors, whether they be bound jointly, or jointly and severally, discharges the others, and may be pleaded in bar, by all. (2 Saund. [48 a] note; 2 Salk. 574; 12 Mod. 550.)[26] That the obligation is joint, or joint and several, then, can make no difference, if there be an actual release. The difference, if there be any, consists in the construction of the instrument. The same words, it may be contended, would amount to a release of a joint obligation, which would not release one which was joint and several.

Has this ever been so determined? I can only say, if it has, I have not found the case. In the absence of authority, the proposition must rest upon its reasonableness, and on analogy.

The reason assigned by the Plaintiff in support of this distinction, is that which is given by the Court in *Lacy* v. *Kynaston.* In case of an obligation which is several as well as joint, the Plaintiff may still sue the obligor, to whom the covenant does not apply, without violating his engagement, or subjecting himself to a suit; whereas, if the obligation be joint only, both obligors must be joined in the action. There is certainly much in this argument which deserves consideration. Without admitting its conclusiveness, which I am far from doing, it is necessary, as an indispensable preliminary to its application to the cause at bar, to shew that the indorsement on the bond of Aylett and Brooke, amounts to an agreement on the part of Campbell, not to sue Aylett on which agreement Aylett might recover damages equivalent to those he had sustained by the suit.

I do not think this is shown. Aylett is no party to the indorsement, and it is only upon the intention, that Campbell can be considered as coming under any stipulation to him. What, then, was his intention? Certainly not to discharge the obligation. The endorsement supposes the obligation to remain in full force, and is received in the confidence, that it does remain in force. It may well be doubted, whether a destruction of the obligation would not also destroy the indorsement; for, Page agrees only to stand in the place of Aylett, in the obligation, and if that be annulled, it is by no means clear, that Page is bound to any thing. Were this even otherwise, it is very certain, that Page would be placed in a situation entirely different from what he intended. If the indorsement is to be considered as a substantive agreement, referring to the obligation, for the sole purpose of ascertaining the sum for which he was bound, and remaining in force after the destruction of that obligation, then Page would be liable to Campbell for the whole debt, without retaining that recourse against Brooke for a moiety of it, which Aylett certainly possessed. He would not then stand in the room of Col. Aylett, as the indorsement imports, but in the room of both Aylett and Brooke, which the indorsement does not import. To construe Campbell's assent to this indorsement, then, as an agreement not to sue Aylett, if the effect of that agreement would be to destroy the obligation, would be to defeat the plain intention of the parties, and effect an object they designed to guard against. This is not to be tolerated, if the act can be otherwise construed. I can perceive no difficulty in doing so. The intention of the indorsement being to secure Col. Aylett, against the claim of William[27] Campbell, and to transfer his liability to Mr. Page, leaving Mr. Brooke still bound, the indorsement must be so construed, as to give full effect to the whole of this intention, so far as its words will justify. Now, if by supposing an agreement on the part of Campbell not to sue Aylett, we plainly defeat the intention of the parties, and probably annul the instrument itself, we ought not to suppose such an agreement, but some other more congenial to their views. Their object would be effected by joining Aylett in the suit on the obligation, and either not proceeding to judgment against him, or not using the judgment when obtained. If it were true, that the suit could never be brought against Brooke without joining Aylett, in the writ, it would be much more rational to suppose that an agreement for his security, omitting to describe the mode by which it was to be effected, was to be carried into execution by means consistent with other objects plainly intended by the parties, than by means which must defeat those objects. The respect which the law, in all such cases, pays to the intention with which an instrument is executed, may receive some illustration from the difference between the construction of a perpetual and of a temporary covenant, not to put a bond in suit; Precisely the same words, which, in a perpetual covenant, is a bar to an action, cannot, if used in a temporary covenant, be pleaded to an action brought during the suspension. Why is this? If the perpetual covenant can bar the action for ever, why may not the temporary covenant be pleaded to an action brought while the suspension exists? The reason of the distinction is founded in the principle, that a personal action once suspended, is gone for ever. Although, therefore, it is the intention of the parties to suspend the action, and although this intention is expressed by their words; yet, as the consequence of giving effect to this intention would be to destroy another more important object; the validity of an instrument not designed to be destroyed, such a covenant is not allowed to constitute, even a temporary bar, but the party injured by its breach, must take his remedy by a cross action upon it.

On general principles, then, I should, in the absence of express authority, be led to the conclusion, that a covenant with one of several joint obligors not to sue him, could not be pleaded as a release. But the very case, has, I think, been decided.

In *Hutton* v. *Eyre,* (1 Marshall, 603, [6 Taunt. 289,]) which was cited by Mr. Call, the action was brought for money paid to the use of the Defendant.[28] The Plaintiff and Defendant being partners, entered into a deed on the 26th August, 1809, to dissolve their partnership, on the 1st of January, 1810; and agreed that neither would in the mean time, contract any debt on the credit of the firm. On the 27th of October, 1810, the Defendant executed an assignment of all his property to Trustees, for the benefit of his creditors; in consideration of which, the creditors covenanted and agreed with the Defendant, not to sue him, on account of any debt due to them from him; and that in case they did sue him, the deed of assignment should be a sufficient release and discharge for him. The Trustees sold the property assigned to them, and paid five shillings in the pound, to the creditors, after which, the Plaintiff paid the residue of certain debts, contracted by the Defendant between the date of the agreement and the time of dissolution, on the credit of the firm, for which this suit was brought. It was contended for the Defendant, that the covenant not to sue him, being perpetual, was a release, not only to him, but to his partner also; and that the payment, being voluntary, gave no cause of action.

It is observable, that this case, is stronger than that under consideration would be, did the indorsement made by Page, on the bond of Aylett and Brooke, even contain a stipulation that no suit should be brought against Aylett, because, the instrument provides expressly, that in case suit should be brought, the deed of assignment should be a sufficient release and discharge.

In delivering the opinion of the Court, Lord Chief Justice Gibbs, noticed the cases of *Lacy* v. *Kynaston,* and *Dean* v. *Newhall;* but observing the circumstance, that those cases were on joint and several obligations, and were, therefore, not direct authority for the case before the Court, he added, "We must look at the principle on which the rule has been applied, that a covenant not to sue, shall operate as a release. Now, where there is only A. on one side, and B. on the other, the intention of the covenant by A. not to sue B. must be taken to mean a release to B. who is accordingly, absolutely discharged from the debt, which A. undertakes never to put in suit against him. The application, therefore, of the principle, in that case, not only acts in prevention of the circuity of action, but, falls in with the clear intention of the parties. But in a case like the present, it is impossible to contend that, by a covenant not to sue the Defendant, it was the intention of the covenantors, to release the Plaintiff, who was able to pay what his partner might be deficient in. It would have been an easier and a shorter method to have given a release, than to make this covenant. The only reason, therefore, for their adopting this course, was, that they did not choose to execute a release to the Defendant, because, that would also, have operated as a release to the Plaintiff; whereas they considered that a bare covenant not to sue the Defendant, would not extend to his partner. As, therefore, the terms of the covenant do not require such a construction, and as such construction would be manifestly against the intention of the parties, we are decidedly of opinion, that it ought not to be permitted so to operate."[29]

I can add nothing to the language of Chief Justice Gibbs, to show farther the direct application of this case to that under the consideration of the Court. That this, was not a joint obligation, but a joint assumpsit, constitutes, I think, no difference in the cases.

In considering a principle of construction, which rests entirely on a technical and positive rule, as defeating a plain intention, it may not be altogether improper to consider the action of other technical principles on the case.

It is clear, that if this indorsement be construed as an agreement between Campbell and Page, who is a stranger to the bond, it cannot release Brooke, the obligor. This is expressly stated by the Court in the case of *Lacy* v. *Kynaston*. But if it be considered as an agreement between Campbell and Aylett, still, it is an agreement by *parol* only, and an agreement by *parol*, cannot release an instrument of writing under seal. This subject is discussed in 2 Saunders, 47, in a note of Mr. Williams.[30] Brooke, does not allege satisfaction of the contract, but a discharge from it. He does not allege performance, but that he is not bound to perform. The instrument which will sustain such a defence, must be of equal dignity, with that which it professes to dissolve.

According to the best view I can take of the question, I cannot consider the indorsement made by Page on the bond of Aylett and Brooke, as implying any agreement on the part of Campbell, which could be used by Brooke, in Law or Equity, as a release.

The next objection to Campbell's claim is, that the estate of Robert Page, ought to be exhausted, before recourse is had to Brooke; because in June, 1792, Braxton mortgaged sundry slaves to Page and White, to indemnify Page, on account of this suretyship, and White, for suretyships entered into by him. Braxton was afterwards taken in execution at the suit of Richard Adams, upon which, Page and White agreed that a sufficient portion of the mortgaged property, should be sold to discharge the execution.[31] It is contended on the part of Brooke, that he has an equal interest with Page, in this mortgage, that it was the duty of Page to see to its application to the discharge of the debt, for which they were both bound, and that he is liable, *first*, for his negligence in allowing the property to be wasted; and *secondly*, for having allowed a part of it to be applied to a different object.

As Campbell was not party or privy to this transaction, it can give Brooke no claim on Campbell, were it even admitted to give him an equity against Page. It is undoubtedly the course of the Court, to Decree in the first instance, against the party who is ultimately responsible; but this is only done, where the parties are before the Court, at the time of the Decree, and their several liabilities, are clearly ascertained. It would be alike unprecedented and unreasonable, to anticipate, in this action, the liability of Page to Brooke, for a transaction not before the Court; and to compel Campbell to resort to that liability, and to forego his direct claim on his immediate debtor, and that without any proof of the competency of Page's estate, to satisfy the unascertained equity of Brooke. The unreasonableness of such a pretension seems so obvious, that I presume it is brought forward only on account of its connexion with a subsequent transaction between Page and Campbell.

On the 6th of June, 1821, articles of agreement were entered into between the representatives of Page, and the Attorney in Fact, of Campbell, in which, Campbell agrees in consideration of one moiety of the whole debt paid by Page's representatives, not to proceed against them, for satisfaction of any part of the Decree which might be obtained against the representatives of Page and Brooke; but this agreement is to be without prejudice to his right to pursue the other Defendants, till the other moiety of the debt should be satisfied, "and the said Campbell farther covenants, that the representatives of Page, shall never be made to contribute any thing to the estate of George Brooke, on account of any payment, the said Brooke's estate may be Decreed to make to the said Campbell."[32]

This agreement, not to levy the Decree, which might be obtained against the representatives of Brook and Page, upon the estate of Page, which had already paid one moiety of the whole debt, is in terms, which exclude the idea of being technically a release of the action, for that is to proceed, as if the agreement had not been made. The representatives of Brooke, can avail themselves of it so far only, as it raises an equity in their favour, against Campbell. What is this equity? It cannot be contended, that receiving one moiety of the debt from Page, is an injury to Brooke; ex parte, *Gifford*, (6 Vesey, Jun. 805;)[33] nor can he be injured by the agreement, not to levy Brooke's moiety, in any possible state of things, on Page. The liability of Brooke cannot be increased, nor his burthen augmented by this transaction. It may be diminished, because his possible liability for more than a moiety of the debt, is removed. Can the covenant that the representatives of Page shall never be made to contribute any thing to the estate of George Brooke on account of any payment the said Brooke's estate may be Decreed to make to the said Campbell, give Brooke an equity against Campbell?

To sustain this, it will be necessary to prove, that the estate of Brooke has an equity against that of Page, and that it is deprived of that equity, by this agreement. The amount of this injury, is the precise extent of Brooke's claim upon Campbell.

Brooke's equity against Page, is founded on the agreement that a part of the property mortgaged to White and Page, might be applied in payment of the debt due from Braxton to Adams, and on the failure of Page to apply the mortgaged property to Campbell's debt.

This mortgage was obtained for the benefit of Page and White, in proportion to their respective responsibilities, and it will not, I presume, be denied, that they are to be completely exonerated, before any equitable claim on the fund, can accrue to Brooke. How far Mr. White may have been relieved, does not appear, nor is it shown that one cent arising from this property, has ever been applied to the use of Mr. Page. Admitting him to be responsible for the sum paid to Adams, his responsibility can be only for the excess of that sum, over the debts the mortgage was intended to secure, and Brooke ought to show that excess. Its existence is not, and cannot be pretended.

As little foundation is there for the claim growing out of the alleged negligence of Page.

It will scarcely be pretended, that one of two sureties who obtains an indemnity for himself, becomes thereby responsible to the other, for that other's moiety of the debt, however insufficient the thing given as an indemnity may be, even to secure himself. If this cannot be pretended, it will certainly be required from the person who claims the residue, to show, that there was a residue, and that it has been lost to him, by the fault of the party whose responsibility he alleges. His difficulties would not, even then, be overcome. The enquiry would still be, why did he not himself proceed to assert his equity, by calling on the mortgagee and mortgagor to apply the fund to its proper object, and thereby relieve him to the extent of his right. But I enter not into this enquiry, because the subject is not, and probably never will be, before the Court. It is enough to say, that this equity cannot be assumed in this suit, to the discharge of Brooke's debt to Campbell.

I will barely add, to prevent my being understood as deciding any thing which might affect a point, not strictly before the Court, that I do not mean to indicate any opinion whether the contract between Campbell and Page, could, or could not, influence any claim of Brooke on Page, growing out of the conduct of Page respecting the mortgage of 1792. In deciding on the right of the plaintiff to demand a specific performance of his contract with Macon, that question must be considered as remaining open.

An additional objection to Campbell's claim on the Mantipike estate, is derived from the length of time which has elapsed, since the Decree, by which his debt was established.

The Decree of affirmance, was entered on the 3d of March, 1800, in the Court of Chancery; and on the 29th of September, in the same year, all attempts to find the mortgaged property having failed, executions were directed by the Court to issue against the estate of Brooke and Page, respectively, in the hands of their respective representatives, who, on the 18th of March, 1801, were ordered to settle their several accounts of administration, before a Commissioner of the Court.[34] From that time, till the 27th of October, 1820, when the supplemental bill was filed, no step whatever has been taken, against Brooke's estate.[35] By this gross negligence, the Plaintiff alleges, that his testator has been greatly injured, if Campbell be now permitted to charge his debt upon Mantipike.

There is, undoubtedly, great weight in this objection; but, the extent of its influence on Campbell's claim, depends on circumstances, the testimony concerning which, is not to be found in the record before the Court. It will form a very material part of the case, in which Keith is Plaintiff. That case, being not ripe for a hearing, the claim of Campbell upon Mantipike, even while it remained in the hands of the devisee, must, for the present, be considered as uncertain. Previous to any discussion of the effect of such a claim, on this contract, the Court will proceed to the *second* point, made by the *Plaintiff*, in the argument, which is, that

Second. If Campbell's is one of George Brooke's just debts, and is chargeable on his lands, still, it cannot charge Mantipike, in the hands of William H. Macon.

In considering this point, I shall assume for the present two propositions:

1st. Had Keith's suit, praying a sale of Mantipike for Campbell's debt, been instituted before the contract between Garnett and Macon, was entered into, the subsequent sale, made by the Executor, without the assent of the Court or creditor, could not have relieved the land from the charge created by George Brooke's Will.

2nd. Had the conveyance been made, and the purchase money been paid, before notice of the claim, the purchaser would not have been affected by it.

It is unquestionably true that, whatever doubts may exist, respecting the liability of a purchaser, for the application of the purchase money, to schedule debts, with which lands are charged, he is exempt from all liability for its application to debts generally. Had the contract then, been fully executed before this claim was asserted, Mantipike would have been clearly exonerated from it.

These propositions are stated, for the purpose of clearing the way, to the very case before the Court; the case of a contract for the purchase of land, equitably charged with the payment of debts, and notice of a debt given to the purchaser between the date of the contract, and the time when it is to be executed.

In considering this case, the question immediately occurs, whether there is any distinction between a charge on lands, which descend to the heir, or pass to a devisee, subject to the charge; and a devise to Executors or other trustees, for the payment of debts.

In Moseley, 96, [Anonymous,] and in Nelson's Ch. Rep. 36, this question was answered in the affirmative by the Court; and it was determined, that where lands were charged with debts generally, they remained liable to creditors in the hands of a purchaser.[36] This distinction was, however, overruled in the case of *Elliot* v. *Merryman,* (Barnard. Ch. R. 78, 81–82,) in which the Master of the Rolls determined, that in such a case the purchaser was not liable for the application of the purchase money, and said that "otherwise, whenever lands are charged with the payment of debts generally, they could never by discharged, without a suit in Chancery, which would be extremely inconvenient."[37]

There were many circumstances in the case of *Elliot* v. *Merryman,* showing that the creditors acquiesced in the sales, and looked to the vendor for their money, which might have had great influence on the mind of the Judge; and, if that case stood alone, the question might not be considered as settled. But it does not stand alone. The principle laid down by the Master of the Rolls, appears to have been followed ever since; and in *Walker* v. *Smalwood,* (Amb. 676,) which was a charge on land for debts generally, the Chancellor said, "the Court has established it as a rule, that where the charge is general, the purchaser is not bound to see to the application of the purchase money."[38] This rule has been pursued invariably in the English Courts for near a century, and may, therefore, be considered as well settled. Although the charge creates no legal estate, it manifests a clear intent that the person in whose favour it is made, shall receive so much out of the land, which a Court of Equity considers as a trust, and converts the owner of the legal estate, into a trustee. The heir or devisee, being once considered as a trustee, and the charge considered as a trust, public convenience and uniformity of decision would lead to an assimilation of these charges, or implied trusts to those which are express; and, in general, where no other question arises, than what relates to the construction of the trust, and the respective duties it imposes on a vendor and vendee, in a case attended with no peculiar circumstances, a Court of Equity perceives no ground of distinction between them. But, if it be admitted as a principle, that in a case of direct and culpable, or of negligent and constructive collusion between the vendor and vendee, by which the trust may be defeated, the purchaser may become responsible for the application of the purchase money; or, in other words, the land may remain charged in his hands; it is possible that there may be a difference in the testimony required to establish this constructive collusion, in the one case and in the other.

If lands be devised to trustees or Executors, to be sold for the payment of debts, the devisee possesses a legal, but not a beneficial estate in the premises. He can sell for the purposes of the trust only; and the vendee can consider him as acting no otherwise, than in the execution of a trust for which he has been selected by the owner of the property. This confidence being placed in him, by the person who had the sole right to dispose of the property, at his will, no other can question the correctness of his proceeding, or can be justifiable in suspecting any intention to violate the trust. The payment of the purchase money, therefore, to the trustee, is an act, which is the regular consequence of the contract; and, if that be made fairly, the purchaser has no right to enquire in what manner the residue of the trust will be executed. He has no right to suspect, that the person who has been selected by the Testator for its execution, will violate the trust reposed in him, and no collusion between him and the trustee, ought to be implied from equivocal acts. The existence of a debt, is the very circumstance which justifies a sale, and notice of its existence, can never excuse the purchaser for withholding the payment of the purchase money.

But where lands descend to the heir, or pass to the devisee, he does not necessarily sell, in execution of the trust, but for his own purposes. The trust is, in a great measure, the creature of a Court of Equity; and the heir, or devisee, is made a trustee by the Court. When he sells, he is not executing a power confided to him for the purpose of paying debts, but is parting with an interest vested in himself, for his own use, which interest is charged with debts. The purchaser does not consider the seller as executing a trust, nor does he so consider himself; but each considers him as acting for his own benefit. If in such a case, the charge still remains unsatisfied, the purchaser, who has notice of it, may be considered as aiding in, and conniving at, a violation of the trust, under circumstances which would not justify the same conclusion, if the trustee professed to act in the execution of his trust.

It becomes, therefore, material to enquire, what degree of connivance on the part of the purchaser, in acts which may defeat the trust, will leave him responsible to the creditor.

It is scarcely necessary to say, that positive fraud, or direct collusion, for the purpose of defeating the trust, will charge the purchaser. It is unnecessary to urge this proposition, because the principle is, I believe, conceded by all, and because too, the transaction before the Court, has no taint of that description. Its moral fairness is not questioned; and the sole enquiry is, whether the purchaser by proceeding with the contract, and paying the purchase money, would have exposed himself to the hazard of such a constructive collusion as to leave him subject to the claim of the creditor.

In pursuing this enquiry, it is proper to recollect, that Mantipike, was devised by George Brooke, to his son Richard, charged with the payment of his debts. This devise gave Richard, an absolute estate at Law, subject to an Equity, which could be asserted only in a Court of Chancery. Richard Brooke, would be considered, in this Court, as a trustee for the creditors of his Father, and had they applied to a Court of Equity, a sale of the property would, if necessary, have been Decreed. Richard, survived his Father, upwards of thirty years, during which time, no claim was asserted on Mantipike; and in his last will, devised his estate to be sold, and the money divided among his children. One clause is supposed to charge his real, as well as personal estate, with his debts.

Although a Court of Equity, will consider the trust with which Mantipike was chargeable in the hands of Richard, as passing with the land to his devisee, yet the devisee might naturally consider himself as acting under the express trust, contained in the will of his immediate testator. The purpose of his sale, would be, to comply with the will of Richard, and any presumption, that he might possibly hold himself bound to pay the debts of George, is prevented, so far as respects Campbell's claim, by the fact, that he denied all liability for that claim. If the purchaser should, after receiving notice of that claim, proceed to pay the purchase money to the seller, who contested its validity, and did not hold himself responsible for it, the question arises, whether payment under such circumstances, might not be considered in a Court of Equity, as so far implicating the purchaser in an act tending to defeat the trust, as to charge him, in the event of a failure on the part of the trustee, with the amount of the debt, so far as the purchase money was liable for it. With full notice of the claim, he pays the money to a person, who receives it, not for the avowed purpose of applying it to the objects of the trust, but of applying it to distinct trusts created by the Will of which he is executor.

This state of things, presents a case entitled to very serious consideration.

It is an old rule, that all persons acquiring property bound by a trust, with notice, shall be considered as trustees. The ancient cases on this point, are collected in Equity Cases Abridged, under the title *Notice*,[39] and the modern decisions, maintain the principle. The purchaser is subject to all the consequences of notice, if he receives it before payment of the purchase money. In one case *Wigg* v. *Wigg*, (1 Atk. 382, 384,) this rule has been carried so far, as to affect the purchaser who had paid his purchase money, but had not received his conveyance.[40] Whatever may be thought of the rule, as applying generally to cases of this description, it has, I believe, never been doubted, that notice after the contract, and before the payment of the purchase money, made the purchaser a trustee.

That the charge created by the clause in George Brooke's will, which subjects his lands to the payment of his debts, is a trust in the view of a Court of Equity, is admitted, and the purchaser, with notice, must take the land clothed with that trust, unless he can bring himself within the principle, that he is not bound to see to the application of the purchase money.

I have, certainly, no disposition to contract this principle within narrower limits than have been heretofore assigned to it. On the contrary, I am strongly inclined to the opinion that, if the instrument by which the trust is created, contains no provision contradicting the presumption, that the person who is to make the sale, is also to execute the trust throughout, it will be found difficult to maintain the *dicta* which are scattered thick through the books, declaring the purchaser bound to see to the application of the purchase money, in cases of scheduled debts, or legacies. The principle, however, which supports this opinion, must be examined, to determine how far it will carry us. The person creating the trust, has confided its execution to the trustee, where he has named one; and it is a part of his duty to sell the trust property, and, generally, to receive the purchase money, and dispose of it for the purposes of the trust. The trust could not be executed without a sale, and sales would be very much embarrassed, if the purchaser, by the mere act of purchase, became a trustee. In all cases, therefore, where the objects are not so defined, as to be brought, at once, to the view of the purchaser, it is settled, that he is not affected by them, and has only to pay the purchase money. The same rule is established in the case of a charge, where the lands descend, or are devised, liable to the payment of debts. In such case, a Court of Equity considers the heir, or devisee, as a trustee, and exercises the same controul over him, as over a trustee named by a testator.

In either case, if there be nothing to show that the trustee is acting in violation of his trust, the purchaser must consider him, as acting in pursuance of it; and as the sale may be a necessary part of it, the purchaser has done every thing incumbent on him, when he pays the purchase money, and is, consequently relieved from the necessity of enquiring into the conduct of the trustee.

But trusts, whether express or implied, are the peculiar objects of care to Courts of Equity, and are guarded from abuse, with great vigilance. In the exercise of this vigilance, they extend their controul, not only over the trustees themselves, but over all those who have transactions with the trustees. Their endeavours to secure the faithful execution of trusts, would often be defeated, if their regulations could not comprehend and bind those who contract for the trust property. To prevent the abuse of trust by the trustee, it is necessary to annul his acts, so far as they constitute an abuse; or, in other words, to consider the property in the hands of a purchaser, who has aided in the abuse, as still charged with the trust. In affirmance of this principle, the Master of the Rolls said, in a late case, [*Balfour* v. *Welland*,] (16 Ves. Jun. 156,) "Where the act is a breach of duty in the trustee, it is very fit, that those who deal with him should be affected by an act, tending to defeat the trust, of which they have notice."[41]

Plain as this principle is, and strictly conformable as it is to the general doctrines of a Court of Equity, there is some difficulty in applying it to particular cases. It is not easy to mark the precise act, which constitutes such a breach of duty in the trustee, as will affect the purchaser. If William Garnett be considered in this court as a trustee for the execution of George Brooke's Will, by the sale of Mantipike, it would defeat the trust to sell that estate for the uses described in Richard Brooke's Will, unless the debts of George Brooke, are to be considered as the debts of Richard Brooke, provided for by that clause in his will, which respects his own debts: And if William Garnett, sold with the avowed purpose of excluding the debts of George Brooke, or if he should proceed to distribute the money according to the will of Richard Brooke, disregarding the claims of George Brooke's creditors, if there be any, the trust, so far as respected those claims, would be defeated; and a purchaser intending to aid in thus defeating the trust, could not be perfectly secure. But if William Garnett sold with the intention of paying George Brooke's creditors first, and then of distributing the residue of the money according to the will of Richard Brooke; the act of sale would be no breach of trust, since a sale would be necessary for its performance. A purchaser, therefore, of the Mantipike estate might be placed in some peril. After receiving notice from a creditor of George Brooke, he might be considered, if he proceeded with the contract, as taking upon himself a responsibility for the subsequent transactions of William Garnett, which was no part of his engagement, and which he did not mean to take.

I very readily admit that if a trustee sells for the payment of debts generally, he is at liberty to contest any particular debt, and no notice to the purchaser can involve him in the contest. But, in such case, the trustee is in the fair execution of his trust, and regular performance of his duty; and the purchaser, having no right to intrude himself into the trust, can not be made responsible for its execution. But if the trustee, not professing to sell under the trust, holds himself absolved from it, and this is made known to the purchaser, the question, whether by completing the purchase, he assists in defeating the trust, and will be held responsible in a Court of Equity, becomes a much more serious enquiry. In pursuing it, all the circumstances must be considered, in order to determine, whether they prove satisfactorily, that the trustee is not acting in pursuance of the trust, but under the opinion that it does not bind him.]

In this case William Garnett is the immediate trustee of Richard Brooke, charged with the execution of his will which directs the sale of Mantipike for the benefit of his children, and probably for the payment of his own debts. Although a Court of Equity will consider the land as charged with any debt due from George Brooke, and treat the devisee of Richard Brooke, as a trustee for such creditor; yet the devisee would assume a very great responsibility, were he to undertake to pay this debt, without the direction of a Court. If the existence of the debt might be presumed, of which great doubts have been suggested at the bar, the extent of his testator's liability for it, is far from being certain. The personal estate of George Brooke ought to have been exhausted, before his real estate became chargeable, and the proportion of the debt with which Mantipike ought, under all circumstances, to be charged, could not safely be settled by the Executor. No counsel could have advised William Garnett, to incur this responsibility. No Court could censure him, for not incurring it. William H. Macon, then, who purchased without suspicion that any creditor of George Brooke remained unsatisfied, had great reason for the apprehension, that Mr. Garnett, not considering himself, as a trustee for the benefit of such creditor, would apply the money to the uses prescribed in the Will of Richard Brooke. This apprehension could not be removed by any enquiry. The bill filed by William Garnett, to enforce a specific performance, alleges expressly, that Campbell's debt was not due from George Brooke, and that if it was, Mantipike is not charged with it. Whether any direct communication took place between the parties, on the subject, is unknown; but as none is stated none can be presumed. The fact, however, is sufficiently obvious, that any enquiry respecting it, must have been answered, by the assurance, that the justice of the claim was denied. Whether going on to complete the contract, by paying the purchase money, under these circumstances, would be considered by a Court of Equity, as such a concurrence in "an act tending to defeat the trust" as would affect the purchaser, is a question of real difficulty. Some light may be thrown upon it by analogies drawn from the liability of the purchaser of lease-hold estates. It is well settled, that the purchaser of a chattel from an Executor, is not liable for the application of the purchase money, although such a chattel may be given in trust for a special purpose, or be itself a specific legacy. [*Elliot* v. *Merryman,*] (Barnard. Ch. R. 78, 81, [2 Atk. 42;]) [*Ewer* v. *Corbet,*] (2 P. Wms. 148;) [*Burting* v. *Stonard,*] (2 P. Wms. 150.)[42] The reason is, that no man can exempt his personal estate from the payment of his debts, or make any disposition of it, which shall prevent its passing to his Executors, to be sold by them, if his debts require it. Consequently, whenever an Executor sells in execution of his trust, the purchaser takes the property, freed from any charge with which the testator may have burthened it by his will. But if the sale be a breach of trust, and the purchaser have notice of the fact, he is affected by it. If the Executor sells to a person who knows that there are no debts, or that all the debts are paid, and that the sale is not a fair execution of the trust, the purchaser may take the property subject to the trust. (2 P. Wms. 148, 150.) So too, if the Executor sells at such under value as to indicate fraud; or for payment of his own debt. [*Crane* v. *Drake,* et al.,] (2 Vern. 616, Ed. *Raithby;*) [*Scott* v. *Tyler,*] (2 Bro. C. C. 433, 477;) [*Andrew* v. *Wrigley,*] (4 Bro. C. C. 125, 130;) [*Hill* v. *Simpson,*] (7 Ves. *jun.* 152, 167;) [*Lowther* v. Ld. *Lowther,*] (13 Ves. *jun.* 95;) [*M'Leod* v. *Drummond,*] (17 Ves. *jun.* 169.)[43]

These cases proceed upon the principle, that the Executor does not sell in pursuance of his trust, but in violation of it; and, that the purchaser knowing this fact, aids him in its execution by making the contract. The purchaser is not bound to make any enquiry. The general power of the Executor to sell, protects him in buying; but if he buys with notice, that the sale is a breach of trust, the property remains charged with it.

I feel much difficulty in resisting the application of this principle, to freehold estates charged with the payment of debts. It would seem to me, as if the enquiry must always be into the fact. The question must always be — is the sale, taking its object into view, a breach of trust? And are the circumstances such as to charge a purchaser, having express notice, with a participation in the breach? The purchaser of a chattel, from an Executor, with notice that no debts are due, or in payment of his own debt, seems to me to present the same questions.

Two cases have been cited by the counsel for the Plaintiff, as bearing very strongly on that, under consideration of the Court. The first is, *Walker* v. *Smalwood*, (Amb. 676.) John Smalwood devised his estate to his son Thomas, charged with the payment of debts; and Thomas, afterwards, mortgaged the estate, and then devised it to his wife, charged with the payment of his debts. The Bill was brought by bond creditors of John and Thomas Smalwood, against the wife and mortgagee. Pending the suit, they joined in selling the land to yeomans, against whom, a supplemental Bill was filed, to set aside the sale. It was set aside, upon the principle, that the execution of the trust had been taken out of the hands of the trustee, and transferred to the Court. The Chancellor said, "Though a general charge does not make a purchaser before the suit see to the application of the money, yet after a suit commenced, I should hold him bound to it; and I hold it as a general rule, that an alienation pending a suit is void." He also states, that actual notice was admitted.[44]

The propositions stated by Lord Camden, in this case, have not, I believe, been questioned, but those propositions do not reach the point now in controversy. A part of the purchase money was applied to the mortgage made by Thomas Smalwood, and the case does not inform us, that any objection was made on this account; but the case does not inform us either, whether this mortgage was made in satisfaction of a private debt due from Thomas, or for money generally, which might have been applied to the debts of the Father, or for a debt actually due by the Father. Notice was admitted, but of what? Probably, of the application of the money, and of the pendency of the suit. But these facts, do not imply a breach of trust, since is it not shown that the mortgage itself, which is an alienation *pro tanto*, was made under circumstances, which could involve the mortgagee in the application of the money. This case then, has no positive application to that at bar.

The other case is, *Hardwick* v. *Mynd*, (1 Anstr. 109.) William Mynd, devised considerable estates to his son Wm. Mynd, charged with certain legacies to his daughters. He also devised other estates to George Mynd and John Roberts, in trust for payment of debts, and appointed them his Executors. George Mynd and John Roberts renounced the Executorship, and conveyed their interest in the freehold estates to William, the son, subject to the trusts of the will. William, mortgaged great part of the estate for his own debts; and, about eleven years after the death of his Father, became a bankrupt.

The creditors of the Father, then filed this Bill for the satisfaction of their demands; and, it was admitted, that the most considerable of the mortgagees took, with notice of the situation of the property.

Eyre, Chief Baron, said, (and it is to be presumed the Court concurred with him) — "If the trustees had made these mortgages, they would not have been disturbed; in fact they are made by them; for they have assigned their whole interest to William Mynd to act for them in the trust."[45]

If the case stopped with this opinion, it would be, perhaps, conclusive, certainly very strong, in favour of the Plaintiff. The mortgagees took with notice of the misapplication of the purchase money, and were yet not held responsible for that misapplication. This decision would certainly go far in showing, that a purchaser, knowing that the sale was made not for the purposes of the trust, but of the trustee, would yet hold the land discharged from the trust. But other points were determined which deduct considerably from the application of this opinion to the case at bar, if they do not entirely destroy it. The Court held the trustees liable to make good the whole deficiency arising from the misapplication of the fund.

This case then, considering the two points which were decided in connexion with each other, amounts to nothing more than this. Where there has been a collusion between the trustee and purchaser, which results in an abuse of the trust, the trustee shall be chargeable in the first instance; but the case does not decide, on the ultimate responsibility of the purchaser, should the trustee prove insolvent. Applying it to the case at bar, it would prove, that had William H. Macon, proceeded, after notice, to complete the contract, and to pay the purchase money; and a suit been brought by the creditors of George Brooke, William Garnett, would have been liable in the first instance; but does not, I think, prove that William H. Macon, would not have been liable, in the event of the trustee's insolvency. The Court professed to found its opinion on the case of *Burt* v. *Dennet*, (2 Bro. C. C. 225.)

Dennet, was trustee in a mortgage deed from Godfrey to Burtenshaw, by which an annuity of £30 *per annum*, was secured to the Plaintiff. Dennet, having transactions with Burtenshaw, assigned the mortgage to him, without the privity of the Plaintiff; and afterwards assigned his property to trustees for payment of his debts. Burtenshaw paid the annuity to the year 1784, after which he stopped the payments, upon which the Plaintiff filed her Bill against Dennet. The Chancellor said, "the Plaintiff ought to have made Burtenshaw and the assignees of Dennet's estate parties, by which she might have gotten the mortgage-deeds: he then should have Decreed Burtenshaw to have paid the annuity, and Dennet to stand as a security, for having broken the trust."[46]

This case is not supposed to be applicable to that at bar, or the assignee of the mortgage, was undoubtedly responsible for the annuity. It is cited solely, because it was referred to by the Court, as an authority for the opinion given in *Hardwick* v. *Mynd,* and may, therefore, tend to explain that opinion. It would countenance the idea, that in the case in which it was cited, the Court did not suppose that the liability of the original trustee discharged the assignee.

Taking together the two parts of the opinion given in *Hardwick* v. *Mynd,* I cannot consider them as showing what would have been the decision of the Court, with respect to the mortgagees, had the trustees been insolvent. The report is very unsatisfactory, in as much as it assigns no reason for the decision, nor does it give the principle on which it stands. If the Bill was dismissed as to the mortgagees, because the receipts of the trustees, or of their agent, even under the circumstances of the case, amounted to an absolute discharge, it would be an express authority for the Plaintiff in the case at bar. If the Bill was dismissed, because the trustees were liable in consequence of their breach of trust, and were able to make up all deficiencies, it does not affect this case. If the Court meant to say, that if the trustees had made these mortgages to secure a debt due from themselves, the mortgagees would yet have held the property discharged from the trust, the decision would appear to me, to be in direct opposition to the principle settled in the sales of chattels by an Executor, and to the general principle, that where the act is a breach of duty in the trustee, those who deal with him, knowing the fact, are affected by it. To mortgage the property to secure their own debt, would seem to me, to be a direct and palpable breach of duty in the trustees, in which the mortgagee must have fully participated; and, I cannot conceive, that the Court meant to say, that such a transaction could be innocent. I must therefore suppose, that the decision turned upon the fact, that the trustee himself, who was before the Court, was of himself unquestionably competent to pay the money, and ought to pay it. It is true, that if the Court proceeded on this idea, the land ought to have been held still responsible; but the report is too defective and unsatisfactory to warrant any confidence in its being full, as to this point.

These cases then, though they have a strong apparent bearing on that under consideration, are too loosely and too carelessly reported, to satisfy the Court that they were decided on principles which they are cited to support. I cannot consider them as proving that land sold for other objects, in exclusion of a debt charged upon it, is relieved by the sale, from that charge, if the purchaser pays with notice of the intended misapplication of the purchase money. I repeat then, that it is a question of fact. Did the circumstances under which Mantipike was sold, prove that the purchase money was to be diverted from the payment of George Brooke's debts, to other objects, with such reasonable certainty as to leave it probable that a purchaser with notice, would be liable for the application of the purchase money; or in other words, that the land would, in the event of misapplication, and the insolvency of the trustee, remain charged in his hands?

These circumstances have already been stated. The most prominent are that William Garnett, was the immediate trustee under Richard Brooke's Will, though considered in a Court of Equity, as being also a trustee for George Brooke's creditors, whose claim was prior to that of Richard Brooke's creditors or legatees, but whose claim the vendor not only did not, but could not safely, mean to satisfy, unless directed by a Court of Equity so to do. The purchaser had, certainly, reason to believe, that the sale was not made with a view to satisfy the charge created by George Brooke's Will, and that the purchase money, if paid before the institution of a suit by Campbell's representative, would be applied to the purposes of Richard Brooke's Will. If a suit should be instituted before the purchase money became due under the contract, or before it was paid, the whole affair would then be transferred to the Court of Chancery, and he would no longer be master of his own conduct. In the one event, he would take upon himself the hazard of paying with full notice of the charge, money which he had reason to believe, was to be diverted to different objects; in the other, he would be involved in a Chancery suit, the course and duration of which, he could not anticipate. Do these difficulties constitute a valid objection to a Decree for a specific performance?

It cannot be doubted, that these difficulties, if presented to the mind of a prudent man, contemplating the purchase of an estate, and desirous of performing his contract according to its terms, might have a serious influence on his conduct, and might deter him from making the purchase. If informed of them, after making the contract, but before its execution by the paying of the purchase money and receiving a conveyance, he would have such strong motives for stopping entirely, or at least, for pausing, until the impediments could be removed, as would, I think, justify him, for so doing, in the opinion of any reasonable man. Had this suit come to a hearing as between the vendor and vendee only, on the day on which it was instituted, could a Court of Equity have pronounced the objections to the title so frivolous, as to Decree that Macon should take it, without having those objections removed? Is the exoneration of the land from Campbell's debt, by a sale to a purchaser, with full notice of all the circumstances which had come to the knowledge of Col. Macon, so perfectly clear, that a Court of Equity ought to decree him to take the land and pay the purchase money, without any security against the future demand of Campbell's representative?

Both on principle and authority, I think it very clear, that a specific performance will not be Decreed on the application of the vendor, unless his ability to make such a title as he has agreed to make, may be unquestionable; [*Marlow* v. *Smith*,] (2 P. Wms. 201;) [*Rose* v. *Calland*,] (5 Ves. jun. 186, 189;) [*Roake* v. *Kidd*,] (5 Ves. jun. 647;) [*Stapylton* v. *Scott*,] (16 Ves. jun. 272;) [*Sloper* v. *Fish*,] (2 Ves. and Beame. 149;)[47] and it is equally clear, that a purchaser, under such a contract as that between Garnett and Macon, had a right to expect that an unincumbered estate in fee simple would be conveyed to him. [*Omerod* v. *Hardman,*] (5 Ves. jun. 722, 734;) [*Flureau* v. *Thornhill,*] (2 Wm. Bl. R. 1078.)[48] In a contract for the purchase of a fee simple estate, if no incumbrance be communicated to the purchaser, or be known to him to exist, he must suppose himself to purchase an unincumbered estate, and a Court of Equity will not impose its extraordinary power of compelling a specific execution of the contract, unless the person demanding it, can himself do all that it is incumbent on him to do. It has been said at the bar, that the declarations of the Chancellors to this effect, have been made in cases where the title itself was doubtful, not where there was a money charge upon the estate, which would not materially affect the purchaser, and which might be paid off by him, without any material change in his contract, and without inconvenience.

This allegation is not, I think, entirely correct. The objection is not entirely confined to cases of doubtful title. It applies to incumbrances of every description, which may, in any manner, embarrass the purchaser in the full and quiet enjoyment of his purchase. In 5 Ves. jun. 189, [*Rose* v. *Calland,*] the property was stated to be free of hay tithe; and there was much reason to believe that the statement was correct. But the point being doubtful, the bill of the vendor praying a specific performance, was dismissed. There is, certainly a difference between a defined and admitted charge, to which the purchase money may, by consent, be applied, when it becomes due, and a contested charge which will involve the purchaser in an intricate and tedious law suit of uncertain duration. There can, I think, be no doubt, that Campbell's claim, controverted as it necessarily was by Brooke's representative, is of this character, and that the continuance of the charge on the land in the hands of a purchaser with full notice of that claim, and of all the circumstances under which the sale was made, was too questionable to be disregarded as entirely frivolous, if alleged in a suit between Garnett and Macon only, for a specific performance. If it could not be entirely disregarded by a Court, Macon was certainly justifiable in refusing to proceed while this cloud hung over the estate. He was certainly justifiable in referring the case to a Court. He was justifiable in refusing to take the title which could have been made in January, 1819.

But although it was not in the power of Garnett to make a perfectly secure title, previous to a Decree which would dispose of Campbell's lien, it is undoubtedly now in his power. All the parties are now before this Court, and, if a specific performance should be decreed, the title which can be made to Macon, will undoubtedly stand clear of Campbell's lien. The question, therefore is, whether the contract ought now to be enforced.

It has been repeatedly declared both in the Courts of England and of this country, that time is not of the essence of a contract; and, that a specific performance ought to be decreed if a good title can be made at the time of the Decree.

This principle is sustained by many decisions, and by the practice of the

Court of Chancery in England to refer it to a Master, to report whether the title be good at the time. But, I do not think that the English Court of Chancery has ever laid down the broad principle, that time was never important, and that an ability to make a clear title at the time of the Decree, arrested all enquiry into the previous state of things. On the contrary, if a person sell an estate, to which he has no title, he cannot, though he should afterwards acquire it, enforce the contract. There is an implied averment in every sale made without explanation, that the vendor is able to do what he contracts to do. If he is not, and the vendee sustains an injury in consequence of this inability, it would seem unreasonable, that the contract should be enforced; it would be the more unreasonable, if the amount of the injury should not be the subject of exact calculation. It is a general rule, that he who asks the aid of a Court of Equity, must take care that his own conduct has been exactly correct. It would be strange, if this general rule should be totally inapplicable to time, in the execution of a contract. If the day be carelessly or accidentally passed over without making a conveyance, and no serious inconvenience result from the omission, the objection would be captious, and would very properly be discountenanced; but if the vendor was unable to clear up the title, until such an alteration had taken place in the state of things, as materially to affect the parties, time, I think, cannot in reason, be deemed unimportant. It is settled, that mere inadequacy of price, is not a sufficient ground for a Court of Equity to refuse its assistance, unless the difference between the sum to be given and the value of the land, be so enormous, as to countenance the idea of fraud or imposition. Yet, if an unreasonable contract be not performed according to its letter, equity will not interfere. (Sugd. on Vend. & Pur. 190, [2 Am. Ed.])[49] Between a contract which is unreasonable when made, and one which has become so before it can be executed, if the application be made by the person in fault, for the aid of the Court against the party who has suffered by his inability, no clear distinction is perceived.

In the case of *Gibson* v. *Patterson* et al. (1 Atk. 12.) Lord Hardwicke, is reported to have paid no regard to the negligence of the vendor in producing his title deeds.[50] But that case is said by subsequent Judges who have inspected the record, to be mis-reported; and if it were not, it does not appear that there was any incumbrance on the estate, or that the condition of the parties had been affected by the delay.

In *Morgan* v. *Shaw*, (2 Meriv. 140,) the Chancellor, said, "The inclination of my opinion is against the old doctrine, that time is in no case of the essence of the contract,"[51] and in 4 Bro. C. C. [*Fordyce* v. *Ford*,] 498, the Master of the Rolls said, ["]I hope it will not be supposed, that a man is to enter into a contract, and think that he is to have his own time to make out his title."[52] In *Harrington* v. *Wheeler*, (4 Ves. jun. 686;) and *Lloyd* et al. v. *Collett*, (4 Bro. C. C. 469,) time was held material.[53]

I think that the present doctrine of the Court of Chancery of England, is clearly in favour of the opinion, that where time is really material to the parties, the right to a specific performance may depend upon it; and I think that the same doctrine prevails in the courts of the United States. *Hepburn* and *Dundas* v. *Colin Auld*, (5 Cranch, 262,) was a suit for a specific performance, which was objected to by the vendee, because 6,000 acres of land, sold by Hepburn and Dundas, was not held by a title in severalty, but was an undivided interest in a much larger tract, and that the time of executing the contract was, in that case, material. On that point the Court says, [p. 276,] "It is not to be denied that circumstances may render the time material; and the Court does not decide that this case is not of that description. But the majority of the Court is of opinion, that the estate is to be considered as an estate held in severalty."[54] It was also said in *Pratt* et al. v. *Law* and *Campbell*, (9 Cranch, 456, 494,) that time is made material to the specific performance of a contract, whenever, from the change of circumstances, a specific performance, such as would answer the ends of justice between the parties, has become impossible.[55]

In *Brashier* v. *Gratz* et al. (6 Wheat. 528,) the case was this: Michael Gratz, residing in Philadelphia, sold in March, 1807, to Walter Brashier, residing in Kentucky, a tract of land lying in Kentucky, which Gratz had purchased, and for the title to which a suit was then depending. Brashier gave his notes for the purchase money, and agreed to attend to the prosecution of the suit, for which service an allowance was made him in the price of the land. The land was sold at 22 dollars 50 cents by the acre, and it was agreed, that if any part of the land should be lost by the decision of the Court, Gratz should re-pay 11 dollars 25 cents for each acre that might be so lost.

The suits were not pressed to a decision, and in 1811, the fees were demanded from Gratz, and were paid by him. In 1811, Brashier came to Philadelphia, and his notes being protested for non-payment, Gratz required that they should be paid, or that the contract should be rescinded. Brashier was unwilling to do either, and the question, whether Gratz was still bound by it, was left to Arbiters, who decided that he was. Brashier became insolvent, and Gratz took the management of the suits into his own hands, which were decided in his favour, in 1813. About this time, the lands rose suddenly in value, on which, Brashier tendered payment of his notes, and demanded a conveyance of the land. Gratz refused, and the Bill was brought for a specific performance. It was dismissed in the Circuit Court, and the Plaintiff appealed to the Supreme Court, where the Decree was affirmed.

It will be readily admitted, that the case of Brashier and Gratz, was a strong one, against the Plaintiff—much stronger, than that, now before this Court; but the principles laid down in its decision, apply to all cases where the party demanding the aid of the Court, has failed to perform his part of the contract, and a change in circumstances, unfavourable to the party resisting the demand has taken place. The court says, [p. 533–

534,] "The rule, that time is not of the essence of a contract, has certainly been recognised in Courts of Equity; and there can be no doubt, that a failure on the part of a purchaser or vendor, to perform his contract on the stipulated day, does not, of itself, deprive him of his right to demand a specific performance at a subsequent day, when he shall be able to comply with his part of the engagement. It may be in the power of the Court to direct compensation for the breach of contract in point of time, and in such case, the object of the parties is effectuated by carrying it into execution. But the rule is not universal. Circumstances may be so changed, that the object of the party can be no longer accomplished, that he who is injured by the failure of the other contracting party, cannot be placed in the situation in which he would have stood, had the contract been performed. Under such circumstances, it would be iniquitous to Decree a specific performance, and a Court of Equity will leave the parties to their remedy at Law."

"If, then, a bill for a specific performance be brought by a party who is himself in fault, the Court will consider all the circumstances of the case, and Decree according to those circumstances."

In re-viewing the circumstances of the case, the Court says, [p. 539–540.] "Another circumstance which ought to have great weight, is the change in the value of the land. It was purchased at 22 dollars 50 cents *per* acre. Mr. Brashier faild to comply, and was unable to comply with his engagements. More than five years after the last payment had become due, the land suddenly rises to the price of 80 dollars *per* acre. Then he tenders the purchase money, and demands a specific performance. Had the land fallen in value, he could not have paid the purchase money. This total want of reciprocity, gives increased influence to the objections to a specific performance, which are furnished by this great alteration in the value of the article."[56]

The change in the value of the article in the case which has been cited, between the time when the money ought to have been paid, and the time when the money was tendered, was certainly enormously great, much greater than can take place in ordinary times; but the principle does not depend entirely on the excessiveness of that change. The principle undoubtedly is, that a very great change in the value of the article, constitutes a serious objection to a Decree for a specific performance, when claimed by the party whose fault it is, that the contract has not been executed.

In the case under consideration, a considerable change has taken place in the value of the article; and that change has been produced by a general declension in the price of lands. It must, therefore materially affect the arrangements to be made by the purchaser for a compliance with his contract. The same property which, if sold in time would probably have enabled him to pay for Mantipike, would not on any reasonable estimate, now enable him to do so. If, then, William Garnett was unable to convey a perfectly safe title in January, 1819, Mr. Macon has sustained an injury by the suspension of his proceedings, the amount of which admits of no certain calculation, and which is probably equivalent to the difference in the value of Mantipike at that time and at this.

Although I am entirely satisfied that there is no moral taint in this transaction, that the omission to give notice of Campbell's debt was not concealment to which blame in a moral point of view, can be attached; yet a Court of Equity considers the vendor as responsible for the title he sells, and is bound to inform himself of its defects. The purchaser in making a contract may be excused for relying on the assurance of the vendor, implied in the transaction itself, that he can perform his agreement.

As I think Campbell's claim, was a cloud lowering over the title Garnett could convey to a purchaser with notice, which justified Macon in refusing to go on with the contract, which cloud cannot be dissipated but by the Decree of a Court of Chancery, and as before such a Decree was attainable, the value of the article has greatly changed, that circumstance creates a strong objection to a specific performance. At the same time, it must be perceived that the vendor, who has committed no moral wrong, and who is now able to perform his contract, will sustain all the loss arising from the depreciation of the property, which he might have sold to another, had not Macon purchased. I felt some hesitation between a Decree dismissing the bill, and a Decree for carrying the contract into execution, considering the vendor who has retained possession of the property as entitled to the profits, and the vendee who was justifiable for not proceeding with his contract, as exempt from the payment of interest. But on reflection I have come to the opinion, that as there is no fault in the purchaser, and as there was some remissness in the seller in not communicating Campbell's claim, that the whole disadvantage ought to fall on the vendor, and that his Bill ought to be dismissed.

The point which has weighed heaviest on my mind, and about which I have felt the greatest difficulty, concerning which I have indeed at different times inclined to different opinions, is whether the sale under the Will of Richard Brooke, is, under all the circumstances of the case, to be considered as such a breach of trust, as respects the creditors of George Brooke, as will involve a purchaser, having notice before the contract of sale is carried into execution, in the consequences. I am rather disposed to the opinion that it is such a breach of trust. At all events, I am satisfied that it wears such a serious aspect, as to justify a purchaser in refusing to proceed.[57]

Printed, *The Opinion of Chief Justice Marshall, in the Case of Garnett, Ex'r of Brooke v. Macon et al.* (Richmond, Va., 1825), 9–60; Daniel Call, *Reports of Cases Argued and Decided in the Court of Appeals of Virginia,* VI (Richmond, Va., 1833), 330–76. Square brackets in the printed text are retained here.

1. Contract, 10 June 1818, U.S. Cir. Ct., Va., Rec. Bk. XVII, 174–75.
2. Receipt, 22 Aug. 1818, ibid., XVII, 175.

3. JM had argued the case of Price v. Campbell in the Court of Appeals (2 Call 110, 116–17).

4. U.S. Cir. Ct., Va., Rec. Bk. XVII, 8–9.

5. Call has "detailed."

6. Subpoena, 26 Dec. 1818; bill in chancery, 28 June 1819, U.S. Cir. Ct., Va., Rec. Bk. XVII, 1–6.

7. Decree, 18 June 1821, ibid., XVII, 180–81.

8. Bill of revivor, 23 Aug. 1823; petition for removal, 27 Feb. 1824, ibid., XVII, 238, 279.

9. Bill in chancery [ca. Mar. 1824], ibid., XVII, 287–91.

10. Call corrected this to "amount."

11. Answer, 15 May 1820, U.S. Cir. Ct., Va., Rec. Bk. XVII, 162–63.

12. A legal term for neglect.

13. Deposition of Thomas G. Smith, 14 Nov. 1820, U.S. Cir. Ct., Va., Rec. Bk. XVII, 176–77.

14. Deposition of James M. Garnett, 15 Nov. 1820, ibid., XVII, 178–79.

15. Will of George Brooke, recorded 13 May 1782, ibid., XVII, 7–8.

16. The decree referred to was in the case of Price v. Campbell (cited in n. 3), decided by the Court of Appeals in 1799, affirming a decree of the High Court of Chancery against Braxton and the representatives of George Brooke (Robert Price and Robert Page).

17. Mutter's Executors v. Munford, 1 Brock. 266 (1814); *PJM*, VIII, 51–61.

18. Mortgage deed, 20 July 1769, U.S. Cir. Ct., Va., Rec. Bk. XVII, 28–29. On the Broadneck property, see Harris, *Old New Kent County,* II, 787–88.

19. Deed, 21 May 1773, U.S. Cir. Ct., Va., Rec. Bk. XVII, 239–40.

20. Bond, 15 Dec. 1775, U.S. Cir. Ct., Va., Rec. Bk. XVII, 33. On William Aylett (1743–1781), see Harris, *Old New Kent County,* II, 827.

21. U.S. Cir. Ct., Va., Rec. Bk. XVII, 33.

22. The editor's subjoined note cites Bacon, *Abridgment,* V, 683.

23. Lacy v. Kynaston, 2 Salk. 575, 91 Eng. Rep. 484; 12 Mod. 548, 88 Eng. Rep. 1510; 1 Raym. Ld. 688, 91 Eng. Rep. 1359 (K.B., 1701).

24. 12 Mod. 551–52, 88 Eng. Rep. 1512.

25. Dean v. Newhall, 8 T.R. 168, 101 Eng. Rep. 1326 (K.B., 1799).

26. Fowell v. Forrest, 2 Wms. Saund. 47, 48 n., 85 Eng. Rep. 646 n. (K.B., 1670); Clayton v. Kynaston, 2 Salk. 574, 91 Eng. Rep. 483 (K.B., 1701); Lacy v. Kynaston, 12 Mod. 550, 88 Eng. Rep. 1511 (K.B., 1701).

27. This should be "Robert."

28. Hutton v. Eyre, 6 Taunt. 289, 128 Eng. Rep. 1046 (C.P., 1815). The case is also reported in Sir Charles Marshall, *Reports of Cases Argued and Determined in the Court of Common Pleas* (2 vols.; London, 1815–17), I, 603 (not reprinted in English Reports).

29. JM quoted from Marshall, *Reports of Cases Argued and Determined in the Court of Common Pleas,* I, 607–8.

30. 2 Wms. Saund. 47 n., 85 Eng. Rep. 646 n.

31. Mortgage deed, 10 June 1792; bond, 14 Apr. 1793, U.S. Cir. Ct., Va., Rec. Bk. XVII, 38–40, 65.

32. Articles of agreement, 6 June 1821, ibid., XVII, 131–32.

33. Ex parte Gifford, 6 Ves. 805, 31 Eng. Rep. 1318 (Ch., 1802).

34. Decree, 3 Mar. 1800; decree, 29 Sept. 1800; decree, 18 Mar. 1801, U.S. Cir. Ct., Va., Rec. Bk. XVII, 71–72, 83.

35. Bill of revivor and supplement, 27 Oct. 1820, ibid., XVII, 119–28.

36. Anonymous, Mos. 96, 25 Eng. Rep. 291 (Ch., 1729); Wentworth v. Young, Nels. 36, 21 Eng. Rep. 783 (Ch., 1639).

37. Elliot v. Merryman, Barn. C. 78, 81–82, 27 Eng. Rep. 562, 563 (Ch., 1734).

38. Walker v. Smalwood, Amb. 676, 677, 27 Eng. Rep. 439 (Ch., 1768).

39. 1 Eq. Ca. Abr. 330–34, 21 Eng. Rep. 1081–84 (s.v., "Notice").

40. Wigg v. Wigg, 1 Atk. 382, 384, 26 Eng. Rep. 244, 245 (Ch., 1739).

41. Balfour v. Welland, 16 Ves. 151, 156, 33 Eng. Rep. 941, 943 (Ch., 1809).

42. Elliot v. Merryman, Barn. C., 78, 81, 27 Eng. Rep. 562, 563 (Ch., 1734); Elliot v. Merriman, 2 Atk. 41, 42, 26 Eng. Rep. 422 (Ch., 1740); Ewer v. Corbet, 2 P. Wms. 148, 24 Eng. Rep. 676 (Ch., 1723); Burting v. Stonard, 2 P. Wms. 150, 24 Eng. Rep. 677 (Ch., 1723).

43. Crane v. Drake, 2 Vern. 616, 23 Eng. Rep. 1004 (Ch., 1708); Scott v. Tyler, 2 Bro. C.C. 431, 433, 477, 29 Eng. Rep. 241, 242, 263 (Ch., 1788); Andrew v. Wrigley, 4 Bro. C.C., 125, 130, 29 Eng. Rep. 812, 814 (Ch., 1792); Hill v. Simpson, 7 Ves. 152, 167, 32 Eng. Rep. 63, 68 (Ch., 1802); Lowther v. Lowther, 13 Ves. 95, 33 Eng. Rep. 230 (Ch., 1806); McLeod v. Drummond, 17 Ves. 152, 169, 34 Eng. Rep. 59, 65–66 (Ch., 1810).

44. Walker v. Smalwood, Amb. 676, 677, 27 Eng. Rep. 439 (Ch., 1768).

45. Hardwick v. Mynd, 1 Anst. 109, 110, 145 Eng. Rep. 815, 816 (Ex., 1792).

46. Burt v. Dennet, 2 Bro. C.C. 225, 29 Eng. Rep. 126 (Ch., 1787).

47. Marlow v. Smith, 2 P. Wms. 198, 201, 24 Eng. Rep. 698, 699–700 (Ch., 1723); Rose v. Calland, 5 Ves. 186, 189, 31 Eng. Rep. 537, 538–39 (Ch., 1800); Roake v. Kidd, 5 Ves. 647, 31 Eng. Rep. 785 (Ch., 1800); Stapylton v. Scott, 16 Ves. 272, 34 Eng. Rep. 988 (Ch., 1809); Sloper v. Fish, 2 Ves. & Bea. 145, 149, 35 Eng. Rep. 274, 275–76 (Ch., 1813).

48. Omerod v. Hardman, 5 Ves. 722, 734, 31 Eng. Rep. 825, 830–31 (Ch., 1801); Flureau v. Thornhill, 2 Black. W. 1078, 96 Eng. Rep. 635 (C.P., 1776).

49. Edward Burtenshaw Sugden, *A Practical Treatise of the Law of Vendors and Purchasers of Estates* (2d Am. ed.; Philadelphia, 1820), 190.

50. Gibson v. Patterson, 1 Atk. 12, 26 Eng. Rep. 8 (Ch., 1737).

51. Morgan v. Shaw, 2 Mer. 138, 140, 35 Eng. Rep. 892, 893 (Ch., 1817).

52. Fordyce v. Ford, 4 Bro. C.C. 494, 498, 29 Eng. Rep. 1007, 1009 (Ch., 1794).

53. Harrington v. Wheeler, 4 Ves. 686, 31 Eng. Rep. 354 (Ch., 1799); Lloyd v. Collett, 4 Bro. C.C. 469, 29 Eng. Rep. 992 (Ch., 1793).

54. Hepburn and Dundas v. Auld, 5 Cranch 262, 276 (1809). JM gave the opinion of the Court.

55. Pratt v. Law and Campbell, 9 Cranch 456, 494 (1815). Johnson gave the opinion of the Court.

56. Brashier v. Gratz, 6 Wheat. 528, 533–34, 539–40 (1821). JM gave the opinion of the Court.

57. The accompanying decree dismissed the plaintiff's bill, each party paying his own costs. On 29 Nov. 1825 Garnett petitioned for an appeal to the Supreme Court, which was granted. After executing an appeal bond, Garnett evidently decided not to pursue the case (U.S. Cir. Ct., Va., Rec. Bk. XVII, 301).

From William B. Giles

SIR: WIGWAM,[1] Nov. 26, 1825.

In the 5th volume, page 722, of the Life of Washington, you have introduced my name in the following words, "In support of this motion, after urging the indelicacy of exulting over the misfortunes of others by contrasting our happiness with their misery, Mr. Giles said:" and immediately follows the speech ascribed to me under marks of quotation.[2] It might possibly be inferred, from this mode of stating these facts, that I had given some authority or sanction to this quotation. Immediately after I first saw this statement, I determined to address a respectful note to you, Sir, upon the subject, requesting some explanation and correction thereof; and had reference to two files of papers, the Aurora and United States' Gazette, the one edited by Mr. Bache, the other by Mr. Fenno, to ascertain whether or not the speech ascribed to me, under marks of quotation, was to be found in either of those papers[3] — And I think (those papers not being before me,) that although both of those editors had published notes of the speech, yet neither of them had used the version quoted. About the time of making this examination, I contemplated writing a work upon the origin and progress of the government of the U.S. with an analysis of the constitution of the U.S. and of the several states, grounded upon legislative interpretations of each, as far as was known to me. This work would necessarily have involved a review of certain parts of "The Life of Washington." In the execution of the contemplated work I should have been enabled to have given the necessary explanations myself in relation to the debate referred to. I retired from public life with this determination; but was arrested in the undertaking by a severe providential visitation.[4] Since that disappointment I have frequently intended to address a note to you upon the same subject, but from various causes I have hitherto deferred it. I am now informed thro' the newspapers, that you are engaged in reviewing "The Life of Washington." If so, it will afford you an opportunity, without much inconvenience, of doing me an act of justice, which I am perfectly confident would afford you pleasure. I, therefore, respectfully ask the favor of you, Sir, to inform the public: 1st, Whether or not you have ever received from me, either directly or indirectly, any authority whatever to ascribe to me the speech under marks of quotation, or whether you have any evidence that I have ever given the smallest sanction whatever to the said speech: 2d, To state to the public the paper or document from which that speech was transcribed into "the Life of Washington." I must presume the speech ascribed to me, was taken from some newspaper unknown to me; but from whatever source it may have come, I now disclaim *every expression* in it, and am perfectly confident that I never used *any expression* imputed to me by the note-taker of that speech, nor any other bearing any just resemblance thereto. The notes of the speech as printed, seem to me, to have been taken by a rude, uncultivated, prejudiced mind, for which I do not feel the least responsibility — so far as regards the language used by the note-taker, and it seems, in this case, that the objections taken to the course I pursued, arise principally from the language used, and not the principles advocated by me on that occasion. If the draft of the answer to the President's speech be critically examined, it will be found to have been made with great ability and address, by the majority of the committee who reported it. It was prepared in times of high party excitement, and was evidently pressed upon the republican party with a view of involving it in some inconsistency by calling for a general and unqualified approbation of the measures of the administration, some of the most prominent of which, had been opposed by the republicans generally, and by myself amongst others, and this inconsistency was to be enforced by the dominant influence of the President's popularity, & the general sensibilities excited by his retiring from public life. I did not feel disposed to yield to this influence, and therefore opposed it; but the opposition was supported by the most decorous and respectful language towards the President, then at my command — I also admit that I did not concur in the general sentiments of regrets and even alarms expressed upon the retirement of the President. These sentiments in the course of debate, were limited only by the want of mental efforts to go further in expressions of adulation, of alarms, & of regrets. So much so, that they appeared to me to be poured forth at the expense both of the people, and the government of the U.S. and particularly of the republican party. Not feeling these emotions myself, I endeavored to state more calmly, but not less respectfully, my impressions on the occasion. They were in substance as follow: That the President has devoted the greatest portion of his life to the public service, and had already rendered services inestimable. That he had already filled up the measure of services that the public could reasonably require of him. That he had frequently expressed the most ardent wishes to be relieved from public services; and to be indulged with a beloved retirement. That the sincerity of these wishes could not be doubted; that I thought them highly honorable to him, and concurred with him in the opinion, that he ought to be indulged in them. That I had no doubt but that he was consulting as well his own happiness, as his own glory, in the determination he had made; and that I sincerely wished him all the enjoyments and happiness he had anticipated in the retired and philosophical retreat of Mount Vernon. I expressly and pointedly stated that I was willing to pour forth unbounded plaudits upon General Washington for his own virtues, his own wisdom, his own patriotism; and the most heartfelt gratitude for his inestimable services; but I thought deserved eulogium, became fulsome adulation when bestowed upon him at the expense of the government and people of the U.S. In the extravagant warmth of debate, produced by the occasion, it having been frequently said, amongst other most sublimated conceptions, that upon the retirement of the President there would be a political chaos if not a natural one, I believe both, I replied in substance that I did not apprehend either; but if these horrible anticipations were well founded, the sooner they were made known the better; because the government of the U.S. was founded upon the principle that man was competent to his own government, and that it did not depend upon the services of any individual, however meritorious and exalted; and that if the people had in fact been mistaken in the great principle upon which they had founded their government, they ought to be offered an opportunity upon discovering the fatal error, to fix upon some other better principle for their future government, and for the better protection of their rights, liberties, and

WILLIAM B. GILES

Oil on canvas by Chester Harding, 1829. *Courtesy of the Virginia Historical Society.*

happiness. But I had no apprehensions that so fatal a misfortune had befallen the people of the U.S., and in illustration observed, that I had no doubt if the President, and every officer of the government, were to retire to private life, a thousand other persons might be found in the U.S. to fill their places with equal advantage to the public. I am perfectly satisfied that the President was not singled out as the only officer to which the observation was applicable. I would not at this time pledge myself as to any particular form of expression used upon the occasion, although the subject has at all times been familiar to my mind, but I will positively pledge myself for the correctness of the principles here stated, and that they were urged with the most perfect respect and decorum of language towards the President, interspersed with the sentimental applauses which appeared to me to be called for by the occasion: as proof positive upon this essential point, it will appear from the debate in reply, as stated in "the Life of Washington," that not the slightest charge of indecorous or disrespectful language was imputed to me by a single debater, although the peculiar character of the debate, and the highly excited emotions produced by it, would necessarily have called forth the most pointed recriminations, if they could have been justified by the course of observations made by myself. Whilst therefore, I disclaim all rude expressions imputed to me by note-takers, and of course all responsibility for them, I acknowledge myself fully responsible for the principles I urged in that debate; and whilst I have never presumptuously set up any pretensions whatever to infallibility, and know I have committed many errors, and have at all times been perfectly disposed to acknowledge them when discovered, yet after nearly nine and twenty years of reconsideration, my conscience stands perfectly justified in the course of conduct I pursued upon the memorable occasion stated in "the Life of Washington."[5]

Be pleased, sir, to accept assurances of my most respectful and friendly considerations, &c.

WM. B. GILES.

Printed, *Enquirer* (Richmond, Va.), 8 Dec. 1825.

1. Giles lived at Wigwam, his estate in Amelia County, Va.

2. Giles's speech of Dec. 1796 was in support of his motion to expunge several laudatory paragraphs from the House's reply to President Washington's message announcing his intention to retire. In this speech as reported by JM in the *Life of Washington*, Giles "said 'that with respect to the wisdom and firmness of the president, he differed in opinion from the answer. . . . He believed on the contrary, that it was from a want of wisdom and firmness that we were brought into our present critical situation' " (*The Life of George Washington* [5 vols.; Philadelphia, 1804–7], V, 722–23).

3. John Fenno edited the *Gazette of the United States;* Benjamin Franklin Bache edited the *Aurora General Advertiser.*

4. Afflicted with ill-health and having become increasingly unpopular within the Republican party, Giles resigned from the U.S. Senate in 1815 (Dice Robins Anderson, *William Branch Giles: A Study in the Politics of Virginia and the Nation from 1790 to 1830* [Menasha, Wis., 1914], 210).

5. Giles's public letter was part of his campaign for election to the U.S. Senate, which was to take place during the meeting of the Virginia General Assembly in December. The pages of the Richmond *Enquirer* and the *Whig* were filled with articles supporting or opposing Giles and John Randolph of Roanoke. Giles was criticised for his inconsistency, as evidenced by the contrasting opinions of Washington expressed in 1796 and most recently in the fourteenth number of his "Political Disquisitions," which appeared in the *Enquirer* on 11 Nov. A long defense of Giles by "Civis" brought JM into the picture by citing the passage from the *Life of Washington* reporting Giles's 1796 speech. "Civis" reported having visited Giles some months before and shown him the passage. Giles, according to "Civis," denied having uttered the expressions attributed to him by the author of the *Life of Washington.* "Civis" went on to speculate about the source relied on by JM. He supposed "the venerable Judge to have drawn on his memory, or to have derived his information from some report of the day. I mean not in either view of the case to throw the slightest imputation of unfairness on the Author of the Life of Washington." Despite this disclaimer, "Civis" insinuated that party bias influenced JM's presentation of Giles's speech (Richmond *Enquirer,* 11, 22, 29 Nov. 1825).

To William B. Giles

DEAR SIR: *Richmond, Nov., 29th.* 1825.

Your letter of the 26th was presented to me yesterday evening by your son. Not mingling in the party politics, or even questions of the day, and entirely free from political or personal animosities, it is with real concern, I perceive myself brought into view as having furnished materials for an attack on any gentlemen whatever, especially on one with whom I have long been in habits of friendly intercourse.[1]

To your enquiry I answer without hesitation, that I never received any authority from you to publish the speech you are stated to have made in the debate which took place in the House of Representatives, on the answer to the address of General Washington to Congress, in Dec. 1796, nor did I ever have any conversation with you respecting it. The speech was extracted from one of the papers of the day, which professed to give the debates of Congress, and was supposed to be as correct as debates ever are, which are not prepared by the speaker for the press, not only because no dissatisfaction was expressed with it, but because also, you about that time frequently & unreservedly declared in public the sentiments which were ascribed to you.

Not having preserved my regular files of papers I cannot at this time say from which of them the speech was copied. I was at that time in possession of the Gazette of the United States, of Dunlop and Claypole's paper, of one edited by Mr. Brown, and had also frequent recourse to the Aurora:[2] From one of them your speech was copied, but I cannot say positively from which. I incline to think it was from Dunlap and Claypole. I shall, however, make the necessary inquiries, which, I presume, may be done in Philadelphia.

The opinions which you there expressed were not peculiar to yourself. They certainly prevailed very extensively among the politicians of Virginia. In a struggle for power men speak and think of a conspicuous individual to whom they are opposed, very differently from what they speak and think of the same individual when the struggle is over, and his memory only lives. If this be inconsistency, it would be difficult to point out a consistent man.

In a debate in the Senate on the numbers of the regular army, which took place soon after the declaration of the late war, a speech purporting to be your's was published, in which you took occasion openly to avow a change of opinion respecting General Washington.[3] I thought the declaration magnanimous and honorable to yourself, and while employed in a revision of the life of Washington, I endeavoured to find it for the purpose of inserting it in a note, unless it should be more desirable to you to omit the speech entirely. On this I intended to consult yourself. While at Washington two years ago, I searched the files of the National Intelligencer for it; but could not find it even with the assistance of Mr. Gales. I therefore relinquished the idea of introducing it in a note, and determined to omit the speech made in Dec. 1796.

You suggest some publication from me. I am certainly unwilling to appear in the papers, especially as a volunteer, but shall make no objection to your publishing your letter to me, with this answer to it, if it be desirable to yourself.

With sincere wishes for the restoration of your health, I am, dear sir, very respectfully your obedient servant,

J. MARSHALL.

Printed, *Enquirer* (Richmond, Va.), 8 Dec. 1825.

1. Before Giles entered Congress in 1790, JM had worked closely with him in his law practice (*PJM*, II, 29, 50, 51, 66, 82, 158).

2. David Claypoole and John Dunlap were the editors of *Dunlap and Claypoole's American Daily Advertiser;* Andrew Brown's paper was the *Philadelphia Gazette.*

3. JM refers to a speech of 29 Jan. 1812, six months before the declaration of war, in which Senator Giles spoke against raising a volunteer corps in favor of increasing the regular army. On this occasion he invoked the authority of Washington, apologizing for his youthful errors in doubting the first president's wisdom as a statesman. He was now "completely convinced," he said, "of the superiority of the talent of this great man as a statesman as well as a soldier." In revising his former opinion, Giles cited passages from the *Life of Washington* (Dice Robins Anderson, *William Branch Giles: A Study in the Politics of Virginia and the Nation from 1790 to 1830* [Menasha, Wis., 1914], 177–79; *Annals of Congress,* 12th Congress, 1st sess., Appendix, 1693–1712).

To Joseph Hopkinson

Dear Sir   Richmond Decr. 3d 1825

It is with real pain I give trouble to my friends but a circumstance, disagreeable enough in itself, has occurred which obliges [me] to ask the aid of some gentleman in Philadelphia & there is no person in such a state of things who occurs to me more readily than Yourself.

The 5th. v. of the Life of Washington p 723 contains a quotation of a speech made by Mr. Giles in the House of Representatives in the course of the debate on that part of the answer to the Presidents speech in Decr. 1796, which communicates his intention to retire to private life. Mr. Giles, who is now understood to be a candidate for the Senate has been attacked on this speech with so much violence that he and his friends have d⟨en⟩ied ⟨it &⟩ have conducted the altercation in such a manner as to question the fidelity of the quotation. This imposes on me the necessity, however desirous of keeping aloof from the contest, of producing the paper from which it was copied; and I, with unpardonable carelessness, have lost it. I think the passage cited was extracted from Dunlop & Claypole; but I was at the time in possession of the papers edited by Fenno Beach, Brown & Cobbett.[1] It may have been in some one of these. The several files of these papers are undoubtedly in possession of those who now hold the respective establishments but I know not who they are, and, of course, cannot apply to them. Will you my dear Sir favour me so far, if you can do so without too much inconvenience &c to look into the debates on this subject, they occurred during the first fortnight in Decr., and give me the result. I wish much for the paper itself; but if this be unattainable, I shall be much gratified by being informed certainly who⟨s⟩e paper, & of what date, contains the words u⟨se⟩d.

I have written also to Mr. Sergeant. I am dear Sir with respectful esteem, Your

J MARSHALL

ALS, Hopkinson Papers, PHi. Addressed to Hopkinson in Philadelphia; postmarked Richmond, 3 Dec.

1. "Beach" is Benjamin Franklin Bache. William Cobbett (1762–1835) wrote under the pseudonym "Peter Porcupine" and edited *Porcupine's Gazette*.

From John Sergeant

Dear Sir,   Philada. Decr. 6. 1825.

I had the pleasure this afternoon at my return from Court to find your letter of the 3d inst., and am really obliged by the opportunity to do any thing that will be agreeable to you.[1] There are complete files of the papers published here, in the Library. Upon examining Dunlap & Clay-poole's of the *16 Decr. 1796,* I have found Mr. Giles's speech reported in the very words used in your fifth volume. Enclosed you will find a copy from the paper. In the Aurora of the *15th.,* there is also a report, profess-ing to be of the same speech, but much stronger.[2] Of this, also, I enclose you a copy, except the last sentence, the person who copied for me, not having had time to finish it before the Library closed. If you wish the whole, be good enough to let me know, and I will send it to you entire, I mean of that from the Aurora, for the other is complete.

The copies are made in pencil, but very legible, and I have thought it better to send them just as they are, than run the risk of losing a post.

If in this, or any other matter, I can be of service, I pray you to com-mand me freely. With the highest respect, Dr. Sir, Yr. most obt.

JOHN SERGEANT.

P.S. I have copied the extract from Dunlap and Claypoole, and enclose my copy instead of the pencil copy.

ALS, Marshall Papers, ViW. Addressed to JM in Richmond; postmarked Philadelphia, [6?] Dec.

1. Letter not found.
2. In the second edition JM cited the source of Giles's speech as *Claypoole's American Daily Advertiser,* 16 Dec. 1796. Noting that "some objection has been made to the accuracy of this speech, as reported in" Claypoole's paper, JM then quoted extracts from the speech as reported in Bache's *Aurora General Advertiser,* "the leading paper of that party, of which Mr. Giles was a conspicuous member" (*The Life of George Washington* [2 vols.; 2d ed.; Phila-delphia, 1838], II, 416–18 and n.).

To Joseph Hopkinson

My dear Sir   Richmond Decr. 11th. 1825

I was much flattered as well as obliged by your prompt & friendly attention to the request contained in my letter of the 3d. The informa-tion you have given is all that I wished.

The election which produced this newspaper war being over, hostilities may probably cease; and I, at least, may be allowed to remain in quiet.[1] It gave me real pain to find myself vouched by some anonymous assailant of Mr. Giles, and, upon his addressing me on the subject I returned an answer in the spirit of conciliation which I felt. Since writing that letter, but before its publication, a card appeared from Mr. Giles in the En-quirer, in which he attacks me for the account given in the Life of Wash-ington of the charge made in the Aurora on the President for drawing money from the Treasury which was not due, with so much asperity, that I almost repented my having written to him in such terms as were employed in my letter. The irritation however which was excited was momentary, & has entirely passed away. Yet I shall endeavour to possess myself of the Calm Observer which, I am told, was published in the pamp[h]let form, and which was the foundation of this charge against General Washington.[2] I am a little surprised at the indiscretion discovered by Mr. Giles in his card. He will certainly be considered by an attentive reader as identifying himself with that accusation, and as admitting that he performed a considerable part in the transaction. He seems to say with Aneas *"Quorum pars magna fui."*[3] While I repeat my thanks for your kindness, I beg leave to add that I am with great truth your respec[t]ful & affectionate

J MARSHALL

ALS, Hopkinson Papers, PHi. Addressed to Hopkinson in Philadelphia; postmarked Richmond, 12 Dec.

1. Along with Giles and Randolph, the other nominees for the U.S. Senate were Henry St. George Tucker and John Floyd. In the balloting in the legislature on 9 Dec., Floyd was dropped after the first ballot and Giles after the second. Although Tucker had the highest number of votes, he withdrew in favor of Randolph (Richmond *Enquirer,* 10 Dec. 1825).

2. Giles's "card" and accompanying communication was a response to a piece in the *Whig* insinuating that Giles was behind the charge against President Washington for unauthorized withdrawals from the Treasury. This charge and other attacks on the president's character arose in the wake of the bitter fight over the ratification of the Jay Treaty in the summer of 1795. The accusations of financial improprieties were advanced in a series of articles by "A Calm Observer" in Bache's *Aurora General Advertiser* in Oct. and Nov. 1795. The writer of these pieces was John Beckley, clerk of the House of Representatives and Republican party operative. Secretary of the Treasury Oliver Wolcott and former secretary Alexander Hamilton replied to "A Calm Observer." JM recounted this episode without citing "A Calm Observer" or identifying particular individuals with the assaults on Washington's character. He stated that Hamilton's answer fully vindicated both the Treasury Department and the president, concluding: "When possessed of the entire fact, the public viewed with just indignation this attempt to defame a character which was the nation's pride. Americans felt themselves affected by this atrocious calumny on their most illustrious citizen, and its propagators were frowned into silence." Giles scorned this account as the product of "party spirit," maintaining that JM "was never more mistaken in the effects, he ascribes to Mr. Hamilton's report, if he made one, on that occasion." He added that he could "not recollect to have known a more impressive example of the delusions produced upon the human mind by the indulgence of human passions, than appears in this case, upon the strong and lucid mind, and the benevolent breast of the author of the Life of Washington" (Richmond *Enquirer,* 6 Dec. 1825; *The Life of George Washington* [5 vols.; Philadelphia, 1804–7], V, 636–38; Edmund Berkeley and Dorothy Smith Berkeley, *John Beckley: Zealous Partisan in a Nation Divided* [Philadelphia, 1973], 120–29).

3. Virgil, *Aeneid,* Bk. II, l. 6: "whereof I was no small part" (H. Rushton Fairclough, trans., *Virgil* [2 vols.; Cambridge, Mass., 1986], I, 294–95).

From Joseph Hopkinson

Dear Sir   Philad. Dec. 12. 1825

Since I had the pleasure of sending you the information you required relative to reports given in our papers of M Giles. speech, I have seen his letter to you in the Richmond Enquirer. It is really as Domina Sampson says, (I suppose you have read Guy Mannering) pro-di-gi-ous.[1] For further satisfaction I have looked at the Debate as given in the United States Gazette. It corresponds with that in the Aurora. But the stronger evidence is to come, and is found throughout the whole debate. In the speeches of Mess: Harper — Ames — Smith of Sou Car — Sitgreaves &c the expressions now denied by M Giles are quoted and remarked upon; & in his reply he does not complain that he has been misquoted or misunderstood. In one of the speeches he is quoted as speaking of Gen: Washington, not as President, but as "the *gentleman.*" I think he wishes the *gentleman* all happiness in his retirement. And yet he *boasts* in his letter of the respectful terms in which he spoke of the President — denies that his speech resembled that given by you; and gives what he calls an outline of his remarks; which is as much like the true speech, as the outline of his person would be like that of the Belvedere Apollo.[2] I am almost provoked at the civility of your reply. I hope you will not omit his speech in your revised edition. But you know better than I or any body what you ought to do on this and every other occasion. Mo truly & respectfuly, Yr

JOS. HOPKINSON

ALS, Collection of the late Mrs. James Robert Green, Markham, Va. Addressed to JM in Richmond; postmarked Philadelphia, 13 Dec. Endorsed by James K. Marshall "Jos. Hopkinson / to my Father."

1. The Rev. Abel "Dominie" Sampson was a main character in Sir Walter Scott's novel *Guy Mannering.* "Pro-di-gi-ous" was Sampson's only emotional expression.

2. The Apollo Belvedere is a Roman copy of a Greek statue of the god Apollo. Discovered in the fifteenth century, it was displayed at Belvedere Court in the Vatican and was long regarded as an art masterpiece and as the standard of male beauty (Ian Chilvers, ed., *The Concise Oxford Dictionary of Art and Artists* [New York, 1990], 16).

Teakle v. Bailey

Opinion and Decree
U.S. Circuit Court, Virginia, 14 December 1825

Lucretia Teackle (Teakle), widow and administratrix of Severn Teackle (1756–1794), filed a bill in chancery on her own behalf and on behalf of her children in November 1820. A native of Accomac County on the Eastern Shore, Severn Teackle had served as an officer of the Virginia Line in the Continental army. He subsequently moved to Easton, Maryland, where his wife and children were still living at the time of this suit. For his service in the Revolution, Teackle was awarded more than four thousand acres of military bounty land in Ohio. No patents for the land had issued before Teackle's death, and a portion of it was later sold for unpaid taxes. In 1807 Lucretia Teackle contracted with Thomas M. Bayly (spelled "Bailey" by Marshall), a prominent Accomac lawyer, to redeem the land sold for taxes and to complete title to the remainder. Over the next several years Bayly carried out this business in return for receiving one-half of the lands so secured. Mrs. Teackle eventually became convinced that Bayly had deceived and defrauded her, particularly in representing that the lands were not valuable. Bayly filed his answer in June 1821. After the taking of depositions and the filing of an amended bill and answer, the cause came up for a hearing at the November 1825 term. Marshall's opinion accompanying his interlocutory decree of 14 December 1825 fully describes the transactions that gave rise to this dispute. Brockenbrough erroneously placed this opinion at the May 1822 term (*DAR Patriot Index* [Washington, D.C., 1966], 669; U.S. Cir. Ct., Va., Rec. Bk. XVII, 534–639; U.S. Cir. Ct., Va., Ord. Bk. XI, 503, 521; XII, 61, 71–72).

Teakle admx & al

v

Thomas M Bailey

This suit is brought by Lucretia Teakle widow and Admx. of Severn ¶1 Teakle deceased and by her children to set aside a contract made in Aug. 1807 by the said Lucretia as admx. of her deceased husband and as guardian of her infant children, and by her eldest daughter Rachael Teakle, with the defendant, stipulating to convey to him a moity of certain lands in the state of Ohio; and also to set aside certain deeds dated the 16th. of April 1812 executed by the said Lucretia & Rachael and also by Elizabeth Teakle purporting to convey a moity of those lands.[1]

Thomas M Bailey the defendant, being in the state of Ohio in the ¶2 summer of 1807 for the purpose [of] locating military land warrants he had previously acquired, was informed by the Auditor of the state that 4000 acres of military lands belonging to Severn Teakle a Captain in the army of the United States had been located in Ohio, and that a considerable part of them had been sold for nonpayment of taxes, and that parts of them would continue to be annually sold unless measures should be taken for the payment of future taxes as they should accrue. By the laws of Ohio the lands of minors sold for nonpayment of taxes were redeemable within 12 months after such minor should attain his age of 21, by payment of the purchase money with interest and by paying also for any improvements which the purchaser might have made on the premises. Redemption was so much a thing of course, that the purchasers usually gave up the land on being satisfied of the fact of minority; and if the establishment of that fact in court was required, this was done without formal proceedings and at a very inconsiderable expense. The only real difficulty lay in the adjustment of the claim for improvements where such claim was made.

¶3   On his return from the state of Ohio Mr. Bailey called on Mrs. Teakle then residing at Easton, a small village on the Eastern shore of Maryland, and communicated to her the situation of the lands of the family, on which the contract of the 2d. of August 1807 was entered into.

¶4   Mr. Bailey proceeded to effect the redemption of the lands which had been sold for nonpayment of taxes.

¶5   Not long after this contract the defendant by looking into the act of the Virginia assembly concerning land bounties to the officers of the Virginia line, discovered that Captain Teakle, having served to the end of the war, was entitled to the additional quantity of 1221 acres. He communicated this fact to Mrs. Teakl[e] and drew the warrant under a power of attorny made by her. Under a contract with Mrs. Teakle this warrant was located by Bailey's agent and the title obtained, for which service Baily receives a moity of this tract also.

¶6   In April 1812 Rachael and Elizabeth having then attained their age of 21 years deeds were executed by Lucretia, Rachael, and Elizabeth purporting to convey a moity of the 4000 acres of land to the defendant.

¶7   Elizabeth afterwards intermarried with   Swan,[2] & Severn Teakle has attained his age of 21 years. He refuses to assent to these contracts, and this bill is brought to set them aside, as having been obtained by misrepresentation and concealment, from persons entirely ignorant of the property they sold, and of the situation in which it was placed.

¶8   The contract of the 2d. of August 1807 will be first considered.[3] This paper after reciting the title of Severn Teakle to 4000 acres of military land which had not been patented, and the descent of the said lands to his widow and children; proceeds thus "And whereas a considerable portion of the said land has been sold for the payment of taxes"; "Now therefore in consideration of the said Thomas M. Bailey undertaking to redeem the portion of land so sold for the payment of taxes, or as much thereof as he can redeem, at his own proper expense and trouble; and also obtaining all the necessary title papers to the said 4000 acres or so much thereof as he can obtain at his own proper cost and trouble, which he doth hereby undertake to do, then in that case we the said Lucretia Teakle in her own right and also as Guardian to the said Elizabeth & Severn Teakle, and also the said Rachael Teakle, do agree to convey to the said Thomas M. Bailey one half of the said 4000 acres of the said land or one half of all which shall have been redeemed as being sold, and the half of that unsold." The agreement then contains a covenant on the part of Lucretia & Rachael Teakle that Elizabeth & Severn Teakle shall when they respectively attain their ages of 21, ratify this agreement and make the necessary conveyances.

¶9   The bill charges that the contract and the deeds which grew out of it originated in mistake and ignorance on the part of the complainants;

and in fraud imposition and misrepresentation and concealment on the part of the said Bailey. They were ignorant the bill states of the value of the land and of the means to be employed for its redemption, and were unable from their narrow circumstances and situation to make the enquiry. The said Bailey represented the land as poor & the difficulties of redemption as considerable and, beleiving him to be their friend, they trusted to his representation. He knew the value of the land and knew that the law of Ohio rendered redemption easy.[4]

The communications made by Mr. Bailey to Mrs. Teakle were entirely verbal, and no person, not of the family, appears to have been present at the time. The proof of misrepresentation or concealment can therefore come only from the parties themselves. ¶10

In his answer Mr. Bailey states the communication made to him by the auditor of the State of Ohio relative to Capt. Teakles land, & adds that he communicated all the information he possessed to Mrs. Teakle.[5] The counsel for the plfs. rely upon the representation made in his answer of the auditors communications as being a representation of his own communications to Mrs. Teakle, & contends that they amount to a misrepresentation. The fact supposed to be misrepresented, is the quantity of land sold for nonpayment of taxes. Mr. Bailey in his answer represents the auditor to have said that more than half had been sold, whereas, in truth, not quite half had been sold. Of the 4000 acres, between 1900 & 2000 acres had been actually sold. ¶11

The answer does not aver in terms that he gave to Mrs. Teakle the precise detail of circumstances which he says was made him by the Auditor; & if he had, we do not think that a mistake of less than 100 acres in the quantity of land actually sold would have made any difference in the course which Mrs. Teakle would have pursued, and ought in prudence to have pursued under the circumstances in which she found herself & her family placed. Great part of the land was actually sold, and the residue would certainly share the same fate, unless some person should be employed for its preservation. And the precise quantity actually sold had no influence on her conduct as is shown by the fact that she gave for saving the unsold land as much as she gave for the redemption of that which had been sold. It is also a circumstance of some weight that the bill does not suggest any misrepresentation in this particular, and that the language of the contract is that "a considerable portion," not that more than one half "of the said land had been sold." ¶12

The bill also charges a great misrepresentation in the value of the land; but of this there is no proof. Indeed it does not appear, nor is there any reason to believe that Bailey had in Aug. 1807 acquired any accurate knowledge of its value, nor is it alleged nor is there reason to believe that, at that time, he made any representation respecting it. ¶13

A point of more consequence is the representation he made respecting the facility of redemption. When we compare the description of the ¶14

difficulties attending redemption, detailed in his answer, with the statement of those difficulties made by lawyers of Ohio whose depositions
have been taken,[6] or with those actually encountered, we must say that it
is highly coloured, that it is calculated to magnify those difficulties; but we
cannot say that they are positively untrue. The account of the value of
improvements was certainly exposed to the hazard which he stated.

¶15   The most important enquiry in this part of the case is Did Mr. Bailey
communicate to Mrs. Teakle the legal right of her Children to redeem
within a limited time after attaining their ages of 21 years, the lands
which might before that time be sold for nonpayment of taxes, or did
he leave her to suppose that it was an affair to be arranged with the
purchasers?

¶16   Mr. Baileys answer must be understood as aver⟨r⟩ing that he did give
her this information because he admits that he possessed it, and avers
that he gave all the information he possessed. On this point too the
answer is to be considered as responsive to the bill and as testimony in the
cause. There are certainly some expressions in the contract which are calculated to attract notice, though they may not be sufficient to countervail
the answer. The language of that instrument is that Lucretia & Rachael
Teakle undertake to convey a moity of the land "in consideration of the
said Thomas M Bailey undertaking to redeem the portion of land sold for
the payment of taxes, *or as much thereof as he can redeem.* " These expressions certainly do not imply an absolute legal right to redeem the whole,
and were not to have been looked for in an instrument prepared with a
knowledge of such absolute legal right. The same language is observable
in that part of the instrument which stipulates for the conveyance from
Lucretia & Rachael Teakle. They "agree to convey to the said Thomas M
Bailey one half of the said 4000 acres of the said lands or one *half of all
which shall have been redeemed as being sold, and the half of that unsold.* " These
latter words would be unnecessary if no doubt existed respecting the
redemption of the whole land; for all the land sold & all the land unsold
must certainly be equal to all the land. This last member of the sentence
then would seem to indicate some apprehension in the mind of the contracting parties that some part of the land sold might not be redeemed,
an apprehension not very consistent with a legal right to redeem the
whole. Yet these expressions may originate in the superabundant caution
of the writer of the contract, and are not thought sufficient to outweigh
the answer.

¶17   The counsel for the plaintiffs contend that Bailey is to be considered as
the agent of Mrs. Teakle & the family before this agreement was made,
and that instead of requiring proof of misrepresentation or concealment
from her, he must show that his own conduct was perfectly fair. This fact,
it is contended shifts the *onus probandi* from her to him; and in proof of
the fact they rely on a letter from Mr. Bailey to his agent of the 28th. of
April 1808.[7]

The court cannot understand the letter otherwise than as asserting this ¶18 agency; but, notwithstanding the declaration it contains, we must consider the agency as commencing with the contract of aug. 1807. There is no allegation in the bill which asserts a prior agency. Consequently that fact is not put in issue. This is not all. Such prior agency would be inconsistent with the whole case as made out by the plfs. and with all the other testimony in the cause. John Edmondson speaks in his deposition of a letter from John Teakle to the plf Lucretia recommending the defendant to her as a person capable of giving her information & of transacting her business.[8] The date of this letter as well as its contents might throw some light on a part of this case; but it is not produced and consequently can have no influence on it.

The defendant being entirely free to contract with the plf Lucretia on ¶19 the 2d. of Aug. 1807, the misrepresentation and concealment alleged in order to set aside that contract must be proved by the plaintiffs, or the court cannot interpose its authority for that purpose. We do not think either has been proved.

The contract of Aug. 1807 then is to be considered as remaining in ¶20 force until cancelled by the parties and the court will proceed to examine the extent of its obligation.

The contract was made with the defendant by Lucretia Teakle, the ¶21 widow and Admx. of Severn Teakle decd. & Guardian of his children, and by Rachael Teakle one of his daughters. The contract of Lucretia could not bind the land beyond her dower right. The contract of Rachael might bind her third part if she was of age when it was executed — not otherwise. This fact is proved satisfactorily not only by the affidavit of the mother to which no objection has been made, but by the deposition of her brother John Edmondson. He produces a book proved to be in the handwriting of Severn Teakle decd. in which he has in his own handwriting inserted the age of his wife, the time of their intermarriage & of the birth of each of their children. The deponent farther swears that to his own knowledge the age of Severn, the youngest is truely stated in the book. It is then sufficiently proved that Rachael was an infant when she executed the contract of the 2d. of August 1807; and her lands could not be bound by it.[9]

That contract then unaided by subsequent transactions, would give the ¶22 defendant recourse against Mrs. Teakle in the event of its nonperformance, but would give him no interest in the lands themselves. Those subsequent transactions therefore must be considered.

The court will pass over the purchase made by the defendant in 1809, ¶23 because the deeds were cancelled at the request of the plaintiffs, and proceed to the contract or deeds of April 1812.[10] By deeds of that date Rachael and Elizabeth Teakle who were then of full age, convey to the defendant one moity of the 4000 acres of land in the State of Ohio, to which the heirs of Severn Teakle were entitled. The effect of this conveyance is to execute the contract of 180   not only so far as respected themselves but so far as respected the interest of their brother, then a minor.

¶24   The plfs. make the same objection to this instrument, as being obtained by misrepresentation and concealment from persons ignorant of their rights as were made to the agreement of 1807; and contend that the objection derives additional strength from the fact that the contract was made with an agent.

¶25   That an agent to sell cannot be himself the purchaser under his power to sell is well settled. Such a purchase is absolutely void. The principle however of those decisions does not apply to a contract between an agent and his employer. Such contracts are not void *per se* but are watched with no inconsiderable jealousy by courts of equity. In general, the information of the principal may be supposed to be derived through the agent, who must also be supposed to possess his confidence. In such a case it is certainly desirable that the circumstances attending the transaction should be so clearly stated as to leave no doubt that the principal entered into the agreement with full knowledge of them, or at least of such of them as were material to the contract into which he had entered. Whether the whole burthen of proof be shifted to the agent or not, it may be stated with some confidence that circumstances which are meerly suspicious, and which would be insufficient to affect a contract between persons unconnected with each other, would be allowed great weight in a case between a principal and agent. The case under consideration is one in which proof that the communications to the principal had been full are peculiarly desirable. The principals resided in the state of Maryland, and were young ladies who had not very long attained their age of 21. The business to which the agency related was transacted in the state of Ohio, and the record furnishes no evidence of their possessing any other knowledge respecting it than was derived from their agent. Were the deeds then of april 1812 an original contract there would be much weight in the argument which insists on proof from the defendant that his communications to the plaintiffs were full as well as fair.

¶26   But those deeds do not constitute an original contract. They amount, in part at least to a confirmation of a contract made for them in their infancy by their guardian. So far as Rachael & Elizabeth convey a moity of their several interests in the lands they only confirm the contract made for them by their mother, to which Rachael while an infant was a party. That contract, as has been already observed, must be allowed to stand, and is obligatory on the mother according to its terms, and on the infants, to the extent of the equity it gives for a liberal remuneration for services performed. Being thus far obligatory, the subsequent contract, so far as it is a meer confirmation of a contract unexceptionable in its origin, made by one of the infants in conjunction with her guardian, and for the other by her guardian, cannot we think be set aside.

But so much of the contract of April 1812 as binds Rachael & Elizabeth   ¶27
farther than that of August 1807 was intended to bind them, is not a
confirmation, but is an original contract, and is unquestionably, in all its
parts, made with a person who was at the time an agent, & is subject to all
the rules which a court of equity applies to purchases made by the agent
from his principal. It has been already said that these rules do not positively annul such a contract, but do subject it to a rigorous and suspicious
examination. This principle is we think to be collected from all the cases
which have been cited, or which are to be found in the books. In 6th. Vez.
626 Ex parte Lacy the court said that a trustee may purchase from Cestuy
que trust. The cestuy que trust may by a new contract dismiss him from
that character, but the act must be watched with infinite & most guarded
jealousy.[11]

In 8th. Vez. 337 Ex parte James the court said that an assignee under a   ¶28
commission of Bankruptcy cannot purchase unless he shakes himself
altogether out of the trust, and not then without a little more than parting with the character. It is the duty of a trustee to acquire all the knowledge he can obtain for the benefit of Cestuy que trust; and no court can
discuss what knowledge he has acquired, and whether he has fairly given
the benefit of that knowledge to the cestuy que trust. In this case the
court refused to let Jones who had been the sollicitor to the commission
of Bankruptcy lay down his sollicitorship & become a purchaser.[12] Although a distinction may be taken between the character of the agency in
the case ex parte James & that of Mr. Bailey, yet the principles laid down
in that case apply to a considerable extent to all agencies in which the
agent may be supposed to acquire information in consequence of his
agency which is not in the possession of his principal.

In 9th. Vez. Coles v Tracothis, an agreement was entered into to convey   ¶29
lands to trustees to be sold for the payment of debts, but the deed was not
executed and the Cestuy que trust acted for himself. The trustee purchased a part of the trust property for his Father from Cestuy que trust,
who, being offered some time afterwards a much more considerable
price for the land refused to convey, & this suit was brought by the purchaser for a specific performance. There were many circumstances in
favour of the purchaser, and a specific performance was decreed; but, in
speaking of purchases made by a trustee from Cestuy que trust the Chancellor said "But though permitted it is a transaction of great delicacy, and
which the court will watch with the utmost diligence, so much that it is
very hazardous for a trustee to engage in such a transaction.["][13]

In Morse v Royal 12 Vez. 355, the counsel for the trustee purchaser   ¶30
admitted the law to be "that it is incumbent on the trustee if the suit be
instituted during his life, to prove that the Cestuy que trust knew, not only
that he was selling to his trustee, but also what he was selling; and that he
had all the information the trustee could give him."[14] The same doctrine
was laid down with great strength by the opposite counsel; and although

the court does not, in terms assent to it, there is no reason to beleive that the doctrine was not entirely familiar.

¶31   In Lowther v Lowther 13th. Vez. the Lord Chancellor states the principle to have been laid down to this effect by Lord Eldon in Coles agt. Trecothis; That an agent to sell shall not convert himself into a purchaser unless he can make it perfectly clear that he furnished his employer with all the knowledge that he himself possessed.[15]

¶32   There is much good sense and moral justice in this rule; and it imposes no hardship on the agent. He may make his contracts in the presence of witnesses who may depose to the extent of his verbal communications, or their extent may be shown by written testimony, either in his correspondence or in the contract itself; or it may be inferred from the relative situation of the parties and of the subject of the contract that every material fact was known to the principal. The case under consideration furnishes no circumstance to enable the court to infer that the principal possessed all the knowledge which had probably been acquired by the agent. The facts of the cause justify the belief that he had received accurate information of the value of the property for which the contract was made. They do not authorize the opinion that Lucretia Teakle or her children possessed any other information than was derived from him, nor that he had communicated to them all that he had acquired which was material to the contract. Our knowledge of Mr. Baily may satisfy us as individuals that he had done all which the strictest morality would require, but courts of equity must be guided by the testimony in the record, not by a good or ill opinion of individuals.

¶33   In this case then we perceive a contract made for an infant brother, by young ladies who had recently attained their ages of twenty one, with an agent who had been employed for them during their infancy, in such transactions as gave him full knowledge of the value of the property which constituted the subject of the contract, and which had also constituted the subject of his agency. We perceive no evidence that he had communicated this information to them, or that they had derived it from any other source; nor was their situation in relation to the property such as to justify the inference that they could be possessed of it. Under these circumstances we cannot think that the contract, so far as it was original ought to stand, against Rachael & Elizabeth, since their brother Severn who has now attained his full age, refuses to affirm it.

¶34   But, although the contract of August 1812 must be set aside as to the moity of Severn Teakles third part of the land, the defendant Baily is unquestionably entitled to claim from him his third of the expenses incurred, and of the pecuniary compensation to which he would have been entitled for the services rendered. The advances of money constitute a proper subject for an account. The compensation which Mr. Baily may claim may be referred to a jury unless the parties can adjust it themselves, or prefer a reference to a commissioner.

[Decree]

Teakle admx. & al
v
Bailey

This cause came on to be heard on the bill answer exhibits and depositions of witnesses and was argued by counsel on consideration whereof
the court suspending any opinion on the validity of the contracts in the
bill mentioned relative to the 4000 acres of land therein also mentioned
for which warrants were issued to Severn Teakle in his lifetime doth
direct one of the commissioners of this court to state and report an
account of the advances of money made by the defendant either for
expenses or otherwise on account of the said lands; and the said Commissioner is further authorized to state the services rendered by the said
Bailey in extinguishing the claims for improvements made by the settlers
on the said land, and to state all such matters specially as he may deem
necessary or as either of the parties may require. It is further ordered that
the plaintiffs assign the works on which the patents for the 4000 acres of
land in the bill mentioned will issue to the Honble Andrew Stevenson, so
that the patents may issue in his name that he may hold the same subject
to the future order of this court.[16]

AD, Marshall Judicial Opinions, PPAmP; printed, John W. Brockenbrough, *Reports of
Cases Decided by the Honourable John Marshall . . . ,* II (Philadelphia, 1837), 44–56. Decree,
AD, Teakle v. Bailey, U.S. Cir. Ct., Va., Ended Cases (Unrestored), 1826, Vi. For JM's dele-
tions and interlineations, see Textual Notes below.

1. The children of Lucretia Teackle were Rachel, Elizabeth, and Severn. At the time the
suit began Elizabeth was married to Philip Wallis, who was also a party to the suit.

2. JM was mistaken. He should have inserted the name of Philip Wallis.

3. The contract of 2 Aug. 1807 was annexed to the bill in chancery as an exhibit (U.S. Cir.
Ct., Va., Rec. Bk. XVII, 537).

4. Bill in chancery (filed Nov. 1820), ibid., XVII, 536.

5. Answer (filed June 1821), ibid., XVII, 553.

6. For the depositions of the Ohio lawyers, see ibid., XVII, 607–18.

7. This letter from Bayly to James Galloway, his agent in Ohio, was extracted as part of
Galloway's deposition, 2 May 1825 (ibid., XVII, 582–83).

8. Deposition of John Edmondson (brother of Lucretia Teackle), 5 June 1821, ibid.,
XVII, 602–3.

9. Ibid., XVII, 604–5. According to this testimony, Rachel was born 26 July 1788; Elizabeth, 21 Nov. 1790; and Severn, 11 Aug. 1793.

10. Copies of the deeds of 16 Apr. 1812 were annexed to the bill in chancery (ibid., XVII,
542–46).

11. Ex parte Lacey, 6 Ves. 625, 626, 31 Eng. Rep. 1228 (Ch., 1802). *Cestui que trust* (he for
whom is the trust), the beneficiary who possessed the equitable right to property, the legal
title to which is vested in a trustee.

12. Ex parte James, 8 Ves. 337, 348–49, 32 Eng. Rep. 385, 389 (Ch., 1803).

13. Coles v. Trecothick, 9 Ves. 234, 244–45, 32 Eng. Rep. 592, 596 (Ch., 1804).

14. Morse v. Royal, 12 Ves. 355, 365–66, 33 Eng. Rep. 134, 138 (Ch., 1806).

15. Lowther v. Lowther, 13 Ves. 95, 103, 33 Eng. Rep. 230, 233 (Ch., 1806).

16. Pursuant to this interlocutory decree, the commissioner submitted a report to the court on 30 May 1826, to which both the plaintiffs and defendants made exceptions. After the commissioner amended his report, the court on 5 June issued a final decree conveying one-third of the four thousand acres to Severn Teackle, one-sixth each to Rachel Teackle and Elizabeth Wallis, and the remaining one-third to Thomas Bayly. The plaintiffs prayed an appeal to the Supreme Court but did not further prosecute the case (U.S. Cir. Ct., Va., Rec. Bk. XVII, 586–602).

Textual Notes

¶ 1 ll. 2–3	and ↑by her children↓ to set aside a contract made ↑in Aug. 1807↓ by
l. 4	children, ~~with the defendant~~ and
l. 5	defendant, [*erasure*] ↑stipulating↓ to
¶ 2 l. 4	Teakle ~~late~~ a
l. 8	they ~~might~~ ↑should↓ accrue.
l. 11	interest ~~& proving the fact of minority~~ ↑and by [*erasure*] paying also↓ for
¶ 5 ll. 1–2	the ~~virginia~~ ↑Virginia↓ assembly
ll. 5–6	power of ~~attorny~~ ↑attorney↓ made
¶ 6 ll. 2–3	years ~~a~~ deeds were executed ↑by Lucretia, Rachael, and Elizabeth↓ purporting to convey a [*erasure*] ↑moity↓ of
¶ 8 ll. 2–3	acres of ↑military↓ land
ll. 3–4	patented, ↑and the descent of the said lands to his widow and children;↓ proceeds
¶ 9 l. 2	the ~~ar~~ part
l. 4	ignorant ↑the bill states↓ of
¶11 l. 2	to ~~Mr.~~ ↑Capt.↓ Teakles
¶12 l. 6	pursued ~~on the~~ under
l. 8	certainly ~~be sold~~ ↑share the same fate,↓ unless
ll. 13–14	the ↑language of the↓ contract
l. 14	not ↑that↓ more
¶13 l. 4	value, [*erasure*] ↑nor↓ is it alleged ↑nor is there reason to believe↓ that,
¶14 l. 4	of ~~them~~ ↑those difficulties↓ made
ll. 5–6	taken, ↑or with those actually encountered,↓ we must say that ~~they are~~ ↑it is↓ highly
l. 7	are ↑positively↓ untrue. The account ↑of the value↓ of
¶15 l. 4	which [*erasure*] might before
¶16 l. 4	considered ~~a~~ as responsive
ll. 12–13	instrument ~~founded on the idea~~ ↑prepared with a knowledge↓ of
l. 18	would ~~certainly~~ be
l. 23	apprehension ~~entirely inconsistent~~ ↑not very↓ consistent
l. 25	are [*erasure*] ↑not↓ thought
¶17 l. 1	contend ↑that Bailey↓ is
l. 2	family [*erasure*] ↑before↓ this
¶18 ll. 5–6	would be ~~consistent~~ ↑inconsistent↓ with
ll. 11–12	can ~~not be noticed.~~ ↑have no influence on it.↓
¶19 l. 5	been ~~sufficiently~~ proved.
¶21 l. 1	made ↑with the defendant↓ by

l. 2   decd. & ~~by R~~ Guardian
ll. 6–8   This fact is ~~not entirely free from doubt in a legal point of view.~~
              ~~If the affidavit of the mother be admissible, she states positively~~
              ~~that Rachael was born July 26th. 1788. She was consequently a~~
              ~~minor in Aug. 1807, and could not bind her land. No objection~~
              ~~has been taken to this affidavit, & the cause has proceeded on~~
              ~~the presumption that the fact of infancy was established.~~
              ↑proved satisfactorily not only by the affidavit of the mother to
              which no objection has been made, but by the deposition of
              her brother John Edmondson.↓ He [*erasure*] produces
ll. 10–11   & of [*erasure*] the birth
l. 10   the ~~time of the birth~~ age
¶22 l. 1   subsequent ↑transactions,↓ would
    l. 2   Teakle ~~to the ex~~ in
¶23 l. 3   of ↑April↓ 1812.
    l. 5   land ↑in the State of Ohio,↓ to
    ll. 6–7   conveyance ↑is↓ to
¶24 l. 3   made ~~as were made~~ to
    l. 3   and ~~contend~~ ↑contend↓ that
¶25 l. 2   settled. ~~The pur~~ Such
    l. 4   void *per* [*erasure*] ↑se↓ but
    l. 9   so ~~fully~~ ↑clearly↓ stated
    l. 10   the ~~contract~~ ↑agreement↓ with
    l. 13   some ~~circumstances~~ ↑confidence↓ that
    l. 14   would ↑be↓ insufficient
    l. 15   would ~~have~~ ↑be allowed↓ great
    l. 24   which ~~requires~~ ↑insists on↓ proof
¶26 ll. 5–6   mother, ↑to which Rachael while an infant was a party.↓ ~~We are~~
              ~~not satisfied~~ That
    l. 8   extent of ~~. . . .~~ ↑the↓ equity
¶27 l. 1   so ~~far as~~ ↑much of↓ the
    l. 1   Rachael & ~~Lucretia~~ Elizabeth
    l. 2   that ~~contract~~ of
    l. 2   them, [*erasure*] ↑is↓ not
    l. 3   contract, ~~. That was~~ ↑and is↓ unquestionably,
    ll. 5–6   to ~~contracts between the prin~~ ↑purchases made by the agent
              from↓ his principal. It ~~is~~ ↑has↓ been
    l. 11   the ~~trustee~~ cestuy
¶29 l. 4   trust [*erasure*] property for
    l. 5   afterwards a ↑much↓ more
    l. 8   of ~~a spe the . . . .~~ the
¶30 l. 6   opposite [*erasure*] counsel;
¶32 ll. 7–8   principal. ~~In the~~ ↑The↓ case under consideration ~~there are~~
              ↑furnishes↓ no
    ll. 10–11 accurate ~~knowledge~~ information of
    l. 13   other [*erasure*] information than
    l. 14   them ~~what~~ ↑all↓ that
    l. 16   all [*erasure*] ↑which↓ the
    l. 18   good ↑or ill↓ opinion

¶33 l. 1   made ↑for an infant brother,↓ by
      l. 2   one, ~~for an infant brother,~~ with
      l. 5   subject of [*erasure*] ↑the↓ contract, and which ↑had↓ also
¶34 ll. 1–2   as to ↑the moity of↓ Severn Teakles ~~moity~~ third

To Joseph Hopkinson

My dear Sir   Richmond Decr. 24th. 1825
    I write to thank you for the communications contained in your letter of
the 12th. and to tell you that I shall retain Mr. Giles's speech in my book.
    When I saw the speech he made in the senate in 1812, which I thought
a magnanimous avowal of a total change in his opinions respecting General Washington, I thought it right to relieve him from the pressure which
his speech being on record would load him within the changed state of
public opinion respecting General Washington. When his speech was
published I have no doubt that Mr. Giles was very well satisfied with the
notice taken of it. It did not then injure his popularity with his own party.
Times are changed, and Mr. Giles' wishes, as to his speech, probably
change with them. I was well disposed to retain only the motion made to
amend the address, with a general statement of the argument used in its
support, omitting any particular quotation of the words made use of. But
I do not think myself now at liberty to take this course. To take it, after the
publication[s] which have been made, might wear the appearance of an
admission that the original publication was inaccurate. That I never suspected; nor do I now suspect it. I shall probably think it necessary instead
of changing the text, to fortify it by a note of further reference & I shall
endeavour to procure the numbers of the "Calm Observer" which I
understand were published in the pamphlet form.
    I have some hope of seeing you in Washington this winter & of having
the pleasure to assure you personally that I am with great esteem &
regard, Your Obedt

                                                    J MARSHALL

    ALS, Hopkinson Papers, PHi. Addressed to Hopkinson in Philadelphia; postmarked
Richmond, 24 Dec.

To Martin P. Marshall

My dear Nephew   Richmond Decr. 27th. 1825
    I received your letter of the 14th. of October just as I was commencing
my circuit.[1] Your brother[2] paid me about the same time two hundred and
twenty dollars for my sister[3] for which I gave him my receipt, and I re-

ceived an additional sum of three hundred dollars a few days past for which also I gave my receipt.

I have not made any calculation of my account with Mr. Marshall, having no doubt of the accuracy of the settlement you will make. It is probable I may look it over at some leisure hour. At present I am occupied with things which interest me a good deal. I will only observe that the difference of exchange for eastern funds does not apply to payments made or money laid out in Kentucky. This however you will of course observe. I do not know whether in the accounts sent to me you have made any statement of the money received by Mr. Marshall from Colonel Davies on account of the slaves sold to him. Without that I could not state my account with Mr. Marshall were I to make the attempt.

In settling the account you will credit the history of Kentucky & the Harbinger[4] for six months. I have been greatly obliged by both and have read them with deep interest.

We have been very much engaged with your political contests in Kentucky & have rejoiced a good deal at the triumph of what we believe to be sound constitutional principles at your late elections. The struggle I perceive is not over and will be renewed at the next elections. It is to be hoped that the people have been too well informed during the late severe political campaign to relapse immediately into the unsound and ruinous system which they have pursued for several years. One would think that experience could not fail to prove the ruinous consequences of an unsound fluctuating paper currency, and that the folly as well as unconstitutionality of removing Judges otherwise than as provided in the constitution could not escape any rational being.[5] But reason can rarely maintain a successful struggle against prejudice, interest & passion. My love to my niece. Your Aunt wishes to be remembered to you. I am my dear Nephew your affectionate

J MARSHALL

I should like to know the state of my claim on Colonel Daviess' estate.

ALS, Montague Collection, NN. Addressed to Marshall in Flemingsburg, Ky.; postmarked Richmond, 27 Dec.

1. Letter not found.
2. Probably Charles C. Marshall.
3. Jane Marshall Taylor.
4. Humphrey Marshall had recently published *The History of Kentucky: Exhibiting an Account of the Modern Discovery; Settlement; Progressive Improvement; Civil and Military Transactions; and the Present State of the Country* (2 vols.; Frankfort, Ky., 1824). This was a completion and revision of his one-volume *History of Kentucky* published in 1812. The *Harbinger* was published weekly in Frankfort from 30 Mar. through 28 Sept. 1825, when it was succeeded by the *Constitutional Advocate* (Winifred Gregory, ed., *American Newspapers, 1821–1936* [New York, 1937], 230).
5. In the fall of 1823 the Kentucky Court of Appeals had declared unconstitutional

Kentucky's replevin law of 1820, which placed restrictions on the sale of property seized for debt payment. In response the relief party, after unsuccessfully attempting to remove the judges by address of the legislature, abolished the court and created a new court of appeals in Dec. 1824. This action split the state into "New Court" and "Old Court" parties, with the latter emerging with a majority in the elections of 1825 (Arndt M. Stickles, *The Critical Court Struggle in Kentucky, 1819–1829* [Bloomington, Ind., 1929], 29–87; George Dangerfield, *The Awakening of American Nationalism, 1815–1828* [New York, 1965], 208–10; Sandra F. VanBurkleo, "Relief Crisis," in John E. Kleber et al., eds., *The Kentucky Encyclopedia* [Lexington, Ky., 1992], 762–63).

To Samuel L. Southard

Dear Sir   Richmond Jany. 1st. 1826
    In the case of the Antelope otherwise called The General Ramirez, the Supreme court, at its last term directed a considerable number of Africans to be delivered up to the United States, & I understood that You had ordered a vessel to be in readiness to receive them & transport them to Africa. The papers have given us no information on this subject & I am uncertain whether these Africans have ever been delivered, in conformity with the decree, to the United States. As the annual meeting of the Auxiliary colonization society at this place approaches some interest will be felt in this augmentation of the colony & I shall be gratified at being enabled to communicate the fact.[1] Will you pardon the trouble I give in asking you to have the goodness to drop me a line giving some information on the subject? With great respect I am Sir your obedt.
                                                        J MARSHALL

    ALS, DNA, RG 45. Addressed to the secretary of the navy in Washington and franked; postmarked Richmond, 1 Jan. Endorsed "ansd. 5 Jan."

    1. JM was president of the Richmond and Manchester Auxiliary of the American Colonization Society. It met in Richmond on 16 Jan. (Richmond *Enquirer,* 26 Jan. 1826).

From Samuel L. Southard

Sir,   Navy Department 5 January 1826.
    I have received your letter of the 1st. inst. requesting information concerning the negroes in Georgia which were on board the Genl. Ramirez. Arrangements were made last summer for carrying into effect the decision of the Supreme Court, by transmitting its mandate to the U.S. District Attorney in Georgia. Some difficulty has arisen in consequence of the Spanish claimant insisting that those decreed to be delivered to him should be determined by lot, instead of by proof on each individual negro. On a reference of the question to the Circuit Court there was a

division of opinion and it was determined to submit it to the Supreme Court.[1] This will cause some delay in the delivery of the Africans to the United States; many of them had been brought into Savannah, by those to whom they were hired, and put into the custody of the Marshal, and the rest were soon expected.

Dr. Peaco, the Agent appointed by the Government, will take passage in the vessel chartered by the Colonization Society, which it is supposed will sail soon, and has been instructed to prepare for their reception immediately on his arrival.[2] No time will be lost in sending these negroes to the agency after the Supreme Court shall have decided upon the mode in which they are to be allotted.[3] I have the honor to be, Very respy &c.

S. L. S.

Letterbook copy, RG 45, DNA.

1. See editorial note to The Antelope, Opinion, 15 Mar. 1825.

2. Dr. John W. Peaco, agent of the American Colonization Society, died in Savannah in 1827 before the departure of the vessel that would transport the Africans to Liberia. His successor was Dr. George P. Todson (John T. Noonan, Jr., *The Antelope* [Berkeley, Calif., 1977], 133–38; Charles Huberich, *The Political and Legislative History of Liberia* [2 vols.; New York, 1947], II, 1705).

3. Southard's letter (with other correspondence) was appended to his annual report as secretary of the navy, communicated to Congress in the president's message, 5 Dec. 1826 (*ASP, Naval Affairs,* II, 726–60 [letter at 750]).

From Timothy Pickering

Salem January 17. 1826.

When, my dear sir, I received, by the hands of Judge Story, the very acceptable present of your concise history of the English Colonies of North America, from their settlement to the commencement of the war which terminated in their Independence, the time seemed distant when, by his hands, I should make my acknowledgements for the favour you conferred: but now it appears a short span — the lapse of a few weeks. I presume that to all persons far advanced in years, time appears to fly with increasing velocity. I still enjoy that vigorous health which was a subject of your gratulation: and I pray you to believe that I cordially reciprocate the kind & affectionate sentiment.

I read your introduction to the life of Washington, some years ago. I have not compared with it your present history: but the latter I have read with great satisfaction. The citizens of each State will doubtless desire minute information of actions and events peculiar to it: while your general history will enable all to trace the progress of the prominent acts and occurrences which brought on our revolution. Here I recollect a sentiment of the celebrated Lord Kames; which, as it is in a book neither on law, nor history, nor literature, is not likely to fall in your way, I will transcribe. It is in his admirable volume on farming, entitled "The Gentleman Farmer." My edition is the second, printed in 1779. It is in the beginning of his plan to constitute "A Board for improving Agriculture."[1]

Lord Kames asks — "Can a British minister embrace any measure more patriotic, than to encourage Agriculture and its professors? No other measure would so effectually aggrandize Britain. A small share of the money & attention bestowed on raising Colonies in America, would have done wonders at home. And yet mark the striking difference: our arts are our own, which we never can be deprived of while industry remains. In the very constitution of our Colonies, on the contrary, there are causes of separation, that grow daily more and more efficacious; a wide extended country, a fertile soil, navigable rivers, and a growing population. I disregard the present rebellion of our Americans: for they will soon be reduced to obedience. But as they derive from Britain high notions of liberty & independence, and as they are daily increasing in power and opulence, the œra of their total separation cannot be at a great distance. It is indeed absurd to think, that a great nation, in the vigour of prosperity and patriotism, can be kept in subjection by a nation not more powerful, enervated by luxury and avarice. Let us not however despond; for if agriculture be carried on but to the perfection that our soil and climate readily admit, it will amply compensate the loss of these colonies." His Lordship lived till December 1782 — more than two months after the capture of Cornwallis's army;[2] and thus probably saw the "rebellion" successful; and the independence of the colonies much nearer than his anticipations had suggested. But if the idea of keeping the Colonies in perpetual subjection was so palpably "absurd" — its absurdity must have been apparent to every discerning British minister: Why then did they attempt to coerce submission? Perhaps they thought with Lord Kames — That the "rebellion" might easily be put down. Yet seeing, for the reasons mentioned by Lord Kames, our separation, at no distant period, was certain, why did they even hazard the expense of some millions, & the loss of some thousands of lives, for our temporary subjugation? Their *resentment* at our unexpected resistance, and not their *reason* — their *pride,* and not their *prudence,* urged them on.

We all rejoice in the *Union of the States;* and generally it seems to be imagined, that it will be perpetual — even when our extended population and additional States shall reach the Pacific Ocean. I, however, do not expect it. The present seat of government will be deemed too much on one side; and then it will be carried westward: or a new confederacy will be formed. The rising generation will not pass away before one or the other of these events takes place. But other causes may break the bond of union. The slave population, as you remark, "has had vast influence on the past, and may affect the future destinies of America, to an extent which human wisdom can neither foresee nor controul."[3]

The swarthy Spaniard finds little difficulty in mixing with the African race: and we have seen the Republic of Colombia consent to set them free.

Before, or about the close of our revolutionary war, in conversation with our friend Colonel Carrington, I asked him what he thought would be the final result of the Negro population, in the slave-holding States. He answered — They will mingle their blood with the Whites. That, of course, would bring slavery to an end. But as Mr. Jefferson remarks — in his Notes on Virginia — there appears to be an utter repugnance, in the Whites, to form such a union (at least a permanent one) with the African race.[4] I can think of no cause of gloomy foreboding so dreadful as the extensive and rapidly increasing population of that race, in a state of slavery. And yet the members of Congress in the slave-holding States, voted — I believe without an exception — to carry it over the Mississippi, and thence, eventually, through this wide continent. The Colonization Society may, perhaps, introduce civil[iz]ation into Africa; and ultimately shed blessings on that great Continent; but give no visible relief to their own country. For while they are transporting to that continent one freedman, a thousand slaves are born.

The sentiments and deportment of governor Troup, as displayed in his published letters and communications, in relation to the enslaved negroes and the Creek Indians, have rendered him alike the object of detestation and contempt: yet he appears to be supported by a majority of the Georgians, who, if they dared, would set the authority of the Union at defiance. That authority, while maintained without physical force, will rest on the purity, the intelligence, and the firmness of the Supreme Federal Judiciary. I pray God you may long continue at its head. With great & affectionate respect, I am, dear sir, most truly yours

TIMOTHY PICKERING

ALS, Marshall Papers, ViW; ALS (draft), Pickering Papers, MHi. ALS addressed to JM in Washington; noted as carried by "Mr. Justice Story."

1. Henry Home, Lord Kames, *The Gentleman Farmer, Being an Attempt to Improve Agriculture by Subjecting It to the Test of Rational Principles* (2d ed.; Edinburgh, 1779), 391–92.

2. Pickering erred in the date of the capture at Yorktown, which occurred in Oct. 1781.

3. *History of the Colonies,* 56.

4. *Notes on the State of Virginia,* ed. William Peden (Chapel Hill, N.C., 1955), 137–43.

To William B. Giles

Dear Sir   Richmond January 18th. 1826

On receiving your letter I requested a friend in Philadelphia to examine the papers which I mentioned to him in order to discover from which of them your speech as it appears in the Life of Washington, is taken. He has done so, and informs me that it is, as I supposed, copied from Dunlop and Claypoles Daily Advertizer of the 16th. of December 1796. Should a second edition of the Life of Washington appear, a reference will undoubtedly be made to the particular paper from which the speech is taken.[1] Very respectfully I am, Your Obedt

J MARSHALL

ALS (advertised for sale by Joseph Rubinfine, West Palm Beach, Fla., 1998). Addressed to Giles at Wigwam, Amelia County; postmarked Richmond, 19 Jan. Endorsed by Giles.

1. See John Sergeant to JM, 6 Dec. 1825 and n. 2.

To Joseph Hopkinson

My dear Sir   Richmond Jany. 20th. 1826

I have had the pleasure of receiving yours of the 10th recommending Judge Griffith for the clerkship of the Supreme court.[1]

I should be mortified if I supposed you could doubt for a moment the confidence I place in your representation of the character and qualifications of any gentleman whose interests you embrace, or my disposition to gratify your wishes. Be assured I feel both in a very high degree. In the particular case you mention I had, without any idea of the value of the office and of the number of persons who would apply for it, assured a friend that I would favour the pretensions of his son, whose capacity I did not doubt, should there be a probability of his success. I am now & have long been convinced that he cannot succeed. Yet I think myself bound by what I have said, until the Judges assemble in February. Should it then appear as I am almost certain it will, that the person to whom I allude cannot succeed, I shall feel myself at perfect liberty to support the pretensions of Judge Griffith. The contest, I am confident will lie between him and young Mr. Caldwell. I wish very sincerely that there was an office for each of them.

If patronage is in all instances as painful as I have found it in this, those who have offices in their gift have claims on our pity at least as strong as on our envy. Yours truely

J MARSHALL

ALS, Hopkinson Papers, PHi. Addressed to Hopkinson in Philadelphia; postmarked Richmond, 21 Jan.

1. Letter not found.

From John McPherson

Dear Sir   Frederick City Jany 20th. 1826[1]
    The bearer James Johnson Esqr is an Applicant for the Office of Clerk
of the supreme Court of the United States, & not being personally acquainted with you, or the Honourable members of your Court, he thinks
it necessary to apply to his friends for letters of recommendation.[2] He is a
Gentleman I have long known, of high standing in this State, regularly
Educated to the profession of the Law, & was in the practice for several
years. He is a nephew of the late Judge Johnson, who was Governor of
Maryland, & personally known to you. It is but Justice to Mr. Johnsons
merit to say that he is a competent Clerk, a Gentleman of amiable, accom-
modating manners, & it is believed would fill the Office, which he solicits,
with dignity & correctness. Feeling a desire that he should succeed in his
application, is my apology for thus addressing you. With sentiments of
great respect, I have the Honor to be Yr. Obedt Servt.
                                                      JOHN MC.PHERSON

ALS, RG 267, DNA. Addressed to JM in Washington. Inside address above salutation.

    1. John McPherson (1760–1829), a Pennsylvania native and Continental army officer,
moved to Frederick, Md., in 1781. He represented Frederick in the House of Delegates in
1788 and 1790 and sat on the Frederick County Orphans' Court from 1813 to 1819
(J. Thomas Scharf, *History of Western Maryland* [2 vols.; 1882; Philadelphia, 1968 reprint], I,
459, 479–81).
    2. James Johnson (b. 1774), nephew of Thomas Johnson, who sat on the first U.S.
Supreme Court, represented Frederick County in the House of Delegates in 1815 (ibid., I,
453; Edward C. Papenfuse et al., eds., *An Historical List of Public Officials of Maryland*, I
[Annapolis, Md., 1990], 209).

From Timothy Pickering

Dear Sir,   Salem January 24. 1826.
    Since the date of my other letter, which Judge Story will hand you with
this, I have seen, in the Richmond Enquirer, of the 7th instant, a publication by Mr. Giles, marked No. 2. new series—of political disquisitions, of
which, it seems, 14 numbers had been before published.[1] The subject of
this new number, is John Quincy Adams; and its object, to exonerate Mr.
Giles's conscience of the burden of error respecting Mr. Adams's political
character, as promulgated in his (Mr. Giles's) speech in the Senate of the
United States (it was in the beginning of December 1808)—to vindicate
the purity of the motives on which Mr. Adams's conversion to *Jeffersonism*
was founded; an error resting on Mr. Adams's own "most solemn and
unequivocal assurances," of the sincerity of his conversion; "exempted
from all views of personal promotion or aggrandizement." Having "made

this public avowal to the world, of his perfect confidence in Mr. Adams's professions of sincerity and disinterestedness, in his avowed political conversion," Mr. Giles "now takes occasion most reluctantly, but most solemnly, in the face of the whole world, *to revoke that avowal";*—and declares that "he is now perfectly convinced—that the chief, if not the sole object of his (Mr. A's) affected conversion, was *his own personal promotion and aggrandizement.*" (On this head, you may suppose that Mr. Giles and I will not contend.) And Mr. Giles offers up his most fervent thankfulness and gratitude to his God, for permitting his little remnant of life to be spun out until Mr. Adams's message appeared before the world; which he thinks not only gave him just occasion, *but called upon him for his solemn disavowal of his former confidence,* and declaration above mentioned.

Seeing Mr. Giles viewed the Message as portentous, indicating intentions to introduce into the government "unlimited powers"—from whence the transition to tyranny would be easy; I had recourse to the message, and again read it.[2] But I discovered nothing, which I had not before observed, to authorize Mr. Giles's fearful forebodings; to wit—an exhibition of his (Mr. A's) views concerning internal improvements—which, while left undefined, explicitly embraced seminaries of learning—a National University—and establishments for promoting Agriculture; *which the first of his predecessors had formerly recommended.* I have no doubt that these expressed objects of improvement, by the authority of the General Government, were mentioned by Mr. Adams, to derive some credit to himself, because they had once been recommended by Washington. But I very much doubt whether Mr. Adams is clear in the opinion, that Congress have a Constitutional power to erect a National University, Astronomical Observatories, &c. &c. It would be an exercise of power—while not expressly authorized—not at all necessary to the execution of any of the powers explicitly vested in the General Government.

I presume you have read Mr. Giles's disquisitions, including No. 2. above referred to. Of the whole 16, I have seen only No. 2; unless some of his pieces on Mr. Monroe's pecuniary claims, now pending, constitute a portion of those disquisitions.[3]

Whether Mr. Giles is or is not a disappointed man, I do not know. For his talents and for his services to the Jefferson Party, he would seem to have had a right to succeed Mr. Madison, in the department of state, when the latter was raised to the Presidency. But to this there were strong objections. From the opinion I had formed of Mr. Giles, able, bold, independent and unmanageable, I should say, that Mr. Madison was afraid to introduce him into his cabinet. In the next place, it would have entirely deranged the plan previously formed by Jefferson, Madison & Monroe.

You will recollect that Monroe took in dudgeon Mr. Jefferson's sending back—*very unceremoniously*—the treaty which, for several years, he had been labouring to form with the British Government, and which, finally, with the aid of William Pinkney's superior intelligence, had been accomplished. He wrote a long letter to Jefferson, on the subject, and desired it might be communicated to Congress. This was done, together with the great mass of documents relating to Great Britain. That long letter of Monroe's I was glad to see; and gave him credit for it. He about that time was set up, in Virginia, the rival candidate to Mr. Madison, for the Presidency. But after a few months, Monroe withdrew; and there was then a long correspondence between him & Mr. Jefferson, ostentatiously published, exhibiting their entire reconciliation. This was of a nature to extinguish the incipient respect I was disposed to entertain for Monroe, on the ground of his letter above mentioned. I then supposed the arrangement was made by the Triumvirate: That Madison should immediately succeed Jefferson, and Monroe follow Madison, in the same high station; and in the meantime be provided for, by some valuable office, as soon as it should be found compatible with the claims of some other aspirants. To the surprize of many, I believe, Robert Smith was appointed to the department of state; and it was during his incumbency, that the printed correspondence was carried on with the British Minister, Mr. Jackson, which terminated in Jackson's dismission. Not long afterwards, Smith ceased to be secretary of state: how his exclusion was effected, I do not remember to have heard. He published a pamphlet on the occasion, reproaching Madison. Upon this, Colvin, a clerk in the Secretary of State's office, came out with a declaration, that he draughted Smith's letter to Jackson.

But anterior to this, Cyrus Griffin, district Judge of Virginia, died. John Tyler was then Governor of Virginia; & him Mr. Madison nominated to fill the vacant office. I was in the Senate. A democratic member near me (he was not a Virginian) gave me this account of Governor Tyler: That he had been a judge of one of your state courts, for many (I think he said above twenty) years — the plague and torment of the Bar: that in order to be rid of him, the lawyers united their forces to get him elected Governor — & succeeded. The nomination was approved, of course, by the Senate. Calling one evening on some members of Congress, at a boarding-house, where a Virginian lawyer (a member of the House of Representatives) was present, I mentioned the nomination of Governor Tyler for the office of district judge. That lawyer exclaimed — "He is the damnedest fool that ever sat on a bench of justice."

Tyler accepted the appointment. Your legislature was then in session. Just at that time, meeting Colo. Tayloe[4] in my walk, I told him that Governor Tyler had been appointed District Judge for Virginia, in order to make room for Mr. Monroe; who, he would see, would be immediately elected governor. The next news from Richmond announced his election. The subsequent removal of Robert Smith, left open to Mr. Monroe the department of state — the vestibule to the President's Palace.

Probably most of the preceding details may be in your recollection. I have recited them as they lie in my memory. If I have committed any mistakes, I shall be thankful for your corrections; while I hope there may be found some new circumstances to compensate for your trouble in reading the letter.

If the appointment to the department of state, before Smith, or after his removal, was to Mr. Giles an object of desire, his animadversions on Monroe, so extremely his inferior, are natural enough. I considered Giles as the ablest *practical* politician of the whole party enlisted under Mr. Jefferson's banners; and for his resolute and steady exertions to support and defend it, entitled to the first executive office under the president. He is not yet tired of public life; for I perceive he has consented to occupy Mr. Randolph's seat in the House. In that body, if elected, he will put himself at the head of the opposition — should there be formed a party opposed — to any of the measures of Mr. Adams's administration.

When Mr. Jefferson received the long laboured treaty with Great Britain, negotiated by Monroe and Pinkney, he immediately sent it back, *without laying it before the Senate, altho' then in session.* He had, I conceive, two motives for this extraordinary conduct. The Senate, notwithstanding his astonishing influence in general, might chance to act with some independence; and on a question of such magnitude as, in its consequences, might involve peace or war, prefer the public welfare to their wonted deference to Mr. Jefferson; and advise the ratification of the treaty. Or if they did not so advise, the discussions in that body, and the nature of the treaty, would become known; and if rejected, hazard public dissatisfaction. For the *informal agreement* of the British ministers, respecting the impressment of seamen from American merchant vessels, was considered by Monroe & Pinkney, as giving, in that regard, equal security & inviolability to our flag, as *a formal treaty stipulation;* which the British ministers declared they could not dare to enter into. It was the expectation of this result, I have not a shadow of doubt, that determined Mr. Jefferson to insist on *a formal stipulation,* in the treaty, as a *sine qua non;* because he did not desire to put an end to our controversies with Great Britain; but on the contrary, to cherish that ill-will towards her which corresponded with popular prejudices, and of course rendered his administration popular. Jefferson, however, would have stopped short of WAR; into which the feebler temper of his successor was driven by the firey popular leaders in the House of Representatives. This brings to my recollection Mr. Joseph Hopkinson's characteristics of the three last Presidents. Jefferson (he said) was respected and loved by his adherents; Madison was loved and not respected; but Monroe had neither their love nor respect. I remain, dear sir, with great respect & esteem, your obedt. servt.

                                                            T. PICKERING.

ALS, Marshall Papers, ViW; ALS (draft), Pickering Papers, MHi. Pickering's endorsement on draft notes that Story carried the original.

1. A "New Series" of essays "by the Author of Political Disquisitions" (William B. Giles) began appearing in the Richmond *Enquirer* on 5 Jan. 1826. It was entitled "The GOLDEN CASKET, or *The President's Message*—or a proclamation of a great civil revolution, in the Governments of 'this Union.' " The second number was published in the *Enquirer* on 7 Jan. Giles's earlier series, "Political Disquisitions," consisted of fourteen numbers that ran in the *Enquirer* from Feb. to Dec. 1825 (Dice Robins Anderson, *William Branch Giles: A Study in the Politics of Virginia and the Nation from 1790 to 1830* [Menasha, Wis., 1914], 217–18).

2. Adams's First Annual Message, delivered on 6 Dec. 1825, outlined an ambitious program of internal improvements, funding for scientific projects, and the creation of a national university (James D. Richardson, *A Compilation of the Messages and Papers of the Presidents, 1789–1897* [10 vols.; Washington, D.C., 1896–99], II, 299–317).

3. "The Golden Casket" was not a continuation of "Political Disquisitions" but a series of twelve essays that ran in the *Enquirer* from Jan. through Mar. 1826. Giles's political writings during this period were later collected in a volume entitled *Political Miscellanies* (Richmond, Va., 1829).

4. Col. John Tayloe III (1771–1828) divided his time between Mount Airy, his plantation on the Rappahannock, and the Octagon, his home in Washington, D.C. (Orlando Ridout V, *Building the Octagon* [Washington, D.C., 1989], 1–2, 104).

To James Barbour

Dear Sir   Richmond Jany. 28th. 1826

I was applied to some time past by Mr. Gibson of this place for a letter to you supporting an application he was about to make for the admission of his son Patrick into the military academy at West Point.[1] I declined writing the letter from a conviction that it could be of no service to him, & stated a conversation with you respecting young Mr. Brown, who had been recommended by the late President Monroe, in which you said that the number of students apportioned to Virginia was more than completed.[2] I have just received a letter from Mr. Henry Gibson who was in Washington, repeating the request made by his Father, and adding that he had understood from yourself that a letter from me would be useful to his brother.[3]

I do not know young Mr. Gibson personally, and of course can say nothing respecting him, but have been long and well acquainted with his Father who is a very amiable and very estimable man. I think it probable that he is not unknown to you. He was for some time a merchant of eminence, and was connected in trade with Mr. Jefferson the Nephew of the former President. That gentleman I am told thinks very favourably of him. In the disastrous times we have passed through his fortune is lost chiefly by surety ships for others. With his loss of fortune he has sustained no loss of character, but his children must look to their own merit for an establishment in life. I shall be happy if I can contribute to aid one of them. With great respect & esteem I am dear Sir, Your Obedt

J MARSHALL

ALS, PHi. Addressed to Barbour in Washington and franked; postmarked Richmond, 28 Jan. Endorsed in two different hands.

1. Patrick Gibson (1775–1827), a Scottish merchant who settled in Richmond before 1800, became a director of the Bank of Virginia and had been in business with George Jefferson, the former president's cousin. For some years he had served as Thomas Jefferson's Richmond factor but was now in financial distress. Gibson had five sons by his first wife Eleanor Sanderson Gibson, who died in the Richmond theater fire of 1811 (*Richmond Portraits*, 80; Dumas Malone, *Jefferson and His Time*, VI: *The Sage of Monticello* [Boston, 1981], 82, 302, 304–5, 308–11, 314–15).

2. See JM to Barbour, 27 Mar. 1825 and n. 1.

3. Letter not found.

To Mary W. Marshall

My dearest Polly   Washington Feby. 5th. 1826

I am now in an excellent room with a good fire and am a day sooner than usual in Washington. My usual practice has been to remain a day in Alexandria, but I came on this morning from a desire to end my journey while the weather is good. Mr. Washington and Mr. Duval are here, and we expect our brothers Story and Thompson today. Judge Johnson unfortunate[ly] took the course by way of Norfolk & cannot, in consequence of it, be here till wednesday or thursday. Mr. Todd is unable to perform the journey.[1]

The roads were not quite so good as they were last winter, but we found them better than usual. We arrived in Alexandria at seven. I have not called on my Aunt Keith for which I am truely sorry, but I could not call without giving up the stage, and as I am under the persecution of the Influenza I was desirous of getting as soon as I conveniently could to the end of my journey.

Tell Mr. Harvie I entirely forgot his overshoes & did not think of them till I was out of town. The weather however continued so moderate that I did not feel the want of them, & I think it extremely probable that, had I brought them, I should not have carried them back to Richmond. I dare not trust myself with any thing which can be lost.

Tomorrow we shall open court & wait on the President; but serious business will not commence till tuesday. Farewell my dearest Polly, I am your ever affectionate

J MARSHALL

ALS, Marshall Papers, ViW. Addressed to Mrs. Marshall in Richmond; postmarked Washington, 6 Feb.

1. Justice Thomas Todd died on 7 Feb. 1826.

To Mary W. Marshall

My dearest Polly   Washington Feb. 12th. 26

I am settled down in my old habits as regularly as if I was still on the right side of seventy. I get up as early as ever, take my walk of three miles by seven, think of you, & then set down to business. I have had a pretty severe attack of the influenza, & the cough & confusion in the head still continue, though the soar throat has left me, & the inflammation of the stomack or lungs has entirely subsided. If you had no other reason to know how old I am you would be reminded of it by my dwelling thus on a trifling indisposition. Our brother Story just arrived today while we were at dinner. He was stopped a week at Philadelphia by the influenza which he has had pretty nearly as bad as myself. It only i⟨n⟩duced me to push forward & not stay a day as usual in Alexandria in order to visit my old and good aunt.

I have not heard a word from Fauquier since leaving Richmond but expect soon to receive a letter from Tom as I have written to inform him that you will advance the 200$ he wants; or rather that I read your wishes so plainly that I had determined to furnish them myself.

I have received three invitations for evening parties this week. See how gay Washington is & how much Miss Jones has lost by her journey to Richmond. If you were here and would go with me I am not sure that my influenza or court business would keep me constantly within doors, but as it is ⟨I do⟩ not feast my eyes with gazing at the ⟨numerous⟩ belles who flock ⟨to⟩ this p⟨lace during the win⟩ters. If Lucy Fisher could persuade ⟨ . . . ⟩ ⟨to be⟩come a candidate for Congress, and ⟨persu⟩ade the people to elect him, she might come and have a charming time of it.[1]

Farewell my dearest Polly. However I may jest about trifles I am always sincere and in earnest when I say that I am most affectionately, Your

J MARSHALL

ALS, McGregor Collection, ViU; Tr, Claudia Hamilton Mason Notebook, Collection of H. Norton Mason, Richmond, Va. Addressed to Mrs. Marshall in Richmond; postmarked Washington, 15 [13?] Feb. Angle brackets enclose words missing or obscured by tear in MS and supplied by Tr.

1. Lucy Marshall Fisher (1807–1874) was the daughter of George Fisher and Ann Ambler Fisher, who was Mrs. Marshall's sister. In 1831 she married Dr. Daniel Norborne Norton (George D. Fisher, *Descendants of Jaquelin Ambler* [Richmond, Va., 1890], 3, 6, 7; *Richmond Portraits*, 148).

To William Rawle and Others

Gentlemen   Washington Feb. 22d. 1826

I have been honoured with your letter of the 15th. inst. enquiring whether I have any materials to furnish or testimony to afford respecting the valedictory address of General Washington, or the doubts which have been raised on the subject of its authorship.[1]

I have no information on the claims which have been made for others to the composition of this address, nor do I know any thing except from public report, which is not in the correspondence that was placed in my hands. I have seen nothing there to induce a suspicion that it was written by any other than its avowed author. With great respect, I am gentlemen your obedt

J MARSHALL

ALS, PHi. Addressed to Rawle, Benjamin R. Morgan, and Charles J. Ingersoll. Endorsed.

1. Rawle (1759–1836), Morgan (1764–1840), and Ingersoll (1782–1862) were prominent Philadelphia lawyers. At a meeting of the Historical Society of Pennsylvania on 6 Feb., they were appointed a special committee to inquire into the authorship of the Farewell Address. The committee on 10 Feb. wrote a letter that was sent to Bushrod Washington, Richard Peters, JM, John Jay, and Rufus King. The letter and replies, along with Jay's letter to Peters of 29 Mar. 1811 and a certificate from David Claypoole, who first printed the address in 1796, constituted the committee's report. The society subsequently published the report in its first volume of proceedings in 1826 (John Hill Martin, *Martin's Bench and Bar of Philadelphia* [Philadelphia, 1883], 295; Victor Hugo Paltsits, ed., *Washington's Farewell Address* [New York, 1935], 89; *Memoirs of the Historical Society of Pennsylvania*, I [1826; Philadelphia, 1864 reprint], 239–67).

From John Randolph

Dear Sir,   Tuesday, last of Feb. [28 February 1826][1]

I send you the last Enquirer — I have not read it & feel no inclination to do so for some days at least I am worn down by disease & labour — I ride indeed, but it is as poor Robert Comistor used to do with Death upon the crupper — Port Equitem Sedet atre Casu.[2]

I date this because I have not done as I wished I have not been to see you of late. Most respectfully & faithfully, Yours

J. R. OF ROANOKE

Printed, Henry B. Dawson, ed., *Historical Magazine,* I (1867), 349. Described as having a pencil endorsement in Randolph's hand "No. 7. in the last paper sent is I think rather flat."

1. Randolph's endorsement confirms that he wrote this note in 1826, while serving in the Senate. "No. 7" refers to the seventh number of William B. Giles's "The Golden Casket," published in the Richmond *Enquirer* of 23 Nov. 1826 (see Pickering to JM, 24 Jan. 1826 and n. 1).

2. The Latin should read "post equitem sedet atra Cura" (black Sorrow sits behind the horseman as he rides his horse) (Horace, *Odes,* bk. III, ode I, l. 40; David Ferry, trans., *The Odes of Horace* [New York, 1997], 158–59).

From John Randolph

My dear Sir,   Monday March 6. [1826]

On arriving at the Senate Chamber this morning, your kind note & the papers (Enqrs) were put into my hands. I thought that I had named 4 oClock in my note to you — or rather ½ past three.

As I have had the temerity to introduce a case, extrajudicially, before your Court I must first purge myself of a contempt, by denying that I called your honours ["]the court below" — but the court below *stairs* — which in no wise impugns your high appellate jurisdiction in the last resort.

2d. I must place my client *rectus in curia.* He is not an African but the African's *son.* Pray read "Suppose that an African enslaved, by this act of Piracy — it is just as much witch-craft as it is Piracy. Congress had the power to make it *felony* but they could not make it piracy[1] — they might as well have declared it to be *Astrology.* Suppose that the son of this African who was torn from his country by this piratical act, sanctioned by the constitution & irrepealable until 1808, should sue for his Liberty. He must claim all his father's rights & character to which he superadds that of native of the U.S "Sue for his liberty? where?" in the federal court. "Why, is he a citizen?" No. "An alien?" no. "An Inhabitant of a different state from his master?" No. Nothing of all this but is it not a case arising under the Const. &c?

This I hope will make you laugh. But I have something better for you. Good news of mr Tazewell for whom I have been on the rack of fear & suspense — & of mrs T. also. I got a letter yesterday dictated by his son. The Casket is a good deal injured I fear (not the "Golden Casket") but the Jewel, the inestimable jewel is in perfect preservation.

Pardon this intrusion on your time. I am most faithfully Your's

J. R. OF R.

ALS, ViW. Addressed to "Mr. Chief Justice / with a Newspaper." Year provided on basis of internal evidence.

1. Randolph placed an asterisk here and wrote in the margin "The King can create a peer but he can't make a gentleman."

To Mary W. Marshall

My dearest Polly   Washington March 12th. 1826

John passed through this city a day or two past & although I did not see him I had the pleasure of hearing from Mr. Washington who saw him as he was about to get into the stage that you were as well as usual. I was particularly glad to hear this as I could not help fearing that the uncommon warmth of the season had relaxed your system so as to distress your feelings. I hope you ride constantly, as exercise will I think be of great advantage to you.

I enjoy my usual health. I am not sure that I have any remnant of the influenza, though I sometimes think that it has not entirely left me. I was in a very great croud the other evening at Mrs. Adams' drawing room, but I see very few persons there whom I know & fewer still in whom I take any interest.[1] A person as old as I am feels that his home is his place of most comfort, and his old wife the companion in the world in whose society he is most happy.

I dined yesterday with Mr. Randolph. He is absorbed in the party politics of the day & seems as much engaged in them as he was twenty five years past. It is very different with me. I long to leave this busy bustling scene & to return to the tranquility of my family & farm. Farewell my dearest Polly. That Heaven may bless you is the unceasing prayer of your ever affectionate

J MARSHALL

ALS, Marshall Papers, ViW. Addressed to Mrs. Marshall in Richmond; postmarked Washington, 14 Mar.

1. JM accepted an invitation to dine with President and Mrs. Adams on 3 Mar. (JM to John Quincy Adams, 27 Feb. 1826, Endicott Autograph Collection, MHi).

To Jared Sparks

Sir[1]   Washington March 16th. 1826

I had the pleasure of receiving your letter of the 26th. of January by Judge Story stating your intention of publishing an edition of all the works of General Washington.[2] Feeling a deep interest in the fame of our illustrious fellow citizen, I am gratified at the expectation of seeing his works ushered to the world by a gentleman whose literary reputation ensures full justice to his memory. I can bestow on the plan only my best wishes for its success, & the feeble aid which is afforded by a subscription to it. The papers are in the possession of Mr. Washington, and are entirely at his disposal. He has shown me the letter addressed by you to him with his answer to it.[3] If the publication he is about to make shall defeat the more enlarged and perfect edition which you propose, it will be a circumstance which I shall regret. It is not the object of Mr. Washington to attach any notes or illustrations to the publication he purposes making, but simply to select some of the most interesting of the letters & to offer them to the public. With very great respect I am Sir, Your Obedt

J MARSHALL

ALS, Sparks Papers, MH. Addressed to Sparks in Boston; noted as carried by Justice Story. Endorsed by Sparks "(Recd. at Washingtn.)" (see n. 2).

1. Jared Sparks (1789–1866), a leading Boston literary figure, was then editor of the *North American Review*. He achieved enduring fame for his historical and editorial works concerning the American Revolution, most notably his twelve-volume edition of *The Writings of George Washington* (1834–37).

2. Letter not found. Sparks was on his way to Washington when JM wrote his letter and received it upon arriving in the capital on 27 Mar. (Herbert B. Adams, *The Life and Writings of Jared Sparks, Comprising Selections from His Journals and Correspondence* [2 vols.; Boston and New York, 1893], I, 415, 416).

3. Sparks also wrote to Bushrod Washington on 26 Jan. outlining his proposal to collect and publish the works of General Washington and seeking Bushrod's cooperation in this endeavor. Bushrod replied on 13 Mar., noting that he and JM had been engaged in a project to publish the general's correspondence and expected to send three volumes to the press in the course of the summer. Sparks had previously learned from Justice Story that Bushrod did "not incline to favor your project." "The truth seems to be," said Story, "that he deems these letters a sort of family inheritance, and that no person ought to be permitted to have anything to do with the publication unless he stands in his own intimate confidence" (ibid., I, 394–401, 402–5, 416–17).

To Timothy Pickering

Dear Sir   Washington March 20th. 26

I had the pleasure of receiving your letters of the 17th. & 23d.[1] of Jany. by Mr. Story & congratulate you very sincerely on the vigorous health which your letters manifest. It is consoling to think that we may look forward to very advanced life with the hope of preserving with health & temperance so large a share of mental & bodily strength as to make life still desirable & agreeable.

I concur with you in thinking that nothing portends more calamity & mischief to the Southern states than their slave population; Yet they seem to cherish the evil and to view with immovable prejudice & dislike every thing which may tend to diminish it. I do not wonder that they should resist any attempt should one be made to interfere with the rights of property, but they have a feverish jealousy of measures which may do good without the hazard of harm that is I think very unwise.

All America I believe will join you in opinion respecting the late intemperate course of the Governour of Georgia. I very much fear that the embarassment into which the purchase from the Creeks has thrown us will be prolonged by a rejection of the last treaty.

You are undoubtedly right in supposing Mr. Giles to be a discontented man. He was unquestionably a very powerful debater on the floor of either branch of the legislature & has seen men placed before him by the party which he has served very effectually to whom he gave precedence very reluctantly. He fell out with Virginia too but seems now determined to write himself again into favour. His health has been for some years very bad, but he is now getting rather better and would be very glad to come forward once more in political life. He is undoubtedly desirous of recommencing his career as a public man. He may probably be successful as he undoubtedly possesses & is beleived to possess considerable talents, and avows opinions which are very popular in Virginia.

Your recollection of events which took place for the last twenty years is very accurate and you replace in my memory many things which I had almost forgotten. There are not many who retain them as fresh as you do, and I am persuaded that they will soon be entirely lost. Those who follow us will know very little of the real transactions of our day, and will have very untrue impressions respecting men & things. Such is the lot of humanity.

Farewell. With sincere wishes for your health & happiness and with great and respectful esteem, I am dear Sir Your Obedt

J Marshall

ALS, Pickering Papers, MHi. Addressed to Pickering in Salem, Mass.; noted as carried by "Mr. Story." Endorsed by Pickering.

1. JM should have written "24th."

To Henry Wheaton

Dear Sir   Washington March 20th. 1826

I have received your letter of the 25th. of Feb. requesting me to say what I think of the practicability & utility of revising & consolidating the statute law of New York on the plan proposed.[1]

The task will undoubtedly be laborious & will require great circumspection in its execution, but is I conceive unquestionably practicable. The attempt has been successfully made in Virginia and of course may succeed in New York. Our statute laws comprehending all the British statutes which were in force, have been collected and arranged in two large octavos.[2] We find or think we find great utility in separating provisions belonging to different subjects, and in bringing together in the same act every thing relating to the same subject. The advantages of methodical arrangement are undoubtedly considerable in every thing & are not less in law than in any other science.

I have perused the act you sent me for establishing the judiciary system of your state, & think it a very favorable specimen of the manner in which the plan will be executed. Very respectfully I am dear Sir, Your obedt

J MARSHALL

ALS, N. Addressed to Wheaton; endorsed by Wheaton.

1. Letter not found. On Wheaton's service as a reviser of the laws of New York, see Elizabeth Feaster Baker, *Henry Wheaton, 1785–1848* (1937; New York, 1971 reprint), 71–73. See also William D. Driscoll, *Benjamin F. Butler: Lawyer and Regency Politician* (New York, 1987), 111–37.

2. JM referred to the 1819 *Revised Code of Va.*

To Henry Lee

Dear Sir   Washington March 21 26

I am just leaving Washington and can spare only a moment for your last letter.[1]

I cannot view the interesting subject you mention in precisely the same light with yourself. I do not think it at all wonderful that two military men under the same circumstances with their minds intently fixed on the same subject should form the same general plan of operation.[2]

My relative situation with the Biographer of General Greene would make it extremely unpleasant to me to enter voluntarily into a controversy with him on a point on which he is probably very sensitive. I shall consequently weigh well what I say should I think it proper to advert in any future edition of the Life of Washington to the counsels in which the movement to the south originated. Very respectfully, I am dear Sir your obedt

J MARSHALL

ALS, ViHi. Addressed to Lee in Washington; postmarked Richmond, 27 Mar.

1. Letter not found.

2. The "interesting subject" was probably the question of who originated the plan to move the southern army to South Carolina after the battle of Guilford Courthouse in Mar. 1781. In his recent book vindicating his father, Lee intimated that Gen. Henry "Light-Horse Harry" Lee devised the plan. In his biography of Gen. Nathanael Greene, William Johnson wrote that the plan had been credited to Lee but was in fact Greene's idea (Henry Lee, *The Campaign of 1781 in the Carolinas; with Remarks Historical and Critical on Johnson's Life of Greene* [1824; Chicago, 1962 reprint], 220–21, 304–5, 398–400; William Johnson, *Sketches of the Life and Correspondence of Nathanael Greene, Major General of the Armies of the United States, in the War of the Revolution* [2 vols.; Charleston, S.C., 1822], II, 32–39).

To William Wirt

Dear Sir   Richmond March 24th. 1826

Under the same cover with this you will receive the letter I mentioned to you from Mr. Lee.[1] I write to him today[2] that I cannot take the liberty to obtrude my recommendations on the President who will undoubtedly make appointments from his own views of propriety, & from information of character given him by those who are now actively engaged in the busy political scenes of the day; but that I will take means through you to have his letter communicated to the President with assurances that his former services & present circumstances, produced chiefly by mistaken confidence, are correctly stated. I do this with reluctance because I know well how much the Executive department is persecuted with applications for office, & am very unwilling to contribute a mite to it: but Mr. Lee, though several years younger than myself was with me at William & Mary; and we were associated together in his early life when his circumstances were easy & he stood higher in public opinion than he now does.[3] There is an appearance of want of feeling in refusing to say one word respecting him in his present situation which would pain me still more than the step I now take. I do not take it in the expectation that it will be of any advantage to him. It will do me no great credit to say that, however little I may serve him, I shall relieve my own feelings.

Mr. Washington would without doubt have joined me but he had left Washington before Mr. Lees letter was received.[4] With great & respectful esteem, I am dear Sir your obedt

J MARSHALL

ALS, Adams Family Papers, MHi. Inside address to Wirt.

1. The letter from Richard Bland Lee to JM has not been found. Wirt forwarded both letters to President Adams on 4 Apr. (Wirt to John Quincy Adams, 4 Apr. 1826, Adams Family Papers, MHi).

2. Letter not found.

3. JM served with "Dick" Lee in the Virginia legislature in the 1780s (*PJM*, I, 121).

4. On 20 Mar. Lee wrote Secretary of State Clay soliciting an appointment as chargé d'affaires to Sweden (James F. Hopkins and Mary W. M. Hargreaves, eds., *The Papers of Henry Clay*, V [Lexington, Ky., 1973], 185).

Catlett v. Marshall
Answer in Chancery, March 1826

EDITORIAL NOTE

Marshall drew the answer in chancery below on behalf of himself and his brother James M. Marshall. The plaintiffs, Charles J. Catlett and his wife Ann, sought payment of an annuity bequeathed in the will of Thomas, sixth Lord Fairfax. As purchasers of the Fairfax manors, the Marshalls were by the terms of the deed of purchase required to pay annuities of £100 sterling a year to each of Lord Fairfax's nieces: Frances Martin, Sibylla Martin, and Anna Susanna Martin. In his will, dated November 1777, Fairfax specified that the annuities were to be charged on his real estate. In a codicil, added in November 1779, Fairfax provided that upon the deaths of Frances, Sibylla, and Anna Susanna Martin, their annuities would go, respectively, to the second, third, and fourth children of Bryan Fairfax.

A second cousin of the sixth Lord who himself became the eighth Lord Fairfax, Bryan Fairfax (1736–1802) had been George Washington's close friend and neighbor in Fairfax County. He had numerous children by his first wife, Elizabeth Cary, and a daughter by his second wife, Jane Dennison (or Donaldson). This daughter was Ann, who in 1806 married Charles Catlett. She now claimed to be the fourth child of Bryan Fairfax and thus entitled to the annuity of Anna Susanna Martin, who died in 1817.[1]

The Catletts filed their bill before Judge Henry St. George Tucker in the Superior Court of Chancery, Frederick County, Winchester, in March 1826. The Marshalls filed their answer at the same time. John Marshall took an active role in this suit, not only in drafting the answer and an amended answer but also in closely advising his nephew James Marshall, who was to argue the case in court. The issue hinged on the construction of Lord Fairfax's will. Was the annuity of Anna Susanna Martin to vest in the fourth child of Bryan Fairfax alive at the time of Lord Fairfax's death? Or was it to vest in the fourth child living at the death of the annuitant? Marshall was reasonably confident that the law supported the former construction, which was the one he and his brother had been following in paying the annuities. The chief justice also sent his nephew an opinion (now lost) he had prepared. "The cause will probably come to the court of Appeals," he wrote, "& the opinion will save me a second laborious search into the ca⟨s⟩es."[2]

Chancellor Tucker ruled in favor of the Marshalls on 21 December 1827, but the Catletts took an appeal to the Virginia Court of Appeals. There the case sat for more than ten years. In drawing his will in 1832 Marshall took note of the appeal and directed his executor to retain sufficient funds to meet the Catletts' claim if so decreed by the Court of Appeals. That court finally heard arguments in November 1838 and in February 1839 affirmed the 1827 Winchester decree.[3]

1. See *A Fairfax Friendship: The Complete Correspondence between George Washington and Bryan Fairfax, 1754–1799* (Fairfax, Va., 1982), 19–36; Fairfax Harrison, *The Proprietors of the Northern Neck: Chapters of Culpeper Genealogy* (Richmond, Va., 1926), 134–35, 145–47; *VMHB*, IX (1901), 207; Charles W. Stetson, *Washington and His Neighbors* (Richmond, Va., 1956), 289–91; Kenton Kilmer and Donald Sweig, *The Fairfax Family in Fairfax County: A Brief History* (Fairfax, Va., 1975), 35–42.

2. Catlett v. Marshall, Amended Answer in Chancery, 24 Aug. 1826; JM to James Marshall, 29 Dec. 1826.

3. Will of John Marshall (copy), 9 Apr. 1832, Office of the Clerk, Fauquier County, Warrenton, Va.; Va. Ct. App. Ord. Bk. XV, 280, 281, 282, 353–54; 10 Leigh 83.

[Answer]

[March 1826]

The Answer in chancery of James M Marshall & John Marshall to the bill of complaint filed in this Honble. court against themselves and the devisees & representatives of Raleigh Colston decd. by Charles J Catlett and Ann his wife.

These respondents saving to themselves every benefit of exception which it may be necessary for the purposes of equity to make to the complainants bill for answer thereto say

That they admit the last will and codicil of Thomas Lord Fairfax as recorded in the court of Frederick county, and that he departed this life about the time in the bill stated.

These respondents admit that they together with Raleigh Colston since deceased became the purchasers of a large portion of the estate held by Thomas Lord Fairfax in his life time and devised by him to his Nephew Denny Martin afterwards called Denny Martin Fairfax, with full notice of his will and codicil; and they submit it to this Honble. court to say how far they are bound to pay the annuities in the bill mentioned.

They also admit that Bryan Fairfax in the bill mentioned was twice married, and they have been informed that the complainant Ann is a daughter by the second marriage which they are informed and believe took place after the date of the codicil, and after the death of Thomas Lord Fairfax. They do not know and consequently do not admit that two of the seven children of the said Bryan Fairfax born of his first marriage died before the date of the codicil to the will of the said Thomas Lord Fairfax, nor that two others of them died before the death of either of the said testator's nieces to whom he had bequeathed the annuities in the bill mentioned; and if these facts be deemed material, proof of them is required. These respondents have not supposed them to be material because they contend that under a sound construction of the codicil of the late Thomas Lord Fairfax the reversionary interest in the annuities bequeathed to the second, third, and fourth children of Bryan Fairfax deceased, vested on the death of the testator in the persons who, at the time, answered the description in the codicil, and not in those who might answer that description at the death of the first annuitants. They insist that there is no expression in the codicil which postpones the vesting of this interest to any future time, and the principle is believed to be well settled that, in such case, it vests immediately. Had the annuity continued to the representatives of the second third or fourth child of Bryan Fairfax it is believed that no question could arise between the representatives of the person who was second third or fourth child at the death of the testator and such person as might happen to be his second third or fourth child at the death of the respective nieces who were the first annuitants; and these respondents humbly insist that the same construction must be put on the words as to the persons designated to take as if a larger interest had been bequeathed.

Should these respondents be mistaken in this opinion, & the plaintiffs be thought entitled to the annuity they claim, it is humbly contended that they can have no pretensions to interest. They have never till very lately, advanced their claim to the annuity and these respondents had not even suspected that such claim existed. They believe that to decree interest under such circumstances would be contrary to the usage of courts. They however rely on the correctness of the construction which has heretofore been universally as they believe put on the codicil in the bill mentioned; and denying all fraud and condemnation[1] pray to be hence dismissed with their costs &c and they will ever pray &c[2]

J MARSHALL

J M. MARSHALL

ADS, Beveridge-Marshall Papers, DLC. JM's signature appears to be in different hand.

1. JM meant to write "combination."

2. After the filing of this answer, the Catletts made an addition to their bill, quoting from the deed to Leeds Manor of 18 Oct. 1806, by which the purchasers undertook to pay the annuities mentioned in Lord Fairfax's will and codicil. In an amended answer (not in JM's hand), evidently filed before the amended answer of 24 Aug. 1826, the Marshalls admitted their liability to pay the annuities but denied the Catletts' construction of the codicil. They recited their payment of the annuities to those who were the second, third, and fourth children of Bryan Fairfax living at the time of Lord Fairfax's death. Accordingly, after the death of Anna Susanna Martin, they paid her annuity to Elizabeth, the fourth child of Bryan Fairfax living at the time of Lord Fairfax's death (Catlett v. Marshall, Amended Answer in Chancery, 24 Aug. 1826).

Interview with Jared Sparks

[Richmond, 1 April 1826]

Called on Chief Justice Marshall; entered his yard through a broken wooden gate, fastened by a leather strap and opened with some difficulty, rang, and an old lady came to the door. I asked if Judge Marshall was at home. "No," said she, "he is not in the house; he may be in the office," and pointed to a small brick building in one corner of the yard. I knocked at the door, and it was opened by a tall, venerable-looking man, dressed with extreme plainness, and having an air of affability in his manners. I introduced myself as the person who had just received a letter from him concerning General Washington's letters, and he immediately entered into conversation on that subject.[1] He appeared to think favorably of my project, but intimated that all the papers were entirely at the disposal of Judge Washington. He said that he had read with care all General Washington's letters in the copies left by him, and intimated that a selection only could with propriety be printed, as there was in many of them a repetition, not only of ideas, but of language. This was a necessary consequence of his writing to so many persons on the same subjects, and nearly at the same time. He spoke to me of the history of Virginia; said Stith's History and Beverly's were of the highest authority, and might be relied on.[2] Of Burk he only remarked that the author was fond of indulging his imagination, "but," he added in a good-natured way, "there is no harm in a little ornament, I suppose."³ He neither censured nor commended the work. He conversed some time on what he calls an error in the history of Virginia as generally received. Robertson states that Virginia recognized King Charles II. before he was proclaimed in England.⁴ Henning, it seems, in his voluminous compilation of Virginia statutes, has denied the fact.⁵ Judge Marshall says that Henning is right in stating that no such act was ever passed formally by the legislature or assembly of the colony, but yet he is mistaken in affirming that such was not the state of feeling among the leading people. Beverly affirms it was, and as he was connected with the leading families of the colony, and acquainted with the circumstances, his testimony ought to be received implicitly. Such and other things were the topics of conversation, till the short hour of a ceremonious visit had run out. I retired much pleased with the urbanity and kindly manners of the Chief Justice. There is consistency in all things about him, his house, grounds, office, himself, bear marks of a primitive simplicity and plainness rarely to be seen combined.

Printed, Herbert B. Adams, *The Life and Writings of Jared Sparks, Comprising Selections from His Journals and Correspondence* (2 vols.; Boston and New York, 1893), I, 421–22.

1. JM to Sparks, 16 Mar. 1826.
2. William Stith, *The History of the First Discovery and Settlement of Virginia* (Williamsburg, Va., 1747); Robert Beverley, *The History and Present State of Virginia* (London, 1705).
3. John Daly Burk, *The History of Virginia, From its First Settlement to the Present Day* (4 vols.; Petersburg, Va., 1804–16).
4. William Robertson, *The History of America,* Books IX and X. *Containing the History of Virginia to the Year 1688; and of New England to the Year 1652* (London, 1796).
5. Hening, *Statutes,* I, xiii.

To Edward Everett

Sir   Richmond Apl. 3d. 1826
    I beg you to receive my acknowledgements for your speech on the proposition to amend the constitution of the United States which reached me two days past. I had previously read with much attention in the National Intelligencer, this eloquent argument, but am not the less gratified at receiving it in a pamphlet form, because it is a flattering mark of your polite attention, & will at the same time enable me to preserve it.¹ With great respect I am Sir, your obedt

                                                    J MARSHALL

ALS, Everett Papers, MHi. Addressed to Everett in Washington and franked; postmarked Richmond, 3 Apr. Endorsed by Everett.

1. Everett's speech of 9 Mar. opposed South Carolina Representative George McDuffie's proposal to eliminate the electoral college in favor of a district-voting system for president.

It appeared in the *Daily National Intelligencer* on 18 Mar. and was then separately printed (*Speech of Mr. Everett, on the Proposition to Amend the Constitution of the United States. Delivered in the House of Representatives, March 9, 1826* [Washington, D.C., 1826]).

To Daniel Webster

Dear Sir   Richmond Apl. 3d. 1826

I had the pleasure of receiving a few days past under cover from you the documents accompanying the late message of the President to the House of Representatives on the Panama mission.[1] We anticipate a tolerably animated discussion of this subject.

I thank you very sincerely for this mark of polite recollection & beg you to believe that I remain with

AL[S], NhHi. Addressed to Webster in Washington and franked; postmarked Richmond, 3 Apr. Endorsed by Webster. Another endorsement below clipped complimentary close and signature: "Cut out for Mr Sprague. / Oct. 13. 1828. / Thomas Davis."

1. The president's message of 15 Mar. 1826 and accompanying documents was entitled *Congress at Panama. Message from the President of the United States, Transmitting the Information Required by a Resolution of the House of Representatives, of 5th Ult. in Relation to the Proposed Congress to be held at Panama* (Washington, D.C., 1826); reprinted in *ASP, Foreign Relations*, V, 882–97. In his first annual message in Dec. 1825 President Adams informed Congress that the U.S. had accepted an invitation to participate in a congress of Latin American countries to be held in Panama. This action provoked bitter partisan opposition in the Senate, which requested public disclosure of the diplomatic documents concerning the Panama mission (Mary W. M. Hargreaves, *The Presidency of John Quincy Adams* [Lawrence, Kans., 1985], 147–53).

To Henry Clay

Dear Sir   Richmond April 26th. 1826

I do not know whether the request is unusual or improper when I ask the favour of you to give a place to the enclosed in some packet made up for France.[1] The letter is from a French gentleman residing in Fauquier who complains that his communications on some business of importance have not reached the person to whom they were addressed, and who has asked my aid in obtaining a conveyance. If, as I fear, the application should be out of the course which such affairs are permitted to take, I beg you to return me the letter. I undertook to make the request from a recollection that I had forwarded such letters myself, and without reflecting that a compliance with such requests might expose the department to inadmissible intrusions. With great respect & esteem, I am dear Sir your obedt

J MARSHALL

ALS, RG 59, DNA. Addressed to Clay in Washington and franked; postmarked Richmond, 27 Apr. Endorsed by Clay as "Recd 29th."

1. In Dec. 1825 the State Department clerk informed a correspondent that Secretary Clay had decided to discontinue the practice of forwarding private letters (James F. Hopkins and Mary W. M. Hargreaves, eds., *The Papers of Henry Clay*, IV [Lexington, Ky., 1972], 903–4).

To Joseph Hopkinson

Dear Sir   Richmond April 30th. 1826

Your favour of the 25th. reached me yesterday & I am greatly obliged by the renewed evidence you have given of your disposition to render me any friendly service which may be in your power.[1]

I have never seen the pamphlet which I was desirous of obtaining & now believe that it never existed; but was told by my coadjutor Mr. Hay last fall that Colonel Monroe had several copies of it.[2] I requested him to ask one for me; and, not having heard from him, desired Mr. Washington when we separated in March, to enquire for it in Philadelphia. Mr. Hay was in Richmond yesterday, and, after receiving your letter, I called on him to enquire what had been the success of his application for me to Colonel Monroe. His answer was that, after the most diligent search, the pamphlet could not be found. I have suspected that he has confounded the essays which he read in the Aurora with the idea of a pamphlet and that the essays never appeared in that form or are no longer to be found in it. I will however trespass on your goodness so far as to ask you to furnish me with a fact which will be some substitute for the essays themselves. It is for the date of the papers in which the first & last are published. I beleive Bache's paper in which they were inserted had then the name it afterwards retained — The Aurora. With the best wishes for your happiness & with sincere esteem, I am your Obedt

J MARSHALL

ALS, Hopkinson Papers, PHi. Addressed to Hopkinson in Philadelphia; postmarked Richmond, 1 May.

1. Letter not found.
2. JM referred to the "Calm Observer" essays (JM to Hopkinson, 11 Dec. 1825 and n. 2).

From John Randolph

My dear Sir,   Washington May 1. 1826

Our old friend Major Scott (I beleive that I may use the possessive pronoun in the plural) used to say that he did not know how far the Truth could be carried at second hand; but that he had ascertained, by actual experiment, during Burr's trial, that it could not travel as far as from the Capitol to the Eagle Tavern.[1]

You will perceive the bearing of this remark when I tell you that altho I took the liberty (which I trust you will beleive that I would not have ventured upon unless I had thought myself entitled to do so) to read an extract from your last letter to me in my place in the Senate; yet I named no names whether in the letter or out of it. I read just so much as expressed your estimation of the speeches which I had sent you — (telling the Senate what speeches they were in my own person) & your opinion of them without reading my friend Berton's[2] name — and also that part of the letter that expresses your inability to decide upon the various points of the P(anama?) question, as evedence that *we* could not be very far wrong & our adversaries not manifestly right; when we maintained & they denied that this was an anomalous embassy obnoxious to the very uncertainty as to the character & functions of the various commissioners, or ministers; & the rules of proceeding in the "assembly of nations" which had suggested itself ⟨ . . . ⟩.[3]

On a former occasion I read a letter in which it was stated that Mr. Adams frequently went to the Senate in Mr. Giles carriage on the growth & improvement of their intimacy which led to Mr. Adam's impeachment of his federal friends. But the newspaper makes me say that he frequently *dined* with Mr. Giles & there is not one word about dinner or dining in the whole letter.

On my return from England in 1822 I was struck with the relaxed fibre & languid appearance of the N. Yorkers who all seemed to be recovering from a bilious fever — the victims of lassitude.

On my last return I was more struck by the intolerable filth of the press. Without the wit of the John Bull it is dirtier even than that notorious Journal. But taken generally the ability & point & spirit of the English press stand in strong & disgraceful contrast to the feebleness & vapid scurrility of ours.

Our editors are generally broken merchants or professional men of too small calibre to get business. They must cater too for a most depraved publick taste. As Cromwell told his soldiers they must shoot *low* to gain the victory. They put in my mouth the most obsurd & inconsistent declarations. They ascribe to me the most stupid & rediculous conduct & after perverting all that I say or do; they then answer their own arguments, if arguments they may be called. It is a subject of mortification to me on his ⟨ . . . ⟩.[4] I should esteem it among ⟨ . . . ⟩[5] of the calamities that can ever befall me in case it should be the result of any indiscretion on my part — but even if it should be brought about by that Pandora's Box of lies the press, I should feel it sensibly & deeply to the latest hour of my life. I am with the truest respect & regard my dear Sir Your obliged and faithful servant

JOHN RANDOLPH OF ROANOKE

Tr, Beveridge-Marshall Papers, DLC. Noted by the transcriber as copied from the original in possession of Mrs. Claudia Jones, Washington, D.C., 30 May 1913.

1. Joseph Scott was the U.S. marshal for Virginia at the time of the Burr trial (*PJM,* VII, 397 n. 1).
2. Should be "Benton." Thomas Hart Benton (1782–1858) was then nearing the end of the first of five consecutive terms as a U.S. Senator from Missouri.
3. Transcriber's note: "page torn."
4. Transcriber's note: "half of page torn away."
5. Transcriber's note: "page torn."

To John Randolph

My dear Sir   Richmond May 5th. 1826

I cannot proceed upon my circuit to North Carolina without acknowledging the receipt of your letter of the first inst. It gave me the first intimation that you had read in your place in the Senate any thing I had written. I have since been told that in some paper which I have not seen, the circumstance has been mentioned as if the letter had been read as being written by me. I have not seen the paper, nor did the gentleman say whether the Editor founded his assertion that I had written it entirely on his own conjectures, or on your statements. However this may be I beg you to believe that I know you too well & rely too implicitly on any statement you may make to have my faith staggered for an instant by any thing I may hear is inserted in the papers. I have not the least doubt of the entire correctness of your representation, and feel the most entire confidence that you have said nothing and will say nothing respecting me to which the most scrupulous delicacy ought to object.

I certainly do not purpose to mingle in the party conflicts of the day, which will be carried on by those whose situation makes it perhaps a duty to engage in them, and who are not restrained by other considerations from performing that duty. Both my age and official character would admonish me to check such a disposition if I could feel it. I do not think any part of my letter was calculated to represent the writer as making himself a party to the question which has been so ably discussed in both houses of Congress. The speeches you were so kind as to forward me might be admired as able arguments by any man who was pleased with sound & acute reasoning whatever he might think of the mission; and the doubts I stated respecting its character I really felt at the time & still feel. I have been lead to these perhaps unnecessary observations by a disposition to express the real quiescent state of my mind on party politics. I am as calm an observer of passing events & controversies as a man can be who feels & to his latest breath will feel an ardent wish for the prosperity of his country. But it is not for the purpose of expressing this sentiment that I now write. I cannot pass over that expression of your letter in which you indicate the pain it would give you to incur the forfeiture of those sentiments which I have long, let me add very long cherished for you. Believe me my dear Sir this is a pain which can never be inflicted by me. Mine I trust is not a bosom from which esteem founded on qualities which may justly claim it in a preeminent degree is to be lightly expelled. A friendship of thirty years standing, cherished by many endearing recollections, not capriciously taken up originally, will not be capriciously laid down. I am too old to form new friendships, & I shall cling too closely to those already formed to allow them to be broken by the trash of Editors about whom I know nothing.

These declarations are perhaps more serious than the occasion requires; but I have not seen the newspaper paragraphs to which you allude, & as you seem to suppose that they may be of a character to make some impression on me I have thought you would excuse the effort to dissipate the suspicion. With real esteem & regard I am dear Sir, Your

J MARSHALL

ALS, ViHi. Addressed to Randolph in Washington and franked; postmarked Richmond, 5 May. Endorsed by Randolph "The last before / my departure."

Interview with Jared Sparks

[Monroe, N.C., 9 May 1826]

Rode all night, and arrived in Richmond at sunset to-day. Met Judge Marshall last evening at the town of Monroe, on the Roanoke River. He was on his way to hold his circuit court in Raleigh, and traveling in a sulky. He said he much preferred the stage for its expedition, but could not travel nights. Passed half an hour very agreeably with him. He spoke of Canova's statue of Washington at Raleigh; and said he was no judge of the art, but was bound to suppose it a *chef d'oeuvre;* he was glad the country had a specimen of art of so high an order, but said it gave no impressions of Washington, it was not like him in any respect what ever. Houdon's statue, in the State House of Virginia, he observed, is a very exact representation of Washington, particularly if you view it in a position so as to look at the figure between the front and left side.[1]

A case of libel is to come on at Raleigh, which the judge seemed to dread exceedingly. It is a case between two clergymen, Mr. Whitaker and Dr. McPheeters.[2] A good deal of excitement exists on the subject, and the decision must involve principles which present legal difficulties and perplexities.

Printed, Herbert B. Adams, *Life and Writings of Jared Sparks, Comprising Selections from His Journals and Correspondence* (2 vols.; Boston and New York, 1893), I, 451.

1. The artist Antonio Canova (1757–1822) was commissioned by the Senate of North Carolina in 1815 to carve a memorial to Washington to be placed in the state capitol. Canova based his sculpture on other likenesses of Washington, never having seen him in person. Although the statue was destroyed by fire sometime after 1826, surviving models indicate that Canova sculpted Washington both as nude and as a Roman general. The final version was undoubtedly very classical and abstract. The statue of Washington executed by Jean Antoine Houdon (1741–1828) in 1788–92, on the other hand, is believed to resemble Washington most closely. It was the result of Houdon's visit to Mount Vernon, where he was able to measure and take casts of Washington's face and figure. The original is located at the Virginia State Capitol in Richmond (David Finn and Fred Licht, *Canova* [New York, 1983], 103–5; Sherwin McRae, *The Houdon Statue, Its History and Value* [Senate Doc. 21; Richmond, Va., 1873], 3).

2. See JM to Story, 31 May 1826 and n. 2.

To Daniel Webster

Dear Sir   Richmond May 20th. 1826

I returned yesterday from North Carolina & had the pleasure of finding your speech on the mission to Panama under cover from yourself.[1] I had previously read it with deep interest but was not on that account the less gratified at this polite mark of your attention. I can preserve it more certainly in the pamphlet form than in that of a newspaper.

Whatever doubts may very fairly be entertained respecting the policy of the mission as an original measure, I think it was not involved in much difficulty when considered as it came before the House of Representatives.

I congratulate you on closing a most laborious session and am with great & respectful esteem, your Obedt

J MARSHALL

ALS, ICU. Addressed to Webster in Washington and franked; readdressed to Boston in another hand; postmarked Richmond, 20 May. Endorsed by Webster.

1. *Speech of Mr. Webster, of Mass., in the House of Representatives, on the Panama Mission: Delivered on the 14th April 1826* (Washington, D.C., 1826). Webster fully supported American participation in the Panama Congress and opposed attempts to attach specific instructions to the House appropriations bill (reprinted in Charles M. Wiltse and Alan R. Berolzheimer, eds., *The Papers of Daniel Webster: Speeches and Formal Writings* [2 vols.; Hanover, N.H., 1986–88], I, 201–35).

To Joseph Story

My dear Sir   Richmond May 31st. 1826

I send you by the General Jackson (because the name must render every part of its cargo valuable in your estimation) a small cask of hams which I hope you will find tolerably good in themselves. They are packed in hiccory ashes; and our Ladies, who are skilful in the management of their Hams, say that they must be taken out on their arrival & put in a cool dry place as the hiccory ashes may probably become lye on the voyage. They will be deposited with Henry Hovey & Co No. 23 Central Wharf, Boston.

I am now engaged in my circuit duties at this place, & shall finish today an issue out of chancery to try the legitimacy of two children of a woman residing in North Carolina in the free indulgence of her natural appetites, whose husband resided in Virginia with another woman whom he married between the two births. Our best lawyers are engaged in it, and yesterday was employed by Stannard in continuation & Johnson. Wickham closes today. Leigh occupied so much of the preceding day as remained after reading the testimony.[1]

I counted on a longer term in North Carolina than I actually had. A cause was for trial between two New England clergymen in which one had charged the other with very serious crimes; and on being sued, had pleaded that the words written, for it is a libel, were true. They have taken the depositions of almost all New England; & I am told by the lawyers that the testimony is very contradictory. All was ready; but the combatants seemed to fear each other, and the cause was continued in the hope that one more effort might produce a reference, if not a compromise. All their former attempts had failed. Notwithstanding my knowledge of the persevering firmness with which gentlemen of th⟨e⟩ sacred profession pursue their objects, I was surprized at this — obstinacy may I call it — till I was informed that it was Presbyterian vs. Unitarian.[2]

I find the bill for multiplying our numbers has failed, although a majority of both houses was in its favour.[3] It will probably pass next session. The chance of such a bill is better the second session of any Congress than the first. I hope the seven Judges will convene at our next term & that the constitutional questions depending before us may be argued and decided. I am glad that our brother Tremble has passed the senate *Maugre* Mr. Rowan.[4]

Our friend & brother Washington seems to have been involved by his respect for the Sabbath in a very unpleasant affair with about thirty members of Congress. I am truely sorry for this casualty. The circumstance I presume could not have occurred had his previous notice & letter to the Captain of the Steamboat been communicated to them.[5]

Edward, who has run away from Cambridge, left us yesterday on an expedition to the mountains, to take possession of his farm & acquire, if he can, a different science from what is taught at college. A drought such as has never been known at this season has affected our crops considerably, but we shall make too much for the demand unless our northern brethren will double their number of manufacturers, or double their appetites. Far[e]well. I am my dear Sir your affectionate

J MARSHALL

ALS, Story Papers, MHi. Addressed to Story in Salem, Mass.; postmarked Richmond,
31 May.

1. See Stegall v. Stegall's Administrator, Opinion, 22 June 1825.

2. The plaintiff in the libel suit was the Rev. Jonathan Whitaker, formerly of Massachusetts
and then residing in Camden, S.C. The defendant was the Rev. Frederick Freeman. A jury
heard the case over four days at the Nov. 1826 term. It found a verdict for the plaintiff for
$1,800, subject to the court's opinion on a reserved question of law. The defendant had
entered two pleas: not guilty and justification. The question was whether the defendant by
pleading justification waived the benefit of the plea of not guilty. JM, in a hurry to attend his
circuit in Richmond, postponed his decision until the next term. In May 1827 he delivered
"a very lucid and elaborate opinion" in the defendant's favor and set aside the verdict. The
court, however, granted the plaintiff's motion for a new trial. At the Nov. 1828 term a
second jury again found for the plaintiff, this time assessing damages of $2,000 and costs.
The court overruled a motion for a new trial and entered judgment for the plaintiff.
Whitaker was also plaintiff in a companion libel case against William McPheeters and
Henry Potter. This suit was dismissed at the 1826 term upon the award of two arbitrators
(U.S. Cir. Ct., N.C., Min. Bk., 12 May 1826, 17 Nov. 1826, 12 May 1827, 13 May 1828, 14
Nov. 1828; Whitaker v. Freeman; Whitaker v. McPheeters and Potter, Records of U.S. Cir.
Ct., N.C., RG 21, GEpFRC; *Raleigh Register,* 19 May 1826, 17, 24 Nov. 1826, 18 May 1827).

3. This was a bill to increase the number of circuits to ten and to add three additional
Supreme Court justices. See Warren, *Supreme Court,* I, 675–83.

4. Robert Trimble (1777–1828) replaced Thomas Todd on the Supreme Court. A Virginia native, Trimble moved to Kentucky at an early age, studied law, and became a leading
practitioner in that state. In 1817 he was appointed judge of the U.S. District Court, where
he sat until his elevation to the Supreme Court. Senator John Rowan (1773–1843) of
Kentucky objected to Trimble's sympathy for federal supremacy and led the fight against
his nomination. The Senate confirmed Trimble by a vote of twenty-seven to five on 9 May
(ibid., I, 684–85).

5. On Sunday, 14 May, a party of congressmen and senators took a steamboat excursion
to Mount Vernon but were prevented from landing under threat of prosecution. Although
this action drew "the most indignant epithets" upon the proprietor, Washington had previously given public notice that the house would be closed on Sundays (Richmond *Enquirer,*
19 May 1826).

To Bushrod Washington

My dear Sir   Richmond May 31st. 26

I had the pleasure of receiving your letter written immediately after
your return from Philadelphia and am much obliged by your kind enquiries for "The Calm Observer."[1] I now believe that those papers were
never in the pamp[h]let form, or, if ever so published, are no longer to be
found. I will thank you, if General Washington ever took & preserved that
precious deposit of democratic patriotism — The Aurora — to examine
those of the summer of 1796, for the essays under the signature of "The
Calm Observer" & let me know the dates of the first and last number.
Indeed I should be very desirous of getting the file. I fear however that
you have not the papers. I wrote to Mr. Hopkinson in April requesting
him to give me this information, but have received no answer & suppose

my letter has miscarried. These essays are alone wanting to complete my revision of the 5th. volume. The preceding volumes are entirely prepared. Should the publication take place I could wish the edition not by any means to exceed the demand. I should think 1000 copies a sufficient number. Mr. Wayne however will judge of this. I presume there will be no difficulty in furnishing us with the number of copies we wish for our friends.

I think it would be better to place such letters to General Washington as you shall select for publication in the order in which it would be desirable to read them. May not this be effected by copying them in a separate volume and affixing to each a note or memorandum referring to the letter next to which the printer is to insert it? If the press be properly superintended I should think this might be done without much hazard of confusion.

I have been sorry to see in the papers your unpleasant altercation with some members of Congress. I think those gentlemen ⟨might?⟩ have been informed of your decision respecting these sunday visits or they would not have attempted a violation of rules your perfect right to establish which can as little be questioned as their propriety. Farewell. I am your affectionate

J MARSHALL

ALS, Marshall Papers, DLC. Addressed to Washington at Mount Vernon; postmarked Richmond, 31 May. Endorsed by Washington.

1. Letter not found.

From Unknown

Sir,   Alexa. D.C. 10. June 1826

Having heard of the death of the Hon. Wm. Griffith of N. Jersey by which event the office of Clerk of the Supreme ⟨Court⟩ ⟨ . . . v⟩acant, ⟨ . . . ⟩ John ⟨ . . . ⟩ place ⟨ . . . ⟩ Charles ⟨ . . . ⟩ daughter of the late Colo. Danl. Carroll Brent; after whose death Mr. Simms removed from Alexa. to a farm in Virga. which descended from, or was devised to his wife by, her father; but it has unexpectedly appear'd that the estate was so much encumber'd as to be worthless to him; and it has, I believe, been sold for the debts of Colo. Brent.[1] Mr. Simms was in good and increasing practice when he left Alexa. — but I am told is now reduced to absolute poverty. His talents are sufficient to enable him to rise again to a very respectable standing at the bar; but how shall he fill the gap between the present moment & that? How support himself, his wife, &, I believe five amiable children, untill he can regain his station in the profession? This is to him a most serious question.

I take the liberty of suggesting these circumstances for the consideration of the Judges; and of assuring them that I believe Mr. Simms to be competent to the discharge of the duties of the office.

I have never heard anything against his moral character & believe it to be irreproachable.

AL[S], RG 267, DNA. MS mutilated owing to clipping of signature.

1. John Douglas Simms, son of the late Charles Simms of Alexandria, married Eleanor Carroll Brent (1787–1846), daughter of the late Daniel Carroll Brent (1759–1814), in 1816. He practiced law in Alexandria before moving to Stafford County in 1818 (Chester Horton Brent, *The Descendants of Collo. Giles Brent, Capt. George Brent and Robert Brent . . .* [Rutland, Vt., 1946], 142–43, 157; T. Michael Miller, comp., *Artisans and Merchants of Alexandria, Virginia: 1780–1820* [2 vols.; Bowie, Md., 1991–92], II, 121–22, 123).

From [Charles F. Mercer]

Dear Sir   Leesburg Loudoun Cy. June 12th. 1826
    You are so well acquainted with the ⟨ . . . ⟩ my friend, Mr Edmund J. Lee, of ⟨ . . . ⟩ sustain his application to your ⟨ . . . ⟩ office of Clerk — lately become vacant, I need not assure You, that for industry, and integrity, no man of my acquaintance stands higher, while the fidelity and ability with which he has fulfilled the duties of his office in Alexandria, are pledges of his capacity to give the Court and the public a satisfaction in the station which he seeks at Washington.[1]

My zeal for his welfare springs from a long and intimate acquaintance with his worth and a knowledge of the fact that his great sacrifices for his relatives and the demands of a large family would render his translation from the Court of Alexandria to the more lucrative station in that of Washington a great releif, not to himself only; but to his highly estimable family and connections.

With this apology for presenting his wishes to your most favourable notice I beg leave to combine the assurance of the very high esteem of ⟨ . . . ⟩.

AL[S], RG 267, DNA. MS mutilated owing to clipping of signature. Mercer's identity confirmed by comparison of handwriting.

1. Edmund Jennings Lee (1772–1843), a lawyer and former mayor of Alexandria (1815–18), was then clerk of the U.S. Circuit Court for D.C., Alexandria (Edmund Jennings Lee, ed., *Lee of Virginia, 1642–1892* [1895; Baltimore, 1974 reprint], 374–82; T. Michael Miller, comp., *Artisans and Merchants of Alexandria, Virginia: 1780–1820* [2 vols.; Bowie, Md., 1991–92], I, 268).

From [William Wirt]

Dear Sir   Washington. June 12. 1826

Mr Griffith, the clerk of the Supreme court, has just died — and I beg to be excused for presenting to you this early, as a candidate for that appointment, Colo. Thomas Randall of this place.[1] He is a young gentleman for whose intellectual and moral character and for all the qualifications requisite for the office, I will answer with the most perfect confidence. He was a public agent for the government in the West India islands and on the Spanish main two or three years ago and discharged his duties in a manner highly honorable to himself and useful to his country. He is a good lawyer, a good writer, steady and correct in all his habits and conduct, and a perfect gentleman in his principles and deportment. An intimate acquaintance has attached me to him very strongly, and, taking as I do a more than common interest in his success, and being perfectly convinced of his entire fitness for the office, you will I am sure excuse the earnestness with which I recommend him to your attention.

AL[S], RG 267, DNA. Addressed to JM in Richmond. Endorsed by JM: "Mr Randall." Signature clipped. Wirt's identity based on handwriting and on internal evidence (see n. 1).

1. Thomas Randall (1792–1877), a native of Annapolis, was Wirt's son-in-law. He was then practicing law in Washington and soon received an appointment as U.S. judge for the Middle District of Florida (*The Biographical Cyclopedia of Representative Men of Maryland and District of Columbia* [Baltimore, 1879], 531; *Journal of the Executive Proceedings of the Senate . . .*, III [Washington, D.C., 1828], 579, 583).

To Samuel Bayard

Dear Sir   Richmond June 15th. 1826

Your letter of the 10th. of June signifying your inclination to become the Clerk of the Supreme court has been received.[1]

I recollect perfectly that we were formerly acquainted with each other, and have not the slightest doubt of your entire competence to the duties of the office you wish.[2] I am quite confident that you would fill it with reputation.

The applicants are numerous, and are gentlemen of great worth. Some considerable division among the Judges may therefore be expected. If we make an appointment it cannot fail to be a good one, and it is my earnest wish that an appointment may be made. Although I may feel a preference, I shall feel it so important to fill the vacancy that I shall enter on the duty without any preengagement, & with a determination to make some sacrifice of inclination in order to effect the object. With very great respect, I am Sir your obedt

J MARSHALL

ALS, NRU. Addressed to Bayard in Princeton, N.J.; postmarked Richmond, 16 June. Endorsed by Bayard.

1. Letter not found.
2. See *PJM*, IV, 60, 265, 328.

From [Joseph Hopkinson]

Dear Sir   Philad. June 30. 1826

My brother in law, Mr Condy, has informed you of his intention of offering himself as a Candidate for the office of Clerk of the Supreme Court.[1] I believe he has the honour of being personally known to you; but as many years have passed since you have seen him; I take the liberty to say, in his behalf, that he stands in the first class of his profession at this bar; and as a man of business, of extensive general learning and acquirements, and high integrity, he is above all exception. If, consistently with other duties and demands upon you on this subject, you can favour his pretensions, I feel assured he will afford no ground hereafter for regret to you.

AL[S], RG 267, DNA. Addressed to JM in Richmond; postmarked Philadelphia, 30 June. Signature clipped. Endorsed by JM "Mr. Condé."

1. Jonathan Williams Condy (1770–1828) was married to Elizabeth Hopkinson, sister of Joseph Hopkinson. A 1786 graduate of the University of Pennsylvania, he was admitted to the Philadelphia bar in 1791. From 1797 to 1800 Condy served as clerk of the U.S. House of Representatives (*Biographical Catalogue of the Matriculates of the College* [Philadelphia, 1894], 26; John Hill Martin, *Martin's Bench and Bar of Philadelphia* [Philadelphia, 1883], 258).

From [Judges of the U.S. Circuit Court, D.C.]

[ca. June 1826]

Understanding that Edmund J. Lee esquire, is an applicant for the Office of Clerk of the supreme Court of the United States, we beg leave to state, that having had long experience of his learning, skill, accuracy, attention and fidelity as Clerk of the Alexandria Circuit Court of this District, as well as of his professional talents and learning, we can, with great confidence recommend him, as perfectly competent to the discharge of the duties of the Office, for which he has applied: and, we have no doubt, that if appointed, he will discharge its duties with entire satisfaction to the court, and with honour to himself.

It would be with great regret that we should lose the Services of Mr. Lee; but, if they should be required by the supreme Court, our respect for that Court, and our regard for Mr. Lee, would induce us cheerfully to acquiesce

AL[S], RG 267, DNA. Addressed to the judges of the Supreme Court in Washington. Signatures clipped. The circuit court judges were William Cranch, chief judge, Buckner Thruston, and James S. Morsell. Cover evidently in Cranch's hand; text in different hand.

To Charles Dabney

My dear Sir   Richmond July 26th. 1826
I send you the certificate you request but fear it will be of no service. There ought certainly to be no distinction between the 1st. & 2d. state regiments & the continental line, but Congress has made engagements to the continental lines only & may be unwilling to extend their liberality to those who have in justice the same claims.[1]

I am much gratified to hear that your health is so perfectly restored and that you still enjoy life. That you may long enjoy it is the wish of him who is with great esteem & regard your obedt

J MARSHALL

ALS (owned by Gerhard A. Gesell, Washington, D.C., 1967); Tr, Charles William Dabney Papers, Southern Historical Collection, NcU. Tr identifies recipient as Col. Charles Dabney of Hanover County, Va.

1. The reference is apparently to an act of 20 May 1826 extending the time for officers and soldiers of the Va. Continental Line to obtain warrants on bounty lands. In 1830 Congress adopted an act concerning military land bounties that extended to the officers, soldiers, sailors, and marines of the Virginia state line (*U.S. Statutes at Large,* IV, 189, 422–24). For Dabney's efforts on behalf of Revolutionary veterans, see Charles William Dabney, "Colonel Charles Dabney of the Revolution: His Service as Soldier and Citizen," *VMHB,* LI (1943), 186–99.

To Joseph Hopkinson

My dear Sir   Richmond July 31st. 1826
I received some time past your letter recommending Mr. Condy as the successor of Judge Griffith. I had before understood from himself that this gentleman was a candidate and had written to him on the subject. That he has your good wishes is with me no inconsiderable addition to his own merit, and should he succeed, I shall see him in the office with pleasure. It is however candid to say that I think the chances against him. The candidates are not only highly respectable in themselves and supported by names of the greatest influence, but have personal claims on individual Judges which are almost irresistable. For myself, I had never so

painful a task to perform as to select among the names who are presented to me. I see on the list many very estimable friends, and the sons of others with whom I was connected in the closest affection. I cannot think of one without remorse & self reproach at the exclusion of several others. If patronage be always so painful those who possess it are much better entitled to our pity than our envy. God in his mercy defend me from being ever again called to its exercise.

I have come to no decision in favour of any individual & shall go to Washington prepared to relinquish any preference I may feel in order to secure an election. Several others must carry with them the same disposition or we shall make no clerk. I say this because I believe several of the Judges, perhaps a majority have fixed on different individuals. I have however no positive knowledge of the decision of more than two. Farewell — with sincere wishes for your happiness, and with great and respectful esteem, I am your Obdt.

J MARSHALL

ALS, Hopkinson Papers, PHi. Addressed to Hopkinson in Philadelphia; postmarked Richmond, 31 July.

To James Monroe

Dear Sir   Richmond July 31st. 1826

I have had the pleasure of receiving your letter recommending Mr. Randall to the vacant office in the clerkship of the Supreme court.[1] I trust I need not say that there is no person whose recommendation can have more influence with me than yours. I feel the utmost confidence in the merit of this gentleman, and that the office, should he receive the appointment, will be well bestowed. To myself personally, though I am not acquainted with him, it will be far from disagreeable.

I have never in my life been required to perform a more painful duty than making this appointment. In addition to the numbers & great respectability of the applicants, a circumstance which of itself would create sufficient difficulty in making a selection, the list exhibits many of my highly valued personal friends, and the sons of others with whom I have been connected by ties of close affection & esteem. I cannot point to one without looking at others, who must be excluded, with extreme regret. Among those too who have supported individual and of course opposing candidates, are the most valued friends I have in the world. In this to me new as well as distressing situation, I have made no positive determination, but have uniformly said that a clerk must be appointed, and that some sacrifice of individual preference must be made to effect this necessary object. That under this conviction I shall go into the election prepared to support that one of the many I could wish to assist, who can unite a sufficient number of votes to secure an appointment. I shall feel much more of chagrin at being compelled to pass by so many deserving men to whom I feel the best disposition, than of pleasure at giving my voice in favour of the successful candidate.

I hope you are not in danger of famine from the drought as many of us are. With great & respectful esteem, I am dear Sir your Obedt

J MARSHALL

ALS, Monroe Papers, DLC. Addressed to Monroe. Endorsed by Monroe.

1. Letter not found.

To Edward Everett

Dear Sir   Richmond Aug. 2d. 1826

I have received and read with attention & much pleasure your oration delivered at Cambridge on the anniversary of our Independence.[1] The theme which has so often employed the eloquence of our countrymen, has not, I perceive, been entirely exhausted. That great event may still be contemplated in points of view which furnish additional subjects for reflection and gratulation.

Allow me to express the peculiar satisfaction I felt at reading your statement of the causes in which our great revolution originated. Our resistance was not made to actual oppression. Americans were not pressed down to the earth by the weight of their chains, nor goaded to resistance by actual suffering. "They were not slaves rising in desperation from beneath the agonies of the lash; but freemen snuffing from afar 'the tainted gale of tyranny.'[2] This view of the subject is not only more consistent with the fact, but is more honorable to the intelligence of those virtuous patriots and sensible men who dared to lead us into the mighty conflict. The long list of tyrannical acts which is found in our declaration of independence, and which swells the papers of the day, was judiciously inserted as tending to produce unanimity, and was justified by the irritated feelings of the moment; but the time is arrived when the truth may be declared, and it is most honorable to our ancestors to declare it. The war was a war of principle, against a system hostile to political liberty, from which oppression was to be dreaded, not against actual oppression.

Allow me to thank you for this flattering mark of your recollection, and to assure you tha⟨t⟩ I am with great respect and esteem, your obedt

J MARSHALL

ALS, Everett Papers, MHi. Addressed to Everett in Boston and franked; postmarked Richmond, (2?) Aug. Endorsed by Everett "7 Aug 26" (date of receipt?).

1. *An Oration Delivered at Cambridge, on the Fiftieth Anniversary of the Declaration of the Independence of the United States of America* (Boston, 1826); reprinted as "Principle of the American Constitutions," in Edward Everett, *Orations and Speeches on Various Occasions* (2d ed.; 2 vols.; Boston, 1850), I, 103–30.
2. Everett, *Orations and Speeches,* I, 105.

Catlett v. Marshall
Amended Answer in Chancery

[24 August 1826]

The amended answer in chancery of John Marshall and James Marshall to the bill of complaint exhibited against themselves & others in the Honble. the High court of Chancery held in Winchester by Chas J Catlett and Ann his wife.[1]

These respondents as an amendment to their answer formerly filed in this cause humbly state that they have understood and beleive that the late Thomas Lord Fairfax in the bill mentioned was very distantly related to Bryan Fairfax in the bill also mentioned, and had very little intercourse with the said Bryan Fairfax or any of his family. That the said Thomas Lord Fairfax was an old & infirm man as they are informed & beleive who for many years before his death mixed but little with the world, was scarcely ever from home, & saw very few persons. They therefore think it probable, and from these circumstances, believe that the said Thomas Lord Fairfax did not know at the time of making his will the names or sex of the particular children of Bryan Fairfax. They are also informed that his will was written by the late Gabriel Jones an eminent lawyer residing in Rockingham, who transacted his law business generally & who was also unacquainted with the said Bryan Fairfax or his family.

J MARSHALL
Js MARSHALL

Fauquier county to wit John Marshall and James Marshall appeared before me a Magistrate for the county aforesaid this 24 day of August 1826 & made oath that the allegations of the foregoing amended answer so far as they are stated to be made on their own knowledge are true and so far as they are stated to be made on the knowledge of others they beleive them to be true

TH. M. AMBLER

ADS, Catlett v. Marshall, Frederick County Superior Court of Chancery, Ended Cases, 1828–016, Vi. Entirely in JM's hand except for signatures of James Marshall and magistrate Thomas M. Ambler. Endorsed as filed 23 Oct. 1826.

1. The amended answer was a response to a further allegation in the Catletts' bill stating that Lord Fairfax long before the making and publication of his will had been "on habits &

terms of friendly intimacy and acquaintance with the said Bryan Fairfax & that he well knew that both the first & second children of Bryan Fairfax were sons" (bill in chancery [filed Mar. 1826], Catlett v. Marshall). The given names of the Catletts were inserted in another hand.

To James Barbour

Dear Sir   Richmond Septr. 7th. 1826

I have been applied to by two of my Nephews to recommend them to you for admission into the seminary at West Point. One is Alexander Keith Marshall the son of Doctor Marshall of Kentucky,[1] and the other Humphry Marshall jr.[2] the son of Mr. John James Marshall of Ohio.[3] Both these young gentleman are of the proper age, and have received the preliminary education which fits them for reception into the institution.

It is with no inconsiderable repugnance that I add to the disagreeable perplexities of office by increasing the number of applicants who are already too numerous to be satisfied. But these young gentlemen have claims upon me which I cannot resist without being thought unkind; and I have informed them that it will be expected that their application should be supported by the members from their respective states or some of them. With great respect & esteem, I am dear Sir your Obedt

J MARSHALL

ALS, RG 94, DNA. Addressed to Barbour in Washington and franked; postmarked Richmond, 9 Sept. Several endorsements in different hands.

1. Alexander Keith Marshall (1808–1884), son of Louis Marshall, apparently did not attend the military academy. He studied medicine and graduated from the medical department of the University of Pennsylvania in 1844. Settling in Nicholasville, he practiced medicine and engaged in politics. He served one term (1855–57) in the House of Representatives as a member of the American, or Know-Nothing, Party.

2. Humphrey Marshall, Jr. (1812–1872), entered the military academy in 1828 and graduated in 1832. The next year he resigned his commission and took up the practice of law, first in Frankfort and then in Louisville. After serving in the Mexican War, he was elected to Congress and sat in the House of Representatives as a Whig from 1849 to 1852 and as a member of the Know-Nothing Party from 1855 to 1859.

3. John James Marshall (1785–1846), son of Humphrey Marshall, may have lived briefly in Ohio, but at the time he resided in Frankfort, Ky. In the margin Barbour or a clerk placed an asterisk and noted at the bottom of the page: "His father says Kentucky, or rather heads his letter Frankford." This is a reference to John J. Marshall's letter to Barbour, 6 Oct. 1826, recommending his son as a candidate for West Point. John J. Marshall served in the Kentucky state senate from 1820 to 1824 and as judge of the Louisville Circuit Court from 1836 to 1846. He also published seven volumes of Kentucky law reports (John J. Marshall to James Barbour, 6 Oct. 1826 [file of Humphrey Marshall], RG 94, DNA; Paxton, *Marshall Family*, 184).

From Augustine Smith, Jr.

Dear Sir[1]   Paris[2] 9th Septr. 1826

I here with send you the lists of Annual rents promised you on your return from over the ridge.[3] I carried them to our last court expecting to have met with you there. I received your letter of the 1st Instant[4] on the receip⟨t of w⟩hich I applied to Mr. George Morehead for the Amount you paid my brother Thomas for him he could not inform me I then Applied to my brother who said he had no account of it.[5] I am now in this place for the purpose of seeing Mr. Murry the Sheriff who had the Execution against Mr. Morehead and find⟨ing⟩ the Amount paid on the 28th day of April 1823 $700.00 of which I paid you $560.0⟨o⟩ the contents of your letter of the 28th of last month shall be attended to.[6] I am dear Sir with much respect, yours &c

AUGUSTINE SMITH JR.

ALS, Collection of the late Mrs. James R. Green, Markham, Va. Addressed to "Genl. John Marshall" in Richmond; postmarked Paris, Va., 9 Sept. Endorsed by JM. Text of letter written below list of rents.

1. Augustine Smith, Jr., was one of the lessees on the list of rents (see n. 3). He was probably a descendant (son or grandson) of the Augustine Smith who married Ann Marshall, JM's aunt (Paxton, *Marshall Family,* 17–18, 36–37; Robert Adams Gaebler, ed., "Descendants of John Adams and Elizabeth Naylor of Charles County, Maryland" [typescript, Fauquier Heritage Society, Marshall, Va., 1984], 9).

2. The town of Paris is in the extreme northwest corner of Fauquier County.

3. This was a "list of Anual Rents due Genl. John Marshall betwen Buck and cobler mountains." It listed the names of the lessees on twenty-two lots of land in Leeds Manor, the acreage, annual rent, and month due.

4. Letter not found.

5. On this business, see *PJM,* IX, 271, 272 n. 2; Articles of Agreement, 9 Sept. 1825 (App. II, Cal.).

6. Letter not found.

To [Samuel] Fay

Dear Sir[1]   Richmond Septr. 15th. 1826

I received a letter from my son Edward, soon after his last arrival in Cambridge, informing me that his addresses to your daughter had been favorably received by her, and that he had been so fortunate as to obtain the approbation of her parents. A second letter written immediately on his return to Virginia repeats this information.[2]

I had feared that the almost entire separation of miss Fay from her natural friends and all the companions of her youth, wou'd be too great a sacrifice to be made; and, if made, would produce permanent unhappiness. That she has been induced to make it chearfully is the best proof of that sincere affection which is I am persuaded, when mutual, the never failing source of feli[c]ity to those who are united under its influence.

My sons situation is far from being splendid, but I hope to make it comfortable with proper exertions on his part; and though he will reside in the country, the neighborhood is far from being ineligible. His wife must be an economist, & will I trust find her truest happiness at home!

I write to assure you of the satisfaction with which I look forward to my sons connexion with a young lady whom he describes as entitled to the strongest sentiments of love and esteem; and that she will be received by his mother and myself as our own daughter, and with that parental affection which is the best though an inadequate substitute for the deep loss she will sustain in parting from Mrs. Fay & yourself. I can promise too for my other sons in the midst of whom Edward will be settled, and for their wives, that she will receive the most affectionate and cordial welcome.

Have the goodness to present Mrs. Marshall's compliments & my own to Mrs. Fay & our future daughter, and to believe that I am with great respect, your obedt

J MARSHALL

ALS (draft), Marshall Papers, ViW. Addressed to Fay in Cambridge, Mass.

1. JM omitted Fay's given name in his address, but the recipient was undoubtedly Samuel Prescott Phillips Fay (1778–1856), judge of the probate court for Middlesex County and a close friend of Joseph Story. He had been a member of the convention for revising the Massachusetts Constitution in 1820 and for many years served on the Board of Overseers of Harvard College. He was married to Harriet Howard, with whom he had eloped in 1801 (Orlin P. Fay, *Fay Genealogy: John Fay of Marlborough and His Descendants* [Cleveland, Ohio, 1898], 68; Christina Hopkinson Baker, *The Story of Fay House* [Cambridge, Mass., 1929], 53–56, 88).

2. Letters not found. The Fays' eldest daughter, Harriet Howard Fay (1810–1885), was a noted beauty who attracted the attentions of the young men of Cambridge. To Oliver Wendell Holmes, a schoolmate, she was " 'the golden blonde.' " "Her abounding natural curls were so full of sunshine, her skin was so delicately white, her smile and her voice were so all-subduing, that half our heads were turned" Her Cambridge neighbor and friend was Margaret Fuller (1810–1850), who later earned literary fame (Fay, *Fay Genealogy,* 68; Baker, *The Story of Fay House,* 64–65; Robert N. Hudspeth, ed., *The Letters of Margaret Fuller. Volume I, 1817–1838* [Ithaca, N.Y., 1983], 31, 129 n., 133, 134 n.).

To James Barbour

Dear Sir   Richmond Septr. 18th. 26

I have received the papers which are herewith transmitted from Colo. Eaton with a request that I would annex to the affidavit such certificate as my memory would enable me to give & forward the papers to you.[1]

He states accurately the company & Regiment to which he says he belonged. The officers were recruiting when he says he enlisted, & the company marched about the time he mentions to Philadelphia whence it marched with some other companies belonging to the same regiment to Princeton.[2]

I am the only surviving officer of the company. I commanded it at & sometime before the time he mentions.

I have a decided impression that there was a soldier in the company named Krystar or Christie, but have no recollection of his christian name.[3] If this information will be of any service to the applicant whom I really believe to have been a soldier in the company I am ready to depose to it. I am dear Sir with great respect, Your obedt

J MARSHALL

[Certificate]

A young man of the name of Krystar or Christie as he was called to the best of my recolle⟨c⟩tion enlisted in the county of Fauquier in Virginia in the fall or in December of the year 1776 in the company commanded by Capt. William Blackwell in the 11th. Virginia Regiment of which Colo. Daniel Morgan was Colonel, Christian Febiger Lieutenant Colonel and William Heth Major. I was then first Lieutenant in the company & soon afterwards commanded it. Every other officer in it is dead & has been dead for some time. Lieutenant James Wright, the survivor of them died three or four years past. The company marched to Philadelphia in the winter, I think in January 1777, and, joind with some other companies of the Regiment marched in the Spring, in March, to Princeton. All the soldiers of the company, and Krystar or Christie with the rest, enlisted for three years or during the war.

I cannot be positive that such a person was in the company, but his name rests in my memory so as to leave as strong an impression as I can have respecting a soldier who never attracted my particular attention, that he was in the company. I believe firmly that he was, and my belief is founded on my recollection.

I have no doubt that he served till regularly discharged.[4]

J MARSHALL
LATE A CAPTAIN IN THE 11TH. VIRGA.
REGT. ON CONTINENTAL ESTABLISHMENT

ALS, RG 15, DNA. Endorsed (by Barbour?) as received 28 Sept.

1. "Col. Eaton" was probably John H. Eaton (1790–1856), then serving in the U.S. Senate from Tennessee. He was a resident of Williamson County, which was the home of John Krytsar, the Revolutionary war veteran whose affidavit was sent to JM. Eaton's covering letter to JM has not been found.

2. Krytsar sought a pension under the act of Congress of 18 Mar. 1818. His affidavit, sworn on 10 Jan. 1826 in the Williamson County Court of Pleas and Quarter Sessions, gives a full account of his military service (pension file of John Krytsar, RG 15, DNA).

3. Muster rolls and payrolls variously record his name as Critser, Cretser, and Crytser (*PJM*, I, 7, 8, 10, 13, 16, 28).

4. An endorsement on Krytsar's file indicates that he was admitted to the pension list (pension file of John Krytsar, RG 15, DNA).

To Bushrod Washington

My dear Sir   Richmond Septr. 28 26

I am satisfied from the enquiries my friends have made for me that The Calm Observer, if ever published in a pamphlet, is no longer to be found in that form. Mr. Hopkinson was kind enough to make the enquiry for me and to communicate the result. In my answer acknowledging the receipt of his letter I requested him to look into the files of the Aurora & to let me know the date of the first & of the last number. He has never noticed this letter, & I have suspect[1] that it has miscarried. This leaves me under some embarassment because if he has received the letter my writing to him again might bear the appearance of impatience at his not attending to my request; & if he has not received it, the appearance will be that I have neglected a letter written by him on my own affairs, and in some measure requiring an answer. Will you my dear Sir have the goodness to inspect the files of the Aurora for the summer of 1796 & note for my use the dates of the first & last number of the Calm Observer. I should be glad to have a number which charges General Washington with peculation or drawing money improperly, copied & the date of the paper from which it is taken noted, & will thank you if convenient to pay for copying it. I am dear Sir truely yours

J MARSHALL

ALS, Marshall Papers, DLC. Addressed to Washington in Philadelphia; postmarked Richmond, 28 Sept. Endorsed by Washington.

1. JM originally wrote "suspected." In deleting the "ed," he forgot to delete "have."

From Richard Peters, Jr.

Dr Sir   Phila. Sepr 30 1826

It has been said and it is believed that Mr Wheaton will be appointed District Judge of the Southern District of New York in which Event the place of Reporter of the Supreme Court will be vacant.[1]

Will you allow me Sir to present myself for your Consideration for the Situant should the vacancy occur. Having for seven years been engaged in the publication of the decisions of the Circuit Court here, I claim a knowledge of the duties which will be imposed upon me, and I trust that with the protecting aid of the Court I can perform them to their Satisfaction and that of the Bar.

I take the liberty to Enclose a letter to you upon this Subject from my father, who has ever felt towards you the warmest regard & the highest respect. With the Highest Confident, I am, your ob st

R. P.

ALS (draft), Cadwalader Collection, PHi. Inside address to JM. Endorsed by Peters.

1. Richard Peters, Jr. (1779–1848), was actively campaigning to succeed Wheaton as Supreme Court reporter. Wheaton did not obtain the federal judgeship but eventually resigned in 1827 after receiving a diplomatic appointment. Peters assumed the duties of reporter at the beginning of the 1828 term and served through the 1842 term (G. Edward White, *The Marshall Court and Cultural Change, 1815–35,* the Oliver Wendell Holmes Devise History of the Supreme Court of the United States, III–IV [New York, 1988], 404–7).

To Richard Peters

Dear Sir   Richmond October 2d. 1826

I received today your letter of the 29th. communicating the wish of your son to succeed Mr. Wheaton as Reporter of the Supreme Court in the event of the removal of that gentleman to a more eligible situation.[1] Your son may be assured of my cordial support. I have received letters on the same subject from my brother Washington & your son.[2] I communicate my answer to you in preference because it furnishes me once more with the opportunity of adding that I am with the truest respect & esteem, Your Obedt

J MARSHALL

ALS, Peters Papers, PHi. Addressed to Peters in Philadelphia; postmarked Richmond, 3 Oct. Endorsed by Peters.

1. Letter not found.
2. Letter from Bushrod Washington not found.

To Martin P. Marshall

My dear Nephew   Richmond Oct. 10th. 1826

Your letter of the 25th. of September has just reached me, & shows me that I have to reproach myself for neglecting to answer your former letter respecting your contract with my sister.[1] If I had felt any delicacy in expressing my opinion in answer to your enquiry I ought to have told you so, & this would certainly have been my course had such been the fact.

But the truth is that I received your letter a short time before my journey to North Carolina & I deferred answering it until I could have some communication with my sister. I called on her in Petersburg & mentioned the contests respecting the title & her consequent liability to refund, with the determination to inform you of the result on my return. The circuit court at this place commences on my return from North Carolina, & I became immediately so engaged that I forgot your business. When my official duties had passed away & I reflected on other matters I really thought I had written to you. This is one of the effects of age. We very often confound what we have determined to do with what we have done, and remembering the resolution think it is executed. I am sorry that this has happened in the present instance.

My sister is unwilling to receive money which she would be liable to refund, & as I believe her expenses equal her receipts, I am sure that she would find repayment very inconvenient. At any rate it would produce unpleasant feelings which neither of you would wish. She would however, I am sure repay were she to live, but should she die I am not sure that some difficulty might not occur. I had intended to mention to you an investment of the money in stock. This would undoubtedly be exposed to some slight hazard as there is some fluctuation in the price, but the banks of this place are believed to be solid, & as you would not be compelled to sell when any casual depression might take place, I think there would not be much danger of serious loss, not at any rate a loss equivalent to the accumulation of interest. I shall see my sister again in November & will again converse with her on the subject and write to you when my deposition is sent out which I shall undoubtedly give as you request.

I wish you would let me know what you think of making this investment. If you approve I can purchase the stock for you as opportunities occur either in your own name or in my own as trustee for you. At any rate my sister would not wish you to pay any money to her agent. It would be charging her unnecessarily with commissions which would be very inconvenient in the event of refunding & be attended with other disadvantages.

You have never said whether the money Mr. Marshall received from Colo. Davies was included in your settlement with him, nor how much he has received.[2] It ought to be a considerable sum & I had supposed he was my debtor on this account. I wish you would mention this subject in your next letter. I will thank you also to say some thing about my sister Pollard.[3] I remitted to my Nephew John[4] 100$ for her & requested that he would draw on me for such farther small sums as he might think reasona⟨bly pro⟩per for her particular situation but I have never heard farther from him. I have great demands on my purse in this country, but I would not neglect my sister if I could serve her when in real want.

We are informed in the papers that the sound party in Kentucky have proved successful at the elections but I have not heard what has been your fate.[5]

JANE MARSHALL TAYLOR
Oil on canvas, artist unknown, ca. 1830. *Courtesy of the Association for Preservation of Virginia Antiquities.*

Your Aunt whose health continues very feeble, sends her love to you & joins me in the same message to our niece.[6] I am my dear Nephew your affectionate Uncle

J MARSHALL

I do not recollect what place in Ohio my Nephew John has removed

ALS (advertised for sale by John Reznikoff, University Archives, Stamford, Conn., 1992). Addressed to Marshall in Flemingsburg, Ky.; postmarked Richmond, 10 Oct. (?).

1. Letters not found. The "sister" was Jane Marshall Taylor.
2. The reference is to Humphrey Marshall and the late Joseph Hamilton Daveiss. On this business, see *PJM*, VIII, 315–16, 364; IX, 62, 241–42.
3. Nancy Marshall Pollard (b. ca. 1781), wife of William Pollard, was previously married to Daveiss (Paxton, *Marshall Family*, 78).
4. John J. Marshall.
5. Marshall then represented Fleming County in the Kentucky legislature, having narrowly won election the previous year as an "Old Court" candidate. In the 1826 election, he lost out to two "New Court" candidates, though the returns as a whole favored the "Old Court" party (*Kentucky Reporter* [Lexington], 22, 29 Aug. 1825, 14 Aug. 1826; JM to Martin P. Marshall, 27 Dec. 1825 and n. 5).
6. Eliza Colston Marshall, wife of Martin Marshall.

To [Samuel] Fay

Dear Sir   Richmond Oct. 15th. 1826
Your letter reached me yesterday.[1] As it conveys a positive and deliberate rejection of my son it would of course terminate our correspondence did I not feel that my letter requires an apology.

It must have appeared very strange to you sir that, while your objections to a connexion between our famili⟨e⟩s remained immoveable, I should treat it —⟨ ⟩ to yourself, as an affair already arranged. I entreat you to believe that I am incapable of knowingly committing such an impropriety, and that I wrote under a total misunderstanding of the actual state of things. I have not seen Edward since May; but his letters to his mother & myself from Cambridge, and one from Alexandria on his return, state his reception with delight, and dwell on his expected union with the lady of his choice, in the language of a young man who sees nothing but felicity before him. He did not indeed say in terms that he had conversed with you and received expressly your consent to his marriage with your daughter, but every thing he said implied that all obstacles were removed, and that the event itself was certain, though the time was not fixed. I could not suppose it possible that he had left Cambridge under these impressions without full exp[l]anations with the Father of the lady he was addressing. Not doubting that you had viewed the attachment, which I then supposed to be mutual, between our children, with as

DRAFT OF LETTER TO SAMUEL FAY

Third page of draft letter to Samuel Fay, 15 October 1826. *Courtesy of the Department of Manuscripts and Rarebooks, Earl Gregg Swem Library, College of William and Mary.*

much indulgence as myself, my heart told me that, as no direct communication had ever been made by me, it could not be displeasing to a Father totally unacquainted with the connexions of the gentleman who was to marry his daughter, and to remove her to a great distance from her friends, to be assured that she would be received with cordial & tender affection by the family into which she was about to enter.

I hope Edward has received notice of your decision, and that it is made with the approbation of Mrs. & Miss Fay. It is kindness to awaken him as soon as possible from the dream of happiness in which he has been too long indulging.[2]

I am far from imputing blame to you or to Mrs. Fay for this misapprehension into which I have been led or for the pain my son will experience at the disappointment of his hopes. That tender solicitude which Parents must feel for their daughter gives them a right to reject the addresses of any man to whom they are unwilling to entrust her, and it is their duty to exercise this right whenever they believe its exercise necessary to her happiness. It is for themselves alone to judge of the correctness of the reasoning by which their minds are led to the conclusion; it is enough for others to know that such is their conclusion. But your objections have intrinsic weight and will be respected independent of their authority. They are such as I anticipated when first informed by my son that he meditated addressing a young lady in Cambridge. I felt the immense sacrifice she would make in leaving her friends to come with him to a land of strangers, and was convinced that misery would follow their marri⟨age⟩ unless warded off by deep rooted love for the person for whom it was made. Under this conviction, when I stated the repinings which this vast change of situation would probably produce, I required Edward should he prosecute his intentions, to disclose his real circumstances that the decision of the family might be made under no mistaken view of the situation in which their daughter would be placed. I wished it to be known that she would live in the country, not even in the neighbourhood of a town, and upon a farm which required industry & economy in its master.

It is not an empty compliment when I say that I am grieved to hear of the feeble state of health in which Miss Fay finds herself. I have accustomed myself to take an interest in what concerns her which I cannot instantly dismiss, and shall enquire respect[ing] her health with the sincere wish to hear that the threatening and obstinate symptoms of which you speak have yi[e]lded to medicine & exercise.[3] With compliments to Mrs. Fay and With great respect for yourself, I am Sir your Obedt

J M

ALS (draft), Marshall Papers, ViW.

1. Letter not found.

2. JM marked the preceding two sentences for insertion at this point, having written them at the end of the MS.

3. Edward C. Marshall married Rebecca Peyton (b. 1810), daughter of John Peyton and Mary Chiswell Lewis Peyton of Gloucester County, in 1829 (Horace Edwin Hayden, *Virginia Genealogies* . . . [Wilkes Barre, Pa., 1891], 478–79). Harriet Fay married William H. Greenough (1795–1854) of New York City in 1831. On the eve of her wedding she wrote to a friend that Greenough was "a gentleman of undisputed integrity and worth and who in all respects is agreeable to my family" (Orlin P. Fay, *Fay Genealogy: John Fay of Marlborough and His Descendants* [Cleveland, Ohio, 1898], 68; Harriet H. Fay to George C. Shattuck, 3 Dec. 1831, G. C. Shattuck Papers, MHi).

From Joseph Hopkinson

My dear Sir   Philad. Octob. 27. 1826
    I have got him at last. The first number of the "Calm Observer" was published in the Aurora of the 23. of *Octob. 1795* — addressed to O. Wolcott, Secretary of the Treasury. The last is on the 5. Nov. 1795 — being four in the whole. They all relate to the charge of an illegal payment of the Presidents Salary; which you know was elaborately and triumphantly answered by M Hamilton. M Wolcott also published a reply.[1]
    Be good enough to give me your further commands on this Subject. I believe these papers were not written by *Giles.*
    I regret to inform you that Judge Washington has been obliged to break up his court, on account of the State of his health. Mo. respectfuly, Yr
                                                    JOS. HOPKINSON

ALS, Marshall Papers, ViW. Addressed to JM in Richmond; postmarked Philadelphia, 27 Oct.

1. Hopkinson wrote the preceding sentence in the left margin.

To Charles Hammond

Dear Sir   Richmond Novr. 7th. 1826
    This will be presented to you by Mr. Price a young gentleman who has studied law in this place and purposes to pursue his profession in Ohio. His connexions are very respectable, & some of them are my particular friends. I, of course, take an interest in his success & shall feel obliged by your giving him as much of your countenance & aid as may comport with your views & situation. I trust they will not be bestowed on an individual who does not merit them. With great respect & esteem, I am your Obedt
                                                    J MARSHALL

ALS, OHi. Addressed to Hammond in Cincinnati. Endorsed by Hammond.

From [Joseph Kent]

Sir,   Annapolis 15th. Novr. 1826[1]

The death of Mr. Griffin has occasioned a vacancy in the Clerks Office of the Supreme Court of the U. States, to fill which I beg leave to recommend my friend and neighbour Colo. E⟨dmun⟩d B. Duvall.[2]

The Colo. had qualified here ⟨ . . . ⟩nd commenced the practice of the law for some time previous to the late war, at the commencement of which he enterd the military service of the Country & continued in it till peace took place, when he returnd to the Country & declined resuming it.

His habits of industry and methodical attention to whatever he undertakes, with his knowledge of business, peculiarly fit him for this appointment, and I have no doubt shou'd he succeed in his application, that the Court will find in him an able, efficient and obliging officer. With sentiments of high respect I have the honor to be

AL[S], RG 267, DNA. Addressed to JM in Richmond. MS mutilated owing to clipping of signature. Endorsed in unknown hand "Jos. Kent."

1. Joseph Kent (1779–1837) was then governor of Maryland, having recently resigned from the U.S. House of Representatives.

2. Edmund Bryce Duvall (d. 1831), son of Justice Gabriel Duvall, had served in the War of 1812 and represented Prince George's County in the Maryland House of Delegates from 1823 to 1826. Duvall suffered from mental illness throughout the 1820s (William M. Marine, *The British Invasion of Maryland, 1812–1815.* Appendix by Louis Henry Dielman [Hatboro, Pa., 1965], 274; Edward C. Papenfuse, et al., eds., *An Historical List of Public Officials of Maryland,* I [Annapolis, Md., 1990], 238; G. Edward White, *The Marshall Court and Cultural Change, 1815–35,* the Oliver Wendell Holmes Devise History of the Supreme Court of the United States, III–IV [New York, 1988], 324–25).

From [James Boon?]

D Sir   Chester Town 18 Nov. 1826

With great deference I beg leave to recommend to your favorable notice the pretensions of my Friend Ed: B Duval Esq. who will be an applicant for the Clerkship of the Supreme Court.[1]

A personal acquaintance with Mr. Duval for several years in the course of which we were fellow-members of the Maryland Legislature has convinced me of his just claims to the high consideration which he sustains amongst his Friends both as a man of intelligence & of exemplary deportment as a gentleman.

Should the Court confer upon him the appointment he solicits the most confident anticipations may I think be indulged that the duties of the Office will be so accurately & industriously discharged as to elicit from the Court & all others having connexion with it the expression of perfect & entire satisfaction.

My solicitude for the advancement of an individual of great merit & the full persuasion that his appointment will secure the services of a valuable officer must plead my apology for this expression of my opinions

AL[S], RG 267, DNA. Addressed to JM in Richmond. Signature clipped.

1. The writer may have been James Boon, a legislator from Kent County whose service overlapped with Duvall's (Edward C. Papenfuse, et al., eds., *An Historical List of Public Officials of Maryland* [Annapolis, Md., 1990], 226).

To Joseph Hopkinson

My dear Sir   Richmond Novr 24th 1826

I had the pleasure of receiving the day on which I commenced my journey to North Carolina your letter informing me that you had at length found the Calm Observer. I postponed making my acknowledgements till my return which did not take place until the night of the 21st. & the Cir court at this place commenced on the 22d. *Voila* my apology for not returning earlier my thanks for the very kind exertions you have made to find a series of essays to which I wish to refer particularly. I never suspected Mr. Giles of being their author. They do not bear his mark, and they were at the time ascribed to Mr. Beckley. My reason for wishing to refer particularly to them is that Mr. Giles has in a card in the Richmond Enquirer made some references to myself which I think not perfectly civil and allusions to the slander on the President for anticipations of his salary which in my opinion misrepresent the publication containing the charge. In that card Mr. Giles has exposed himself to the suspicion of being in a conspiracy for the fabrication of the attack though he did not himself make it. I am desirous of procuring the letter of General Hamilton which you mention, and have searched my broken files of the gazette of the United States for it but cannot find it. If I did not fear to trespass too much on your kindness I would ask a copy of it. I recollect that it put an end to the Calm Observer & was I thought at the time a full vindication of President Washington from the malignant charge made in the Aurora; but I have lost it.

I was gratified highly by receiving on my return from Raleigh your oration in Philadelphia before your law academy.[1] I have read it with great pleasure, & wish the sentiments it contains & inculcates were universally felt by students & acted on by the whole profession.

I am tolerably busy with the court & therefore will only add that I have received today your letter enquiring into the safe arrival of that making your communications respecting the Calm Observer[2] and that I am with respectful & affectionate esteem, Your Obedt

J MARSHALL

ALS, Hopkinson Papers, PHi. Addressed to Hopkinson in Philadelphia; postmarked Richmond, 24 Nov.

1. Joseph Hopkinson, *An Address Delivered before the Law Academy of Philadelphia, at the Opening of the Session of 1826–7* (Philadelphia, 1826). Hopkinson, vice provost of the academy, delivered this address on 2 Nov. 1826.

2. Letter not found.

To Joseph Story

MY DEAR SIR: Richmond, November 26th, 1826.

I have deferred thanking you for the copy of your Discourse before the Society of Phi Beta Kappa, until there was some probability that my letter might find you at Salem. . . .[1]

But it is time to return to your discourse. I have read it with real pleasure, and am particularly gratified with your eulogy on the ladies. It is matter of great satisfaction to me to find another Judge, who, though not as old as myself, thinks justly of the fair sex, and commits his sentiments to print. I was a little mortified, however, to find that you had not admitted the name of Miss Austen into your list of favorites.[2] I had just finished reading her novels when I received your discourse, and was so much pleased with them that I looked in it for her name, and was rather disappointed at not finding it. Her flights are not lofty, she does not soar on eagle's wings, but she is pleasing, interesting, equable, and yet amusing. I count on your making some apology for this omission. . . . Farewell. With esteem and affection, I am yours,

J. MARSHALL.

Printed, William W. Story, ed., *Life and Letters of Joseph Story,* I (Boston, 1851), 505–6.

1. Joseph Story, *A Discourse Pronounced before the Phi Beta Kappa Society, at the Anniversary Celebration, on the Thirty First Day of August 1826* (Boston, 1826), reprinted in William Story, ed., *The Miscellaneous Writings of Joseph Story* (1852; New York, 1972 reprint), 340–78.

2. Story's list of female authors included Elizabeth Smith, Elizabeth Carter, Hannah More, Anna Letitia Aikin Barbauld, Lucy Aikin (niece of Mrs. Barbauld), Frances Burney (Madame D'Arblay), Ann Ward Radcliffe, Felicia Dorothea Browne Hemans, and Maria Edgeworth (Story, ed., *Miscellaneous Writings of Joseph Story,* 350).

From Jared Sparks

[1 December 1826]

On the following pages you will find a copy of a letter which I wrote some weeks ago to Judge Washington. He informs me that he has written to consult you on the proposal therein contained; and as I have thought it possible that it might not occur to him to send you a copy of the letter, I take the liberty to forward it for your consideration.[1]

Since I saw you in Richmond, I have visited all the old States, and carefully examined the public offices in each, and procured copies of all the important papers relating to the Revolution, and, among others, all the letters of General Washington. I have also had access to the papers of many of the officers of the army, among whom are Sullivan, Lord Stirling, Steuben, Clinton, Lincoln, and I am now busily engaged, with a copyist constantly employed in pursuing my investigations. In most cases I am favored with the loan of all papers not contained in public offices, which I retain till I have examined them thoroughly, and taken copies of all that are important. I shall pursue this through all the Revolutionary papers in the country to which I can obtain access, and I have not yet met one instance in which this was not cheerfully granted. Among the masses of papers which have already passed through my hands, I have of course found great numbers of General Washington's letters. My success, in short, has been such that I have resolved to execute an edition of his works in as perfect a manner as I can, and to use the materials I am collecting in making appropriate illustrations.

I need not repeat to you how important it will be to the entire success of the undertaking, for me to have the use of the papers in Judge Washington's possession. My views on this subject you will see in the letter annexed. As I know Judge Washington has entire confidence in your judgment, I cannot but hope that you will see the thing in the same light as myself, and will encourage him to accept the proposal which I have made. This offer is in itself a highly liberal one, especially considering the vast pains I have taken in collecting materials from other quarters.

Feeling assured that you will cordially promote this object, as far as you will think it consistent with all the merits of the case, I am . . .

Printed, Herbert B. Adams, *The Life and Writings of Jared Sparks, Comprising Selections from His Journals and Correspondence* (2 vols.; Boston and New York, 1893), I, 410–11.

1. Sparks to Bushrod Washington, 12 Sept. 1826; Washington to Sparks, 24 Nov. 1826 (ibid., I, 406–10). Undeterred by Washington's previous refusal to provide access to the Mount Vernon papers, Sparks renewed his appeal for cooperation, offering an equal division of the property of the copyright and of the profits of sale.

To Jared Sparks

Sir   Richmond Decr. 10th 1826

Your letter of the 1st. inst. reached me yesterday just as I was on my way to court. Mr. Washington had previously communicated your proposal to me, & I had instantly advised his acceptance of it.[1] I cannot doubt your having received a letter from him on the subject early in this month.

I have always believed that the correspondence of General Washington would appear to more advantage if published according to your views of the subject, under the superintendence of a gentleman who can devote a sufficient portion of his time to the work and is qualified to do it justice. Neither Judge Washington nor myself were in a situation to do this, and his purpose did not extend beyond a selection and a publication of the letters selected unaccompanied by comment or notes of any description. I wish you all the success you anticipate and am with great respect and esteem, Your obedt

J MARSHALL

ALS, Sparks Papers, MH. Addressed to Sparks in Boston; postmarked Richmond, 11 Dec. Endorsed by Sparks.

1. In his letter to Sparks of 24 Nov. 1826, Washington indicated that he would write to JM on the same day. This letter has not been found. JM answered Washington's letter immediately on receiving it (as he later explained), but his reply miscarried (Herbert B. Adams, *The Life and Writings of Jared Sparks, Comprising Selections from His Journals and Correspondence* [2 vols.; Boston and New York, 1893], I, 409–10; JM to Washington, 27 Dec. 1826).

Gallego v. Gallego's Executor
Opinion
U.S. Circuit Court, Virginia, 11 December 1826

Manuela Grivegnee Gallego, a Spanish subject and wife of Henry Newman, sued by her next friend for the full share of a legacy bequeathed by her uncle, the late Richmond merchant Joseph Gallego. Newman had according to Spanish law formally renounced his marital right to this legacy and conferred full power on her to receive the legacy and to hold it to her own separate use. Peter J. Chevallié (1791–1837), executor and principal heir of Joseph Gallego, withheld payment of this legacy because Newman owed $2,000 to Gallego's estate and because of a pending suit in the state Superior Court of Chancery to attach so much of the legacy to satisfy a debt of $1,600 owed by Newman. The case was argued on 7 June 1826, when Marshall decreed in part that the plaintiff should be paid the surplus of the legacy over and above the two debts owed by Newman. The court left for future consideration the questions whether the sum of $2,000 should be deducted from the legacy and whether the sum of $1,600 was liable to be attached. Marshall's opinion of 11 December 1826 accompanied an interlocutory decree that decided the first of these questions (bill in chancery; answer of Peter J. Chevallié, 15 May 1826, Gallego v. Chevallié, U.S. Cir. Ct., Va., Ended Cases [Unrestored, 1829], Vi; U.S. Cir. Ct., Va., Ord. Bk. XII, 110–11, 133–34; *Richmond Portraits*, 39).

Manuela Grivignie y Galliego wife of Henry Newman by her next friend

v

Peter J. Chevallie surviving exr. of Joseph Galliego decd.

¶1   The plaintiff who resides in Spain, claims a legacy bequeathed to her by Joseph Galliego decd.

¶2   The Exr. admits assetts, and submits the question to the court whether the plaintiff as a married woman can properly demand this legacy:

¶3   The demand is supported by an instrument of writing executed by the husband, in which he transfers all his marital rights in this legacy to his wife, and gives her full authority to receive it. Under these circumstances the course of a court of equity is to sustain the bill of a married woman brought by her next friend, and to decree that the legacy shall be paid to herself.

¶4   But, admitting her right to sue, the exr. contends that her husband was indebted to his testator, & that this debt ought to be deducted from the legacy. He also says that a creditor of the husband has attached a part of this money in his hands in the court of the state, and he submits it to the court to say whether he is not bound to retain a sum sufficient to answer this demand.

¶5   This defence makes it necessary to enquire into the right of the husband to a legacy bequeathed to his wife, and into the rights of the creditors of the husband to such legacy.

¶6   The common law of England identifies the wife so entirely with her husband as scarcely to tolerate the idea of her separate existence while they live together. She cannot acquire personal property by a direct conveyance to herself. Her interest is by act of law in almost every instance, transferred to her husband and becomes vested in him. But this rule does not apply to personal estate to which a female is entitled before marriage and which has not been reduced to possession. This remains her property, and does not vest in the husband by the marriage. The marital right does not extend to the property while a chose in action, but enables the husband to reduce it to possession, and thereby to acquire it.[1] The property becomes his, not upon the marriage, but on the fact of his obtaining possession.

¶7   The right of the legatee does not originate in the common law, and is not governed by the old rule which disables the wife from taking for her own benefit. It is a right which cannot be asserted at common law, and can be sustained only in a court of equity. The personal estate of the testator vests in the exr. for the payment of debts, who is a trustee for the legatee, after the primary trust for creditors shall be satisfied. As courts of equity grew up under the controul of civilians they have adopted the principles of the civil law which views the rights of married women with much more liberality than the common law. Legacies therefore bequeathed to a married woman have never been classed with conveyances at common law, but with choses in action, and vest an equity in the wife herself, in which the husband participates so far only as to assert her title in a court of equity. The property does not become his, nor is it subject to the liabilities which attach to that which is his, until it shall be reduced to possession. Til then, his creditors have no claim to it. If he dies living the wife, before reducing it to possession, his power is not transmissible to his representatives, but dies with him. Since the claim of the creditor extends only to the property of the debtor, it cannot reach a legacy until it becomes his property. It follows then not only because meer rights cannot be taken in execution without the aid of some special legislative provision, but because also there is no title in the husband to the thing itself, that a legacy not reduced to possession is not liable for his debts. Can a court of equity subject it to them.

The books furnish no case in which this naked question has been ¶8 brought before a court. This is of itself a strong, we think a conclusive argument against the right. That a creditor has never applied to a court of chancery to interpose in his favour and subject the choses in action, or the equitable rights of the wife to his claim against the husband demonstrates the universality of the opinion that equity affords no aid in such a case. It is true that the assignees of a Bankrupt are permitted to assert this right. But it is equally true that they represent the Bankrupt as well as his creditors, and that all the marital rights of the husband are transferred to them. When they come into a court of equity asserting a claim on the equitable interests of the wife, they exercise the marital right to reduce those interests to possession, not any preexisting right of the creditors. In such a case the court grants its aid on such conditions as its own rules prescribe, and will never permit the husband or his assignees to receive the property of the wife but on such terms, on making out of it for herself & children, such provision as, on a view of all the circumstances of the case, may be deemed equitable. This uniform course of a court of equity would be incompatible with a previously existing right in the creditors. This rule has never been recognized so far as we are informed in the courts of Virginia; but it has never been denied, & we can conceive no principle on which it should be denied. That those who ask equity should do equity is a fundamental principle of that court which enters into, and mingles with all its decisions; & that the property of a married woman should not be taken from her without making some provision for her, is as equitable in Virginia as elsewhere. Our statute of distributions does not we think alter the case, by making the husband a purchaser of equitable interests which may come to the wife during marriage.[2] We can find no case in which a husband has been considered as a purchaser of the equitable interests or *choses in action* of the wife without some specific agreement by which he becomes so; and the act of assembly contains no declaration to that effect. It would be unreasonable to put this construction on it by implication because the consideration supposed to be given by law for her estate remains in the power of the husband. The court of Chancery will not enable a Freeman of London to obtain the personal estate of his wife without a settlement on her.[3] Suits have been brought to assert the marital right of reducing her property into possession, but in no case that we have seen has her equitable right for a maintenance been doubted. Were this a suit by the husband & wife for her legacy, the court would, certainly on the application of the wife, in England without such application, direct a reasonable provision for her maintainance. As this case stands, the husband has relinquished his marital rights in this subject, and the question is whether a court of equity will disregard, or controul this relinquishment in favour of creditors. As a general question, we can find no precedent for doing so. The husband has no interest in the legacy; he has only a power to make it his by reducing it to possession. Till this power be exercised, the property remains hers. We can find no case in which creditors have required the aid of the court to compel the husband to reduce it to possession, or in which a court has restrained the effect of a previous relinquishment of this marital right on the part of the husband. As a general proposition we should consider this relinquishment valid against creditors; and if it is not so on the present occasion, its invalidity must be produced by the particular circumstances of the case.

¶9   What are those circumstances?

¶10   In August 1814 Henry Newman, the husband of the plaintiff drew bills on Joseph Galliego the testator for $2000 and at the same time addressed a letter to him soliciting his acceptance of them and promising repayment.[4] These bills with the letter of Mr. Newmann were presented to Mr. Galliego in Baltimore in June 1815, who accepted them & made arrangements for their payment in Richmond. He communicated the transaction to Mr. Poitou his partner in this place, in a letter which contains this sentence "Be so good as to debit Mr. Henry Newmann senr. to notes payable for the sake of form, and that the amount may appear against him or his heirs when I am no more to be deducted out of the share coming to the family."[5]

¶11   It also appears that this debt was charged to Newmann on the books of the testator, and remained on his books till his death. His will was made in the year 1818.[6]

¶12   Some objection was made to the admission of the letter from Mr. Galliego to Mr. Poitou, the plaintiff considering it as irrelevant, since parol & extrinsic testimony cannot affect the construction of the will.

¶13   It is undoubtedly true that this letter cannot affect the construction of the will, nor does the court look in to it with that view. If it has any bearing on the question under consideration, it is on an entirely distinct part of it.

¶14   Although the legacy given to the wife does not become the property of the husband unless reduced to possession, yet he has a right to reduce it to possession, and may demand the aid of a court of equity for that purpose, which aid will be afforded as of course, unless the court be restrained from affording it by considerations which are never disregarded. These considerations are extrinsic of the will, and depend on parol testimony. Such testimony must be admitted for this purpose. In cases where the husband does not voluntarily relinquish his claim to a legacy bequeathed to his wife, but asserts that claim in equity, if a distinct claim be also asserted for the wife, the court does not, as a matter of course, settle the whole on the wife as her separate property, but secures the whole or part of it to her, according to circumstances. Where, as in this case, the husband voluntarily relinquishes his marital rights, the court will undoubtedly sustain that relinquishment unless it be made in fraud of the rights of others.

¶15 In this case there is reason to beleive that the husband is insolvent, and that he has relinquished to his wife that she may receive & enjoy the legacy bequeathed to her secured from his creditors. In this there is no injustice. His creditors trusted to his own resources for payment of their claims, & had no right to count on the fortune of Mrs. Galliego.[7] Creditors generally therefore cannot compel him to reduce the legacy of his wife to possession for their benefit. But the application of this rule to a creditor who is in rightful possession of the legacy, and has probably trusted the husband in the confidence that the means to secure repayment are in his own hands, is very much questioned. The relinquishment of the husband and the consequent separate claim of the wife may be considered as parts of the same transaction; and if the relinquishment was iniquitous, the claim so far as it depends on that relinquishment, cannot be supported. If it was perfectly clear that the testator at the time of making his will or at the time of his death intended this advance to the husband to be set off against the legacy to the wife, the court would feel great difficulty in disappointing such intention. But this is not perfectly clear. The debt is due from Newmann, the legacy is given not to him but to his wife. The debt therefore may still exist, & yet not be a set off against the legacy. Had the money been advanced subsequent to the date of the will there would have been more reason for considering it as satisfaction in part for the legacy; but even then it would not necessarily be so considered.[8] But this advance being made anterior to the will gives countenance to the opinion that the testator did not intend it as a deduction from the legacy. The will being subsequent and to a different person furnishes probability to the opinion that if a provision for the debt had been in the mind of the testator, his will would have given some indication of his intention respecting it. It is also a consideration not to be disregarded that the fund out of which this legacy is to be paid does not comprehend the debt due from Newmann.

¶16 The circumstances of the parties, and indeed the two letters introduced into the cause lead to the opinion that the testator made frequent advances to his relations and that this particular advance might not be in his mind when his will was made.

¶17   The court does not perceive in the case any satisfactory evidence that equity ought to restrain the full operati⟨on⟩ of the instrument by which Henry Newman relinquishes his marital rights in this legacy to his wife, and is therefore of opinion that it ought to be allowed its full effect.[9]

AD, Marshall Judicial Opinions, PPAmP; printed, John W. Brockenbrough, *Reports of Cases Decided by the Honourable John Marshall . . .*, II (Philadelphia, 1837), 286–92. For JM's deletions and interlineations, see Textual Notes below.

1. *Chose in action* (thing in action) is a personal right not reduced into possession but is recoverable by a suit at law.

2. The reference is to the act concerning wills, distribution of intestates' estates, and the duty of executors and administrators, first enacted in 1785 (*Revised Code of Va.*, I, 382).

3. Adams v. Pierce, 3 P. Wms. 11, 24 Eng. Rep. 948 (Ch., 1724).

4. Henry Newman to Joseph Gallego, 9 Aug. 1814, Gallego v. Chevallié (in Spanish, with English translation).

5. Extract of letter from Joseph Gallego to Michael B. Poitiaux, 27 June 1815, ibid.

6. In his answer, Chevallié stated he was ready to produce Newman's bills at the trial and that it appeared by his testator's books that they were charged as a debt (answer of Peter J. Chevallié, 15 May 1826, ibid.).

7. JM should have said Mrs. Newman.

8. Shudal v. Jekyll, 2 Atk. 516, 26 Eng. Rep. 710 (Ch., 1742).

9. The court accordingly ordered Chevallié to pay the additional sum of $2,000 to the plaintiff, leaving open the question of whether the sum of $1,600 attached in a pending suit in the state chancery court was to be deducted from the legacy. After the state chancery court in Jan. 1829 decreed that Chevallié pay the debt of $1,600 out of the legacy, the federal court on 29 May 1829 dismissed the plaintiff's bill as to that amount (U.S. Cir. Ct., Va., Ord. Bk. XII, 133–34, 300).

Textual Notes

¶ 1 l. 1   plaintiff ↑who resides in Spain,↓ claims
¶ 2 ll. 1–2   whether ↑the plaintiff↓ as a married woman ~~the legacy~~ can ~~be~~ properly demand ~~demanded by him~~ this legacy:
¶ 3 ll. 2–3   legacy to his ↑wife,↓ and
   ll. 4–5   equity is to ~~authorise~~ ↑sustain the bill of↓ a married woman ~~to . . .~~ ↑brought↓ by her
   ll. 5–6   and to ~~recover the property for her separate use~~ ↑decree that the legacy shall be paid to herself.↓
¶ 4 ll. 1–2   was indebted to ~~the~~ ↑his↓ testator, &
¶ 6 l. 4   by act of law ↑in almost every instance,↓ transferred
   ll. 5–6   But ~~the civil law pays more regard to the rights of the wife~~ ↑this rule does not apply to personal estate to which a female is entitled↓ before
   ll. 8–9   marital right ↑does not extend↓ ~~extends to not~~ to the property
   l. 11   but on ↑the fact of↓ his obtaining
¶ 7 ll. 5–6   legatee, after ~~debts shall~~ the primary
   l. 13   his, nor ~~become~~ ↑is it↓ subject to
   l. 14   attach to ~~the property~~ ↑that which is his,↓ until it
   l. 15   he dies ↑living the wife,↓ before
¶ 8 l. 1 beg.   ~~The books furnish no case in as to freeman 3 PW . . .~~ The books

l. 2	a court ~~of equity~~. This is
l. 2	a strong, ~~I~~ ↑we↓ think
l. 14	will never ~~direct~~ ↑permit↓ the
l. 19	so far as ~~I am~~ ↑we are↓ informed
l. 20	denied, & ~~I~~ ↑we↓ can
ll. 25–26	does not ~~I~~ ↑we↓ think
l. 27	marriage. ~~I~~ ↑We↓ can find
l. 33	by law for ~~the~~ ↑her↓ estate
l. 33	husband. ~~In the~~ ↑The↓ court
ll. 34–35	to obtain the ↑personal↓ estate of
l. 37	case that ~~I~~ ↑we↓ have seen
ll. 42–43	equity will ↑disregard, or↓ controul
ll. 43–44	question, ~~I~~ ↑we↓ can find
l. 46	hers. ~~I~~ ↑We↓ can find
l. 50	proposition ~~I~~ ↑we↓ should
ll. 51–52	occasion, ~~it~~ ↑its invalidity↓ must be
¶10 l. 2	the same ↑time↓ addressed
ll. 6–7	transaction ~~in a letter~~ to Mr. Poitou his ~~agent~~ ↑partner↓ in this
l. 11	the family." ~~Some objection was made to the admissibility of the testimony showing the circumstances atten~~
¶11 l. 1	to Newmann [*erasure*] on the
¶12 ll. 2–3	since parol ↑& extrinsic↓ testimony
¶14 l. 6	will, and ~~are to~~ ↑depend↓ on
l. 7	testimony ~~is of course to~~ ↑must↓ be
ll. 9–10	in equity, ↑if ~~the separate~~ a distinct claim be also asserted for the wife,↓ the
l. 12	the whole or ~~such~~ part of it
¶15 ll. 4–5	his own ~~fortune~~ ↑resources for payment of their claims,↓ & had
l. 7	benefit. But ~~it may well be questioned~~ the application
l. 17	disappointing ~~their~~ such intention
l. 20	the legacy [*erasure*]. Had the
l. 28	not to be ~~entirely~~ disregarded

To Edward Everett

Dear Sir   Richmond Decr. 16th. 1826

I had the pleasure of receiving this morning a copy of the Presidents message transmitted by you.[1] To my thanks for this flattering mark of your polite attention permit me to add that I am, with great and respectful esteem, your obedt.

J MARSHALL

ALS, Everett Papers, MHi. Addressed to Everett in Washington. Endorsed by Everett.

1. *Message of the President of the United States, Communicated to the Senate and House of Representatives. . . .* (Washington, D.C., 1826). The message and documents are reprinted in *ASP, Foreign Relations*, VI, 207–93.

To Charles F. Mercer

My dear Sir   Richmond Decr. 16th. 1826

I had the pleasure of re[c]eiving this morning the message of the President with the accompanying documents transmitted by you.[1] I thank you for this polite mark of your friendly attention.

The correspondence with Mr. Canning is particularly interesting. The state of our commerce with the British West indies is a subject of real importance to that portion of our country which furnishes either breadstuff or lumber. Its suspension will I fear be seriously felt.[2] I do not pretend to say that the present embarassment grows out of any fault on our part, but I may be permitted seriously to regret it.

I have seen with great pleasure the report of your central convention on the Chesapeake & ohio canal.[3] It furnishes ground for the hope that this work to a great and beneficial extent may be executed at an expense not exceeding the means which may be wisely and prudently applied to the object. With great respect & esteem I am dear Sir, Your Obedt

J Marshall

ALS, Collins Collection, CoCCC. Addressed to Mercer in Washington and franked; postmarked Richmond, 17 Dec. Endorsed by Mercer.

1. See JM to Everett, 16 Dec. 1826 and n. 1.

2. The reference is to correspondence between British Foreign Secretary George Canning and American minister to Great Britain Albert Gallatin in August and September of 1826 (*ASP, Foreign Relations,* VI, 249–56). On British and U.S. relations concerning the West Indies, see George Dangerfield, *The Awakening of American Nationalism, 1815–1828* (New York, 1965), 258–65; F. Lee Benns, *The American Struggle for the British West India Carrying-Trade, 1815–1830* (1923; Clifton, N.J., 1972 reprint), 121–62.

3. Mercer was the driving force behind the Chesapeake and Ohio Canal Company, which held a convention of delegates in Washington from 6 to 9 Dec. 1826. The proceedings of the convention were reported in the Washington *Daily National Intelligencer* on 7, 8, 9 and 11 Dec. (reprinted in the Richmond *Enquirer,* 14 Dec.). See Douglas R. Egerton, *Charles Fenton Mercer and the Trial of National Conservatism* (Jackson, Miss., 1989), 197–207.

To Samuel L. Southard

Dear Sir   Richmond Decr. 21st. 1826

I have been applied to by a friend of young Mr. Jefferson Nelson[1] who is a candidate for admission into our navy as a midshipman, to state to you the character and services of his grand Fathers on the sides of both the Father and Mother. General Thomas Nelson his paternal[2] Grand Father was at the commencement of the revolution one of the most distinguished gentlemen of Virginia and took an early and decided part in the revolution, his exertions during which greatly impaired his then large fortune. He was Governour of Virginia in the year 1781, and his very valuable services during the siege of Yorktown were such as to entitle him to the thanks of the commander in chief.

Mr. John Page Mr. Nelsons maternal[3] grand Father was one of his Majesty's Privy Counsel at the commencement of the war and took an early and decided part in the revolution. He has been a member of Congress and Governour of Virginia, and has always been considered as one of our most distinguished and valuable citizens. Mr. Jefferson Nelson is too young to be personally known to me, but there is no person in whose family Virginia takes a deeper interest than in that to which he belongs. With great respect and esteem, I am dear Sir your Obedt

J MARSHALL

ALS, ViHi. Addressed to Southard in Washington and franked; postmarked Richmond, 21 Dec. Endorsed by Southard: "Answ — & promise respl. con / sidn. when oppy. offers."

1. Here and throughout his letter JM mistakenly referred to Thomas Jefferson Page as Jefferson Nelson. Someone (Southard?) corrected "Nelson" to "Page." Page (1808–1899) entered the navy as a midshipman in 1827 and led a distinguished career. During the Civil War he served in the Confederate navy, commanding an ironclad. After the war he lived in Argentina and Italy.

2. Corrected to read "maternal."

3. Corrected to read "paternal."

From Samuel L. Southard

Sir,   Navy Dep'mt., 23. Dec. 1826.

I have received your letter of the 21st. inst. in behalf of young Page, an applicant for an appointment as Midshipman, and have placed the same on file. His case shall receive respectful attention the first favorable opportunity. I am, respectfully, &c.

S. L. S.

Letterbook copy, RG 45, DNA.

To Bushrod Washington

My dear Sir   Decr. 27th. 1826

Your letter of the 21st. has just reached me.[1] I am astonished at the failure of my letter in answer to that which contained the proposition of Mr. Sparks. I answered the day of its reception and expressed unequivocally my opinion that his offer should be accepted.[2] In addition to the obvious reasons for accepting it stated by yourself I suggested others of a nature somewhat delicate which I would not willingly submit to any eye but yours. I also mentioned an idea respecting the second edition of The Life of Washington which I will state to you when we meet. This letter was addressed to you at Mount Vernon. I shall send this to Alexandria, lest the address to Mount Vernon should not secure the conveyance to the proper post office.

Soon after writing to you I received a letter from Mr. Sparks which I answered by informing him that I had received a letter from you communicating his offer which I had answered by advising its acceptance.[3] With great esteem & affection, I am dear Sir Your Obedt

J MARSHALL

ALS, Marshall Papers, DLC. Addressed to Washington at Mount Vernon, "via Alexandria"; postmarked Richmond, 27 Dec. Endorsed by Washington.

1. Letter not found.
2. See JM to Jared Sparks, 10 Dec. 1826 and n. 1.
3. Washington wrote to Sparks on 2 Jan. 1827 that he and JM accepted the proposal (Herbert B. Adams, *The Life and Writings of Jared Sparks, Comprising Selections from His Journals and Correspondence* [2 vols.; Boston and New York, 1893], I, 412).

From [Richard Stockton]

Dear Sir   Princeton N J Decr: 27: 1826[1]
Although my Friend Mr Bayard has the honor of a slight personal acquaintance with you — still I take great pleasure in stating the complete and perfect knowledge which I have, of his Talents — Habits of business — general Character, and standing in the particular community to which he belongs.[2]

This Gentleman has been well known to me from his Youth. He has been my next Neighbour for twenty years — and I can truly say, that there can be no Man who more fully possesses the affection, and confidence, ⟨ . . . ⟩ than Mr Bayard. His Talents ⟨ . . . ⟩ order. He was regularly educa⟨ted . . . ⟩ice of Mr Bradford once Attorney General of the United States.

He practiced Law with reputation both in the City of Philadelphia, of which He is a native, and also in the City of New York, on his return from England where he had been in the employ of the Government for some years. He removed to this place some twenty years ago for the purpose of educating his Sons — during all this time he has not been idle. In addition to the indulgence of his habits of general reading — as a Trustee, and Treasurer of the College — as a Leading Member of most of our Charitable, and Religious, Institutions, his time has been well employed in doing good. His habits of business originally well formed, remain fresh, and unimpaired.

If you, and your honorable Companions, should think proper to bestow upon him the Clerkship of your Court, I feel every assurance that he would execute the office in such manner as to give entire satisfaction, to the Bench — the Bar, and the Country. I have the honor to be, with the highest respect & Veneration, your Obt: servt

AL[S], RG 267, DNA. Addressed to JM in Washington. Noted as carried by Samuel Bayard. MS mutilated owing to clipping of signature. Endorsed by JM "Mr. Bayard." Stockton's identity based on comparison of handwriting and family connection (see n. 2).

1. Richard Stockton (1764–1828), a graduate of the College of New Jersey, resided at his family's estate near Princeton. A lawyer and Federalist politician, he had served in the Senate (1796–99) and in the House of Representatives (1813–15).

2. Bayard was connected to the Stockton family through his wife Martha, daughter of Lewis Pintard and Susanna Stockton Pintard (George Adams Boyd, *Elias Boudinot: Patriot and Statesman, 1740–1821* [1952; New York, 1969 reprint], 36 and n. 12).

From Thomas S. Hinde

Kentucky, Campbell County,
Dear sir,   Newport Decr. 28th 1826
   Perhaps as you may have been apprized of the fact, of my being a Candidate for the appointment of Clerk to the Supreme Court of the United States, it will become necessary that I should present you documents in regard to my qualifications as clerk — you have documents on that subject, herewith enclosed.[1] I ⟨am⟩ sir with great respect, your Obt Sert:
                                                    TH: SPOTSWOOD HINDE

ALS, RG 267, DNA. Addressed to JM in Washington.

1. Thomas S. Hinde (1785–1846), son of a British naval surgeon who settled in Virginia, was born in Hanover County and moved with his family to Kentucky in 1797. After serving as clerk of the Ohio House of Representatives, 1807–10, he became a Methodist circuit preacher. In addition to his ministerial activities, he engaged in a variety of business and journalistic pursuits in Ohio, Kentucky, and Illinois. He was a founder of Mount Carmel, Ill., and in his later years settled in that town (*Combined History of Edwards, Lawrence and Wabash Counties, Illinois* [Philadelphia, 1883], 189–90, 236–37; Josephine L. Harper, *Guide to the Draper Manuscripts* [Madison, Wis., 1983], 120–21).

To James Marshall

My dear Nephew[1]   Richmond Decr. 29th. 1826
   Your letter of the 14th. of Novr. reached me about the commencement of the session of the circuit court at this place, & I deferred answering it until the pressure of business should pass away.[2] The term continued till christmass and my letter was consequently delayed till christmass should be over.

You undoubtedly state the question truely when you say it is, what person is designated by the codicil as the fourth child of Bryan Fairfax?[3] If that person was in esse at the death of the testator, the annuity would I think undoubtedly vest in him in point of interest had it not been charged on land. If it did not vest because it was charged on land, this circumstance cannot transfer the gift to another. The 5th. child cannot become the 4th. because the annuity was prevented from vesting in the 4th. by the operation of a principle introduced solely for the benefit of the land holder and to the prejudice of the legatee. If the annuity would have vested had it not been charged on land then the words designate the person to take, and consequently those cases which prove that it would have vested in the one case prove with equal certainty in the other that the person to take is designated. The controversies which have arisen respecting the person to take have almost universally turned on the question whether the legacy vested or was contingent as to the person, and as the language which would be sufficient to vest a legacy is of course sufficient to describe the person the enquiry has carelessly been in this case whether the annuity vested in the person who answered the description at the death of the testator when in truth it ought to have [been] whether the person who was the 2d. child &c at the death of the testator is or is not the person who is to take by the description of the 2d. child &c. It is undoubtedly more advisable to use accurate language and to contend for the description of the person in terms, using the cases in which it has been decided that a legacy not charged on land would have vested if given by similar words as proving that they sufficiently describe the person to take.

The cases of strict settlement, & the case you mention from Vernon are undoubtedly in point to show that the description may fix on the person although the interest does not vest. So is every case of an executory devise or contingent remainder where the contingency depends on an uncertain event.

Although I have no idea of embarassing this case with the question whether this annuity was prevented from vesting by its being charged on land I am far from being satisfied on that point. I am not satisfied that the doctrine relative to a particular estate and a remainder does not apply to it. It is unquestionably true that "a remainder necessarily presupposes an estate in the grantor or devisor coextensive with the remainder and the particular estate supporting it"; and that "the first annuities to the Miss Martins were created de novo"; but it is not so certain that "their existence" though created by the will, "terminated with the lives of the Miss Martins.["] They were created by the will for a single life but were prolonged by the codicil for a second life, and if the will & codicil are to be taken together, the whole may be considered as an annuity for two lives that is for the life of Frances Martin remainder to the 2d. child of Bryan Fairfax for his life, and so of the others. This however is of no real importance, since if the legacy would have vested had it been payable out of personal estate, it must be because the words sufficiently describe the person; and if that be the case, no other can be substituted for him. So far as the question depends on decided cases I had relied much on the principle that a will must always take effect on the death of the testator unless its words plainly direct the contrary; and that in pursuance of this principle, if there was at the death of the testator, a person in being who answered the description, that person would take. The cases I had seen in which after born children were held to take were all bequests to an aggregate of persons by words which could not be satisfied without comprehending those born afterwards. But my brother has mentioned the case West v. The Lord Primate of Ireland in Cox's cases which you consider as strongly supporting the right of Thomas Fairfax, and in which I find an after born child took as the youngest child of Lord Cantelupe.[4] This case is reported in a very unsatisfactory manner; and it is remarkable that it is not cited either by Maddox or by Gwillim in his edition of Bacon.[5] It does not give the argument of counsel and with holds the principle on which the Chancellor decided. His decree undoubtedly turned on the peculiar language of the will and w⟨e⟩ are left to conjecture what view he took of those words. It is probable that he understood the bequest as if it had been expressed "for the use of his seventh child, or if he should not have a seventh *now* living then for the use of his youngest child." Had the bequest been direct to Lord Cantalupe and thus expressed I should have thought that the youngest child living at the death of Sir Septimius would have been entitled. We are not told on what principle the claim put in for him was rejected, but I should suppose that this rejection was founded on the circumstance that the testator instead of bequeathing himself in his own will to Lord Cantalupe directs that his executor should make the bequest. This may have been considered as indicating an intention that the state of things existing when the will of the exr. should be made was to govern the bequest & designate the person to take. It was a power to be executed at a future time; and the state of things when it was to be executed was to be regarded. In this view of the case the decision that the person who was then the seventh should not be regarded as the seventh according to the will of Sir Septimius Robinson is certainly a very strong case in favour of the right of Thomas Fairfax. I cannot discover any other reason for this decision than that the description in the will must be understood as applying to the children in the order of their birth, but I am strongly impressed with the idea that this opinion was formed on the particular language of the clause, & would have been changed by a very slight variation in the language. The introduction of the word "living" makes it prob⟨able⟩ that the testator knew a seventh child had been born to Lord Cantalupe a⟨nd t⟩hat the legacy was intended for that seventh child if then alive. The seventh not being alive the legacy was then transferred to the youngest he should have. The Chancellor understood the will as intending to describe a person who had been in existence but of whose continuing ex⟨ist⟩ence the testator was uncertain, and if the intended legatee should not be living then to substitute for him the youngest child of Lord Cantalupe at the death of his executor when the power was to be executed. This from the imperfection of the report, is a case which it is difficult to apply. We are left to grope in the dark for its principle, and it may operate for or against us according to the reason assigned by the Chancellor for his opinion. The case which I most fear is Godfrey v Davis 6 Vez. 49.[6] I have no doubt of its being used by Catletts counsel and I have as little doubt that the general expressions used in it were not used in the broad sense which the language of the chancellor imports. They must be restrained to the case itself. Every case of a bequest to an aggregate of individuals in which the representations of one dying before distribution of the fund have been held to take is I think decidedly in our favor, but that which I think most directly in point is Danvers v The Earl of Clarendon 1st. Vernon 35.[7]

I shall send you the opinion I had prepared in the case under cover by Mr. Powell.[8] I will thank you to preserve it & return it to me when I visit Happy Creek. The cause will probably come to the court of Appeals & the opinion will save me a second laborious search into the ca⟨s⟩es. Your father will take care of it for me. I am my dear Nephew your affectionate

J MARSHALL

Since writing this letter I have looked at West vs The Lord Primate of Ireland in 3. Brown & find it still more imperfectly reported than by Coxe. "The youngest child living at the death of the testator is not noticed as a party to the suit.["] The Chancellor however says that the 8th. child cannot take as the 7th. which is strongly in favour of the claim of T. Fairfax. I still believe that the decision must have turned on the language of the will.

ALS, William Keeney Bixby Collection, MoSW. Addressed to Marshall in Winchester; postmarked Richmond, 9 Jan.

1. James Marshall (1802–1880), third son of James M. Marshall, practiced law in Winchester (Paxton, *Marshall Family*, 139).

2. Letter not found.

3. JM referred to the case of Catlett v. Marshall (see Answer in Chancery, Mar. 1826).

4. West v. Lord Primate of Ireland, 2 Cox 258, 30 Eng. Rep. 120 (Ch., 1790); 3 Bro. C.C. 148, 29 Eng. Rep. 459.

5. Henry Maddock, *A Treatise on the Principles and Practice of the High Court of Chancery* (3d Am. ed.; 2 vols.; Hartford, Conn., 1827). Henry Gwillim was the editor of the sixth London edition (in seven volumes) of Bacon's *Abridgment*.

6. Godfrey v. Davis, 6 Ves. 43, 31 Eng. Rep. 929 (Ch., 1801).

7. Danvers v. Earl of Clarendon, 1 Vern. 35, 23 Eng. Rep. 290 (Ch., 1681).

8. Possibly Alfred H. Powell (1781–1831), a prominent Winchester lawyer who was then serving in the U.S. House of Representatives. See David Holmes Conrad, "Early History of Winchester," in *Annual Papers of the Winchester Virginia Historical Society,* I (1931), 208, 224.

From Unknown

Dear Sir   Washington Decr 30th. 1826

You will pardon the liberty I take in recommending to you Mr. John R Livingston Jnr as a competent & well educated young Gentleman to fill the office of Clk of the supreme Court of the United States.[1]

Mr. Livingston has a respectable standing at the Bar in our State his Character is fair & his connections most respectable. With respect, Your Hm Servt

AL[S], RG 267, DNA. Addressed to JM in Richmond. Endorsed by JM "Livingstone." Signature clipped.

1. John R. Livingston, Jr. (1803–1871), was a son of John R. Livingston (1754–1851) and nephew of Robert R. Livingston and Edward Livingston. The elder John R. Livingston was a prominent member of New York's steamboat monopoly (George Dangerfield, *Chancellor Robert R. Livingston of New York, 1746–1813* [New York, 1960], 409, 416; Howland Davis and Arthur Kelly, comps., *A Livingston Genealogical Register* [Rhinebeck, N.Y., 1995], Chart D10). The writer was presumably a senator or congressman from New York. The hand does not match that of Senator Martin Van Buren; the other New York senator was Nathan Sanford.

From [Alfred H. Powell?]

Dear Sir   Washington Jany. 3. 1827.

Among the candidates for the office of Clerk of the Supreme Court, is John D. Simms the son of my old friend and patron the late Colo. Simms of Alexandria.[1] Altho' I have already made to you a communication in behalf of another highly respectable candidate I see no impropriety in my doing justice to the claims of Mr. Simms for this office.

Mr. Simms has been educated to the profession of the law, and commenced his professional life in Alexandria, with fair prospects of success in the progress of his business having a growing family and believing that he could do better for them by removing to a farm in the Country, he did so, and settled himself in the County of Stafford in Virga. This unfortunate step has been attended with his ruin. He has totally faild in his agricultural persuits and is now not only in poverty but in distress for the common necessaries of life.

Mr. Simms is a worthy and amiable man — Intirely adequate to perform the duties of a clerk and I have no hesitation in recommending him as a fit person for that station.

AL[S], RG 267, DNA. Addressed to JM. Signature clipped.

1. The writer may have been Alfred H. Powell, then serving in the U.S. House of Representatives, who had studied law with Charles Simms (T. Michael Miller, comp., *Artisans and Merchants of Alexandria, Virginia: 1780–1820* [2 vols.; Bowie, Md., 1991–92], II, 49).

From Unknown

Senate Chamber, Jany 5th 1827.[1]

William W Carroll having informed me of his willingness to Accept and his wish to obtain the Appointment of Clerk of the Supreme court, I take great pleasure in stating that in my opinion he is qualified to discharge the duties of the office, and would give entire satisfaction to all connected with the business of the Court.[2] Your's very respectfully

AL[S], RG 267, DNA. Addressed to the Supreme Court justices. Signature clipped.

1. The writer was presumably one of the U.S. Senators from Maryland, Samuel Smith or Ezekiel Chambers (1788–1867). The handwriting does not match samples of Smith's known hand.

2. William T. Carroll (1802–1863), a lawyer and professor with William Cranch at the short-lived law school associated with Columbian College, was appointed clerk on 20 Jan. 1827 (Robert F. McNamara, "In Search of the Carrolls of Belle Vue," *Maryland Historical Magazine*, LXXX [1985], 108–9; U.S. Sup. Ct. Minutes, 20 Jan. 1827).

From Humphrey Marshall

Dr. Sir,   Janry 7th. 1827.

I am about doing, what I never did for myself, for a son — it is to request your interposition with the president of the United States, in favour of Thos. A. Marshall, who is an applicant for the office of Attorney for the U.S. in Kentucky:[1] the office being vacant, by the appointment of Mr. Bibb, to our court of Appeals.[2] I have only to say for Thos. that he's able, and honest. I know, that, in general, (speaking of occurrences here) these are but incompetent recommendations to office. Yet, knowing the father, of the president, and thinking the son, something like him, I cannot think they will be turned into objections. In truth, was not Mr. Clay, in the cabinet, to whom the president can refer for information, and who knows the applicant, I should have no expectation of his getting the appointment. I know him to be backward — and although I could mention that he was, in written documents, recommended strongly, to the Governor for a circuit Judgeship — yet I could not turn out to procure their renewal, or others, of a similar kind. No appointments are made here, but of partizans, of a particular character, and of the Governors creed — of course no Judgeship was confered on a Marshall.

Doubtless, it is of great importance to any administration, to fill vacant offices, with friends, and presume, that, while Mr. Adams is attentive to other qualifications, he is not forgetfull of this. It is a fact, not unworthy of notice, by the by, that in general, our *relief party*, are Jacksonites.

If I may be allowed, to say a word, as to myself, having suffered, by the ill will of this state, towards the former president Adams, I should feel some compensation, were his son, to place mine, in a situation where he could serve both his country, and himself.[3] Yours respectfully,

H. MARSHALL

ALS, RG 59, DNA. Addressed to JM in Washington; postmarked Frankfort, Ky., 8 Jan. Enclosed in JM to Henry Clay, 20 Jan. 1827.

1. Thomas A. Marshall (1794–1871), a graduate of Yale (1815), was then practicing law in Paris, Ky. He later served in the U.S. Congress and for many years sat on the Kentucky Court of Appeals.

2. George M. Bibb (1776–1859), a native of Prince Edward County, Va., graduated from both Hampden-Sydney and the College of William and Mary. He began practicing law in Virginia before moving to Kentucky in 1798. After serving in the U.S. Senate from 1811 to 1814, he practiced law and figured prominently in Kentucky politics. Appointed chief justice of the state court of appeals in 1827, he resigned the next year and returned to the U.S. Senate, where he served until 1835. His last public office was a brief stint as secretary of the treasury, 1844–45.

3. The appointment of federal attorney for Kentucky went to John J. Crittenden (1787–1863), a graduate of William and Mary (1807), who led a distinguished career in state and national politics.

To Edward Livingston

Dear Sir   [ca. 15 January 1827?]

Two cases St. Amand v Brandege have been put into the hands of the court as cases in which the plf. in errour probably did not mean to oppose an affirmance.[1] On looking into the record I can scarcely believe that the plf intended to abandon them & therefore ask whether you are employed in them. Your obedt

J MARSHALL

ALS, MB. Addressed to Livingston and endorsed by him.

1. The cases of St. Amand v. Brandegee, from the U.S. District Court for Eastern Louisiana, were filed in the Supreme Court in Mar. 1824. Livingston represented the appellant St. Amand and filed an assignment of errors in the first case on 15 Jan. 1827. Both cases were dismissed by consent of the parties on 1 Mar. 1828 (St. Amand v. Brandegee, App. Cas. Nos. 1296, 1297).

From Littleton W. Tazewell

Sir;   Washington. Jany. 18. 1827

Not having been present in the Supreme Court, when the opinion was deliver'd in the case of the Palmyra, I yesterday asked of Mr. Justice Story (by whom I understood it had been read) to allow me the favour of perusing it.[1] This application he granted me to day. In reading this opin-

LITTLETON W. TAZEWELL

Oil on canvas by Cephas Thompson, date unknown. *Courtesy of the Virginia Historical Society.*

ion I find in it the following sentence. "The other point of objection is of a far more subtle and novel nature."

Had these expressions been used in the heat and animation of debate, however singular the *coincidence* of the language with that which has been used elsewhere, it would not have attracted my observation. Could I consider them as only the words of Mr. Justice Story, they would not certainly have excited any other feeling, than that of mere regret. But when they are handed out as the deliberate, written, judicial language of the Supreme Court, I think I have the right to call the attention of the other Judges to the terms employed, to the end they may not go forth to the world, without being noticed and approved by at least a majority of them. Such, Sir, is the single purpose of this letter.

You will not I hope misunderstand me as intending to utter any *complaint*, as to the manner in which the Supreme Court may choose to exert the undoubted power it possesses in such cases. This is not my object. In becoming an advocate at its bar, I voluntarily submitted myself to this power; and altho' I had no reason then to expect, that it would ever be exercised in this mode, yet I am perfectly willing to abide the result.

I would not have troubled you with this letter, but under the hope, that the expressions I have quoted, might probably have escaped the observation of yourself and of some of your associates, in the pressure of the other engagements which occupy the time of the Judges. I am very respectfully, your mo: obdt. servt.

L. W. TAZEWELL

ALS (copy), Wickham Family Papers, 1766–1945, ViHi. Inside address to JM.

1. Tazewell represented the Spanish government, respondent in the case of The Palmyra, which had been argued on 9 Jan. Story delivered the opinion of the Court on 15 Jan. (12 Wheat. 1–18).

To Littleton W. Tazewell

Dear Sir   Jany. 19th. 27

Your letter of yesterday just reached me as the argument of today opened. I very much regret that any expression should have found its way into any opinion given by the court which wounds any gentleman of the bar. There is certainly no member of the bench who would not wish very seriously to avoid such a circumstance. I do not understand you when you speak of the "singular *coincidence* of the words used with those which have been used elsewhere." I did not know that similar words had been used elsewhere in reference to any argument of yours, nor do I believe that any thing offensive to you came into the mind of Mr. Story when he employed them.[1]

Without enquiring however into this circumstance, or whether I should have myself felt equal sensitiveness on a similar occasion, it is enough for me that the words pain you & I shall apply to Mr. Story without showing him your letter to expunge them. With great respect & esteem, I am your obedt

J MARSHALL

ALS, ICABF; copy, Wickham Family Papers, 1766–1945, ViHi. ALS addressed to Tazewell "of the Senate." Endorsed by Tazewell.

1. In a letter to John Wickham enclosing copies of his correspondence with the chief justice, Tazewell explained more fully why he was upset by Justice Story's use of the expression "subtle and novel nature" in reference to Tazewell's argument in The Palmyra. "These very words," he said, "have been often applied to my political arguments." As a member of the Senate, Tazewell was a leading critic of the policies of the Adams administration, particularly the Panama Mission. Administration newspapers, he complained, regularly characterized him as " 'an intellectual gladiator' — 'a most ingenious sophist' — 'a subtle reasoner' — 'a practised lawyer trained to make the worse appear the better cause.' " As political criticism such words did not bother him, he said, but he "did not think it fair for the Judges to echo such terms, when it was neither usual necessary or decorous to do so" (Tazewell to Wickham, 21 Jan. 1827, Wickham Family Papers, 1766–1945, ViHi).

To Henry Clay

Dear Sir   Washington Jany. 20th. 27
I have this instant received the enclosed letter requesting me to apply to the President in favour of my Nephew Thomas A Marshall who is a candidate for the office of District Attorney in Kentucky. You are a much better Judge of his fitness than I am.

I have much repugnance to solicit for my friends, especially where the office is in a different State from that in which I reside, and shall not venture to make an application to the President; but if you think the communication of the enclosed letter can be of any service to my Nephew and are yourself inclined to favour his pretensions, you will oblige me by laying it before him. I submit the affair entirely to your judgement & am, dear Sir with great respect & esteem, Your obedt.

J MARSHALL

ALS, RG 59, DNA. Addressed to Clay. Endorsed by clerk: "recommends Thos. A. / Marshall as Atto U.S. for / Kentucky District." Encloses Humphrey Marshall to JM, 7 Jan. 1827.

To Littleton W. Tazewell

Dear Sir   Jany. 20th. 1827

On my return from court yesterday I informed Mr. Story that you had been much hurt at an expression used in the opinion he had delivered in the case of the Palmyra. He expressed equal surprize and regret on the occasion, and declared that the words which had given offence were not used or understood by him in an offensive sense. He assented without hesitation to such modification of them as would render them in your view entirely unexceptionable.[1] When I mentioned your allusion to the coincidence of the language with what had been used elsewhere, he declared his entire ignorance of the matter to which the allusion pointed. With great respect, Your Obedt

J MARSHALL

ALS (owned by Thomas B. Marshall, West Chester, Pa., 1967). Addressed to Tazewell in the "Senate Chamber." Endorsed by Tazewell.

1. In place of "The other point of objection is of a far more subtle and novel nature," the opinion in The Palmyra was changed to read: "The other point of objection is of a far more important and difficult nature" (12 Wheat. 14).

From Littleton W. Tazewell

Dear Sir;   Washington. Jany. 20. 1827

Engagements I could not dispense with, have prevented me from acknowledging at an earlier hour, the receipt of your kind letter of yesterday, for which I now beg leave to render you my sincere and very grateful acknowledgments. You mistake entirely the feelings which dictated mine, if you suppose (as seems to be the case) that in calling your attention to the expressions used in the opinion of the Court I felt either pained or wounded by them. I thought it possible, that this language might "have found its way" into the opinion, without being sought for even by its author; and very probable that in adopting it as their own, the other Judges had either not noticed it particularly, or been aware of the construction which might be put upon it, or the use to which it might be applied. I believed moreover, that should this be the case, they might hereafter feel regret at such an occurrence; and therefore felt it right to call their attention specially to the words used, to the end I then stated. But I think I said, and am very certain I meant to say, that I had no cause of complaint in any terms by which the Court might think proper to characterize my arguments or opinions offer'd to them, whether these terms were "regardant" as of ancient right in its own usages, or had been merely "impounded" into one of its opinions, as "estrays" from another manor. In either case I am well content that they should remain, provided they are still approved by the Judges, when their attention has been thus drawn to them. I am with great respect, and much esteem, your mo: obdt. sevt.

L. W. TAZEWELL

ALS (copy), Wickham Family Papers, 1766–1945, ViHi. Inside address to JM.

To Joseph Hopkinson

Dear Sir   Washington Feb. 3d. 1827
I have received your letter of the 28th. of January[1] and am much obliged by your kind notice of an error in the Life of Washington respecting the route pursued by the American army in its march from Trenton to Princeton. I was informed of it and corrected it when the edition was published only in part. Many copies of the work however contained the error, and yours unfortunately is one of them. I do not know to what extent the publication was made when the mistake was detected and corrected, but the copy in my possession is right.[2]

I thank you for the information respecting the particular paper which contains Hamiltons vindication of President Washington against the calumnies of the Calm Observer. If it is copied, be so obliging as to send it to me. If it is not you need not direct the copy to be made. With real esteem & regard, I am dear Sir your

J MARSHALL

ALS, Hopkinson Papers, PHi. Addressed to Hopkinson in Philadelphia; postmarked Washington, 3 Feb.

1. Letter not found.
2. JM's account of the battles of Trenton and Princeton appears in vol. II, ch. 8, of the first edition of the *Life of Washington*. In Oct. 1804, after the publication of the volume, an anonymous correspondent supplied publisher Caleb P. Wayne with a detailed list of corrections, which Wayne then passed on to JM. The author used this information in revising his account for the 1805 second printing (*PJM*, VI, 340–41 and nn. 2, 3).

From Timothy Pickering

My Dear Sir,   Salem Feby. 14. 1827.[1]
I must suppose you have given some attention to the controversy in which your *judicial* associate, Judge Johnson, has been a good while engaged, relative to General Pulaski and the battle of Germantown. I had

read his Sketches of the Life of General Greene; but only a few of the controversial papers and pamphlets, to which those Sketches had given rise, when I wrote a letter to Mr. Sparks, the Editor of the North American Review, in answer to his queries about Pulaski and that battle, and which was published in that Review (No. 53) last October.[2] I did not expect, & certainly did not desire, to be thereby involved in a controversy with the Judge. Our respective politics, I knew, were *antipodes:* but all political feeling had for many years subsided. Two or three years ago, some very civil letters were interchanged; & he was so obliging, as to make a very modest tender of his Sketches; which I thankfully accepted. He sent me the two volumes, handsomely bound. Greene's letters (I wished they had composed a still larger portion of the work) developed more of the character, and raised higher the opinion I had long entertained, of that eminent soldier and statesman. Johnson places him above all other Generals of our revolution; excepting Washington, "whom none can equal." The four last words are Johnson's: and yet he elsewhere says, that every day, Washington was asking counsel of Greene. In a word, notwithstanding the sentiment above quoted, and other *wholesale* expressions of eulogy, I think an impartial judge would rise, from reading the Sketches, impressed with the idea, that *Washington* was in *leading-strings,* and that these were held by *Greene.*

When I read your Life of Washington, I noticed your expression, in summing up his character; that while some were disposed to ascribe to him, as his distinguished excellence, uncommon Prudence, you, as the result of your investigation, thought him a *Great Man.* I, without an occasion, or the means of investigation, under the influence of common & universal fame, had entertained the same opinion; until I went into the army, in the campaign of 1777. What I then *saw*—what I *knew*, as *a present witness* and *actor*—formed & fixed my opinion. No subsequent event, down to the capture of York, and I consider the surrender of the whole British army, under Lord Cornwallis, as terminating the war, furnished me with any reason to change that opinion.

There is a vast difference, however, between a *military* and a *civil* administration; for while the latter admits of delay; to reflect, to consult, and to obtain advice, the former demands *quick discernment,* and *instant decision;* qualities which, in Washington, a few well knew, and lamented to see, were strikingly deficient. In my late reply to Judge Johnson, I refer to two instances.[3] And it was that reference which has now induced me to address you on this subject: for having written the Life of Washington, and placed him on high ground, you would naturally feel a desire, there to sustain him. The diligence, the judgement, and the fidelity of the Historian are concerned. But if these rest on all the known data within the reach of the writer, there can be no room for censure.

From the commencement of the revolution-war, to the autumn of

1776, I continued to reside in Salem (the place of my birth) holding various offices, in the town, in the county, & in the state. After the disasters of the campaign of 1776, there was a call for a large body of Massachusetts militia. I then held the commission of colonel in the militia. To encourage others, in that gloomy period, I pledged myself to go with them. In december, I marched the quota of Essex — a regiment of seven hundred men — first to Providence — then through Rhode-Island and Connecticut, to New-York State; and was, with other corps of militia, on the fruitless expedition to the enemy's posts near Kingsbridge, under General Heath, as chief in command. General Lincoln commanded the militia of Massachusetts. Soon afterwards we were ordered to march into New-Jersey; and, taking post at Bound-Brook, there our campaign ended. This was in March 1777. After my return home, and I had resumed my civil employments, I received a letter from General Washington, inviting me to take the office of adjutant general.

While a captain in the militia, some years before, I had read a few military books; and had even formed a plan of discipline for the militia, which was in the press just at the commencement of the war. And in my absence, on the winter campaign above mentioned, a second edition was published; by the government of Massachusetts, and ordered to be used for the instruction of the militia.[4]

Thinking very humbly of myself, and therefore unaspiring, I was not ambitious of military fame, or of any other distinction. I had a little family to support, and my various public offices satisfied me. It was, therefore, only from a sense of duty, that I accepted the office to which the commander-in-chief had called me. I joined the army in the middle of June; while it lay encamped at Middlebrook.

At Brandywine, just as the General was leaving his quarters, to repair to the right, where, at a late hour, it was discovered that the enemy had crossed the river, and were marching downward, he sent me with a verbal order to General Nash, at Chad's Ford. I delivered the order; & there falling in with colonel Fitzgerald (one of the General's aids) we rode together to the right. On our way, we heard a very heavy fire of musketry, in that quarter; and before our arrival, our right wing had been defeated. Proceeding on, I found the General near the southeastern quarter of a very large clear field; at the farther side of which, I saw the enemy advancing in line. The sun shone, and was perhaps 15 or 20 minutes above the horizon. A few rods in our front, was a small rising in the ground; and General Knox asked — "Will your Excellency have the artillery (I think he said the park of artillery) drawn up here?" I heard no answer; nor did I see any body of infantry to support it. We retired. Some of our troops were formed behind a rail fence. The enemy continued to advance. A shot from their artillery I saw cut down a file of those troops. We retreated farther. Col. R. K. Mead, one of the General's aids, rode up to him about this time, and asked "if Weedon's (or Muhlenberg's) brigade, which had not yet been engaged, should be ordered up?" I do not know what answer was given. Very soon after, I saw Colo. Walter Stewart's Pennsylvania regiment (which, if I do not mistake, belonged to one of those two brigades) engaged with the enemy. That regiment was close up to the edge of a thick wood in its front, and firing briskly; Stewart on foot, in its rear, animating his men. But although I was within 30 or 40 yards of this regiment, I could not see any troops of the enemy at whom they were firing. Very soon after this, the General retired still farther. The sun had for some time disappeared: it began to grow dusky: and as we proceeded, in retiring, the General said to me — "Why 'tis a perfect rout."

I have given these minute details, in order to preserve them (for, as well as I recollect, I have never before committed them to paper;) and to accompany them with this remark: That in this part of the action (and it was all I saw of the battle of Brandywine) I observed no original orders from the General; but that whatever orders were given, they appeared to be in answer to leading questions. I state one more fact. In the morning of that day, as early, at least, as nine o'clock, I was by the General's side, on a hill to the right of and near to Chad's Ford; where the enemy were firing their field artillery apparently without doing us any harm; and where the fire was returned by the American artillery. This *idle* interchange of round shot being continued for some time, without any movement on the part of the enemy, to pass the ford, I perfectly remember making to the General a remark to this effect; and I think nearly in these words: 'If the principal attack were intended at this place, the enemy would not waste time in this ineffectual fire; which is kept up merely to amuse us; while the main body is marching to cross elsewhere.' The General made no answer. I well remember the embarrassment arising from the want of correct information concerning the enemy, and the varied accounts of their situation & movements; and that at one time, General Greene was preparing to cross the Brandywine, to attack the enemy at Chad's ford; when further information prevented it.

The army having retreated, by the way of Chester, to Philadelphia, passed on, and encamped near the Falls of Schuylkill, for about two days; then marched higher up, and recrossed the river, at a place then called Matson's Ford. The water appeared to be two feet deep, & the current so swift, that the men of each platoon locked their arms, the better to resist its force. During this advance, with the intention again to face the enemy, I saw no sign of discouragement; but all seemed willing to renew the fight.

On the 16th of September, in the morning, while I was on the grand parade, with the new guards, to relieve those of the preceding day, it appeared that the enemy were on the march towards us. The guards being sent off, I returned to Head Quarters. The troops were under arms. The General on seeing me, directed me to proceed to the right of our army, to assist in forming them for battle. I went thither: they appeared ready for action; & I returned immediately to the General. He, with many officers about him, appeared to be in consultation. At this time the enemy's van, and the portions of our own troops detached to keep them in check, were briskly engaged. The report of the musketry induced me to think the enemy continued to advance; while on our part, every thing appeared to be in suspense. This rendering me extremely uneasy, I pressed up my horse, that I might learn the cause of the inaction; and I found this question under discussion: Whether to receive the enemy on the present ground, or to retire to the high ground on the other side of the valley, which was just in our rear. For it was said the bottom of the valley was miry; and that in case of a defeat, the artillery would be lost, from the difficulty, or impracticability, of dragging it across the valley; excepting the pieces with the left wing, through which there was a firm road. During this time the skirmishing with the enemy continued, and was apparently drawing nearer. At this critical moment (such it seemed to me) I addressed the General in this manner: 'Sir, the sound of the musketry shows that the enemy is advancing: the order of battle is not yet completed: if we are to fight the enemy on this ground, no time is to be lost in completing it. If we are to take the high ground on the other side of the valley, we ought to march immediately; or the enemy may fall upon us in the midst of our movement: *Pray, sir, decide.*' "Let us move" was the General's instant answer; and the movement immediately took place.

This is the first of the two instances referred to, in my reply to Judge Johnson; in which, as I there remark, "my opinion gave an impulse and determination to the General's mind previously in suspense." It was stated in a letter I wrote to Governor Sullivan, in April 1808, and published, with the rest of my correspondence with him, in a pamphlet printed in Boston, in that year.[5] This letter closed that correspondence: and as it was designed for the press, I dashed out the words *pray sir decide* (because of their obvious implication) before I sent it to Boston. I was at that time in the Senate of the United States, at Washington.

The other instance occurred at Whitemarsh. There the army, reinforced by some of Gates's victorious brigades, had encamped, in November. The range of hills was commanding. The front line was posted near their brow; and was protected by a good abbatis: but by the expiration of that month, the troops, suffering from the cold, had burnt up the whole of it, the small brush excepted. In the beginning of December, Sir William Howe marched in great force, from Philadelphia, and took post on Chesnut Hill, about three miles from us. During two days (on the first of which there was some skirmishing with the Pennsylvania militia) he viewed our position; and on the morning of the third day, advanced with his whole army, with the design and determination (as every body supposed) to make a general attack. Our army was drawn up in three lines to receive him. General Washington rode along in the rear of the front line. It happened that I alone was then with him. The firing of the advanced guards and Morgan's rifle corps, in our front, had begun; but a close wood concealed them and the enemy from our view. As we rode along, the General directed me to speak (which I did) to each officer commanding a regiment, *to caution his men not to fire too high, when the enemy should be advancing up the hill.* As we proceded towards the left, & the firing continuing, the General addressed me precisely in the following words: "I wonder now whether it will be best to reinforce Morgan, or not?" Instantly I answered 'If a small reinforcement be sent, they must soon give way: if a large force be detached, a great breach will be made in the line of defence; and this body must retire before the whole force of the enemy; & if they retreat in disorder, they will hazard throwing the whole army into confusion.' "That is true" — was the General's reply. After a little more skirmishing, Howe retired, and marched back to Philadelphia. Our own army then soon decamped, marched to, and hutted at Valley Forge.

On the 28th of July, 1783, Congress, then sitting at Princeton, requested General Washington to attend them.

On the 7th of August, "on motion of A. Lee, seconded by Mr. Bland," it was "Resolved (unanimously, ten states being present) That an equestrian statue of General Washington be erected at the place where the residence of Congress shall be established." And Arthur Lee, Mr. Ellsworth, & General Mifflin, were appointed a committee to prepare the plan of it. On their report, it was Resolved, That the statue should be of Bronze, &c. and be supported by a marble pedestal, on which should be represented five principal events of the war; to wit: The evacuation of Boston — the capture of the Hessians at Trenton — the battle of Princeton — the action of Monmouth — and the surrender of York.

It is the usual course, you know, to ascribe to the commander-in-chief of an army, the honour of all its achievements; although these may have been proposed, and successfully conducted by subordinate officers. The *world,* however, believing that Washington possessed military talents of a high order, have attributed to him the acquisition of all the victories gained by the army under his immediate command. But facts will not justify the public opinion; not even in one of the five cases before mentioned: or, if any exception be admitted, and that appears to me at least a doubtful one, it will apply only to the battle of Monmouth. I was then a member of the Board of War, sitting with Congress, at York in Pennsylvania. But I have carefully read the voluminous trial of General Charles Lee, spread over sixty folio pages of small print, in which may be seen the *origin,* and *progress,* and *issue* of that battle.[6] It is five years since I read it. The impressions left on my memory, from its perusal, are to the following effect.

Before the army left Valley Forge, a Council of War was assembled, to consider and advise the measures proper to be taken, consequent on the expected evacuation of Philadelphia, by the British army. In regard to a general action with the enemy, the Council were nearly unanimous in opposing it; Major General Charles Lee, in particular, being most decisively opposed. Subsequently, at another council of war (after they had left Valley Forge) the opposition to a general action was not materially changed. Baron Steuben, Inspector General, and well knowing the imperfect discipline of the troops, was also in the opposition. Washington himself, however, manifested a strong inclination to bring on a general action; in which General Wayne was also zealous; and that this should be effected, by attacking the rear of the British army, on the first favourable occasion, in its retreat. To account for Washington's inclination, I offer the following conjectures.

1. The battles between Gates's army & Burgoyne's, in the preceding campaign, were brought on by partial engagements, supported by detachments, until the actions became general; ending in Gates's complete success.

2. That success was the basis of an intrigue, in the winter of 1777–8, for superseding Washington, and placing Gates at the head of the army. Stung, I presume, with this attempt to disgrace him, he seemed eager to seize the opportunity then presenting, to remove, as he must have confidently hoped, the ground of a disadvantageous comparison. For although Washington was not naturally ambitious; and therefore preferred a private to a public life; yet perhaps no man was more sensible to reproach; the injustice of which he keenly felt, from the consciousness that he faithfully exerted all his faculties, and devoted his life, to the performance of the duties of his station.

3. Some opinions seem to have been afloat (broached, or entertained, by some men certainly incompetent to judge in this matter, however distinguished they might be as politicians) that Washington was too cautious; and that more fighting was necessary, to bring the war to a speedy and successful conclusion.

4. To these motives may perhaps be added, the influence of some of the young gentlemen of his family — his aids de camp — full of ardor and ambition. Perhaps, too, some of them (I except Hamilton, whose correct and elevated mind was above it) perceiving the General's earnest inclination, might, *for that reason*, be induced to manifest a concurring opinion.

No. 1. With regard to the action of Monmouth, Lee's retreat appeared to me justifiable and proper; to escape from bad grounds, where, if assailed by a very superior force, a safe retreat would have been impracticable. And he seems to have fallen back to tenable grounds, just when the commander-in-chief came up, and accosted him in terms, and in a manner, which the able and experienced veteran could not brook. The consequences are too well known to be recited. I shall only remark, that the sentence of the court-martial was a strange one. They found Lee guilty of a disobedience of orders, *which in fact were placed in his discretion* — of an unnecessary, and in some instances a disorderly retreat — and of disrespect to the commander-in-chief: And yet only suspended him from command for one year! Whereas, if really guilty of disobedience of orders, in a case of such magnitude, he ought to have been broken, if not shot.

If when Washington met Lee, his wonted equanimity and prudence had forsaken him; if, without first calmly asking the cause of the retreat, he abruptly accosted Lee, in the manner which the latter deemed so offensive; may it not be thus accounted for? With his whole heart set on a general action, he saw, or thought he saw, in Lee's retreat, his fond hopes frustrated: and the warmth of his resentment corresponding with his extreme disappointment, produced the harsh and precipitate rebuke.

No. 2. Capture of the Hessians at Trenton.

Of the honour of this event, colonel Joseph Reed, adjutant general, claimed a full share. In Gordon's history is an extract of his letter to Washington (Reed was then on some duty at Bristol) most earnestly urging the crossing of the army into New-Jersey, as a measure of the highest importance, & assigning his reasons. The letter was dated the 22d of December. Washington answered it on the 23d, in perfect accordance with Reed's ideas.[7] The army crossed in the night of the 25th, and in the morning of the 26th, the Hessians were captured. In 1782, Reed being assailed, unjustly as he thought, from the press (I believe it was by General John Cadwallader) he published his vindication in a pamphlet, in the preface of which, Reed says: "The letter [of December 22d to Washington] I have great reason to believe, was influential on the determination which was followed by the surprize of the Hessians at Trenton; an event (continues Reed) which though brilliant and highly honourable to all concerned, would not, I conceive, have been attended with decisive effects to America, had it not been followed by the return of the army to New Jersey, and the subsequent successes at Princeton and in East Jersey."[8] It was the permanent occupancy of some part of New Jersey, by the army, that seemed to Reed so highly important.

No. 3. The battle of Princeton. Of this I have given an account in my late reply to Judge Johnson; and shown that it was the consequence of a movement suggested by General St. Clair; a stroke of generalship alike admirable and important. It saved the army from impending ruin; while it presented a fair prospect of destroying the enemy's great deposite of stores at Brunswick, and of seizing their military chest. The march to Brunswick was prevented by the battle of Princeton; where the victory, however, was more than an equivalent to the advantages expected from the intended attack on Brunswick. The timely and salutary escape from Princeton, with the prisoners and captured property, was also due to St. Clair.

No. 4. The capture of Cornwallis & his army at York.

The combined American and French armies having marched from the North, united again in Virginia. A number of French corps had previously arrived from the West-Indies. The whole marched down, and took their stations before York. The first or second morning after, the General sent for me, to accompany him in reconnoitring the enemy's positions, *and the ground proper for our encampment.* At that moment I was engaged in some necessary business in my department; which having quickly despatched, I mounted my horse, and rode to meet the General. The reconnoitring respected only the American troops; & the space they were to occupy being of small extent, the General, attended by General Knox and some other officers (probably their aids only) had nearly gone over the ground when I met them. As soon as I came up, they halted: and Knox thus accosted me. "Colonel Pickering, the General thinks we ought to move, and encamp nearer to the enemy's works: what is your opinion?" I answered instantly — expressing precisely the following ideas; and nearly, I am sure, in these words: 'The duties of troops at a siege are severe. Those off duty ought to be so situated as to take their rest in security. We must look for repeated sallies from the enemy; and if any of these are made in great force, they will beat the guards of the trenches, and compel them to retreat. If the camp be near, the soldiers will not have time to rouse from sleep, and to recollect themselves, before the enemy will be upon them. Shot from the enemy's out-works reach us where we now are. For these reasons I think we are near enough.' – "Well, but we must invest the place" said General Washington. I think my countena[n]ce must have indicated, that I thought this a strange remark; for I well remember having a peculiar feeling on hearing it. However, without a moment's hesitation, I replied. 'The object of an investment of a fortified place, is to prevent the besieged from receiving succours, or making their escape. The American army now extends so as to command the ground from York river below the town, round to the morass on our left. Above the town, the French army commands the ground from the morass to the river. Duke Lauzun's legion, and General Weedon's brigade of Virginia militia are at Gloucester Point,* opposite to Yorktown; and Count de Grasse, with his fleet, commands the mouth of the river. No passage is open, except that up the river; and Lord Cornwallis will not attempt an escape by marching into the heart of the country. So I think, Sir, that the place is completely invested already.' The General made no reply: and the troops continued, during the siege, on the ground they then occupied.

Now, my dear sir, you will recollect that this was the seventh year of the war; and after the siege of the city of New-York had been once, if not

---

*This was a mistake: it afterwards appeared, that the British occupied the *Point;* & that Duke Lauzun and Weedon were in the town of Gloucester, back of the Point.

twice, in contemplation. And yet it is obvious that General Washington had not yet formed any distinct idea, even of the first step for besieging a fortified place, its investment. How much merit, then, can he be presumed to have had in conducting the siege to a successful issue?

No. 5 The evacuation of Boston.

This stands first in Arthur Lee's resolve, as it was the first in order of time, of the "principal events of the war, in which General Washington commanded in person." And here I put the question: If so little can be ascribed to the military talents of Washington, for the successes in the other principal events of the war, the last in its *seventh* year, how much less must be placed to his account, for the military measures which induced, or compelled, Sir William Howe to evacuate Boston, in the *first* year of the war?

I have seen, by the news papers, that you and judge Washington pronounced Rembrandt Peele's portrait of General Washington, to be the best likeness of him that you had ever met with: and my old friend Judge Peters (a friend now of forty nine years standing) in his letter to Peele, concurs with you.[9] But not content with general eulogy, he supererogates; and makes this extraordinary declaration: "Meritorious as were all others of our revolutionary patriots, without a *Washington* their exertions would have been vain." I, on the contrary, venture to assert, that without the agency of many citizens, of talents far surpassing Washington's, the revolution would never have been accomplished. My opinion of him, in his military character, was formed on what I *saw:* the *facts* I could not mistake: and the *inference* was unavoidable. In regard to Judge Peters, well might his intimate friend and admirer, Baron Steuben, say to him (as he did, very good-naturedly) "Damn you, Peters, you are an Idolater!" His declaration above-mentioned, I would tell my friend, is a libel on the eminent citizens and patriots who began the revolution, who conducted its affairs with distinguished wisdom & firmness, and brought it to a happy conclusion. Certainly the army was an essential instrument; and if we had very few able captains to direct its operations (Greene was the ablest) happily for the United States, our enemy was but poorly furnished. Lord Rawdon appeared to me superior to any of his brethren. I once asked Colo. Carrington what he thought of Lord Cornwallis; & received for answer "He is a damned fool." But great Generals are rare. In a whole century, Britain can boast of three: Marlborough — Wolfe — Wellington. I was a boy when Wolfe fell on the Plains of Abraham: his death was deeply lamented. He was a young man — only thirty three. Had he survived, he, probably, would have commanded the armies sent to reduce the Colonies. And if these had finally obtained the victory, the contest would have been vastly more arduous. He would have been only fifty one years old when our revolution-war commenced.

I know not, my highly respected friend, what you will think of this letter.

But a mind enlightened like yours, must be superior to prejudice; and above the pride of opinion, when new views, on new evidence, shall prove it to have been in any degree erroneous. One reader of my Review of the Adams and Cunningham Correspondence, said, that "I had lessened the lustre of Washington's character:" Yet I went no further than Hamilton's, Greene's, Steuben's, and Ramsay's opinions warranted. Washington's *Virtues* were *his own:* his important *official acts were rendered illustrious by others' aids;* and did he not shine with borrowed lustre?

Such are the opinions I have long entertained of Washington: and the series of facts now exhibited, are, I presume, sufficient to justify them. Endure me a little longer, while I refer to Mr. Wirt's Life of Patrick Henry.

After serving in the Indian & French wars, from 1754 to 1758, Washington resigned his commission. He was then elected a member of your House of Burgesses. The House directed their Speaker to express to him their thanks, for his services. This was done in an affecting style. Washington rose to make his acknowledgements; but "blushed, stammered, and trembled; and could not utter a word." (See page 45.)[10] Here was an early instance of his characteristic *unreadiness.*

At page 113, Mr. Wirt gives an anecdote which cannot be correct. Washington and Henry were two of the Virginia delegates to the Congress which sat at Philadelphia, in September and October, 1774. On his return home, some of Henry's neighbours gathered about him; and, with a natural curiosity, inquired who in that assembly were the greatest men. Henry pronounced John Rutledge to be the greatest orator: but that "for solid information and sound judgement, Washington was unquestionably the greatest man on that floor."[11] Now, my dear sir, if Henry pronounced such an opinion, you cannot think it correct: but you cannot believe either. Henry never pronounced that opinion. If he uttered such a sentiment at all, it must have been of some other member; and by mistake applied by one of the audience to Washington. The idea will be repelled by every man of information who looks over the list of the eminent lawyers and politicians who were members of that assembly. It is also utterly inconsistent with the opinion expressed by Henry, in August 1796, in a letter to his daughter Aylett, at page 386. There, referring to the abusive treatment which Washington, as President of the United States, had received, Henry says: "Nor are his long and great services remembered, as any apology for his mistakes *in an office to which he was totally unaccustomed.*" Then pronouncing "his character, as our leader during the war, as above all praise," he adds "I ever wished he might keep himself clear of the office he bears, and its attendant difficulties."[12] But why thus wish? The "solid information and sound judgement" ascribed by Henry to "the greatest man on the floor of that Congress" if possessed by Washington, designated him, above all others, to become the President of the United States; and there Mr. Henry must have wished to see him placed. His opinion of Washington's *military* character, is of no value. Great and admirable as were Henry's civic talents, he could not, nor could any man, who had not been with Washington in the army, form a correct opinion of his talents for war. But of his political talents — of his character as a *statesman,* Henry had many opportunities, and certainly was very competent to judge: and how he judged, the letter to his daughter Aylett sufficiently shows.

But it is time for me to stop — for my own sake as well as yours. In all that I have ever said or written on this subject, I have been influenced solely by a regard to historic truth, and the justice due to others. I have never considered my country honoured by those who ascribed everything to Washington; and held up to the world the idea, that during our revolution, the United States really possessed but *one* man. From our hyperbolic eulogies on Washington, foreigners have admitted that idea as substantially correct; and thence have inferred and said, That Washington gave to his country its independence. For myself I claim nothing; and have so little ambition, that I should not be disturbed were my name to be blotted from the page of history. To have found it there, would once have given me great surprize.

Always thinking myself honoured by your friendship, and feeling towards you respect and esteem alike great & sincere, you will allow me to subscribe myself, Your friend,

TIMOTHY PICKERING.

ALS (copy), Pickering Papers, MHi. Caption supplied by Pickering at head of first sheet: "To John Marshall. (Chief Justice of the United States, / & Author of the Life of Washington)."

1. In an "Advertisement" written on a separate sheet Pickering explained the circumstances that produced this letter. Noting his long and cordial friendship with JM and the chief justice's high opinion of George Washington, Pickering stated that he held a "different opinion" and had expressed such views in his recent public controversy with Justice Johnson. He then added: "I thought that candour towards so excellent a man, & my friend, as well as a regard to my own reputation, required me to state explicitly to Judge Marshall, some principal facts on which my opinion of Washington's military character was formed; and also to glance at some incidents, tending to show, that he was not endowed with the talents of a Statesman; as I knew that he did not possess those of a General. These considerations gave birth to the following letter."

2. William Johnson's *Sketches of the Life and Correspondence of Nathanael Greene* (Charleston, S.C., 1822) provoked a series of hostile reviews to which the author had replied in a separate pamphlet. The most recent publication was a review in the *North American Review* of Johnson, *Remarks, Critical and Historical, on an Article in the Forty-seventh Number of the North American Review, Relating to Count Pulaski* (Charleston, S.C., 1825) and of Paul Bentalou, *A Reply to Judge Johnson's Remarks on an Article in the North American Review, Relating to Count Pulaski* (Baltimore, 1826). The review included Pickering's letter to Jared Sparks of 23 Aug. 1826, prefaced by the editor's comments that Pickering "was present at the battle of Germantown, by the side of Washington, and, from his station, had as good an opportunity of knowing the events of the day, as any other person" (Donald G. Morgan, *Justice William*

Johnson: The First Dissenter [Columbia, S.C., 1954], 152 and n. 23; "Judge Johnson and Count Pulaski," *North American Review* [Oct. 1826], 414–40, esp. 425–30).

3. The "late reply" was Pickering's letter addressed to the editor of the *North American Review* and dated 5 Jan. 1827. It was published in the Washington *Daily National Intelligencer,* 30 Jan. 1827 (and in a supplement to the 27 Jan. issue of the country edition). Pickering was responding to Johnson's letter, dated Nov. 1826, published in the *Intelligencer* of 4 Dec. 1826 (and also in the 5 Dec. issue of the country edition). Johnson's letter, in turn, had been provoked by the reprinting (in the *Intelligencer* of 12 Oct. 1826) of Pickering's letter of 23 Aug. 1826 lately published in the *North American Review* (see n. 2).

4. *An Easy Plan of Discipline for a Militia* (Salem, Mass., 1775; 2d ed.; Boston, 1776).

5. *Interesting Correspondence between His Excellency Governour Sullivan and Col. Pickering* (Boston, 1808), 20–21.

6. *Proceedings of a General Court-martial, Held at Brunswick, . . . for the Trial of Major General Lee, July 4, 1778* (Cooperstown, N.Y., 1823). Pickering apparently referred to an earlier edition.

7. William Gordon, *The History of the Rise, Progress, and Establishment of the Independence of the United States of America* (3 vols.; 3d Am. ed.; New York, 1801). Reed's letter to Washington, 22 Dec. 1776, and the latter's response on 23 Dec., are printed in vol. II, 151.

8. Joseph Reed, *Remarks on a Late Publication in the Independent Gazetteer* (Philadelphia, 1783).

9. See JM to Rembrandt Peale, 10 Mar. 1824; Richard Peters to Peale, 24 June 1824, Lillian B. Miller, et al., eds., *The Selected Papers of Charles Willson Peale and His Family,* IV (New Haven, Conn., 1996), 420–21.

10. William Wirt, *Sketches of the Life and Character of Patrick Henry* (Philadelphia, 1817), 45. Pickering's quote is not verbatim.

11. Ibid., 113.

12. Ibid., 386.

Ogden v. Saunders
Opinion
U.S. Supreme Court, 19 February 1827

EDITORIAL NOTE

The Supreme Court's decisions in *Sturgis* v. *Crowninshield* and *McMillan* v. *McNeill* in 1819 had not fully resolved the constitutional status of state bankruptcy laws. The former established that retrospective laws discharging a debtor from a contract made before the enactment of the law were repugnant to the contract clause of the Constitution. The latter held that a bankruptcy law of one state could not operate extraterritorially to affect a contract executed in another state, whether or not the law was enacted before or after the contract. Still unsettled was whether a prospective law releasing a debtor from a contract made within the same state was constitutional. This question presented itself in *Ogden* v. *Saunders* and produced Chief Justice Marshall's first and only dissent in an important constitutional case.

The case began in the U.S. District Court for Louisiana in May 1814 when Lewis Sanders of Kentucky sued George M. Ogden for payment on five bills of exchange amounting to $2,200.[1] Sanders (1781–1861) was a Lexington merchant, manufacturer, and livestock breeder who had dealings with Henry Clay. The transactions on which the case later arose occurred in 1806, the result of Sanders's financial support for the dubious enterprise of Aaron Burr, who visited Lexington that year. The bills of exchange, all dated 30 September 1806, had been drawn in Sanders's favor by John Jordan, Burr's agent in Lexington, and directed to Ogden (1779–1824), a New York City merchant on whose firm Burr drew numerous bills to cover his expenses in the West. While on a trip east to buy goods for his Lexington store, Sanders presented the bills to Ogden, who accepted them for payment in expectation of receiving funds from Burr's associates. Sanders never received payment, however, and Ogden soon thereafter entered debtor's prison, from which he was released in 1808 after obtaining a certificate of discharge under New York's 1801 insolvent law. In 1810 Ogden moved to New Orleans, resuming his mercantile business in partnership with Peter V. Ogden, his younger brother (also a former Burr agent). Sanders evidently learned of Ogden's removal and subsequent recovery and determined to pursue him in the federal court at New Orleans.[2]

In November 1816, more than two years after the suit began, Ogden entered several pleas, including his certificate of discharge under New York's insolvent law. This was the "three-fourths" law, so called because it enabled a debtor, by request of so many creditors who had debts owed to them amounting to three-fourths of all the debts owed, to be released from prison. A jury returned a special verdict in May 1817, which was argued in June 1818 and on which Judge Dominick A. Hall gave judgment for the plaintiff Sanders in December 1819. The case came by writ of error to the Supreme Court in February 1820.[3]

After languishing on the docket for four years, the appeal was finally set down for argument at the 1824 term. The chief justice's absence from court owing to his injury postponed the hearing until late in the session. The case was argued over three days, 3–5 March, with Clay, David B. Ogden, and Charles G. Haines, a New York lawyer, appearing for Ogden, and Daniel Webster and Henry Wheaton representing Sanders. The Court adjourned without a decision at this and the following two terms. As became evident the Court was unable to decide the case in 1825 and 1826 because the six attending justices were evenly divided.[4] The Court directed a reargument at the 1827 term, when all seven justices were present, including the newest member, Robert Trimble. The case was reargued on 18, 19, and 20 January 1827 by Ogden and Edward Livingston for Ogden and by Wheaton and Webster for Sanders.[5]

Several other insolvency cases besides *Ogden* were also on the Court's docket: *Pearson and Carter* v. *Harison and Lewis* and *Starr and Smith* v. *Benedict and Richardson*, both of which came up from the New York Court for the Trial of Impeachments and Correction of Errors; and *Shaw* v. *Robins*, from the Ohio Supreme Court.[6] In each of these cases the state courts had sustained the constitutionality of prospective bankruptcy laws, following earlier precedents. The principal New York case was *Mather* v. *Bush*, decided in May 1819; the leading Ohio precedent was *Smith* v. *Parsons*, decided in December 1823. Both the New York and Ohio courts carefully distinguished their cases from *Sturgis* and *McMillan*, not wishing to extend the authority of the Supreme Court's precedents beyond their particular facts.[7]

While *Ogden* and the other state bankruptcy cases were pending, Congress was nearing the conclusion of debate on a national bankruptcy bill, which had been on the legislative agenda for nearly ten years.[8] The debate proceeded in full awareness of what was occurring in the courtroom below. Senator Hayne, for example, urged adoption of the bill on the ground that relief from debts could only come from the federal government. He interpreted the Supreme Court's earlier bankruptcy decisions as denying to the states the power of passing laws absolving debts. He believed there was "hardly a chance" the Court would sustain prospective laws, but even if such laws were upheld they could not apply to creditors who lived in another state. Senator Reed, on the other hand, was fully confident that the power of the states to pass prospective laws would "escape unhurt, through the ordeal of the judiciary tribunals of this country." The Court had not yet denied this power, he noted, and even though such a case was now pending, "we cannot wait, in the exercise of our high powers, upon the movements of that tribunal." Congress rejected the bankruptcy bill early in February 1827, soon after the argument but before the Court announced its decision in *Ogden*.[9]

In argument both sides invoked the rules of construction to affirm or deny the validity of prospective bankruptcy laws. The case hinged, however, on the meaning of the phrase "obligation of contract." One side maintained that prospective bankruptcy laws merely annexed conditions that entered "into the contract, and form a part of it as completely as if they had been expressly stipulated by the parties themselves."[10] The parties form contracts with the knowledge of such laws and thereby tacitly assent to the condition that the contract shall be discharged by a surrender of property in case of insolvency. The obligation of contract, according to this argument, was a legal obligation arising from the laws under which a contract is made and the remedies provided by those laws for enforcing performance of the contract. Bankruptcy laws fell into this class of legislation, not being in principle different from laws against usury, gambling laws, statutes of limitation, or any other ordinary regulation of contract. The obligation of contract was not intrinsic to the contract itself but arose from the external action of municipal legislation regulating and enforcing the contract. So long as such legislation was prospective and formed part of the contract, it could not be said to impair the obligation.

Wheaton and Webster for the other side denied that the obligation of contract originated solely in municipal law, contending that it sprang "from a higher source: from those great principles of universal law, which are binding on societies of men as well as on individuals." This natural-law basis for the obligation of contract was supported by the weighty authority of the great writers on natural law and the law of nations: Grotius, Burlamaqui, Vattel, Pothier, and Rutherforth. Municipal law did not enter into the contract but rather, said Webster, acted "upon the contract only when it is broken, or to discharge the party from its obligation after it is broken." Taken to its extreme, the argument that the law formed part of the contract would render the contract clause nugatory. If a state enacted a general law that henceforth contracts would be subject to legislative control, this law would become part of the contract and enable the legislature to interfere with contracts "for any and all purposes, wholly uncontrolled by the constitution of the United States." Obligation, founded in natural law, inhered in the contract and was distinct from the remedy given by municipal law to enforce it. A state's power to modify the remedy could not extend to impairing or destroying the obligation.[11]

On 19 February the Court upheld the constitutionality of prospective bankruptcy laws by a vote of four to three. The majority justices, Washington, Johnson, Thompson, and Trimble, delivered their opinions seriatim in order of seniority. In sustaining the New York insolvency statute, Washington adhered to the opinion he had uttered on circuit in 1814.[12] Although then and now he believed that Congress's power over bankruptcy was exclusive and effectively withdrew that subject from the states, the Court had rejected this view in *Sturgis*. So far as the contract clause applied to such laws, it voided only those that operated retrospectively. Conceding that obligation of contract derived from natural law and that this was the obligation acknowledged in compacts among sovereign nations or in contracts made on a desert island, Washington denied that the framers intended this to be the exclusive meaning of the phrase. It also included the municipal laws of the state where the contract was formed. Natural law obligation, furthermore, was to be understood as strictly subordinate to the obligation defined by municipal legislation.

In their various ways Justices Johnson, Thompson, and Trimble agreed with Washington that a state had authority to regulate, modify, or control the operation of universal law within its jurisdiction. State laws created a civil obligation that, at least as to private contracts, superseded natural law, and it was this civil obligation that the Constitution was meant to protect. To concede a state's power to outlaw usury and gambling contracts, to adopt statutes of frauds and limitation, was to "surrender" the whole argument, said Johnson, for it admitted "the right of the government to limit and define the power of contracting, and the extent of the creditor's remedy against his debtor."[13]

Chief Justice Marshall spoke for the minority, which also included Story and Duvall. If their view had prevailed, the effect would have been to prohibit all state bankruptcy laws, that is, those which discharged the debtor from future liability. Perhaps the chief justice regarded such a prohibition as good policy, believing that bankruptcy was a national responsibility that should be entrusted to Congress. On the other hand, in view of the perennial failure to enact national legislation, he might well have concluded that state laws, by providing relief for honest debtors and reasonable protection for creditors, could serve the laudable goals of encouraging commercial enterprise and promoting economic expansion. Expediency might well have inclined him to adopt the majority's view.

No matter which course expediency might have dictated, Marshall believed this to be a case of constitutional principle that allowed no room for compromise. Indeed, given his earlier judicial construction of the contract clause, which held that the Constitution protected both "executed" and "executory" contracts, public contracts as well as private, it is difficult to conceive how he could have admitted a distinction between retrospective and prospective bankruptcy legislation that restricted the clause's reach only to the former. The whole thrust of his interpretation of the contract clause had been to elucidate its comprehensive scope, to show that it embodied a general principle of the sanctity of contracts that was the vital essence of the Constitution. Consistent with this understanding, the chief justice insisted that the contract clause was not directed at particular laws or a particular class of laws. He never expressly declared that it prohibited all bankruptcy laws, only those that impaired the obligation of contract. Traditional insolvency laws that released a debtor from prison but did not discharge his debt were constitutional. The distinction between bankruptcy and insolvency laws was not a workable criterion of constitutionality, however, because, as Marshall had pointed out in *Sturgis*, there was no bright line of demarcation between the two kinds of laws.[14] In this case, for example, the New York law was called an insolvency law.

Marshall's *Ogden* dissent was his last major exposition of the contract clause and embodied his most deeply held convictions about its meaning and the principles of constitutional construction for discerning its intention. No other opinion better reveals the extent to which natural law principles informed his constitutional jurisprudence. For Marshall natural law provided the broad foundation for explicating the meaning and intention of the Constitution, particularly the contract clause. He read into that clause a manifest intention to provide ample protection for the fundamental rights of property and contract. The phrase "obligation of contract" could only be understood in terms of natural law, he believed, for the act of making a contract occurred independently of society and government. Contract preceded legislation, which therefore could not be the source of the right to contract. Municipal law could not create the obligation but could only act upon an intrinsic, preexisting obligation. Marshall, of course, recognized that individuals in forming society surrender their natural liberty in return for civil liberty protected and enforced by government. He denied, however, that the natural obligation of contract was thereby converted into a civil obligation. The right surrendered to society was not the right to contract but only the natural right of coercion.

Here was the nub of the issue. To what extent did government's right to regulate and control the remedy on broken contracts affect the obligation? Did not withholding the remedy effectually destroy the obligation? The chief justice devoted the greater part of his opinion to maintaining the distinction between obligation, which originated in the act of the parties, and remedy, which was provided by a subsequent act of government. There was no absurdity, he insisted, in leaving the states in full possession of the power over the remedy while prohibiting them from impairing the obligation of contracts. The Constitution presumed these governments would act responsibly and in good faith to enforce the performance of contracts.

Marshall's reliance on natural law in *Ogden* was fully consistent with his text-based, positive law conception of judicial review. Natural law in this case was not an external standard for reviewing state laws but rather was embodied in the positive law of the Constitution. The chief justice had no doubt that the framers of the Constitution attached a definite natural-law meaning to "obligation of contract."[15]

Although the Court upheld the validity of the New York law, final judgment in this case was postponed pending determination of a reserved point. The question concerned the validity of a discharge under a state law with respect to a creditor who was a citizen of another state and where the discharge was pleaded in a federal court or another state court.[16] On 13 March the Court affirmed the lower court's ruling in favor of the creditor Sanders. Washington, Thompson, and Trimble dissented from this judgment, in which the unpredictable Johnson joined Marshall, Story, and Duvall. Johnson, speaking for the new majority, concluded that the power of states over contracts, once they had become the subject of a lawsuit, was limited to controversies between the state's own citizens. The actual holding in *Ogden*, then, affected only those creditors who sued in a state court and where the debtor pleaded a discharge under a law of that state. Creditors who were citizens of another state could sue in federal court, where a certificate of discharge under a state law would not bar the action. On the same principle the Court (again speaking through Johnson) in the companion case of *Shaw v. Robins* further held that the plea of discharge was not sufficient to bar an action brought in a different state court. In this case the creditor sued in an Ohio state court, and the debtor pleaded a New York discharge.[17]

The restricted scope of *Ogden* explains in part why there was no immediate enactment of state bankruptcy legislation in the aftermath of the decision. Many state legislators also continued to believe that bankruptcy legislation constitutionally belonged to Congress. Moreover, the same considerations of principle and interest that prevented adoption of a national bankruptcy law also operated at the state level. Many Americans disapproved of the idea of discharging debts despite its constitutional sanction. Those who accepted bankruptcy in principle were sharply divided on whether such legislation should be confined to merchants and traders or extended to all debtors. In addition, bankruptcy was a subject of such technical complexity that no agreement could be reached on the principles and procedures to be included in legislation.[18]

1. All the official records spell the party's name as "Sanders." He became "Saunders" in Wheaton's report and has remained so in subsequent citations of the case.

2. Ogden v. Sanders, record on appeal, App. Cas. No. 1036; Anna Virginia Parker, "Lewis Sanders of Grass Hill," in *Papers of the Christopher Gist Historical Society* (Covington, Ky.), III (1951–52), 1–9; Mary-Jo Kline and Joanne Wood Ryan, eds., *Political Correspondence and Public Papers of Aaron Burr,* II (Princeton, N.J., 1983), 955–56, 991, 994–95, 1033.

3. Ogden v. Saunders, record on appeal, App. Cas. No. 1036.

4. Todd was absent in 1825; Trimble, his successor, was not appointed until after the 1826 term.

5. U.S. Sup. Ct. Minutes, 3, 4, 5 Mar. 1824; 18, 19, 20 Jan. 1827. In addition to Ogden and Livingston, the reporter Wheaton states that Wirt, Walter Jones, and Sampson argued for the constitutionality of prospective bankruptcy laws. They were counsel in other cases involving the same question that were argued along with Ogden v. Saunders (12 Wheat. 214).

6. Pearson and Carter v. Harison and Lewis, App. Cas. No. 1171; Starr and Smith v. Benedict and Richardson, App. Cas. No. 1185; Shaw v. Robins, App. Cas. No. 1250. The first two cases were not reported; Shaw v. Robins is briefly reported in a note at the end of the report of Ogden v. Saunders (12 Wheat. 369 n.).

7. Mather v. Bush, 16 Johns. 233 (N.Y. Sup. Ct., 1819); Smith v. Parsons, 1 Ohio 249 (Ohio Sup. Ct., 1823).

8. Charles Warren, *Bankruptcy in United States History* (Cambridge, Mass., 1935), 22–45.

9. Speech of Robert Y. Hayne, 25 Jan. 1827; speech of Thomas B. Reed, 26 Jan. 1827 (*Register of Debates in Congress, Comprising the Leading Debates and Incidents of the Second Session of the Nineteenth Congress* [Washington, D.C., 1829], III, 117, 125–26).

10. 12 Wheat. 231. Wheaton did not report counsel's arguments for the plaintiff individually.

11. 12 Wheat. 222, 240, 244, 246.

12. Golden v. Prince, 10 Fed. Cas. 542–47 (U.S. Cir. Ct., Pa., 1814).

13. 12 Wheat. 291.

14. 4 Wheat. 194–95; *PJM*, VIII, 245.

15. Warren B. Hunting, *The Obligation of Contracts Clause of the United States Constitution* (1919; New York, 1977 reprint), 42, 43.

16. 12 Wheat. 357; U.S. Sup. Ct. Minutes, 10 Mar. 1827.

17. 12 Wheat. 358–69 and n.

18. Peter J. Coleman, *Debtors and Creditors in America: Insolvency, Imprisonment for Debt, and Bankruptcy, 1607–1900* (Madison, Wis., 1974), 34–36.

OPINION

It is well known that the Court has been divided in opinion on this case. Three Judges, Mr. Justice DUVALL, Mr. Justice STORY, and myself, do not concur in the judgment which has been pronounced. We have taken a different view of the very interesting question which has been discussed with so much talent, as well as labour, at the bar, and I am directed to state the course of reasoning on which we have formed the opinion that the discharge pleaded by the defendant is no bar to the action.

The single question for consideration, is, whether the act of the State of New-York is consistent with or repugnant to the constitution of the United States?

This Court has so often expressed the sentiments of profound and respectful reverence with which it approaches questions of this character, as to make it unnecessary now to say more than that, if it be right that the power of preserving the constitution from legislative infraction, should reside any where, it cannot be wrong, it must be right, that those [on] whom the delicate and important duty is conferred should perform it according to their best judgment.

Much, too, has been said concerning the principles of construction which ought to be applied to the constitution of the United States.

On this subject, also, the Court has taken such frequent occasion to declare its opinion, as to make it unnecessary, at least, to enter again into an elaborate discussion of it. To say that the intention of the instrument must prevail; that this intention must be collected from its words; that its words are to be understood in that sense in which they are generally used by those for whom the instrument was intended; that its provisions are neither to be restricted into insignificance, nor extended to objects not comprehended in them, nor contemplated by its framers — is to repeat what has been already said more at large, and is all that can be necessary.

As preliminary to a more particular investigation of the clause in the constitution, on which the case now under consideration is supposed to depend, it may be proper to inquire how far it is affected by the former decisions of this Court.

In *Sturges* v. *Crowninshield,* it was determined, that an act which discharged the debtor from a contract entered into previous to its passage, was repugnant to the constitution. The reasoning which conducted the

Court to that conclusion might, perhaps, conduct it farther; and with that reasoning, (for myself alone this expression is used,) I have never yet seen cause to be dissatisfied. But that decision is not supposed to be a precedent for *Ogden* v. *Saunders,* because the two cases differ from each other in a material fact; and it is a general rule, expressly recognised by the Court in *Sturges* v. *Crowninshield,* that the positive authority of a decision is co-extensive only with the facts on which it is made. In *Sturges* v. *Crowninshield,* the law acted on a contract which was made before its passage; in this case, the contract was entered into after the passage of the law.

In *M'Neil* v. *M'Millan,* the contract, though subsequent to the passage of the act, was made in a different State, by persons residing in that State, and, consequently, without any view to the law, the benefit of which was claimed by the debtor.

The *Farmers' and Mechanics' Bank of Pennsylvania* v. *Smith* differed from *Sturges* v. *Crowninshield* only in this, that the plaintiff and defendant were both residents of the State in which the law was enacted, and in which it was applied. The Court was of opinion that this difference was unimportant.

It has then been decided, that an act which discharges the debtor from pre-existing contracts is void; and that an act which operates on future contracts is inapplicable to a contract made in a different State, at whatever time it may have been entered into.

Neither of these decisions comprehends the question now presented to the Court. It is, consequently, open for discussion.

The provision of the constitution is, that "no State shall pass any law" "impairing the obligation of contracts." The plaintiff in error contends that this provision inhibits the passage of retrospective laws only — of such as act on contracts in existence at their passage. The defendant in error maintains that it comprehends all future laws, whether prospective or retrospective, and withdraws every contract from State legislation, the obligation of which has become complete.

That there is an essential difference in principle between laws which act on past, and those which act on future contracts; that those of the first description can seldom be justified, while those of the last are proper subjects of ordinary legislative discretion, must be admitted. A constitutional restriction, therefore, on the power to pass laws of the one class, may very well consist with entire legislative freedom respecting those of the other. Yet, when we consider the nature of our Union; that it is intended to make us, in a great measure, one people, as to commercial objects; that, so far as respects the intercommunication of individuals, the lines of separation between States are, in many respects, obliterated; it would not be matter of surprise, if, on the delicate subject of contracts once formed, the interference of State legislation should be greatly abridged, or entirely forbidden. In the nature of the provision, then, there seems to be nothing which ought to influence our construction of the words; and, in making that construction, the whole clause, which consists of a single sentence, is to be taken together, and the intention is to be collected from the whole.

The first paragraph of the tenth section of the first article, which comprehends the provision under consideration, contains an enumeration of those cases in which the action of the State legislature is entirely prohibited. The second enumerates those in which the prohibition is modified. The first paragraph, consisting of total prohibitions, comprehends two classes of powers. Those of the first are political and general in their nature, being an exercise of sovereignty without affecting the rights of individuals. These are, the powers "to enter into any treaty, alliance, or confederation; grant letters of marque or reprisal, coin money, emit bills of credit."

The second class of prohibited laws comprehends those whose operation consists in their action on individuals. These are, laws which make any thing but gold and silver coin a tender in payment of debts, bills of attainder, *ex post facto* laws, or laws impairing the obligation of contracts, or which grant any title of nobility.

In all these cases, whether the thing prohibited be the exercise of mere political power, or legislative action on individuals, the prohibition is complete and total. There is no exception from it. Legislation of every description is comprehended within it. A State is as entirely forbidden to pass laws impairing the obligation of contracts, as to make treaties, or coin money. The question recurs, what is a law impairing the obligation of contracts?

In solving this question, all the acumen which controversy can give to the human mind, has been employed in scanning the whole sentence, and every word of it. Arguments have been drawn from the context, and from the particular terms in which the prohibition is expressed, for the purpose, on the one part, of showing its application to all laws which act upon contracts, whether prospectively or retrospectively; and, on the other, of limiting it to laws which act on contracts previously formed.

The first impression which the words make on the mind, would probably be, that the prohibition was intended to be general. A contract is commonly understood to be the agreement of the parties; and, if it be not illegal, to bind them to the extent of their stipulations. It requires reflection, it requires some intellectual effort, to efface this impression, and to come to the conclusion, that the words contract and obligation, as used in the constitution, are not used in this sense. If, however, the result of this mental effort, fairly made, be the correction of this impression, it ought to be corrected.

So much of this prohibition as restrains the power of the States to punish offenders in criminal cases, the prohibition to pass bills of attainder and *ex post facto* laws, is, in its very terms, confined to pre-existing cases. A bill of attainder can be only for crimes already committed; and a law is not *ex post facto,* unless it looks back to an act done before its passage. Language is incapable of expressing, in plainer terms, that the mind of the Convention was directed to retroactive legislation. The thing forbidden is retroaction. But that part of the clause which relates to the civil transactions of individuals, is expressed in more general terms; in terms which comprehend, in their ordinary signification, cases which occur after, as well as those which occur before, the passage of the act. It forbids a State to make any thing but gold and silver coin a tender in payment of debts, or to pass any law impairing the obligation of contracts. These prohibitions relate to kindred subjects. They contemplate legislative interference with private rights, and restrain that interference. In construing that part of the clause which respects tender laws, a distinction has never been attempted between debts existing at the time the law may be passed, and debts afterwards created. The prohibition has been considered as total; and yet the difference in principle between making property a tender in payment of debts, contracted after the passage of the act, and discharging those debts without payment, or by the surrender of property, between an absolute right to tender in payment, and a contingent right to tender in payment, or in discharge of the debt, is not clearly discernible. Nor is the difference in language so obvious, as to denote plainly a difference of intention in the framers of the instrument. "No State shall make any thing but gold and silver coin a tender in payment of debts." Does the word "debts" mean, generally, those due when the law applies to the case, or is it limited to debts due at the passage of the act? The same train of reasoning which would confine the subsequent words to contracts existing at the passage of the law, would go far in confining these words to debts existing at that time. Yet, this distinction has never, we believe, occurred to any person. How soon it may occur is not for us to determine. We think it would, unquestionably, defeat the object of the clause.

The counsel for the plaintiff insist, that the word "impairing," in the present tense, limits the signification of the provision to the operation of the act at the time of its passage; that no law can be accurately said to impair the obligation of contracts, unless the contracts exist at the time. The law cannot impair what does not exist. It cannot act on nonentities.

There might be weight in this argument, if the prohibited laws were such only as operated of themselves, and immediately on the contract. But insolvent laws are to operate on a future, contingent, unforeseen event. The time to which the word "impairing" applies, is not the time of the passage of the act, but of its action on the contract. That is, the time present in contemplation of the prohibition. The law, at its passage, has no effect whatever on the contract. Thus, if a note be given in New-York for the payment of money, and the debtor removes out of that State into

Connecticut, and becomes insolvent, it is not pretended that his debt can be discharged by the law of New-York. Consequently, that law did not operate on the contract at its formation. When, then, does its operation commence? We answer, when it is applied to the contract. Then, if ever, and not till then, it acts on the contract, and becomes a law impairing its obligation. Were its constitutionality, with respect to previous contracts, to be admitted, it would not impair their obligation until an insolvency should take place, and a certificate of discharge be granted. Till these events occur, its impairing faculty is suspended. A law, then, of this description, if it derogates from the obligation of a contract, when applied to it, is, grammatically speaking, as much a law impairing that obligation, though made previous to its formation, as if made subsequently.

A question of more difficulty has been pressed with great earnestness. It is, what is the original obligation of a contract, made after the passage of such an act as the insolvent law of New-York? Is it unconditional to perform the very thing stipulated, or is the condition implied, that, in the event of insolvency, the contract shall be satisfied by the surrender of property? The original obligation, whatever that may be, must be preserved by the constitution. Any law which lessens, must impair it.

All admit, that the constitution refers to, and preserves, the legal, not the moral obligation of a contract. Obligations purely moral, are to be enforced by the operation of internal and invisible agents, not by the agency of human laws. The restraints imposed on States by the constitution, are intended for those objects which would, if not restrained, be the subject of State legislation. What, then, was the original legal obligation of the contract now under the consideration of the Court?

The plaintiff insists, that the law enters into the contract so completely as to become a constituent part of it. That it is to be construed as if it contained an express stipulation to be discharged, should the debtor become insolvent, by the surrender of all his property for the benefit of his creditors, in pursuance of the act of the legislature.

This is, unquestionably, pressing the argument very far; and the establishment of the principle leads inevitably to consequences which would affect society deeply and seriously.

Had an express condition been inserted in the contract, declaring that the debtor might be discharged from it at any time by surrendering all his property to his creditors, this condition would have bound the creditor. It would have constituted the obligation of his contract; and a legislative act annulling the condition would impair the contract. Such an act would, as is admitted by all, be unconstitutional, because it operates on pre-existing agreements. If a law authorizing debtors to discharge themselves from their debts by surrendering their property, enters into the contract, and forms a part of it, if it is equivalent to a stipulation between the parties, no repeal of the law can affect contracts made during its existence. The effort to give it that effect would impair their obligation. The counsel for the plaintiff perceive, and avow this consequence, in effect, when they contend, that to deny the operation of the law on the contract under consideration, is to impair its obligation. Are gentlemen prepared to say, that an insolvent law, once enacted, must, to a considerable extent, be permanent? That the legislature is incapable of varying it so far as respects existing contracts?

So, too, if one of the conditions of an obligation for the payment of money be, that on the insolvency of the obligor, or on any event agreed on by the parties, he should be at liberty to discharge it by the tender of all, or part of his property, no question could exist respecting the validity of the contract, or respecting its security from legislative interference. If it should be determined, that a law authorizing the same tender, on the same contingency, enters into, and forms a part of the contract, then, a tender law, though expressly forbidden, with an obvious view to its prospective, as well as retrospective operation, would, by becoming the contract of the parties, subject all contracts made after its passage to its control. If it be said, that such a law would be obviously unconstitutional and void, and, therefore, could not be a constituent part of the contract, we answer, that if the insolvent law be unconstitutional, it is equally void, and equally incapable of becoming, by mere implication, a part of the contract. The plainness of the repugnancy does not change the question. That may be very clear to one intellect, which is far from being so to another. The law now under consideration is, in the opinion of one party, clearly consistent with the constitution, and, in the opinion of the other, as clearly repugnant to it. We do not admit the correctness of that reasoning which would settle this question by introducing into the contract a stipulation not admitted by the parties.

This idea admits of being pressed still farther. If one law enters into all subsequent contracts, so does every other law which relates to the subject. A legislative act, then, declaring that all contracts should be subject to legislative control, and should be discharged as the legislature might prescribe, would become a component part of every contract, and be one of its conditions. Thus, one of the most important features in the constitution of the United States, one which the state of the times most urgently required, one on which the good and the wise reposed confidently for securing the prosperity and harmony of our citizens, would lie prostrate, and be construed into an inanimate, inoperative, unmeaning clause.

Gentlemen are struck with the enormity of this result, and deny that their principle leads to it. They distinguish, or attempt to distinguish, between the incorporation of a general law, such as has been stated, and the incorporation of a particular law, such as the insolvent law of New-York, into the contract. But will reason sustain this distinction? They say, that men cannot be supposed to agree to so indefinite an article as such a general law would be, but may well be supposed to agree to an article, reasonable in itself, and the full extent of which is understood.

But the principle contended for does not make the insertion of this new term or condition into the contract, to depend upon its reasonableness. It is inserted because the legislature has so enacted. If the enactment of the legislature becomes a condition of the contract because it is an enactment, then it is a high prerogative, indeed, to decide, that one enactment shall enter the contract, while another, proceeding from the same authority, shall be excluded from it.

The counsel for the plaintiff illustrates and supports this position by several legal principles, and by some decisions of this Court, which have been relied on as being applicable to it.

The first case put is, interest on a bond payable on demand, which does not stipulate interest. This, he says, is not a part of the remedy, but a new term in the contract.

Let the correctness of this averment be tried by the course of proceeding in such cases.

The failure to pay, according to stipulation, is a breach of the contract, and the means used to enforce it constitute the remedy which society affords the injured party. If the obligation contains a penalty, this remedy is universally so regulated that the judgment shall be entered for the penalty, to be discharged by the payment of the principal and interest. But the case on which counsel has reasoned is a single bill. In this case, the party who has broken his contract is liable for damages. The proceeding to obtain those damages is as much a part of the remedy as the proceeding to obtain the debt. They are claimed in the same declaration, and as being distinct from each other. The damages must be assessed by a jury; whereas, if interest formed a part of the debt, it would be recovered as part of it. The declaration would claim it as a part of the debt; and yet, if a suitor were to declare on such a bond as containing this new term for the payment of interest, he would not be permitted to give a bond in evidence in which this supposed term was not written. Any law regulating the proceedings of Courts on this subject, would be a law regulating the remedy.

The liability of the drawer of a bill of exchange, stands upon the same principle with every other implied contract. He has received the money of the person in whose favour the bill is drawn, and promises that it shall be returned by the drawee. If the drawee fail to pay the bill, then the promise of the drawer is broken, and for this breach of contract he is liable. The same principle applies to the endorser. His contract is not written, but his name is evidence of his promise that the bill shall be paid, and of his having received value for it. He is, in effect, a new drawer, and has made a new contract. The law does not require that this contract shall be in writing; and, in determining what evidence shall be sufficient to prove it, does not introduce new conditions not actually made by the parties. The same reasoning applies to the principle which requires notice. The original contract is not written at large. It is founded on the acts of the parties, and its extent is measured by those acts. A. draws on B. in favour of C., for value received. The bill is evidence that he has received value, and has promised that it shall be paid. He has funds in the hands of the drawer, and has a right to expect that his promise will be performed. He has, also, a right to expect notice of its non-performance, because his conduct may be materially influenced by this failure of the drawee. He ought to have notice that *his* bill is disgraced, because this notice enables him to take measures for his own security. It is reasonable that he should stipulate for this notice, and the law presumes that he did stipulate for it.

A great mass of human transactions depends upon implied contracts; upon contracts which are not written, but which grow out of the acts of the parties. In such cases, the parties are supposed to have made those stipulations, which, as honest, fair, and just men, they ought to have made. When the law assumes that they have made these stipulations, it does not vary their contract, or introduce new terms into it, but declares that certain acts, unexplained by compact, impose certain duties, and that the parties had stipulated for their performance. The difference is obvious between this and the introduction of a new condition into a contract drawn out in writing, in which the parties have expressed every thing that is to be done by either.

The usage of banks, by which days of grace are allowed on notes payable and negotiable in bank, is of the same character. Days of grace, from their very term, originate partly in convenience, and partly in the indulgence of the creditor. By the terms of the note, the debtor has to the last hour of the day on which it becomes payable, to comply with it; and it would often be inconvenient to take any steps after the close of day. It is often convenient to postpone subsequent proceedings till the next day. Usage has extended this time of grace generally to three days, and in some banks to four. This usage is made a part of the contract, not by the interference of the legislature, but by the act of the parties. The case cited from 9 *Wheat. Rep.* 581. is a note discounted in bank.[1] In all such cases the bank receives, and the maker of the note pays, interest for the days of grace. This would be illegal and usurious, if the money was not lent for these additional days. The extent of the loan, therefore, is regulated by the act of the parties, and this part of the contract is founded on their act. Since, by contract, the maker is not liable for his note until the days of grace are expired, he has not broken his contract until they expire. The duty of giving notice to the endorser of his failure, does not risc, until the failure has taken place; and, consequently, the promise of the bank to give such notice is performed, if it be given when the event has happened.

The case of the *Bank of Columbia* v. *Oakley,* (4 *Wheat. Rep.* 235.) was one in which the legislature had given a summary remedy to the bank for a broken contract, and had placed that remedy in the hands of the bank itself.[2] The case did not turn on the question whether the law of Maryland was introduced into the contract, but whether a party might not, by his own conduct, renounce his claim to the trial by jury in a particular case. The Court likened it to submissions to arbitration, and to stipulation and forthcoming bonds. The principle settled in that case is, that a party may renounce a benefit, and that *Oakley* had exercised this right.

The cases from *Strange* and *East* turn upon a principle, which is generally recognised, but which is entirely distinct from that which they are cited to support.[3] It is, that a man who is discharged by the tribunals of his own country, acting under its laws, may plead that discharge in any other country. The principle is, that laws act upon a contract, not that they enter into it, and become a stipulation of the parties. Society affords a remedy for breaches of contract. If that remedy has been applied, the claim to it is extinguished. The external action of law upon contracts, by administering the remedy for their breach, or otherwise, is the usual exercise of legislative power. The interference with those contracts, by introducing conditions into them not agreed to by the parties, would be a very unusual and a very extraordinary exercise of the legislative power, which ought not to be gratuitously attributed to laws that do not profess to claim it. If the law becomes a part of the contract, change of place would not expunge the condition. A contract made in New-York would be the same in any other State as in New-York, and would still retain the stipulation originally introduced into it, that the debtor should be discharged by the surrender of his estate.

It is not, we think, true, that contracts are entered into in contemplation of the insolvency of the obligor. They are framed with the expectation that they will be literally performed. Insolvency is undoubtedly a casualty which is possible, but is never expected. In the ordinary course of human transactions, if even suspected, provision is made for it, by taking security against it. When it comes unlooked for, it would be entirely contrary to reason to consider it as a part of the contract.

We have, then, no hesitation in saying that, however law may act upon contracts, it does not enter into them, and become a part of the agreement. The effect of such a principle would be a mischievous abridgment of legislative power over subjects within the proper jurisdiction of States, by arresting their power to repeal or modify such laws with respect to existing contracts.

But, although the argument is not sustainable in this form, it assumes another, in which it is more plausible. Contract, it is said, being the creature of society, derives its obligation from the law; and, although the law may not enter into the agreement so as to form a constituent part of it, still it acts externally upon the contract, and determines how far the principle of coercion shall be applied to it; and this being universally understood, no individual can complain justly of its application to himself, in a case where it was known when the contract was formed.

This argument has been illustrated by references to the statutes of frauds, of usury, and of limitations. The construction of the words in the constitution, respecting contracts, for which the defendants contend, would, it has been said, withdraw all these subjects from State legislation. The acknowledgment, that they remain within it, is urged as an admission, that contract is not withdrawn by the constitution, but remains under State control, subject to this restriction only, that no law shall be passed impairing the obligation of contracts in existence at its passage.

The defendants maintain that an error lies at the very foundation of this argument. It assumes that contract is the mere creature of society, and derives all its obligation from human legislation. That it is not the stipulation an individual makes which binds him, but some declaration of the supreme power of a State to which he belongs, that he shall perform what he has undertaken to perform. That though this original declaration may be lost in remote antiquity, it must be presumed as the origin of the obligation of contracts. This postulate the defendants deny, and, we think, with great reason.

It is an argument of no inconsiderable weight against it, that we find no trace of such an enactment. So far back as human research carries us, we find the judicial power as a part of the executive, administering justice by the application of remedies to violated rights, or broken contracts. We find that power applying these remedies on the idea of a pre-existing obligation on every man to do what he has promised on consideration to do; that the breach of this obligation is an injury for which the injured party has a just claim to compensation, and that society ought to afford him a remedy for that injury. We find allusions to the mode of acquiring property, but we find no allusion, from the earliest time, to any supposed act of the governing power giving obligation to contracts. On the contrary, the proceedings respecting them of which we know any thing, evince the idea of a pre-existing intrinsic obligation which human law enforces. If, on tracing the right to contract, and the obligations created by contract, to their source, we find them to exist anterior to, and independent of society, we may reasonably conclude that those original and pre-existing principles are, like many other natural rights, brought with man into society; and, although they may be controlled, are not given by human legislation.

In the rudest state of nature a man governs himself, and labours for his own purposes. That which he acquires is his own, at least while in his possession, and he may transfer it to another. This transfer passes his right to that other. Hence the right to barter. One man may have acquired more skins than are necessary for his protection from the cold; another more food than is necessary for his immediate use. They agree each to supply the wants of the other from his surplus. Is this contract without obligation? If one of them, having received and eaten the food he needed, refuses to deliver the skin, may not the other rightfully compel him to deliver it? Or two persons agree to unite their strength and skill to hunt together for their mutual advantage, engaging to divide the animal they shall master. Can one of them rightfully take the whole? or, should he attempt it, may not the other force him to a division? If the answer to these questions must affirm the duty of keeping faith between these parties, and the right to enforce it if violated, the answer admits the obligation of contracts, because, upon that obligation depends the right to enforce them. Superior strength may give the power, but cannot give the right. The rightfulness of coercion must depend on the pre-existing obligation to do that for which compulsion is used. It is no objection to the principle, that the injured party may be the weakest. In society, the wrong-doer may be too powerful for the law. He may deride its coercive power, yet his contracts are obligatory; and, if society acquire the power of coercion, that power will be applied without previously enacting that his contract is obligatory.

Independent nations are individuals in a state of nature. Whence is derived the obligation of their contracts? They admit the existence of no superior legislative power which is to give them validity, yet their validity is acknowledged by all. If one of these contracts be broken, all admit the right of the injured party to demand reparation for the injury, and to enforce that reparation of it be withheld. He may not have the power to enforce it, but the whole civilized world concurs in saying, that the power, if possessed, is rightfully used.

In a state of nature, these individuals may contract, their contracts are obligatory, and force may rightfully be employed to coerce the party who has broken his engagement.

What is the effect of society upon these rights? When men unite together and form a government, do they surrender their right to contract, as well as their right to enforce the observance of contracts? For what purpose should they make this surrender? Government cannot exercise this power for individuals. It is better that they should exercise it for themselves. For what purpose, then, should the surrender by made? It can only be, that government may give it back again. As we have no evidence of the surrender, or of the restoration of the right; as this operation of surrender and restoration would be an idle and useless ceremony, the rational inference seems to be, that neither has ever been made; that individuals do not derive from government their right to contract, but bring that right with them into society; that obligation is not conferred on contracts by positive law, but is intrinsic, and is conferred by the act of the parties. This results from the right which every man retains to acquire property, to dispose of that property according to his own judgment, and to pledge himself for a future act. These rights are not given by society but are brought into it. The right of coercion is necessarily surrendered to government, and this surrender imposes on government the correlative duty of furnishing a remedy. The right to regulate contracts, to prescribe rules by which they shall be evidenced, to prohibit such as may be deemed mischievous, is unquestionable, and has been universally exercised. So far as this power has restrained the original right of individuals to bind themselves by contract, it is restrained; but beyond these actual restraints the original power remains unimpaired.

This reasoning is, undoubtedly, much strengthened by the authority of those writers on natural and national law, whose opinions have been viewed with profound respect by the wisest men of the present, and of past ages.

Supposing the obligation of the contract to be derived from the agreement of the parties, we will inquire how far law acts externally on it, and may control that obligation. That law may have, on future contracts, all the effect which the counsel for the plaintiff in error claim, will not be denied. That it is capable of discharging the debtor under the circumstances, and on the conditions prescribed in the statute which has been pleaded in this case, will not be controverted. But as this is an operation which was not intended by the parties, nor contemplated by them, the particular act can be entitled to this operation only when it has the full force of law. A law may determine the obligation of a contract on the happening of a contingency, because it is the law. If it be not the law, it cannot have this effect. When its existence as law is denied, that existence cannot be proved by showing what are the qualities of a law. Law has been defined by a writer, whose definitions especially have been the theme of almost universal panegyric, "to be a rule of civil conduct prescribed by the supreme power in a State."[4] In our system, the legislature of a State is the supreme power, in all cases where its action is not restrained by the constitution of the United States. Where it is so restrained, the legislature ceases to be the supreme power, and its acts are not law. It is, then, begging the question to say, that, because contracts may be discharged by a law previously enacted, this contract may be discharged by this act of the legislature of New-York; for the question returns upon us, is this act a law? Is it consistent with, or repugnant to, the constitution of the United States? This question is to be solved only by the constitution itself.

In examining it, we readily admit, that the whole subject of contracts is under the control of society, and that all the power of society over it resides in the State legislatures, except in those special cases where restraint is imposed by the constitution of the United States. The particular restraint now under consideration is on the power to impair the obligation of contracts. The extent of this restraint cannot be ascertained by showing that the legislature may prescribe the circumstances, on which the original validity of a contract shall be made to depend. If the legislative will be, that certain agreements shall be in writing, that they shall be sealed, that they shall be attested by a certain number of witnesses, that they shall be recorded, or that they shall assume any prescribed form before they become obligatory, all these are regulations which society may rightfully make and which do not come within the restrictions of the constitution, because they do not *impair* the obligation of the contract. The obligation must exist before it can be impaired; and a prohibition to impair it, when made, does not imply an inability to prescribe those circumstances which shall create its obligation. The statutes of frauds, therefore, which have been enacted in the several States, and which are acknowledged to flow from the proper exercise of State sovereignty, prescribe regulations which must precede the obligation of the contract, and, consequently, cannot impair that obligation. Acts of this description, therefore, are most clearly not within the prohibition of the constitution.

The acts against usury are of the same character. They declare the contract to be void in the beginning. They deny that the instrument ever became a contract. They deny it all original obligation; and cannot impair that which never came into existence.

Acts of limitations approach more nearly to the subject of consideration, but are not identified with it. They defeat a contract once obligatory, and may, therefore, be supposed to partake of the character of laws which impair its obligation. But a practical view of the subject will show us that the two laws stand upon distinct principles.

In the case of *Sturges* v. *Crowninshield,* it was observed by the Court, that these statutes relate only to the remedies which are furnished in the Courts; and their language is generally confined to the remedy. They do not purport to dispense with the performance of a contract, but proceed on the presumption that a certain length of time, unexplained by circumstances, is reasonable evidence of a performance. It is on this idea alone that it is possible to sustain the decision, that a bare acknowledgment of the debt, unaccompanied with any new promise, shall remove that bar created by the act. It would be a mischief not to be tolerated, if contracts might be set up at any distance of time, when the evidence of payment might be lost, and the estates of the dead, or even of the living, be subjected to these stale obligations. The principle is, without the aid of a statute, adopted by the Courts as a rule of justice. The legislature has enacted no statute of limitations as a bar to suits on sealed instruments. Yet twenty years of unexplained silence on the part of the creditor is evidence of payment. On parol contracts, or on written contracts not under seal, which are considered in a less solemn point of view than sealed instruments, the legislature has supposed that a shorter time might amount to evidence of performance, and has so enacted. All have acquiesced in these enactments, but have never considered them as being of that class of laws which impair the obligation of contracts. In prescribing the evidence which shall be received in its Courts, and the effect of that evidence, the State is exercising its acknowledged powers. It is likewise in the exercise of its legitimate powers, when it is regulating the remedy and mode of proceeding in its Courts.

The counsel for the plaintiff in error insist, that the right to regulate the remedy and to modify the obligation of the contract are the same; that obligation and remedy are identical, that they are synonymous — two words conveying the same idea.

The answer given to this proposition by the defendant's counsel seems to be conclusive. They originate at different times. The obligation to perform is coeval with the undertaking to perform; it originates with the contract itself, and operates anterior to the time of performance. The remedy acts upon a broken contract, and enforces a pre-existing obligation.

If there be any thing in the observations made in a preceding part of this opinion respecting the source from which contracts derive their obligation, the proposition we are now considering cannot be true. It was shown, we think satisfactorily, that the right to contract is the attribute of a free agent, and that he may rightfully coerce performance from another free agent who violates his faith. Contracts have, consequently, an intrinsic obligation. When men come into society, they can no longer exercise this original and natural right of coercion. It would be incompatible with general peace, and is, therefore, surrendered. Society prohibits the use of private individual coercion, and gives in its place a more safe and more certain remedy. But the right to contract is not surrendered with the right to coerce performance. It is still incident to that degree of free agency which the laws leave to every individual, and the obligation of the contract is a necessary consequence of the right to make it. Laws regulate this right, but, where not regulated, it is retained in its original extent. Obligation and remedy, then, are not identical; they originate at different times, and are derived from different sources.

But, although the identity of obligation and remedy be disproved, it may be, and has been urged, that they are precisely commensurate with each other, and are such sympathetic essences, if the expression may be allowed, that the action of law upon the remedy is immediately felt by the obligation — that they live, languish, and die together. The use made of this argument is to show the absurdity and self-contradiction of the construction which maintains the inviolability of obligation, while it leaves the remedy to the State governments.

We do not perceive this absurdity or self-contradiction.

Our country exhibits the extraordinary spectacle of distinct, and, in many respects, independent governments over the same territory and the same people. The local governments are restrained from impairing the obligation of contracts, but they furnish the remedy to enforce them, and administer that remedy in tribunals constituted by themselves. It has been shown that the obligation is distinct from the remedy, and, it would seem to follow, that law might act on the remedy without acting on the obligation. To afford a remedy is certainly the high duty of those who govern to those who are governed. A failure in the performance of this duty subjects the government to the just reproach of the world. But the constitution has not undertaken to enforce its performance. That instrument treats the States with the respect which is due to intelligent beings, understanding their duties, and willing to perform them; not as insane beings, who must be compelled to act for self-preservation. Its language is the language of restraint, not of coercion. It prohibits the States from passing any law impairing the obligation of contracts; it does not enjoin them to enforce contracts. Should a State be sufficiently insane to shut up or abolish its Courts, and thereby withhold all remedy, would this annihilation of remedy annihilate the obligation also of contracts? We know it would not. If the debtor should come within the jurisdiction of any Court of another State, the remedy would be immediately applied, and the inherent obligation of the contract enforced. This cannot be ascribed to a renewal of the obligation; for passing the line of a state cannot re-create an obligation which was extinguished. It must be the original obligation derived from the agreement of the parties, and which exists unimpaired though the remedy was withdrawn.

But, we are told, that the power of the State over the remedy may be used to the destruction of all beneficial results from the right; and hence it is inferred, that the construction which maintains the inviolability of the obligation, must be extended to the power of regulating the remedy.

The difficulty which this view of the subject presents, does not proceed from the identity or connexion of right and remedy, but from the existence of distinct governments acting on kindred subjects. The constitution contemplates restraint as to the obligation of contracts, not as to the application of remedy. If this restraint affects a power which the constitution did not mean to touch, it can only be when that power is used as an instrument of hostility to invade the inviolability of contract, which is placed beyond its reach. A State may use many of its acknowledged powers in such manner as to come in conflict with the provisions of the constitution. Thus the power over its domestic police, the power to regulate commerce purely internal, may be so exercised as to interfere with regulations of commerce with foreign nations, or between the States. In such cases, the power which is supreme must control that which is not supreme, when they come in conflict. But this principle does not involve any self-contradiction, or deny the existence of the several powers in the respective governments. So, if a State shall not merely modify, or withhold a particular remedy, but shall apply it in such manner as to extinguish the obligation without performance, it would be an abuse of power which could scarcely be misunderstood, but which would not prove that remedy could not be regulated without regulating obligation.

The counsel for the plaintiff in error put a case of more difficulty, and urge it as a conclusive argument against the existence of a distinct line dividing obligation from remedy. It is this. The law affords remedy by giving execution against the person, or the property, or both. The same power which can withdraw the remedy against the person, can withdraw that against the property, or that against both, and thus effectually defeat the obligation. The constitution, we are told, deals not with form, but with substance; and cannot be presumed, if it designed to protect the obligation of contracts from State legislation, to have left it thus obviously exposed to destruction.

The answer is, that if the law goes farther, and annuls the obligation without affording the remedy which satisfies it, if its action on the remedy be such as palpably to impair the obligation of the contract, the very case arises which we suppose to be within the constitution. If it leaves the obligation untouched, but withholds the remedy, or affords one which is merely nominal, it is like all other cases of misgovernment, and leaves the debtor still liable to his creditor, should he be found, or should his property be found, where the laws afford a remedy. If that high sense of duty which men selected for the government of their fellow citizens must be supposed to feel, furnishes no security against a course of legislation which must end in self-destruction; if the solemn oath taken by every member, to support the constitution of the United States, furnishes no security against intentional attempts to violate its spirit while evading its letter — the question how far the constitution interposes a shield for the protection of an injured individual, who demands from a Court of justice that remedy which every government ought to afford, will depend on the law itself which shall be brought under consideration. The anticipation of such a case would be unnecessarily disrespectful, and an opinion on it would be, at least, premature. But, however the question might be decided, should it be even determined that such a law would be a successful evasion of the constitution, it does not follow, that an act which operates directly on the contract after it is made, is not within the restriction imposed on the States by that instrument. The validity of a law acting directly on the obligation, is not proved by showing that the constitution has provided no means for compelling the States to enforce it.

We perceive, then, no reason for the opinion, that the prohibition "to pass any law impairing the obligation of contracts," is incompatible with the fair exercise of that discretion, which the State legislatures possess in common with all governments, to regulate the remedies afforded by their own Courts. We think, that obligation and remedy are distinguishable from each other. That the first is created by the act of the parties, the last is afforded by government. The words of the restriction we have been considering, countenance, we think, this idea. No State shall "pass any law impairing the obligation of contracts." These words seem to us to import, that the obligation is intrinsic, that it is created by the contract itself, not that it is dependent on the laws made to enforce it. When we advert to the course of reading generally pursued by American statesmen in early life, we must suppose, that the framers of our constitution were intimately acquainted with the writings of those wise and learned men, whose treatises on the laws of nature and nations have guided public opinion on the subjects of obligation and contract. If we turn to those treatises, we find them to concur in the declaration, that contracts possess an original intrinsic obligation, derived from the acts of free agents, and not given by government. We must suppose, that the framers of our constitution took the same view of the subject, and the language they have used confirms this opinion.

The propositions we have endeavoured to maintain, of the truth of which we are ourselves convinced, are these:

That the words of the clause in the constitution which we are considering, taken in their natural and obvious sense, admit of a prospective, as well as of a retrospective operation.

That an act of the legislature does not enter into the contract, and become one of the conditions stipulated by the parties; nor does it act externally on the agreement, unless it have the full force of law.

That contracts derive their obligation from the act of the parties, not from the grant of government; and that the right of government to regulate the manner in which they shall be formed, or to prohibit such as may be against the policy of the State, is entirely consistent with their inviolability after they have been formed.

That the obligation of a contract is not identified with the means which government may furnish to enforce it; and that a prohibition to pass any law impairing it, does not imply a prohibition to vary the remedy; nor does a power to vary the remedy, imply a power to impair the obligation derived from the act of the parties.

We cannot look back to the history of the times when the august spectacle was exhibited of the assemblage of a whole people by their representatives in Convention, in order to unite thirteen independent sovereignties under one government, so far as might be necessary for the purposes of union, without being sensible of the great importance which was at that time attached to the tenth section of the first article. The power of changing the relative situation of debtor and creditor, of interfering with contracts, a power which comes home to every man, touches the interest of all, and controls the conduct of every individual in those things which he supposes to be proper for his own exclusive management, had been used to such an excess by the State legislatures, as to break in upon the ordinary intercourse of society, and destroy all confidence between man and man. The mischief had become so great, so alarming, as not only to impair commercial intercourse, and threaten the existence of credit, but to sap the morals of the people, and destroy the sanctity of private faith. To guard against the continuance of the evil was an object of deep interest with all the truly wise, as well as the virtuous, of this great community, and was one of the important benefits expected from a reform of the government.

To impose restraints on State legislation as respected this delicate and interesting subject, was thought necessary by all those patriots who could take an enlightened and comprehensive view of our situation; and the principle obtained an early admission into the various schemes of government which were submitted to the Convention. In framing an instrument, which was intended to be perpetual, the presumption is strong, that every important principle introduced into it is intended to be perpetual also; that a principle expressed in terms to operate in all future time, is intended so to operate. But if the construction for which the plaintiff's counsel contend be the true one, the constitution will have imposed a restriction in language indicating perpetuity, which every State in the Union may elude at pleasure. The obligation of contracts in force, at any given time, is but of short duration; and, if the inhibition be of retrospective laws only, a very short lapse of time will remove every subject on which the act is forbidden to operate, and make this provision of the constitution so far useless. Instead of introducing a great principle, prohibiting all laws of this obnoxious character, the constitution will only suspend their operation for a moment, or except from it pre-existing cases. The object would scarcely seem to be of sufficient importance to have found a place in that instrument.

This construction would change the character of the provision, and convert an inhibition to pass laws impairing the obligation of contracts, into an inhibition to pass retrospective laws. Had this been the intention of the Convention, is it not reasonable to believe that it would have been so expressed? Had the intention been to confine the restriction to laws which were retrospective in their operation, language could have been found, and would have been used, to convey this idea. The very word would have occurred to the framers of the instrument, and we should have probably found it in the clause. Instead of the general prohibition to pass any "law impairing the obligation of contracts," the prohibition would have been to the passage of any retrospective law. Or, if the intention had been not to embrace all retrospective laws, but those only which related to contracts, still the word would have been introduced, and the State legislatures would have been forbidden "to pass any *retrospective* law impairing the obligation of contracts," or "to pass any law impairing the obligation of contracts previously made." Words which directly and plainly express the cardinal intent, always present themselves to those who are preparing an important instrument, and will always be used by them. Undoubtedly there is an imperfection in human language, which often exposes the same sentence to different constructions. But it is rare, indeed, for a person of clear and distinct perceptions, intending to convey one principal idea, so to express himself as to leave any doubt respecting that idea. It may be uncertain whether his words comprehend other things not immediately in his mind; but it can seldom be uncertain whether he intends the particular thing to which his mind is specially directed. If the mind of the Convention, in framing this prohibition, had been directed, not generally to the operation of laws upon the obligation of contracts, but particularly to their retrospective operation, it is scarcely conceivable that some word would not have been used indicating this idea. In instruments prepared on great consideration, general terms, comprehending a whole subject, are seldom employed to designate a particular, we might say, a minute portion of that subject. The general language of the clause is such as might be suggested by a general intent to prohibit State legislation on the subject to which that language is applied — the obligation of contracts; not such as would be suggested by a particular intent to prohibit retrospective legislation.

It is also worthy of consideration, that those laws which had effected all that mischief the constitution intended to prevent, were prospective as well as retrospective, in their operation. They embrace future contracts, as well as those previously formed. There is the less reason for imputing to the Convention an intention, not manifested by their language, to confine a restriction intended to guard against the recurrence of those mischiefs, to retrospective legislation. For these reasons, we are of opinion, that, on this point, the District Court of Louisiana has decided rightly.[5]

Printed, Henry Wheaton, *Reports of Cases Argued and Adjudged in the Supreme Court of the United States . . .* , XII (New York, 1827), 332–57.

1. Renner v. Bank of Columbia, 9 Wheat. 581 (1824).

2. Bank of Columbia v. Okely, 4 Wheat. 235. (1819).

3. These cases, as cited by counsel at 12 Wheat. 232, are Burrows v. Jemino, 2 Str. 733, 93 Eng. Rep. 815 (Ch., 1726); Smith v. Buchanan, 1 East 6, 102 Eng. Rep. 3 (K.B., 1800); Potter v. Brown, 5 East 124, 102 Eng. Rep. 1016 (K.B., 1804).

4. Blackstone, *Commentaries*, I, 44.

5. The ultimate judgment in this case, as given on 13 Mar. 1827, affirmed the judgment below in favor of Sanders. By this time Sanders had assigned his debt, which now had several claims upon it. See Robert Scott to Henry Clay, 27 Sept. 1827, James F. Hopkins and Mary W. M. Hargreaves, eds., *The Papers of Henry Clay*, VI (Lexington, Ky., 1981), 1081–82.

Bank of the United States v. Dandridge
Opinion
U.S. Supreme Court, 28 February 1827

This was a writ of error to a judgment of the U.S. Circuit Court for Virginia in June 1823. Chief Justice Marshall on circuit had decided in favor of the defendants, who were sureties on a performance bond executed by Julius B. Dandridge as cashier of the Richmond branch of the Bank of the United States. At the trial Marshall sustained defense counsel's motion to exclude the bond and the handwriting of the sureties as evidence by which a jury could infer the delivery of the bond and its acceptance by the board of directors of the bank. He ruled that by the law incorporating the bank the directors were to keep minutes of their proceedings and that their approval and acceptance of the bond could only be proved by this record. Bills of exceptions were filed to this opinion, which were the basis of the appeal to the Supreme Court. The bank had large amounts of money riding on the outcome of this case and retained Webster and Wirt as counsel. The appeal, which appeared too late on the docket to be heard at the 1826 term, was argued on 3, 5, 6, and 7 February 1827 by Webster and Wirt and by Tazewell for the defendants. While the decision was pending, Webster wrote to Nicholas Biddle, president of the bank: "As to Dandridge, we hear nothing from the Court yet. The Ch. Jus. I fear will *die hard.* Yet I hope that, as to this question, he is *moribundus.*" Webster acknowledged "having spoken somewhat more freely than usually befits the mouth of an humble attorney at law, like myself, of the 'manifest errors' in the opinion of the Great Chief." Story on 28 February delivered the opinion of the Court reversing the lower court's judgment and remanding the case to Virginia. Marshall followed with his opinion, not so much to register a dissent but to explain the reasons for a judgment that he believed had given "general surprize" to the legal profession (*PJM,* IX, 324–26, 330–31, 332–33; Bank of the U.S. v. Dandridge, App. Cas. No. 1283; U.S. Sup. Ct. Minutes, 3, 5, 6, 7, 28 Feb. 1827; Webster to Biddle, 21 Mar. 1826, 28 Dec. 1826, Charles M. Wiltse and Harold D. Moser, eds., *The Papers of Daniel Webster: Correspondence, Volume 2, 1825–1829* [Hanover, N.H., 1976], 96, 144; Webster to Biddle, 20 Feb. 1827, quoted in Warren, *Supreme Court,* I, 698).

I should now, as is my custom, when I have the misfortune to differ from this Court, acquiesce silently in its opinion, did I not believe that the judgment of the Circuit Court of Virginia gave general surprize to the profession, and was generally condemned. A full conviction that the commission of even gross error, after a deliberate exercise of the judgment, is more excusable than the rash and hasty decision of an important question, without due consideration, will, I trust, constitute some apology for the time I consume in stating the reasons and the imposing authorities which guided the Circuit Court in the judgment that has been reversed.

The case before that Court depended on the question whether the official bond of the cashier, on which the suit was brought, bound the defendants.

As preliminary to the investigation of this question, I shall state some propositions belonging to it, which are supposed to be incontrovertible. All admit that delivery is essential to the validity of a deed, and that acceptance is essential to a complete delivery. If this be true, they must be proved in every case where they are put in issue by the pleadings. This proof varies according to circumstances. If there be subscribing witnesses to the instrument, it can be proved only by them, if attainable. If unattainable, or if there be no subscribing witnesses, other proof may be admitted; but, in every case, a delivery and acceptance must be legally proved.

If, in transactions between individuals, where a deed is without a subscribing witness, proof of the signature of the maker, accompanied with the facts that the instrument has passed out of his hands, and is in the possession of the person for whose benefit it was made, be *prima facie* evidence of its delivery, it is because delivery by mere manual tradition, without witnesses, is good; and the assertion of title under it is proof of acceptance, because that requires only the assent of the mind, which assent is legally manifested by asserting a claim to it. That a plaintiff may maintain his action by this evidence, does not show that delivery and acceptance are unnecessary, or that proof of them can be dispensed with; but that, in ordinary cases, this evidence amounts to such proof. If, however, a case should occur in which the possession of the instrument by the party claiming under it, does not afford legal *prima facie* evidence of delivery and acceptance, because such party is incapable of receiving and assenting to the instrument in a form which can be legally proved or inferred from those facts, then such other facts must be shown on the trial as will establish a lawful delivery and acceptance.

I state these legal axioms, at the hazard of being thought tedious, because they appear to me to have a direct bearing on the case before the Court.

The plaintiff is a corporation aggregate; a being created by law; itself impersonal, though composed of many individuals. These individuals change at will; and, even while members of the corporation, can, in virtue of such membership, perform no corporate act, but are responsible in their natural capacities, both while members of the corporation, and after they cease to be so, for every thing they do, whether in the name of the corporation or otherwise. The corporation being one entire impersonal entity, distinct from the individuals who compose it, must be endowed with a mode of action peculiar to itself, which will always distinguish its transactions from those of its members. This faculty must be exercised according to its own nature.

Can such a being speak, or act otherwise than in writing? Being destitute of the natural organs of man, being distinct from all its members, can it communicate its resolutions, or declare its will, without the aid of some adequate substitute for those organs? If the answer to this question must be in the negative, what is that substitute? I can imagine no other than writing. The will to be announced is the aggregate will. The voice which utters it must be the aggregate voice. Human organs belong only to individuals. The words they utter are the words of individuals. These individuals must speak collectively to speak corporately, and must use a collective voice. They have no such voice, and must communicate this collective will in some other mode. That other mode, as it seems to me, must be by writing.

A corporation will generally act by its agents; but those agents have no self-existing power. It must be created by law, or communicated by the body itself. This can be done only by writing.

If, then, corporations were novelties, and we were required now to devise the means by which they should transact their affairs, or communicate their will, we should, I think, from a consideration of their nature, of their capacities and disabilities, be compelled to say, that where other means were not provided by statute, such will must be expressed in writing.

But they are not novelties. They are institutions of very ancient date; and the books abound with cases, in which their character, and their means of action, have been thoroughly investigated. In *Brooke's Abridgement,* (title *Corporation,*) we find many cases, cited chiefly from the *Year Books,* from which the general principle is to be extracted, that a corporation aggregate can neither give nor receive, nor do any thing of importance, without deed.[1] Lord Coke, in his commentary on *Littleton,* (66 b.) says, "But no corporation aggregate of many persons capable can do homage." "And the reason is, because homage must be done in person, and a corporation aggregate of many cannot appear in person; for, albeit, the bodies natural, whereupon the body politique consists, may be seen, yet the body politique or corporate, itself, cannot be seen, *nor do any act,* but by attorney."[2] So, too, a corporation is incapable of attorning otherwise than by deed, (6 *Co.* 386.)[3] or of surrendering a lease for years, (10 *Co.* 676.)[4] or of presenting a clerk to a living, (*Br. Corp.* 83.)[5] or of appointing a person to seize forfeited goods, (1 *Vent.* 47.)[6] or agreeing to a disseisin to their use. (*Br. Corp.* 34.)[7] These incapacities are founded on the impersonal character of a corporation aggregate, and the principle must be equally applicable to every act of a personal nature.

Sir William Blackstone, in his *Commentaries,* (v. 1. p. 475.) enumerates, among the incidents to a corporation, the right "to have a common seal." "For," he adds, "a corporation being an invisible body, cannot manifest its intention by any personal act or oral discourse. It therefore acts and speaks only by a common seal. For though the particular members may express their private consents to any acts, by words, or signing their names, yet this does not bind the corporation; it is the fixing of the seal, and that only, which unites the several assents of the individuals who compose the community, and makes one joint assent of the whole."[8]

Though this general principle, that the assent of a corporation can appear only by its seal, has been in part overruled, yet it has been overruled so far only as respects the seal. The corporate character remains what Blackstone states it to be. The reasons he assigns for requiring their seal as the evidence of their acts, are drawn from the nature of corporations, and must always exist. If the seal may be exchanged for something else, that something must yet be of the same character, must be equally capable of "uniting the several assents of the individuals who compose the community, and of making one joint assent of the whole." The declaration, that a seal is indispensable, is equally a declaration of the necessity of writing; for the sole purpose of a seal is to give full faith and credit to the writing to which it is appended. The seal in itself, not affixed to an instrument of writing, is nothing; is meant as nothing, and can operate nothing. The writing is the substance, and the seal appropriates it to the corporation.

Though the rule stated by Blackstone may not be so universal as his language indicates, it is certainly of extensive application, and the exceptions prove its extent. Mr. Hargrave, in his notes on *Co. Litt.* (99.) says, "In general, a corporation aggregate cannot take or pass away any interest in lands, *or do any act of importance,* without deed, but there are several exceptions to the rule."[9] The question before the Court depends very much on the extent of these exceptions, and on the manner in which this invisible impersonal being must act and speak, when it may act and speak without using its seal.

It is stated in the old books, (*Br. Corp.* 49.) that a corporation may have a ploughman, butler, cook, &c. without retaining them by deed; and, in the same book, (50.) Wood says, "small things need not be in writing, as to light a candle, make a fire, and turn cattle off the land." Fairfax said, "A corporation cannot have a servant but by deed. Small things are admissible on account of custom, and the trouble of a deed in such cases, not by strict law."[10] Some subsequent cases show that officers may be appointed without deed, but not that they may be appointed without writing. Every instrument under seal was designated as a deed, and all writings not under seal were considered as acts by parol. Consequently, when the old books say a thing may be done without deed, or by parol, nothing more is intended than it may be done without a sealed instrument. It may still require to be in writing. In 2 *Bac. Abr.* 13. it is said, "Aggregate corporations, consisting of a constant succession of various persons, can regularly do no act without writing; therefore, gifts by and to them, must be by deed." In page 340, it is said, "if a corporation aggregate disseise to the use of another, they are disseisors in their natural capacity," "as a corporation they can regularly do no act without writing."[11]

In the case of *The King* v. *Bigg,* (*Strange,* 18.) the prisoner was convicted for erasing an endorsement on a bank note. The indictment and verdict are set forth at large by *Peere Williams,* (v. 3. p. 419.) and it appears that the note was signed by Joshua Adams, who was intrusted and employed by the Bank of England to sign bank notes, *but not under their common seal.* It was contended by Peere Williams, in an able argument, that the appointment was not valid, because not made under their common seal; and his argument contains an enumeration of decisions previously made, which go far in support of his proposition. The prisoner, however, was condemned, and, consequently, the appointment was held valid. But there is no reason to suppose that it was not made by writing. The verdict finds "that he was intrusted and employed by the governor and company of the Bank of England, *but not under their common seal.*" Consequently his employment was evidenced by writing, if it was necessary; and the negative finding that it was not under their common seal, strengthens the presumption that it was in writing. Peer Williams has reported his argument, and would certainly have taken this objection, had the case afforded it. I consider the appointment of Adams, then, as having been made in writing, though not under seal.[12]

Mr. *Fonblanque* says, (vol. 1. p. 296. note *o*,) "And the agreement of the major part of the corporation, being entered in the corporation books, though not under the corporate seal, will be decreed in equity."[13] The inference is strong that it will not be decreed unless it be entered on the corporation books. Consequently, unless it be so entered, it is not an agreement, for every lawful agreement which is in itself equitable, will be decreed in equity.

In the *Mayor of Thetford's case*, (1 *Salk.* 192.) Lord Holt said, that though a corporation cannot do an act *in pais* without their common seal, they may do an act on record, and that is the case with the city of London, which makes an attorney in Court annually by warrant; and the reason is, they are estopped by the record. Upon the same principle, a return to a mandamus is good, though not under the common seal. In these exceptions to the general rule, the substitute for the common seal must be writing; and the exceptions are stated in terms which exclude every idea that the act can be evidenced otherwise.[14]

Yarborough v. *The Bank of England*, (16 *East*, 6.) was an action of trover and conversion, in which, after verdict for the plaintiff, it was moved in arrest of judgment, that the action would not lie, because a corporation was incapable of committing a tort. The action was sustained; and Lord Ellenborough, in delivering the opinion of the Court, said, that a corporation can act only through the instrumentality of others; and wherever they can act, or order any act to be done on their behalf, which, as by their common seal they may do, they are liable to the consequences of such acts. "A corporation cannot be aiding to a trespass, nor give a warrant for a trespass, without writing." His lordship cited several old cases, showing the incompetency of a corporation to act in important matters otherwise than by deed; and added, "But many little things require no special command, as to chase cattle out of their land. Those things are incident to the appointment." Several cases are put, in which a corporation may be liable for a trespass; but they are all consistent with his first proposition, that the liability of a corporation must be founded on writing. "If," he says, "the mayor and commonalty disseise me, and I release to 20 or 200 of the commonalty, this will not save the corporation, and the reason is, because the disseisin is in their corporate character, and the release to individuals." So in trespass against the mayor and commonalty of York, they cannot justify under a right of the inhabitants to common, because the right in natural persons gave no right to a corporation. Nor could the corporation give a warrant without writing, to commit a trespass.[15] The foundation of this action is, was the authority in writing given by the corporation? It stands on the same principle with the action of assumpsit made by an agent acting under a written power. The idea that their seal was indispensable to the validity of all corporate acts, which is laid down in such strong terms by Blackstone, and by others, on whom he relied, probably grew out of the state of the times in which it originated; seals were then more frequent and better known than signatures. An instrument was much more certainly authenticated by the seal, than by the name of the maker. This circumstance would bring seals into common use; and as every corporation possessed a seal of extensive notoriety, and any other mode of authenticating its acts would, in those simple times, be attended with difficulties and perplexities, it is not matter of surprise that this rule should prevail. As writing has become more common, and seals are less distinguishable from each other, the good sense of mankind gradually receives the writing without the seal, in all the less formal and less important transactions of the corporate body. All the reasons derived from the corporate character, which have been assigned for requiring the seal, are satisfied by the writing without it.

The English cases on this subject are very well summed up by Mr. *Kyd,* (p. 259.)[16] The result of the whole appears to be, that in England the general rule is, that a corporation acts and speaks by its common seal, at least so far as respects the appointment of officers, whose duties and powers are important. In those transactions, where the use of the seal would be unnecessary, and extremely inconvenient, it is frequently dispensed with; but in all of them, I think, writing is indispensable. In almost every case which I can imagine, there ought to be, and is, a record in the corporation books. With respect to the necessity of a seal, the difference is certainly great between ancient and modern times; and between corporations, whose principal transactions respected land, and those which are commercial in their character. This distinction may, and ought to influence the use of the seal, but not the use of writing. The inability of a corporation aggregate to speak or act otherwise than by writing, is constitutional, and must be immutable, unless it be endowed by the legislature with other qualities than belong to the corporate character. The English cases, so far as I have had an opportunity of examining them, concur in the principle, that a corporation aggregate can act only by writing. A case from 4 *Barnw. & Cresw.* has been cited at the bar, and undoubtedly deserves attention. I regret that it has not been in my power to examine it. As far, however, as I could judge of it from the statement made at the bar, I did not think that it had overturned what appears to me to be the settled law of England.[17]

I will now inquire whether the decisions of this Court vary in principle from those of England.

Head & Amory v. *The Providence Insurance Company,* (2 *Cranch,* 127.) was an action on a policy of insurance, which the defendants contended had been vacated by a subsequent agreement; and the validity of this agreement constituted the sole question in the cause.[18]

The plaintiffs had proposed terms for vacating the policy, and some communications had taken place through Brown & Ives, their correspondents, which showed a misunderstanding between the parties, and that mutual propositions had been mistaken by the plaintiffs for an acceptance of the terms they had proposed. This produced a letter from the plaintiffs, of the 3d of September, 1800, which was understood by the defendants, and was considered by the Court, as amounting to a renewal of propositions for vacating the policy. The secretary of the company delivered to Brown & Ives, on the 6th of September, the following note:

"Sept. 6th, 1800.

"As there appears to have been a misunderstanding in the business as it respects the first propositions of the company, the directors are willing to accede to Messrs. Head & Amory's proposition, (viz.) to settle the policy on the merchandise at 25 per cent., although it was their intention and expectation to have both policies included in the settlement. Messrs. Head & Amory will please to forward the policy, and have it annulled immediately. Premium due 12 — 15 September.

"You will please to govern yourself accordingly, and we will attend to your wishes."

This paper was in the handwriting of the secretary, but without signature.

Testimony was given at the trial to show the usage of the insurance companies, to consider an agreement to do an act as equivalent to the performance of the act.

This paper was forwarded by Brown & Ives, on the 9th of September, to the house of Head & Amory, in Boston, and its receipt was acknowledged by their clerks on the 12th. they being at the time absent. On the 17th of September, the plaintiffs wrote to Brown & Ives, informing them that, previous to their seeing the letter of the 9th, intelligence was received of the capture of the vessel, which would, of course, prevent any farther negotiation on the subject.

The Circuit Court determined that the agreement to vacate the policy was complete; and the jury found for the defendants. The judgment was brought before this Court, and was reversed; because this informal paper did not amount to an acceptance of the terms proposed by the plaintiffs. The act incorporating the company, enacted, "that policies of insurance, and other instruments, made and signed by the president of the said company, or any other officer thereof, according to the ordinance, by-laws," &c. "shall be good and effectual," &c. The Court considered the company as the mere creature of the incorporating act, and as being capable of exerting its faculties only in the manner which the act authorizes. This paper, not being executed in the form prescribed by law, could not be considered as the act of the company.

On the testimony of the witness concerning usage, the Court observed, that "if he was to be understood as stating that an assent to the formation or dissolution of a policy, if manifested according to the forms required by law, is as binding as the performance of the act agreed to be done, it is probable that the practice he alludes to is correct. But if he means to say that this assent may be manifested by parol, the practice cannot receive the sanction of this Court. It would be to dispense with the formalities required by law for valuable purposes, and to enable these artificial bodies to act and to contract, in a manner essentially different from that prescribed for them by the legislature."

"An individual," the Court added, "has an original capacity to contract and bind himself in such a manner as he pleases." "He who acts by another, acts by himself. He who authorizes another to make a writing for him, makes it himself; but with these bodies, which have only a legal existence, it is otherwise. The act of incorporation is, to them, an enabling act. It gives them all the power they possess. It enables them to contract; and when it prescribes to them a mode of contracting, they must observe that mode, or the instrument no more creates a contract than if the body had never been incorporated."[19]

The Court considered the note of the 6th of September "as a mere informal paper, which might perhaps amount to notice of an act, if such act was really performed, but which is not in itself an act of any legal obligation on the company. That if the proposition contained in the letter of the 3d of September, had been regularly accepted, this note might possibly have been considered as notice of that acceptance, but is not in itself an acceptance."[20]

I have gone the more fully into this case, because, both the decision itself, and the reasoning by which it is supported, appear to me to apply throughout to the case now before the Court.

This subject came on to be again considered in *The Bank of Columbia* v. *Patterson's Administrators,* (7 *Cranch,* 299.)[21] That was an action of assumpsit brought by Patterson's administrators for work and labour done by their intestate for the bank. It was founded on an agreement in writing between Patterson and "a duly authorized committee of the directors of the bank," in their own names. Judgment was given in favour of the administrators, upon which the cause was brought by a writ of error into this Court; and, among other objections to the proceedings below, it was contended, that a corporation aggregate could not promise otherwise than under its seal.

In considering this objection, the Court did not controvert the ancient rule.[22] But this rule, if it ever existed to the extent claimed by the plaintiffs in error, had been relaxed; and it seems at length to have been established, that though corporations could not contract directly, except under their corporate seal, yet they might, by mere vote, or other corporate act, not under their corporate seal, appoint an agent, whose acts and contracts, within the scope of his authority, would be binding on the corporation. It being conceded that the committee were authorized to make agreements, there could be no doubt that a contract made by them in the name of the corporation, would be binding on the corporation. But as this promise is made in their own names, if the principle stopped here, the remedy would be only against the committee.

The Court proceeds to consider it as a sound rule of law, that wherever a corporation is acting within the scope of the legitimate purposes of its institution, all parol contracts made by its authorized agents are express promises of the corporation.

In applying this rule of law to the case then under consideration, the Court reviewed the evidence from which the jury might legally infer, "that the corporation had adopted the contracts of the committee, and had voted to pay the whole sum which should become due under the contracts, and that the plaintiffs' intestate had accepted the engagement."

The Bank of Columbia v. *Patterson's Administrators,* differed from the case of the *Providence Insurance Company* v. *Head & Amory,* in two essential circumstances. The contract which was sustained against the bank was made through the instrumentality of a legally constituted agent; that which the insurance company attempted to set up, purported to be a direct contract between the company and the plaintiffs in the cause. In the case of *The Bank of Columbia,* the Court said, "At length it seems to have been established, that though they (corporations) could not contract directly, except under their corporate seal, yet they might, by mere vote, or other corporate act, not under their corporate seal, appoint an agent, whose acts and contracts, within the scope of his authority, would be binding on the corporation."[23]

The obligation on which this suit was instituted, if it be an obligation, purports to be a direct contract between the bank and the individuals who signed the instrument. It is not alleged that any agent was authorized to act for the bank.

Another very essential difference between the two cases cited from *Cranch* is this: In that of the *Providence Insurance Company,* the corporation attempted to set up an agreement, which, if it existed, was in its own possession. It claimed to imply that an act had been performed by itself, the evidence of which was in its own possession, and might be produced. The Court disallowed this implication.

In the case of *The Bank of Columbia,* as in that of the insurance company, the act to be implied was an act performed by the corporation in its own office, without witnesses, the evidence of which remained in its own possession; but it was set up against, not by the corporation. The Court was not of opinion that the suit could be maintained without the existence of this act. No such idea is indicated. On the contrary, the language of the opinion shows very clearly that the act was necessary. If, in order to charge the bank, it was necessary that the corporation should have "adopted the contracts of the committee," and should have "voted to pay the whole sum which should become due under the contracts." The Court enumerates circumstances which were deemed sufficient to justify a jury in implying against the corporation that the bank had performed these acts.

In the case at bar, the suit is brought by the corporation, and the corporation asks the Court to imply that it has performed those acts which are necessary to the validity of the bond on which it sues, although the evidence of its having performed them is in its own possession.

Fleckner v. *The Bank of the United States*, (8 *Wheat. Rep.* 338.) was a writ of error to a judgment given by the Court of the United States for the District of Louisiana, in favour of the bank, in a suit instituted against Fleckner on a note given by him, and endorsed to the Bank of the United States by the President, Directors and Company of the Planters' Bank of New-Orleans, through their cashier, as their agent.[24] One of the errors alleged in the proceedings of the Court below was, that the cashier of the Planters' Bank had no authority to make the transfer. The authority was given by a vote of the board of directors to the president and cashier, and the act itself was afterwards affirmed by an instrument of writing under the corporate seal. It was contended that the original vote, empowering the president and cashier to perform the act, ought to have been a power under the corporate seal. In noticing this objection, the Court said, "Whatever may be the original correctness of this doctrine as applied to corporations existing by the common law, in respect even to which it has been certainly broken in upon in modern times, it has no application to corporations created by statute, whose charters contemplate the business of the corporation to be transacted exclusively by a special body or board of directors. And the acts of such body or board, evidenced by a written vote, are as completely binding upon the corporation, and as complete authority to their agents, as the most solemn acts under the corporate seal."[25]

The Court then proceeded, in a very elaborate and well digested opinion to maintain that the endorsement was within the official duty of the cashier, that it was within the original power given to the president and cashier, and that, were this otherwise, it was sanctioned by the concluding act under the corporate seal. The whole of this case, as of the two preceding cases, turns upon the idea, that a writing, in due form, on the part of the corporation, is indispensable to the validity of its contracts.

According to the decisions of the Courts of England, then, and of this Court, a corporation, unless it be in matters to which the maxim *de minimis non curat lex*[26] applies, can act or speak, and, of course, contract, only by writing. This principle, which seems to be an essential ingredient of its very being, has been maintained by all the judges who have ever discussed the subject. Upon this principle, and the authority of these cases, I have supposed that a corporation cannot receive and assent to a deed of any description, unless this assent be expressed regularly in writing. It ought to be entered on the books of the corporation.

The counsel for the plaintiffs in error insist, that the proof offered in the Circuit Court was sufficient to establish the full execution of the bond; and they support this proposition upon principle, upon convenience, upon usage, and upon the authority of cases decided in the different States of the Union.

It is, we are told, a general rule, that acceptance by a corporation is a fact which may be proved before a jury, and the acceptance of a new charter is mentioned to illustrate the rule.

Without question, acceptance is a fact, and is to be proved before a jury; but the inquiry is, by what evidence may it be proved? I have supposed that it must be proved by testimony which shows that the corporation has acted in the form in which alone it is capable of acting; that it has expressed its acceptance in the mode in which such a being is capable of expressing it. I receive readily the case put of the acceptance of a new charter as an apt illustration of the principle we are investigating, and should be surprised, indeed, if a new charter were to be accepted without a vote of acceptance entered upon the record. The case cited from 1 *Term Rep.* 575. does not appear to me to sanction the doctrine it is adduced to support.[27]

We are told, too, that there was never a time when a corporation might not take by a deed poll. But, if this be admitted, I cannot perceive its influence on the case. A deed poll is in writing, and there is the same necessity that its acceptance should be evidenced by writing as if it were an indenture. The general assertion which we find in all the books, that a corporation can take only by deed, that is, as I understand it, that the act of taking must be by deed, applies as well to conveyances by deed poll, as by indenture.

We have been also referred to a time anterior to writing, and are asked how corporations then acquired property?

We have no knowledge of such a time. Since Europe was subdued and civilized by the arms and literature of Rome, the science of writing, though rare, has never been entirely lost. So much of it as remained was found most generally in corporate bodies. If the corporation was not entirely ecclesiastical, which in early times was most frequent, yet there can be little reason to doubt their having, among themselves, or being able to command, a scribe. Be this as it may, the earliest information we have on the subject tells us that corporations aggregate could only take or grant by deed, under their corporate seal. Even when land passed from man to man by livery, a corporation could not so grant or take. Livery could not be made by, or to, a corporation aggregate, because they are personal acts, and it is an impersonal being. These acts were to be performed through the agency of an individual having a power to perform them under the corporate seal.

We are also told, that the title of the bank to the ground purchased for a banking house, and to all mortgages taken for the security of its debts, will be put in hazard by the principle which I have endeavoured to maintain; that it is probable not a single conveyance will stand the test by which the defendant in error proposes to try its validity, and that the usage is, to receive and deposit them among the papers of the institution without taking any notice of them on its records.

I can scarcely suppose it possible that so loose a practice can have prevailed. I can scarcely suppose it possible, that, on points of such vital importance, and of such rare occurrence, the plain requisites of law can have been so entirely disregarded. Deeds of mortgage, as well as of ground for necessary buildings, are conveyances of lands, and if any one legal proposition is laid down without a single exception, it is this, that a corporation aggregate cannot take lands otherwise than by deed. To me it would appear very incautious to take such conveyances otherwise than as is prescribed in the books, that is, by appointing an attorney under the corporate seal to receive them; but, however this may be, I can scarcely suppose it possible, that an act so easily performed as to enter their assent in their own books, should be habitually neglected. That the current business of the bank should sometimes want the requisite forms, might be excused, but that the same failure should take place in single transactions, which seldom take place, and are yet of great importance, seems to me to be scarcely possible. I should not be inclined to act judicially on the presumption that the fact exists. If it does, the mischief may be corrected by correcting the practice.

The counsel for the plaintiff rely very much on the cases which have been decided in the States of Pennsylvania, New-York, and Massachusetts.

In the case mentioned at the bar, from Pennsylvania, a demurrer was filed to a plea in bar of the action on a cashier's bond, which brought up the very question in consideration before this Court. The argument was opened by the counsel for the plaintiff, but he stopped in the midst of it, and withdrew his demurrer without submitting the point to the Court.[28]

The cases in New-York have not, I think, gone farther than *The Bank of Columbia* v. *Patterson's Administrators.* Those of Massachusetts have, I admit, gone the full length for which the plaintiffs contend, and the point is probably settled in that State. It would be presumptuous in me to place my understanding of those decisions in opposition to that of professional gentlemen from that State, but to me it seems, that even there the doctrine has not been uniformly maintained. *Bigelow's Digest* of Massachusetts cases contains this passage: "Aggregate corporations cannot make a parol contract, unless by the intervention of some agent or attorney duly authorized by a corporate vote to contract on their part, because there is no other way in which they can express their assent." He cites 7 *Mass. Rep.* 102. in which Chief Justice Parsons said, "We cannot admit that a corporation can make a parol contract unless by the intervention of some agent or attorney duly authorized to contract on their part."[29]

In the *Essex Turnpike Company* v. *Collins,* (8 *Mass. Rep.* 292.) the Court said, "Aggregate corporations cannot contract without vote, because there is no other way in which they can express their assent."[30]

In the case of *Hayden* v. *The Middlesex Turnpike Corporation,* (10 *Mass. Rep.* 397.) the work for which the action was brought was performed on the road. The committee appointed to contract for, and superintend it, was frequently present while it was going on, and directed the workmen. Other directors were also present, and one of them swore that he supposed the work to be going on by order of the directors. But the contract was not in exact conformity with the written authority under which the committee acted. A verdict taken for the plaintiff, subject to the opinion of the Court, was set aside, and the Court said, "No individual member can represent the corporation in their aggregate capacity, but in consequence of their consent. The requisite evidence of this, at common law, was a deed under the seal of the corporation. Aggregate corporations, established by statute, are not restricted to that formality. They have power given them to order their affairs, and to appoint and employ agents by votes, or in such other manner as the corporation may by their by-laws appoint."[31] Again: "Nor can a parol declaration, made to the corporators at a corporate meeting, by any individual, amount to a contract between such individual and the corporation."[32]

In *The Proprietors of the Canal Bridge* v. *Gordon,* (1 *Pick. Rep.* 297.) the Court decided, that a corporation could be bound without a vote, by implication from corporate acts.[33] This, however, was in a suit brought against a corporation, and attended with circumstances extremely well calculated to strengthen every presumption against them. The corporation might have passed the vote, though it was not in the power of the plaintiff to produce it, and their acts afforded the strongest probability in favour of the implication that they had passed it. I should not consider this case as conclusive evidence that the same Court would have drawn the same inference from the same circumstances, in a case in which the corporation was plaintiff. But, in the case of *The Inhabitants of the First Parish in Sutton* v. *Cole,* the corporation was plaintiff, and the validity of an entry into land was one of the points made in the cause.[34] The corporation had appointed two agents for the purpose, but the entry was made by one only. This entry was held to be made not in pursuance of the authority, but it was also held, that the action brought by the corporation was a ratification of the entry. This I admit to be a decision expressly in point. But, thinking it a case in opposition to the whole course of decisions in England, as well as in this Court, and not supported by decisions in other States, or by a long course of decisions even in the State of Massachusetts, I should not, perhaps, highly respectable as it undoubtedly is, and as I certainly think it, have felt myself warranted in yielding to it, had it even been known to me.

It has been contended, that the act of Congress incorporating the bank, does not, in terms, require that it shall keep a record of its proceedings; and from this omission, it has been inferred, that a record is unnecessary. I cannot assent to the correctness of this inference.

When a being is created without the organs of speech, and endowed only with the faculty of communicating its will by writing, we need not look in the laws given by its creator, for a prohibition to speak, or a mandate to write. These are organic laws which it is compelled to observe. If we find, in the act of its creation, an enumeration of duties and powers which are to be performed and exercised by writing, it is evidence that the creator considered it as certain that the creature would write, and that the evidence of its conformity to the will of the creator would be found in writing. It is equivalent to a declaration that it shall act by writing.

Let the charter be examined with this principle in our minds.[35]

The 8th section empowers the stockholders to choose directors for the management of their affairs, but does not require that the election shall be evidenced by writing. Is it to be believed, that Congress could have intended that an act, on which all the operations of the corporation depended, which might be controverted in every action it should institute, might rest upon the uncertain, and, perhaps, contradictory recollection of the individuals who were present.

The fairness of an election may be contested; the mode of voting is prescribed by law. Can it be that Congress supposed no provision was made which secured written testimony, by which such contests might be tried?

The directors are to elect one of their body as president; is no record to be kept of this election? Can we presume so much carelessness in Congress, as to suppose it possible that matters of such consequence should be left to the loose proof which the memory of individuals might furnish? The act prescribes the notice which shall be given of the time and place of holding the election; and adds, "it shall be lawful for such election to be then and there made." The legality of the election depends on time and place. Did Congress mean that these facts should rest on memory?

The 10th section empowers the directors, for the time being, to appoint officers, and to allow them a compensation; and to exercise such other powers for the well governing of the officers of the corporation, as shall be prescribed by its laws. May all these acts be found only in the frail memory of individuals?

The 4th rule of the fundamental articles provides, that not less than seven directors, of whom the president, or some person deputed by him, shall be one, shall constitute a board for the transaction of business; but there is no clause in the charter requiring a board. Can it be pretended, that not less than seven directors may make a board, and yet, that the directors may act without being assembled as a board? Congress has not thought it necessary to forbid their acting otherwise than as a board, because the whole law of corporations forbids it.

In the event of making unlawful loans, the directors are made personally responsible; but those are exempted who were absent, or who dissented from the resolution or act whereby the same was so contracted or created.

No clause in the charter directs that loans shall be created only by writing. The bond of the debtor may be said to be sufficient. Yet this clause is obviously drawn in the idea, that all the proceedings on the subject would necessarily be in writing. The absentees and dissentients are excused. How is this absence or dissent to be proved? Is it to depend on vague and uncertain memory?

The same observations apply to the limitations and restrictions which are found in the 9th and 10th rules of the fundamental articles.

The 13th rule declares, that semi-annual dividends shall be made, but does not direct that they shall be declared in writing. May the bank so manage its affairs, that no trace of these dividends shall be found on its books?

The 16th rule declares, that no stockholder, unless he be a citizen of the United States, shall vote in the choice of directors, but does not direct that written lists shall be taken. May they be dispensed with? Is the question who has voted to depend on recollection solely?

The 23d section subjects the books of the corporation to the inspection of a committee of either house of Congress.

But there is no clause in the charter which directs the corporation to keep any books. May this be set up as an excuse for not opening books containing their transactions for the inspection of a committee of Congress?

How are we to account for all these strange omissions? Strange and unaccountable they would certainly be, on any other hypothesis, than that the law of its being, required that it should speak and act by writing. Aware of this, Congress did not deem it necessary to enjoin upon it, that it should act in the only mode in which its organs enabled it to act, and that it should abstain from what its organs did not enable it to do.

It may be said, that although certain things ought to appear in writing, it is not necessary that all the transactions of a bank should so appear; and the assent of the directors to the bonds given by their cashiers, need not appear. Such grave acts or omissions as may justify the suing out a *scire facias,* to vacate the charter, ought to be evidenced by their records; but such unimportant acts as taking bonds from their officers, need not appear. These may be inferred.

I do not concur in this proposition. I neither admit the distinction which has been alleged, nor do I admit that the bond of a cashier is to be classed with unimportant transactions. Congress has not prescribed the intrinsic importance which shall entitle any transaction of a bank to a place on its record, but has legislated on the idea that a record of its proceedings will be kept. And if such a distinction could be found, the bonds of officers, intrusted with all the money of the bank, are among the most interesting of its duties. Congress has manifested this opinion, by enacting, that "Each cashier or treasurer, before he enters upon the duties of his office, shall be required to give bond, with two or more sureties, to the satisfaction of the directors, in a sum not less than 50,000 dollars, with a condition for his good behaviour, and the faithful performance of his duties to the corporation."[36]

Congress, then, considered the bonds to be given by the cashiers as a subject of real importance; and Congress was right in this opinion. It requires very little knowledge of the interior of banks, to know that the interests of the stockholders are committed, to a very great extent, to these and other officers. It was, and ought to have been, the intention of Congress to secure the government, which took a deep interest in this institution, and to secure individuals, who embarked their fortunes in it, on the faith of government, as far as possible, from the mal-practices of its officers. One of the means employed for this purpose is the bond required from the cashier. Are the directors at liberty to dispense with this requisition? I think they are not.

Should a committee of Congress, on inspecting the books of the corporation, find that cashiers were acting without bonds, would not such gross negligence, such utter disregard of the positive mandate of the law, furnish serious cause for a *scire facias* to vacate the charter?

It has been urged, that the rule for which the defendants contend, would break in upon all the usages of the bank, invalidate all the notes they have discounted, and destroy their liability for deposits.

I do not think so. I do not profess to understand banking operations; but I think the counsel for the defendants has plainly shown, that not a single note is discounted, without evidence, in writing, on the note itself, or on the books of the bank, or on both. It is admitted, that the official acts of the officers of the bank are binding, and, of course, written memorandums made by such officer, in pursuance of orders of the board, whether on the note itself, or in a book, is a corporate act, is written evidence of such order of the board of directors as the writing imports. The counsel for the defendant has, I think, shown from "the rules and regulations for conducting the business of the Bank of the United States," as well as from the practice under those rules, that all transactions of that character are, as they ought to be, in writing. He has shown also, conclusively, as I think, that full provision is made both for general and special deposits, and, in my judgment, every difficulty of this description is removed by the 23d rule, which shows that a regular record is, as it ought to be, kept of all the proceedings of the board of directors. So much of that rule as applies to this subject is in these words:

"The proceedings of the board of directors, when conducting their business as a deliberative body, shall be governed by the following articles:

"1st. When the president takes the chair, the members shall take their seats.["]

"2d. The minutes of the preceding meeting shall be read before the board proceeds to any other business; and no debate shall be admitted, nor question taken at such reading, except as to errors and inaccuracies. The state of the bank shall then be read, and the discounts settled."[37]

The board, then, does act as a deliberative body, and does keep a minute of its proceedings, which are to be read over and corrected. On what subject does the board deliberate, if not on the measures which are to be taken for the security of its debts, and on the sufficiency of the sureties in the bonds given by the officers who have the management of its funds? Most especially is it bound to deliberate on the bonds to be given by the cashiers of the bank. This is a subject on which the directors are particularly commanded to exercise their judgment by one of the fundamental articles of the constitution of the corporation. That article requires, that "each cashier or treasurer, before he enters upon the duties of his office, shall be required to give bond, with two or more sureties, to the satisfaction of the directors, in the sum of 50,000 dollars, with a condition," &c. Is not the sufficiency of this bond, then, most especially a subject for deliberation? If it be, how is this deliberation to be conducted? The rules prescribe the mode with precision, and go so far as to direct, that "at the request of any two of the board, the names of the members who make and second a motion, shall be entered on the minutes."[38] The bond must be offered, and the question ought to be put, and must be put, whether it shall be accepted. The acceptance is necessary to the completion of delivery, and is the only proof which can be given of that fact, unless it be delivered to an attorney, previously appointed by a board to receive it. Acceptance, undoubtedly, includes approbation, but is the deliberate act of the board, and must appear in their minutes. If it must, a copy of those minutes is, in a suit brought by the bank, the only admissible evidence of the fact.

I think it worthy of remark, that among these rules and regulations, not one is found which ordains that a record shall be kept, in which the proceedings of the directors shall be inserted. They are framed upon the idea, that one must be kept. We find them speaking of the minutes, as if their existence was indispensable, and need not be prescribed. Imitating the charter, in this respect, it was deemed unnecessary to ordain that a being should write, whose organization gave it not the means of transacting business otherwise than by writing.

The counsel for the plaintiffs has sought to escape the almost insuperable difficulties which must attend any attempt to maintain the proposition, that a corporation aggregate can act without writing, by insisting that the directors are not the corporation, but are to be considered merely as individuals who are its agents.

If this proposition can be successfully maintained, it becomes a talisman, by whose magic power the whole fabric which the law has erected respecting corporations, is at once dissolved. In examining it, we encounter a difficulty in the commencement. Agents are constituted for special purposes, and the extent of their power is prescribed, in writing, by the corporate body itself. The directors are elected by the stockholders, and manage all their affairs, in virtue of the power conferred by the election. The stockholders impart no authority to them, except by electing them as directors. But, we are told, and are told truly, that the authority is given in the charter. The charter authorizes the directors to manage all the business of the corporation. But do they act as individuals, or in a corporate character? If they act as a corporate body, then the whole law applies to them as to other corporate bodies. If they act as individuals, then we have a corporation which never acts in its corporate character, except in the instances of electing its directors, or instructing them. The corporation possesses many important powers, and is, as a corporation, to perform many important acts, scarcely one of which is to be performed in a corporate character. They are all to be performed by agents, acting as individuals, under general powers conferred by the charter.

It cannot escape notice, that this rule, if it be one, would apply to almost all corporations aggregate, and would abolish the distinction which has been taken between those which act by an individual, and those which act by an aggregate of persons. The first partakes of the qualities of a sole corporation, the last of a corporation aggregate.

This rule would apply to almost every corporation aggregate which exists, or which ever has existed. The exceptions are the very few in which all the members are active, or in which the corporation acts by a single individual who is its head. All others act by boards usually described in the charter. If the president and directors of the Bank of the United States act as individuals, then it would seem, that the managers of every other corporation, being in like manner created by charter, and being in like manner empowered by charter to transact all the affairs of the corporation, would likewise act as individuals, and the whole doctrines of the law upon the subject, would find nothing to which they are applicable.

But these doctrines grow out of adjudged cases, and Courts have always considered those official agents, whose powers are described in the charter, and who act collectively, as acting in a corporate character. The idea has, I believe, never before been suggested, that their acts were to be treated as the acts of individuals. They do not appear as individual acts; they are not in the name of individuals, but of the corporate body. In all the cases which have come before this Court, that of *The Bank of Columbia* v. *Patterson's Administrators*, as well as all others, directors are considered as acting in their corporate character. In the cases in England, where the Bank of England has been a party, and in all others, the same view has always been taken of the subject.

The president and directors form, by the charter, a select body, in which the general powers of the corporation are placed. This body is, I think, the acting corporation; and, according to the 4th article of the fundamental rules, seven of them, including the president, or the director deputed by the president, are necessary to constitute a board. The act of the major part of the board, is the act of the whole, and binds the corporation; but this act must, on general principles, be done at one and the same time, and at a regular meeting held for the purpose. (*Kyd. Corp.* 309.)[39] Its validity depends on the legal constitution of the board, and on its being the act of the body. These essential requisites must be shown; and to show them, the board must keep a record of its proceedings. Were the by-laws silent on the subject, this would be, as I think, rendered indispensable, by the fact, that it is the act of a corporation aggregate.

If there must be a record of their proceedings, and, even were this necessity not absolute, if the by-laws show that there is one, it follows that this record, not the oral testimony of the members, or of bystanders, must prove their acts. Their acceptance of any deed, or their assent to any contract, if it be their own act, must appear on this record; if it be by agents, authorized for the purpose, the vote giving the authority must appear in like manner.

The 6th article of the fundamental rules directs, that "each cashier or treasurer, before he enters upon the duties of his office, shall be required to give bond, with two or more sureties, to the satisfaction of the directors, in a sum not less than 50,000 dollars, with a condition," &c.

As the bond is to be given before the cashier enters upon the duties of his office, it must be given before he can rightfully perform any official act; and it will be admitted, that the sureties to an official bond are responsible only for the official acts of the officer. This bond cannot be given till it is received, for they are different, and equally necessary parts of one and the same act; but, if it could, the law specially requires that it shall be "to the satisfaction of the directors." The "satisfaction" must be as to the sufficiency of the sureties, for the amount of the penalty is fixed by law. This is a subject on which the judgment of the directors must be exercised, and it can be exercised only at a regular meeting of a board, legally constituted. This must appear by the record. Any opinion given otherwise, is the opinion of individual members, but is not the corporate opinion of the board, is not a corporate act binding on the corporation, or of which the corporation can avail itself.

It appears to me, that the bond must be received and approved by the board, before the cashier can regularly perform any official act. This reception and approbation are required by the law which enables the corporation to act. They cannot be dispensed with. That they have been performed must be proved or presumed. If they have been performed, they are upon record, for the very act of performance places them upon record. This record, or an authentic copy of it, must, according to the rules of evidence be produced, that it may prove itself.

May its existence be presumed in this case?

The corporation, which claims this presumption, keeps the record, and is now in possession of it, if its exists. No rule of evidence is more familiar to the profession, than that a paper cannot be presumed under such circumstances.

I have stated the view which was taken by the Circuit Court of this case. I have only to add, that the law is now settled otherwise, perhaps to the advancement of public convenience. I acquiesce, as I ought, in the decision which has been made, though I could not concur in it.[40]

Printed, Henry Wheaton, *Reports of Cases Argued and Adjudged in the Supreme Court of the United States . . .* , XII (New York, 1827), 90–116.

1. Sir Robert Brooke, *La Graunde Abridgement . . .* (London, 1586), tit. "Corporations & Capacities." This work, in law French, was first published in 1568, the last edition in 1586 (Sir William Holdsworth, *A History of English Law,* II [1936; London, 1971 reprint], 545).

2. Edward Coke, *The First Part of the Institutes of the Laws of England; or, A Commentary upon Littleton . . .* , I (16th ed.; London, 1809), 66b.

3. Bellamy's Case, 6 Co. Rep. 38b, 77 Eng. Rep. 309–10 (C.P., 1605).

4. The Case of the Churchwardens of St. Saviour in Southwark, 10 Co. Rep. 66b, 67b, 77 Eng. Rep. 1025, 1026 (K.B., 1613).

5. Brooke, *La Graunde Abridgement,* tit. "Corporations & Capacities," par. 83.

6. Horn v. Ivy, 1 Vent. 47, 48, 86 Eng. Rep. 33, 34 (K.B., 1669).

7. Brooke, *La Graunde Abridgement,* tit. "Corporations & Capacities," par. 34.

8. Blackstone, *Commentaries,* I, 475.

9. Coke, *Institutes: Commentary upon Littleton,* III, Note 99 (keyed to ibid., II, 94b). Francis Hargrave and Charles Butler were the editors of Coke's *Institutes.* Their notes appear in the third volume, entitled *Notes on Lord Coke's First Institute, or Commentary upon Littleton.*

10. Brooke, *La Graunde Abridgement,* tit. "Corporations & Capacities," pars. 49, 50.

11. Bacon, *Abridgment,* II, 13, 340.

12. Rex v. Bigg, 1 Str. 18, 93 Eng. Rep. 357 (K.B., 1717); 3 P. Wms. 419–38, 24 Eng. Rep. 1127–33 (Ch., 1717).

13. John Fonblanque, *A Treatise of Equity* [Henry Ballow] (1793–94; 2 vols. in 1; New York, 1979 reprint), I, 296 n.

14. Mayor of Thetford's Case, 1 Salk. 192, 91 Eng. Rep. 173–74 (K.B., 1703).

15. Yarborough v. Bank of England, 16 East 6, 7, 9, 10–11, 104 Eng. Rep. 991, 992, 993 (K.B., 1812).

16. Stewart Kyd, *A Treatise on the Law of Corporations* (1793–94; 2 vols.; New York, 1978 reprint), I, 259.

17. Harper v. Charlesworth, 4 Barn. & Cress. 574, 107 Eng. Rep. 1174 (K.B., 1825). Wheaton did not report the arguments of counsel, but Story cited this case in his opinion (12 Wheat. 68).

18. Head & Amory v. Providence Insurance Co., 2 Cranch 127 (1804).

19. 2 Cranch 168–69. JM gave the opinion of the Court.

20. 2 Cranch 166–67.

21. Bank of Columbia v. Patterson's Administrators, 7 Cranch 299 (1813).

22. Here and in the three succeeding paragraphs JM paraphrased Story's opinion for the Court at 7 Cranch 305–7.

23. 7 Cranch 305.

24. Fleckner v. Bank of the U.S., 8 Wheat. 338 (1823).

25. 8 Wheat. 357. Story delivered the opinion of the Court.

26. The law does not concern itself about trifles.

27. The King v. Amery, 1 T.R. 575, 99 Eng. Rep. 1259 (K.B., 1787); 2 T.R. 515, 100 Eng. Rep. 278 (K.B., 1788).

28. Bank of the Northern Liberties v. Cresson, 12 S & R 306, 308 (Pa. Sup. Ct., 1824), cited by Story at 12 Wheat. 89.

29. Lewis Bigelow, *A Digest of the Reported Cases Argued and Determined in the Supreme Judicial Court of the Commonwealth of Massachusetts* (Boston, 1825), 219, citing Andover and Medford Turnpike Corporation v. Hay, 7 Mass. 102, 107 (1810). The passage in Bigelow is under the title "Corporation," pt. D: "How a corporation may contract."

30. Essex Turnpike Corporation v. Collins, 8 Mass. 292, 298–99 (1811).

31. Hayden v. Middlesex Turnpike Corporation, 10 Mass. 397, 403 (1813).

32. Bigelow, *Digest*, 219, citing Proprietors of the Canal Bridge v. Gordon, 1 Pick. 297 (Mass., 1823).

33. Proprietors of the Canal Bridge v. Gordon, 1 Pick. (18 Mass. 297) (1823).

34. Inhabitants of the First Parish in Sutton v. Cole, 8 Mass. 96 (1811).

35. For the 1816 act incorporating the Bank of the United States, see *U.S. Statutes at Large*, III, 266–77.

36. Ibid., III, 271.

37. *The Rules and Regulations for Conducting the Business of the Bank of the United States* (Philadelphia, 1816). The rules are reprinted in Ralph C. H. Catterall, *The Second Bank of the United States* (Chicago, Ill., 1903), 490–98 (Rule 23 at 497).

38. JM quoted article 10 under Rule 23 (Catterall, *Second Bank of the United States*, 498).

39. Kyd, *A Treatise on the Law of Corporations*, I, 309.

40. The Supreme Court mandate remanded the case to the U.S. Circuit Court in Richmond for a new trial. For more than two weeks in June 1827 a jury heard evidence and arguments of counsel, Wirt for the bank and Benjamin W. Leigh and Chapman Johnson for the defendants. After the close of arguments, JM "charged the Jury at considerable length as to the points of law." On 26 June, after deliberating less than an hour, the jury reported its inability to agree on a verdict assessing damages for the plaintiff. The jurors were accordingly discharged and the case continued, lingering on the docket for another six years. In the meantime, Dandridge, the former cashier, died in Apr. 1828 from a fall into "a deep ravine." A coroner's inquest ruled the death accidental. At the May 1833 term a jury assessed damages of $5,000 for the plaintiff (U.S. Cir. Ct., Va., Ord. Bk. XII, 177–88, 243, 274, 408; *Enquirer* [Richmond], 29 June 1827, 29 Apr. 1828; Bank of the U.S. v. Dandridge, U.S. Cir. Ct., Va., Ended Cases [Unrestored], 1833, Vi).

Brown v. Maryland
Opinion and Judgment
U.S. Supreme Court, 12 March 1827

EDITORIAL NOTE

Eight years earlier the Supreme Court in *McCulloch* v. *Maryland* invalidated a Maryland law imposing a tax on the Bank of the United States. In the present case the Court considered the validity of another tax enacted by the legislature of that state. By a law adopted in 1821 importers and other wholesalers of foreign imports were required to take out a license costing fifty dollars. At issue was whether this license fee infringed the constitutional restriction on the power of the states to lay imposts or duties on imports or interfered with Congress's power to regulate interstate and foreign commerce.

The Baltimore merchants had strenuously opposed the license law, which a commentator described as "one of that class which is perpetually planning to tax *Baltimore city*, for the benefit of the *state of Maryland*."[1] Doubts about the constitutionality of the law induced the leading merchant of the city, Alexander Brown (1764–1834), to test its validity in the courts. A native of Ireland, Brown had set up a linen trading business in Baltimore in late 1800. Over the years, in partnership with his sons George Brown (1787–1859), John A. Brown (1788–1872), and James Brown (1791–1877), he expanded his business from importing linens to the exporting of tobacco and cotton and also to banking and shipping. The firm of Alexander Brown & Sons eventually established branches in Philadelphia, New York, and Boston.[2] In November 1822 Brown and his sons, having refused to purchase a license, were indicted in the Baltimore City Court for importing and selling a package of foreign dry goods. After the court rendered judgment against them, the Browns appealed to the state Court of Appeals, which in June 1824 affirmed the judgment. The defendants then obtained a writ of error and filed their case in the Supreme Court in February 1825.[3]

The Court heard arguments on 28 February and 1 March 1827. Representing the Browns were William M. Meredith (1799–1873), a Pennsylvania lawyer and politician and future secretary of the treasury, and William Wirt. Counsel for the state of Maryland were Roger B. Taney (1777–1864), the future chief justice of the United States and then attorney general of Maryland, and Reverdy Johnson (1796–1876), a distinguished Baltimore lawyer who later served in the U.S. Senate and as U.S. Attorney General.[4] Meredith focused primarily on showing that the license fee violated the express restriction on the states to lay duties on imports. He denied that there were any substantial differences between this fee and a direct tax on imports, particularly that the former merely taxed the privilege of selling while the latter taxed the privilege of importing. These privileges were "indissolubly connected," he insisted; "the right to sell is a necessary incident to the right of importing."[5] Meredith further contended that the Maryland law interfered with the federal government's exclusive right to raise revenue from import duties. The principle of federal supremacy implied a restriction on a state's concurrent power of taxation when, as in this case, the state tax operated to undermine or destroy the policy of the federal revenue laws.

Wirt centered his argument on the commerce clause, citing *Gibbons* v. *Ogden* (1824) as having determined that the power of regulating interstate and foreign commerce was "exclusively vested in Congress." Since Congress had the exclusive right to prescribe the terms on which commerce was to be carried on, the states were "incompetent . . . to add other terms."[6] The Maryland law was just such an attempt to prescribe those terms, for in effect it added to the costs of importation. If permitted to regulate to this extent, the states in principle could prohibit importation altogether and indeed defeat the beneficial exercise of the commerce power. He buttressed his argument by reciting the *McCulloch* maxim that the taxing power involves "a power to destroy."[7]

Taney and Johnson insisted that the license tax was not a duty on imports but a tax on the occupation of selling by wholesale, no different in principle from "the usual taxes on retailers, or innkeepers, or hawkers and pedlars, or upon any other trade exercised within the State." Once the act of importation was complete, the imported goods became subject to state law. If the privilege of selling was inseparable from that of importing, they argued, the consequence would be that the importer would have an "absolute and unconditional right" derived from the general government to sell anywhere and in whatever manner he chose — such as selling "gunpowder in the heart of a city."[8] There was nothing in the Constitution to confine this privilege to selling by wholesale. In short, the states could exercise no control or regulation over property that had been imported. The same conse-

ALEXANDER BROWN
Engraving by Samuel Sartain, after the original by Sarah Peale, ca. 1830.
Courtesy of the Maryland Historical Society.

quence would result from holding that the license tax was repugnant to the commerce clause. If Congress under the power to regulate commerce could confer the right to sell, then the states would have surrendered many important powers of taxation besides those of taxing imports and exports explicitly denied by the Constitution. Indeed, many of the state's regulatory and police powers would "exist only by the permission of Congress." The proper rule of construction of the Constitution, they urged by citations to *The Federalist*, was that the states retain their full powers of taxation except as to imports and exports. No real inconvenience or danger to the federal revenue could arise from the license tax, for the people of a state would not impose "heavy burthens upon themselves, for the purpose of thwarting or embarrassing the general government."[9]

On 12 March the Supreme Court invalidated the Maryland license tax by a vote of six to one, Justice Thompson dissenting. Chief Justice Marshall devoted the greater part of his opinion for the Court to demonstrating that the state law fell within the Constitution's prohibition on the states to lay imposts or duties on imports. He refashioned the arguments of Brown's counsel in a way that served this purpose while answering the various objections raised by counsel for Maryland. Where counsel for the most part endeavored to show that the Maryland law was or was not a tax on imports, Marshall focused his analysis on the words of the prohibitory clause, employing the rules of statutory construction to expound the Constitution. Turning first to the "literal meaning of the words" and then to "the general objects to be accomplished by the prohibitory clause," the chief justice discerned a clear intent on the part of the framers to give a comprehensive scope to the clause sufficient to bring the Maryland license tax within the prohibition.[10] The more difficult question was to determine the point at which the prohibition ceased to operate and the imported article became subject to state taxation. Observing that the time was not ripe to formulate a rule that was "universal in its application," he was satisfied at present to say that while the import remained the importer's property in its "original form or package," a tax laid on it was "too plainly a duty on imports to escape the prohibition in the constitution."[11]

Although the prohibitory clause was sufficient to invalidate the Maryland license fee on importers, Marshall did briefly consider the effect of the commerce clause on this case as well. This discussion added little to what he had previously stated in *Gibbons*, namely, that the commerce power was plenary and penetrated to the interior of a state. Again, he carefully avoided converting this affirmative power into an absolute prohibition on state legislative activity in the field of interstate and foreign commerce. He also acknowledged a state's "sacred" power of taxation over persons and property within its territory. As in *Gibbons*, the chief justice refrained from holding the state law to be repugnant to the commerce clause but found it to be in collision with an actual exercise of the commerce power. Congress, by its tariff legislation, authorized not only the importation but also the sale of goods "as a component part of the power to regulate commerce." Maryland's exercise of its taxing power in this instance was thus in direct conflict with Congress's exercise of the commerce power. In terms reminiscent of *McCulloch*, he denied that the degree of taxation entered "into the inquiry concerning" the existence of the conflict.[12]

1. *Niles' Weekly Register* (Baltimore), 17 Mar. 1827.
2. The parent company and its branches (now separate) continue to operate as banking

and financial services institutions. Following a recent merger with Bankers Trust, the name of the original firm survives as BT Alex. Brown.

3. Brown v. Maryland, App. Cas. No. 1350.
4. U.S. Sup. Ct. Minutes, 28 Feb., 1 Mar. 1827.
5. Brown v. Maryland, 12 Wheat. 422.
6. 12 Wheat. 433, 434.
7. 12 Wheat. 433.
8. 12 Wheat. 425, 427.
9. 12 Wheat. 431, 432.
10. Opinion and Judgment, 12 Mar. 1827 (400, below).
11. Opinion and Judgment, 12 Mar. 1827 (403, below).
12. Opinion and Judgment, 12 Mar. 1827 (407, 408, below).

OPINION

This is a writ of error to a judgment rendered in the court of appeals of Maryland, affirming a judgment of the city court of Baltimore, on an indictment found in that court against the plaintiffs in error, for violating an act of the legislature of Maryland. The indictment was founded on the second section of that act, which is in these words: "And be it enacted, that all importers of foreign articles or commodities, of dry goods, wares or merchandise, by bale or package, or of wine, rum, brandy, whiskey, and other distilled spiritous liquors, &c. and other persons selling the same by wholesale, bale or package, hogshead, barrel, or tierce, shall before they are authorized to sell, take out a license, as by the original act is directed, for which they shall pay fifty dollars: and in case of neglect or refusal to take out such license, shall be subject to the same penalties and forfeitures as are prescribed by the original act to which this is a supplement." The indictment charges the plaintiffs in error with having imported and sold one package of foreign dry goods without having license to do so. A judgment was rendered against them on demurrer for the penalty which the act prescribes for the offence, and that judgment is now before this court.

The cause depends entirely on the question, whether the legislature of a state can constitutionally require the importer of foreign articles to take out a license from the state, before he shall be permitted to sell a bale or package so imported.

It has been truly said, that the presumption is in favor of every legislative act, and that the whole burthen of proof lies on him who denies its constitutionality. The plaintiffs in error take the burthen upon themselves, and insist that the act under consideration is repugnant to two provisions in the constitution of the United States.

1. To that which declares that "no state shall, without the consent of Congress, lay any imposts, or duties on imports or exports, except what may be absolutely necessary for executing its inspection laws."

2. To that which declares that Congress shall have power "to regulate commerce with foreign nations, and among the several states, and with the Indian tribes."

1. The first inquiry is into the extent of the prohibition upon states "to lay any imposts or duties on imports or exports." The counsel for the state of Maryland would confine this prohibition to laws imposing duties on the act of importation or exportation. The counsel for the plaintiffs in error give them a much wider scope.

In performing the delicate and important duty of construing clauses in the constitution of our country, which involve conflicting powers of the government of the union, and of the respective states, it is proper to take a view of the literal meaning of the words to be expounded, and their connexion with other words, and of the general objects to be accomplished by the prohibitory clause, or by the grant of power.

What, then, is the meaning of the words, "imposts, or duties on imports or exports?"

An impost, or duty on imports, is a custom or a tax levied on articles brought into a country, and is most usually secured before the importer is allowed to exercise his rights of ownership over them, because evasions of the law can be prevented more certainly by executing it while the articles are in custody. It would not, however, be less an impost or duty on the articles, if it were to be levied on them after they were landed. The policy and consequent practice of levying or securing the duty before, or on entering the port, does not limit the power to that state of things, nor, consequently, the prohibition, unless the true meaning of the clause so confines it. What, then, are "imports?" The lexicons inform us, they are "things imported." If we appeal to usage for the meaning of the word, we shall receive the same answer. They are the articles themselves which are brought into the country. "A duty on imports" then, is not merely a duty on the act of importation, but it is a duty on the thing imported. It is not, taken in its literal sense, confined to a duty levied while the article is entering the country, but extends to a duty levied after it has entered the country. The succeeding words of the sentence which limit the prohibition, show the extent in which it was understood. The limitation is, "except what may be absolutely necessary for executing its inspection laws." Now, the inspection laws, so far as they act upon articles for exportation, are generally executed on land, before the article is put on board the vessel; so far as they act upon importations, they are generally executed upon articles which are landed. The tax or duty of inspection, then, is a tax which is frequently, if not always paid for service performed on land, while the article is in the bosom of the country. Yet this tax is an exception to the prohibition on the states to lay duties on imports or exports. The exception was made because the tax would otherwise have been within the prohibition.

If it be a rule of interpretation to which all assent, that the exception of a particular thing from general words, proves that, in the opinion of the lawgiver, the thing excepted would be within the general clause, had the exception not been made, we know no reason why this general rule should not be as applicable to the constitution as to other instruments. If it be applicable, then this exception in favour of duties for the support of inspection laws, goes far in proving that the framers of the constitution classed taxes of a similar character with those imposed for the purposes of inspection, with duties on imports and exports, and supposed them to be prohibited.

If we quit this narrow view of the subject, and passing from the literal interpretation of the words, look to the objects of the prohibition, we find no reason for withdrawing the act under consideration from its operation.

From the vast inequality between the different states of the confederacy, as to commercial advantages, few subjects were viewed with deeper interest, or excited more irritation, than the manner in which the several states exercised, or seemed disposed to exercise, the power of laying duties on imports. From motives which were deemed sufficient by the statesmen of that day, the general power of taxation, indispensably necessary as it was, and jealous as the states were of any encroachment on it, was so far abridged as to forbid them to touch imports or exports, with the single exception which has been noticed. Why are they restrained from imposing these duties? Plainly, because, in the general opinion, the interest of all would be best promoted by placing that whole subject under the control of Congress. Whether the prohibition to "lay imposts, or duties on imports or exports," proceeded from an apprehension that the power might be so exercised as to disturb that equality among the states which was generally advantageous, or that harmony between them which it was desirable to preserve, or to maintain unimpaired, our commercial connexions with foreign nations, or to confer this source of revenue on the government of the union, or whatever other motive might have induced the prohibition, it is plain that the object would be as completely defeated by a power to tax the article in the hands of the importer the instant it was landed, as by a power to tax it while entering the port. There is no difference, in effect, between a power to prohibit the sale of an article, and a power to prohibit its introduction into the country. The one would be a necessary consequence of the other. No goods would be imported if none could be sold. No object of any description can be accomplished by laying a duty on importation, which may not be accomplished with equal certainty by laying a duty on the thing imported in the hands of the importer. It is obvious, that the same power which imposes a light duty, can impose a very heavy one, one which amounts to a prohibition. Questions of power do not depend on the degree to which it may be exercised. If it may be exercised at all, it must be exercised at the will of those in whose hands it is placed. If the tax may be levied in this form by a state, it may be levied to an extent which will defeat the revenue by impost, so far as it is drawn from importations into the particular state. We are told, that such wild and irrational abuse of power is not to be apprehended, and it is not to be taken into view when discussing its existence. All power may be abused; and if the fear of its abuse is to constitute an argument against its existence, it might be urged against the existence of that[1] which is indispensable to the general safety. The states will never be so mad as to destroy their own commerce, or even to lessen it.

We do not dissent from those general propositions. We do not suppose any state would act so unwisely. But we do not place the question on that ground.

These arguments apply with precisely the same force against the whole prohibition. It might, with the same reason, be said, that no state would be so blind to its own interests as to lay duties on importation which would either prohibit or diminish its trade. Yet the framers of our constitution have thought this a power which no state ought to exercise. Conceding, to the full extent which is required, that every state would, in its legislation on this subject, provide judiciously for its own interest, it cannot be conceded, that each would respect the interests of others. A duty on imports is a tax on the article which is paid by the consumer. The great importing states would thus levy a tax on the non-importing states, which would not less be[2] a tax because their interest would afford ample security against its ever being so heavy as to expel commerce from their ports. This would necessarily produce countervailing measures on the part of those states whose situation was less favorable to importation. For this, among other reasons, the whole power of laying duties on imports was, with a single and slight exception, taken from the states. When we are inquiring whether a particular act is within this prohibition, the question is not, whether the state may so legislate as to hurt itself, but whether the act is within the words and mischief of the prohibitory clause. It has already been shown, that a tax on the article in the hands of the importer, is within its words; and we think it too clear for controversy, that the same tax is within its mischief. We think it unquestionable, that such a tax has precisely the same tendency to enhance the price of the article, as if imposed upon it while entering the port.

The counsel for the state of Maryland insist, with great reason, that if the words of the prohibition be taken in their utmost latitude, they will abridge the power of taxation, which all admit to be essential to the states, to an extent which has never yet been suspected, and will deprive them of resources which are necessary to supply revenue, and which they have heretofore been admitted to possess. These words must, therefore, be construed with some limitation; and, if this be admitted, they insist, that entering the country is the point of time when the prohibition ceases, and the power of the state to tax commences.

It may be conceded, that the words of the prohibition ought not to be pressed to their utmost extent; that in our complex system, the object of the powers conferred on the government of the union, and the nature of the often conflicting powers which remain in the states, must always be taken into view, and may aid in expounding the words of any particular clause. But, while we admit that sound principles of construction ought to restrain all courts from carrying the words of the prohibition beyond the object the constitution is intended to secure, that there must be a point of time when the prohibition ceases, and the power of the state to tax commences; we cannot admit that this point of time is the instant that the articles enter the country. It is, we think, obvious, that this construction would defeat the prohibition.

The constitutional prohibition on the states to lay a duty on imports, a prohibition which a vast majority of them must feel an interest in preserving, may certainly come in conflict with their acknowledged power to tax persons and property within their territory. The power, and the restriction on it though quite distinguishable when they do not approach each other, may yet, like the intervening colors between white and black, approach so nearly as to perplex the understanding, as colors perplex the vision in marking the distinction between them. Yet the distinction exists, and must be marked as the cases arise. Till they do arise, it might be premature to state any rule as being universal in its application. It is sufficient for the present to say, generally, that when the importer has so acted upon the thing imported, that it has become incorporated and mixed up with the mass of property in the country, it has, perhaps, lost its distinctive character as an import, and has become subject to the taxing power of the state; but while remaining the property of the importer, in his warehouse, in the original form or package in which it was imported, a tax upon it is too plainly a duty on imports to escape the prohibition in the constitution.

The counsel for the plaintiffs in error contend, that the importer purchases, by payment of the duty to the United States, a right to dispose of his merchandize, as well as to bring it into the country; and certainly the argument is supported by strong reason, as well as by the practice of nations, including our own. The object of importation is sale; it constitutes the motive for paying the duties; and if the United States possess the power of conferring the right to sell, as the consideration for which the duty is paid, every principle of fair dealing requires that they should be understood to confer it. The practice of the most commercial nations conforms to this idea. Duties, according to that practice, are charged on those articles only which are intended for sale or consumption in the country. Thus, sea stores, goods imported and re-exported in the same vessel, goods landed and carried over land for the purpose of being re-exported from some other port, goods forced in by stress of weather, and landed, but not for sale, are exempted from the payment of duties. The whole course of legislation on the subject shows, that, in the opinion of the legislature, the right to sell is connected with the payment of duties.

The counsel for the defendant in error have endeavored to illustrate their proposition, that the constitutional prohibition ceases the instant the goods enter the country, by an array of the consequences which they suppose must follow the denial of it. If the importer acquires the right to sell by the payment of duties he may, they say, exert that right when, where, and as he pleases, and the state cannot regulate it. He may sell by retail, at auction, or as an itinerant pedlar. He may introduce articles, as gunpowder, which endanger a city, into the midst of its population; he may introduce articles which endanger the public health, and the power of self-preservation is denied. An importer may bring in goods, as plate, for his own use, and thus retain much valuable property exempt from taxation.

These objections to the principle, if well founded, would certainly be entitled to serious consideration. But we think, they will be found, on examination, not to belong necessarily to the principle, and consequently, not to prove, that it may not be resorted to with safety as a criterion by which to measure the extent of the prohibition.

This indictment is against the importer for selling a package of dry goods in the form in which it was imported without a license. This state of things is changed if he sells them, or otherwise mixes them with the general property of the state, by breaking up his packages, and travelling with them as an itinerant pedlar. In the first case, the tax intercepts the import, as an import, in its way to become incorporated with the general mass of property, and denies it the privilege of becoming so incorporated until it shall have contributed to the revenue of the state. It denies to the importer the right of using the privilege which he has purchased from the United States, until he shall have also purchased it from the state. In the last cases, the tax finds the articles already incorporated with the mass of property by the act of the importer. He has used the privilege he had purchased, and has himself mixed them up with the common mass, and the law may treat them as it finds them. The same observations apply to plate, or other furniture used by the importer.

So, if he sells by auction. Auctioneers are persons licensed by the state, and if the importer chooses to employ them, he can as little object to paying for this service, as for any other for which he may apply to an officer of the state. The right of sale may very well be annexed to importation, without annexing to it also, the privilege of using the officers licensed by the state to make sales in a peculiar way.

The power to direct the removal of gunpowder is a branch of the police power, which unquestionably remains, and ought to remain, with the states. If the possessor stores it himself out of town, the removal cannot be a duty on imports, because it contributes nothing to the revenue. If he prefers placing it in a public magazine, it is because he stores it there, in his own opinion, more advantageously than elsewhere. We are not sure that this may not be classed among inspection laws. The removal or destruction of infectious or unsound articles is undoubtedly, an exercise of that power, and forms an express exception to the prohibition we are considering. Indeed, the laws of the United States expressly sanction the health laws of a state.

The principle, then, for which the plaintiffs in error contend, that the importer acquires a right, not only to bring the articles into the country, but to mix them with the common mass of property, does not interfere with the necessary power of taxation which is acknowledged to reside in the states, to that dangerous extent which the counsel for the defendants in error seem to apprehend. It carries the prohibition in the constitution no farther than to prevent the states from doing that which it was the great object of the constitution to prevent.

But if it should be proved, that a duty on the article itself would be repugnant to the constitution, it is still argued, that this is not a tax upon the article, but on the person. The state, it is said, may tax occupations, and this is nothing more.

It is impossible to conceal from ourselves, that this is varying the form, without varying the substance. It is treating a prohibition which is general, as if it were confined to a particular mode of doing the forbidden thing. All must perceive, that a tax on the sale of an article, imported only for sale, is a tax on the article itself. It is true, the state may tax occupations generally, but this tax must be paid by those who employ the individual, or is a tax on his business. The lawyer, the physician, or the mechanic, must either charge more on the article in which he deals, or the thing itself is taxed through his person. This the state has a right to do, because no constitutional prohibition extends to it. So, a tax on the occupation of an importer is, in like manner, a tax on importation. It must add to the price of the article, and be paid by the consumer, or by the importer himself, in like manner as a direct duty on the article itself would be made. This the state has not a right to do, because it is prohibited by the constitution.

In support of the argument, that the prohibition ceases the instant the goods are brought into the country, a comparison has been drawn between the opposite words export and import. As, to export, it is said, means only to carry goods out of the country; so, to import, means only to bring them into it. But, suppose we extend this comparison to the two prohibitions. The states are forbidden to lay a duty on exports, and the United States are forbidden to lay a tax or duty on articles exported from any state. There is some diversity in language, but none is perceivable in the act which is prohibited. The United States have the same right to tax occupations which is possessed by the states. Now, suppose the United States should require every exporter to take out a license, for which he should pay such tax as Congress might think proper to impose; would government be permitted to shield itself from the just censure to which this attempt to evade the prohibitions of the constitution would expose it, by saying, that this was a tax on the person, not on the article, and that the legislature had a right to tax occupations? Or, suppose revenue cutters were to be stationed off the coast for the purpose of levying a duty on all merchandise found in vessels which were leaving the United States for foreign countries; would it be received as an excuse for this outrage, were the government to say that exportation meant no more than carrying goods out of the country, and as the prohibition to lay a tax on imports, or things imported, ceased the instant they were brought into the country, so the prohibition to tax articles exported ceased when they were carried out of the country?

We think, then, that the act under which the plaintiffs in error were indicted, is repugnant to that article of the constitution which declares, that "no State shall lay any impost or duties on imports or exports."

2. Is it also repugnant to that clause in the constitution which empowers "congress to regulate commerce with foreign nations, and among the several states, and with the Indian tribes?"

The oppressed and degraded state of commerce previous to the adoption of the constitution can scarcely be forgotten. It was regulated by foreign nations with a single view to their own interests; and our disunited efforts to counteract their restrictions were rendered impotent by want of combination. Congress, indeed, possessed the power of making treaties; but the inability of the federal government to enforce them had become so apparent as to render that power in a great degree useless.

Those who felt the injury arising from this state of things, and those who were capable of estimating the influence of commerce on the prosperity of nations, perceived the necessity of giving the control over this important subject to a single government. It may be doubted whether any of the evils proceeding from the feebleness of the federal government, contributed more to that great revolution which introduced the present system, than the deep and general conviction, that commerce ought to be regulated by congress. It is not, therefore, matter of surprise, that the grant should be as extensive as the mischief, and should comprehend all foreign commerce, and all commerce among the states. To construe the power so as to impair its efficacy, would tend to defeat an object, in the attainment of which the American public took, and justly took, that strong interest which arose from a full conviction of its necessity.

What, then, is the just extent of a power to regulate commerce with foreign nations, and among the several states?

This question was considered in the case of *Gibbons* v. *Ogden*, (9 *Wheat. Rep.* 1.) in which it was declared to be complete in itself, and to acknowledge no limitations other than are prescribed by the constitution. The power is co-extensive with the subject on which it acts, and cannot be stopped at the external boundary of a state, but must enter its interior.

We deem it unnecessary now to reason in support of these propositions. Their truth is proved by facts continually before our eyes, and was, we think, demonstrated, if they could require demonstration, in the case already mentioned.

If this power reaches the interior of a state, and may be there exercised, it must be capable of authorizing the sale of those articles which it introduces. Commerce is intercourse: one of its most ordinary ingredients is traffic. It is inconceivable, that the power to authorize this traffic, when given in the most comprehensive terms, with the intent that its efficacy should be complete, should cease at the point when its continuance is indispensable to its value. To what purpose should the power to allow importation be given, unaccompanied with the power to authorize a sale of the thing imported? Sale is the object of importation, and is an essential ingredient of that intercourse, of which importation constitutes a part. It is as essential an ingredient, as indispensable to the existence of the entire thing, then, as importation itself. It must be considered as a component part of the power to regulate commerce. Congress has a right, not only to authorize importation, but to authorize the importer to sell.

If this be admitted, and we think it cannot be denied, what can be the meaning of an act of congress which authorizes importation, and offers the privilege for sale at a fixed price to every person who chooses to become a purchaser? How is it to be construed, if an intent to deal honestly and fairly, an intent as wise as it is moral, is to enter into the construction? What can be the use of the contract, what does the importer purchase, if he does not purchase the privilege to sell?

What would be the language of a foreign government, which should be informed that its merchants, after importing according to law, were forbidden to sell the merchandise imported? What answer would the United States give to the complaints and just reproaches to which such an extraordinary circumstance would expose them? No apology could be received, or even offered. Such a state of things would break up commerce. It will not meet this argument to say that this state of things will never be produced; that the good sense of the states is a sufficient security against it. The constitution has not confided this subject to that good sense. It is placed elsewhere. The question is, where does the power reside? not, how far will it be probably abused. The power claimed by the state is, in its nature, in conflict with that given to congress; and the greater or less extent in which it may be exercised, does not enter into the inquiry concerning its existence.

We think, then, that if the power to authorize a sale exists in congress, the conclusion that the right to sell is connected with the law permitting importation, as an inseparable incident, is inevitable.

If the principles we have stated be correct, the result to which they conduct us cannot be mistaken. Any penalty inflicted on the importer for selling the article in his character of importer, must be in opposition to the act of congress which authorizes importation. Any charge on the introduction and incorporation of the articles into and with the mass of property, in the country, must be hostile to the power given to congress to regulate commerce, since an essential part of that regulation, and principal object of it, is to prescribe the regular means for accomplishing that introduction and incorporation.

The distinction between a tax on the thing imported, and on the person of the importer, can have no influence on this part of the subject. It is too obvious for controversy, that they interfere equally with the power to regulate commerce.

It has been contended, that this construction of the power to regulate commerce, as was contended in construing the prohibition to lay duties on imports, would abridge the acknowledged power of a state to tax its own citizens, or their property within its territory.

We admit this power to be sacred; but cannot admit that it may be used so as to obstruct the free course of a power given to congress. We cannot admit, that it may be used so as to obstruct or defeat the power to regulate commerce. It has been observed, that the powers remaining with the states may be so exercised as to come in conflict with those vested in congress. When this happens that which is not supreme must yield to that which is supreme. This great and universal truth is inseparable from the nature of things, and the constitution has applied it to the often interfering powers of the general and state governments, as a vital principle of perpetual operation. It results, necessarily, from this principle, that the taxing power of the states must have some limits. It cannot reach and restrain the action of the national government within its proper sphere. It cannot reach the administration of justice in the courts of the union, or the collection of the taxes of the United States, or restrain the operation of any law which congress may constitutionally pass. It cannot interfere with any regulation of commerce. If the states may tax all persons and property found on their territory, what shall restrain them from taxing goods in their transit through the state from one port to another, for the purpose of re-exportation? The laws of trade authorize this operation, and general convenience requires it. Or what should restrain a state from taxing any article passing through it from one state to another, for the purpose of traffic? or from taxing the transportation of articles passing from the state itself to another state, for commercial purposes? These cases are all within the sovereign power of taxation, but would obviously derange the measures of congress to regulate commerce, and affect materially the purpose for which that power was given. We deem it unnecessary to press this argument farther, or to give additional illustrations of it, because the subject was taken up, and considered with great attention in *M'Culloch* vs. *The state of Maryland,* (4. *Wheat. Rep.* 316.) the decision in which case is, we think, entirely applicable to this.

It may be proper to add that we suppose the principles laid down in this case, to apply equally to importations from a sister state. We do not mean to give any opinion on a tax discriminating between foreign and domestic articles.

We think there is error in the judgment of the court of appeals of the state of Maryland, in affirming the judgment of the Baltimore city court, because the act of the legislature of Maryland, imposing the penalty for which the said judgment is rendered, is repugnant to the constitution of the United States, and, consequently, void. The judgment is to be reversed, and the cause remanded to that court, with instructions to enter judgment in favour of the appellants.[3]

[Judgment]

Alexander Brown and others   writ of errour to
                                the Court of appeals of the
The State of Maryland   State of Maryland

This cause came on to be heard on the transcript of the record of the Court of Appeals held for the Western shore of the State of Maryland, and was argued by counsel, on consideration whereof this court is of opinion that there is errour in the judgement rendered by the said court of appeals in this, that the judgement of the city court of Baltimore condemning the said Alexander Brown George Brown John A Brown and James Brown to pay the penalty therein mentioned, ought not to have been so rendered against them because the Act of the state of Maryland entitled "A supplement to the act to the act laying duties on Licences to the retailers of dry goods and for other purposes" on which the indictment on which the said judgement was rendered is founded, so far as it enacts "that all importers of foreign articles or commodoties [sic] of dry goods, wares, or merchandise by bale or package, or of wine, rum, brandy, whisky, and other distilled spirituous liquors &c., selling the same by wholesale bale or package hoxhead barrel or tierce, shall, before they are authorized to sell, take out a licence as by the original act is directed, for which they shall pay fifty dollars; and, in case of neglect or refusal to take out such licence, shall be subject to the same penalties and forfeitures as are prescribed by the original act to which this is a supplement" is repugnant to the constitution of the United States and void; wherefore the said court of appeals held for the Western shore of the State of Maryland before whom the said judgement of the said city court of Baltimore was brought by appeal ought not to have affirmed but should have reversed the same. Wherefore it is considered by this court that the said judgement of the said court of Appeals held for the Western shore of the state of Maryland affirming the said judgement of the city court of Baltimore be reversed and annulled, and that the cause be remanded to the said court of Appeals with directions to reverse the same.

Printed, *Niles' Weekly Register* (Baltimore), 23 June 1827. Judgment, AD, Brown v. Maryland, Appellate Case No. 1350, RG 267, DNA.

1. Wheaton's text inserts the following phrase at this point: "which is universally acknowledged, and."

2. Wheaton's text reads "not be less."

3. In his dissenting opinion, Thompson denied that the Maryland license tax infringed the commerce clause, contending that it related only to the purely internal trade of the state. External commerce, he said, ended with the importation of the foreign article. Nor was a license to sell an import duty within the meaning of that term as used in the Constitution. The principle that payment of an import duty conferred a right to sell was unsound, he added, for it could be applied to deprive the states of all taxing power over imported goods. Nothing in the Constitution supported extending the exemption from state taxation only to wholesalers of foreign imports and not retailers as well (12 Wheat. 449–59).

To Tench Ringgold

Dear Sir[1]   Washington March 13th. 27
    The Judges have agreed to relinquish to Mr. Carrol the use of the room 23 which has been assigned to them. You will please to deliver him the key that he may take possession, Your Obedt

                                                                J MARSHALL

ALS, RG 46, DNA. Addressed to the "Marshal of the District." Endorsed by clerk.

1. Tench Ringgold (1776–1844), was U.S. marshal for the District of Columbia from 1818 to 1827 (Wilhelm Bogardus Bryan, *The History of the National Capital* [2 vols.; New York, 1914–16], I, 527; Frank Metcalf and George Martin, *Marriages and Deaths: 1800–1820; from the National Intelligencer* [Washington, D.C., 1968], 74; *Journal of the Executive Proceedings of the Senate* [3 vols.; Washington, D.C., 1828], III, 142, 150, 315, 329, 552, 558).

To Jared Sparks

                                        [Washington, ca. 13 March 1827]
    Mr. Marshall will thank Mr Sparks for a copy of the orders which preceded the battle of Germantown and which contain the order of battle. They were I think issued and are dated on the 3d. of October 1777. It is possible they may be dated the 2d.

AL, Sparks Papers, MH. For dating, see n. 1.

1. JM evidently wrote this note while he and Sparks were still in Washington. Sparks left Washington for Alexandria on 13 Mar. and the next day proceeded to Mount Vernon, where he spent several weeks examining Washington's papers. He wrote to JM on 3 Apr. from Mount Vernon, enclosing a copy of the order JM requested (Herbert B. Adams, *The Life and Writings of Jared Sparks, Comprising Selections from His Journals and Correspondence* [2 vols.; Boston and New York, 1893], II, 10–11, 13–14).

To Timothy Pickering

My dear Sir   Washington March 15th. 1827

I was much obliged by your favour of the 14th. of Feby. through our friend Mr. Mercer. I am always gratified at being recollected by my old friends, for I find myself incapable of making new ones.

I have seen in the papers the discussions between my brother Johnson and yourself respecting Count Pulaski and the battle of Germantown. It is not a little gratifying to us who are treading close upon your heels to observe how firmly you step, & how perfectly you retain your recollection. You are a little before me and I find myself almost alone in the world. With the exception of Judge Peters yourself & Mr. Wolcot I can scarcely find any person who was conspicuous on the great theatre of our country when I first began to mix in public affairs. Things are very much changed as well as men.

Is it probable that you will ever travel as far south as Washington? Few things would give me so much pleasure as to see you, but that is a pleasure which I scarcely dare promise myself. It is probable that the line which circumscribes your movements to the south will never intersect that which bounds me on the north.

You give a great many interesting anecdotes of General Washington which serve to develope his character. Your opportunities of personal observation enable you to take a near view of the man. I have seen him only at a distance. I have looked at him through those actions which were the result of mature deliberation, and consultation with those to whom he gave his confidence. The conclusion to which this view of him has conducted me is extremely favourable to his judgement, his wisdom and his virtue. If he did not possess that rapidity of decision which distinguishes many men of genius, there seems to have been a solidity in his mind which fitted him in a peculiar manner for occupying the high place he filled in the United States in the critical times in which he filled it. No feature in his character was more conspicuous that his firmness.[1] Though prizing popular favour as highly as it ought to be prized, he never yielded principle to obtain it, or sacrificed his judgement on its altar. This firmness of character added to his acknowledged virtue enabled him to stem a torrent which would have overwhelmed almost any other man, and did I believe save his country.

Such is my impression of Washington, an impression certainly not formed on a near view of him, but on a very attentive consideration of his character his conduct, and his papers. You could take a closer view of him, especially as a military man than was in my power, and have consequently better means of judging correctly than I possess.

With the best wishes for your health and happiness, and with sincere and respectful esteem, I am dear Sir your Obedt.

J MARSHALL

ALS, Pickering Papers, MHi. Addressed to Pickering in Salem, Mass. Noted as carried by Joseph Story.

1. Pickering here placed an asterisk keyed to the following note written at the end of the letter: "[* I recollect that when, on some question of importance, Washington was consulting the heads of departments, of whom I was one, He said, 'Let me see my way clear, and no consideration shall turn me aside;' or used words to that effect; manifesting that firmness in the performance of his official duties to which Judge Marshall here refers. T Pickering.]."

Postmaster General v. Early
Opinion
U.S. Supreme Court, 15 March 1827

This case originated in the U.S. Circuit Court for Georgia, brought in the name of the Postmaster General against Eleazer Early, postmaster at Savannah, and others on a performance bond executed in June 1820. The defendants pleaded to the jurisdiction of the federal court, contending that the suit was not one in which the United States was a party and that the debt sued on was not one contracted under a law of the United States. In December 1825 Justice Johnson and U.S. District Judge Cuyler divided on the question whether the court had jurisdiction, and the case was certified to the Supreme Court for final decision. The case was argued on 9 and 10 March 1827, Wheaton and Wirt for the plaintiff and Berrien and Webster for the defendants. Marshall delivered the opinion of the court on 15 March (Postmaster General v. Early, App. Cas. No. 1369; U.S. Sup. Ct. Minutes, 9, 10 Mar. 1827).

The post office department was established at the commencement of the revolution, under the superintendence of a Post Master General, who was authorized to appoint his deputies, and was made responsible for their conduct. Soon after the adoption of the present government, in September, 1789, Congress passed a temporary act, directing that a Post Master General should be appointed, and that his powers, and the regulations of his office, should be the same as they last were, "under the resolutions and ordinances of the last Congress."[1] The power of appointing deputies, therefore, and the responsibility for their conduct, still remained with the Post Master General.

This act was continued until the first day of June, 1792. In February, 1792, an act was passed detailing the duties and powers of the Post Master General, and fixing the rates of postage.[2] It directs his deputies to settle at the end of every three months, and to pay up the moneys in their hands; on failure to do which, it becomes the duty of the Post Master General "to cause a suit to be commenced against the person or persons so neglecting or refusing. And if the Post Master General shall not cause such suit to be commenced within three months from the end of every such three months, the balances due from every such delinquent shall be charged to and recoverable from him." This act was to take effect on the first of June, 1792, and to continue for two years. In May, 1794, a permanent act was passed.[3] It retains the provision requiring the Post Master General to settle quarterly with his deputies, but omits that which makes it his duty to cause suits to be instituted within three months after failure.

In March, 1799, the subject was again taken up, and Congress passed an act, which retains the clause making it the duty of the deputy post masters to settle their accounts quarterly, and reinstates that which directs the Post Master General to cause suits to be instituted against delinquents; substituting six months in the place of three, after the expiration of the quarter, under the penalty of being himself chargeable with the arrears due from such delinquent.[4] This act declares, that all causes of action arising under it may be sued before the judicial Courts of the several States, and of the several territories of the United States.

In April, 1810, Congress passed an act for regulating the post office establishment, which enacts, among other things, that all suits thereafter to be brought for the recovery of debts or balances due to the general post office, should be instituted in the name of "the Post Master General of the United States."[5] This act also authorizes all causes of action arising under it to be sued in the Courts of the States and territories.

In March, 1815, Congress passed "an act to vest more effectually in the State Courts, and in the District Courts of the United States, jurisdiction in the cases therein mentioned."

This act enables the State Courts to take cognizance of all suits arising under any law for the collection of any direct tax or internal duties of the United States. The 4th section contains this clause: "And be it further enacted, that the District Court of the United States shall have cognizance, concurrent with the Courts and magistrates of the several States, and the Circuit Courts of the United States, of all suits at common law where the United States, or any officer thereof, under the authority of any act of Congress, shall sue, although the debt, claim, or other matter in dispute, shall not amount to one hundred dollars."[6] On these several acts the question of jurisdiction depends.

The suit is brought for money due to the United States; and, at any time previous to the act of 1810, the suit for the money, had no bond been taken, might have been brought in the name of the United States. It is not certain that, independent of the bond, it could have been instituted in the name of any other party. The Courts of the United States, had, of course, jurisdiction. The laws make it the duty of the Post Master General to "cause suits to be instituted," not to bring them; and it was not until March, 1799, that Congress authorized these suits to be instituted in the State Courts. It is obvious, that the right to institute them in those Courts, anterior to the passage of that act, was doubted; at any rate, was not exercised; for it could not have been deemed necessary to give expressly the power to sue in those Courts, had the power been admitted to exist, and been commonly exercised. We must suppose, then, that these suits were usually instituted in the Courts of the United States; and no doubt could be entertained on the question of jurisdiction, if they were brought, as they certainly might have been, in the name of the United States.

The act of 1810 directed, that all suits for debts, or balances due to the general post office, should be brought in the name of the Post Master General. The manner in which this change in the style of the suit might affect jurisdiction, was not noticed, and no provision was made for this new state of things. These debts and balances which were due to the general post office, were not due to the officer personally, but to the office, and were to be sued for, and collected for the United States. The money belonged to the nation, not to the individual by whose agency it was to be brought into the treasury. The whole course of opinion, and of legislation, on this subject, is, that, although for convenience, and to save expense to the debtors, recourse may be had to the State Courts for the recovery of small sums, yet a right to resort to the Courts of the Union in suits for money due to the United States, was never intended to be relinquished. If the effect of any provision in a statute be to abolish this jurisdiction, it must be an effect which was neither intended nor foreseen. That construction which will produce a consequence so directly opposite to the whole spirit of our legislation, ought to be avoided, if it can be avoided without a total disregard of those rules by which Courts of justice must be governed.

If the question had rested solely on the act of 1810, it is probable that the aid of the legislature might have been thought indispensable to the jurisdiction of the federal Courts, over suits brought for the recovery of debts and balances due to the general post office. But it does not rest solely on that act. The act of 1815 contains a clause which does, we think, confer this jurisdiction. It cannot be doubted that this clause vests jurisdiction expressly in the District Courts, in all suits at common law where any officer of the United States sues under the authority of any act of Congress. The Post Master General is an officer of the United States, who sues under the authority of the act of 1810, which makes it his duty to sue for debts and balances due to the office he superintends, and obliges him to sue in his own name.

It has been contended, that this clause, if it gives jurisdiction, gives it only where the demand is under one hundred dollars. We do not think the words will sustain this criticism.

The right to take cognizance of suits brought by any officer of the United States, under authority of any act of Congress, is first given in general words, comprehending sums to any amount. The limitation which follows is not a proviso that the sum shall not exceed the sum of one hundred dollars; it is no restriction on the previous grant, but an enlargement of it, if an enlargement should be thought necessary. This act might be construed, in connexion with the Judiciary Act of 1789, and a general clause giving jurisdiction might be limited as to amount to the sum mentioned in the 9th section of that act. The subsequent words, therefore, of the section we are considering, were introduced for the purpose of obviating this construction, and removing the doubt, which might otherwise exist, of the right to take cognizance of sums less than one hundred dollars. After giving the jurisdiction generally, the words are, "*although the debt, claim, or other matter in dispute, shall not amount to one hundred dollars.*" These words do not confine the jurisdiction previously given to one hundred dollars, but prevents it from stopping at that sum.

The jurisdiction of the District courts, then, over suits brought by the Post Master General for debts and balances due the general post office, is unquestionable. Has the Circuit Court jurisdiction?

The language of the act is, ["]that the District Court shall have cognizance concurrent with the Courts and magistrates of the several States, and the Circuit Courts of the United States, of all suits," &c. What is the meaning and purport of the words "concurrent with" the Circuit Courts of the United States? Are they entirely senseless? Are they to be excluded from the clause in which the legislature has inserted them, or are they to be taken into view, and allowed the effect of which they are capable?

The words are certainly not senseless. They have a plain and obvious meaning. And it is, we think, a rule, that words which have a meaning, are not to be entirely disregarded in construing a statute. We cannot understand this clause as if these words were excluded from it. They, perhaps, manifest the opinion of the legislature, that the jurisdiction was in the Circuit Courts; but ought, we think, to be construed to give it, if it did not previously exist. Any other construction would destroy the effect of those words. The District Court cannot take cognizance concurrent with the Circuit Courts, unless the Circuit Courts can take cognizance of the same suits. For one body to do a thing concurrently with another, is to act in conjunction with that other; it is equivalent to saying, that one may act *together with* the other. The phrase may imply, that power was previously given to that other; but if, in fact, it had not been given, the words are capable of imparting it. If they are susceptible of this construction, they ought to receive it, because they will otherwise be totally inoperative, or will contradict the other parts of the sentence, which show plainly the intention, that the District Court shall have cognizance of the subject, and shall take it to the same extent with the Circuit Courts.

It has been said, and perhaps truly, that this section was not framed with the intention of vesting jurisdiction in the Circuit Courts. The title of the act, and the language of the sentence, are supposed to concur in sustaining this proposition. The title speaks only of State and District Courts. But it is well settled, that the title cannot restrain the enacting clause. It is true that the language of the section indicates the opinion, that jurisdiction existed in the Circuit Courts, rather than an intention to give it; and a mistaken opinion of the legislature concerning the law, does not make law.

But if this mistake is manifested in words competent to make the law in future, we know of no principle which can deny them this effect. The legislature may pass a declaratory act, which, though inoperative on the past, may act in future. This law expresses the sense of the legislature on the existing law, as plainly as a declaratory act, and expresses it in terms capable of conferring the jurisdiction. We think, therefore, that in a case plainly within the judicial power of the federal Courts, as prescribed in the constitution, and plainly within the general policy of the legislature, the words ought to receive this construction.

So far as the suits brought by the Post Master General were referred to in argument, in the case of *The Bank of the United States* v. *Osborn,* this construction was assumed as unquestionable. As the act was referred to for the sole purpose of illustrating the argument on the point then under consideration, it was not examined with the attention which has since been bestowed upon it; but the opinion then expressed, that the section we have been considering conferred jurisdiction on the Courts of the United States over suits brought by the Post Master General was correct.

Had this suit been brought to recover the balance due from the deputy post master, on his original liability to pay the money in his hands, no doubt would have been felt respecting the jurisdiction of the Court. The act of 1810 gives the Post Master General a right to sue for such balances, and the act of 1815 enables him to sue in the Circuit or District Courts of the United States. But it is contended that he has no right to secure such balances by bond; and, consequently, the bond being unauthorized, the act of Congress cannot be construed to authorize a suit upon it.

Were it even true that an official bond cannot be taken in a case where it is not expressly directed by law, we do not think that a bond taken to secure the payment of a sum of money is void, because it is also an official bond. Even supposing this bond to be void, so far as it is intended to stipulate for the performance of official duties, it is not necessarily void, so far as it stipulates for the payment of money of the United States, which might come to the hands of the deputy post master. That part of the condition which shows the bond was taken to secure the payment of money which should be received for the United States, is not vitiated by that part of it which shows that it was also taken to secure the general official conduct of the deputy. Now, a part of the condition is expressly "that if he shall pay all moneys that shall come to his hands, for the postages of whatsoever is by law chargeable with postage," then the obligation is to be void. The obligation itself, on which the suit is brought, was intended to secure the payment of money collected for the United States, as well as the official conduct of the deputy; and as no law prohibited such an official bond, we cannot think, although it might not in itself be valid, that it would destroy an obligation taken for a legitimate purpose. As the breach assigned is altogether in the non-payment of the money collected, we do not think that, if a bond would be good, taken for this single object, it is made bad by being extended also to the official conduct of the obligor.

The inquiry then is, whether, under a fair construction of the acts of Congress, the Post Master General may take bonds to secure the payment of money due, or which may become due, to the general post office.

All the acts relative to the post office, make it the duty of the Post Master General to superintend the department, to regulate the conduct and duties of his deputies, and to collect the moneys received by them for the general post office. May not these powers extend to taking bonds to the officer who is to perform them? May not these bonds be considered as means proper to be used in the collection of debts, and in securing them?

If this interpretation of the words should be too free for a judicial tribunal, yet if the legislature has made it, if Congress has explained its own meaning too unequivocally to be mistaken, their Courts may be justified in adopting that meaning.

The 22d section of the act of 1799, after directing the Post Master General to sue for all balances due from his deputies, within six months after the expiration of the three months within which they ought to have been paid, enacts, "that all suits, which shall be hereafter commenced for the recovery of debts or balances due to the general post office, whether they appear by *bond or obligations* made in the name of the existing or any preceding Post Master General, or otherwise, shall be instituted in the name of the Post Master General of the United States."

These words follow immediately the clause which makes it the duty of the Post Master General to sue for the money due from his deputies, and are obviously applied to the moneys in their hands. They show the sense of legislature, that this money may be a "debt" or a "balance," may "appear by bond or obligation," or otherwise; and are, we think, a legislative exposition of the words, describing the power and duty of the Post Master General in the superintendence of his department, and the means he may employ for collecting the money due from his deputies.

The 31st section of the same act, repeals the previous laws for establishing the post office department, after the 1st day of the ensuing May; and adds a proviso to the repealing clause, that as to "all bonds, contracts, debts, demands, rights, penalties, or punishments, which have been made, have arisen, or have been incurred," &c. "the said acts shall have the same effect, as if this act had not been made."

It is said by the counsel for the defendants, that these words do not give efficacy to the bonds to which they refer, but leave them as they were anterior to the repealing act. This is true. But they explain the sense of the legislature, respecting the powers of the Post Master General, and the manner in which he might execute those powers.

An additional proviso extends even to official bonds. After continuing the Post Master General and all his deputies in office, it adds, "and also the bonds which they or either of them have or may give for the faithful execution of their several duties, shall continue to have the same force and effect, to all intents and purposes, after the 1st day of May next, as though this act had not been made."

This proviso, also, is no more than a recognition of the validity of those bonds; but it is a recognition of it, and goes the full extent of showing the legislative opinion that they might be taken. The act of 1810 repeals former acts, and contains the same provisions on this subject with the act of 1799.

The Court has felt the pressure of this part of the case. There is always difficulty in extending the operation of words beyond their plain import; but the cardinal rule of construction is, that where any doubt exists, the intent of the legislature, if it can be plainly perceived, ought to be pursued. It is also a rule, that the whole law is to be taken together, and one part expounded by any other, which may indicate the meaning annexed by the legislature itself to ambiguous phrases. The words describing the power and duty of the Post Master General, may be expounded by other parts of the act showing the legislative opinion as to their extent; and if this be true, the sections which have been cited cannot be misunderstood. They show plainly that the legislature supposed it had given the Post Master General authority to take these bonds.

A case cannot exist, in which effect may be given to the legislative intent more safely than in this. The bonds are taken in a case where no doubt can exist respecting the right and propriety of giving authority to take them; they are for money due to the United States; and the opinion of the legislature that authority was given, is expressed in as plain words as can be used. The acts of Congress sustain the opinion, that they have been taken with the knowledge and approbation of the legislature, from the first establishment of the offices; and provision is made by law for their being put in suit. The Courts of the United States have, until very lately, uniformly given judgments on them.

Under these circumstances, we think ourselves justified in continuing to sustain them, and to certify, in this case, that the Circuit Court has jurisdiction of the cause.

Printed, Henry Wheaton, *Reports of Cases Argued and Adjudged in the Supreme Court of the United States . . .* , XII (New York, 1827), 144–52.

1. *U.S. Statutes at Large*, I, 70.
2. Ibid., I, 232–39.
3. Ibid., I, 354–66.
4. Ibid., I, 733–41.
5. Ibid., II, 592–604.
6. Ibid., III, 244–45.

To John Quincy Adams

Sir   Washington March 16th. 1827

I have heard it said that the venerable and estimable Gentleman who has so long performed the duties of District Judge in the state of Pennsylvania is about to retire from office. If I take the liberty to bring to your notice a person who stands high in his profession, as one well qualified to be his successor, I must hope to find an apology in my conviction of the importance you attach to the judicial department, and of your desire to fill all vacancies which may occur in it with gentlemen in all respects entitled to the public confidence.

I have been long and intimately acquainted with Mr. Joseph Hopkinson, and think highly of his legal attainments, as well as of his fitness in all other respects for the office. I have heard him argue several important causes in the Supreme Court of the United States, in which he has always displayed accurate knowledge of his subject, and very considerable power of mind. I forbear to speak of him otherwise than professionally, because I believe he is personally known to you.[1] With very great respect, I am Sir your Obedt. Servt.

J Marshall

ALS, Hopkinson Papers, PHi. Addressed to the president.

1. Richard Peters continued to sit as district judge until his death in Aug. 1828. Adams made a recess appointment of Hopkinson and nominated him at the ensuing session of Congress on 11 Dec. 1828. The Senate confirmed the nomination on 23 Feb. 1829. JM probably sent this letter under cover with his letter of this day to Hopkinson, who apparently decided not to send it on to the president (*Journal of the Executive Proceedings of the Senate* [3 vols.; Washington, D.C., 1828], III, 621, 650).

To Joseph Hopkinson

My dear Sir   Washington March 16th. 1827

Our friend Mr. Story informs me that you are not unwilling to retire from the bustle of the bar, and that an office which will probably soon become vacant would be acceptable to you. I cannot boast of my influence with the President, and fear that it is not in my power to be of any service to you. I cannot however hesitate to contribute my endeavours, feeble as they certainly are, to the promotion of your views. With real esteem I am dear Sir Your Obedt

J Marshall

ALS, Hopkinson Papers, PHi. Addressed to Hopkinson in Philadelphia. Noted as carried by Joseph Story.

To Jared Sparks

Dear Sir   Richmond March 28th. 27

The steam boat Potowmack will carry up to Allexandria next week, copies of the letters written by General Washington from 1755 to 1759 in a box addressed to the care of Mr. Cazenove of that place.[1] The same box contains a book of letters written in 1787, which I have retained by accident. I write to Mr. Cazenove informing him that the box may be opened and the contents taken out by you.[2] With great respect, I am your Obedt

J MARSHALL

ALS, Sparks Papers, MH. Addressed to Sparks "now at Mount Vernon / near Alexandria." Endorsed by Sparks as received 1 Apr.

1. By the terms of their agreement executed on 7 Mar., JM and Bushrod were to deliver to Sparks, free of charge, copies of Washington's correspondence they had caused to be made (Articles of Agreement, 7 Mar. 1827 [App. II, Cal.]).

2. Letter not found.

APPENDICES

Appendix I
Opinions Delivered by Chief Justice John Marshall
in the U.S. Supreme Court
1824–1827

The calendar below lists in chronological order all the opinions delivered by Chief Justice Marshall from the 1824 term through the 1827 term of the Supreme Court. Of the fifty-four opinions, two were on motions for a mandamus; four were in cases coming up by certificate of division; and the remainder were in cases coming up by appeal or by writ of error. For a brief discussion of federal appellate procedure under the judicial statutes of 1789, 1802, and 1803, see the *Papers of John Marshall,* VI, 537–38.

In addition to the date of the opinion and the name of the case, the calendar provides the following information: the citation to the printed report; the type of appeal; the name of the court of origin; the appellate case number; and the date(s) of arguments by counsel. This information has been compiled from the printed reports and the Supreme Court minutes, dockets, and appellate case files belonging to Record Group 267 in the National Archives. The style of the case is that used by the reporter Henry Wheaton, unless other sources indicate that he was mistaken. The existence of an original manuscript opinion in Marshall's hand is also noted.

1824

3 February	Taylor v. Mason, 9 Wheat. 339–53. Appeal from U.S. Circuit Court, Md. Appellate Case No. 1058. Argued 2–5 Mar. 1823.
16 February	Kirk v. Smith, 9 Wheat. 256–94. Error to U.S. Circuit Court, Pa. Appellate Case No. 1140. Argued 10–13 Mar. 1823.
17 February	Baits v. Peters and Stebbins, 9 Wheat. 557. Error to U.S. District Court, Ala. Appellate Case No. 1150. Argued 17 Feb. 1824.
17 February	McIver v. Wattles, 9 Wheat. 650. Error to U.S. Circuit Court, D.C., Alexandria. Appellate Case No. 1153. Argued 13 Feb. 1824.
18 February	Stephens v. McCargo, 9 Wheat. 502–15. Appeal from U.S. Circuit Court, Ky. Appellate Case No. 1114. Argued 8, 10 Feb. 1823
2 March	Gibbons v. Ogden, 9 Wheat. 186–222. Appeal from Court for the Trial of Impeachments and Correction of Errors, N.Y. Appellate Case No. 1148. Argued 4–7, 9 Feb. 1824.
3 March	Smith v. McIver, 9 Wheat. 532–37. Appeal from U.S. Circuit Court, W. Tenn. Appellate Case No. 1136. Argued 12–13 Feb. 1824.
3 March	Meredith v. Picket, 9 Wheat. 574–75. Appeal from U.S. Circuit Court, Ky. Appellate Case No. 1170. Argued 14 Feb. 1824.
3 March	Walden v. Craig, 9 Wheat. 577–78. Error to U.S. Circuit Court, Ky. Appellate Case No. 1155. Argued 13 Feb. 1824.

10 March   Mollan v. Torrance, 9 Wheat. 538–40. Error to U.S. District
             Court, Miss. Appellate Case No. 1152. Argued 13 Feb., 6 Mar.
             1824.
12 March   Peyton v. Robertson, 9 Wheat. 527–28. Error to U.S. Circuit
             Court, D.C. Appellate Case No. 1295. No date found for
             argument.
17 March   Ex Parte Burr, 9 Wheat. 529–31. Motion for mandamus to U.S.
             Circuit Court, D.C. Argued 16 Mar. 1824.
19 March   Osborn v. Bank of the United States, MS opinion, 9 Wheat.
             816–71. Appeal from U.S. Circuit Court, Ohio. Appellate Case
             No. 1135. Argued 10–11 Feb., 10–11 Mar. 1824.
22 March   Bank of the United States v. Planters' Bank of Georgia, 9 Wheat.
             904–10. Certificate of division from U.S. Circuit Court, Ga.
             Appellate Case No. 1270. Argued 10–12 Mar. 1824.
23 March   Dodderidge v. Thompson, 9 Wheat. 470–83. Error to U.S. Circuit
             Court, Ohio. Appellate Case No. 1075. Argued 6 Mar. 1824.

1825

19 February Carneal v. Banks, Banks v. Carneal, 10 Wheat. 182–92. Appeal
             from U.S. Circuit Court, Ky. Appellate Case Nos. 1156, 1157.
             Argued 9 Feb. 1825.
19 February The Palmyra, 10 Wheat. 503–4. Appeal from U.S. Circuit
             Court, S.C. Appellate Case No. 1211. Argued 19 Feb. 1825.
23 February Day v. Chism, 10 Wheat. 450–54. Error to U.S. Circuit Court,
             W. Tenn. Appellate Case No. 1200. Argued 11 Feb. 1825.
1 March   Wayman v. Southard, 10 Wheat. 20–50. Certificate of division
             from U.S. Circuit Court, Ky. Appellate Case No. 1164. Argued
             17–19 Mar. 1824.
3 March   McDowell v. Peyton, 10 Wheat. 455–64. Appeal from U.S. Circuit
             Court, Ky. Appellate Case No. 1144. Argued 19, 21, Feb. 1825.
7 March   The Dos Hermanos, 10 Wheat. 310–11. Appeal from U.S. District
             Court, La. Appellate Case No. 1204. Argued 5 Mar. 1825.
10 March   Elmendorf v. Taylor, 10 Wheat. 157–77. Appeal from U.S. Circuit
             Court, Ky. Appellate Case No. 1055. Argued 22–23 Feb. 1825.
15 March   The Antelope, 10 Wheat. 114–32. Appeal from U.S. Circuit
             Court, Ga. Appellate Case Nos. 1161, 1162. Argued 26, 28 Feb.,
             1–3 Mar. 1825.
21 March   Brent v. Davis, 10 Wheat. 396–405. Error to U.S. Circuit Court,
             D.C. Appellate Case No. 1224. Argued 14–15 Mar. 1825.
21 March   The Corporation of Washington v. Young, 10 Wheat. 406–10.
             Error to U.S. Circuit Court, D.C. Appellate Case No. 1223.
             Argued 14–15 Mar. 1825.

1826

11 February Wetzell v. Bussard, 11 Wheat. 310–16. Error to U.S. Circuit
             Court, D.C. Appellate Case No. 1241. Argued 7 Feb. 1826.
20 February Brooks v. Marbury, 11 Wheat. 79–99. Error to U.S. Circuit
             Court, D.C. Appellate Case No. 1259. Argued 10–11 Feb. 1826.

23 February   Taylor's Devisee v. Owings, 11 Wheat. 226–36. Error to U.S. Circuit Court, Ky. Appellate Case No. 1081. Argued 14 Feb. 1826.

2 March   Finley v. Bank of the United States, 11 Wheat. 304–9. Appeal from U.S. Circuit Court, Ky. Appellate Case No. 1254. Argued 24–25 Feb. 1826.

4 March   Armstrong v. Toler, 11 Wheat. 267–79. Error to U.S. Circuit Court, Pa. Appellate Case No. 1206. Argued 24 Feb. 1826.

10 March   Walker v. Griffin's Heirs, 11 Wheat. 375–79. Appeal from U.S. Circuit Court, Ky. Appellate Case No. 1251. Not argued.

11 March   Harding v. Handy, Handy v. Harding, 11 Wheat. 119–33. Appeal from U.S. Circuit Court, R.I. Appellate Case Nos. 1244, 1245. Argued 23–25 Feb. 1826.

14 March   Williams v. Bank of the United States, 11 Wheat. 415. Error to U.S. Circuit Court, Ohio. Appellate Case No. 1271. Argued 7–8 Mar. 1826.

14 March   Barnes v. Williams, 11 Wheat. 416–17. Certificate of division from U.S. Circuit Court, W. Tenn. Appellate Case No. 1268. Argued 10, 11, 13 Mar. 1826.

14 March   Miller's Heirs v. McIntyre, 11 Wheat. 442–45. Appeal from U.S. Circuit Court, Ky. Appellate Case No. 1257. Argued 3 Mar. 1826.

16 March   Etting v. Bank of the United States, 11 Wheat. 73–78. Error to U.S. Circuit Court, Md. Appellate Case No. 1266. Argued 8–11 Mar. 1826.

21 March   Carnochan and Mitchell v. Christie, 11 Wheat. 447–67. Appeal from U.S. Circuit Court, Ga. Argued 15–17 Mar. 1826.

1827

19 January   Williams v. Norris, 12 Wheat. 117–29. Error to Supreme Court of Errors and Appeals, Tenn. Appellate Case No. 1217. Argued 11–12 Jan. 1827.

23 January   Rankin & Schatzell v. Scott, 12 Wheat. 178–80. Error to U.S. District Court, Mo. Appellate Case No. 1253. Argued 15 Mar. 1826, 15 Jan. 1827.

7 February   Clark v. Corporation of Washington, 12 Wheat. 52–63. Error to U.S. Circuit Court, D.C., Alexandria. Appellate Case No. 1358. Argued 26–27, 29–30 Jan. 1827.

9 February   Potter v. Gardner, 12 Wheat. 499–505. Appeal from U.S. Circuit Court, R.I. Appellate Case No. 1290. Argued 1–3 Feb. 1827.

17 February   Dunlap v. Dunlap, 12 Wheat. 574–81. Appeal from U.S. Circuit Court, Ohio. Appellate Case No. 1340. Argued 9–10 Feb. 1827.

19 February   Ogden v. Saunders, 12 Wheat. 332–57. Error to U.S. District Court, La. Appellate Case No. 1036. Argued 3–5 Mar. 1824, 18–20 Jan. 1827.

20 February   Parker v. Judges of the U.S. Circuit Court for Maryland, 12 Wheat. 562–65. Motion for mandamus to U.S. Circuit Court, Md. Argued 10 Feb. 1827.

22 February McConnell v. The Town of Lexington, 12 Wheat. 582–86.
             Appeal from U.S. Circuit Court, Ky. Appellate Case No. 1304.
             Printed briefs submitted, 13 Feb. 1827.
23 February The United States v. Barker, 12 Wheat. 560–61. Error to U.S.
             Circuit Court, Pa. Appellate Case Nos. 1322–25. Printed briefs
             submitted, 16 Feb. 1827.
28 February Bank of the United States v. Dandridge, 12 Wheat. 90–116.
             Error to U.S. Circuit Court, Va. Appellate Case No. 1283.
             Argued 3, 5–7 Feb. 1827.
2 March   Ramsay v. Allegre, 12 Wheat. 613–14. Appeal from U.S. Circuit
             Court, Md. Appellate Case No. 1348. Argued 20 Feb. 1827.
7 March   Henderson v. Poindexter, 12 Wheat. 530–45. Error to U.S.
             District Court, Miss. Appellate Case No. 1311. Argued 16–17
             Feb. 1827.
7 March   Thompson v. Peter, 12 Wheat. 566–67. Error to U.S. Circuit
             Court, D.C. Appellate Case No. 1331. Argued 2 Mar. 1827.
8 March   Davidson v. Taylor, 12 Wheat. 604. Error to U.S. Circuit Court,
             D.C. Appellate Case No. 1308. Argued 31 Jan. 1827.
12 March   Brown v. The State of Maryland, 12 Wheat. 436–49. Error to
             Court of Appeals, Western Shore, Md. Appellate Case No. 1350.
             Argued 28 Feb., 1 Mar. 1827.
15 March   Postmaster General v. Early, 12 Wheat. 144–52. Certificate of
             division from U.S. Circuit Court, Ga. Appellate Case No. 1369.
             Argued 9–10 Mar. 1827.
16 March   Daniel v. Williamson, 12 Wheat. 569–70. Appeal from U.S.
             Circuit Court, Ga. Appellate Case No. 1371. Argued 12 Mar.
             1827.

Appendix II
Calendar of Miscellaneous Papers
and Letters Not Found

Beginning with Volume VI, the editors adopted a policy of presenting calendar summaries in a separate appendix. Any inconvenience resulting from this separation is more than offset, they believe, by keeping the main body of the volume reserved for documents selected for printing in full. In this volume calendar entries have been prepared for routine correspondence with Secretary of State Henry Clay, in which the secretary transmits copies of printed public documents and requests acknowledgment of receipt; certificates, letters, and toasts composed for various purposes; and contracts for selling land and for publishing Jared Sparks's edition of George Washington's correspondence. Entries have also been prepared for letters not found whose contents are at least partly known from extracts or summaries in the catalogs of auction houses and autograph dealers. Most of these letters, if extant, would be printed in full.

All calendar entries begin with the dateline in italics, followed by information (in parentheses) describing the document and its location. The contents of the document are then stated in summary style; however, extracts from letters not found are quoted in full. Where necessary, footnotes have been subjoined to calendar entries.

Circular

12 January 1824, Richmond (ALS, ViHi). As president of the local branch of the American Colonization Society, JM writes that "a meeting of the managers of the auxiliary colonization society of Richmond is desired on wednesday evening next at four, in the office of the Clerk of the House of Delegates."[1]

1. JM had been elected president of the auxiliary society on 4 Nov. 1823 and was reelected at each annual meeting through 1835 ("Minutes of the Virginia Branch American Colonization Society, 4 Nov. 1823–5 Feb. 1859," Papers of the Colonization Society of Virginia, ViHi).

To John Randolph

17 January 1824, Richmond (ALS, ViU). Thanks Randolph for report of secretary of the treasury.[1]

1. Secretary of the Treasury William H. Crawford delivered his annual report on 5 Jan. 1824 (*ASP, Finances,* IV, 374–90).

To John Page

7 May 1824, Richmond (summary of ALS in American Art Association, Catalog [New York, 1928], item 452). Writes to Page in Williamsburg; refers to a bond and speaks of Page's son, James.

Toast

19 October 1824, Yorktown (printed, *Enquirer* [Richmond, Va.], 22 Oct. 1824). "The Patriot soldier whose youth, whose manhood and whose age have been devoted to the battles of Liberty."[1]

1. JM arrived in Williamsburg on Sunday, 17 Oct., and was a member of the welcoming party on board the steamboat *Virginia* that met Lafayette at the mouth of the York River on 18 Oct. and conducted him to Yorktown. At a "Grand Civic and Military Dinner" in the general's honor on the 19th, JM was one of eighteen "volunteers" who offered toasts. The next day he accompanied Lafayette and his party to Williamsburg (Robert D. Ward, *An Account of General La Fayette's Visit to Virginia, in the Years 1824–25* [Richmond, Va., 1881], 15, 21–22; Edgar Ewing Brandon, ed., *Lafayette Guest of the Nation: A Contemporary Account of the "Triumphal Tour" of General Lafayette* [3 vols.; Oxford, Ohio, 1957], III, 51–52, 61–62, 68).

Toast

26 October 1824, Richmond (printed, *Enquirer* [Richmond, Va.], 29 Oct. 1824). "Rational liberty—The cause of mankind. Its friends cannot despair when they behold its champions."[1]

1. JM gave this toast at a dinner at the Eagle Hotel on the first day of Lafayette's visit to Richmond.

To Samuel L. Southard

27 October 1824, Richmond (summary of ALS in Dawson's Book Shop, Catalog No. 78 [Los Angeles, 1931], 28–29). Recommends William Leigh for appointment as midshipman.

Toast

28 October 1824, Richmond (printed, *Enquirer* [Richmond, Va.], 2 Nov. 1824). "The sports of the turf—Virginia must be indebted to them for their Cavalry."[1]

1. JM offered this toast at the Jockey Club dinner held on the third day of Lafayette's visit to Richmond.

Certificate

30 October 1824, Richmond (DS, Foundation José et René de Chambrun, La Grange, France). As president of the local colonization society, JM certifies that $10 was contributed by members of Harmony Hall Academy, in Richmond, making Lafayette member for life of "The Richmond and Manchester Society auxiliary to the American Society for colonizing the free people of colour on the coast of Africa."

Certificate

[Ca. 20 December 1824, Richmond] (ADS, RG 94, DNA). JM subscribes to letter from John H. Cocke to Secretary of War Calhoun, 19 Dec. 1824, recommending Wirt Robinson (spelled "Robertson" by JM) for appointment to the U.S. Military Academy. Although not personally acquainted with the applicant, JM has "known his Father long and intimately."[1]

1. JM's certificate appears below that of James Pleasants, dated Richmond, 20 Dec. 1824. Wirt Robinson was the son of Anthony Robinson (1771–1851), who had served as a court clerk in Richmond and Williamsburg and was then second teller of the Bank of Virginia (*Richmond Portraits*, 172–73).

From Samuel L. Southard

16 February 1825, Washington (letterbook copy, RG 45, DNA). Secretary of navy writes that JM's letter of 12 Feb.[1] will "receive that consideration to which it is entitled, when appointments are to be made."

1. Letter not found.

To Thomas Tunney, James Carson, and Humphry Peake

16 February 1825, Washington (summary of ALS, Walter R. Benjamin Autographs, Inc., *Collector* [New York, 1952], 78). Regrets that official duties make it impossible to accept dinner invitation for 21 Feb. " 'in honour of our distinguished brother General Lafayette.' "[1]

1. The occasion was a Masonic dinner held at Clagett's Hotel in Alexandria (Edgar Ewing Brandon, ed., *Lafayette Guest of the Nation: A Contemporary Account of the "Triumphal Tour" of General Lafayette* [3 vols.; Oxford, Ohio, 1957], III, 246–50).

To St. George Tucker

23 May 1825, [Richmond] (printed extract of ALS, Kingston Galleries, Inc., Catalog No. 4 [Somerville, Mass., 1962]). "Nothing in particular requires your attention, and I think it would be harassing yourself unnecessarily to come to Richmond. I should rejoice to see you . . . but do not think the state of the docket requires any extraordinary exertion."[1]

1. Beset by "various infirmities, and particularly my almost total loss of Hearing," Tucker resigned his commission as U.S. District Judge on 30 June 1825. To succeed Tucker, President Adams made a recess appointment of George Hay, whose nomination was ultimately confirmed by the Senate on 31 Mar. 1826 (Tucker to Henry Clay [copy], 30 June 1825, in "Cases in the Courts of the United States, 25 February 1813–November 1824," No. 3, p. 159, Tucker-Coleman Papers, ViW; *Journal of the Executive Proceedings of the Senate*, III [Washington, D.C., 1828], 449, 502, 525).

To Ralph R. Gurley

27 July 1825, Richmond (printed extract of ALS, Charles Hamilton Autographs, Inc., Catalog No. 61 [New York, 1972], 45). "I thank you for your polite attention in sending me your discourse delivered . . . in Washington, and have read it with much pleasure.[1] Your views on the subject of our infant colony, and of the objects of the society, are I think perfectly just. Your efforts to promote those objects will I trust be as successful as they are meretorious."

1. Ralph Randolph Gurley, *A Discourse, Delivered on the Fourth of July, 1825, in the City of Washington* (Washington, D.C., 1825). Gurley (1797–1872) was associated with the American Colonization Society for fifty years. He was appointed secretary of the society in June 1825 after returning from Liberia, where he worked with Jehudi Ashmun to regain the trust of the colonists (P. J. Staudenraus, *The African Colonization Movement, 1816–1865* [New York, 1961], 94–99).

Articles of Agreement

9 September 1825, [Fauquier] (ADS, owned by Mrs. James Robert Green, Markham, Va., 1971). George Morehead of Fauquier County agrees to sell part of lease held by assignment from Thomas Simpson for $5 per acre, of which Morehead acknowledges receiving $700 from JM. Morehead is to deliver up the land on 1 Sept. 1826.[1]

1. On Morehead, see *PJM*, IX, 270–71, 272 n. 2.

To Bushrod Washington

[11 October] 1825, Richmond (printed extract of ALS, Walter R. Benjamin Autographs, Inc., *Collector* [New York, 1894], 118). "I want half a dozen copies of my history of the colonies, and as I wish to dispose of three or four in Washington, one to our brother Todd should he join us, I shall be much obliged by your putting them in your baggage."

From Henry Clay

20 October 1825, Washington (letterbook copy, RG 59, DNA). State Department has sent box containing documents of Seventeenth and Eighteenth Congresses.

To Henry Clay

29 October 1825, Richmond (ALS, DLC). Acknowledges receipt of box of documents from State Department.

To Henry Clay

4 March 1826, [Washington] (noted as missing in Register of Miscellaneous Letters Received, RG 59, DNA). Recommends John D. Simms for appointment.

To Martin P. Marshall

15 April 1826, Richmond (ALS, Parke-Bernet Galleries, Inc., Auction Catalog [New York, 1958], item 261). Advises nephew on reading law with Scott, instructing him to do as much of Mr. Scott's office business as possible and outlining the work.

Toast

23 June 1826, Richmond (printed, *Enquirer* [Richmond, Va.], 27 June 1826). "Our late important acquisitions in the South and West: The American people can never forget the statesmen, whose wise policy extended our territory to the Gulph of Mexico and the Pacific without violating the rights of others."[1]

1. JM's was one of a number of toasts by "volunteers" at a dinner at the Eagle Hotel in honor of James Monroe.

From Unknown

21 July 1826, St. Louis. (AL[S], RG 267, DNA). Forwards letter of applicant (not found) and states that his "sympathies are on the side of the application."[1]

1. The signature to the letter and also to the frank have been clipped. The writer was a member of Congress, but the hand does not match that of Sen. Thomas Hart Benton, who lived in St. Louis. Missouri's other Senator, David Barton, was also a St. Louis resident. An endorsement on the cover reads "Polk," but again the hand does not match that of James K. Polk, then a Representative from Tennessee.

Answer in Chancery

1826, Fauquier County, Va. (AD, owned by Mrs. James Robert Green, Markham, Va., 1971). Drawn on behalf of James K. Marshall and wife Claudia H. Marshall, defendants in suit brought by Israel Pleasants and John P. Pleasants against John H. Blair, administrator of Nathaniel Burwell, and others in superior court of chancery at Williamsburg. Plaintiffs seek recovery from heirs and representatives of Burwell, who as high sheriff of Gloucester was alleged to be liable for debt incurred by deputy sheriff. Defendants do not admit liability but if proved to be ultimately liable insist that deputy sheriff's estate sufficient to satisfy claim.[1]

1. Claudia H. Marshall was Nathaniel Burwell's only surviving child (*PJM*, IX, 202 n. 1). No further details on this suit are available owing to the destruction of the Williamsburg chancery court's records.

Articles of Agreement

7 March 1827, [Washington, D.C.] (DS, NjMoHiP). Jared Sparks, Bushrod Washington, and JM sign articles of agreement whereby Sparks proposes to publish an edition of George Washington's writings in return for having free access to all the papers in Bushrod's possession at Mount Vernon. The two parties, Sparks of the first part, Bushrod and JM of the second, to have an equal interest in the copyright and profits of sales.[1]

1. The signing took place in Justice Washington's rooms at ten o'clock. Afterwards, Sparks had the following conversation with JM: " 'I should be glad to beg one favor of you, sir, which is, to be allowed to mention you on all proper occasions as cordially approving this plan, and disposed to aid it in any way that may be in your power; and particularly to insert your name in the public notices and prospectuses.' He replied: 'I have no objection; you can use my name as you please.' 'Not that I expect to pledge you to anything,' said I, 'but merely to impress it strongly on the public that my labors in this business meet your approbation, and will receive your support.' He answered: 'I understand you; the thing will be properly done; I shall feel no concern' " (Herbert B. Adams, *The Life and Writings of Jared Sparks, Comprising Selections from His Journals and Correspondence* [2 vols.; Boston and New York, 1893], II, 8–9).

INDEX

In addition to persons and subjects, this index includes the titles of all cases mentioned in the documents and in the accompanying annotation. Persons are identified on pages cited below in italics. If a person has been identified in an earlier volume, the volume number and page reference follow the name in parentheses.